C Programming
A MODERN APPROACH

C Programming
A MODERN APPROACH

K. N. King
Georgia State University

W • W • Norton & Company
New York • London

Printed in the United States of America.

Library of Congress Cataloging-in-Publication Data

King, K. N. (Kim N.)
    C programming : a modern approach / K.N. King.
      p.   cm.
    Includes bibliographical references and index.
    1. C (Computer program language)   I. Title.
  QA76.73.C15K49   1996
  005.13'3—dc20   96-1484

ISBN 0-393-96945-2

W. W. Norton & Company, Inc.
500 Fifth Avenue, New York, N.Y. 10110

W. W. Norton & Company Ltd.
10 Coptic Street, London WC1A 1PU

    4 5 6 7 8 9 0

BRIEF CONTENTS

CONTENTS

PREFACE

*In computing, turning the obvious into the useful
is a living definition of the word "frustration."*

Let me get this off my chest right at the start: I've had a love/hate relationship with C for years. I love the ease with which I can write C programs. I love the development environments that come with many of today's C compilers. But I hate the ease with which I can make mistakes. I hate the attention to picky details that C programming often requires. And, above all, I hate the way many C programmers disparage other languages. Let's face it: C isn't the ultimate programming language. (C++ isn't, either.) It is, however, a language with which every software developer should become familiar. It has become, for better or for worse, the *lingua franca* of the computer world.

I first used C in 1975, when it was new and somewhat immature. I then lost touch with the language for some years. Once C was standardized, I decided to take another look at it. To my relief, I found that some of its worst flaws had been corrected during standardization. (Of course, there are enough left to keep life interesting!) I decided to write a book that would take a fresh look at C, while at the same time tapping into the collective wisdom that C programmers have accumulated over the past quarter of a century.

Goals

Here are some of the goals I've tried to accomplish in this book:

- *Be clear, readable, and possibly even entertaining.* Many C books are too concise for the average reader. Others are badly written or just plain dull. I've tried to give clear, thorough explanations, leavened with enough humor to hold the reader's interest.

- *Be accessible to a broad range of readers.* I assume that the reader has a minimal amount of previous programming experience, but I don't assume knowledge of a particular language. I've tried to keep jargon to a minimum and to define the terms that I use. I've also attempted to separate advanced material from more elementary topics, so that the beginner won't get discouraged.

■ *Be authoritative without being pedantic.* To avoid reader frustration, I've tried to cover all the features of the Standard C language and library, including signals, `setjmp/longjmp`, variable-length argument lists, and international features. At the same time, I've tried to avoid burdening the reader with unnecessary detail.

■ *Be organized for easy learning.* My experience in teaching C underscores the importance of presenting the features of C gradually. I use a spiral approach, in which difficult topics are introduced briefly, then revisited one or more times later in the book with details added each time. Pacing is deliberate, with each chapter building gradually on what has come before. For most students, this is probably the best approach: it avoids the extremes of boredom on the one hand, or "information overload" on the other.

■ *Motivate language features.* Instead of just describing each feature of the language and giving a few simple examples of how the feature is used, I've tried to motivate each feature and discuss how it's used in practical situations.

■ *Emphasize style.* It's important for every C programmer to develop a consistent style. Rather than dictating what this style should be, though, I usually describe a few possibilities and let the reader choose the one that's most appealing. Knowing alternative styles is a big help when reading other people's programs (which programmers often spend a great deal of time doing).

■ *Avoid dependence on a particular machine, compiler, or operating system.* Since C is available on such a wide variety of platforms, I've tried to avoid dependence on any particular machine, compiler, or operating system. Of course, with a language like C, it's impossible to skip machine details completely. When such discussions are unavoidable, I give examples for both 16-bit and 32-bit architectures. When examples depend on a particular operating system, I discuss both DOS and UNIX.

■ *Use illustrations to clarify key concepts.* I've tried to put in as many figures as I could, since I think these are crucial for understanding many aspects of C. In particular, I've tried to "animate" algorithms whenever possible by showing snapshots of data at different points in the computation.

What's So Modern about *A Modern Approach?*

One of my most important goals has been to take a "modern approach" to C. Here are some of the ways I've tried to achieve this goal:

■ *Put C in perspective.* Instead of treating C as the only programming language worth knowing, I treat it as one of many useful languages. I discuss what kind of applications C is best suited for; I also show how to capitalize on C's strengths while minimizing its weaknesses.

- *Emphasize Standard C.* I pay minimal attention to older versions of the language. There are just a few scattered references to Classic (K&R) C in the chapters, mostly in Q&A sections. Appendix C lists the major differences between Standard C and Classic C.

- *Debunk myths.* Today's compilers are often at odds with commonly held assumptions about C. I don't hesitate to debunk some of the myths about C or challenge beliefs that have long been part of the C folklore (for example, the belief that pointer arithmetic is always faster than array subscripting). I've re-examined the old conventions of C, keeping the ones that are still helpful.

- *Emphasize software engineering.* I treat C as a mature software engineering tool, emphasizing how to use it to cope with issues that arise during programming-in-the-large. I stress making programs readable, maintainable, reliable, and portable, and I put special emphasis on information hiding.

- *Postpone C's low-level features.* These features, although handy for the kind of systems programming originally done in C, are not as relevant now that C is used for a great variety of applications. Instead of introducing them in the early chapters, as most C books do, I postpone them until Chapter 20.

- *De-emphasize "manual optimization."* Many books teach the reader to write nonobvious code in order to gain small savings in program efficiency. With today's abundance of optimizing C compilers, these techniques are often no longer necessary; in fact, they can result in programs that are less efficient.

- *Emphasize compatibility with C++.* I'll have more to say about this later.

Q&A Sections

Each chapter ends with a "Q&A section"—a series of questions and answers related to material covered in the chapter. Topics addressed in these sections include:

- *Frequently asked questions.* I've tried to answer questions that come up frequently in my own courses, in other books, and on newsgroups related to C.

- *Additional discussion and clarification of tricky issues.* Although readers with experience in a variety of languages may be satisfied with a brief explanation and a couple of examples, readers with less experience need more.

- *Side issues that don't belong in the main flow.* Some questions raise technical issues that won't be of interest to all readers.

- *Material too advanced or too esoteric to interest the average reader.* Questions of this nature are marked with an asterisk (*). Curious readers with a fair bit of programming experience may wish to delve into these questions immediately; others should definitely skip them on a first reading. *Warning:* These questions often refer to topics covered in later chapters.

- *Common differences among C compilers.* I discuss some frequently used (but nonstandard) features that are provided by DOS and UNIX compilers.

Q&A   Some questions in Q&A sections relate directly to specific places in the chapter; these places are marked by a special icon to signal the reader that additional information is available.

Other Features

In addition to Q&A sections, I've included a number of useful features, many of which are marked with simple but distinctive icons (shown at left).

cross-references ➤*Preface*

- **Warnings** alert readers to common pitfalls. C is famous for its traps; documenting them all is a hopeless—if not impossible—task. I've tried to pick out the pitfalls that are most common and/or most important.
- **Cross-references** provide a hypertext-like ability to locate information. Although many of these are pointers to topics covered later in the book, some point to previous topics that the reader may wish to review.

idiom
- **Idioms**—code patterns frequently seen in C programs—are marked for quick reference.

portability tip
- **Portability tips** give hints for writing programs that are independent of a particular machine, compiler, or operating system.
- **Sidebars** cover topics that aren't strictly part of C but that every knowledgeable C programmer should be aware of, including unsigned integers, the IEEE floating-point standard, and Unicode. (See "Source Code" at the bottom of this page for an example of a sidebar.)
- **Appendices** provide valuable reference information.

Programs

Choosing illustrative programs isn't an easy job. If programs are too brief and artificial, readers won't get any sense of how the features are used in the real world. On the other hand, if a program is *too* realistic, its point can easily be lost in a forest of details. I've chosen a middle course, using small, simple examples to make concepts clear when they're first introduced, then gradually building up to complete programs. I haven't included programs of great length; it's been my experience that instructors don't have the time to cover them and students don't have the patience to read them. I don't ignore the issues that arise in the creation of large programs, though—Chapter 15 (Writing Large Programs) and Chapter 19 (Program Design) cover them in detail.

Source Code

Source code for all programs in this book is available via the World-Wide Web at *http://www.gsu.edu/~matknk/cbook*. Updates, corrections, and news about the book are also available through this Web page.

Coverage of C++

C Programming: A Modern Approach was designed from the beginning to be completely compatible with C++, so that readers won't develop habits they must unlearn later. It prepares readers for C++ in three ways:

- By stressing modern design principles such as information hiding.
- By scattering brief discussions of C++—each tagged with a special "C++" icon—throughout the text.
- By providing a detailed overview of C++ in Chapter 19.

C++ is complex enough to warrant its own book. Coincidentally, I just happen to have one in preparation. For more information, feel free to contact me, or watch my Web page for news.

Audience

This book is designed as a primary text for a C course at the undergraduate level. Previous programming experience in a high-level language or assembler is helpful, but not necessary for a computer-literate reader (an "adept beginner," as my editor likes to put it).

Since the book is self-contained and usable for reference as well as learning, it makes an excellent companion text for a course in data structures, compiler design, operating systems, computer graphics, or other courses that use C for project work. It's also suitable for use as one of several books in a "survey of programming languages" course.

Thanks to its Q&A sections and emphasis on practical problems, the book will also appeal to readers who are enrolled in a training class or who are learning C by self-study.

Organization

The book is divided into four parts:

- *Basic Features of C.* Chapters 1–10 cover enough of C to allow the reader to write single-file programs using arrays and functions.
- *Advanced Features of C.* Chapters 11–20 build on the material in the earlier chapters. The topics become a little harder in these chapters, which provide in-depth coverage of pointers, strings, the preprocessor, structures, unions, enumerations, and low-level features of C. In addition, two chapters (15 and 19) offer guidance on program design.
- *The Standard C Library.* Chapters 21–26 focus on the C library, a large collection of functions that come with every compiler. These chapters are most likely to be used as reference material, although portions are suitable for lectures.

■ *Reference.* Appendix A covers the complete syntax of C, with annotations to explain some of the more obscure points. Appendix B gives a complete list of C operators. Appendix C describes the differences between Standard C and Classic C. Appendix D is an alphabetical listing of all functions in the C library, with a thorough description of each. Appendix E lists the ASCII character set. An annotated bibliography points the reader toward other sources of information.

A full-blown course on C should cover Chapters 1–20 in sequence, with topics from Chapters 21–26 added as needed. A shorter course can omit the following topics without losing continuity: Section 9.6 (recursive functions), Section 12.4 (pointers and multidimensional arrays), Section 14.5 (miscellaneous directives), Section 17.7 (pointers to functions), Chapter 19 (program design), Section 20.2 (bit-fields in structures), and Section 20.3 (other low-level techniques).

Exercises

Having a variety of good exercises is obviously essential for a textbook. I've provided over 300 exercises at a variety of skill levels. Some are brief drill questions. Although these exercises aren't the most exciting (in fact, they can be downright boring), I consider them essential for developing skill in C, in the same way that vocabulary drill is needed in a foreign-language text or math problems in an algebra text. In addition to drill questions, I've included a number of short-answer questions and programming exercises. Short-answer questions require more thought than drill questions, although answers are usually brief. Programming exercises ask the reader to write a short program or a piece of a larger program.

A few exercises have nonobvious answers (some individuals uncharitably call these "trick questions"—the nerve!). Since C programs often contain abundant examples of such code, I feel it's necessary to provide some practice. However, I'll play fair by marking these exercises with an asterisk (*). Be careful with a starred exercise: either pay close attention and think hard or skip it entirely.

Errors, Lack of (?)

I've taken great pains to ensure the accuracy of this book. Inevitably, however, any book of this size contains a few errors. If you spot one, please send e-mail to *knking@gsu.edu* or write to me at the following address:

K. N. King
Department of Mathematics and Computer Science
Georgia State University
University Plaza
Atlanta, GA 30303-3083

I'd also appreciate hearing about which features you found especially helpful, which ones you could do without, and what you'd like to see added.

Acknowledgments

First, I'd like to thank my editor at Norton, Joe Wisnovsky, whose wisdom and good taste was much appreciated, and my former editor, Jim Jordan, who believed—rightly, I hope—that the world needed another C book. Another Norton person, Deborah Gerish, deserves many thanks for her skill in copyediting the manuscript.

The predecessor to this book was the tutorial that I wrote to accompany the TopSpeed C compiler. I thank Karin Ellison and Niels Jensen for the opportunity to write that tutorial and for permission to reuse material in this book.

The following colleagues were kind enough to review some or all of the manuscript:

Susan Anderson-Freed and Lisa J. Brown, Illinois Wesleyan University
Manuel E. Bermudez, University of Florida
Steven C. Cater, University of Georgia
Patrick Harrison, United States Naval Academy
Brian Harvey, University of California, Berkeley
Henry H. Leitner, Harvard University
Darrell Long, University of California, Santa Cruz
Arthur B. Maccabe, University of New Mexico
Carolyn Rosner, University of Wisconsin
Patrick Terry, Rhodes University

Brian Harvey and Pat Terry deserve special mention for going above and beyond the call of duty. I appreciate their detailed comments more than they'll ever know, and I promise to forgive them for the occasional scathing remark.

I also received much valuable feedback from friends and colleagues in Atlanta, including Geoff George, who was always willing to discuss the details of C and C++, Marge Hicks, who caught a number of mistakes in the final manuscript, and Scott Owen, who made many useful comments on an early draft. The support and encouragement of my department chair, Fred Massey, was especially appreciated. A number of students provided feedback, including Terry Turner, who read early drafts with a keen eye, Nina Dalal, Jay Schneider, and Michael Sigmond.

Susan Cole not only read the entire manuscript with great care but created the kind of home environment that was conducive to writing. Without her love and understanding, I might never have finished the book. I must also acknowledge the assistance of our cats, Bronco and Dennis, who were always eager to provide company during the book-writing process.

Finally, I'd like to acknowledge the late Alan J. Perlis, whose epigrams appear at the beginning of each chapter. I had the privilege of studying briefly under Alan at Yale in the mid-70s. I think he'd be amused at finding his epigrams in a C book.

1 Introducing C

*When someone says "I want a programming language in which
I need only say what I wish done," give him a lollipop.* *

What is C? The simple answer—a widely used programming language developed
in the early 1970s at Bell Laboratories—conveys little of C's special flavor. Before
we become immersed in the details of the language, let's take a look at where C
came from, what it was designed for, and how it has changed over the years (Section 1.1). We'll also discuss C's strengths and weaknesses and see how to get the
most out of the language (Section 1.2).

1.1 History of C

The history of C dates back to the computing field's Paleozoic era: the late 1960s.
Let's take a quick look at C's history, from its origins at Bell Laboratories, to its
coming of age as a standardized language, to its influence on recent languages.

Origins

C is a by-product of the UNIX operating system, which was developed at Bell
Laboratories by Ken Thompson, Dennis Ritchie, and others. Thompson single-
handedly wrote the original version of UNIX, which ran on the DEC PDP-7 computer, an early minicomputer with only 8K words of main memory (this was 1969,
after all!).

Like other operating systems of the time, UNIX was written in assembly language. Programs written in assembly language are usually painful to debug and

---

*The epigrams at the beginning of each chapter are from "Epigrams on Programming" by Alan J. Perlis
(*ACM SIGPLAN Notices* (September, 1982): 7–13).

1

Q&A

hard to enhance, and UNIX was no exception. Thompson decided that a higher-level language was needed for the further development of UNIX, so he designed a small language named B. Thompson based B on BCPL, a systems programming language developed in the mid-1960s. BCPL, in turn, traces its ancestry to Algol 60, one of the earliest (and most influential) programming languages.

Ritchie soon joined the UNIX project and began programming in B. In 1970, Bell Labs acquired a PDP-11 for the UNIX project. Once B was up and running on the PDP-11, Thompson rewrote a portion of UNIX in B. By 1971, it became apparent that B was not well-suited to the PDP-11, so Ritchie began to develop an extended version of B. He called his language NB ("New B") at first, and then, as it began to diverge more from B, he changed the name to C. The language was stable enough by 1973 that UNIX could be rewritten in C. The switch to C provided an important benefit: portability. By writing C compilers for other computers at Bell Labs, the team could get UNIX running on those machines as well.

Standardization

C continued to evolve during the 1970s, especially between 1977 and 1979. It was during this period that the first book on C appeared. *The C Programming Language*, written by Brian Kernighan and Dennis Ritchie and published in 1978, quickly became the bible of C programmers. In the absence of an official standard for C, this book—known as K&R or the "White Book" to aficionados—served as a *de facto* standard.

During the 1970s, there were relatively few C programmers, and most of them were UNIX users. By the 1980s, however, C had expanded beyond the narrow confines of the UNIX world. C compilers became available on a variety of machines running under different operating systems. In particular, C began to establish itself on the fast-growing IBM PC platform.

With C's increasing popularity came problems. Programmers who wrote new C compilers relied on K&R as a reference. Unfortunately, K&R was fuzzy about some language features, so compilers often treated these features differently. Also, K&R failed to make a clear distinction between which features belonged to C and which were part of UNIX. To make matters worse, C continued to change after K&R was published, with new features being added and a few older features removed.

The need for a thorough, precise, and up-to-date description of the language soon became apparent. Without such a standard, numerous dialects would have arisen, threatening one of C's major strengths—program portability.

The development of a U.S. standard for C began in 1983 under the auspices of the American National Standards Institute (ANSI). After many revisions, the standard was completed in 1988 and formally approved in December 1989 as ANSI standard X3.159-1989. In 1990, it was approved by the International Standards Organization (ISO) as international standard ISO/IEC 9899-1990. The language described in these standards is known as "ANSI C," "ANSI/ISO C," or just "Standard C," the term we'll use in this book.

Although the version of C described in the first edition of K&R is often called K&R C, this name is no longer appropriate since the second edition of K&R, published in 1988, reflects the changes made in the ANSI standard. We'll refer to the older language as "Classic C"; this terminology (a play on "Coke Classic") is becoming common in the C world.

The description of C in this book is based on the ANSI/ISO standard. However, we can't completely ignore Classic C, since many of the "real-world" programs written in the older language are still in use. Appendix C lists the major differences between Standard C and Classic C; if you should encounter older C programs, this appendix will help you understand them.

C++

Although C itself hasn't changed since the ANSI/ISO standard was adopted, its evolution continues, in a sense, with the creation of newer languages based on C. Of these languages, which include Concurrent C and Objective C, the most notable is C++. C++, designed by Bjarne Stroustrup of Bell Labs, extends C in a variety of ways. In particular, C++ adds features to support object-oriented programming.

C++ is rapidly gaining popularity; there's an excellent chance that you'll be writing in C++ in the future. In that case, why bother to learn C? First, C++ is much harder to learn than C; it's best to master C before tackling the complexities of C++ (or any of the other languages derived from C). Second, there's a lot of C code around; it's likely that you'll need to read and maintain this code. Third, not everyone is likely to switch to C++. People who write relatively small programs, for example, will derive little benefit from C++.

The primary argument in favor of learning C++ first is that you'll avoid picking up C habits that have to be "unlearned" when using C++. You'll find that this book sidesteps the problem by emphasizing data abstraction, information hiding, and other principles that play a large role in C++. C++ includes all of the features of C, so you'll be able to use everything you learn from this book when you later tackle C++.

We won't ignore C++, although it's not a major focus of this book. Brief references to C++ will crop up from time to time, marked with the **C++** symbol. We'll also take a detailed look at C++ in Section 19.4.

1.2 Strengths and Weaknesses of C

Like any other programming language, C has strengths and weaknesses. Both stem from the language's intended use (writing operating systems and other systems software) and its underlying philosophy:

- *C is a low-level language.* To serve as a suitable language for systems programming, C provides access to machine-level concepts (bytes and addresses, for example) that other programming languages try to hide. Moreover, C provides operations that correspond closely to a computer's built-in instructions, so that programs can be fast. Since application programs rely on it for input/output, storage management, and numerous other services, an operating system can't afford to be slow.

- *C is a small language.* C provides a more limited set of features than many languages. (The reference manual in the second edition of K&R covers the entire language in 49 pages.) To keep the number of features small, C relies heavily on a "library" of standard *functions*. (A "function" is similar to what other programming languages would call a "procedure" or "subroutine.")

- *C is a permissive language.* C assumes that you know what you're doing, so it allows you a wider degree of latitude than many languages. Moreover, C doesn't mandate the detailed error-checking found in other languages.

Strengths

C's strengths help explain why the language has become so popular:

- *Efficiency.* Efficiency has been one of C's advantages from the beginning. Since C was intended for applications where assembly language had traditionally been used, it was crucial that C programs could run quickly and in limited amounts of memory.

- *Portability.* Although program portability wasn't a primary goal of C, it has turned out to be one of the language's strengths. When a program must run on computers ranging from PCs to supercomputers, it is often written in C. One reason for the portability of C programs is that—thanks to C's early association with UNIX and the later ANSI/ISO standard—the language hasn't splintered into incompatible dialects. Another is that C compilers are small and easily written, which has helped make them widely available. Finally, C itself has features that support portability (although there's nothing to prevent programmers from writing nonportable programs).

- *Power.* C's large collection of data types and operators help make it a powerful language. In C, it is often possible to accomplish quite a bit in just a few lines of code.

- *Flexibility.* Although C was originally designed for systems programming, it has no inherent restrictions that limit it to this arena. C is now used for applications of all kinds, from embedded systems to commercial data processing. Moreover, C imposes very few restrictions on the use of its features; operations that would be illegal in other languages are often permitted in C. For example, C allows a character to be added to an integer value (or, for that matter, a floating-point number). This flexibility can make programming easier, although it may allow some bugs to slip through.

■ *Standard library.* One of C's great strengths is its standard library, which contains hundreds of functions for input/output, string handling, storage allocation, and other useful operations.

■ *Integration with UNIX.* C is particularly powerful in combination with UNIX. In fact, some UNIX tools assume that the user knows C.

Weaknesses

C's weaknesses arise from the same source as many of its strengths: C's closeness to the machine. If we think of languages like Pascal or Ada as "high-level languages," then C is more accurately described as a "low-level language" or even a "structured assembly language."

Here are a few of C's most notorious problems:

■ *C programs can be error-prone.* C's flexibility makes it an error-prone language. Programming mistakes that would be caught in many other languages can't be detected by a C compiler. In this respect, C is a lot like assembly language, where most errors aren't detected until the program is run. To make matters worse, C contains a number of pitfalls for the unwary. In later chapters, we'll see how an extra semicolon can create an infinite loop or a missing & can cause a program crash.

■ *C programs can be difficult to understand.* Although C is a small language by most measures, it has a number of features that aren't found in other common languages (and consequently are often misunderstood). These features can be combined in a great variety of ways, many of which—although obvious to the original author of a program—can be hard for others to understand. Another problem is the terse nature of C programs. C was designed at a time when interactive communication with computers was tedious at best. As a result, C was purposefully kept terse to minimize the time required to enter and edit programs. C's flexibility can also be a negative factor; programmers who are too clever for their own good can make programs almost impossible to understand.

■ *C programs can be difficult to modify.* Large programs written in C can be hard to change if they haven't been designed with maintenance in mind. Modern programming languages usually provide a language feature called a "module" (or "unit" or "package") that supports the division of a large program into more manageable pieces. C, unfortunately, lacks such a feature.

Obfuscated C

Even C's most ardent admirers admit that C code can be hard to read. The annual International Obfuscated C Code Contest actually encourages contestants to write the most confusing C programs possible. The winners are truly baffling, as 1991's "Best Small Program" shows:

```
int v,i,j,k,l,s,a[99];
main()
{
    for(scanf("%d",&s);*a-s;v=a[j*=v]-a[i],k=i<s,j+=
(v=j<s&&(!k&&!!printf(2+"\n\n%c"-(!1<<!j),"  #Q"[1^v?(
1^j)&1:2])&&++1||a[i]<s&&v&&v-i+j&&v+i-j&&v+i-j))&&!(
1%=s),v||(i==j?a[i+=k]=0:++a[i])>=s*k&&++a[--i])
                    ;
}
```

This program, written by Doron Osovlanski and Baruch Nissenbaum, prints all solutions to the Eight Queens problem (the problem of placing eight queens on a chessboard in such a way that no queen attacks any other queen). In fact, it works for any number of queens between four and 99. Other winning programs can be found in the book *Obfuscated C and Other Mysteries* by Don Libes (New York: Wiley, 1993).

Effective Use of C

Using C effectively requires taking advantage of C's strengths while avoiding its weaknesses. Here are a few suggestions:

- **Learn how to avoid C pitfalls.** Hints for avoiding pitfalls are scattered throughout this book—just look for the △ symbol. For a more extensive list of pitfalls, see Andrew Koenig's *C Traps and Pitfalls* (Reading, Mass.: Addison-Wesley, 1989). Modern compilers will detect common pitfalls and issue warnings, but no compiler spots them all.

Q&A
- **Use software tools to make programs more reliable.** C programmers are prolific tool builders (and users). One of the most famous C tools is named lint. lint, which is traditionally provided with UNIX, can subject a program to a more extensive error analysis than most C compilers. If lint (or a similar program) is available, it's a good idea to use it. Another useful tool is a debugger. Because of the nature of C, many bugs can't be detected by a C compiler; these show up instead in the form of run-time errors or incorrect output. Consequently, using a good debugger is practically mandatory for C programmers.

- **Take advantage of existing code libraries.** One of the benefits of using C is that so many other people also use it; it's a good bet that they've written code you can employ in your own programs. C code is often bundled into libraries (collections of functions); obtaining a suitable library is a good way to reduce errors—and save considerable programming effort. Libraries for common tasks, including user-interface development, graphics, communications, database management, and networking, are readily available. Some libraries are in the public domain while others are sold commercially.

- **Adopt a sensible set of coding conventions.** A coding convention is a style rule that a programmer has decided to adopt even though it is not enforced by the language. Well-chosen conventions help make programs more uniform, easier to read, and easier to modify. Conventions are important when using any programming language, but especially so with C. As noted above, C's highly flexible nature makes it possible for programmers to write code that is all but unreadable. The programming examples in this book follow one set of conventions, but there are other, equally valid, conventions in use. (We'll discuss some of the alternatives from time to time.) Which set you use is less important than adopting *some* conventions and sticking to them.

■ *Avoid "tricks" and overly complex code.* C encourages programming tricks. There are usually several ways to accomplish a given task in C; programmers are often tempted to choose the method that's most concise. Don't get carried away; the shortest solution is often the hardest to comprehend. In this book, I'll illustrate a style that's reasonably concise but still understandable.

■ *Use Standard C rather than Classic C.* Standard C is more than just a better-defined version of Classic C. It actually adds features that allow compilers to detect errors that go unnoticed in Classic C.

■ *Avoid nonportable features.* Most C compilers provide features and library functions that aren't part of the C standard. It's best to avoid using these unless they're absolutely necessary.

Q & A

Q: What is this Q & A section anyway?

A: Glad you asked. The Q & A section, which appears at the end of each chapter, serves several purposes.

The primary purpose of Q & A is to tackle questions that are frequently asked by students learning C. The reader can participate in a dialogue (more or less) with the author, much the same as if you were attending one of my C classes.

Another purpose of Q & A is to provide additional information about topics covered in the chapter. Readers of this book will likely have widely varying backgrounds. Some will be experienced in other programming languages, while others will be learning to program for the first time. Readers with experience in a variety of languages may be satisfied with a brief explanation and a couple of examples, while readers with less experience need more. The bottom line: If you find the coverage of a topic to be sketchy, check Q & A for more details.

Some of the questions in Q&A cover material too advanced or too esoteric to interest the average reader; questions of this nature are marked with an asterisk (*). *Warning:* These questions often refer to material covered in later chapters. Curious readers with a fair bit of programming experience may wish to delve into these questions immediately; others should definitely skip them on a first reading.

On occasion, Q & A will discuss common differences among C compilers. For example, we'll cover some frequently used (but nonstandard) features that are provided by DOS and UNIX compilers.

Q: Besides C, are there any other modern-day descendants of Algol 60? [p. 2]

A: Yes. Algol 60 is the ancestor of Pascal, Ada, and Modula-2, among others. These languages are the cousins of C; although they may look different from C, they have much in common with it.

Q: What does `lint` do? [p. 6]

A: `lint` checks a C program for potential errors. It produces a list of diagnostic messages, which the programmer must then sift through. The advantage of using `lint` is that it can detect errors that are missed by the compiler. On the other hand, you've got to remember to use `lint`; it's all too easy to forget about it. Worse still, `lint` can produce messages by the hundreds, of which only a fraction refer to actual errors.

Q: Where did `lint` get its name?

A: Unlike the names of many other UNIX tools, `lint` isn't an acronym; it got its name from the way it picks up pieces of "fluff" from a program.

Q: How do I get a copy of `lint`?

A: If you're using UNIX, then you automatically have access to `lint`, which is a standard UNIX utility. If you rely on another operating system, then you probably don't have `lint`. Fortunately, versions of `lint` are available from third parties.

*Q: I've heard that `gcc` (the GNU C compiler) can check a program as thoroughly as `lint`. Is this true?

A: When it's run with the `-Wall` option, `gcc` does indeed perform a thorough check of the program. It still misses some problems that `lint` can spot, however.

*Q: I'm interested in making my program as reliable as possible. Are there any other tools available besides `lint` and debuggers?

A: Yes. Other common tools include "bounds-checkers" and "leak-finders." C doesn't require that array subscripts be checked; a bounds-checker adds this capability. A leak-finder helps locate "memory leaks": blocks of memory that are dynamically allocated but never deallocated.

2 C Fundamentals

One man's constant is another man's variable.

This chapter introduces several basic concepts, including *preprocessor directives*, *functions, variables,* and *statements,* that we'll need in order to write even the simplest programs. Later chapters will cover these topics in much greater detail.

To start off, Section 2.1 presents a small C program and describes how to compile and link it. Section 2.2 then discusses how to generalize the program, and Section 2.3 shows how to add explanatory remarks, known as *comments.* Section 2.4 introduces variables, which store data that may change during the execution of a program, and Section 2.5 shows how to use the scanf function to read data into variables. Constants—data that won't change during program execution—can be given names, as Section 2.6 shows. Finally, Section 2.7 explains C's rules for creating names (*identifiers*) and Section 2.8 gives the rules for laying out a program.

2.1 Writing a Simple Program

In contrast to programs written in some languages, C programs require little "boilerplate"—a complete program can be as short as a few lines.

PROGRAM **Printing a Pun**

The first program in Kernighan and Ritchie's classic *The C Programming Language* is extremely short; it does nothing but write the message hello, world. Unlike other C authors, I won't use this program as my first example. I will, however, uphold another C tradition: the bad pun. Here's the pun:

```
To C, or not to C: that is the question.
```

The following program, which we'll name `pun.c,` displays this message each time it is run.

pun.c

```
#include <stdio.h>

main()
{
  printf("To C, or not to C: that is the question.\n");
}
```

Section 2.2 explains the form of this program in some detail. For now, I'll just make a few brief observations. The line

```
#include <stdio.h>
```

is necessary to "include" information about the C standard input/output library. The program's executable code goes inside `main`, which represents the "main" program. The only line inside `main` is a command to display the desired message. `printf` is a function from the standard I/O library that can produce nicely formatted output. The `\n` code tells `printf` to advance to the next line after printing the message.

Compiling and Linking

Despite its brevity, getting `pun.c` to run is more involved than you might expect. First, we need to create a file named `pun.c` containing the program (any editor will do). The name of the file doesn't matter, but the `.c` extension is often required by compilers.

Next, we've got to convert the program to a form that the machine can execute. For a C program, that usually involves three steps:

- *Preprocessing.* The program is first given to a *preprocessor*, which obeys commands that begin with # (known as *directives*). A preprocessor is a bit like an editor; it can add things to the program and make modifications.

- *Compiling.* The modified program now goes to a *compiler*, which translates it into machine instructions (*object code*). The program isn't quite ready to run yet, though.

- *Linking.* In the final step, a *linker* combines the object code produced by the compiler with any additional code needed to yield a complete executable program. This additional code includes library functions (like `printf`) that are used in the program.

Fortunately, this process is often automated, so you won't find it too onerous. In fact, the preprocessor is usually integrated with the compiler, so you probably won't even notice it at work.

The commands necessary to compile and link vary, depending on the compiler and operating system. Under UNIX, the C compiler is usually named `cc`. To compile and link the `pun.c` program, enter the following command:

```
% cc pun.c
```

(The % character is the UNIX prompt.) Linking is automatic when using cc; no separate link command is necessary.

After compiling and linking the program, cc leaves the executable program in a file named a.out by default. cc has many options; one of them (the -o option) allows us to choose the name of the file containing the executable program. For example, if we want the executable version of pun.c to be named pun, we would enter the following command:

```
% cc -o pun pun.c
```

The GNU C Compiler

One of the most popular UNIX compilers is gcc ("GNU C compiler"), which is available for a wide variety of platforms. gcc comes from the Free Software Foundation, an organization set up by Richard M. Stallman as a protest against the restrictions (and high cost) of licensed UNIX software. The Foundation's GNU project has rewritten much traditional UNIX software from scratch and made it publicly available at no charge. GNU, which stands for "GNU's Not UNIX!," is pronounced *guh-new*, by the way.

If you're using gcc, it's a good idea to use the -Wall option when compiling:

```
% gcc -Wall -o pun pun.c
```

The -Wall option causes gcc to check the program more thoroughly than usual and warn of possible problems.

On a personal computer, there are often at least two ways to compile and link a program: we can either use the command line as in UNIX or we can use an "integrated development environment" that allows us to edit, compile, link, execute, and even debug a program without leaving the environment.

2.2   The General Form of a Simple Program

Let's take a closer look at pun.c and see how we can generalize it a bit. Simple C programs have the form

directives

```
main()
{
    statements
}
```

In this template, and in similar templates elsewhere in this book, items printed in Courier would appear in a C program exactly as shown; items in *italics* represent text to be supplied by the programmer.

Notice how the braces show where main begins and ends. C uses { and } in much the same way that other languages use words like begin and end. This illustrates a general point about C: it relies heavily on abbreviations and special symbols, one reason that C programs are concise (or—less charitably—cryptic).

Q&A

Even the simplest C programs rely on three key language features: *directives* (editing commands that modify the program prior to compilation), *functions* (named blocks of executable code, of which main is an example), and *statements* (commands to be performed when the program is run). We'll take a closer look at these features now.

Directives

Before a C program is compiled, it is first edited by a ***preprocessor***. Commands intended for the preprocessor are called ***directives***. We'll cover these in detail later. For now, we're interested only in the #include directive.

The pun.c program begins with the line

```
#include <stdio.h>
```

This directive states that the information in <stdio.h> is to be "included" into the program before it is compiled. <stdio.h> contains information about C's standard input/output library. C has a number of ***headers*** like <stdio.h>; each contains information about some part of the standard library. The reason we're including <stdio.h> is that C, unlike many programming languages, has no built-in "read" and "write" commands. The ability to perform I/O is provided instead by functions in the standard library.

headers ➤ 15.2

Directives always begin with a # character, which distinguishes them from other items in a C program. By default, directives are one line long; there's no semicolon or other special marker at the end of a directive.

Functions

Functions are like "procedures" or "subroutines" in other programming languages—they're the building blocks from which programs are constructed. In fact, a C program is little more than a collection of functions. Functions fall into two categories: those written by the programmer and those provided as part of the C implementation. I'll refer to the latter as ***library functions***, since they belong to a "library" of functions that are supplied with the compiler.

The term "function" comes from mathematics, where a function is a rule for computing a value when given one or more arguments:

$$f(x) = x + 1$$
$$g(y, z) = y^2 - z^2$$

C uses the term "function" more loosely. In C, a function is simply a series of statements that have been grouped together and given a name. Some functions compute a value; some don't. A function that computes a value uses the `return` statement to specify what value it "returns." For example, a function that adds 1 to its argument might execute the statement

```
return x + 1;
```

while a function that computes the difference of the squares of its arguments might execute the statement

```
return y * y - z * z;
```

 Although a C program may consist of many functions, only the `main` function is mandatory. `main` is special: it gets called automatically when the program is executed. Until Chapter 9, where we'll learn how to write other functions, `main` will be the only function in our programs.

⚠ The name `main` is critical; it can't be `begin` or `start` or even `MAIN`.

If `main` is a function, does it return a value? Yes: it returns a status code that is given to the operating system when the program terminates. We'll have more to say about `main`'s return value in a later chapter. For now, we'll always have `main` return the value 0, which indicates normal program termination.

return value of main ➤9.5

Q&A

In the interest of simplicity, I omitted the `return` statement from the original version of `pun.c`. Here's the program with `return` added:

```
#include <stdio.h>

main()
{
  printf("To C, or not to C: that is the question.\n");
  return 0;
}
```

Q&A It's a good idea to end `main` with a `return` statement such as this one; some compilers will generate a warning message otherwise.

Statements

A *statement* is a command to be executed when the program runs. We'll be exploring statements later in the book, primarily in Chapters 5 and 6. The `pun.c` program uses only two kinds of statements. One is the `return` statement; the other is the *function call*. Asking a function to perform its assigned task is known as *calling* the function. The `pun.c` program, for example, calls the `printf` function to display a string on the screen:

```
printf("To C, or not to C: that is the question.\n");
```

compound statement ➤ 5.2

C requires that each statement end with a semicolon. (As with any good rule, there's one exception: the compound statement, which we'll encounter later.) The semicolon shows the compiler where the statement ends; since statements can continue over several lines, it's not always obvious where they end. Directives, on the other hand, are one line long, and they *don't* end with a semicolon.

Printing Strings

printf is a powerful function that we'll explore in Chapter 3. So far, we've only used printf to display a *string literal*—a series of characters enclosed in double quotation marks. When printf displays a string literal, it doesn't show the quotation marks.

printf doesn't automatically advance to the next output line when it finishes printing. To instruct printf to advance one line, we must include \n (the *new-line character*) in the string to be printed. Writing a new-line character terminates the current output line; subsequent output goes onto the next line. To illustrate this point, consider the effect of replacing the statement

```
printf("To C, or not to C: that is the question.\n");
```

by two calls of printf:

```
printf("To C, or not to C: ");
printf("that is the question.\n");
```

The first call of printf writes To C, or not to C: . The second call writes that is the question. and advances to the next line. The net effect is the same as the original printf; the user can't tell the difference.

The new-line character can appear more than once in a string literal. To display the message

```
Brevity is the soul of wit.
  --Shakespeare
```

we could write

```
printf("Brevity is the soul of wit.\n  --Shakespeare\n");
```

2.3 Comments

Our pun.c program still lacks something important: documentation. Every program should contain identifying information: the program name, the date written, the author, the purpose of the program, and so forth. In C, this information is placed in *comments*. The symbol /* marks the beginning of a comment and the symbol */ marks the end:

```
/* This is a comment */
```

Comments may appear almost anywhere in a program, either on separate lines or on the same lines as other program text. Here's what pun.c might look like with comments added at the beginning:

```
/* Name: pun.c                */
/* Purpose: Prints a bad pun. */
/* Author: K. N. King         */
/* Date written: 5/21/95      */

#include <stdio.h>

main()
{
  printf("To C, or not to C: that is the question.\n");
  return 0;
}
```

Comments can extend over more than one line; once it has seen the /* symbol, the compiler reads (and ignores) whatever follows until it encounters the */ symbol. If we like, we can combine a series of short comments into one long comment:

```
/* Name: pun.c
   Purpose: Prints a bad pun.
   Author: K. N. King
   Date written: 5/21/95 */
```

A comment like this can be hard to read, though: someone reading the program can't easily tell where the comment ends. Putting */ on a line by itself helps:

```
/* Name: pun.c
   Purpose: Prints a bad pun.
   Author: K. N. King
   Date written: 5/21/95
*/
```

Even better, we can form a "box" around the comment to make it stand out:

```
/**********************************************************
 * Name: pun.c                                            *
 * Purpose: Prints a bad pun.                             *
 * Author: K. N. King                                     *
 * Date written: 5/21/95                                  *
 **********************************************************/
```

Some programmers simplify boxed comments by omitting three of the sides:

```
/*
 * Name: pun.c
 * Purpose: Prints a bad pun.
 * Author: K. N. King
 * Date written: 5/21/95
 */
```

A short comment can go on the same line with other program code:

```
main()    /* Beginning of main program */
```

A comment like this is sometimes called a "winged comment."

Forgetting to terminate a comment may cause the compiler to ignore part of your program. Consider the following example:

```
printf("My ");     /* forgot to close this comment...
printf("cat ");
printf("has ");    /* so it ends here */
printf("fleas");
```

Because we've neglected to terminate the first comment, this example prints My fleas; the compiler ignores the middle two statements.

2.4 Variables and Assignment

Few programs are as simple as the one in Section 2.1. Most programs need to perform a series of calculations before producing output, and thus need a way to store data temporarily during program execution. In C, as in most programming languages, these storage locations are called *variables*.

Types

Every variable must have a *type*, which specifies what kind of data it will hold. C has a wide variety of types. For now, we'll limit ourselves to just two: int and float. Choosing the proper type is critical, since the type affects how the variable is stored and what operations can be performed on the variable. The type of a numeric variable determines the largest and smallest numbers that the variable can store; it also determines whether or not digits are allowed after the decimal point.

A variable of type int (short for *integer*) can store a whole number, like 0, 1, 392, or –2553. The range of possible values is limited, though. On some computers, the largest int value is only 32,767.

range of int values ➤7.1

A variable of type float (short for *floating-point*) can store much larger numbers than an int variable. Furthermore, a float variable can store numbers with digits after the decimal point, like 379.125. float variables have drawbacks, however. They require more space than int variables. Arithmetic on float numbers is usually slower than arithmetic on int numbers. Moreover, the value of a float variable is often just an approximation of the number that was stored in it. If we store 9,999,999,999 in a float variable, we may later find that the variable has the value 10,000,000,000, thanks to rounding error.

Declarations

Variables must be *declared*—described for the benefit of the compiler—before they can be used. To declare a variable, we first specify the *type* of the variable, then its *name*. (Variable names are chosen by the programmer, subject to the rules described in Section 2.7.) For example, we might declare variables `height` and `profit` as follows:

```
int height;
float profit;
```

The first declaration states that `height` is a variable of type `int`, meaning that `height` can store an integer value. The second declaration says that `profit` is a variable of type `float`.

If several variables have the same type, their declarations can be combined:

```
int height, length, width, volume;
float profit, loss;
```

Notice that each complete declaration ends with a semicolon.

Our first template for `main` didn't include declarations. When `main` contains declarations, these must precede the statements:

```
main()
{
    declarations
    statements
}
```

As a matter of style, it's a good idea to leave a blank line between the declarations and the statements.

Assignment

A variable can be given a value by means of *assignment*. For example, the statements

```
height = 8;
length = 12;
width = 10;
```

assign the values 8, 12, and 10 to `height`, `length`, and `width`, respectively.

Once a variable has been assigned a value, it can be used to help compute the value of another variable:

```
volume = height * length * width;
```

In C, `*` represents the multiplication operator, so this statement multiplies the values stored in `height`, `length`, and `width`, then assigns the result to the variable `volume`. In general, the right side of an assignment can be a formula (or *expression*, in C terminology) involving constants, variables, and operators.

Printing the Value of a Variable

We can use `printf` to display the current value of a variable. For example, to write the message

```
Height: n
```

where *n* is the current value of the `height` variable, we'd use the following call of `printf`:

```
printf("Height: %d\n", height);
```

`%d` is a placeholder indicating where the value of `height` is to be filled in during printing. Note the placement of `\n` just after `%d`, so that `printf` will advance to the next line after printing the value of `height`.

`%d` works only for `int` variables; to print a `float` variable, we'd use `%f` instead. By default, `%f` displays a number with six digits after the decimal point. To force `%f` to display *n* digits after the decimal point, we can put `.n` between `%` and `f`. For example, to print the line

```
Profit: $2150.48
```

we'd call `printf` as follows:

```
printf("Profit: $%.2f\n", profit);
```

There's no limit to the number of variables that can be printed by a single call of `printf`. To display the values of both the `height` and `length` variables, we could use the following call of `printf`:

```
printf("Height: %d  Length: %d\n", height, length);
```

PROGRAM ## Computing the Dimensional Weight of a Box

Shipping companies don't especially like boxes that are large but very light, since they take up valuable space in a truck or airplane. In fact, companies often charge extra for such a box, basing the fee on its volume instead of its weight. The usual method is to divide the volume by 166 (the allowable number of cubic inches per pound). If this number—the box's "dimensional" or "volumetric" weight—exceeds its actual weight, the shipping fee is based on the dimensional weight.

Let's say that you've been hired by a shipping company to write a program that computes the dimensional weight of a box. Since you're new to C, you decide to start off by writing a program that calculates the dimensional weight of a particular box that's 12″ × 10″ × 8″. Division is represented by / in C, so the obvious way to compute the dimensional weight would be

```
weight = volume / 166;
```

where `weight` and `volume` are integer variables representing the box's weight and volume. Unfortunately, this formula isn't quite what we need. In C, when one integer is divided by another, the answer is "truncated": all digits after the decimal point are lost. The volume of a $12'' \times 10'' \times 8''$ box will be 960 cubic inches. Dividing by 166 gives the answer 5 instead of 5.783, so we have in effect rounded *down* to the next lowest pound; the shipping company expects us to round *up*. One solution is to add 165 to the volume before dividing by 166:

```
weight = (volume + 165) / 166;
```

A volume of 166 would give a weight of 331/166, or 1, while a volume of 167 would yield 332/166, or 2. Calculating the weight in this fashion gives us the following program.

dweight.c

```
/* Computes the dimensional weight of a 12" x 10" x 8" box */

#include <stdio.h>

main()
{
  int height, length, width, volume, weight;

  height = 8;
  length = 12;
  width = 10;
  volume = height * length * width;
  weight = (volume + 165) / 166;

  printf("Dimensions: %dx%dx%d\n", length, width, height);
  printf("Volume (cubic inches): %d\n", volume);
  printf("Dimensional weight (pounds): %d\n", weight);

  return 0;
}
```

The output of the program is

```
Dimensions: 12x10x8
Volume (cubic inches): 960
Dimensional weight (pounds): 6
```

Initialization

variable initialization ➤ *18.5*
Some variables are automatically set to zero when a program begins to execute, but most are not. As a result, we can't usually predict what the value of a variable will be initially; it might be 2568, –30891, or some equally strange number.

We can always give a variable an initial value by using assignment, of course. But there's an easier way: put the initial value of the variable in its declaration. For example, we can declare the height variable and initialize it in one step:

```
int height = 8;
```

In C jargon, the value 8 is said to be an ***initializer***.

Any number of variables can be initialized in the same declaration:

```
int height = 8, length = 12, width = 10;
```

Notice that each variable requires its own initializer. In the following example, the initializer 10 is good only for the variable width, not for height or length (whose values remain unknown):

```
int height, length, width = 10;
```

Printing Expressions

printf isn't limited to displaying numbers stored in variables; it can display the value of *any* numeric expression. Taking advantage of this property can simplify a program and reduce the number of variables. For instance, the statements

```
volume = height * length * width;
printf("%d\n", volume);
```

could be replaced by

```
printf("%d\n", height * length * width);
```

printf's ability to print expressions illustrates one of C's general principles: *Wherever a value is needed, any expression of the same type will do.*

2.5   Reading Input

The dweight.c program isn't especially useful, since it only calculates the dimensional weight of one box. To improve the program, we'll need to allow the user to enter the dimensions.

To obtain input, we'll use the scanf function, the C library's counterpart to printf. The f in scanf, like the f in printf, stands for "formatted"; both scanf and printf require the use of a *format string* to specify the appearance of the input or output data. scanf needs to know what form the input data will take, just as printf needs to know how to display output data.

To read an int value, we'd use scanf as follows:

```
scanf("%d", &i);    /* reads an integer; stores into i */
```

& operator ➤ 11.2

The "%d" string tells scanf to read input that represents an integer; i is an int variable into which we want scanf to store the input. The & symbol is hard to explain at this point; for now, I'll just note that it is usually (but not always) required when using scanf.

Reading a float value requires a slightly different call of scanf:

```
scanf("%f", &x);    /* reads a float value; stores into x */
```

%f works only with variables of type float, so I'm assuming that x is a float variable. The "%f" string tells scanf to look for an input value in float format (the number may contain a decimal point, but doesn't have to).

PROGRAM   **Computing the Dimensional Weight of a Box (Revisited)**

Here's an improved version of the dimensional weight program in which the user enters the dimensions. Note that each call of scanf is immediately preceded by a call of printf. That way, the user will know when to enter input and what input to enter.

dweight2.c
```
/* Computes the dimensional weight of a box */
/* from input provided by the user          */

#include <stdio.h>

main()
{
  int height, length, width, volume, weight;

  printf("Enter height of box: ");
  scanf("%d", &height);
  printf("Enter length of box: ");
  scanf("%d", &length);
  printf("Enter width of box: ");
  scanf("%d", &width);
  volume = height * length * width;
  weight = (volume + 165) / 166;

  printf("Volume (cubic inches): %d\n", volume);
  printf("Dimensional weight (pounds): %d\n", weight);

  return 0;
}
```

The output of the program has the following appearance (input entered by the user is underlined):

```
Enter height of box: 8
Enter length of box: 12
Enter width of box: 10
Volume (cubic inches): 960
Dimensional weight (pounds): 6
```

2.6   **Defining Constants**

When a program contains *constants*—values that don't change during execution—it's often a good idea to give them names. The dweight.c and dweight2.c programs rely on the constant 166, whose meaning may not be at all clear to someone reading the program later. Using a feature known as ***macro definition***, we can name this constant:

```
#define CUBIC_IN_PER_LB 166
```

`#define` is a preprocessor directive, just as `#include` is, so there's no semicolon at the end of the line.

When a program is compiled, the preprocessor replaces each macro by the value that it represents. For example, the statement

```
weight = (volume + CUBIC_IN_PER_LB - 1) / CUBIC_IN_PER_LB;
```

will become

```
weight = (volume + 166 - 1) / 166;
```

giving the same effect as if we'd written the latter statement in the first place.

A macro can also be defined in terms of an expression:

```
#define SCALE_FACTOR (5.0 / 9.0)
```

parentheses in macros ➤ *14.3*   When it contains operators, the expression should be enclosed in parentheses.

Notice that we've used only upper-case letters in names of constants. This is a convention that most C programmers follow, not a requirement of the language. (Still, C programmers have been doing this for decades; you wouldn't want to be the first to deviate.)

PROGRAM   **Converting from Fahrenheit to Celsius**

The following program prompts the user to enter a Fahrenheit temperature; it then prints the equivalent Celsius temperature. The output of the program will have the following appearance (as usual, input entered by the user is underlined):

```
Enter Fahrenheit temperature: 212
Celsius equivalent: 100.0
```

The program will allow temperatures that aren't integers; that's why the Celsius temperature is displayed as `100.0` instead of `100`. Let's look first at the entire program, then see how it's put together.

celsius.c
```
/* Converts a Fahrenheit temperature to Celsius */

#include <stdio.h>

#define FREEZING_PT 32.0
#define SCALE_FACTOR (5.0 / 9.0)

main()
{
  float fahrenheit, celsius;
```

```
    printf("Enter Fahrenheit temperature: ");
    scanf("%f", &fahrenheit);

    celsius = (fahrenheit - FREEZING_PT) * SCALE_FACTOR;

    printf("Celsius equivalent: %.1f\n", celsius);

    return 0;
}
```

The statement

```
celsius = (fahrenheit - FREEZING_PT) * SCALE_FACTOR;
```

converts the Fahrenheit temperature to Celsius. Since FREEZING_PT stands for 32.0 and SCALE_FACTOR stands for (5.0 / 9.0), the compiler sees this statement as

```
celsius = (fahrenheit - 32.0) * (5.0 / 9.0);
```

Defining SCALE_FACTOR to be (5.0 / 9.0) instead of (5 / 9) is important, because C truncates the result when two integers are divided. The value of (5 / 9) would be 0, which definitely isn't what we want.

The call of printf writes the Celsius temperature:

```
printf("Celsius equivalent: %.1f\n", celsius);
```

Notice the use of %.1f to display celsius with just one digit after the decimal point.

2.7 Identifiers

As we're writing a program, we'll have to choose names for variables, functions, macros, and other entities. These names are called *identifiers*. In C, an identifier may contain letters, digits, and underscores, but must begin with a letter or underscore. Here are some examples of legal identifiers:

```
times10   get_next_char   _done
```

The following are *not* legal identifiers:

```
10times   get-next-char
```

The symbol 10times begins with a digit, not a letter or underscore. get-next-char contains minus signs, not underscores.

C is *case-sensitive:* it distinguishes between upper-case and lower-case letters in identifiers. For example, the following identifiers are all different:

```
job   joB   jOb   jOB   Job   JoB   JOb   JOB
```

These eight identifiers could all be used simultaneously, each for a completely different purpose. (Talk about obfuscation!) Sensible programmers try to make identifiers look different unless they're somehow related.

Since case matters in C, many programmers follow the convention of using only lower-case letters in identifiers (other than macros), with underscores inserted when necessary for legibility:

```
symbol_table   current_page   name_and_address
```

Other programmers avoid underscores, instead using an upper-case letter to begin each word in an identifier:

```
SymbolTable   CurrentPage   NameAndAddress
```

Other reasonable conventions exist; just be sure to capitalize an identifier the same way each time it appears in a program.

Standard C places no limit on the maximum length of an identifier, so don't be afraid to use long, descriptive names. A name such as current_page is a lot easier to understand than a name like cp.

Keywords

In Standard C, the *keywords* in Table 2.1 have special significance to the compiler and therefore can't be used as identifiers.

Table 2.1
Keywords

auto	double	int	struct
break	else	long	switch
case	enum	register	typedef
char	extern	return	union
const	float	short	unsigned
continue	for	signed	void
default	goto	sizeof	volatile
do	if	static	while

Because of C's case-sensitivity, keywords must appear in programs exactly as shown in Table 2.1, with all letters in lower case. Names of functions in the standard library (such as printf) contain only lower-case letters also. Avoid the plight of the unfortunate programmer who enters an entire program in upper case, only to find that the compiler can't recognize keywords and calls of library functions.

restrictions on identifiers ➤*21.1*

Watch out for other restrictions on identifiers. Some compilers treat certain identifiers (asm, far, and near, for example) as additional keywords. Identifiers that belong to the standard library are restricted as well. Accidentally using one of these names can cause an error during compilation or linking. Identifiers that begin with an underscore are also restricted.

2.8 Layout of a C Program

tokens ➤ *Appendix A* We can think of a C program as a series of *tokens:* groups of characters that can't be split up without changing their meaning. Identifiers and keywords are tokens. So are operators like + and –, punctuation marks such as the comma and semicolon, and string literals. For example, the statement

```
printf("Height: %d\n", height);
```

consists of seven tokens:

```
printf    (      "Height: %d\n"     ,     height     )     ;
  ①       ②            ③            ④       ⑤        ⑥     ⑦
```

Tokens ① and ⑤ are identifiers, token ③ is a string literal, and tokens ②, ④, ⑥, and ⑦ are punctuation.

The amount of space between tokens in a program isn't critical in most cases. At one extreme, tokens can be crammed together with no space between them at all, except where this would cause two tokens to merge into a third token. For example, we could delete most of the space in the celsius.c program of Section 2.6, provided that we leave space between tokens such as float and fahrenheit.

```
/* Converts a Fahrenheit temperature to Celsius */
#include <stdio.h>
#define FREEZING_PT 32.0
#define SCALE_FACTOR (5.0/9.0)
main(){float fahrenheit,celsius;printf(
"Enter Fahrenheit temperature: ");scanf("%f", &fahrenheit);
celsius=(fahrenheit-FREEZING_PT)*SCALE_FACTOR;
printf("Celsius equivalent: %.1f\n", celsius);return 0;}
```

In fact, if the page were wider, we could put the entire main function on a single line. We can't put the whole *program* on one line, though, because each preprocessor directive requires a separate line.

Compressing programs in this fashion isn't a good idea. In fact, adding spaces and blank lines to a program can make it easier to read and understand. Fortunately, C allows us to insert any amount of space—blanks, tabs, and new-line characters—between tokens. This rule has several important consequences for program layout:

■ *Statements can be divided* over any number of lines. The following statement, for example, is so long that it would be hard to squeeze it onto a single line:

```
printf("Dimensional weight (pounds): %d\n",
   (volume + CUBIC_IN_PER_LB - 1) / CUBIC_IN_PER_LB);
```

- *Space between tokens* makes it easier for the eye to separate them. For this reason, I usually put a space before and after each operator:

```
volume = height * length * width;
```

I also put a space after each comma. Some programmers go even further, putting spaces around parentheses and other punctuation.

Q&A

- *Indentation* can make nesting easier to spot. For example, we should indent declarations and statements to make it clear that they're nested inside `main`.
- *Blank lines* can divide a program into logical units, making it easier for the reader to discern the program's structure. A program with no blank lines is as hard to read as a book with no chapters.

The `celsius.c` program of Section 2.6 illustrates several of these guidelines. Let's take a closer look at the `main` function in that program:

```
main()
{
  float fahrenheit, celsius;

  printf("Enter Fahrenheit temperature: ");
  scanf("%f", &fahrenheit);

  celsius = (fahrenheit - FREEZING_PT) * SCALE_FACTOR;

  printf("Celsius equivalent: %.1f\n", celsius);

  return 0;
}
```

First, observe how the space around =, –, and * makes these operators stand out. Second, notice how the indentation of declarations and statements makes it obvious that they all belong to `main`. Finally, note how blank lines divide `main` into five parts: (1) declaring the `fahrenheit` and `celsius` variables; (2) obtaining the Fahrenheit temperature; (3) calculating the value of `celsius`; (4) printing the Celsius temperature; and (5) returning to the operating system.

While we're on the subject of program layout, notice how I've placed the { token underneath `main()` and put the matching } on a separate line, aligned with {. Putting } on a separate line lets us insert or delete statements at the end of the function; aligning it with { makes it easy to spot the end of `main`.

A final note: Although extra spaces can be added *between* tokens, it's not possible to add space *within* a token without changing the meaning of the program or causing an error. Writing

```
fl oat fahrenheit, celsius;    /*** WRONG ***/
```

or

```
fl
oat fahrenheit, celsius;        /*** WRONG ***/
```

produces an error when the program is compiled. Putting a space inside a string literal is allowed, although it changes the meaning of the string. Putting a new-line character in a string (in other words, splitting the string over two lines) is illegal, though:

```
printf("To C, or not to C:
that is the question.\n");     /*** WRONG ***/
```

Continuing a string from one line to the next requires a special technique that we'll learn in a later chapter.

continuing a string ➤ *13.1*

Q & A

Q: **Why is C so terse? It seems as though programs would be more readable if C used `begin` and `end` instead of { and }, `integer` instead of `int`, and so forth. [p. 12]**

A: Legend has it that the brevity of C programs is due to the environment that existed in Bell Labs at the time the language was developed. The first C compiler ran on a DEC PDP-11 (an early minicomputer); programmers used a teletype—essentially a typewriter connected to a computer—to enter programs and print listings. Since teletypes were very slow (they could print only 10 characters per second), minimizing the number of characters in a program was clearly advantageous.

Q: **In some C books, the `main` function ends with `exit(0)` instead of `return 0`. Are these the same? [p. 13]**

A: When they appear inside `main`, these statements are indeed equivalent: both terminate the program, returning the value 0 to the operating system. Which one to use is mostly a matter of taste.

Q: **What happens if a program terminates without executing a `return` statement? [p. 13]**

A: *Some* value will be returned to the operating system, but there's no guarantee what it will be. As long as the program's status is never tested once it terminates, there shouldn't be any problem.

Q: **Does the compiler remove a comment entirely or replace it with blank space?**

A: Some older C compilers simply delete all the characters in each comment, making it possible to write

```
a/**/b = 0;
```

and have the compiler interpret it as

```
ab = 0;
```

According to the C standard, however, the compiler must replace each comment by a single space character, so this trick doesn't work. Instead, we'd end up with the following (illegal) statement:

```
a b = 0;
```

Q: How can I tell if my program has an unterminated comment?

A: If you're lucky, the program won't compile because the comment has rendered the program illegal. If the program does compile, there are several techniques that you can use. Stepping through the program line by line with a debugger will reveal if any lines are being skipped. Some development environments display programs in color, with comments in a different color to distinguish them from the surrounding code. If you're using such an environment, you can easily spot unterminated comments, since program text will have a different color if it's accidentally included in a comment. A program such as `lint` can also help.

lint ➤*1.2*

Q: Is it legal to nest one comment inside another?

A: Not in Standard C. For instance, the following code is illegal:

```
/*
   /*** WRONG ***/
*/
```

The `*/` symbol on the second line matches the `/*` symbol on the first line, so the compiler will flag the `*/` symbol on the third line as an error.

C's prohibition against nested comments can sometimes be a problem. Suppose we've written a long program containing many short comments. To disable a portion of the program temporarily (during testing, say), our first impulse is to "comment out" the offending lines with `/*` and `*/`. Unfortunately, this method won't work if the lines contain comments. As we'll see later, there's a better way to disable portions of a program.

disabling code ➤*14.4*

Q: I've seen C programs containing comments that begin with `//` instead of `/*`, and don't have `*/` at the end:

```
// This is a comment.
```

Is this practice legal?

A: Not in Standard C. Using `//` to begin a comment is a C++ practice that some C compilers also allow. Avoid the urge to use `//`; other compilers may not support it, so you'll end up with a nonportable program.

Q: Where does the `float` type get its name? [p. 16]

A: `float` is short for "floating-point," a technique for storing numbers in which the decimal point "floats." A `float` value is usually stored in two parts: the ***fraction*** (or ***mantissa***) and the ***exponent***. The number 12.0 might be stored as 1.5×2^3, for example, where 1.5 is the fraction and 3 is the exponent. Some programming languages call this type `real` instead of `float`.

*Q: **Is it really true that there's no limit on the length of an identifier? [p. 24]**

A: Yes and no. The C standard says that identifiers may be arbitrarily long. However, compilers are only required to remember the first 31 characters. Thus, if two names begin with the same 31 characters, a compiler might be unable to distinguish between them.

external linkage ➤ *18.2* To make matters even more complicated, the C standard has special rules for identifiers with external linkage; most function names fall into this category. Since these names must be made available to the linker, and since some older linkers can handle only short names, the standard says that only the first six characters are significant. Moreover, the case of letters doesn't matter. As a result, ABCDEFG and abcdefh might be treated as the same name.

Most compilers and linkers are more generous than the standard, so these rules aren't a problem in practice. Don't worry about making identifiers too long—worry about making them too short.

Q: **How many spaces should I use for indentation? [p. 26]**

A: That's a tough question. Leave too little space, and the eye has trouble detecting indentation. Leave too much, and lines run off the screen (or page). Many C programmers indent nested statements eight spaces (one tab stop), but four is also common. Indenting eight spaces is probably too much, especially when some screens and printers are limited to 80 columns. Studies have shown that the optimum amount of indentation is three spaces. I'll use two spaces in this book, however, so that programs will fit within the margins.

Exercises

Section 2.1

1. Create and run Kernighan and Ritchie's famous "hello, world" program:

```
#include <stdio.h>

main()
{
  printf("hello, world\n");
}
```

Do you get a warning message from the compiler? If so, what's needed to make it go away?

Section 2.2

2. Consider the following program:

```
#include <stdio.h>

main()
{
  printf("Parkinson's Law:\nWork expands so as to ");
  printf("fill the time\n");
  printf("available for its completion.\n");
  return 0;
}
```

(a) Identify the directives and statements in this program.

(b) What output does the program produce?

3. Write a program that uses `printf` to display the following picture on the screen:

Section 2.4

4. Condense the `dweight.c` program by (1) replacing the assignments to `height`, `length`, and `width` with initializers and (2) removing the `weight` variable, instead calculating `(volume + 165) / 166` within the last `printf`.

5. Write a program that computes the volume of a sphere with a 10-meter radius, using the formula $v = 4/3\pi r^3$. Write the fraction 4/3 as `4.0/3.0`. (Try writing it as `4/3`. What happens?)

6. Write a program that declares several `int` and `float` variables—without initializing them—and then prints their values. Is there any pattern to the values? (Usually there isn't.)

Section 2.5

7. Modify the program of Exercise 5 so that it prompts the user to enter the radius of the sphere.

8. Write a program that asks the user to enter a dollar amount, then displays the amount with 5% tax added:

```
Enter a dollar amount: 100.00
With tax added: 105.00
```

Section 2.6

9. Modify Exercise 7 by making `PI` a macro that represents the value of π.

Section 2.7

10. Which of the following are not legal C identifiers?

(a) `100_bottles`

(b) `_100_bottles`

(c) `one__hundred__bottles`

(d) `bottles_by_the_hundred_`

11. Which of the following are keywords in C?

(a) `for`

(b) `If`

(c) `main`

(d) `printf`

(e) `while`

Section 2.8

12. How many tokens are there in the following statement?

```
a=(3*q-p*p)/3;
```

13. Insert spaces between the tokens in Exercise 12 to make the statement easier to read.

3 Formatted Input/Output

In seeking the unattainable, simplicity only gets in the way.

scanf and printf, which support formatted reading and writing, are two of the most frequently used functions in C. As this chapter shows, both are powerful but tricky to use properly. Section 3.1 describes printf, and Section 3.2 covers scanf. Neither section gives complete details, which will have to wait until Chapter 22.

3.1 The printf Function

The printf function is designed to display the contents of a string, the *format string,* with values possibly inserted at specified points in the string. When it is called, printf must be supplied with the format string, followed by any values that are to be inserted into the string during printing:

printf(*string*, *expr*$_1$, *expr*$_2$, ...);

The values displayed can be constants, variables, or more complicated expressions. There's no limit on the number of values that can be printed by a single call of printf.

The format string may contain both ordinary characters and *conversion specifications*, which begin with the % character. A conversion specification is a placeholder representing a value to be filled in during printing. The information that follows the % character *specifies* how the value is *converted* from its internal form (binary) to printed form (characters)—that's where the term "conversion specification" comes from. For example, the conversion specification %d specifies that printf is to convert an int value from binary to a string of decimal digits, while %f does the same for a float value.

Ordinary characters in a format string are printed exactly as they appear in the string; conversion specifications are replaced by the values to be printed. Consider the following example:

```
int i, j;
float x, y;

i = 10;
j = 20;
x = 43.2892;
y = 5527.0;

printf("i = %d, j = %d, x = %f, y = %f\n", i, j, x, y);
```

This call of `printf` produces the following output:

```
i = 10, j = 20, x = 43.289200, y = 5527.000000
```

The ordinary characters in the format string are simply copied to the output line. The four conversion specifications are replaced by the values of the variables i, j, x, and y, in that order.

 C compilers don't check that the number of conversion specifications in a format string matches the number of output items. The following call of `printf` has more conversion specifications than values to be printed:

```
printf("%d %d\n", i);    /*** WRONG ***/
```

`printf` will print the value of i correctly, then print a second (meaningless) integer value. A call with too few conversion specifications has similar problems:

```
printf("%d\n", i, j);    /*** WRONG ***/
```

In this case, `printf` prints the value of i but doesn't show the value of j.

Furthermore, there's no check that a conversion specification is appropriate for the type of item being printed. If the programmer uses an incorrect specification, the program will simply produce meaningless output. Consider the following call of `printf`, in which the int variable i and the float variable x are in the wrong order:

```
printf("%f %d\n", i, x);    /*** WRONG ***/
```

Since `printf` must obey the format string, it will dutifully display a float value, followed by an int value. Unfortunately, both will be meaningless.

Conversion Specifications

Conversion specifications give the programmer a great deal of control over the appearance of output. On the other hand, they can be complicated and hard to read. In fact, describing conversion specifications in complete detail is too arduous a task to tackle this early in the book. Instead, we'll just take a brief look at some of their more important capabilities.

In Chapter 2, we saw that a conversion specification can include formatting information. In particular, we used `%.1f` to display a `float` value with one digit after the decimal point. More generally, a conversion specification can have the form `%m.pX` or `%-m.pX`, where m and p are integer constants and X is a letter. Both m and p are optional; if p is omitted, the period that separates m and p is also dropped. In the conversion specification `%10.2f`, m is 10, p is 2, and X is f. In the specification `%10f`, m is 10 and p (along with the period) is missing, but in the specification `%.2f`, p is 2 and m is missing.

The ***minimum field width***, m, specifies the minimum number of characters to print. If the value to be printed requires fewer than m characters, the value is right-justified within the field. (In other words, extra spaces precede the value.) For example, the specification `%4d` would display the number 123 as •123. (I'm using • to represent the space character.) If the value to be printed requires more than m characters, the field width automatically expands to the necessary size. Thus, the specification `%4d` would display the number 12345 as 12345—no digits are lost. Putting a minus sign in front of m causes left justification; the specification `%-4d` would display 123 as 123•.

The meaning of the ***precision***, p, isn't as easily described, since it depends on the choice of X, the ***conversion specifier***. X indicates which conversion should be applied to the value before it is printed. The most common conversion specifiers for numbers are:

Q&A

- d—displays an integer in decimal (base 10) form. p indicates the minimum number of digits to display (extra zeros are added to the beginning of the number if necessary); if p is omitted, it is assumed to have the value 1.

- e—displays a floating-point number in exponential format (scientific notation). p indicates how many digits should appear after the decimal point (the default is 6). If p is 0, the decimal point is not displayed.

- f—displays a floating-point number in "fixed decimal" format, without an exponent. p has the same meaning as for the e specifier.

- g—displays a floating-point number in either exponential format or fixed decimal format, depending on the number's size. p indicates the maximum number of significant digits (*not* digits after the decimal point) to be displayed. Unlike the f conversion, the g conversion won't show trailing zeros. Furthermore, if the value to be printed has no digits after the decimal point, g doesn't display the decimal point.

The g specifier is especially useful for displaying numbers whose size can't be predicted when the program is written or that tend to vary widely in size. When used to print a moderately large or moderately small number, the g specifier uses fixed decimal format. But when used to print a very large or very small number, the g specifier switches to exponential format so that the number will require fewer characters.

specifiers for integers ➤ *7.1*
specifiers for floats ➤ *7.2*
specifiers for characters ➤ *7.3*
specifiers for strings ➤ *13.3*

There are many other specifiers besides `%d`, `%e`, `%f`, and `%g`. I'll gradually introduce many of them in subsequent chapters. For the full list, and for a complete explanation of the other capabilities of conversion specifications, consult Section 22.3.

PROGRAM   # Using `printf` to Format Numbers

The following program illustrates the use of `printf` to print integers and floating-point numbers in various formats.

tprintf.c

```
/* Prints int and float values in various formats */

#include <stdio.h>

main()
{
  int i;
  float x;

  i = 40;
  x = 839.21;

  printf("|%d|%5d|%-5d|%5.3d|\n", i, i, i, i);
  printf("|%10.3f|%10.3e|%-10g|\n", x, x, x);

  return 0;
}
```

The `|` characters in the `printf` format strings are there merely to help show how much space each number occupies when printed; unlike `%` or `\`, the `|` character has no special significance to `printf`. The output of this program is:

```
|40|   40|40   |  040|
|   839.210| 8.392e+02|839.21    |
```

Let's take a closer look at the conversion specifications used in this program:

- `%d`—displays `i` in decimal form, using a minimum amount of space.
- `%5d`—displays `i` in decimal form, using a minimum of five characters. Since `i` requires only two characters, three spaces were added.
- `%-5d`—displays `i` in decimal form, using a minimum of five characters; since the value of `i` doesn't require five characters, the spaces are added afterward (that is, `i` is left-justified in a field of length five).
- `%5.3d`—displays `i` in decimal form, using a minimum of five characters overall and a minimum of three digits. Since `i` is only two digits long, an extra zero was added to guarantee three digits. The resulting number is only three characters long, so two spaces were added, for a total of five characters (`i` is right-justified).

- %10.3f—displays x in fixed decimal form, using ten characters overall, with three digits after the decimal point. Since x requires only seven characters (three before the decimal point, three after the decimal point, and one for the decimal point itself), three spaces precede x.
- %10.3e—displays x in exponential form, using ten characters overall, with three digits after the decimal point. x requires nine characters altogether (including the exponent), so one space precedes x.
- %-10g—displays x in either fixed decimal form or exponential form, using ten characters overall. In this case, printf chose to display x in fixed decimal form. The presence of the minus sign forces left justification, so x is followed by four spaces.

Escape Sequences

escape sequences ➤ 7.3

The \n code that we often use in format strings is called an ***escape sequence***. Escape sequences enable strings to contain characters that would otherwise cause problems for the compiler, including nonprinting (control) characters and characters that have a special meaning to the compiler (such as "). We'll provide a complete list of escape sequences later; for now, here's a sample:

alert (bell)	\a
backspace	\b
new line	\n
horizontal tab	\t

When they appear in printf format strings, these escape sequences represent actions to perform upon printing. Printing \a causes an audible beep on most machines. Printing \b moves the cursor back one position. Printing \n advances the cursor to the beginning of the next line. Printing \t moves the cursor to the next tab stop.

A string may contain any number of escape sequences. Consider the following printf example, in which the format string contains six escape sequences:

```
printf("Item\tUnit\tPurchase\n\tPrice\tDate\n");
```

Executing this statement prints a two-line heading:

```
Item    Unit    Purchase
        Price   Date
```

Another common escape sequence is \", which represents the " character. Since the " character marks the beginning and end of a string, it can't appear within a string without the use of this escape sequence. Here's an example:

```
printf("\"Hello!\"");
```

This statement produces the following output:

```
"Hello!"
```

Incidentally, you can't just put a single \ character in a string; the compiler will assume that it's the beginning of an escape sequence. To print a single \ character, put two \ characters in the string:

```
printf("\\");    /* prints one \ character */
```

3.2 The `scanf` Function

Just as `printf` prints output in a specified format, `scanf` reads input according to a particular format. A `scanf` format string, like a `printf` format string, may contain both ordinary characters and conversion specifications. The conversions allowed with `scanf` are essentially the same as those used with `printf`.

In many cases, a `scanf` format string will contain only conversion specifications, as in the following example:

```
int i, j;
float x, y;

scanf("%d%d%f%f", &i, &j, &x, &y);
```

Suppose that the user enters the following input line:

```
1 -20 .3 -4.0e3
```

`scanf` will read the line, converting its characters to the numbers they represent, and then assign 1, –20, 0.3, and –4000.0 to `i`, `j`, `x`, and `y`, respectively. "Tightly packed" format strings like `"%d%d%f%f"` are common in `scanf` calls. `printf` format strings are less likely to have adjacent conversion specifications.

`scanf`, like `printf`, contains several traps for the unwary. When using `scanf`, the programmer must check that the number of conversion specifications matches the number of input variables and that each conversion is appropriate for the corresponding variable—as with `printf`, the compiler doesn't check for a possible mismatch. Another trap involves the `&` symbol, which normally precedes each variable in a `scanf` call. The `&` is usually (but not always) required, and it's the programmer's responsibility to remember to use it.

Forgetting to put the `&` symbol in front of a variable in a call of `scanf` will have unpredictable—and possibly disastrous—results. A program crash is a common outcome. At the very least, the value that is read from the input won't be stored in the variable; instead, the variable will retain its old value (which may be meaningless if the variable wasn't given an initial value). Omitting the `&` is an extremely common error—be careful! Some compilers can spot this error, but usually not all the time. If the variable that is missing the `&` (`i`, say) hasn't yet been assigned a value, you may get a warning such as *"Possible use of 'i' before definition."* If you get this warning, check for a missing `&`.

Calling scanf is a powerful but unforgiving way to read data. Many professional C programmers avoid scanf, instead reading all data in character form and converting it to numeric form later. We'll use scanf quite a bit, especially in the early chapters of this book, because it provides a simple way to read numbers. Be aware, however, that many of our programs won't behave properly if the user enters unexpected input. As we'll see later, it's possible to have a program test whether scanf successfully read the requested data (and attempt to recover if it didn't). Such tests are impractical for the programs in this book—they would add too many statements and obscure the point of the examples.

detecting errors in scanf ➤ 22.3

How scanf Works

scanf can actually do much more than I've indicated so far. It is essentially a "pattern-matching" function that tries to match up groups of input characters with conversion specifications.

Like printf, scanf is controlled by the format string. When it is called, scanf begins processing the information in the string, starting at the left. For each conversion specification in the format string, scanf tries to locate an item of the appropriate type in the input data, skipping blank space if necessary. scanf then reads the item, stopping when it encounters a character that can't possibly belong to the item. If the item was read successfully, scanf continues processing the rest of the format string. If any item is not read successfully, scanf returns immediately without looking at the rest of the format string (or the remaining input data).

As it searches for the beginning of a number, scanf ignores *white-space* characters (the space, horizontal and vertical tab, form-feed, and new-line characters). As a result, numbers can be put on a single line or spread out over several lines. Consider the following call of scanf:

```
scanf("%d%d%f%f", &i, &j, &x, &y);
```

Suppose that the user enters three lines of input:

```
   1
-20    .3
    -4.0e3
```

scanf sees one continuous stream of characters:

••1¤-20•••.3¤•••-4.0e3¤

(I'm using • to represent the space character and ¤ to represent the new-line character.) Since it skips over white-space characters as it looks for the beginning of each number, scanf will be able to read the numbers successfully. In the following diagram, an s under a character indicates that it was skipped, and an r indicates it was read as part of an input item:

```
••1¤-20•••.3¤•••-4.0e3¤
ssrsrrrssssrrssssrrrrrr
```

`scanf` "peeks" at the final new-line character without actually reading it. This new-line will be the first character read by the next call of `scanf`.

What rules does `scanf` follow to recognize an integer or a floating-point number? When asked to read an integer, `scanf` first searches for a digit, plus sign, or minus sign; it then reads digits until it reaches a nondigit. When asked to read a floating-point number, `scanf` looks for

> a *plus* or *minus* sign (optional), followed by
> a series of *digits* (possibly containing a decimal point), followed by
> an *exponent* (optional). An exponent consists of the letter e (or E), an optional sign, and one or more digits.

The `%e`, `%f`, and `%g` conversions are interchangeable when used with `scanf`; all three follow the same rules for recognizing a floating-point number.

Q&A When `scanf` encounters a character that can't be part of the current item, the character is "put back" to be read again during the scanning of the next input item or during the next call of `scanf`. Consider the following (admittedly pathological) arrangement of our four numbers:

```
1-20.3-4.0e3¤
```

Let's use the same call of `scanf` as before:

```
scanf("%d%d%f%f", &i, &j, &x, &y);
```

Here's how `scanf` would process the new input:

- Conversion specification: `%d`. The first nonblank input character is 1; since integers can begin with 1, `scanf` then reads the next character, −. Recognizing that − can't appear inside an integer, `scanf` stores 1 into i and puts the − character back.
- Conversion specification: `%d`. `scanf` then reads the characters −, 2, 0, and . (period). Since an integer can't contain a decimal point, `scanf` stores −20 into j and puts the . character back.
- Conversion specification: `%f`. `scanf` reads the characters ., 3, and −. Since a floating-point number can't contain a minus sign after a digit, `scanf` stores 0.3 into x and puts the − character back.
- Conversion specification: `%f`. Lastly, `scanf` reads the characters −, 4, ., 0, e, 3, and ¤ (new-line). Since a floating-point number can't contain a new-line character, `scanf` stores -4.0×10^3 into y and puts the new-line character back.

In this example, `scanf` was able to match every conversion specification in the format string with an input item. Since the new-line character wasn't read, it will be left for the next call of `scanf`.

Ordinary Characters in Format Strings

The concept of pattern-matching can be taken one step further by writing format strings that contain ordinary characters in addition to conversion specifications. The action that scanf takes when it processes an ordinary character in a format string depends on whether or not it is a white-space character.

- **White-space characters.** When it encounters one or more consecutive white-space characters in a format string, scanf repeatedly reads white-space characters from the input until it reaches a non-white-space character (which is "put back"). The number of white-space characters in the format string is irrelevant; one white-space character in the format string will match any number of white-space characters in the input. In a format string, all white-space characters are equivalent; a space character or white-space escape sequence in a format string can match any number of spaces, new-lines, or other white-space characters.

- **Other characters.** When it encounters a non-white-space character in a format string, scanf compares it with the next input character. If the two characters match, scanf discards the input character and continues processing the format string. If the characters don't match, scanf puts the offending character back into the input, then aborts without further processing the format string or reading characters from the input.

For example, suppose that the format string is "%d/%d". If the input is

•5/•96

scanf skips the first space while looking for an integer, matches %d with 5, matches / with /, skips a space while looking for another integer, and matches %d with 96. On the other hand, if the input is

•5•/•96

scanf skips one space, matches %d with 5, then attempts to match the / in the format string with a space in the input. There's no match, so scanf puts the space back; the •/•96 characters remain to be read by the next call of scanf. To allow spaces after the first number, we should use the format string "%d /%d" instead.

Confusing printf with scanf

Although calls of scanf and printf may appear similar, there are significant differences between the two functions; ignoring these differences can be hazardous to the health of your program.

One common mistake is to put & in front of variables in a call of printf:

```
printf("%d %d\n", &i, &j);   /*** WRONG ***/
```

Fortunately, this mistake is fairly easy to spot: printf will display a couple of odd-looking numbers instead of the values of i and j.

Since scanf normally skips white-space characters when looking for data items, there's often no need for a format string to include characters other than conversion specifications. Incorrectly assuming that scanf format strings should resemble printf format strings—another common error—may cause scanf to behave in unexpected ways. Let's see what happens when the following call of scanf is executed:

```
scanf("%d, %d", &i, &j);
```

scanf will first look for an integer in the input, which it stores in the variable i. scanf will then try to match a comma with the next input character. If the next input character is a space, not a comma, scanf will terminate without reading a value for j.

 Although printf format strings often end with \n, putting a new-line character at the end of a scanf format string is usually a bad idea. To scanf, a new-line character in a format string is equivalent to a space; both cause scanf to advance to the next non-white-space character. For example, if the format string is "%d\n", scanf will skip white space, read an integer, then skip to the next non-white-space character. A format string like this can cause an interactive program to "hang" until the user enters a nonblank character.

PROGRAM   **Computing the Value of Stock Holdings**

Stock prices are usually expressed as dollar amounts, possibly including a fraction: 4 1/2, 63 17/32, and the like. If we own 100 shares, each worth 4 1/2, the value of our holdings would be $450. If we own 1000 shares at 63 17/32, our holdings are worth $63,531.25. The following program uses scanf to read a stock price and a number of shares, then it displays the value of the stock holdings.

stocks.c

```
/* Computes the value of stock holdings */

#include <stdio.h>

main()
{
  int price, shares;
  float num, denom, value;

  printf("Enter share price (must include a fraction): ");
  scanf("%d%f/%f", &price, &num, &denom);
  printf("Enter number of shares: ");
  scanf("%d", &shares);

  value = (price + num / denom) * shares;

  printf("Value of holdings: $%.2f\n", value);
  return 0;
}
```

A session with this program might have the following appearance:

```
Enter share price (must include a fraction): 63 17/32
Enter number of shares: 1000
Value of holdings: $63531.25
```

Note that the user *must* enter a fraction as part of the stock price. Note also that num and denom are declared to be float rather than int. Treating num and denom as integers would cause a problem, since the / operator truncates when dividing integers; 17/32 would have the value 0.

Q & A

Q: **I've seen the %i conversion used to read and write integers. What's the difference between %i and %d? [p. 33]**

A: When used in a printf format string, there's no difference. In a scanf format string, however, %d can only match an integer written in decimal (base 10) form, while %i can match an integer expressed in octal (base 8), decimal, or hexadecimal (base 16). If an input number has a 0 prefix (as in 056), %i treats it as an octal number; if it has a 0x or 0X prefix (as in 0x56), %i treats it as a hex number. Using %i instead of %d to read a number can have surprising results if the user should accidentally put 0 at the beginning of the number. Because of this trap, I recommend sticking with %d.

Q: **If printf treats % as the beginning of a conversion specification, how can I print the % character?**

A: If printf encounters two consecutive % characters in a format string, it prints a single % character. For example, the statement

```
printf("Net profit: %d%%\n", profit);
```

might print

```
Net profit: 10%
```

Q: **The \t escape is supposed to cause printf to advance to the next tab stop. How do I know how far apart tab stops are? [p. 35]**

A: You don't. The effect of printing \t isn't defined in Standard C; it depends on what your operating system does when asked to print a tab character. Tab stops are typically eight characters apart, but C makes no guarantee.

Q: **What does scanf do if it's asked to read a number but the user enters nonnumeric input?**

A: Let's look at the following example:

```
printf("Enter a number: ");
scanf("%d", &i);
```

Suppose that the user enters a valid number, followed by nonnumeric characters:

```
Enter a number: 23foo
```

In this case, scanf reads the 2 and the 3, storing 23 in i. The remaining characters (foo) are left to be read by the next call of scanf (or some other input function). On the other hand, suppose that the input is invalid from the beginning:

```
Enter a number: foo
```

In this case, the value of i is undefined and foo is left for the next scanf.

What can we do about this sad state of affairs? Later, we'll see how to test

detecting errors in scanf ➤22.3

whether a call of scanf has succeeded. If the call fails, we can have the program either terminate or try to recover, perhaps by discarding the offending input and asking the user to try again. (Ways to discard bad input are discussed in the Q&A section at the end of Chapter 22.)

Q: **I don't understand how scanf can "put back" characters and read them again later. [p. 38]**

A: As it turns out, programs don't read user input as it is typed. Instead, input is stored in a hidden buffer, to which scanf has access. It's easy for scanf to put characters back into the buffer for subsequent reading. Chapter 22 discusses input buffering in more detail.

Q: **What does scanf do if the user puts punctuation marks (commas, for example) between numbers?**

A: Let's look at a simple example. Suppose that we try to read a pair of integers using scanf:

```
printf("Enter two numbers: ");
scanf("%d%d", &i, &j);
```

If the user enters

```
4,28
```

scanf will read the 4 and store it in i. As it searches for the beginning of the second number, scanf encounters the comma. Since numbers can't begin with a comma, scanf returns immediately. The comma and the second number are left for the next call of scanf.

Of course, we can easily solve the problem by adding a comma to the format string if we're sure that the numbers will *always* be separated by a comma:

```
printf("Enter two numbers, separated by a comma: ");
scanf("%d,%d", &i, &j);
```

Exercises

Section 3.1

1. What output do the following calls of `printf` produce?

    (a) `printf("%6d,%4d", 86, 1040);`
    (b) `printf("%12.5e", 30.253);`
    (c) `printf("%.4f", 83.162);`
    (d) `printf("%-6.2g", .0000009979);`

2. Write calls of `printf` that display a `float` variable x in the following formats.

    (a) Exponential notation; left-justified in a field of size 8; one digit after the decimal point.
    (b) Exponential notation; right-justified in a field of size 10; six digits after the decimal point.
    (c) Fixed decimal notation; left-justified in a field of size 8; three digits after the decimal point.
    (d) Fixed decimal notation; right-justified in a field of size 6; no digits after the decimal point.

Section 3.2

3. For each of the following pairs of `scanf` format strings, indicate whether or not the two strings are equivalent. If they're not, show how they can be distinguished.

    (a) `"%d"`   versus `" %d"`
    (b) `"%d-%d-%d"` versus `"%d -%d -%d"`
    (c) `"%f"`   versus `"%f "`
    (d) `"%f,%f"`   versus `"%f, %f"`

4. Write a program that accepts a date from the user in the form *mm/dd/yy* and then displays it in the form *yymmdd*:

    ```
    Enter a date (mm/dd/yy): 2/17/96
    You entered the date 960217
    ```

5. Write a program that formats product information entered by the user. A session with the program should look like this:

    ```
    Enter item number: 583
    Enter unit price: 13.5
    Enter purchase date (mm/dd/yy): 10/24/95

    Item          Unit          Purchase
                  Price         Date
    583           $  13.50      10/24/95
    ```

    The item number and date should be left justified; the unit price should be right justified. Allow dollar amounts up to $9999.99. *Hint:* Use tabs to line up the columns.

6. Books are identified by an International Standard Book Number (ISBN) such as 0-393-30375-6. The first digit specifies the language in which the book was written (for example, 0 is English and 3 is German). The next group of digits designates the publisher (393 is the code for W. W. Norton), and the one after it is a number assigned by the publisher to identify the book (30375 is the code for Stephen Jay Gould's *The Flamingo's Smile*). The number ends with a "check digit" that is used to verify the accuracy of the preceding digits. Write a program that breaks down an ISBN entered by the user:

```
Enter ISBN: 0-393-30375-6
Language: 0
Publisher: 393
Book number: 30375
Check digit: 6
```

Test your program with actual ISBN values (usually found on the back cover of a book and on the copyright page).

*7. Suppose that we call scanf as follows:

```
scanf("%d%f%d", &i, &x, &j);
```

If the user enters

```
10.3 5 6
```

what will be the values of i, x, and j after the call? (Assume that i and j are int variables and x is a float variable.)

*8. Suppose that we call scanf as follows:

```
scanf("%f%d%f", &x, &i, &y);
```

If the user enters

```
12.3 45.6 789
```

what will be the values of x, i, and y after the call? (Assume that x and y are float variables and i is an int variable.)

---

*Starred exercises are tricky—the correct answer is usually not the obvious one. Read the question thoroughly, review the relevant section if necessary, and be careful!

4 Expressions

*One does not learn computing by using a hand
calculator, but one can forget arithmetic.*

One of C's distinguishing characteristics is its emphasis on ***expressions***—formulas
that show how to compute a value—rather than statements. The simplest expressions are variables and constants. A variable represents a value to be computed as
the program runs; a constant represents a value that doesn't change. More complicated expressions apply operators to operands (which are themselves expressions).
In the expression a + (b * c), the + operator is applied to the operands a and
(b * c), both of which are expressions in their own right.

Operators are the basic tools for building expressions, and C has an unusually
rich collection of them. To start off, C provides the rudimentary operators that are
found in most programming languages:

- ***Arithmetic operators,*** including addition, subtraction, multiplication, and
  division.
- ***Relational operators*** to perform comparisons such as "i is *greater than* 0."
- ***Logical operators*** to build conditions such as "i is greater than 0 *and* i is less
  than 10."

But C doesn't stop here; it goes on to provide dozens of other operators. There are
so many operators, in fact, that we'll need to introduce them gradually over the
first twenty chapters of this book. Mastering so many operators can be a chore, but
it's essential to become proficient at C.

In this chapter, we'll cover some of C's most fundamental operators: the arithmetic operators (Section 4.1), the assignment operators (Section 4.2), and the
increment and decrement operators (Section 4.3). In addition to discussing the
arithmetic operators, Section 4.1 explains operator precedence and associativity,
which are important for expressions that contain more than one operator. Section
4.4 describes how C expressions are evaluated; in some cases—which I'll discuss

how to avoid—the value of an expression may depend on which C compiler you use. Finally, Section 4.5 introduces the *expression statement*, an unusual feature that allows any expression to serve as a statement.

4.1   Arithmetic Operators

The *arithmetic operators*—operators that perform addition, subtraction, multiplication, and division—are the workhorse of many programming languages, including C. Table 4.1 shows C's arithmetic operators.

Table 4.1
Arithmetic Operators

Unary	*Binary*	
	Additive	*Multiplicative*
+ unary plus – unary minus	+ addition – subtraction	* multiplication / division % remainder

The additive and multiplicative operators are said to be **binary** because they require *two* operands. The **unary** operators require *one* operand:

```
i = +1;    /* + used as a unary operator */
j = -i;    /* - used as a unary operator */
```

The unary + operator does nothing; in fact, it doesn't exist in Classic C. It's used primarily to emphasize that a numeric constant is positive.

The binary operators probably look familiar. The only one that might not is %, the remainder operator; in other programming languages, % often has a name such as mod (modulus) or rem (remainder). The value of i % j is the remainder when i is divided by j. For example, the value of 10 % 3 is 1, and the value of 12 % 4 is 0.

Q&A   The binary operators in Table 4.1—with the exception of %—allow either integer or floating-point operands, with mixing allowed. When int and float operands are mixed, the result has type float. Thus, 9 + 2.5 has the value 11.5, and 6.7 / 2 has the value 3.35.

The / and % operators require special care:

- The / operator can produce surprising results. When both of its operands are integers, / truncates the result by dropping the fractional part. Thus, the value of 1 / 2 is 0, not 0.5.

- The % operator requires integer operands; if either operand is not an integer, the program won't compile.

- When / and % are used with negative operands, the result depends on the implementation. If either operand is negative, the result of a division can be rounded either up or down. (For example, the value of –9 / 7 could be either –1 or –2). If i or j is negative, the sign of i % j depends on the implementation. (For example, the value of –9 % 7 could be either 2 or –2).

"Implementation-Defined"

The term ***implementation-defined*** will arise often enough that it's worth taking a moment to discuss it. The C standard deliberately leaves parts of the language unspecified, with the understanding that an "implementation"—the software needed to compile, link, and execute programs on a particular platform—will fill in the details. As a result, the behavior of the program may vary somewhat from one implementation to another. The behavior of the / and % operators for negative operands is an example of implementation-defined behavior.

Leaving parts of the language unspecified may seem odd or even dangerous, but it reflects C's philosophy. One of the language's goals is to achieve efficiency, which often means matching the way that hardware behaves. Some machines may yield −1 when −9 is divided by 7, while others produce −2; the standard simply reflects this fact of life.

It's best to avoid writing programs that depend on implementation-defined behavior. If that's not possible, at least check the manual carefully—the C standard requires that implementation-defined behavior be documented.

Operator Precedence and Associativity

When an expression contains more than one operator, its interpretation may not be immediately clear. For example, does i + j * k mean "add i and j, then multiply the result by k," or does it mean "multiply j and k, then add i"? One solution to this problem is to add parentheses, writing either (i + j) * k or i + (j * k). As a general rule, C allows the use of parentheses for grouping in all expressions.

What if we don't use parentheses, though? Will the compiler interpret i + j * k as (i + j) * k or i + (j * k)? C, like many other languages, uses *operator precedence* rules to resolve this potential ambiguity. The arithmetic operators have the following relative precedence:

```
highest:   +   -  (unary)
           *   /  %
lowest:    +   -  (binary)
```

When two or more operators appear in the same expression, we can determine how the compiler will interpret the expression by repeatedly putting parentheses around subexpressions, starting with high-precedence operators and working down to low-precedence operators. The following examples illustrate the result:

```
i + j * k      is equivalent to    i + (j * k)
-i * -j        is equivalent to    (-i) * (-j)
+i + j / k     is equivalent to    (+i) + (j / k)
```

Operator precedence rules alone aren't enough when an expression contains two or more operators at the same level of precedence. In this situation, the *associativity* of the operators comes into play. An operator is said to be *left associative* if it groups from left to right. The binary arithmetic operators (*, /, %, +, and –) are all left associative, so

```
i - j - k       is equivalent to     (i - j) - k
i * j / k       is equivalent to     (i * j) / k
```

An operator is **right associative** if it groups from right to left. The unary arithmetic operators (+ and –) are both right associative, so

```
- + i           is equivalent to     -(+i)
```

Precedence and associativity rules are important in many languages, but especially so in C. However, C has so many operators (almost fifty!) that few programmers bother to memorize the precedence and associativity rules. Instead, they consult a table of operators when in doubt or just use plenty of parentheses.

table of operators ➤*Appendix B*

PROGRAM   **Computing a UPC Check Digit**

For a number of years, manufacturers of goods sold in supermarkets have put a bar code on each product. This code, known as the Universal Product Code (UPC), identifies both the manufacturer and the product. By scanning the bar code on a product, a supermarket can determine what price to charge for the item. Each bar code represents a twelve-digit number, which is usually printed underneath the bars. For example, the 26-ounce package of Morton iodized salt has the digits

```
0   24600 01003   0
```

underneath its bar code. The first digit identifies the type of item (0 for most grocery items, 2 for items that must be weighed, 3 for drugs and health-related merchandise, and 5 for coupons). The first group of five digits identifies the manufacturer. The second group of five digits identifies the product (including package size). The final digit is a "check digit," whose only purpose is to help identify an error in the preceding digits. If the UPC is scanned incorrectly, the first 11 digits probably won't be consistent with the last digit, and the supermarket scanner will reject the entire code.

Here's one method of computing the check digit:

Add the first, third, fifth, seventh, ninth, and eleventh digits.
Add the second, fourth, sixth, eighth, and tenth digits.
Multiply the first sum by 3 and add it to the second sum.
Subtract 1 from the total.
Compute the remainder when the adjusted total is divided by 10.
Subtract the remainder from 9.

Using the Morton salt example, we get $0 + 4 + 0 + 0 + 0 + 3 = 7$ for the first sum and $2 + 6 + 0 + 1 + 0 = 9$ for the second sum. Multiplying the first sum by 3 and adding the second yields 30. Subtracting 1 gives 29. The remainder upon dividing by 10 is 9. When the remainder is subtracted from 9, the result is 0. Here are a couple of other UPCs, in case you want to try your hand at computing the check digit (raiding the kitchen cabinet for the answer is *not* allowed):

Jif creamy peanut butter (18 oz.):   0   37000 00407   ?
Ocean Spray jellied cranberry sauce (8 oz.): 0   31200 01005   ?

The answers appear at the bottom of the page.

Let's write a program that calculates the check digit for an arbitrary UPC. We'll ask the user to enter the first 11 digits of the UPC, then we'll display the corresponding check digit. To avoid confusion, we'll ask the user to enter the number in three parts: the single digit at the left, the first group of five digits, and the second group of five digits. Here's what a session with the program will look like:

```
Enter the first (single) digit: 0
Enter first group of five digits: 24600
Enter second group of five digits: 01003
Check digit: 0
```

Instead of reading each digit group as a *five*-digit number, we'll read it as five *one*-digit numbers. Reading the numbers as single digits is more convenient; also, we won't have to worry that one of the five-digit numbers is too large to store in an int variable. (Some compilers limit int variables to 32,767.) To read single digits, we'll use scanf with the %1d conversion specification, which matches a one-digit integer.

upc.c

```c
/* Computes a Universal Product Code check digit */

#include <stdio.h>

main()
{
  int d, i1, i2, i3, i4, i5, j1, j2, j3, j4, j5,
      first_sum, second_sum, total;

  printf("Enter the first (single) digit: ");
  scanf("%1d", &d);
  printf("Enter first group of five digits: ");
  scanf("%1d%1d%1d%1d%1d", &i1, &i2, &i3, &i4, &i5);
  printf("Enter second group of five digits: ");
  scanf("%1d%1d%1d%1d%1d", &j1, &j2, &j3, &j4, &j5);

  first_sum = d + i2 + i4 + j1 + j3 + j5;
  second_sum = i1 + i3 + i5 + j2 + j4;
  total = 3 * first_sum + second_sum;

  printf("Check digit: %d\n", 9 - ((total - 1) % 10));

  return 0;
}
```

The missing check digits are 3 (Jif) and 6 (Ocean Spray).

4.2 Assignment Operators

Once the value of an expression has been computed, we'll often need to store it in a variable for later use. C's = (**simple assignment**) operator is used for that purpose. For updating a value already stored in a variable, C provides an assortment of **compound assignment** operators.

Simple Assignment

The effect of the assignment *v* = *e* is to evaluate the expression *e* and copy its value into *v*. As the following examples show, *e* can be a constant, a variable, or a more complicated expression:

```
i = 5;              /* i is now 5  */
j = i;              /* j is now 5  */
k = 10 * i + j;     /* k is now 55 */
```

If *v* and *e* don't have the same type, then the value of *e* is converted to the type of *v* as the assignment takes place:

```
int i;
float f;

i = 72.99;    /* i is now 72 */
f = 136;      /* f is now 136.0 */
```

conversion during assignment ➤7.5 We'll return to the topic of type conversion later.

In many programming languages, assignment is a *statement*; in C, however, assignment is an *operator*, just like +. In other words, the act of assignment produces a result, just as adding two numbers produces a result. The value of an assignment *v* = *e* is the value of *v* *after* the assignment. Thus, the value of i = 72.99 is 72 (not 72.99).

Side Effects

We don't normally expect operators to modify their operands, since operators in mathematics don't. Writing i + j doesn't modify either i or j; it simply computes the result of adding i and j.

Most C operators don't modify their operands, but some do. We say that these operators have **side effects**, since they do more than just compute a value. The simple assignment operator is the first operator we've seen that has side effects; it modifies its left operand. Evaluating the expression i = 0 produces the result 0 and—as a side effect—assigns 0 to i.

Since assignment is an operator, several assignments can be chained together:

```
i = j = k = 0;
```

The = operator is right associative, so this assignment is equivalent to

```
i = (j = (k = 0));
```

The effect is to assign 0 first to `k`, then to `j`, and finally to `i`.

 Watch out for unexpected results in chained assignments as a result of type conversion:

```
int i;
float f;

f = i = 33.3;
```

`i` is assigned the value 33, then `f` is assigned 33.0 (not 33.3, as you might think).

In general, an assignment of the form *v* = *e* is allowed wherever a value of type *v* would be permitted. In the following example, the expression `j = i` copies `i` to `j`; the new value of `j` is then added to `1`, producing the new value of `k`:

```
i = 1;
k = 1 + (j = i);
printf("%d %d %d\n", i, j, k);   /* prints "1 1 2" */
```

Using the assignment operator in this fashion usually isn't a good idea, though. For one thing, "embedded assignments" can make programs hard to read. They can also be a source of subtle bugs, as we'll see in Section 4.4.

Lvalues

Most C operators allow their operands to be variables, constants, or expressions containing other operators. The assignment operator, however, requires an *lvalue* as its left operand. An lvalue (pronounced "L-value") represents an object stored in computer memory, not a constant or the result of a computation. Variables are lvalues; expressions such as `10` or `2 * i` are not. At this point, variables are the only lvalues that we know about; other kinds of lvalues will appear in later chapters.

Since the assignment operator requires an lvalue as its left operand, it's illegal to put any other kind of expression on the left side of an assignment expression:

```
12 = i;        /*** WRONG ***/
i + j = 0;     /*** WRONG ***/
-i = j;        /*** WRONG ***/
```

The compiler will detect errors of this nature, and you'll get an error message such as *"Lvalue required."*

Compound Assignment

Assignments that use the old value of a variable to compute its new value are common in C programs. The following statement, for example, adds 2 to the value stored in i:

```
i = i + 2;
```

C's **compound assignment operators** allow us to shorten this statement and others like it. Using the += operator, we simply write:

```
i += 2;    /* same as i = i + 2; */
```

The += operator adds the value of the right operand to the variable on the left.

There are nine other compound assignment operators, including the following:

```
-=    *=    /=    %=
```

other assignment operators ➤20.1 (We'll cover the remaining compound assignment operators in a later chapter.) All compound assignment operators work in much the same way:

> v += e adds v to e, storing the result in v
> v −= e subtracts e from v, storing the result in v
> v *= e multiplies v by e, storing the result in v
> v /= e divides v by e, storing the result in v
> v %= e computes the remainder when v is divided by e, storing the result in v

Note that I've been careful not to say that v += e is "equivalent" to $v = v + e$. One problem is operator precedence: i *= j + k isn't the same as i = i * j + k. There are also rare cases in which v += e differs from $v = v + e$ because v itself has a side

  effect. Similar remarks apply to the other compound assignment operators.

When using the compound assignment operators, be careful not to switch the two characters that make up the operator. Switching the characters may yield an expression that is acceptable to the compiler but that doesn't have the intended meaning. For example, if you meant to write i += j but typed i =+ j instead, the program will still compile. Unfortunately, the latter expression is equivalent to i = (+j), which merely copies the value of j into i.

The compound assignment operators have the same properties as the = operator. In particular, they're right associative, so the statement

```
i += j += k;
```

means

```
i += (j += k);
```

4.3 Increment and Decrement Operators

Two of the most common operations on a variable are "incrementing" (adding 1) and "decrementing" (subtracting 1). We can, of course, accomplish these tasks by writing

```
i = i + 1;
j = j - 1;
```

The compound assignment operators allow us to condense these statements a bit:

```
i += 1;
j -= 1;
```

But C allows increments and decrements to be shortened even further, using the ++ (*increment*) and -- (*decrement*) operators.

At first glance, the increment and decrement operators are simplicity itself: ++ adds 1 to its operand, while -- subtracts 1. Unfortunately, this simplicity is misleading—the increment and decrement operators can be tricky to use. One complication is that ++ and -- can be used as *prefix* operators (++i and --i, for example) or *postfix* operators (i++ and i--). The correctness of a program may hinge on picking the proper version.

Another complication is that, like the assignment operators, ++ and -- have side effects: they modify the values of their operands. Evaluating the expression ++i (a "pre-increment") yields i + 1 and—as a side effect—increments i:

```
i = 1;
printf("i is %d\n", ++i);    /* prints "i is 2" */
printf("i is %d\n", i);      /* prints "i is 2" */
```

Evaluating the expression i++ (a "post-increment") produces the result i, but causes i to be incremented afterwards:

```
i = 1;
printf("i is %d\n", i++);    /* prints "i is 1" */
printf("i is %d\n", i);      /* prints "i is 2" */
```

The first printf shows the original value of i, before it is incremented. The second printf shows the new value. As these examples illustrate, ++i means "increment i immediately," while i++ means "use the old value of i for now, but increment i later." How much later? The C standard doesn't specify a precise time, but it's safe to assume that i will be incremented before the next statement is executed.

The -- operator has similar properties:

```
i = 1;
printf("i is %d\n", --i);    /* prints "i is 0" */
printf("i is %d\n", i);      /* prints "i is 0" */
```

```
i = 1;
printf("i is %d\n", i--);    /* prints "i is 1" */
printf("i is %d\n", i);      /* prints "i is 0" */
```

When ++ or -- is used more than once in the same expression, the result can often be hard to understand. Consider the following statements:

```
i = 1;
j = 2;
k = ++i + j++;
```

What are the values of i, j, and k after these statements are executed? Since i is incremented *before* its value is used, but j is incremented *after* it is used, the last statement is equivalent to

```
i = i + 1;
k = i + j;
j = j + 1;
```

so the final values of i, j, and k are 2, 3, and 4, respectively. In contrast, executing the statements

```
i = 1;
j = 2;
k = i++ + j++;
```

will give i, j, and k the values 2, 3, and 3, respectively.

For the record, the postfix versions of ++ and -- have higher precedence than unary plus and minus and are left associative. The prefix versions have the same precedence as unary plus and minus and are right associative.

4.4   Expression Evaluation

Table 4.2 summarizes the operators we've seen so far. (Appendix B has a similar table that shows *all* operators.) The first column shows the precedence of each

Table 4.2
A Partial List of C
Operators

Precedence	Name	Symbol(s)	Associativity
1	increment (postfix) decrement (postfix)	++ --	left
2	increment (prefix) decrement (prefix) unary plus unary minus	++ -- + -	right
3	multiplicative	* / %	left
4	additive	+ -	left
5	assignment	= *= /= %= += -=	right

operator relative to the other operators in the table (the highest precedence is 1; the lowest is 5). The last column shows the associativity of each operator.

Table 4.2 (or its larger cousin in Appendix B) has a variety of uses. Let's look at one of these. Suppose that we run across a complicated expression such as

```
a = b += c++ - d + --e / -f
```

as we're reading someone's program. This expression would be easier to understand if there were parentheses to show how the expression is constructed from subexpressions. With the help of Table 4.2, adding parentheses to an expression is easy: After examining the expression to find the operator with highest precedence, we put parentheses around the operator and its operands, indicating that it should be treated as a single operand from that point onwards. We then repeat the process until the expression is fully parenthesized.

In our example, the operator with highest precedence is ++, used here as a postfix operator, so we put parentheses around ++ and its operand:

```
a = b += (c++) - d + --e / -f
```

We now spot a prefix -- operator and a unary minus operator (both precedence 2) in the expression:

```
a = b += (c++) - d + (--e) / (-f)
```

Note that the other minus sign has an operand to its immediate left, so it must be a subtraction operator, not a unary minus operator.

Next, we notice the / operator (precedence 3):

```
a = b += (c++) - d + ((--e) / (-f))
```

The expression contains two operators with precedence 4, subtraction and addition. Whenever two operators with the same precedence are adjacent to an operand, we've got to be careful about associativity. In our example, - and + are both adjacent to d, so associativity rules apply. The - and + operators group from left to right, so parentheses go around the subtraction first, then the addition:

```
a = b += (((c++) - d) + ((--e) / (-f)))
```

The only remaining operators are = and +=. Both operators are adjacent to b, so we must take associativity into account. Assignment operators group from right to left, so parentheses go around the += expression first, then the = expression:

```
(a = (b += (((c++) - d) + ((--e) / (-f)))))
```

The expression is now fully parenthesized.

Order of Subexpression Evaluation

The rules of operator precedence and associativity allow us to break any C expression into subexpressions—to determine uniquely where the parentheses would go if the expression were fully parenthesized. Paradoxically, these rules don't always allow us to determine the value of the expression, which may depend on the order in which its subexpressions are evaluated.

logical *and* and *or* operators ➤5.1
conditional operator ➤5.2
comma operator ➤6.3

C doesn't define the order in which subexpressions are evaluated (with the exception of subexpressions involving the logical *and*, logical *or*, conditional, and comma operators). Thus, in the expression (a + b) * (c – d) we don't know whether (a + b) will be evaluated before (c – d).

Most expressions have the same value regardless of the order in which their subexpressions are evaluated. However, this may not be true when a subexpression modifies one of its operands. Consider the following example:

```
a = 5;
c = (b = a + 2) - (a = 1);
```

After these statements have been executed, the value of c will be either 6 or 2. If the subexpression (b = a + 2) is evaluated first, b is assigned the value 7 and c is assigned 6. But if (a = 1) is evaluated first, b is assigned 3 and c is assigned 2.

An expression whose value depends on the order in which its subexpressions are evaluated is a sort of time bomb set to go off in the future. The program may work as expected when originally written but misbehave when compiled later with a different compiler.

To prevent problems, it's a good idea to avoid using the assignment operators in subexpressions; instead, use a series of separate assignments. For example, the statements above could be rewritten as

```
a = 5;
b = a + 2;
a = 1;
c = b - a;
```

The value of c will always be 6 after these statements are executed.

Besides the assignment operators, the only operators that modify their operands are increment and decrement. When using these operators, be careful that your expressions don't depend on a particular order of evaluation. In the following example, j may be assigned one of two values:

```
i = 2;
j = i * i++;
```

It's natural to assume that j is assigned the value 4. However, j could just as well be assigned 6 instead. Here's the scenario: (1) The second operand (the original value of i) is fetched, then i is incremented. (2) The first operand (the new value of i) is fetched. (3) The new and old values of i are multiplied, yielding 6.

4.5 Expression Statements

C has the unusual rule that *any* expression can be used as a statement. That is, any expression—regardless of its type or what it computes—can be turned into a statement by appending a semicolon. For example, we could turn the expression `++i` into a statement:

```
++i;
```

When this statement is executed, `i` is first incremented, then the new value of `i` is fetched (as though it were to be used in an enclosing expression). However, since `++i` isn't part of a larger expression, its value is discarded and the next statement executed. (The change to `i` is permanent, of course.)

Since its value is discarded, there's little point in using an expression as a statement unless the expression has a side effect. Let's look at three examples. In the first example, 1 is stored into `i`, then the new value of `i` is fetched but not used:

```
i = 1;
```

In the second example, the value of `i` is fetched but not used; however, `i` is decremented afterwards:

```
i--;
```

In the third example, the value of the expression `i * j - 1` is computed and then discarded:

```
i * j - 1;
```

Since `i` and `j` aren't changed, this statement has no effect.

A slip of the finger can easily create a "do-nothing" expression statement. For example, instead of entering

```
i = j;
```

we might accidentally type

```
i + j;
```

(This kind of error is more common than you might expect, since the = and + characters usually occupy the same key.) Some compilers can detect meaningless expression statements; you'll get a warning such as *"Code has no effect."*

Q & A

Q: **I notice that C has no exponentiation operator. How can I raise a number to a power?**

A: Raising an integer to a small positive integer power is best done by repeated multiplication (`i * i * i` is `i` cubed). To raise a number to a noninteger power, call the

pow function ➤23.3 `pow` function.

Q: **I want to apply the `%` operator to a floating-point operand, but my program won't compile. What can I do? [p. 46]**

fmod function ➤23.3 **A:** The `%` operator requires integer operands. Try the `fmod` function instead.

Q: **If C has lvalues, does it also have rvalues? [p. 51]**

A: Yes, indeed. An *l*value is an expression that can appear on the *left* side of an assignment; an *r*value is an expression that can appear on the *right* side. Thus, an rvalue could be a variable, constant, or more complex expression. In this book, as in the C standard, we'll use the term "expression" instead of "rvalue."

*Q: **You said that *v* += *e* isn't equivalent to *v* = *v* + *e* if *v* has a side effect. Can you explain? [p. 52]**

A: Evaluating *v* += *e* causes *v* to be evaluated only once; evaluating *v* = *v* + *e* causes *v* to be evaluated twice. Any side effect caused by evaluating *v* will occur twice in the latter case. In the following cxample, `i` is incremented once:

```
a[i++] += 2;
```

If we use = instead of +=, however, `i` is incremented twice:

```
a[i++] = a[i++] + 2;
```

Q: **Why does C provide the `++` and `--` operators? Are they faster than other ways of incrementing and decrementing, or they are just more convenient? [p. 53]**

A: C inherited `++` and `--` from Ken Thompson's earlier B language. Thompson apparently created these operators because his B compiler could generate a more compact translation for `++i` than for `i = i + 1`. These operators have became a deeply ingrained part of C (in fact, many of C's most famous idioms rely on them). With modern compilers, using `++` and `--` won't make a compiled program any smaller or faster; the continued popularity of these operators stems mostly from their brevity and convenience.

Q: **Do `++` and `--` work with `float` variables?**

A: Yes; the increment and decrement operations are defined for all numeric types. In practice, however, it's fairly rare to increment or decrement a `float` variable.

*Q: **When I use the postfix version of ++ or −−, just when is the increment or decrement performed? [p. 53]**

A: That's an excellent question. Unfortunately, it's also a difficult one to answer. The C standard introduces the concept of "sequence point" and says that "updating the stored value of the operand shall occur between the previous and the next sequence point." There are various kinds of sequence points in C; statements are one variety. By the end of a statement, all increments and decrements within the statement must have been performed; the next statement can't begin to execute until this condition has been met.

Consider the following example:

```
i = 1;
j = i++ + i++;
```

By the time the second statement has been executed, i will have been incremented twice. However, we don't know whether both increments were done after i was added to itself (giving j the value 2), or whether one of the occurrences of i was incremented earlier (giving j the value 3).

Certain operators that we'll encounter in later chapters (logical *and*, logical *or*, conditional, and comma) also impose sequence points. So do function calls: the arguments in a function call must be fully evaluated before the call can be performed. If an argument happens to be an expression containing a ++ or −− operator, the increment or decrement must occur before the call can take place.

Q: **What do you mean when you say that the value of an expression statement is discarded? [p. 57]**

A: By definition, an expression represents a value. If i has the value 5, for example, then evaluating i + 1 produces the value 6. Let's turn i + 1 into a statement by putting a semicolon after it:

```
i + 1;
```

When this statement is executed, the value of i + 1 is computed. Since we have failed to save this value—or at least use it in some way—it is lost.

Q: **But what about statements like i = 1;? I don't see what is being discarded.**

A: Don't forget that = is an operator in C and produces a value just like any other operator. The assignment

```
i = 1;
```

assigns 1 to i. The value of the entire expression is 1, which is discarded. Discarding the expression's value is no great loss, since the reason for writing the statement in the first place was to modify i.

Exercises

1. Show the output produced by each of the following code fragments. Assume that i, j, and k are int variables.

    (a) `i = 5; j = 3;`
        `printf("%d %d", i / j, i % j);`
    (b) `i = 2; j = 3;`
        `printf("%d", (i + 10) % j);`
    (c) `i = 7; j = 8; k = 9;`
        `printf("%d", (i + 10) % k / j);`
    (d) `i = 1; j = 2; k = 3;`
        `printf("%d", (i + 5) % (j + 2) / k);`

*2. If i and j are positive integers, does `(-i)/j` always have the same value as `-(i/j)`? Justify your answer.

3. Write a program that asks the user to enter a two-digit number, then prints the number with its digits reversed. A session with the program should have the following appearance:

    `Enter a two-digit number: `<u>28</u>
    `The reversal is: 82`

    Read the number using %d, then break it into two digits. *Hint:* If n is an integer, then n % 10 is the last digit in n and n / 10 is n with the last digit removed.

4. Extend the program in Exercise 3 to handle *three*-digit numbers.

5. Rewrite the program in Exercise 4 so that it prints the reversal of a three-digit number without using arithmetic to split the number into digits. *Hint:* Review the upc.c program.

6. Show the output produced by each of the following code fragments. Assume that i, j, and k are int variables.

    (a) `i = 7; j = 8;`
        `i *= j + 1;`
        `printf("%d %d", i, j);`
    (b) `i = j = k = 1;`
        `i += j += k;`
        `printf("%d %d %d", i, j, k);`
    (c) `i = 1; j = 2; k = 3;`
        `i -= j -= k;`
        `printf("%d %d %d", i, j, k);`
    (d) `i = 2; j = 1; k = 0;`
        `i *= j *= k;`
        `printf("%d %d %d", i, j, k);`

*7. Show the output produced by each of the following code fragments. Assume that i, j, and k are int variables.

    (a) `i = 1;`
        `printf("%d ", i++ - 1);`
        `printf("%d", i);`

```
(b) i = 10; j = 5;
    printf("%d ", i++ - ++j);
    printf("%d %d", i, j);
(c) i = 7; j = 8;
    printf("%d ", i++ - --j);
    printf("%d %d", i, j);
(d) i = 3; j = 4; k = 5;
    printf("%d ", i++ - j++ + --k);
    printf("%d %d %d", i, j, k);
```

8. Only one of the expressions ++i and i++ is exactly the same as (i += 1); which is it? Justify your answer.

Section 4.4 9. Supply parentheses to show how a C compiler would interpret each of the following expressions.

```
(a) a * b - c * d + e
(b) a / b % c / d
(c) - a - b + c - + d
(d) a * - b / c - d
```

*10. How many possible values are there for the expression (i++) + (i--)? What are those values, assuming that i has the value 1 initially?

Section 4.5 11. Describe the effect of executing each of the following expression statements. (Assume that i has the value 1 initially and j has the value 2.)

```
(a) i += j;
(b) i--;
(c) i * j / i;
(d) i % ++j;
```

5 Selection Statements

Programmers are not to be measured by their ingenuity and their logic but by the completeness of their case analysis.

return statement ➤2.2
expression statement ➤4.5

Although C has many operators, it has relatively few statements. We've encountered just two so far: the `return` statement and the expression statement. Most of C's remaining statements fall into one of three categories, depending on how they affect the order in which statements are executed:

- **Selection statements.** The `if` and `switch` statements allow a program to select a particular execution path from a set of alternatives.
- **Iteration statements.** The `while`, `do`, and `for` statements support iteration (looping).
- **Jump statements.** The `break`, `continue`, and `goto` statements cause an unconditional jump to some other place in the program. (The `return` statement belongs in this category, as well.)

The only other statements in C are the **compound statement**, which groups several statements into a single statement, and the **null statement**, which performs no action.

This chapter discusses the selection statements and the compound statement. (Chapter 6 covers the iteration statements, the jump statements, and the null statement.) Section 5.2 explains the `if` statement and compound statement, as well as introducing the **conditional operator** (`?:`), which can test a condition within an expression. Section 5.3 describes the `switch` statement. Before we can use the `if` statement, however, we'll need **logical expressions:** conditions that `if` statements can test. Section 5.1 explains how logical expressions are built from the **relational operators** (`<`, `<=`, `>`, and `>=`), the **equality operators** (`==` and `!=`), and the **logical operators** (`&&`, `||`, and `!`).

5.1 Logical Expressions

Several of C's statements, including the `if` statement, must test the value of an expression to see if it's "true" or "false." For example, an `if` statement might need to test the expression `i < j`; a true value would indicate that `i` is less than `j`. In many programming languages, an expression such as `i < j` would have a special "Boolean" or "logical" type. Such a type would have only two values, *false* and *true*. C has no such type. Instead, a comparison such as `i < j` yields an integer: either 0 (false) or 1 (true). With this in mind, let's look at the operators that are used to build logical expressions.

Relational Operators

C's *relational operators* (Table 5.1) correspond to the $<$, $>$, $\leq$, and $\geq$ operators of

Table 5.1
Relational Operators

Symbol	Meaning
<	less than
>	greater than
<=	less than or equal to
>=	greater than or equal to

mathematics, except that they produce 0 (false) or 1 (true) when used in expressions. For example, the value of `10 < 11` is 1; the value of `11 < 10` is 0.

The relational operators can be used to compare integers and floating-point numbers, with operands of mixed types allowed. Thus, `1 < 2.5` has the value 1, while `5.6 < 4` has the value 0.

The precedence of the relational operators is lower than that of the arithmetic operators; for example, `i + j < k - 1` means `(i + j) < (k - 1)`. The relational operators are left associative.

The expression

`i < j < k`

is legal in C, but doesn't have the meaning that you might expect. Since the < operator is left associative, this expression is equivalent to

`(i < j) < k`

In other words, the expression first tests whether `i` is less than `j`; the 1 or 0 produced by this comparison is then compared to `k`. The expression does *not* test whether `j` lies between `i` and `k`. (We'll see later in this section that the correct expression would be `i < j && j < k`.)

Equality Operators

Although the relational operators are denoted by the same symbols as in many other programming languages, the **equality operators** have a unique appearance (Table 5.2). The "equal to" operator is two adjacent = characters, not one, since a

Symbol	Meaning
==	equal to
!=	not equal to

single = character represents the assignment operator. The "not equal to" operator is also two characters: ! and =.

Like the relational operators, the equality operators are left associative and produce either 0 (false) or 1 (true) as their result. However, the equality operators have *lower* precedence than the relational operators. For example, the expression

```
i < j == j < k
```

is equivalent to

```
(i < j) == (j < k)
```

which is true if $i < j$ and $j < k$ are both true or both false.

Clever programmers sometimes exploit the fact that the relational and equality operators return integer values. For example, the value of the expression (i >= j) + (i == j) is either 0, 1, or 2, depending on whether i is less than, greater than, or equal to j, respectively. Tricky coding like this generally isn't a good idea, however; it makes programs hard to understand.

Logical Operators

More complicated logical expressions can be built from simpler ones by using the **logical operators:** *and*, *or*, and *not* (Table 5.3). The ! operator is unary, while && and || are binary.

Symbol	Meaning
!	logical negation
&&	logical *and*
||	logical *or*

The logical operators produce either 0 or 1 as their result. Often, the operands will have values of 0 or 1, but this isn't a requirement; the logical operators treat any nonzero operand as a true value and any zero operand as a false value.

The logical operators behave as follows:

- ! *expr* has the value 1 if *expr* has the value 0.
- *expr1* && *expr2* has the value 1 if the values of *expr1* and *expr2* are both nonzero.

- *expr1* || *expr2* has the value 1 if either *expr1* or *expr2* (or both) has a nonzero value.

In all other cases, these operators produce the value 0.

Both && and || perform "short-circuit" evaluation of their operands. That is, these operators first evaluate the left operand, then the right operand. If the value of the expression can be deduced from the value of the left operand alone, then the right operand isn't evaluated. Consider the following expression:

```
(i != 0) && (j / i > 0)
```

To find the value of this expression, we must first evaluate (i != 0). If i isn't equal to 0, then we'll need to evaluate (j / i > 0) to determine whether the entire expression is true or false. However, if i is equal to 0, then the entire expression must be false, so there's no need to evaluate (j / i > 0). The advantage of short-circuit evaluation is apparent—without it, evaluating the expression would have caused a division by zero.

Be wary of side effects in logical expressions. Thanks to the short-circuit nature of the && and || operators, side effects in operands may not always occur. Consider the following expression:

```
i > 0 && ++j > 0
```

Although j is apparently incremented as a side effect of evaluating the expression, that isn't always the case. If i > 0 is false, then ++j > 0 is not evaluated, so j isn't incremented. The problem can be fixed by changing the condition to ++j > 0 && i > 0 or, even better, by incrementing j separately.

The ! operator has the same precedence as the unary plus and minus operators. The precedence of && and || is lower than that of the relational and equality operators; for example, i < j && k == m means (i < j) && (k == m). The ! operator is right associative; && and || are left associative.

5.2 The if Statement

The if statement allows a program to choose between two alternatives by testing the value of an expression. In its simplest form, the if statement has the form

if statement
                                    if (*expression*) *statement*

Notice that the parentheses around the expression are mandatory; they're part of the if statement, not part of the expression. Also note that the word then doesn't come after the parentheses, as it would in some languages.

When an if statement is executed, the expression in the parentheses is evaluated; if the value of the expression is nonzero—which C interprets as true—the statement after the parentheses is executed. Here's an example:

```
if (line_num == MAX_LINES)
  line_num = 0;
```

The statement line_num = 0; is executed if the condition line_num == MAX_LINES is true (has a nonzero value).

Don't confuse == (equality) with = (assignment). The statement

```
if (i == 0) …
```

tests whether i is equal to 0. However, the statement

```
if (i = 0) …
```

assigns 0 to i, then tests whether the *result* is nonzero. In this case, the test always fails.

Confusing == with = is perhaps the most common C programming error, probably because = means "is equal to" in mathematics (and in many other programming languages). Some compilers issue a warning such as "*Possibly incorrect assignment*" if they notice = where == would normally appear.

Often the expression in an if statement will test whether a variable falls within a range of values. To test whether $0 \le i < n$, for example, we'd write

idiom
```
if (0 <= i && i < n) …
```

To test the *opposite* condition (i is outside the range), we'd write

idiom
```
if (i < 0 || i >= n) …
```

Note the use of the || operator instead of the && operator.

Compound Statements

In our if statement template, notice that *statement* is singular, not plural:

```
if ( expression ) statement
```

What if we want an if statement to control *two* statements or more? That's where the ***compound statement*** comes in. A compound statement has the form

compound statement

{ *statements* }

By putting braces around a group of statements, we can force the compiler to treat it as a single statement.

Here's an example of a compound statement:

```
{ line_num = 0; page_num++; }
```

For clarity, I'll usually put a compound statement on several lines, with one statement per line:

```
{
  line_num = 0;
  page_num++;
}
```

Notice that each inner statement still ends with a semicolon, but the compound statement itself does not.

Here's what a compound statement would look like when used inside an `if` statement:

```
if (line_num == MAX_LINES) {
  line_num = 0;
  page_num++;
}
```

Compound statements are also common in loops and other places where the syntax of C requires a single statement, but we want more than one.

The `else` Clause

An `if` statement may have an `else` clause:

`if` statement with `else` clause

> `if (` *expression* `)` *statement* `else` *statement*

The statement that follows the word `else` is executed if the expression in parentheses has the value 0.

Here's an example of an `if` statement with an `else` clause:

```
if (i > j)
  max = i;
else
  max = j;
```

Notice that both "inner" statements end with a semicolon.

When an `if` statement contains an `else` clause, a layout issue arises: where should the `else` be placed? Many C programmers align it with the `if` at the beginning of the statement, as in the previous example. The inner statements are usually indented, but if they're short they can be put on the same line as the `if` and `else`:

```
if (i > j) max = i;
else max = j;
```

There arc no restrictions on what kind of statements can appear inside an if statement. In fact, it's not unusual for if statements to be nested inside other if statements:

```
if (i > j)
  if (i > k)
    max = i;
  else
    max = k;
else
  if (j > k)
    max = j;
  else
    max = k;
```

if statements can be nested to any depth. Notice how aligning each else with the matching if makes the nesting easier to see. If you still find the nesting confusing, don't hesitate to add braces:

```
if (i > j) {
  if (i > k)
    max = i;
  else
    max = k;
} else {
  if (j > k)
    max = j;
  else
    max = k;
}
```

Adding braces to statements—even when they're not necessary—is like using parentheses in expressions: both techniques help make a program more readable while at the same time avoiding the possibility that the compiler won't understand the program the way we thought it did.

Cascaded if Statements

We'll often need to test a series of conditions, stopping as soon as one of them is true. A "cascaded" if statement is often the best way to write such a series of tests. For example, the following cascaded if statement tests whether n is less than 0, equal to 0, or greater than 0:

```
if (n < 0)
  printf("n is less than 0\n");
else
  if (n == 0)
    printf("n is equal to 0\n");
  else
    printf("n is greater than 0\n");
```

Although the second `if` statement is nested inside the first, C programmers don't usually indent it. Instead, they align each `else` with the original `if`:

```
if (n < 0)
  printf("n is less than 0\n");
else if (n == 0)
  printf("n is equal to 0\n");
else
  printf("n is greater than 0\n");
```

This arrangement gives the cascaded `if` a distinctive appearance:

```
if ( expression )
  statement
else if ( expression )
  statement
...
else if ( expression )
  statement
else
  statement
```

The last two lines (`else` *statement*) aren't always present, of course. This way of indenting the cascaded `if` statement avoids the problem of excessive indentation when the number of tests is large. Moreover, it assures the reader that the statement is nothing more than a series of tests.

Keep in mind that a cascaded `if` statement is not some new kind of statement; it's just an ordinary `if` statement that happens to have another `if` statement as its `else` alternative (and *that* `if` statement has another `if` statement as its `else` alternative, *ad infinitum*).

PROGRAM   **Calculating a Broker's Commission**

When stocks are sold or purchased through a broker, the broker's commission is often computed using a sliding scale that depends upon the value of the stocks traded. Let's say that a broker charges the amounts shown in the following table:

Transaction size	Commission rate
Under $2,500	$30 + 1.7%
$2,500–$6,250	$56 + 0.66%
$6,250–$20,000	$76 + 0.34%
$20,000–$50,000	$100 + 0.22%
$50,000–$500,000	$155 + 0.11%
Over $500,000	$255 + 0.09%

The minimum charge is $39. Our next program asks the user to enter the amount of the trade, then displays the amount of the commission:

```
Enter value of trade: 30000
Commission: $166.00
```

The heart of the program is a cascaded if statement that determines which range the trade falls into.

broker.c

```
/* Calculates a broker's commission */

#include <stdio.h>

main()
{
  float commission, value;

  printf("Enter value of trade: ");
  scanf("%f", &value);

  if (value < 2500.00)
    commission = 30.00 + .017 * value;
  else if (value < 6250.00)
    commission = 56.00 + .0066 * value;
  else if (value < 20000.00)
    commission = 76.00 + .0034 * value;
  else if (value < 50000.00)
    commission = 100.00 + .0022 * value;
  else if (value < 500000.00)
    commission = 155.00 + .0011 * value;
  else
    commission = 255.00 + .0009 * value;

  if (commission < 39.00)
    commission = 39.00;

  printf("Commission: $%.2f\n", commission);

  return 0;
}
```

The "Dangling **else**" Problem

When if statements are nested, we've got to watch out for the notorious "dangling else" problem. Consider the following example:

```
if (y != 0)
  if (x != 0)
    result = x / y;
else
  printf("Error: y is equal to 0\n");
```

To which if statement does the else clause belong? The indentation suggests that it belongs to the outer if statement. However, C follows the rule that an else clause belongs to the nearest if statement that hasn't already been paired with an else. In this example, the else clause actually belongs to the inner if statement, so a correctly indented version would look like this:

```
if (y != 0)
  if (x != 0)
    result = x / y;
  else
    printf("Error: y is equal to 0\n");
```

To make the else clause part of the outer if statement, we can enclose the inner if statement in braces:

```
if (y != 0) {
  if (x != 0)
    result = x / y;
} else
    printf("Error: y is equal to 0\n");
```

This example illustrates the value of braces; if we'd used them in the original if statement, we wouldn't have gotten into this situation in the first place.

Conditional Expressions

C's if statement allows a program to perform one of two actions depending on the value of a condition. C also provides an *operator* that allows an expression to produce one of two *values* depending on the value of a condition.

The **conditional operator** consists of the symbols ? and :, which must be used together in the following way:

conditional expression

$$expr1 \ ? \ expr2 \ : \ expr3$$

expr1, *expr2*, and *expr3* can be expressions of any type. The resulting expression is said to be a **conditional expression**. The conditional operator is unique among C operators in that it requires *three* operands instead of one or two. For this reason, it is often referred to as a **ternary** operator.

The conditional expression *expr1* ? *expr2* : *expr3* should be read "if *expr1* then *expr2* else *expr3*." The expression is evaluated in stages: *expr1* is evaluated first; if its value isn't zero, then *expr2* is evaluated, and its value is the value of the entire conditional. If the value of *expr1* is zero, then the value of *expr3* is the value of the entire conditional.

The following example illustrates the conditional operator:

```
int i, j, k;

i = 1;
j = 2;
k = i > j ? i : j;          /* k is now 2 */
k = (i >= 0 ? i : 0) + j;   /* k is now 3 */
```

In the first assignment to k, the i > j comparison fails, so the value of the conditional expression i > j ? i : j is 2, which is assigned to k. In the second assignment to k, the i >= 0 comparison succeeds; the conditional expression (i >= 0 ? i : 0) has the value 1, which is then added to j to produce 3. The parentheses are necessary, by the way; the precedence of the conditional operator is less than that of the other operators we've discussed so far, with the exception of the assignment operators.

Conditional expressions tend to make programs shorter but harder to understand, so it's probably best to avoid them. There are, however, a few places in which they're tempting; one is the return statement. Instead of writing

```
if (i > j)
  return i;
else
  return j;
```

many programmers would write

```
return (i > j ? i : j);
```

Calls of printf can sometimes benefit from condition expressions. Instead of

```
if (i > j)
  printf("%d\n", i);
else
  printf("%d\n", j);
```

we could simply write

```
printf("%d\n", i > j ? i : j);
```

conditional expressions in
macro definitions ➤ 14.3

Conditional expressions are also common in certain kinds of macro definitions.

Boolean Values

C's lack of a proper Boolean type can be annoying, since many programs need variables that can store either *false* or *true*. (Recognizing this problem, newer versions of C++ provide a built-in Boolean type.) We can always simulate a Boolean variable by declaring an int variable, then assigning it 0 or 1:

```
int flag;

flag = 0;
...
flag = 1;
```

Although this scheme works, it doesn't contribute much to program readability. It's not obvious that flag is to be assigned only Boolean values and that 0 and 1 represent false and true.

macros ➤ 2.6

To make programs more understandable, it's a good idea to define macros with names such as TRUE and FALSE:

```
#define TRUE 1
#define FALSE 0
```

Assignments to flag now have a more natural appearance:

```
flag = FALSE;
...
flag = TRUE;
```

To test whether flag is true, we can write

```
if (flag == TRUE) ...
```

or just

```
if (flag) ...
```

To test whether flag is false, we can write

```
if (flag == FALSE) ...
```

or

```
if (!flag) ...
```

Carrying this idea one step further, we might even define a macro that can be used as a type:

```
#define BOOL int
```

BOOL can take the place of int when declaring Boolean variables:

```
BOOL flag;
```

It's now clear that flag isn't an ordinary integer variable, but instead represents a Boolean condition. (The compiler still treats flag as an int variable, of course.) In later chapters, we'll discover better ways to set up a Boolean type.

type definitions ➤ 7.6
enumerations ➤ 16.5

5.3 The switch Statement

In everyday programming, we'll often need to compare an expression against a series of values to see which one it currently matches. We saw in Section 5.2 that a cascaded if statement can be used for this purpose. For example, the following cascaded if statement prints the English word that corresponds to a numerical grade:

```
if (grade == 4)
  printf("Excellent");
else if (grade == 3)
  printf("Good");
else if (grade == 2)
  printf("Average");
else if (grade == 1)
```

```
      printf("Poor");
else if (grade == 0)
  printf("Failing");
else
  printf("Illegal grade");
```

As an alternative to this kind of cascaded `if` statement, C provides the `switch` statement. The following `switch` is equivalent to our cascaded `if`:

```
switch (grade) {
  case 4:  printf("Excellent");
           break;
  case 3:  printf("Good");
           break;
  case 2:  printf("Average");
           break;
  case 1:  printf("Poor");
           break;
  case 0:  printf("Failing");
           break;
  default: printf("Illegal grade");
           break;
}
```

When this statement is executed, the value of the variable `grade` is tested against 4, 3, 2, 1, and 0. If it matches 4, for example, the message `Excellent` is printed, then the `break` statement transfers control to the statement following the switch. If the value of `grade` doesn't match any of the choices listed, the `default` case applies, and the message `Illegal grade` is printed.

break statement ➤6.4

A `switch` statement is often easier to read than a cascaded `if` statement. Moreover, `switch` statements are often faster than `if` statements, especially when there are more than a handful of cases.

Q&A

In its most common form, the `switch` statement has the form

switch statement

```
switch ( expression ) {
  case constant-expression : statements
  ...
  case constant-expression : statements
  default : statements
}
```

The `switch` statement is fairly complex; let's look at its components one by one:

- ***Controlling expression.*** The word `switch` must be followed by an integer expression in parentheses. Characters are treated as integers in C and thus can be tested in `switch` statements. Floating-point numbers and strings don't qualify, however.

characters ➤7.3

- ***Case labels.*** Each case begins with a label of the form

```
case constant-expression :
```

A *constant expression* is much like an ordinary expression except that it can't contain variables or function calls. Thus, 5 is a constant expression, and 5 + 10 is a constant expression, but n + 10 isn't a constant expression (unless n is a macro that represents a constant). The constant expression in a case label must evaluate to an integer (characters are also acceptable).

- *Statements.* After each case label comes any number of statements. No braces are required around the statements. (Enjoy it—this is one of the few places in C where braces aren't required.) The last statement in each group is normally break.

Duplicate case labels aren't allowed. The order of the cases doesn't matter; in particular, the default case doesn't need to come last.

Only one constant expression may follow the word case; however, several case labels may precede the same group of statements:

```
switch (grade) {
  case 4:
  case 3:
  case 2:
  case 1:  printf("Passing");
           break;
  case 0:  printf("Failing");
           break;
  default: printf("Illegal grade");
           break;
}
```

To save space, programmers sometimes put several case labels on the same line:

```
switch (grade) {
  case 4: case 3: case 2: case 1:
           printf("Passing");
           break;
  case 0:  printf("Failing");
           break;
  default: printf("Illegal grade");
           break;
}
```

Unfortunately, there's no way to write a case label that specifies a range of values, as there is in some programming languages.

A switch statement isn't required to have a default case. If default is missing and the value of the controlling expression doesn't match any of the case labels, control simply passes to the next statement after the switch.

The Role of the **break** Statement

Now, let's take a closer look at the mysterious break statement. As we've seen, executing a break statement causes the program to "break" out of the switch statement; execution continues at the next statement after the switch.

The reason that we need `break` has to do with the fact that the `switch` statement is really a form of "computed jump." When the controlling expression is evaluated, control jumps to the case label matching the value of the `switch` expression. A case label is nothing more than a marker indicating a position within the `switch`. When the last statement in the case has been executed, control "falls through" to the first statement in the following case; the case label for the next case is ignored. Without `break` (or some other jump statement), control will flow from one case into the next. Consider the following `switch` statement:

```
switch (grade) {
  case 4:  printf("Excellent");
  case 3:  printf("Good");
  case 2:  printf("Average");
  case 1:  printf("Poor");
  case 0:  printf("Failing");
  default: printf("Illegal grade");
}
```

If the value of `grade` is 3, the message printed is

```
GoodAveragePoorFailingIllegal grade
```

Forgetting to use `break` is a common error. Although omitting `break` is sometimes done intentionally to allow several cases to share code, it's usually just an oversight.

Since deliberately falling through from one case into the next is rare, it's a good idea to point out any deliberate omission of `break`:

```
switch (grade) {
  case 4: case 3: case 2: case 1:
          num_passing++;
          /* FALL THROUGH */
  case 0: total_grades++;
          break;
}
```

Without the comment, someone might later fix the "error" by adding an unwanted `break` statement.

Although the last case in a `switch` statement never needs a `break` statement, it's common practice to put one there anyway to guard against a "missing `break`" problem if cases should later be added.

PROGRAM ## Printing a Date in Legal Form

Contracts and other legal documents are often dated in the following way:

Dated this _____ day of _____ , 19__ .

Let's write a program that displays dates in this form. We'll have the user enter the date in month/day/year form, then we'll display the date in "legal" form:

```
Enter date (mm/dd/yy): 7/19/96
Dated this 19th day of July, 1996.
```

We can get `printf` to do most of the formatting. However, we're left with two problems: how to add "th" (or "st" or "nd" or "rd") to the day, and how to print the month as a word instead of a number. Fortunately, the `switch` statement is ideal for both situations; we'll have one `switch` print the day suffix and another print the month name.

date.c

```c
/* Prints a date in legal form */

#include <stdio.h>

main()
{
  int month, day, year;

  printf("Enter date (mm/dd/yy): ");
  scanf("%d /%d /%d", &month, &day, &year);

  printf("Dated this %d", day);
  switch (day) {
    case 1: case 21: case 31:
      printf("st"); break;
    case 2: case 22:
      printf("nd"); break;
    case 3: case 23:
      printf("rd"); break;
    default: printf("th"); break;
  }
  printf(" day of ");

  switch (month) {
    case 1:  printf("January");   break;
    case 2:  printf("February");  break;
    case 3:  printf("March");     break;
    case 4:  printf("April");     break;
    case 5:  printf("May");       break;
    case 6:  printf("June");      break;
    case 7:  printf("July");      break;
    case 8:  printf("August");    break;
    case 9:  printf("September"); break;
    case 10: printf("October");   break;
    case 11: printf("November");  break;
    case 12: printf("December");  break;
  }

  printf(", 19%.2d.\n", year);
  return 0;
}
```

Note the use of `%.2d` to display the last two digits of the year. If we had used `%d` instead, single-digit years would be displayed incorrectly (1900 would be printed as `190`).

Q & A

Q: My compiler doesn't give a warning when I use = instead of ==. Is there some way to force the compiler to notice the problem? [p. 67]

A: Here's a trick that some programmers use: instead of writing

```
if (i == 0) …
```

they habitually write

```
if (0 == i) …
```

Now suppose that the `==` operator is accidentally written as `=`:

```
if (0 = i) …
```

The compiler will produce an error message, since it's not possible to assign a value to 0. I don't use this trick, because I think it makes programs look unnatural. Also, it can be used only when one of the operands in the test condition isn't an lvalue.

Q: C books seem to use several different styles of indentation and brace placement for compound statements. Which style is best?

A: According to *The New Hacker's Dictionary* (Cambridge, Mass.: MIT Press, 1993), there are four common styles of indentation and brace placement:

- The *K&R style*, used in Kernighan and Ritchie's *The C Programming Language*, is the one I've chosen for the programs in this book. In the K&R style, the left brace appears at the end of a line:

  ```
  if (line_num == MAX_LINES) {
    line_num = 0;
    page_num++;
  }
  ```

  The K&R style keeps programs compact by not putting the left brace on a line by itself. It's also similar to indentation styles used in many modern languages. A disadvantage: the left brace can be hard to find. (I don't consider this a problem, since the indentation of the inner statements makes it clear where the left brace should be.)
- The *Allman style*, named after Eric Allman (the author of `sendmail` and other UNIX utilities), resembles the way programs are laid out in Pascal:

```
if (line_num == MAX_LINES)
{
  line_num = 0;
  page_num++;
}
```

Each brace is on a separate line, making it easy to check that they match.

■ The *Whitesmiths style*, popularized by the Whitesmiths C compiler, dictates that braces be indented:

```
if (line_num == MAX_LINES)
  {
  line_num = 0;
  page_num++;
  }
```

■ The *GNU style*, used in the GNU software distributed by the Free Software Foundation, indents the braces, then further indents the inner statements:

```
if (line_num == MAX_LINES)
  {
    line_num = 0;
    page_num++;
  }
```

Which style you use is mainly a matter of taste; there's no proof that one style is clearly better than the others. In any event, choosing the right style is less important than applying it consistently.

The New Hacker's Dictionary claims that the Allman and Whitesmiths styles are the most widely used, followed by the K&R style; the GNU style is the rarest. Arguments over style can still be found in the C community, although they often degenerate into "holy wars." Fans of the K&R style, for example, often refer to it as the "One True Brace Style."

Q: **If i is an int variable and f is a float variable, what is the type of the conditional expression (i > 0 ? i : f)?**

A: When int and float values are mixed in a conditional expression, as they are here, the expression has type float. If i > 0 is true, the value of the expression will be the value of i after conversion to float type.

Q: **The template given for the switch statement described it as the "most common form." Are there other forms? [p. 75]**

A: The switch statement is a bit more general than described in this chapter. For
labels ►6.4   example, it can contain labels that aren't preceded by the word case, which leads to an amusing (?) trap. Suppose that we accidentally misspell the word default:

```
switch (…) {
  …
  defualt: …
}
```

The compiler won't detect the error, since it assumes that defualt is an ordinary label.

Although I've omitted a few details about the switch statement, the form described in the chapter is general enough for virtually all programs. Appendix A gives a more precise description of the statement.

Q: **I've seen several methods of indenting the switch statement. Which way is best?**

A: There are at least two common methods. One is to put the statements in each case *after* the case label:

```
switch (coin) {
  case 1:  printf("Cent");
           break;
  case 5:  printf("Nickel");
           break;
  case 10: printf("Dime");
           break;
  case 25: printf("Quarter");
           break;
}
```

If each case consists of a single action (a call of printf, in this example), the break statement could even go on the same line as the action:

```
switch (coin) {
  case 1:  printf("Cent"); break;
  case 5:  printf("Nickel"); break;
  case 10: printf("Dime"); break;
  case 25: printf("Quarter"); break;
}
```

The other method is to put the statements *under* the case label, indenting the statements to make the case label stand out:

```
switch (coin) {
  case 1:
    printf("Cent");
    break;
  case 5:
    printf("Nickel");
    break;
  case 10:
    printf("Dime");
    break;
  case 25:
    printf("Quarter");
    break;
}
```

In one variation of this scheme, each case label is aligned under the word switch.

The first method is fine when the statements in each case are short and there are relatively few of them. The second method is better for large `switch` statements in which the statements in each case are complex and/or numerous.

Exercises

Section 5.1

1. The following code fragments illustrate the relational and equality operators. Show the output produced by each, assuming that i, j, and k are int variables.

    (a) `i = 2; j = 3;`
        `k = i * j == 6;`
        `printf("%d", k);`
    (b) `i = 5; j = 10; k = 1;`
        `printf("%d", k > i < j);`
    (c) `i = 3; j = 2; k = 1;`
        `printf("%d", i < j == j < k);`
    (d) `i = 3; j = 4; k = 5;`
        `printf("%d", i % j + i < k);`

2. The following code fragments illustrate the logical operators. Show the output produced by each, assuming that i, j, and k are int variables.

    (a) `i = 10; j = 5;`
        `printf("%d", !i < j);`
    (b) `i = 2; j = 1;`
        `printf("%d", !!i + !j);`
    (c) `i = 5; j = 0; k = -5;`
        `printf("%d", i && j || k);`
    (d) `i = 1; j = 2; k = 3;`
        `printf("%d", i < j || k);`

*3. The following code fragments illustrate the short-circuit behavior of logical expressions. Show the output produced by each, assuming that i, j, and k are int variables.

    (a) `i = 3; j = 4; k = 5;`
        `printf("%d ", i < j || ++j < k);`
        `printf("%d %d %d", i, j, k);`
    (b) `i = 7; j = 8; k = 9;`
        `printf("%d ", i - 7 && j++ < k);`
        `printf("%d %d %d", i, j, k);`
    (c) `i = 7; j = 8; k = 9;`
        `printf("%d ", (i = j) || (j = k));`
        `printf("%d %d %d", i, j, k);`
    (d) `i = 1; j = 1; k = 1;`
        `printf("%d ", ++i || ++j && ++k);`
        `printf("%d %d %d", i, j, k);`

*4. Write a single expression whose value is either -1, 0, or $+1$, depending on whether i is less than, equal to, or greater than j, respectively.

Section 5.2

5. Write a program that determines the number of digits in a number:

```
Enter a number: 374
The number 374 has 3 digits
```

You may assume that the number has no more than four digits. *Hint:* Use if statements to test the number. For example, if the number is between 0 and 9, it has one digit. If the number is between 10 and 99, it has two digits.

6. Write a program that asks the user for a 24-hour time, then displays the time in 12-hour form:

```
Enter a 24-hour time: 21:11
Equivalent 12-hour time: 9:11 PM
```

Be careful not to display 12:00 as 0:00.

7. Modify the broker.c program by making both of the following changes:

(a) Ask the user to enter the number of shares and the price per share, instead of the value of the trade.

(b) Add statements that compute the commission charged by a rival broker ($33 plus 3¢ per share for fewer than 2000 shares; $33 plus 2¢ per share for 2000 shares or more). Display the rival's commission as well as the commission charged by the original broker.

8. Here's a simplified version of the Beaufort scale, which is used to measure wind force:

Velocity (knots)	Description
Less than 1	Calm
1–3	Light air
4–27	Breeze
28–47	Gale
48–63	Storm
Above 63	Hurricane

Write a program that asks the user to enter a wind velocity (in knots), then displays the corresponding description.

9. In one state, single residents are subject to the following income tax:

Income	Amount of tax
Not over $750	1% of income
$750–$2,250	$7.50 plus 2% of amount over $750
$2,250–$3,750	$37.50 plus 3% of amount over $2,250
$3,750–$5,250	$82.50 plus 4% of amount over $3,750
$5,250–$7,000	$142.50 plus 5% of amount over $5,250
Over $7,000	$230.00 plus 6% of amount over $7,000

Write a program that asks the user to enter the amount of taxable income, then displays the tax due.

10. Modify the upc.c program of Section 4.1 so that it checks whether a UPC is valid. After the user enters a UPC, the program will display either VALID or NOT VALID.

*11. Is the following if statement legal in C?

```
if (n >= 1 <= 10)
  printf("n is between 1 and 10\n");
```

If so, what does it do when n is equal to 0?

*12.   Is the following if statement legal in C?

```
if (n == 1-10)
   printf("n is between 1 and 10\n");
```

If so, what does it do when n is equal to 5?

13.   What does the following statement print if i has the value 17? What does it print if i has the value –17?

```
printf("%d\n", i >= 0 ? i : -i);
```

Section 5.3   14.   Using the switch statement, write a program that converts a numerical grade into a letter grade:

```
Enter numerical grade: 84
Letter grade: B
```

Use the following grading scale: A = 90–100, B = 80–89, C = 70–79, D = 60–69, F = 0–59. Print an error message if the grade is larger than 100 or less than 0. *Hint:* Break the grade into two digits, then use a switch statement to test the ten's digit.

15.   Write a program that asks the user for a two-digit number, then prints the English word for the number:

```
Enter a two-digit number: 45
You entered the number forty-five.
```

Hint: Break the number into two digits. Use one switch statement to print the word for the first digit ("twenty," "thirty," and so forth). Use a second switch statement to print the word for the second digit. Don't forget that the numbers between 11 and 19 require special treatment.

*16.   What output does the following program fragment produce? (Assume that i is an integer variable.)

```
i = 1;
switch (i % 3) {
  case 0: printf("zero");
  case 1: printf("one");
  case 2: printf("two");
}
```

6 Loops

A program without a loop and a structured
variable isn't worth writing.

Chapter 5 covered C's selection statements, if and switch. In this chapter, we'll introduce C's iteration statements, which allow us to set up loops.

A *loop* is a statement whose job is to repeatedly execute some other statement (the *loop body*). In C, every loop has a *controlling expression*. Each time the loop body is executed (an *iteration* of the loop), the controlling expression is evaluated; if the expression is true—has a value that's not zero—the loop continues to execute.

C provides three iteration statements: while, do, and for, which are covered in Sections 6.1, 6.2, and 6.3, respectively. The while statement is used for loops whose controlling expression is tested *before* the loop body is executed. The do statement is used if the expression is tested *after* the loop body is executed. The for statement is convenient for loops that increment or decrement a counting variable. Section 6.3 also introduces the comma operator, which is used primarily in for statements.

The last two sections of this chapter are devoted to C features that are used in conjunction with loops. Section 6.4 describes the break, continue, and goto statements. break jumps out of a loop and transfers control to the next statement after the loop, continue skips the rest of a loop iteration, and goto jumps to any statement within a function. Section 6.5 covers the null statement, which can be used to create loops with empty bodies.

6.1 The while Statement

Of all the ways to set up loops in C, the while statement is the simplest and most fundamental. The while statement has the form

while statement   while (*expression*) *statement*

The expression inside the parentheses is the controlling expression; the statement after the parentheses is the loop body. Here's an example:

```
while (i < n)     /* controlling expression */
  i = i * 2;      /* loop body */
```

Note that the parentheses are mandatory and that nothing goes between the right parenthesis and the loop body. (Some languages require the word do.)

When a while statement is executed, the controlling expression is evaluated first. If its value is nonzero (true), the loop body is executed and the expression is tested again. The process continues in this fashion—first testing the controlling expression, then executing the loop body—until the controlling expression eventually has the value zero.

The following example uses a while statement to compute the smallest power of 2 that's greater than or equal to a number n:

```
i = 1;
while (i < n)
  i = i * 2;
```

Suppose that n has the value 10. The following trace shows what happens when the while statement is executed:

```
i = 1;        i is now 1.
Is i < n?     Yes; continue.
i = i * 2;    i is now 2.
Is i < n?     Yes; continue.
i = i * 2;    i is now 4.
Is i < n?     Yes; continue.
i = i * 2;    i is now 8.
Is i < n?     Yes; continue.
i = i * 2;    i is now 16.
Is i < n?     No; exit from loop.
```

Notice how the loop keeps going as long as the controlling expression (i < n) is true. When the expression is false, the loop terminates, and i is greater than or equal to n, as desired.

Although the loop body must be a single statement, that's merely a technicality; if we want more than one statement, we can just use braces to create a single compound statement:

```
while (i > 0) {
  printf("T minus %d and counting\n", i);
  i--;
}
```

Some programmers always use braces, even when they're not strictly necessary:

```
while (i < n) {    /* braces allowed, but not required */
  i = i * 2;
}
```

As a second example, let's trace the execution of the following statements, which display a series of "countdown" messages:

```
i = 10;
while (i > 0) {
  printf("T minus %d and counting\n", i);
  i--;
}
```

Before the while statement is executed, the variable i is assigned the value 10. Since 10 is greater than 0, the loop body is executed, causing the message T minus 10 and counting to be printed and i to be decremented. The condition i > 0 is then tested again. Since 9 is greater than 0, the loop body is executed once more. This process continues until the message T minus 1 and counting is printed and i becomes 0. The test i > 0 then fails, causing the loop to terminate.

The "countdown" example leads us to make several observations about the while statement:

- The controlling expression is false when a while loop terminates. Thus, when a loop controlled by the expression i > 0 terminates, i must be less than or equal to 0. (Otherwise, we'd still be executing the loop!)
- The body of a while loop may not be executed at all. Since the controlling expression is tested *before* the loop body is executed, it's possible that the body isn't executed even once. If i has a negative or zero value when the "countdown" loop is first entered, the loop will do nothing.
- A while statement can often be written in a variety of ways. For example, we could make the "countdown" loop more concise by decrementing i inside the call of printf:

Q&A

```
while (i > 0) printf("T minus %d and counting\n", i--);
```

Infinite Loops

A while statement won't terminate if the controlling expression always has a nonzero value. In fact, C programmers sometimes deliberately create an infinite loop by using a nonzero constant as the controlling expression:

idiom   `while (1) ...`

A while statement of this form will execute forever unless its body contains a statement that transfers control out of the loop (break, goto, return) or calls a function that causes the program to terminate.

PROGRAM   **Printing a Table of Squares**

Let's write a program that prints a table of squares. The program will first prompt the user to enter a number *n*. It will then print *n* lines of output, with each line containing a number between 1 and *n* together with its square:

```
This program prints a table of squares.
Enter number of entries in table: 5
         1         1
         2         4
         3         9
         4        16
         5        25
```

Let's have the program store the desired number of squares in a variable named n. We'll need a loop that repeatedly prints a number i and its square, starting with i equal to 1. The loop will repeat as long as i is less than or equal to n. We'll have to make sure to add 1 to i each time through the loop.

We'll write the loop as a while statement. (Frankly, we haven't got much choice, since the while statement is the only kind of loop we've covered so far.) Here's the finished program:

See pg. 95

square.c

```c
/* Prints a table of squares using a while statement */

#include <stdio.h>

main()
{
  int i, n;

  printf("This program prints a table of squares.\n");
  printf("Enter number of entries in table: ");
  scanf("%d", &n);

  i = 1;
  while (i <= n) {
    printf("%10d%10d\n", i, i * i);
    i++;
  }

  return 0;
}
```

Note how square.c displays numbers in neatly aligned columns. The trick is to use a conversion specification like %10d instead of just %d, taking advantage of the fact that printf right-justifies numbers when a field width is specified.

PROGRAM   **Summing a Series of Numbers**

As a second example of the while statement, let's write a program that sums a series of integers entered by the user. Here's what the user will see:

```
This program sums a series of integers.
Enter integers (0 to terminate): 8 23 71 5 0
The sum is: 107
```

Clearly we'll need a loop that uses scanf to read a number and then adds the number to a running total.

Letting n represent the number just read and sum the total of all numbers previously read, we end up with the following program:

sum.c

```
/* Sums a series of numbers */

#include <stdio.h>

main()
{
  int n, sum = 0;

  printf("This program sums a series of integers.\n");
  printf("Enter integers (0 to terminate): ");

  scanf("%d", &n);
  while (n != 0) {
    sum += n;
    scanf("%d", &n);
  }
  printf("The sum is: %d\n", sum);

  return 0;
}
```

Notice that the condition n != 0 is tested just after a number is read, allowing the loop to terminate as soon as possible.

6.2 The do Statement

The do statement is closely related to the while statement; in fact, the do statement is essentially just a while statement whose controlling expression is tested *after* each execution of the loop body. The do statement has the form

do statement

> do *statement* while (*expression*) ;

As with the while statement, the body of a do statement must be one statement (possibly compound, of course) and the controlling expression requires parentheses.

When a do statement is executed, the loop body is executed first, then the controlling expression is evaluated. If the value of the expression is nonzero, the loop body is executed again and then the expression is evaluated once more. Execution of the do statement terminates when the controlling expression has the value 0 *after* the loop body has been executed.

Let's rewrite our "counting down" example, using a do statement this time:

```
i = 10;
do {
  printf("T minus %d and counting\n", i);
  --i;
} while (i > 0);
```

When the do statement is executed, the loop body is first executed, causing the message T minus 10 and counting to be printed and i to be decremented. The condition i > 0 is now tested. Since 9 is greater than 0, the loop body is executed a second time. This process continues until the message T minus 1 and counting is printed and i becomes 0. The test i > 0 now fails, causing the loop to terminate. As this example shows, the do statement is often indistinguishable from the while statement. The difference between the two is that the body of a do statement is always executed at least once; the body of a while statement is skipped entirely if the controlling expression is 0 initially.

Incidentally, many C programmers use braces in *all* do statements, whether or not they're needed, because a do statement without braces can easily be mistaken for a while statement:

```
do printf("T minus %d and counting\n", i--);
while (i > 0);
```

A careless reader might think that the word while was the beginning of a while statement.

PROGRAM   ## Calculating the Number of Digits in an Integer

Although the while statement appears in C programs much more often than the do statement, the latter is handy for loops that must execute at least once. To illustrate this point, let's write a program that calculates the number of digits in an integer entered by the user:

```
Enter a nonnegative integer: 60
The number has 2 digit(s).
```

Our strategy will be to divide the user's input by 10 repeatedly until it becomes 0; the number of divisions performed is the number of digits. Clearly we'll need some kind of loop, since we don't know how many divisions it will take to reach 0. But should we use a while statement or a do statement? The do statement turns out to be more attractive, because every integer—even 0—has at least *one* digit. Here's the program:

numdigit.c   `/* Calculates the number of digits in an integer */`

`#include <stdio.h>`

```
main()
{
  int digits = 0, n;

  printf("Enter a nonnegative integer: ");
  scanf("%d", &n);

  do {
    n /= 10;
    digits++;
  } while (n > 0);

  printf("The number has %d digit(s).\n", digits);

  return 0;
}
```

To see why the do statement is the right choice, let's see what would happen if we were to replace the do loop by a similar while loop:

```
while (n > 0) {
  n /= 10;
  digits++;
}
```

If n is 0 initially, this loop won't execute at all, and the program would print

```
The number has 0 digit(s).
```

6.3 The for Statement

We now come to the last, and most powerful, of C's loops: the for statement. Don't be discouraged by the for statement's apparent complexity; it's actually the best way to write many loops. The for statement is ideal for loops that have a "counting" variable, but it's versatile enough to be used for other kinds of loops as well.

The for statement has the form

for statement

> for (*expr1* ; *expr2* ; *expr3*) *statement*

where *expr1*, *expr2*, and *expr3* are expressions. Here's an example:

```
for (i = 10; i > 0; i--)
  printf("T minus %d and counting\n", i);
```

When this for statement is executed, the variable i is initialized to 10, then i is tested to see if it's greater than 0. Since it is, the message T minus 10 and counting is printed, then i is decremented. The condition i > 0 is then tested again. The loop body will be executed 10 times in all, with i varying from 10 down to 1.

Q&A The for statement is closely related to the while statement. In fact, except in a few rare cases, a for loop can always be replaced by an equivalent while loop:

```
expr1;
while ( expr2 ) {
  statement
  expr3;
}
```

As this expansion shows, *expr1* is an initialization step that's performed only once, before the loop begins to execute, *expr2* controls loop termination (the loop continues executing as long as the value of *expr2* is nonzero), and *expr3* is an operation to be performed at the end of each loop iteration. Applying this expansion to our previous for loop example, we arrive at the following:

```
i = 10;
while (i > 0) {
  printf("T minus %d and counting\n", i);
  i--;
}
```

Studying the equivalent while statement can help us understand the fine points of a for statement. For example, suppose that we replace i-- by --i in our for loop example:

```
for (i = 10; i > 0; --i)
  printf("T minus %d and counting\n", i);
```

How does this change affect the loop? Looking at the equivalent while loop, we see that it has no effect:

```
i = 10;
while (i > 0) {
  printf("T minus %d and counting\n", i);
  --i;
}
```

Since the first and third expressions in a for statement are executed as statements, their values are irrelevant—they're useful only for their side effects. Consequently, these two expressions are usually assignments or increment/decrement expressions.

for Statement Idioms

The for statement is usually the best choice for loops that "count up" (increment a variable) or "count down" (decrement a variable). A for statement that counts up or down a total of n times will usually have one of the following forms:

- *Counting up from 0 to n–1:*

idiom
```
for (i = 0; i < n; i++) …
```

- *Counting up from 1 to n:*

idiom
```
for (i = 1; i <= n; i++) …
```

- *Counting down from n–1 to 0:*

idiom
```
for (i = n-1; i >= 0; i--) …
```

- *Counting down from n to 1:*

idiom
```
for (i = n; i > 0; i--) …
```

Imitating these patterns will help you avoid some of the errors that beginning C programmers often make:

- Using < instead of > (or vice versa) in the controlling expression. Notice that "counting up" loops use the < or <= operator, while "counting down" loops rely on > or >=.
- Using == in the controlling expression instead of <, <=, >, or >=. A controlling expression needs to be true at the beginning of the loop, then later become false so that the loop can terminate. A test such as i == n doesn't make much sense, because it won't be true initially.
- "Off-by-one" errors such as writing the controlling expression as i <= n instead of i < n.

Omitting Expressions in a `for` Statement

The for statement is even more flexible than we've seen so far. Some for loops may not need all three of the expressions that normally control the loop, so C allows us to omit any or all of the expressions.

If the *first* expression is omitted, no initialization is performed before the loop is executed:

```
i = 10;
for (; i > 0; --i)
  printf("T minus %d and counting\n", i);
```

In this example, i has been initialized by a separate assignment, so we've omitted the first expression in the for statement. (Notice that the semicolon between the first and second expressions remains. The two semicolons must always be present, even when we've omitted some of the expressions.)

If we omit the *third* expression in a for statement, the loop body is responsible for ensuring that the value of the second expression eventually becomes false. Our for statement example could be written like this:

```
for (i = 10; i > 0;)
  printf("T minus %d and counting\n", i--);
```

To compensate for omitting the third expression, we've arranged for i to be decremented inside the loop body.

When the *first* and *third* expressions are both omitted, the resulting loop is nothing more than a while statement in disguise. For example, the loop

```
for (; i > 0;)
  printf("T minus %d and counting\n", i--);
```

is the same as

```
while (i > 0)
  printf("T minus %d and counting\n", i--);
```

The while version is clearer and therefore preferable.

If the *second* expression is missing, it defaults to a true value, so the for statement doesn't terminate (unless stopped in some other fashion). For example, some programmers use the following for statement to establish an infinite loop:

idiom

```
for (;;) …
```

The Comma Operator

On occasion, we might like to write a for statement with two (or more) initialization expressions or one that increments several variables each time through the loop. We can do this by using a ***comma expression*** as the first or third expression in the for statement.

A comma expression has the form

comma expression

expr1 , *expr2*

where *expr1* and *expr2* are any two expressions. A comma expression is evaluated in two steps: First, *expr1* is evaluated and its value discarded. Second, *expr2* is evaluated; its value is the value of the entire expression. Evaluating *expr1* should always have a side effect; if it doesn't, then *expr1* serves no purpose.

For example, suppose that i and j have the values 1 and 5, respectively. When the comma expression ++i,i+j is evaluated, i is first incremented, then i+j is evaluated, so the value of the expression is 7. (And, of course, i now has the value 2.) The precedence of the comma operator is less than that of all other operators, by the way, so there's no need to put parentheses around ++i and i+j.

Occasionally, we'll need to chain together a series of comma expressions, just as we sometimes chain assignments together. The comma operator is left associative, so the compiler interprets

```
i = 1, j = 2, k = i + j
```

as

```
((i = 1), (j = 2)), (k = (i + j))
```

As a result, we're guaranteed that the expressions $i = 1$, $j = 2$, and $k = i + j$ are evaluated from left to right.

The comma operator is provided for situations where C requires a single expression, but we'd like to have two or more expressions. In other words, the comma operator allows us to "glue" two expressions together to form a single expression. (Note the similarity to the compound statement, which allows us to treat a group of statements as a single statement.)

The need to glue expressions together doesn't arise that often. Certain kinds of macros can benefit from the comma operator, as we'll see in a later chapter. The `for` statement is the only other place where the comma operator is likely to be found. For example, suppose that we want to initialize two variables when entering a `for` statement. Instead of writing

macros ➤ 14.3

```
sum = 0;
for (i = 1; i <= N; i++)
  sum += i;
```

we can write

```
for (sum = 0, i = 1; i <= N; i++)
  sum += i;
```

The expression $sum = 0$, $i = 1$ first assigns 0 to `sum`, then assigns 1 to `i`. With additional commas, the `for` statement could initialize more than two variables.

PROGRAM   **Printing a Table of Squares (Revisited)**

The `square.c` program (Section 6.1) can be improved by converting its `while` loop to a `for` loop:

square2.c
```
/* Prints a table of squares using a for statement */

#include <stdio.h>

main()
{
  int i, n;

  printf("This program prints a table of squares.\n");
  printf("Enter number of entries in table: ");
  scanf("%d", &n);

  for (i = 1; i <= n; i++)
    printf("%10d%10d\n", i, i * i);

  return 0;
}
```

We can use this program to illustrate an important point about the `for` statement. The `for` statement in C is more powerful than the `for` statement in similar programming languages—and potentially more confusing—because C places no restrictions on the three expressions that control its behavior. Although these expressions usually initialize, test, and update the same variable, there's no requirement that they be related in any way. Consider the following version of the same program:

square3.c

```
/* Prints a table of squares using an odd method */

#include <stdio.h>

main()
{
  int i, n, odd, square;

  printf("This program prints a table of squares.\n");
  printf("Enter number of entries in table: ");
  scanf("%d", &n);

  i = 1;
  odd = 3;
  for (square = 1; i <= n; odd += 2) {
    printf("%10d%10d\n", i, square);
    ++i;
    square += odd;
  }

  return 0;
}
```

The `for` statement in this program initializes one variable (`square`), tests another (`i`), and increments a third (`odd`). `i` is the number to be squared, `square` is the square of `i`, and `odd` is the odd number that must be added to the current square to get the next square (allowing the program to compute consecutive squares without performing any multiplications).

The tremendous flexibility of the `for` statement can sometimes be useful; we'll find it to be a great help when working with linked lists. The `for` statement can easily be misused, though, so don't go overboard. The `for` loop in `square3.c` would be a lot clearer if we rearranged its pieces so that the loop is clearly controlled by `i`; in fact, you're asked to do just that in an exercise.

linked lists ➤ 17.5

6.4   Exiting from a Loop

We've seen how to write loops that have an exit point before the loop body (using `while` and `for` statements) or after it (using `do` statements). Occasionally, however, we'll need a loop with an exit point in the middle. We may even want a loop to have more than one exit point. The `break` statement makes it possible to write either kind of loop.

After we've examined the break statement, we'll look at a couple of related statements: continue and goto. The continue statement makes it possible to skip part of a loop iteration without jumping out of the loop. The goto statement allows a program to jump from one statement to another. Thanks to the availability of statements such as break and continue, the goto statement is rarely used.

The break Statement

We've already discussed how a break statement can transfer control out of a switch statement. The break statement can also be used to jump out of a while, do, or for loop.

Suppose that we're writing a program that checks whether a number n is prime. Our plan is to write a for statement that divides n by the numbers between 2 and n − 1. We can break out of the loop as soon as any divisor is found; there's no need to try the remaining possibilities. After the loop has terminated, we can use an if statement to determine whether termination was premature (hence n isn't prime) or normal (n is prime):

```
for (d = 2; d < n; d++)
  if (n % d == 0) break;
if (d < n)
  printf("%d is divisible by %d\n", n, d);
else
  printf("%d is prime\n", n);
```

The break statement is particularly useful for writing loops in which the exit point is in the middle of the body rather than at the beginning or end. Loops that read user input, terminating when a particular value is entered, often fall into this category:

```
for (;;) {
  printf("Enter a number (enter 0 to stop): ");
  scanf("%d", &n);
  if (n == 0) break;
  printf("%d cubed is %d\n", n, n*n*n);
}
```

A break statement transfers control out of the *innermost* enclosing while, do, for, or switch statement. Thus, when these statements are nested, the break statement can escape only one level of nesting. Consider the case of a switch statement nested inside a while statement:

```
while (…) {
  switch (…) {
    …
    break;
    …
  }
}
```

The `break` statement transfers control out of the `switch` statement, but not out of the `while` loop. I'll return to this point later.

The `continue` Statement

The `continue` statement doesn't really belong here, because it doesn't exit from a loop. It's similar to `break`, though, so its inclusion in this section isn't completely arbitrary. `break` transfers control just *past* the end of a loop, while `continue` transfers control to a point just *before* the end of the loop body. With `break`, control leaves the loop; with `continue`, control remains inside the loop. There's another difference between `break` and `continue`: `break` can be used in `switch` statements and loops (`while`, `do`, and `for`), whereas `continue` is limited to loops.

The following example, which reads a series of numbers and computes their sum, illustrates a simple use of `continue`. The loop terminates when 10 nonzero numbers have been read. Whenever the number 0 is read, the `continue` statement is executed, skipping the rest of the loop body (the statements `sum += i;` and `n++;`) but remaining inside the loop.

```
n = 0;
sum = 0;
while (n < 10) {
  scanf("%d", &i);
  if (i == 0) continue;
  sum += i;
  n++;
  /* continue jumps to here */
}
```

If `continue` were not available, we could have written the example as follows:

```
n = 0;
sum = 0;
while (n < 10) {
  scanf("%d", &i);
  if (i != 0) {
    sum += i;
    n++;
  }
}
```

The `goto` Statement

`break` and `continue` are jump statements: they transfer control from one point in the program to another. Both are restricted, however; the target of a `break` is a point just *beyond* the end of the enclosing loop, while the target of a `continue` is a point just *before* the end of the loop. The `goto` statement, on the other hand, is capable of jumping to *any* statement in a function, provided that the statement has a *label*.

A label is just an identifier placed at the beginning of a statement:

labeled statement

> *identifier* : *statement*

A statement may have more than one label. The goto statement itself has the form

goto statement

> goto *identifier* ;

Executing a goto statement transfers control to the statement that follows the label, which must be in the same function as the goto statement itself.

If C didn't have a break statement, here's how we might use a goto statement to exit prematurely from a loop:

```
for (d = 2; d < n; d++)
  if (n % d == 0) goto done;
done:
if (d < n)
  printf("%d is divisible by %d\n", n, d);
else
  printf("%d is prime\n", n);
```

exit function ➤9.5

The goto statement, a staple of older programming languages, is rarely needed in everyday C programming. The break, continue, and return statements—which are essentially restricted goto statements—and the exit function are sufficient to handle most situations that might require a goto in other programming languages.

Nonetheless, the goto statement can be helpful once in a while. Consider the problem of exiting a loop from within a switch statement. As we saw earlier, the break statement doesn't quite have the desired effect: it exits from the switch, but not from the loop. A goto statement solves the problem:

```
while (…) {
  switch (…) {
    …
    goto loop_done;    /* break won't work here */
    …
  }
}
loop_done: …
```

The goto statement is also useful for exiting from nested loops.

PROGRAM **Balancing a Checkbook**

Many simple interactive programs are menu-based: they present the user with a list of commands to choose from. Once the user has selected a command, the program performs the desired action, then prompts the user for another command. This process continues until the user selects an "exit" or "quit" command.

The heart of such a program will obviously be a loop. Inside the loop will be statements that prompt the user for a command, read the command, then decide what action to take:

```
for (;;) {
    prompt user to enter command;
    read command;
    execute command;
}
```

Executing the command will require a switch statement (or cascaded if statement):

```
for (;;) {
    prompt user to enter command;
    read command;
    switch (command) {
        case command₁: perform operation₁; break;
        case command₂: perform operation₂; break;
        ...
        case commandₙ: perform operationₙ; break;
        default: print error message; break;
    }
}
```

To illustrate this arrangement, let's develop a program that maintains a checkbook balance. The program will offer the user a menu of choices: clear the account balance, credit money to the account, debit money from the account, display the current balance, and exit the program. The choices are represented by the integers 0, 1, 2, 3, and 4, respectively. Here's what a session with the program will look like:

```
*** ACME checkbook-balancing program ***
Commands: 0=clear, 1=credit, 2=debit, 3=balance, 4=exit

Enter command: 1
Enter amount of credit: 1042.56
Enter command: 2
Enter amount of debit: 133.79
Enter command: 1
Enter amount of credit: 1754.32
Enter command: 2
Enter amount of debit: 1400
Enter command: 2
Enter amount of debit: 68
Enter command: 2
Enter amount of debit: 50
Enter command: 3
Current balance: $1145.09
Enter command: 4
```

When the user enters the command 4 (exit), the program needs to exit from the `switch` statement *and* the surrounding loop. The `break` statement won't help, and we'd prefer not to use a `goto` statement. Instead, we'll have the program execute a `return` statement, which will cause it to terminate and return to the operating system.

checking.c

```
/* Balances a checkbook */

#include <stdio.h>

main()
{
  int cmd;
  float balance = 0.0, credit, debit;

  printf("*** ACME checkbook-balancing program ***\n");
  printf("Commands: 0=clear, 1=credit, 2=debit, ");
  printf("3=balance, 4=exit\n\n");
  for (;;) {
    printf("Enter command: ");
    scanf("%d", &cmd);
    switch (cmd) {
      case 0:
        balance = 0.0;
        break;
      case 1:
        printf("Enter amount of credit: ");
        scanf("%f", &credit);
        balance += credit;
        break;
      case 2:
        printf("Enter amount of debit: ");
        scanf("%f", &debit);
        balance -= debit;
        break;
      case 3:
        printf("Current balance: $%.2f\n", balance);
        break;
      case 4:
        return 0;
      default:
        printf("Commands: 0=clear, 1=credit, 2=debit, ");
        printf("3=balance, 4=exit\n\n");
        break;
    }
  }
}
```

Note that the `return` statement is not followed by a `break` statement. A `break` immediately following a `return` can never be executed, and many compilers will issue a warning message.

6.5   The Null Statement

A statement can be ***null***—devoid of symbols except for the semicolon at the end. Here's an example:

```
i = 0; ; j = 1;
```

This line contains three statements: an assignment to i, a null statement, and an assignment to j.

Q&A   The null statement is primarily good for one thing: writing loops whose bodies are empty. As an example, recall the prime-finding loop of Section 6.4:

```
for (d = 2; d < n; d++)
  if (n % d == 0) break;
```

If we move the n % d == 0 condition into the loop's controlling expression, the body of the loop becomes empty:

```
for (d = 2; d < n && n % d != 0; d++)
  ;    /* empty body */
```

Each time through the loop, the condition d < n is tested first; if it is false, the loop terminates. Otherwise, the condition n % d != 0 is tested, and if it is false, the loop terminates. (In the latter case, n % d == 0 must be true; in other words, we've found a divisor of n.)

Note how we've put the null statement on a line by itself, instead of writing

```
for (d = 2; d < n && n % d != 0; d++);
```

Q&A   C programmers customarily put the null statement on a line by itself. Otherwise, someone reading the program might get confused about whether the statement after the for was actually its body:

```
for (d = 2; d < n && n % d != 0; d++);
if (d < n)
  printf("%d is divisible by %d\n", n, d);
```

Converting an ordinary loop into one with an empty body doesn't buy much: the new loop is often more concise but usually no more efficient. In a few cases, though, a loop with an empty body is clearly superior to the alternatives. For *reading characters* ➤ *7.3*   example, we'll find these loops to be handy for reading character data.

The null statement is responsible for an entire class of pitfalls. Accidentally putting a semicolon after the parentheses in an if, while, or for statement ends the statement prematurely; the compiler can't detect an error of this kind.

- In an `if` statement, putting a semicolon after the parentheses creates an `if` statement that apparently performs the same action regardless of the value of its controlling expression:

```
if (d == 0);                                /*** WRONG ***/
  printf("Error: Division by zero\n");
```

The call of `printf` isn't inside the `if` statement, so it's performed regardless of whether `d` is equal to 0.

- In a `while` statement, putting a semicolon after the parentheses may create an infinite loop:

```
i = 10;
while (i > 0);                              /*** WRONG ***/
{
  printf("T minus %d and counting\n", i);
  --i;
}
```

Another possibility is that the loop terminates, but the statement that should be the loop body is executed only once, after the loop has terminated:

```
i = 11;
while (--i > 0);                            /*** WRONG ***/
  printf("T minus %d and counting\n", i);
```

This example prints the message

```
T minus 0 and counting
```

- In a `for` statement, putting a semicolon after the parentheses causes the statement that should be the loop body to be executed only once:

```
for (i = 10; i > 0; i--);                   /*** WRONG ***/
  printf("T minus %d and counting\n", i);
```

This example also prints the message

```
T minus 0 and counting
```

Q & A

Q: **The following loop appears in Section 6.1:**

```
while (i > 0) printf("T minus %d and counting\n", i--);
```

Why not shorten the loop even more by removing the "> 0" test?

```
while (i) printf("T minus %d and counting\n", i--);
```

This version will stop when i reaches 0, so it should be just as good as the original. [p. 87]

A: The new version is certainly more concise, and many C programmers would write the loop in just this way. It does have drawbacks, though.

First, the new loop is not as easy to read as the original. It's clear that the loop will terminate when i reaches 0, but it's not obvious whether we're counting up or down. In the original loop, that information can be deduced from the controlling expression, i > 0.

Second, the new loop behaves differently than the original if i should happen to have a negative value when the loop begins to execute. The original loop terminates immediately, but the new loop doesn't.

Q: **Section 6.3 says that *most* for loops can be converted to while loops using a standard pattern. Why isn't this true for *all* for loops? [p. 92]**

A: When the body of a for loop contains a continue statement, the while pattern shown in Section 6.3 is no longer valid. Consider the following example from Section 6.4:

```
n = 0;
sum = 0;
while (n < 10) {
   scanf("%d", &i);
   if (i == 0) continue;
   sum += i;
   n++;
}
```

At first glance, it looks as though we could convert the while loop into a for loop:

```
sum = 0;
for (n = 0; n < 10; n++) {
   scanf("%d", &i);
   if (i == 0) continue;
   sum += i;
}
```

Unfortunately, this loop isn't equivalent to the original. When i is equal to 0, the original loop doesn't increment n, but the new loop does.

Q: **Which form of infinite loop is preferable, while (1) or for (;;)? [p. 94]**

A: C programmers have traditionally preferred for (;;) for reasons of efficiency; older compilers would often force programs to test the 1 condition each time through the while loop. With modern compilers, however, there should be no difference in performance.

Q: **I've heard that programmers should never use the continue statement. Is this true?**

A: It's true that `continue` statements are rare. Still, `continue` is handy once in a while. Suppose we're writing a loop that reads some input data, checks that it's valid, and, if so, processes the input in some way. If there are a number of validity tests, or if they're complex, `continue` can be helpful. The loop would look something like this:

```
for (;;) {
    read data;
    if (data fails first test)
        continue;
    if (data fails second test)
        continue;
    ...
    if (data fails last test)
        continue;
    process data;
}
```

Q: What's so bad about the `goto` statement? [p. 99]

A: The `goto` statement isn't inherently evil; it's just that we usually have better alternatives. Programs that use more than a few `goto` statements can quickly degenerate into "spaghetti code," with control blithely jumping from here to there. Spaghetti code is hard to understand and hard to modify.

`goto` statements make programs hard to read because they can jump either forward or backward. (In contrast, `break` and `continue` only jump forward.) A program that contains `goto` statements often requires the reader to jump back and forth in an attempt to follow the flow of control.

`goto` statements can make programs hard to modify, since they make it possible for a section of code to serve more than one purpose. For example, a statement that is preceded by a label might be reachable either by "falling through" from the previous statement or by executing one of several `goto` statements.

Q: Does the null statement have any uses besides indicating that the body of a loop is empty? [p. 102]

A: Very few. Since the null statement can appear wherever a statement is allowed, there are many *potential* uses for the null statement. In practice, however, there's only one other use of the null statement, and it's rare.

Suppose that we need to put a label at the end of a compound statement. A label can't stand alone; it must always be followed by a statement. Putting a null statement after the label solves the problem:

```
{
    ...
    goto end_of_stmt;
    ...
    end_of_stmt: ;
}
```

Q: **Are there any other ways to make an empty loop body stand out besides putting the null statement on a line by itself? [p. 102]**

A: Some programmers use a dummy `continue` statement:

```
for (d = 2; d < n && n % d != 0; d++)
  continue;
```

Others use an empty compound statement:

```
for (d = 2; d < n && n % d != 0; d++)
  {}
```

Exercises

Section 6.1

1.   Write a program that finds the largest in a series of numbers entered by the user. The program must prompt the user to enter numbers one by one. When the user enters 0 or a negative number, the program must display the largest nonnegative number entered:

```
Enter a number: 60
Enter a number: 38.3
Enter a number: 4.89
Enter a number: 100.62
Enter a number: 75.2295
Enter a number: 0
```

not sure how to print max.

```
The largest number entered was 100.62
```

Notice that the numbers aren't necessarily integers.

2.   Write a program that asks the user to enter two integers, then calculates and displays their greatest common divisor (GCD):

```
Enter two integers: 12 28
Greatest common divisor: 4
```

Hint: The classic algorithm for computing the GCD, known as Euclid's algorithm, goes as follows: Let m and n be variables containing the two numbers. Divide m by n. Save the divisor in m, and save the remainder in n. If n is 0, then stop: m contains the GCD. Otherwise, repeat the process, starting with the division of m by n.

3.   Write a program that asks the user to enter a fraction, then converts the fraction to lowest terms:

```
Enter a fraction: 6/12
In lowest terms: 1/2
```

Hint: To convert a fraction to lowest terms, first compute the GCD of the numerator and denominator. Then divide both the numerator and denominator by the GCD.

4.   Add a loop to the `broker.c` program of Section 5.2 so that the user can enter more than one trade and the program will calculate the commission on each. The program should terminate when the user enters 0 as the trade value:

```
Enter value of trade: 30000
Commission: $166.00
```

```
Enter value of trade: 20000
Commission: $144.00

Enter value of trade: 0
```

Section 6.2 5. Exercise 3 in Chapter 4 asked you to write a program that displays a two-digit number with its digits reversed. Generalize the program so that the number can have one, two, three, or more digits. *Hint:* Use a do loop that repeatedly divides the number by 10, stopping when it reaches 0.

Section 6.3 6. Write a program that prompts the user to enter a number *n*, then prints all even squares between 1 and *n*. For example, if the user enters 100, the program should print the following:

```
4
16
36
64
100
```

7. Rearrange the square3.c program so that the for loop initializes i, tests i, and increments i. Don't rewrite the program; in particular, don't use any multiplications.

8. Write a program that prints a one-month calendar. The user specifies the number of days in the month and the day of the week on which the month begins:

```
Enter number of days in month: 31
Enter starting day of the week (1=Sun, 7=Sat): 3

         1  2  3  4  5
 6  7  8  9 10 11 12
13 14 15 16 17 18 19
20 21 22 23 24 25 26
27 28 29 30 31
```

Hint: This program isn't as hard as it looks. The most important part is a for statement that uses a variable i to count from 1 to n, where n is the number of days in the month, printing each value of i. Inside the loop, an if statement tests whether i is the last day in a week; if so, it prints a new-line character.

*9. What output does the following for statement produce?

```
for (i = 5, j = i - 1; i > 0, j > 0; --i, j = i - 1)
  printf("%d ", i);
```

10. Which one of the following statements is not equivalent to the other two (assuming that the loop bodies are the same)?

(a) `for (i = 0; i < 10; i++) …`
(b) `for (i = 0; i < 10; ++i) …`
(c) `for (i = 0; i++ < 10; ) …`

11. Which one of the following statements is not equivalent to the other two (assuming that the loop bodies are the same)?

(a) `while (i < 10) {…}`
(b) `for (; i < 10;) {…}`
(c) `do {…} while (i < 10);`

Section 6.4   12.   Show how to replace a `continue` statement by an equivalent `goto` statement.

13.   What output does the following program fragment produce?

```
sum = 0;
for (i = 0; i < 10; i++) {
  if (i % 2) continue;
  sum += i;
}
printf("%d\n", sum);
```

14.   The following "prime-testing" loop appeared in Section 6.4 as an example:

```
for (d = 2; d < n; d++)
  if (n % d == 0) break;
```

This loop isn't very efficient. It's not necessary to divide n by all numbers between 2 and n − 1 to determine whether it's prime. In fact, we need only check divisors up to the square root of n. Modify the loop to take advantage of this fact. *Hint:* Don't try to compute the square root of n; instead, compare d * d with n.

Section 6.5   *15.   Rewrite the following loop so that its body is empty:

```
for (n = 0; m > 0; n++)
  m /= 2;
```

*16.   Find the error in the following program fragment and fix it.

```
if (n % 2 == 0);
  printf("n is even\n");
```

7 Basic Types

*Make no mistake about it: Computers process numbers—
not symbols. We measure our understanding (and control)
by the extent to which we can arithmetize an activity.*

So far, we've used only two of C's **basic** (built-in) **types:** int and float. This chapter describes the rest of the basic types and, in the process, provides additional information about the int and float types. Section 7.1 reveals the full range of integer types, including long integers, short integers, and unsigned integers. Section 7.2 introduces the double and long double types, which provide a larger range of values and greater precision than float. Section 7.3 covers the char (character) type, which we'll need in order to work with character data. Section 7.4 describes the sizeof operator, which measures the amount of storage required for a type. Section 7.5 tackles the important issue of converting a value of one type to an equivalent value of another. Finally, Section 7.6 shows how to use typedef to define new type names.

7.1 Integer Types

C supports two fundamentally different kinds of numeric types: **integer** types and **floating** types. Values of an integer type are whole numbers, while values of a floating type can have a fractional part as well. The integer types, in turn, are divided into two categories: **signed** and **unsigned**.

Signed and Unsigned Integers

Integers are typically stored in either 16 bits or 32 bits. In a **signed** number, the left-most bit (the **sign bit**) is 0 if the number is positive or zero, 1 if it's negative. Thus, the largest 16-bit integer has the binary representation

0111111111111111

which has the value 32,767 ($2^{15} - 1$). The largest 32-bit integer is

01111111111111111111111111111111

which has the value 2,147,483,647 ($2^{31} - 1$). An integer with no sign bit (the leftmost bit is considered part of the number's magnitude) is said to be **unsigned**. The largest 16-bit unsigned integer is 65,535 ($2^{16} - 1$), and the largest 32-bit unsigned integer is 4,294,967,295 ($2^{32} - 1$).

By default, integer variables are signed in C—the leftmost bit is reserved for the sign. To tell the compiler that a variable has no sign bit, we declare it to be `unsigned`. Unsigned numbers are primarily useful for systems programming and low-level, machine-dependent applications. We'll discuss typical applications for unsigned numbers in Chapter 20; until then, we'll generally avoid them.

C's integer types come in different sizes. The `int` type is the "natural size" for integers on a given computer (usually 16 bits or 32 bits). Since a 16-bit integer—with its upper limit of 32,767—may be too limited for many applications, C also provides *long* integers. At times, we may need to save space by instructing the compiler to store a number in less space than normal; such a number is called a *short* integer.

To construct an integer type that exactly meets our needs, we can specify that a variable is `long` or `short`, `signed` or `unsigned`. We can even combine specifiers (e.g., `long unsigned int`). However, only the following six combinations actually produce different types:

```
short int
unsigned short int

int
unsigned int

long int
unsigned long int
```

Other combinations are synonyms for one of these six types. (For example, `long signed int` is the same as `long int`, since integers are always signed unless otherwise specified.) Incidentally, the order of the specifiers doesn't matter; `unsigned short int` is the same as `short unsigned int`.

C allows us to abbreviate the names of integer types by dropping the word `int`. For example, `unsigned short int` may be abbreviated to `unsigned short`, and `long int` may be abbreviated to just `long`.

The range of values represented by each of the six integer types varies from one machine to another. However, there are a couple of rules that all compilers must obey. First, the C standard requires that `short int`, `int`, and `long int` each cover a certain minimum range of values. Second, the standard requires that `int` not be shorter than `short int`, and `long int` not be shorter than `int`.

However, it's possible that `short int` represents the same range of values as `int`; also, `int` may have the same range as `long int`.

Table 7.1 shows the usual range of values for the integer types on a 16-bit

Table 7.1
Integer Types on a
16-bit Machine

Type	Smallest Value	Largest Value
short int	−32,768	32,767
unsigned short int	0	65,535
int	−32,768	32,767
unsigned int	0	65,535
long int	−2,147,483,648	2,147,483,647
unsigned long int	0	4,294,967,295

machine; note that `short int` and `int` have identical ranges. Table 7.2 shows

Table 7.2
Integer Types on a
32-bit Machine

Type	Smallest Value	Largest Value
short int	−32,768	32,767
unsigned short int	0	65,535
int	−2,147,483,648	2,147,483,647
unsigned int	0	4,294,967,295
long int	−2,147,483,648	2,147,483,647
unsigned long int	0	4,294,967,295

the usual ranges on a 32-bit machine; here `int` and `long int` have identical ranges. Macros that define the smallest and largest values of each integer type can be found in the `<limits.h>` header, which is part of the standard library.

`<limits.h> header ➤23.2`

Notice that the `short` and `long` integer types have the same ranges for both 16-bit and 32-bit machines. This observation leads to our first portability tip:

portability tip

For maximum portability, use `int` *(or* `short int`*) for integers that won't exceed 32,767 and* `long int` *for all other integers.*

Don't use long integers indiscriminately, however, since operations on long integers may require more time than operations on smaller integers.

Integer Constants

Let's turn our attention to *constants*—numbers that appear in the text of a program, not numbers that are read, written, or computed. C allows integer constants to be written in decimal (base 10), *octal* (base 8), or *hexadecimal* (base 16).

Octal and Hexadecimal Numbers

An octal number is written using only the digits 0 through 7. Each position in an octal number represents a power of 8 (just as each position in a decimal number represents a power of 10). Thus, the octal number 237 represents the decimal number $2 \times 8^2 + 3 \times 8^1 + 7 \times 8^0 = 128 + 24 + 7 = 159$.

A hexadecimal (or hex) number is written using the digits 0 through 9 plus the letters A through F, which stand for 10 through 15, respectively. Each position in a hex number represents a power of 16; the hex number 1AF has the decimal value $1 \times 16^2 + 10 \times 16^1 + 15 \times 16^0 = 256 + 160 + 15 = 431$.

- *Decimal* constants contain digits between 0 and 9, but must not begin with a zero:

  ```
  15   255   32767
  ```

- *Octal* constants contain only digits between 0 and 7, and *must* begin with a zero:

  ```
  017   0377   077777
  ```

- *Hexadecimal* constants contain digits between 0 and 9 and letters between a and f, and always begin with 0x:

  ```
  0xf   0xff   0x7fff
  ```

The letters in a hexadecimal constant may be either upper or lower case:

```
0xff   0xfF   0xFf   0xFF   0Xff   0XfF   0XFf   0XFF
```

Keep in mind that octal and hexadecimal are nothing more than an alternative way of writing numbers; they have no effect on how the numbers are actually stored. (Integers are always stored in binary, regardless of what notation we've used to express them.) We can switch from one notation to another at any time, and even mix them: 10 + 015 + 0x20 has the value 55 (decimal). Octal and hex are most convenient for writing low-level programs; we won't use these notations much until Chapter 20.

When an integer constant appears in a program, the compiler treats it as an ordinary integer if it falls within the range of the int type and as a long integer otherwise. To force the compiler to treat a constant as a long integer, just follow it with the letter L (or l):

```
15L   0377L   0x7fffL
```

To indicate that a constant is unsigned, put the letter U (or u) after it:

```
15U   0377U   0x7fffU
```

L and U may be used in combination to show that a constant is both long *and* unsigned: 0xffffffffUL. (The order of the L and U doesn't matter, nor does their case.)

Reading and Writing Integers

Q&A

Suppose that we've got a program that's not working because one of its int variables is "overflowing"—the program is assigning the variable a value that's too large to be stored in an `int`. Our first thought is to change the type of the variable from `int` to `long int`. But we're not done yet; we've got to see how the change will affect the rest of the program. In particular, we'll need to check whether the variable is used in a call of `printf` or `scanf`. If so, the format string in the call will need to be changed, since the `%d` conversion works only for `int` values.

Reading and writing unsigned, short, and long integers requires several new conversion specifiers:

Q&A

- When reading or writing an *unsigned* integer, use the letter u, o, or x instead of d in the conversion specification. If the u specifier is present, the number is read (or written) in decimal notation; o indicates octal notation, and x indicates hexadecimal notation.

```
unsigned int u;

scanf("%u", &u);     /* reads   u in base 10 */
printf("%u", u);     /* writes  u in base 10 */
scanf("%o", &u);     /* reads   u in base  8 */
printf("%o", u);     /* writes  u in base  8 */
scanf("%x", &u);     /* reads   u in base 16 */
printf("%x", u);     /* writes  u in base 16 */
```

- When reading or writing a *short* integer, put the letter h in front of d, o, u, or x:

```
short int s;

scanf("%hd", &s);
printf("%hd", s);
```

- When reading or writing a *long* integer, put the letter l in front of d, o, u, or x:

```
long int l;

scanf("%ld", &l);
printf("%ld", l);
```

PROGRAM **Summing a Series of Numbers (Revisited)**

In Section 6.1, we wrote a program that sums a series of integers entered by the user. One problem with this program is that the sum (or one of the input numbers) might exceed the largest value allowed for an `int` variable. Here's what might happen if the program is run on a machine whose integers are 16 bits long:

```
This program sums a series of integers.
Enter integers (0 to terminate): 10000 20000 30000 0
The sum is: -5536
```

The sum was 60,000, which wouldn't fit in an `int` variable, so we got a nonsense answer instead. To improve the program, let's switch to `long int` variables.

sum2.c   `/* Sums a series of numbers (using long int variables) */`

```
#include <stdio.h>

main()
{
  long int n, sum = 0;

  printf("This program sums a series of integers.\n");
  printf("Enter integers (0 to terminate): ");

  scanf("%ld", &n);
  while (n != 0) {
    sum += n;
    scanf("%ld", &n);
  }
  printf("The sum is: %ld\n", sum);

  return 0;
}
```

The change was fairly simple: we declared n and `sum` to be `long int` variables instead of `int` variables, then we changed the conversion specifications in `scanf` and `printf` to `%ld` instead of `%d`.

7.2 Floating Types

The integer types aren't suitable for all applications. Sometimes we'll need variables that can store numbers with digits after the decimal point, or numbers that are exceedingly large or small. Numbers like these are stored in *floating-point* format (so called because the decimal point "floats"). C provides three *floating* types, corresponding to different floating-point formats:

`float`	single-precision floating-point
`double`	double-precision floating-point
`long double`	extended-precision floating-point

Which type to use depends on the amount of precision (and the magnitude) required. `float` is suitable when the amount of precision isn't critical (calculating temperatures to one decimal point, for example). `double` provides greater precision—enough for most programs. `long double`, which supplies the ultimate in precision, is rarely used.

The C standard doesn't state how much precision the `float`, `double`, and `long double` types provide, since different computers may store floating-point numbers in different ways. Most modern PCs and workstations follow the specifications in IEEE Standard 754, so we'll use it as an example.

The IEEE Floating-Point Standard

The IEEE standard, developed by the Institute of Electrical and Electronics Engineers, provides two primary formats for floating-point numbers: single precision (32 bits) and double precision (64 bits). Numbers are stored in a form of scientific notation, with each number having three parts: a **sign**, an **exponent**, and a **fraction**. The number of bits reserved for the exponent determines how large (or small) numbers can be, while the number of bits in the fraction determines the precision. In single-precision format, the exponent is 8 bits long, while the fraction occupies 23 bits. As a result, a single-precision number has a maximum value of approximately 3.40×10^{38}, with a precision of about 6 decimal digits.

The IEEE standard also describes two other formats, single extended precision and double extended precision. The standard doesn't specify the number of bits in these formats, although it requires that the single extended type occupy at least 43 bits and the double extended type at least 79 bits. For more information about the IEEE standard and floating-point arithmetic in general, see "What every computer scientist should know about floating-point arithmetic" by David Goldberg (*ACM Computing Surveys*, vol. 23, no. 1 (March 1991): 5–48).

Table 7.3 shows the characteristics of the floating types when implemented

Table 7.3
Floating Type
Characteristics
(IEEE Standard)

Type	Smallest Positive Value	Largest Value	Precision
float	1.17×10^{-38}	3.40×10^{38}	6 digits
double	2.22×10^{-308}	1.79×10^{308}	15 digits

according to the IEEE standard. The `long double` type isn't shown in the table, since its length varies from one machine to another, with 80 bits and 128 bits being the most common sizes. On computers that don't follow the IEEE standard, Table 7.3 won't be valid. In fact, on some machines, `float` may have the same set of values as `double`, or `double` may have the same values as `long double`. Macros that define the characteristics of the floating types can be found in the `<float.h>` header.

<float.h> header ➤23.1

Floating Constants

Floating constants can be written in a variety of ways. The following constants, for example, are all valid ways of writing the number 57.0:

```
57.0  57.  57.0e0  57E0  5.7e1  5.7e+1  .57e2  570.e-1
```

A floating constant must contain a decimal point and/or an exponent; the exponent indicates the power of 10 by which the number is to be scaled. If an exponent is present, it must be preceded by the letter E (or e). An optional + or – sign may appear after the E (or e).

By default, floating constants are stored as double-precision numbers. In other words, when a C compiler finds the constant 57.0 in a program, it arranges for the number to be stored in memory in the same format as a double variable. This rule generally causes no problems, since double values are converted automatically to float when necessary.

On rare occasions, it may be necessary to force the compiler to store a floating constant in float or long double format. To indicate that only single precision is desired, put the letter F (or f) at the end of the constant (for example, 57.0F). To indicate that a constant should be stored in long double format, put the letter L (or l) at the end (57.0L).

Reading and Writing Floating-Point Numbers

As we've discussed, the conversion specifications %e, %f, and %g are used for reading and writing single-precision floating-point numbers. Values of types double and long double require slightly different conversions:

■ When *reading* a value of type double, put the letter l in front of e, f, or g:

```
double d;

scanf("%lf", &d);
```

Note: Use l only in a scanf format string, not a printf string. In a printf format string, the e, f, and g conversions can be used to write either float or double values.

■ When reading or writing a value of type long double, put the letter L in front of e, f, or g:

```
long double ld;

scanf("%Lf", &ld);
printf("%Lf", ld);
```

7.3 Character Types

 The only remaining basic type is char, the character type. The values of type char can vary from one computer to another, because different machines may have different underlying character sets.

Character Sets

ASCII character set ➤ *Appendix E* Today's most popular character set is ASCII (American Standard Code for Information Interchange), a 7-bit code capable of representing 128 characters. In ASCII, the digits 0 to 9 are represented by the codes 0110000–0111001, and the uppercase letters A to Z are represented by 1000001–1011010. Some computers extend ASCII to an 8-bit code so that it can represent 256 characters.

Unicode ➤25.2 Other computers use entirely different character sets. IBM mainframes, for example, rely on an older code named EBCDIC. Future machines may use Unicode, a 16-bit code capable of representing 65,536 characters.

A variable of type `char` can be assigned any character that the computer can represent:

```
char ch;
```

```
ch = 'a';    /* lower-case a */
ch = 'A';    /* upper-case A */
ch = '0';    /* zero         */
ch = ' ';    /* space        */
```

Notice that character constants are enclosed in single quotes, not double quotes.

Working with characters in C is simple, because of one fact: *C treats characters as small integers.* After all, characters are encoded in binary, and it doesn't take much imagination to view these binary codes as integers. In ASCII, for example, character codes range from 0000000 to 1111111, which we can think of as the integers from 0 to 127. The character 'a' has the value 97, 'A' has the value 65, '0' has the value 48, and ' ' has the value 32.

When a character appears in a computation, C simply uses its integer value. Consider the following examples, which assume the ASCII character set:

```
char ch;
int i;
```

```
i = 'a';       /* i is now 97   */
ch = 65;       /* ch is now 'A' */
ch = ch + 1;   /* ch is now 'B' */
ch++;          /* ch is now 'C' */
```

Characters can be compared, just as numbers can. The following `if` statement checks whether `ch` contains a lower-case letter; if so, it converts `ch` to upper case.

```
if ('a' <= ch && ch <= 'z')
  ch = ch - 'a' + 'A';
```

Comparisons such as 'a' <= ch are done using the integer values of the characters involved. These values vary depending on the character set in use, so programs that use <, <=, >, and >= to compare characters may not be portable.

The fact that characters have the same properties as numbers has some advantages. For example, we can easily write a `for` statement whose control variable steps through all the upper-case letters:

```
for (ch = 'A'; ch <= 'Z'; ch++) …
```

On the other hand, treating characters as numbers can lead to various programming errors that won't be caught by the compiler, and lets us write meaningless expressions such as 'a' * 'b' / 'c'. It can also hamper portability, since our programs may be based on assumptions about the underlying character set. (Our `for` loop, for example, assumes that the letters A to Z have consecutive codes.)

Since C allows characters to be used as integers, it shouldn't be surprising that the `char` type—like the integer types—exists in both signed and unsigned versions. Signed characters normally have values between –128 and 127, while unsigned characters have values between 0 and 255.

The C standard doesn't specify whether ordinary `char` is a signed or an unsigned type; some compilers treat it as a signed type, while others treat it as an unsigned type. (Some even allow the programmer to select, via a compiler option, whether `char` should be signed or unsigned.)

Q&A

Most of the time, we don't really care whether `char` is signed or unsigned. Once in a while, though, we do, especially if we're using a character variable to store a small integer. For this reason, Standard C allows the use of the words `signed` and `unsigned` to modify `char`:

```
signed char sch;
unsigned char uch;
```

portability tip   *Don't assume that* `char` *is either signed or unsigned by default. If it matters, use* `signed char` *or* `unsigned char` *instead of* `char`.

In light of the close relationship between characters and integers, I'll use the term ***integral types*** to include both the integer types and the character types.

Escape Sequences

A character constant is usually one character enclosed in single quotes, as we've seen in previous examples. However, certain special characters—including the new-line character—can't be written in this way, because they're invisible (non-printing) or because they can't be entered from the keyboard. So that programs can deal with every character in the underlying character set, C provides a special notation, the ***escape sequence***.

There are two kinds of escape sequences: ***character escapes*** and ***numeric escapes***. We saw a partial list of character escapes in Section 3.1; Table 7.4 gives the complete set. The `\a`, `\b`, `\f`, `\r`, `\t`, and `\v` escapes represent common

Q&A

ASCII control characters. The `\n` escape represents the ASCII line-feed character. The `\\` escape allows a character constant or string to contain the `\` character. The `\'` escape allows a character constant to contain the `'` character, while the `\"`

Q&A

escape allows a string to contain the `"` character. The `\?` escape is rarely used.

Character escapes are easy to use, but they have a problem: the list of character escapes doesn't include all the nonprinting ASCII characters, just the most common. Character escapes are also useless for representing characters beyond the basic 128 ASCII characters. (Some computers—the IBM PC family is a notable example—provide an extended ASCII character set.) Numeric escapes, which can represent *any* character, are the solution to this problem.

Table 7.4
Character Escapes

Name	Escape Sequence
Alert (bell)	\a
Backspace	\b
Form feed	\f
New line	\n
Carriage return	\r
Horizontal tab	\t
Vertical tab	\v
Backslash	\\
Question mark	\?
Single quote	\'
Double quote	\"

To write a numeric escape for a particular character, first look up the character's octal or hexadecimal value in a table like the one in Appendix E. For example, the ASCII escape character (decimal value: 27) has the value 33 in octal and 1B in hex. Either of these codes can be used to write an escape sequence:

- An *octal escape sequence* consists of the \ character followed by an octal number with at most three digits. (This number must be representable as an unsigned character, so its maximum value is normally 377 octal.) For example, the escape character could be written \33 or \033. Octal numbers in escape sequences—unlike octal numbers in general—don't have to begin with 0.

- A *hexadecimal escape sequence* consists of \x followed by a hexadecimal number. Although Standard C places no limit on the number of digits in the hexadecimal number, it must be representable as an unsigned character (hence it can't exceed FF if characters are eight bits long). Using this notation, the escape character would be written \x1b or \x1B. The x must be in lower case, but the hex digits (such as b) can be upper or lower case.

When used as a character constant, an escape sequence must be enclosed in single quotes. For example, a constant representing the escape character would be written '\33' (or '\x1b'). Escape sequences tend to get a bit cryptic, so it's often a good idea to give them names using #define:

```
#define ESC '\33'    /* ASCII escape character */
```

Escape sequences can be embedded in strings as well, as we saw in Section 3.1.

Escape sequences aren't the only special notations used for representing characters. Several others were added to C in the 1980s as part of an effort to make it a more international language. *Trigraph sequences* are codes for ASCII characters that are unavailable on some computers outside the U.S. *Multibyte characters* and *wide characters* are used for character sets whose codes are too large to store in a single byte.

trigraph sequences ➤25.3

multibyte characters ➤25.2

wide characters ➤25.2

Character-Handling Functions

Earlier in this section, we saw how to write an `if` statement that converts a lower-case letter to upper-case:

```
if ('a' <= ch && ch <= 'z')
  ch = ch - 'a' + 'A';
```

This isn't the best method, though. A faster—and more portable—way to convert case is to call C's `toupper` library function:

```
ch = toupper(ch);   /* converts ch to upper case */
```

When it's called, `toupper` checks whether its argument (`ch` in this case) is a lower-case letter. If so, it returns the corresponding upper-case letter. Otherwise, `toupper` returns the value of the argument. In our example, we've used the assignment operator to store the return value of `toupper` back into the `ch` variable, although we could just as easily have done something else with it—stored it in another variable, say, or tested it in an `if` statement:

```
if (toupper(ch) == 'A') …
```

Programs that call `toupper` need to have the following `#include` directive at the top:

```
#include <ctype.h>
```

`toupper` isn't the only useful character-handling function in the C library. Section 23.4 describes them all and gives examples of their use.

Reading and Writing Characters

The `%c` conversion specification allows `scanf` and `printf` to read and write single characters:

```
char ch;

scanf("%c", &ch);   /* reads a single character */
printf("%c", ch);   /* writes a single character */
```

`scanf` doesn't skip white-space characters before reading a character. If the next unread character is a space, then the variable `ch` in the previous example will contain a space after `scanf` returns. To force `scanf` to skip white space before reading a character, put a space in its format string just before `%c`:

```
scanf(" %c", &ch);   /* skips white space, then reads ch */
```

Recall from Section 3.2 that a blank in a `scanf` format string means "skip zero or more white-space characters."

Since `scanf` doesn't normally skip white space, it's easy to detect the end of an input line: check to see if the character just read is the new-line character. For example, the following loop will read and ignore all remaining characters in the current input line:

```
do {
  scanf("%c", &ch);
} while (ch != '\n');
```

When scanf is called the next time, it will read the first character on the next input line.

C provides other ways to read and write single characters. In particular, we can use the getchar and putchar functions instead of calling scanf and printf. Each time getchar is called, it reads one character, which it returns. In order to save the character that getchar returns, we must use assignment to store it in a variable:

```
ch = getchar();   /* reads a character and stores it in ch */
```

Like scanf, getchar doesn't skip white-space characters as it reads. putchar writes a single character:

```
putchar(ch);
```

Using getchar and putchar (rather than scanf and printf) saves time when the program is executed. getchar and putchar are fast for two reasons. First, they're much simpler than scanf and printf, which are designed to read and write many kinds of data in a variety of formats. Second, getchar and putchar are usually implemented as macros for additional speed.

getchar has another advantage over scanf: because it returns the character that it reads, getchar lends itself to various C idioms, including loops that search for a character or skip over all occurrences of a character. Consider the scanf loop that we used to skip the rest of an input line:

```
do {
  scanf("%c", &ch);
} while (ch != '\n');
```

Rewriting this loop using getchar gives us the following:

```
do {
  ch = getchar();
} while (ch != '\n');
```

Moving the call of getchar into the controlling expression allows us to condense the loop:

```
while ((ch = getchar()) != '\n')
  ;
```

This loop reads a character, stores it into the variable ch, then tests if ch is not equal to the new-line character. If the test succeeds, the loop body (which is empty) is executed, then the loop test is performed once more, causing a new character to be read. Actually, we don't even need the ch variable; we can just compare the return value of getchar with the new-line character:

idiom   ```
while (getchar() != '\n')   /* skips rest of line */
    ;
```

The resulting loop is a well-known C idiom that's cryptic but worth learning.

getchar is useful in loops that skip characters as well as loops that search for characters. Consider the following statement, which uses getchar to skip an indefinite number of blank characters:

**idiom**     ```
while ((ch = getchar()) == ' ')    /* skips blanks */
    ;
```

When the loop terminates, ch will contain the first nonblank character that getchar encountered.

 Be careful if you mix getchar and scanf in the same program. scanf has a tendency to leave behind characters that it has "peeked" at but not read, including the new-line character. Consider what happens if we try to read a number first, then a character:

```
printf("Enter an integer: ");
scanf("%d", &i);
printf("Enter a command: ");
command = getchar();
```

The call of scanf will leave behind any characters that weren't consumed during the reading of i, including (but not limited to) the new-line character. getchar will fetch the first leftover character, which wasn't what we had in mind.

PROGRAM   ## Determining the Length of a Message

To illustrate how characters are read, let's write a program that calculates the length of a message. After the user enters the message, the program displays the length:

```
Enter a message: Brevity is the soul of wit.
Your message was 27 character(s) long.
```

The length includes spaces and punctuation, but not the new-line character at the end of the message.

We'll need a loop whose body reads a character and increments a counter. The loop will terminate as soon as a new-line character turns up. We could use either scanf or getchar to read characters; most C programmers would choose getchar. Using a straightforward while loop, we might end up with the following program:

length.c `/* Determines the length of a message */`

```
#include <stdio.h>

main()
{
  char ch;
  int len = 0;

  printf("Enter a message: ");
  ch = getchar();
  while (ch != '\n') {
    len++;
    ch = getchar();
  }
  printf("Your message was %d character(s) long.\n", len);

  return 0;
}
```

Recalling our discussion of idioms involving `while` loops and `getchar`, we realize that the program can be shortened:

length2.c `/* Determines the length of a message */`

```
#include <stdio.h>

main()
{
  int len = 0;

  printf("Enter a message: ");
  while (getchar() != '\n')
    len++;
  printf("Your message was %d character(s) long.\n", len);

  return 0;
}
```

7.4   The `sizeof` Operator

The `sizeof` operator allows a program to determine how much memory is required to store values of a particular type. The value of the expression

`sizeof` expression

$$\texttt{sizeof (} \textit{type-name} \texttt{)}$$

is an unsigned integer representing the number of bytes required to store a value belonging to *type-name*. `sizeof(char)` is always 1, but the sizes of the other types may vary. On a 16-bit machine, `sizeof(int)` is normally 2; on most 32-

bit machines, `sizeof(int)` is 4. Note that `sizeof` is a rather unusual operator, since the compiler itself can determine the value of a `sizeof` expression.

The `sizeof` operator can also be applied to constants, variables, and expressions in general. If `i` and `j` are `int` variables, then `sizeof(i)` is 2 on a 16-bit machine, as is `sizeof(i+j)`. When applied to an expression—as opposed to a type—`sizeof` doesn't require parentheses; we could write `sizeof i` instead of `sizeof(i)`. However, parentheses may be needed anyway because of operator precedence. The compiler would interpret `sizeof i + j` as `(sizeof i) + j`, because `sizeof`—a unary operator—takes precedence over the binary + operator. To avoid problems, I always use parentheses in `sizeof` expressions.

Printing a `sizeof` value requires care, because the type of a `sizeof` expression is implementation-defined. The trick is to convert the value of the expression to a known type before printing it. Since `sizeof` returns an unsigned integer type, it's safest to convert a `sizeof` expression to `unsigned long` (the largest of the unsigned types) and then print it using the `%lu` conversion. Converting an expression to a different type requires "casting," a technique that's described in the next section. Here's how we'd use a cast to help display the size of the `int` type:

```
printf("Size of int: %lu\n", (unsigned long) sizeof(int));
```

The notation `(unsigned long)` tells the compiler to convert the value of the expression that follows (`sizeof(int)`, in this case) to an unsigned long integer.

7.5 Type Conversion

Computers tend to be more restrictive than C when it comes to arithmetic. For a computer to perform an arithmetic operation, the operands must usually be of the same size (the same number of bits) and be stored in the same way. A computer may be able to add two 16-bit integers directly, but not a 16-bit integer and a 32-bit integer or a 32-bit integer and a 32-bit floating-point number.

C, on the other hand, allows the basic types to be mixed in expressions. We can combine integers, floating-point numbers, and even characters in a single expression. The C compiler may then have to generate instructions that convert some operands to different types so that the hardware will be able to evaluate the expression. If we add a 16-bit `int` and a 32-bit `long int`, for example, the compiler will arrange for the `int` value to be converted to 32 bits. If we add an `int` and a `float`, the compiler will arrange for the `int` to be converted to `float` format. This conversion is a little more complicated, since `int` and `float` values are stored in different ways.

Since the compiler handles these conversions automatically, without the programmer's involvement, they're known as *implicit conversions*. C also allows the programmer to perform *explicit conversions*, using the *cast* operator. I'll discuss implicit conversions first, postponing explicit conversions until later in the section. Unfortunately, the rules for performing implicit conversions are somewhat complex, primarily because C has so many different basic types (six integer types and three floating types, not to mention the character types).

Implicit conversions are performed on the following occasions:

- When the operands in an arithmetic or logical expression don't have the same type. (C performs what are known as the ***usual arithmetic conversions***.)
- When the type of the expression on the right side of an assignment doesn't match the type of the variable on the left side.
- When the type of an argument in a function call doesn't match the type of the corresponding parameter.
- When the type of the expression in a `return` statement doesn't match the function's return type.

We'll discuss the first two cases now and save the others for Chapter 9.

The Usual Arithmetic Conversions

The usual arithmetic conversions are applied to the operands of most binary operators, including the arithmetic, relational, and equality operators. For example, let's say that x has type `float` and i has type `int`. The usual arithmetic conversions will be applied to the operands in the expression x + i, because their types aren't the same. Clearly it's safer to convert i to type `float` (matching x's type) rather than convert x to type `int` (matching i's type). An integer can always be converted to `float`; the worst that can happen is a minor loss of precision. Converting a floating-point number to `int`, on the other hand, would cost us the fractional part of the number. Worse still, we'd get a completely meaningless result if the original number were larger than the largest possible integer or smaller than the smallest integer.

The strategy behind the usual arithmetic conversions is to convert operands to the "narrowest" type that will safely accommodate both values. (Roughly speaking, one type is narrower than another if it requires fewer bytes to store.) The types of the operands can often be made to match by converting the operand of the narrower type to the type of the other operand (this act is known as ***promotion***). Among the most common promotions are the ***integral promotions***, which convert a character or short integer to type `int` (or to `unsigned int` in some cases).

Q&A

We can divide the rules for performing the usual arithmetic conversions into two cases:

- ***The type of either operand is a floating type.*** Use the following diagram to promote the operand whose type is narrower:

$$\begin{array}{c} \texttt{long double} \\ \uparrow \\ \texttt{double} \\ \uparrow \\ \texttt{float} \end{array}$$

That is, if one operand has type `long double`, then convert the other operand to type `long double`. Otherwise, if one operand has type `double`, convert the other operand to type `double`. Otherwise, if one operand has type `float`, convert the other operand to type `float`. Note that these rules cover mixtures of integer and floating types: if one operand has type `long int`, for example, and the other has type `double`, the `long int` operand is converted to `double`.

■ *Neither operand type is a floating type.* First perform integral promotion on both operands (guaranteeing that neither operand will be a character or short integer). Then use the following diagram to promote the operand whose type is narrower:

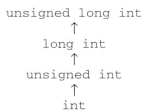

$$
\begin{array}{c}
\texttt{unsigned long int} \\
\uparrow \\
\texttt{long int} \\
\uparrow \\
\texttt{unsigned int} \\
\uparrow \\
\texttt{int}
\end{array}
$$

There's one special case, but it occurs only when `long int` and `unsigned int` have the same length (32 bits, say). Under these circumstances, if one operand has type `long int` and the other has type `unsigned int`, both are converted to `unsigned long int`.

When a signed operand is combined with an unsigned operand, the signed operand is "converted" to an unsigned value by treating the sign bit as part of the number's magnitude. This rule can cause obscure programming errors.

Suppose that the `int` variable i has the value –10 and the `unsigned int` variable u has the value 10. If we compare i and u using the < operator, we might expect to get the result 1 (true). Before the comparison, however, i is converted to `unsigned int`. Since a negative number can't be represented as an unsigned integer, the converted value won't be –10, but a large positive number (the result of interpreting the bits in i as an unsigned number). The comparison i < u will therefore produce 0.

Because of traps like this one, it's best to use unsigned integers as little as possible and, especially, never mix them with signed integers.

The following example shows the usual arithmetic conversions in action:

```
char c;
short int s;
int i;
unsigned int u;
long int l;
unsigned long int ul;
```

```
float f;
double d;
long double ld;

i = i + c;     /* c is converted to int              */
i = i + s;     /* s is converted to int              */
u = u + i;     /* i is converted to unsigned int      */
l = l + u;     /* u is converted to long int          */
ul = ul + l;   /* l is converted to unsigned long int */
f = f + ul;    /* ul is converted to float            */
d = d + f;     /* f is converted to double            */
ld = ld + d;   /* d is converted to long double       */
```

Conversion During Assignment

The usual arithmetic conversions don't apply to assignment. Instead, C follows the simple rule that the expression on the right side of the assignment is converted to the type of the variable on the left side. If the variable's type is at least as "wide" as the expression's, this will work without a snag. For example:

```
char c;
int i;
float f;
double d;

i = c;   /* c is converted to int   */
f = i;   /* i is converted to float */
d = f;   /* f is converted to double */
```

Other cases are problematic. Assigning a floating-point number to an integer variable drops the fractional part of the number:

```
int i;

i = 842.97;    /* i is now 842 */
i = -842.97;   /* i is now -842 */
```

Moreover, assigning a value to a variable of a narrower type will give a meaningless result (or worse) if the value is outside the range of the variable's type:

```
c = 10000;    /*** WRONG ***/
i = 1.0e20;   /*** WRONG ***/
f = 1.0e100;  /*** WRONG ***/
```

Q&A

An assignment of this kind may elicit a warning from the compiler or from `lint`.

Casting

Although C's implicit conversions are convenient, we sometimes need a greater degree of control over type conversion. For this reason, C provides *casts*. A cast expression has the form

cast expression

(*type-name*) *expression*

type-name specifies the type to which the expression should be converted.

The following example shows how to use a cast expression to compute the fractional part of a `float` value:

```
float f, frac_part;

frac_part = f - (int) f;
```

The cast expression `(int) f` represents the result of converting the value of `f` to type `int`. C's usual arithmetic conversions then require that `(int) f` be converted back to type `float` before the subtraction can be performed. The difference between `f` and `(int) f` is the fractional part of `f`, which was dropped during the cast.

Cast expressions enable us to document type conversions that would take place anyway:

```
i = (int) f;   /* f is converted to int */
```

They also enable us to overrule the compiler and force it to do conversions that we want. Consider the following example:

```
float quotient;
int dividend, divisor;

quotient = dividend / divisor;
```

As it's now written, the result of the division—an integer—will be converted to `float` form before being stored in `quotient`. We probably want `dividend` and `divisor` converted to `float` *before* the division, though, so that we get a more exact answer. A cast expression will do the trick:

```
quotient = (float) dividend / divisor;
```

`divisor` doesn't need a cast, since casting `dividend` to `float` forces the compiler to convert `divisor` to `float` also.

Incidentally, C regards (*type-name*) as a unary operator. Unary operators have higher precedence than binary operators, so the compiler interprets

```
(float) dividend / divisor
```

as

```
((float) dividend) / divisor
```

If you find this confusing, note that there are other ways to accomplish the same effect:

```
quotient = dividend / (float) divisor;
```

or

```
quotient = (float) dividend / (float) divisor;
```

Casts are sometimes necessary to avoid overflow. Consider the following example:

```
long int i;
int j = 1000;

i = j * j;    /*** WRONG ***/
```

At first glance, this statement looks fine. The value of j * j is 1,000,000, and i is a long int, so it can easily store values of this size, right? The problem is that when two int values are multiplied, the result will have int type. But j * j is too large to represent as an int on some machines. On such a machine, i would be assigned a nonsense value. Fortunately, using a cast avoids the problem:

```
i = (long int) j * j;
```

Since the cast operator takes precedence over *, the first j is converted to long int type, forcing the second j to be converted as well. Note that the statement

```
i = (long int) (j * j);    /*** WRONG ***/
```

wouldn't work, since the overflow would already have occurred by the time of the cast.

7.6 Type Definitions

In Section 5.2, we used the #define directive to create a macro that could be used as a Boolean type:

```
#define BOOL int
```

Q&A   There's a better way to set up a Boolean type, though, using a feature known as a *type definition:*

```
typedef int Bool;
```

Notice that the name of the type being defined comes *last*. Note also that I've capitalized the word Bool. Capitalizing the first letter of a type name isn't required; it's just a convention that some C programmers employ.

Using typedef to define Bool causes the compiler to add Bool to the list of type names that it recognizes. Bool can now be used in the same way as the built-in type names—in variable declarations, cast expressions, and elsewhere. For example, we might use Bool to declare variables:

```
Bool flag;    /* same as int flag; */
```

The compiler treats Bool as a synonym for int; thus, flag is really nothing more than an ordinary int variable.

Type definitions can make a program more understandable (assuming that the programmer has been careful to choose meaningful type names). For example, suppose that the variables cash_in and cash_out will be used to store dollar amounts. Declaring Dollars as

```
typedef float Dollars;
```

and then writing

```
Dollars cash_in, cash_out;
```

is more informative than just writing

```
float cash_in, cash_out;
```

Type definitions can also make a program easier to modify. If we later decide that Dollars should really be defined as double, all we need do is change the type definition:

```
typedef double Dollars;
```

The declarations of Dollars variables need not be changed. Without the type definition, we would need to locate all float variables that store dollar amounts (not necessarily an easy task) and change their declarations.

Type definitions are an important tool for writing portable programs. One of the problems with moving a program from one computer to another is that types may have different ranges on different machines. If i is an int variable, an assignment like

```
i = 100000;
```

is fine on a machine with 32-bit integers, but will fail on a machine with 16-bit integers.

portability tip   *For greater portability, consider using* typedef *to define new names for integer types.*

Suppose that we're writing a program that needs variables capable of storing product quantities in the range 0–50,000. We could use long int variables for this purpose (since they're guaranteed to be able to hold numbers up to at least 2,147,483,647), but we'd rather use int variables, since arithmetic on int values may be faster than operations on long int values; also, int variables may take up less space.

Instead of using the int type to declare quantity variables, we can define our own "quantity" type:

```
typedef int Quantity;
```

and use this type to declare variables:

```
Quantity q;
```

When we transport the program to a machine with shorter integers, we'll change the definition of Quantity:

```
typedef long int Quantity;
```

This technique doesn't solve all our problems, unfortunately, since changing the definition of Quantity may affect the way Quantity variables are used. At the very least, calls of printf and scanf that use Quantity variables will need to be changed, with %d conversion specifications replaced by %ld.

The C library itself uses typedef to create names for types that can vary from one C implementation to another; these types often have names that end with _t, such as ptrdiff_t, size_t, and wchar_t. One compiler might have the following type definitions in its library:

```
typedef int ptrdiff_t;
typedef unsigned size_t;
typedef char wchar_t;
```

Other compilers might define these types in different ways; for example, ptrdiff_t might be long int on some machines.

Q & A

Q: **What happens if "overflow" occurs—for example, we add two numbers and the result is too large to store? [p. 112]**

A: That depends on whether the numbers were signed or unsigned. When overflow occurs during an operation on signed numbers, the result is "undefined," according to the C standard. We can't reliably say what the result is, since that depends on the behavior of the machine. The program could even abort (a typical response to division by zero).

When overflow occurs during an operation on *unsigned* numbers, though, the result *is* defined: we get the correct answer modulo 2^n, where n is the number of bits used to store the result. For example, if we add 1 to the unsigned 16-bit number 65,535, the result is guaranteed to be 0.

Q: **Section 7.1 says that %o and %x are used to write unsigned integers in octal and hex notation. How do I write ordinary (signed) integers in octal or hex? [p. 113]**

A: You can use %o and %x to print a signed integer as long as its value isn't negative. These conversions cause printf to treat a signed integer as though it were unsigned; in other words, printf will assume that the sign bit is part of the number's magnitude. As long as the sign bit is 0, there's no problem. If the sign bit is 1, `printf` will print an unexpectedly large number.

Q: **But what if the number *is* negative? How can I write it in octal or hex?**

A: There's no direct way to print a negative number in octal or hex. Fortunately, the need to do so is pretty rare. You can, of course, test whether the number is negative and print a minus sign yourself:

```
if (i < 0)
  printf("-%x", -i);
else
  printf("%x", i);
```

Q: **Why are floating constants stored in `double` form rather than `float` form? [p. 116]**

A: For historical reasons, C gives preference to the `double` type; `float` is treated as a second-class citizen. Consider, for instance, the discussion of `float` in Kernighan and Ritchie's *The C Programming Language*: "The main reason for using `float` is to save storage in large arrays, or, less often, to save time on machines where double-precision arithmetic is particularly expensive." Classic C goes so far as to mandate that all floating-point arithmetic be done in double precision. (Standard C has no such requirement.)

*Q: **Why do we use `%lf` to read a `double` value but `%f` to print it? [p. 116]**

A: This is a tough question to answer. First, notice that `scanf` and `printf` are unusual functions in that they aren't restricted to a fixed number of arguments. We say that `scanf` and `printf` have ***variable-length argument lists***. When functions with variable-length argument lists are called, the compiler arranges for `float` arguments to be converted automatically to type `double`. As a result, `printf` can't distinguish between `float` and `double` arguments. This explains why `%f` works for both `float` and `double` arguments in calls of `printf`.

variable-length argument lists
➤26.1

    `scanf`, on the other hand, is passed a *pointer* to a variable. `%f` tells `scanf` to store a `float` value at the address passed to it, while `%lf` tells `scanf` to store a `double` value at that address. The distinction between `float` and `double` is crucial here. If given the wrong conversion specification, `scanf` will likely store the wrong number of bytes (not to mention the fact that the bit pattern for a `float` probably isn't the same as that for a `double`).

Q: **What's the proper way to pronounce `char`? [p. 116]**

A: There's no universally accepted pronunciation. Some people pronounce `char` in the same way as the first syllable of "character." Others say "char," as in

```
char broiled;
```

Q: **When does it matter whether a character variable is signed or unsigned? [p. 118]**

A: If we store only 7-bit characters in the variable, it doesn't matter, since the sign bit will be zero. If we plan to store 8-bit characters, however, we'll probably want the variable to have `unsigned char` type. Consider the following example:

```
ch = '\xdb';
```

If `ch` has been declared to have type `char`, the compiler may choose to treat it as a signed character (many compilers do). As long as `ch` is used only as a character, there won't be any problem. But if `ch` is ever used in a context that requires the compiler to convert its value to an integer, we're likely to have trouble: the resulting integer will be negative, since `ch`'s sign bit is 1.

Here's another situation: In some kinds of programs, it's customary to use `char` variables to store one-byte integers. If we're writing such a program, we'll have to decide whether each variable should be `signed char` or `unsigned char`, just as we must decide whether ordinary integer variables should have type `int` or `unsigned int`.

Q: **I don't understand how the new-line character can be the ASCII line-feed character. When a user enters input and presses the return key, doesn't the program read this as a carriage return character or a carriage return plus a line feed? [p. 118]**

A: Nope. As part of C's UNIX heritage, it always regards the end of a line as being marked by a single line-feed character. (In UNIX text files, a single line-feed character—but no carriage return—appears at the end of each line.) The C library takes care of translating the user's keypress into a line-feed character. When a program reads from a file, the I/O library translates the file's end-of-line marker (whatever it may be) into a single line-feed character. The same transformations occur—in reverse—when output is written to the screen or to a file. (See Section 22.1 for details.)

Although these translations may seem confusing, they serve an important purpose: insulating programs from details that may vary from one operating system to another.

*Q: **What's the purpose of the \? escape sequence? [p. 118]**

A: The \? escape is related to trigraph sequences, which begin with ??. If you should

trigraph sequences ➤*25.3*   put ?? in a string, there's a possibility that the compiler will mistake it for the beginning of a trigraph. Replacing the second ? by \? fixes the problem.

Q: **If `getchar` is faster, why would we ever want to use `scanf` to read individual characters? [p. 121]**

A: Although it's not as fast as `getchar`, the `scanf` function is more flexible. As we saw previously, the `"%c"` format string causes `scanf` to read the next input character; `" %c"` causes it to read the next non-white-space character. Also, `scanf` is good at reading characters that are mixed in with other kinds of data. Let's say that our input data consists of an integer, then a single nonnumeric character, then another integer. By using the format string `"%d%c%d"`, we can get `scanf` to read all three items.

*Q: Under what circumstances do the integral promotions convert a character or short integer to `unsigned int`? [p. 125]

A: The integral promotions yield an `unsigned int` if the `int` type isn't large enough to include all possible values of the original type. Since characters are usually eight bits long, they are almost always converted to `int`, which is guaranteed to be at least 16 bits long. Signed short integers can always be converted to `int` as well. Unsigned short integers are problematic. If short integers have the same length as ordinary integers (as they do on a 16-bit machine), then unsigned short integers will have to be converted to `unsigned int`, since the largest unsigned short integer (65,535 on a 16-bit machine) is larger than the largest `int` (32,767).

Q: Exactly what happens if I assign a value to a variable that's not large enough to hold it? [p. 127]

A: Roughly speaking, if the value is of an integral type and the variable is of an unsigned type, the extra bits are thrown away; if the variable has a signed type, the result is *implementation-defined*. Assigning a floating-point number to a variable—integer or floating—that's too small to hold it produces *undefined* behavior: anything can happen, including program termination.

*Q: Why does C bother to provide type definitions? Isn't defining a `BOOL` macro just as good as defining a `Bool` type using `typedef`? [p. 129]

A: There are two important differences between type definitions and macro definitions. First, type definitions are more powerful than macro definitions. In particular, array and pointer types can't be defined as macros. Suppose that we try to use a macro to define a "pointer to integer" type:

```
#define PTR_TO_INT int *
```

The declaration

```
PTR_TO_INT p, q, r;
```

will become

```
int * p, q, r;
```

after preprocessing. Unfortunately, only p is a pointer; q and r are ordinary integer variables. Type definitions don't have this problem.

Second, `typedef` names are subject to the same scope rules as variables; a `typedef` name defined inside a function body wouldn't be recognized outside the function. Macro names, on the other hand, are replaced by the preprocessor wherever they appear.

Exercises

Section 7.1

1. Give the decimal value of each of the following integer constants.
   - (a) `077`
   - (b) `0x77`
   - (c) `0XABC`

2. The `square2.c` program of Section 6.3 will fail (usually by printing strange answers) if `i * i` exceeds the maximum `int` value. Run the program and determine the smallest value of n that causes failure. Try changing the type of `i` to `short int` and running the program again. (Don't forget to update the conversion specifications in the call of `printf`!) Then try `long int`. From these experiments, what can you conclude about the number of bits used to store integer types on your machine?

Section 7.2

3. Which of the following are not legal numbers in C? Classify each legal number as either integer or floating-point.
   - (a) `010E2`
   - (b) `32.1E+5`
   - (c) `0790`
   - (d) `100_000`
   - (e) `3.978e-2`

4. Which of the following are not legal types in C?
   - (a) `short unsigned int`
   - (b) `short float`
   - (c) `long double`
   - (d) `unsigned long`

5. Modify the `sum2.c` program (Section 7.1) to sum a series of `double` values.

Section 7.3

6. If c is a variable of type `char`, which one of the following statements is illegal?
   - (a) `i += c;   /* i has type int */`
   - (b) `c = 2 * c - 1;`
   - (c) `putchar(c)`
   - (d) `printf(c);`

7. Which one of the following is not a legal way to write the number 65? (Assume that the character set is ASCII.)
   - (a) `'A'`
   - (b) `0b1000001`
   - (c) `0101`
   - (d) `0x41`

8. Modify the `square2.c` program of Section 6.3 so that it pauses after every 24 squares and displays the following message:

   `Press Enter to continue...`

   After displaying the message, the program should use `getchar` to read a character.

getchar won't allow the program to continue until the user presses the Enter (or Return) key.

9.   Write a program that translates an alphabetic phone number into numeric form:

```
Enter phone number: CALLATT
2255288
```

(In case you don't have a telephone nearby, here are the letters on the keys: 2=ABC, 3=DEF, 4=GHI, 5=JKL, 6=MNO, 7=PRS, 8=TUV, 9=WXY.) If the original phone number contains nonalphabetic characters (digits or punctuation, for example), leave them unchanged:

```
Enter phone number: 1-800-COL-LECT
1-800-265-5328
```

You may assume that any letters entered by the user are upper case.

10.   In the SCRABBLE Crossword Game, players form words using small tiles, each containing a letter and a face value. The face value varies from one letter to another, based on the letter's rarity. (Here are the face values: 1: AEILNORSTU, 2: DG, 3: BCMP, 4: FHVWY, 5: K, 8: JX, 10: QZ.) Write a program that computes the value of a word by summing the values of its letters:

```
Enter a word: pitfall
Scrabble value: 12
```

Your program should allow any mixture of lower-case and upper-case letters in the word. *Hint:* Use the toupper library function.

11.   Airline tickets are assigned lengthy identifying numbers, such as 47715497443. To be valid, the last digit of the number must match the remainder when the other digits—as a group—are divided by 7. (For example, 4771549744 divided by 7 yields the remainder 3.) Write a program that checks whether or not an airline ticket number is valid:

```
Enter ticket number: 47715497443
VALID
```

Hint: Don't attempt to read the number in a single step. Instead, use getchar to obtain its digits one by one. Carry out the division one digit at a time, being careful not to include the last digit in the division.

Section 7.4   12.   Write a program that prints the values of sizeof(int), sizeof(short int), sizeof(long int), sizeof(float), sizeof(double) and sizeof(long double).

Section 7.5   13.   Suppose that i and j are variables of type int. What is the type of the expression i / j + 'a'?

14.   Suppose that i is a variable of type int, j is a variable of type long int, and k is a variable of type unsigned int. What is the type of the expression i + (int) j * k?

15.   Suppose that i is a variable of type int, f is a variable of type float, and d is a variable of type double. What is the type of the expression i * f / d?

16.   Suppose that i is a variable of type int, f is a variable of type float, and d is a variable of type double. Explain what conversions take place during the execution of the following statement:

```
d = i + f;
```

17. Assume that a program contains the following declarations:

```
char c = '\1';
short int s = 2;
int i = -3;
long int m = 5;
float f = 6.5;
double d = 7.5;
```

Give the value and the type of each expression listed below.

(a) c * i   (c) f / c   (e) f - d

(b) s + m   (d) d / s   (f) (int) f

18. Does the following statement always compute the fractional part of f correctly (assuming that f and frac_part are float variables)?

```
frac_part = f - (int) f;
```

If not, what's the problem?

Section 7.6   19. Use typedef to create types named Int8, Int16, and Int32. Define the types so that they represent 8-bit, 16-bit, and 32-bit integers on your machine.

8 Arrays

If a program manipulates a large amount of data,
it does so in a small number of ways.

structures ➤ 16.1

So far, the only variables we've seen are *scalar:* capable of holding a single data item. C also supports *aggregate* variables, which can store collections of values. There are two kinds of aggregates in C: *arrays* and *structures* (records). This chapter shows how to declare and use arrays, both one-dimensional (Section 8.1) and multidimensional (Section 8.2). We'll focus on one-dimensional arrays, which play a much bigger role in C than do multidimensional arrays. Later chapters (Chapter 12 in particular) provide additional information about arrays; Chapter 16 covers structures.

8.1 One-Dimensional Arrays

An *array* is a data structure containing a number of data values, all of which have the same type. These values, known as *elements*, can be individually selected by their position within the array.

The simplest kind of array has just one dimension. The elements of a one-dimensional array are conceptually arranged one after another in a single row (or column, if you prefer). Here's how we might visualize a one-dimensional array named a:

To declare an array, we must specify the *type* of the array's elements and the *number* of elements. For example, to declare that the array a has 10 elements of type int, we would write

```
int a[10];
```

constant expressions ➤5.3 The elements of an array may be of any type; the length of the array can be specified by any (integer) constant expression. Since array lengths may need to be
adjusted when the program is later changed, using a macro to define the length of
an array is an excellent practice:

```
#define N 10

int a[N];
```

Array Subscripting

Q&A

To access a particular element of an array, we write the array name followed by an
integer value in square brackets (this is referred to as *subscripting* or *indexing* the
array). Array elements are always numbered starting from 0, so the elements of an
array of length *n* are indexed from 0 to *n* − 1. For example, if a is an array with ten
elements, they're designated by a[0], a[1], ..., a[9], as the following figure
shows:

```
a[0] a[1] a[2] a[3] a[4] a[5] a[6] a[7] a[8] a[9]
```

lvalues ➤4.2 Expressions of the form a[i] are lvalues, so they can be used in the same way as
ordinary variables:

```
a[0] = 1;
printf("%d\n", a[5]);
++a[i];
```

Arrays and `for` loops go hand-in-hand. Many programs contain `for` loops
whose job is to perform some operation on every element in an array. Here are a
few examples of typical operations on an array a of length N:

idiom
```
for (i = 0; i < N; i++)
    a[i] = 0;                    /* clears a */
```

idiom
```
for (i = 0; i < N; i++)
    scanf("%d", &a[i]);          /* reads data into a */
```

idiom
```
for (i = 0; i < N; i++)
    sum += a[i];                 /* sums the elements of a */
```

Notice that we must use the & symbol when calling `scanf` to read an array element, just as we would with an ordinary variable.

 C doesn't require that subscript bounds be checked; when a subscript goes out of
range, the program may behave unpredictably. One cause of a subscript going out

of bounds: forgetting that an array with *n* elements is indexed from 0 to *n* − 1, not 1 to *n*. (As one of my professors liked to say, "In this business, you're always off by one." He was right, of course.) The following example illustrates a bizarre effect that can be caused by this common blunder:

```
int a[10], i;

for (i = 1; i <= 10; i++)
  a[i] = 0;
```

With some compilers, this innocent-looking `for` statement causes an infinite loop! When i reaches 10, the program stores 0 into a[10]. But a[10] doesn't exist, so 0 goes into memory immediately after a[9]. If the variable i follows a[9] in memory—as might be the case—then i will be reset to 0, causing the loop to start over.

An array subscript may be any integer expression:

```
a[i+j*10] = 0;
```

The expression can even have side effects:

```
i = 0;
while (i < N)
  a[i++] = 0;
```

Let's trace this code. After i is set to 0, the `while` statement checks whether i is less than N. If it is, 0 is assigned to a[0], i is incremented, and the loop repeats. Note that a[++i] wouldn't be right, because 0 would be assigned to a[1] during the first loop iteration.

 Be careful when an array subscript has a side effect. For example, the following loop—which is supposed to copy the array b into the array a—may not work properly:

```
i = 0;
while (i < N)
  a[i] = b[i++];
```

Before each assignment to a[i], the memory locations corresponding to a[i] and b[i++] must be determined. If we're lucky, the location corresponding to a[i] will be determined first, so that b[i] is copied to a[i]. If we're not, the location corresponding to b[i++] is determined first, i is incremented, and b[i] is copied to a[i+1]. Of course, we can easily avoid the problem by removing the increment from the subscript:

```
for (i = 0; i < N; i++)
  a[i] = b[i];
```

PROGRAM   **Reversing a Series of Numbers**

Our first array program prompts the user to enter a series of numbers, then writes the numbers in reverse order:

```
Enter 10 numbers: 34 82 49 102 7 94 23 11 50 31
In reverse order: 31 50 11 23 94 7 102 49 82 34
```

Our strategy will be to store the numbers in an array as they're read, then go through the array backwards, printing the elements one by one. In other words, we won't actually reverse the elements in the array, but we'll make the user think we did.

reverse.c
```c
/* Reverses a series of numbers */

#include <stdio.h>

#define N 10

main()
{
  int a[N], i;

  printf("Enter %d numbers: ", N);
  for (i = 0; i < N; i++)
    scanf("%d", &a[i]);

  printf("In reverse order:");
  for (i = N - 1; i >= 0; i--)
    printf(" %d", a[i]);
  printf("\n");

  return 0;
}
```

This program shows just how useful macros can be in conjunction with arrays. The macro N is used four times in the program: in the declaration of a, in the `printf` that displays a prompt, and in both `for` loops. Should we later decide to change the size of the array, we need only edit the definition of N and recompile the program. Nothing else will need to be altered; even the prompt will still be correct.

Array Initialization

An array, like any other variable, can be given an initial value at the time it's declared. The rules are somewhat tricky, though, so we'll cover some of them now *initializers ➤ 18.5* and save others until later.

The most common form of ***array initializer*** is a list of constant expressions enclosed in braces and separated by commas:

```c
int a[10] = {1, 2, 3, 4, 5, 6, 7, 8, 9, 10};
```

If the initializer is *shorter* than the array, the remaining elements of the array are given the value 0:

```
int a[10] = {1, 2, 3, 4, 5, 6};
  /* initial value of a is {1, 2, 3, 4, 5, 6, 0, 0, 0, 0} */
```

Using this feature, we can easily initialize an array to all zeros:

```
int a[10] = {0};
  /* initial value of a is {0, 0, 0, 0, 0, 0, 0, 0, 0, 0} */
```

It's illegal for an initializer to be completely empty, so we've put a single 0 inside the braces. It's also illegal for an initializer to be *longer* than the array it initializes.

If an initializer is present, the length of the array may be omitted:

```
int a[] = {1, 2, 3, 4, 5, 6, 7, 8, 9, 10};
```

The compiler uses the length of the initializer to determine how long the array is. The array still has a fixed number of elements (ten, in this example), just as if we had specified the length explicitly.

PROGRAM

Checking a Number for Repeated Digits

Our next program checks whether any of the digits in a number appear more than once. After the user enters a number, the program prints either `Repeated digit` or `No repeated digit`:

```
Enter a number: 28212
Repeated digit
```

The number 28212 has a repeated digit (2); a number like 9357 doesn't.

The program uses an array of Boolean values to keep track of which digits appear in a number. The array, named `digit_seen`, is indexed from 0 to 9 to correspond to the ten possible digits. Initially, every element of the array is 0 (false). When given a number n, the program examines n's digits one at a time, storing each into the `digit` variable and then using it as an index into `digit_seen`. If `digit_seen[digit]` is true, then `digit` appears at least twice in n. On the other hand, if `digit_seen[digit]` is false, then `digit` hasn't been seen before, so the program sets `digit_seen[digit]` to TRUE and keeps going.

repdigit.c

```
/* Checks numbers for repeated digits */

#include <stdio.h>

#define TRUE 1
#define FALSE 0

typedef int Bool;
```

```
main()
{
  Bool digit_seen[10] = {0};
  int digit;
  long int n;

  printf("Enter a number: ");
  scanf("%ld", &n);

  while (n > 0) {
    digit = n % 10;
    if (digit_seen[digit])
      break;
    digit_seen[digit] = TRUE;
    n /= 10;
  }

  if (n > 0)
    printf("Repeated digit\n\n");
  else
    printf("No repeated digit\n\n");

  return 0;
}
```

Notice that n has type `long int`, allowing the user to enter numbers up to 2,147,483,647 (or more, on some machines).

Using the `sizeof` Operator with Arrays

The `sizeof` operator can determine the size of an array (in bytes). If a is an array of ten integers, then `sizeof(a)` is typically either 20 (if integers are 16 bits long) or 40 (if integers are 32 bits long).

We can also use `sizeof` to measure the size of an array element. Dividing the array size by the element size gives the length of the array:

```
sizeof(a) / sizeof(a[0])
```

Some programmers use this expression when the length of the array is needed. To clear the array a, for example, we could write

```
for (i = 0; i < sizeof(a) / sizeof(a[0]); i++)
  a[i] = 0;
```

With this technique, the loop doesn't have to be modified if the array length should change at a later date. Using a macro to represent the array length has the same advantage, of course, but the `sizeof` technique is slightly better, since there's no macro name to remember (and possibly get wrong).

The expression `sizeof(a) / sizeof(a[0])` is a bit unwieldy; defining a macro that represents it is often helpful:

```
#define SIZE (sizeof(a) / sizeof(a[0]))

for (i = 0; i < SIZE; i++)
  a[i] = 0;
```

If we're back to using a macro, though, what's the advantage of `sizeof`? We'll answer that question in a later chapter (the trick is to add a "parameter" to the macro).

parameterized macros ➤ 14.3

PROGRAM   **Computing Interest**

Our next program prints a table showing the value of $100 invested at different rates of interest over a period of years. The user will enter an interest rate and the number of years the money will be invested. The table will show the value of the money at one-year intervals—at that interest rate and the next four higher rates—assuming that interest is compounded once a year. Here's what a session with the program will look like:

```
Enter interest rate: 6
Enter number of years: 5

Years    6%    7%    8%    9%    10%
  1    106.00 107.00 108.00 109.00 110.00
  2    112.36 114.49 116.64 118.81 121.00
  3    119.10 122.50 125.97 129.50 133.10
  4    126.25 131.08 136.05 141.16 146.41
  5    133.82 140.26 146.93 153.86 161.05
```

Clearly, we can use a `for` statement to print the first row. The second row is a little trickier, since its values depend on the numbers in the first row. Our solution is to store the first row in an array as it's computed, then use the values in the array to compute the second row. Of course, this process can be repeated for the third and later rows. We'll end up with two `for` statements, one nested inside the other. The outer loop will count from 1 to the number of years requested by the user. The inner loop will increment the interest rate from its lowest value to its highest value.

interest.c
```
/* Prints a table of compound interest */

#include <stdio.h>

#define NUM_RATES (sizeof(value)/sizeof(value[0]))
#define INITIAL_BALANCE 100.00

main()
{
  int i, low_rate, num_years, year;
  float value[5];
```

```
      printf("Enter interest rate: ");
      scanf("%d", &low_rate);
      printf("Enter number of years: ");
      scanf("%d", &num_years);

      printf("\nYears");
      for (i = 0; i < NUM_RATES; i++) {
        printf("%6d%%", low_rate+i);
        value[i] = INITIAL_BALANCE;
      }
      printf("\n");

      for (year = 1; year <= num_years; year++) {
        printf("%3d    ", year);
        for (i = 0; i < NUM_RATES; i++) {
          value[i] += (low_rate+i) / 100.0 * value[i];
          printf("%7.2f", value[i]);
        }
        printf("\n");
      }

      return 0;

    }
```

Note the use of NUM_RATES to control two of the `for` loops. If we later change the size of the `value` array, the loops will adjust automatically.

8.2 Multidimensional Arrays

An array may have any number of dimensions. For example, the following declaration creates a two-dimensional array (or *matrix*, in mathematical terminology):

```
int m[5][9];
```

The array m has 5 rows and 9 columns. Rows and columns are both indexed from 0, as the following figure shows:

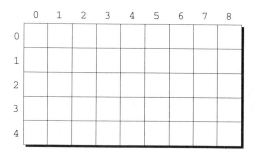

To access the element of m in row i, column j, we must write m[i][j]. The expression m[i] designates row i of m, and m[i][j] then selects element j in this row.

comma operator ➤6.3

Resist the temptation to write m[i,j] instead of m[i][j]. C treats the comma as an operator in this context, so m[i,j] is the same as m[j].

Although we visualize two-dimensional arrays as tables, that's not the way they're actually stored in computer memory. C stores arrays in *row-major* order, with row 0 first, then row 1, and so forth. For example, here's how the m array is stored:

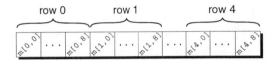

We'll usually ignore this detail, but sometimes it will affect our code.

Just as for loops go hand-in-hand with one-dimensional arrays, nested for loops are ideal for processing multidimensional arrays. Consider, for example, the problem of initializing an array for use as an *identity matrix*. (In mathematics, an identity matrix has 1's on the main diagonal, where the row and column index are the same, and 0's everywhere else.) We'll need to visit each element in the array in some systematic fashion. A pair of nested for loops—one that steps through every row index and one that steps through each column index—is perfect for the job:

```
#define N 10

float ident[N][N];
int row, col;

for (row = 0; row < N; row++)
  for (col = 0; col < N; col++)
    if (row == col)
      ident[row][col] = 1.0;
    else
      ident[row][col] = 0.0;
```

Multidimensional arrays play a lesser role in C than in many other programming languages, primarily because C provides a more flexible way to store multidimensional data: arrays of pointers.

arrays of pointers ➤13.7

Initializing a Multidimensional Array

We can create an initializer for a two-dimensional array by nesting one-dimensional initializers:

```
int m[5][9] = {{1, 1, 1, 1, 1, 0, 1, 1, 1},
               {0, 1, 0, 1, 0, 1, 0, 1, 0},
               {0, 1, 0, 1, 1, 0, 0, 1, 0},
               {1, 1, 0, 1, 0, 0, 0, 1, 0},
               {1, 1, 0, 1, 0, 0, 1, 1, 1}};
```

Each inner initializer provides values for one row of the matrix. Initializers for higher-dimensional arrays are constructed in a similar fashion.

C provides a variety of ways to abbreviate initializers for multidimensional arrays:

- If an initializer isn't large enough to fill a multidimensional array, the remaining elements are given the value 0. For example, the following initializer fills only the first three rows of m; the last two rows will contain zeros:

```
int m[5][9] = {{1, 1, 1, 1, 1, 0, 1, 1, 1},
               {0, 1, 0, 1, 0, 1, 0, 1, 0},
               {0, 1, 0, 1, 1, 0, 0, 1, 0}};
```

- If an inner list isn't long enough to fill a row, the remaining elements in the row are initialized to 0:

```
int m[5][9] = {{1, 1, 1, 1, 1, 0, 1, 1, 1},
               {0, 1, 0, 1, 0, 1, 0, 1},
               {0, 1, 0, 1, 1, 0, 0, 1},
               {1, 1, 0, 1, 0, 0, 0, 1},
               {1, 1, 0, 1, 0, 0, 1, 1, 1}};
```

- We can even omit the inner braces:

```
int m[5][9] = {1, 1, 1, 1, 1, 0, 1, 1, 1,
               0, 1, 0, 1, 0, 1, 0, 1, 0,
               0, 1, 0, 1, 1, 0, 0, 1, 0,
               1, 1, 0, 1, 0, 0, 0, 1, 0,
               1, 1, 0, 1, 0, 0, 1, 1, 1};
```

Once the compiler has seen enough values to fill one row, it begins filling the next.

  Omitting the inner braces in a multidimensional array initializer can be risky, since an extra element (or even worse, a missing element) will affect the rest of the initializer. Leaving out the braces causes some compilers to produce a warning message such as *"Initialization is only partially bracketed."*

Constant Arrays

Any array, whether one-dimensional or multidimensional, can be made "constant" by starting its declaration with the word `const`:

```
const int months[] =
    {31, 28, 31, 30, 31, 30, 31, 31, 30, 31, 30, 31};
```

An array that's been declared `const` should not be modified by the program; the compiler will detect direct attempts to modify an element.

Declaring an array to be `const` has a couple of primary advantages. It documents that the program won't change the array, which can be valuable information for someone reading the program later. It also helps the compiler catch errors, by informing it that we don't intend to modify the array.

const type qualifier ➤ 18.3   `const` isn't limited to arrays; it works with any variable, as we'll see later. However, `const` is frequently used in conjunction with arrays, because they often contain reference information that won't change during program execution.

PROGRAM   **Dealing a Hand of Cards**

Our next program illustrates both two-dimensional arrays and constant arrays. The program deals a random hand from a standard deck of playing cards. (In case you haven't had time to play games recently, each card in a standard deck has a *suit*—clubs, diamonds, hearts, or spades—and a *rank*—two, three, four, five, six, seven, eight, nine, ten, jack, queen, king, or ace.) We'll have the user specify how many cards should be in the hand:

```
Enter number of cards in hand: 5
Your hand: 7c 2s 5d as 2h
```

It's not immediately obvious how we'd write such a program. How do we pick cards randomly from the deck? And how do we avoid picking the same card twice? Let's tackle these problems separately.

time function ➤26.3   To pick cards randomly, we'll use several C library functions. The `time` function (from `<time.h>`) returns the current time, encoded in a single number. The srand function ➤26.2   `srand` function (from `<stdlib.h>`) initializes C's random number generator. Passing the return value of `time` to `srand` prevents the program from dealing the rand function ➤26.2   same cards every time we run it. The `rand` function (from `<stdlib.h>`) produces an apparently random number each time it's called. By using the `%` operator, we can scale the return value from `rand` so that it falls between 0 and 3 (for suits) or between 0 and 12 (for ranks).

To avoid picking the same card twice, we'll need to keep track of which cards have already been chosen. For that purpose, we'll use an array named `in_hand` that has four rows (one for each suit) and 13 columns (one for each rank). In other words, each element in the array corresponds to one of the 52 cards in the deck. All elements of the array will be 0 (false) to start with. Each time we pick a card at random, we'll check whether the element of `in_hand` corresponding to that card is true or false. If it's true, we'll have to pick another card. If it's false, we'll store 1 in that card's array element to remind us later that this card has already been picked.

Once we've verified that a card is "new"—not already selected—we'll need to translate its numerical rank and suit into characters and then display the card. To

translate the rank and suit to character form, we'll set up two arrays of characters—one for the rank and one for the suit—then use the numbers to subscript the
arrays. These arrays won't change during program execution, so we may as well
declare them to be const.

deal.c   /* Deals a random hand of cards */

```c
#include <stdio.h>
#include <stdlib.h>
#include <time.h>

#define NUM_SUITS 4
#define NUM_RANKS 13
#define TRUE 1
#define FALSE 0

typedef int Bool;

main()
{
  Bool in_hand[NUM_SUITS][NUM_RANKS] = {0};
  int num_cards, rank, suit;
  const char rank_code[] = {'2','3','4','5','6','7','8',
                            '9','t','j','q','k','a'};
  const char suit_code[] = {'c','d','h','s'};

  srand((unsigned) time(NULL));

  printf("Enter number of cards in hand: ");
  scanf("%d", &num_cards);

  printf("Your hand:");
  while (num_cards > 0) {
    suit = rand() % NUM_SUITS;      /* picks a random suit */
    rank = rand() % NUM_RANKS;      /* picks a random rank */
    if (!in_hand[suit][rank]) {
      in_hand[suit][rank] = TRUE;
      num_cards--;
      printf(" %c%c", rank_code[rank], suit_code[suit]);
    }
  }
  printf("\n");

  return 0;
}
```

Notice the initializer for the in_hand array:

```c
Bool in_hand[NUM_SUITS][NUM_RANKS] = {0};
```

Even though in_hand is a two-dimensional array, C allows us to use a single pair
of braces. Also, we've supplied only one value in the initializer, knowing that C
will fill in 0 for the other elements.

Q & A

Q: **Why do array subscripts start at 0 instead of 1? [p. 140]**

A: Having subscripts begin at 0 simplifies the compiler a bit. Also, it can make array subscripting marginally faster.

Q: **What if I want an array with subscripts that go from 1 to 10 instead of 0 to 9?**

A: Here's a common trick: declare the array to have 11 elements instead of 10. The subscripts will go from 0 to 10, but you can just ignore element 0.

Q: **Is it possible to use a character as an array subscript?**

A: Yes, because C treats characters as integers. You'll probably need to "scale" the character before you use it as a subscript, though. Let's say that we want the `letter_count` array to keep track of a count for each letter in the alphabet. The array will need 26 elements, so we'd declare it in the following way:

```
int letter_count[26];
```

However, we can't use letters to subscript `letter_count` directly, because their integer values don't fall between 0 and 25. To scale a lower-case letter to the proper range, we can simply subtract `'a'`; to scale an upper-case letter, we'll subtract `'A'`. For example, if `ch` contains a lower-case letter, we'd write

```
letter_count[ch-'a'] = 0;
```

to clear the count that corresponds to `ch`.

Q: **The compiler gives me an error message if I try to copy one array into another by using the assignment operator. What's wrong?**

A: Although it looks quite plausible, the assignment

```
a = b;   /* a and b are arrays */
```

is indeed illegal. The reason for its illegality isn't obvious; it has to do with the peculiar relationship between arrays and pointers in C, a topic we'll explore in Chapter 12.

The simplest way to copy one array into another is to use a loop that copies the elements, one by one:

```
for (i = 0; i < N; i++)
  a[i] = b[i];
```

memcpy function ➤23.5 Another possibility is to use the `memcpy` ("memory copy") function from the `<string.h>` header. `memcpy` is a low-level function that simply copies bytes from one place to another. To copy the array `b` into the array `a`, use `memcpy` as follows:

```
memcpy(a, b, sizeof(a));
```

Many programmers prefer `memcpy`, especially for large arrays, because it's potentially faster than an ordinary loop.

Exercises

Section 8.1

1. Modify the `repdigit.c` program so that it shows which digits (if any) were repeated:

   ```
   Enter a number: 939577
   Repeated digit(s): 7 9
   ```

2. Modify the `repdigit.c` program so that it prints a table showing how many times each digit appears in the number:

   ```
   Enter a number: 41271092
   Digit:        0  1  2  3  4  5  6  7  8  9
   Occurrences:  1  2  2  0  1  0  0  1  0  1
   ```

3. Modify the `repdigit.c` program so that the user can enter more than one number to be tested for repeated digits. The program should terminate when the user enters a number that's less than or equal to 0.

4. We discussed using the expression `sizeof(a) / sizeof(a[0])` to calculate the number of elements in an array. The expression `sizeof(a) / sizeof(t)`, where *t* is the type of a's elements, would also work, but it's considered an inferior technique. Why?

5. Modify the `reverse.c` program to use the expression `sizeof(a) / sizeof(a[0])` (or a macro with this value) for the array length.

6. Modify the `interest.c` program so that it compounds interest *monthly* instead of *annually*. The form of the output shouldn't change; the balance should still be shown at annual intervals.

7. One of the celebrities of the on-line movement is a fellow named B1FF, who has a unique way of writing messages. Here's a typical B1FF communiqué:

   ```
   H3Y DUD3, C 15 R1LLY C00L!!!!!!!!!!
   ```

   Write a "B1FF filter" that reads a message entered by the user and translates it into B1FF-speak:

   ```
   Enter message: Hey dude, C is rilly cool
   In B1FF-speak: H3Y DUD3, C 15 R1LLY C00L!!!!!!!!!!
   ```

   Your program should convert the message to upper-case letters, substitute digits for certain letters (A→4, B→8, E→3, I→1, O→0, S→5), and then append ten or so exclamation marks. *Hint:* Store the original message in an array of characters, then go back through the array, translating and printing characters one by one.

8. The Q&A section shows how to use a *letter* as an array subscript. Describe how to use a *digit* (in character form) as a subscript.

Section 8.2

9. Calculators, watches, and other electronic devices often rely on ***seven-segment displays*** for numerical output. To form a digit, such devices "turn on" some of the seven segments while leaving others "off":

```
 _        _    _    _     _     _          _     _
| |    |  _|   _|  |_|   |_    |_     _|  |_|   |_|
|_|    | |_    _|    |   _|    |_|    |   |_|    _|
```

Suppose that we want to set up an array that remembers which segments should be "on" for each digit. Let's number the segments as follows:

```
  _0_
5|   |1
  _6_
4|   |2
  _3_
```

Here's what the array might look like, with each row representing one digit:

```
const int segments[10][7] = {{1, 1, 1, 1, 1, 1, 0}, ...};
```

I've given you the first row of the initializer; fill in the rest.

10. Using the shortcuts described in Section 8.2, shrink the initializer for the `segments` array (Exercise 9) as much as you can.

11. Write a program that reads a 5 × 5 array of integers and then prints the row sums and the column sums:

```
            0  1  2  3  4
Enter row 1: 8  3  9  0 10
Enter row 2: 3  5 17  1  1
Enter row 3: 2  8  6 23  1
Enter row 4:15  7  3  2  9
Enter row 5: 6 14  2  6  0

Row totals: 30 27 40 36 28
Column totals: 34 37 37 32 21
```

12. Modify Exercise 11 so that it prompts for five quiz grades for each of five students, then computes the total score and average score for each *student*, and the average score, high score, and low score for each *quiz*.

13. Write a program that generates a "random walk" across a 10 × 10 array. The array will contain characters (all '.' initially). The program must randomly "walk" from element to element, always going up, down, left, or right by one element. The elements visited by the program will be labeled with the letters A though Z, in the order visited. Here's an example of the desired output:

```
A . . . . . . . . .
B C D . . . . . . .
. F E . . . . . . .
H G . . . . . . . .
I . . . . . . . . .
J . . . . . . Z .
K . . R S T U V Y .
L M P Q . . . W X .
. N O . . . . . . .
. . . . . . . . . .
```

Hint: Use the `srand` and `rand` functions (see `deal.c`) to generate random numbers. After generating a number, look at its remainder when divided by 4. There are four possible values for the remainder—0, 1, 2, and 3—indicating the direction of the next move. Before performing a move, check that (a) it won't go outside the array, and (b) it doesn't take us to an element that already has a letter assigned. If either condition is violated, try moving in another direction. If all four directions are blocked, the program must terminate. Here's an example of premature termination:

```
A  B  G  H  I  .  .  .  .  .
.  C  F  .  J  K  .  .  .  .
.  D  E  .  M  L  .  .  .  .
.  .  .  .  N  O  .  .  .  .
.  .  W  X  Y  P  Q  .  .  .
.  .  V  U  T  S  R  .  .  .
.  .  .  .  .  .  .  .  .  .
.  .  .  .  .  .  .  .  .  .
.  .  .  .  .  .  .  .  .  .
.  .  .  .  .  .  .  .  .  .
```

Y is blocked on all four sides, so there's no place to put Z.

9 Functions

*If you have a procedure with ten
parameters, you probably missed some.*

We saw in Chapter 2 that a *function* is simply a series of statements that have been grouped together and given a name. Although the term "function" comes from mathematics, C functions don't always resemble math functions. In C, a function doesn't necessarily have arguments, nor does it necessarily compute a value. (In some programming languages, a "function" returns a value, whereas a "procedure" doesn't. C lacks this distinction.)

Functions are the building blocks of C programs. Each function is essentially a small program, with its own declarations and statements. Using functions, we can divide a program into small pieces that are easier for us—and others—to understand and modify. Functions can take some of the tedium out of programming by allowing us to avoid duplicating code that's used more than once. Moreover, functions are reusable: we can take a function that was originally part of one program and use it in others.

Our programs so far have consisted of just one function—main—although they've called library functions. In this chapter, we'll focus on writing our own functions. Section 9.1 shows how to define and call functions. Section 9.2 then discusses function *declarations* and how they differ from function *definitions*. Next, Section 9.3 examines how arguments are passed to functions. The remainder of the chapter covers the return statement (Section 9.4), the related issue of program termination (Section 9.5), and functions that are *recursive* (Section 9.6).

9.1 Defining and Calling Functions

Before we go over the formal rules for defining a function, let's look at three simple programs that define functions.

155

PROGRAM   **Computing Averages**

Suppose we often need to compute the average of two `float` values. The C library doesn't have an "average" function, but we can easily define our own. Here's what it would look like:

```
float average(float a, float b)
{
  return (a + b) / 2;
}
```

The word `float` at the beginning is `average`'s ***return type:*** the type of data that the function returns each time it's called. The identifiers a and b (the function's

Q&A

parameters) represent the two numbers that will be supplied when `average` is called. Each parameter must have a type (just like every variable has a type); we've selected `float` as the type of a and b. (I know it looks odd, but the word `float` must appear twice, once for a and once for b.) A function parameter is essentially a variable whose initial value will be supplied later, when the function is called.

Every function has an executable part, called the ***body***, which is enclosed in braces. The body of `average` consists of a single `return` statement. Executing this statement causes the function to "return" to the place from which it was called; the value of (a + b) / 2 will be the value returned by the function.

To activate (***call***) a function, we write the function name, followed by a list of ***arguments***: `average(x, y)`, for example. Arguments are used to supply information to a function; in this case, `average` needs to know which two numbers to average. The effect of the call `average(x, y)` is to copy the values of x and y into the parameters a and b, then execute the body of `average`. An argument doesn't have to be a variable, by the way; any expression of the proper type will do, allowing us to write `average(5.1, 8.9)` or `average(x/2, y/3)`.

We'll put the call of `average` in the place where we need to use the return value. For example, we could write

```
printf("Average: %g\n", average(x, y));
```

to compute the average of x and y and then print it. This statement has the following effect:

1. It calls the `average` function, passing x and y as arguments.
2. `average` executes its `return` statement, returning the average of x and y.
3. `printf` prints the value that `average` returns. (The return value of `average` becomes one of `printf`'s arguments.)

Note that the return value of `average` isn't saved anywhere; the program prints it and then discards it. If we had needed the return value later in the program, we could have captured it in a variable:

```
avg = average(x, y);
```

This statement calls average, then saves its return value in the variable avg.

Now, let's use the average function in a complete program. The following program reads three numbers and computes their averages, one pair at a time:

```
Enter three numbers: 3.5 9.6 10.2
Average of 3.5 and 9.6: 6.55
Average of 9.6 and 10.2: 9.9
Average of 3.5 and 10.2: 6.85
```

Among other things, this program shows that a function can be called as often as we need.

```
/* Computes pairwise averages of three numbers */

#include <stdio.h>

float average(float a, float b)
{
  return (a + b) / 2;
}

main()
{
  float x, y, z;

  printf("Enter three numbers: ");
  scanf("%f%f%f", &x, &y, &z);
  printf("Average of %g and %g: %g\n", x, y, average(x, y));
  printf("Average of %g and %g: %g\n", y, z, average(y, z));
  printf("Average of %g and %g: %g\n", x, z, average(x, z));

  return 0;
}
```

Notice that I've put the definition of average before main. We'll see in Section 9.2 that putting average after main causes problems. For now, we'll simply play it safe and define our functions before main.

PROGRAM   **Printing a Countdown**

Not every function returns a value. For example, a function whose job is to produce output may not need to return anything. To indicate that a function has no return value, we specify that its return type is void. (In C, the word void is used as a placeholder, much like the message "This page intentionally left blank" found in computer manuals.) Consider the following function, which prints the message T minus *n* and counting, where *n* is supplied when the function is called:

```
void print_count(int n)
{
  printf("T minus %d and counting\n", n);
}
```

print_count has one parameter, n, of type int. It returns nothing, so we've specified void as the return type and omitted the return statement. Since print_count doesn't return a value, we can't call it in the same way we call average. A call of print_count must be a *statement*, not an *expression:*

```
print_count(i);
```

Here's a program that calls print_count ten times inside a loop:

countdwn.c

```
/* Prints a countdown */

#include <stdio.h>

void print_count(int n)
{
  printf("T minus %d and counting\n", n);
}

main()
{
  int i;

  for (i = 10; i > 0; --i)
    print_count(i);
  return 0;
}
```

Initially, i has the value 10. As the call of print_count begins, i is copied into n, so that n takes on the value 10 as well. As a result, the first call of print_count will print

```
T minus 10 and counting
```

print_count then returns to the point at which it was called, which happens to be the body of a for statement. The for statement resumes where it left off, decrementing i to 9 and testing whether it's greater than 0. It is, so print_count is called again, this time printing

```
T minus 9 and counting
```

Each time print_count is called, i is different, so print_count will print ten different messages.

PROGRAM **Printing a Pun (Revisited)**

Some functions have no parameters at all. Consider print_pun, which prints a bad pun each time it's called:

```
void print_pun(void)
{
  printf("To C, or not to C: that is the question.\n");
}
```

The word `void` in parentheses indicates that `print_pun` has no arguments. (Again, we're using `void` as a placeholder that means "nothing goes here.")

To call a function with no arguments, we write the function's name, followed by parentheses:

```
print_pun();
```

The parentheses *must* be present, even though there are no arguments.

Here's a tiny program that tests the `print_pun` function:

pun2.c

```
/* Prints a bad pun */

#include <stdio.h>

void print_pun(void)
{
  printf("To C, or not to C: that is the question.\n");
}

main()
{
  print_pun();
  return 0;
}
```

The execution of this program begins with the first statement in `main`, which happens to be a call of `print_pun`. `print_pun` now begins to execute, calling `printf` to display a string. When `printf` returns, `print_pun` returns to `main`.

Function Definitions

Now that we've seen several examples, let's look at the general form of a function definition:

function definition

> *return-type function-name* (*parameters*)
> {
>   *declarations*
>   *statements*
> }

The "return type" of a function is the type of value that the function returns. The following rules govern the return type:

- Functions may not return arrays, but there are no other restrictions on the return type.
- If the return type is omitted, the function is presumed to return a value of type `int`.

- Specifying that the return type is void indicates that the function doesn't return a value.

It's good practice to specify an explicit return type for every function. Classic C lacked the concept of void, so programmers would often omit the return type if there was no return value:

```
print_count(int n)
{
  printf("T minus %d and counting\n", n);
}
```

I'd recommend that you avoid this practice, since it's not immediately clear whether the function returns nothing or whether it actually returns an int value.

By the way, some programmers put the return type *above* the function name:

```
float
average(float a, float b)
{
  return (a + b) / 2;
}
```

Putting the return type on a separate line is especially useful if the return type is lengthy, like unsigned long int.

Q&A   After the function name comes a list of parameters. Each parameter is preceded by a specification of its type; parameters are separated by commas. If the function has no parameters, the word void should appear between the parentheses. *Note:* A separate type must be specified for each parameter, even when several parameters have the same type:

```
float average(float a, b)    /*** WRONG ***/
{
  return (a + b) / 2;
}
```

The body of a function may include both declarations and statements. For example, the average function could be written

```
float average(float a, float b)
{
  float sum;            /* declaration */

  sum = a + b;          /* statement */
  return sum / 2;       /* statement */
}
```

Variables declared in the body of a function belong exclusively to that function; they can't be examined or modified by other functions.

The body of a function can be empty:

```
void print_pun(void)
{
}
```

Leaving the body empty may make sense during program development; we can leave room for the function without taking the time to complete it, then come back later and write the body.

Function Calls

A function call consists of a function name followed by a list of arguments, enclosed in parentheses:

```
average(x, y)
print_count(i)
print_pun()
```

If the parentheses are missing, the function won't get called:

```
print_pun;    /*** WRONG ***/
```

The result is a legal (albeit meaningless) expression statement that looks correct, but has no effect. Some compilers issue a warning such as *"Code has no effect."*

A call of a `void` function is a *statement*, so it's always followed by a semicolon:

```
print_count(i);
print_pun();
```

A call of a non-`void` function, on the other hand, is an *expression*—it produces a value that can be stored in a variable, tested, printed, or used in some other way:

```
avg = average(x, y);
if (average(x, y) > 0) printf("Average is positive\n");
printf("The average is %g\n", average(x, y));
```

The value returned by a non-`void` function can always be discarded if desired:

```
average(x, y);    /* discards return value */
```

expression statements ➤4.5 This call of `average` is an example of an expression statement: a statement that computes a value, but doesn't save it.

Discarding the return value of `average` is an odd thing to do, of course, since that's what we were after when we called the function. In some cases, however, it makes sense to discard a function's return value. The `printf` function, for example, returns the number of characters that it prints. After the following call, `num_chars` will have the value 9:

```
num_chars = printf("Hi, Mom!\n");
```

Since we're probably not interested in the number of characters printed, we'll normally discard `printf`'s return value:

```
printf("Hi, Mom!\n");    /* discards return value */
```

To make it clear that we're deliberately discarding the return value of a function, C allows us to put (void) before the call:

```
(void) printf("Hi, Mom!\n");
```

casting ➤ 7.5   What we're doing is casting (converting) the return value of printf to type void. (In C, "casting to void" is a polite way of saying "throwing away.") Using (void) makes it clear to others that you deliberately discarded the return value, not just forgot that there was one. Unfortunately, there are a great many functions in the C library whose values are routinely discarded; using (void) when calling them all can get tiresome, so I haven't done so in this book.

PROGRAM   ## Testing Whether a Number Is Prime

To see how functions can make programs easier to understand, let's write a program that tests whether a number is prime. The program will prompt the user to enter the number, then respond with a message indicating whether or not the number is prime:

```
Enter a number: 34
Not prime
```

Instead of putting the prime-testing details in main, we'll define a separate function that returns TRUE if its parameter is a prime number, FALSE if it isn't. When given a number n, the is_prime function will divide n by each of the numbers between 2 and the square root of n; if the remainder is ever 0, we know that n isn't prime.

prime.c
```
/* Tests whether a number is prime */

#include <stdio.h>

#define TRUE 1
#define FALSE 0

typedef int Bool;

Bool is_prime(int n)
{
  int divisor;

  if (n <= 1) return FALSE;
  for (divisor = 2; divisor * divisor <= n; divisor++)
    if (n % divisor == 0)
      return FALSE;
  return TRUE;
}
```

```
main()
{
  int n;

  printf("Enter a number: ");
  scanf("%d", &n);
  if (is_prime(n))
    printf("Prime\n");
  else
    printf("Not prime\n");

  return 0;
}
```

Notice that `main` contains a variable named `n` even though `is_prime`'s parameter is named `n`. An identifier used as the name of a parameter or variable in one function can be reused in other functions; the uses need not be related. (Section 10.1 discusses this issue in more detail.)

As this program demonstrates, a function may have more than one `return` statement. Of course, we can execute just one `return` statement during a given call of the function.

9.2 Function Declarations

In our programs in Section 9.1, we were always careful to put the definition of a function *above* the point at which it was called. Actually, C doesn't require that the definition of a function precede its calls. Suppose that we rearrange the `average.c` program (Section 9.1) by putting the definition of `average` *after* the definition of `main`:

```
#include <stdio.h>

main()
{
  float x, y, z;

  printf("Enter three numbers: ");
  scanf("%f%f%f", &x, &y, &z);
  printf("Average of %g and %g: %g\n", x, y, average(x, y));
  printf("Average of %g and %g: %g\n", y, z, average(y, z));
  printf("Average of %g and %g: %g\n", x, z, average(x, z));

  return 0;
}

float average(float a, float b)
{
  return (a + b) / 2;
}
```

When the compiler encounters the first call of average in main, it has no information about average: it doesn't know how many parameters average has, what the types of these parameters are, or what kind of value average returns. Instead of producing an error message, though, the compiler instead makes a few assumptions about average. It assumes that average returns an int value (recall from Section 9.1 that the return type of a function is int by default). It assumes that we're passing average the right number of arguments. Finally, it assumes that the arguments—after promotion—have the proper type. Since some of these assumptions about average are wrong, the program won't work.

 default argument promotions ➤9.3

One way to avoid the problem of call-before-definition is to arrange the program so that the definition of each function precedes all its calls. Unfortunately, such an arrangement doesn't always exist, and even when it does, it may make the program harder to understand by putting its function definitions in an unnatural order.

Fortunately, C offers a better solution: **declare** each function before calling it. A function declaration provides the compiler with a brief glimpse at a function whose full definition will appear later. A function declaration resembles the first line of a function definition with a semicolon added at the end:

function declaration

> *return-type function-name (parameters) ;*

Needless to say, the declaration of a function must be consistent with the function's definition.

Here's how our program would look with a declaration of average added:

```
#include <stdio.h>

float average(float a, float b);    /* DECLARATION */

main()
{
    float x, y, z;

    printf("Enter three numbers: ");
    scanf("%f%f%f", &x, &y, &z);
    printf("Average of %g and %g: %g\n", x, y, average(x, y));
    printf("Average of %g and %g: %g\n", y, z, average(y, z));
    printf("Average of %g and %g: %g\n", x, z, average(x, z));

    return 0;
}

float average(float a, float b)    /* DEFINITION */
{
    return (a + b) / 2;
}
```

Q&A Function declarations of the kind we've been discussing are known as *function prototypes* to distinguish them from Classic C's function declarations. A prototype provides a complete description of how to call a function: how many arguments to supply, what their types should be, and what type of result will be returned.

Incidentally, a function prototype doesn't have to specify the *names* of the function's parameters, as long as their *types* are present:

```
float average(float, float);
```

It's usually best not to omit the parameter names, however, since they help document the purpose of each parameter and remind the programmer of the order in which arguments must appear when the function is called.

9.3 Arguments

Let's review the difference between a *parameter* and an *argument.* **Parameters** appear in function *definitions;* they're dummy names that represent values to be supplied when the function is called. **Arguments** are expressions that appear in function *calls.* When the distinction between *argument* and *parameter* isn't important, I'll sometimes use *argument* to mean either.

In C, arguments are **passed by value:** when a function is called, each argument is evaluated and its value assigned to the corresponding parameter. Changes made to the parameter during the execution of the function don't affect the value of the argument. In effect, each parameter behaves like a variable initialized to the value of the matching argument.

The fact that arguments are passed by value has both advantages and disadvantages. Since a parameter can be modified without affecting the corresponding argument, we can use parameters as variables within the function, thereby reducing the number of genuine variables needed. Consider the following function, which raises a number x to a power n:

```
int power(int x, int n)
{
  int i, result = 1;

  for (i = 1; i <= n; i++)
    result = result * x;
  return result;
}
```

Since n is a *copy* of the original exponent, we can modify it inside the function, thus removing the need for i:

```
int power(int x, int n)
{
  int result = 1;

  while (n-- > 0)
    result = result * x;
  return result;
}
```

Unfortunately, C's requirement that arguments be passed by value makes it difficult to write certain kinds of functions. For example, suppose that we need a function that will decompose a `float` value into an integer part and a fractional part. Since a function can't *return* two numbers, we might try passing a pair of variables to the function and having it modify them:

```
void decompose(float x, int int_part, float frac_part)
{
  int_part = (int) x;    /* drops the fractional part of x */
  frac_part = x - int_part;
}
```

Suppose that we call the function in the following way:

```
decompose(3.14159, i, f);
```

At the beginning of the call, 3.14159 is copied into `x`, `i`'s value is copied into `int_part`, and `f`'s value is copied into `frac_part`. The statements inside `decompose` then assign 3 to `int_part` and .14159 to `frac_part`, and the function returns. Unfortunately, `i` and `f` weren't affected by the assignments to `int_part` and `frac_part`, so they have the same values after the call as they did before the call. With a little extra effort, `decompose` can be made to work, as we'll see in Section 11.4. However, we'll need to cover more of C's features first.

Argument Conversions

C allows function calls in which the types of the arguments don't match the types of the parameters. The rules governing how the arguments are converted depend on whether or not the compiler has seen a prototype for the function (or the function's full definition) prior to the call:

- **The compiler has encountered a prototype prior to the call.** The value of each argument is implicitly converted to the type of the corresponding parameter as if by assignment. For example, if an `int` argument is passed to a function that was expecting a `float`, the argument is converted to `float` automatically.

- **The compiler has not encountered a prototype prior to the call.** The compiler performs the **default argument promotions:** (1) `float` arguments are converted to `double`. (2) The integral promotions are performed (`char` and `short` arguments are converted to `int`).

The default argument promotions may not produce the desired result. Consider the following example:

```
main()
{
  int i;

  printf("Enter number to be squared: ");
  scanf("%d", &i);
  printf("The answer is %g\n", square(i));    /*** WRONG ***/

  return 0;
}

double square(double x)
{
  return x * x;
}
```

At the time `square` is called, the compiler hasn't seen a prototype yet, so it doesn't know that `square` expects an argument of type `double`. Instead, the compiler performs the default argument promotions on `i`, with no effect. Since it's expecting an argument of type `double` but has been given an `int` value instead, `square` will produce an invalid result. The problem can be fixed by declaring `square` before calling it or by casting `i` to the proper type:

```
printf("The answer is %g\n", square((double) i));
```

The fact that the default argument promotions don't always have the desired effect makes it even more imperative that we always declare functions before calling them.

Array Arguments

Arrays are often used as arguments. When a parameter is a one-dimensional array, the length of the array can be (and is normally) left unspecified:

```
int f(int a[])    /* no length specified */
{
  ...
}
```

The argument can be any one-dimensional array whose elements are of the proper type. There's just one problem: how will `f` know how long the array is? Unfortunately, C doesn't provide any easy way for a function to determine the length of an array passed to it. Instead, we'll have to supply the length—if the function needs it—as an additional argument.

Although we can use the `sizeof` operator to help determine the length of an array *variable*, it doesn't give the correct answer for an array *parameter:*

```c
int f(int a[])
{
  int len = sizeof(a) / sizeof(a[0]);    /*** WRONG ***/
  ...
}
```

Section 12.3 explains why.

The following function illustrates the use of one-dimensional array arguments. When given an array a of `int` values, `sum_array` returns the sum of the elements in a. Since `sum_array` needs to know the length of a, we must supply it as a second argument.

```c
int sum_array(int a[], int n)
{
  int i, sum = 0;

  for (i = 0; i < n; i++)
    sum += a[i];

  return sum;
}
```

The prototype for `sum_array` has the following appearance:

```c
int sum_array(int a[], int n);
```

As usual, we can omit the parameter names if we wish:

```c
int sum_array(int [], int);
```

When `sum_array` is called, the first argument will be the name of an array, and the second will be its length. For example:

```c
#define LEN 100

main()
{
  int b[LEN], total;
  ...
  total = sum_array(b, LEN);
  ...
}
```

Notice that we don't put brackets after an array name when passing it to a function:

```c
total = sum_array(b[], LEN);    /*** WRONG ***/
```

An important point about array arguments: A function has no way to check that we've passed it the correct array length. We can exploit this fact by telling the function that the array is smaller than it really is. Suppose that we've only stored 50 numbers in the b array, even though it can hold 100. We can sum just the first 50 elements by writing

```
total = sum_array(b, 50);   /* sums first 50 elements */
```

sum_array will ignore the other 50 elements. (Indeed, it won't know that they even exist!)

Be careful not to tell a function that an array argument is *larger* than it really is:

```
total = sum_array(b, 150);   /*** WRONG ***/
```

In this example, sum_array will go past the end of the array; as a result, total will include the values of 50 nonexistent array elements.

Q&A   When a parameter is a multidimensional array, only the length of the first dimension may be omitted. For example, if we revise the sum_array function so that a is a two-dimensional array, we must specify the number of columns in a, although we don't have to indicate the number of rows:

```
#define LEN 10

int sum_array(int a[][LEN], int n)
{
  int i, j, sum = 0;

  for (i = 0; i < n; i++)
    for (j = 0; j < LEN; j++)
      sum += a[i][j];

  return sum;
}
```

arrays of pointers ➤ *13.7*

Not being able to pass multidimensional arrays with an arbitrary number of columns can be a nuisance. Fortunately, we can often work around this difficulty by using arrays of pointers.

9.4 The return Statement

A non-void function must use the return statement to specify what value it will return. The return statement has the form

return statement

```
return expression ;
```

The expression is often just a constant or variable:

```
return 0;
return status;
```

More complex expressions are possible. It's not unusual to see the conditional operator used in a return expression:

```
return i > j ? i : j;
```

If the type of the expression in a `return` statement doesn't match the function's return type, the expression will be implicitly converted to the return type. For example, if a function is declared to return an `int`, but the `return` statement contains a `float` expression, the value of the expression is converted to `int`.

`return` statements may appear in functions whose return type is `void`, provided that no expression is given:

```
return;    /* return in a void function */
```

(Putting an expression in such a `return` statement will get you a compile-time error.) In the following example, the `return` statement causes the function to return immediately when given a negative argument:

```
void print_int(int i)
{
  if (i < 0) return;
  printf("%d", i);
}
```

A `return` statement at the end of a `void` function causes no harm:

```
void print_pun(void)
{
  printf("To C, or not to C: that is the question.\n");
  return;    /* OK, but not needed */
}
```

Using `return` is unnecessary, though, since a function will return automatically after its last statement has been executed.

If a non-`void` function should ever reach the end of its body, the value returned is undefined. Needless to say, this practice is not recommended. Some compilers will issue a message such as *"Function should return a value"* if they detect the possibility of a non-`void` function "falling off" the end of its body.

9.5 Program Termination

Since `main` is a function, it must have a return type. We've never specified `main`'s return type, which means that it's `int` by default. We can make the return type explicit if we choose:

```
int main()
{
  ...
}
```

The value returned by `main` is a status code that—in some operating systems—can be tested when the program terminates. `main` should return 0 if the program terminates normally; to indicate abnormal termination, `main` should return a value other than 0. (Actually, there's no rule to prevent us from using the return value for other purposes.) It's good practice to make sure that every C program returns a status code, even if there are no plans to use it, since someone running the program later may decide to test it.

The `exit` Function

Executing a `return` statement in `main` is one way to terminate a program. Another is calling the `exit` function, which belongs to `<stdlib.h>`. The argument passed to `exit` has the same meaning as `main`'s return value: both indicate the program's status at termination. To indicate normal termination, we'd pass 0:

```
exit(0);                /* normal termination */
```

Since 0 is a bit cryptic, C allows us to pass EXIT_SUCCESS instead (the effect is the same):

```
exit(EXIT_SUCCESS);   /* normal termination */
```

Passing EXIT_FAILURE indicates abnormal termination:

```
exit(EXIT_FAILURE);   /* abnormal termination */
```

EXIT_SUCCESS and EXIT_FAILURE are macros defined in `<stdlib.h>`. The values of EXIT_SUCCESS and EXIT_FAILURE are implementation-defined; typical values are 0 and 1, respectively.

As methods of terminating a program, `return` and `exit` are closely related. In fact, the statement

```
return expression;
```

in `main` is equivalent to

```
exit(expression);
```

The difference between `return` and `exit` is that `exit` can be called from any function, not just from `main`. Some programmers use `exit` exclusively so that a pattern-matching program can easily locate all exit points in a program.

9.6   Recursive Functions

A function is *recursive* if it calls itself. For example, the following function computes $n!$ recursively, using the formula $n! = n \times (n-1)!$:

```
int fact(int n)
{
  if (n <= 1)
    return 1;
  else
    return n * fact(n-1);
}
```

Some programming languages rely heavily on recursion, while others don't even allow it. C falls somewhere in the middle: it allows recursion, but most C programmers don't use it that often.

To see how recursion works, let's trace the execution of the statement

```
i = fact(3);
```

Here's what happens:

fact(3) finds that 3 is not less than or equal to 1, so it calls
    fact(2), which finds that 2 is not less than or equal to 1, so it calls
        fact(1), which finds that 1 *is* less than or equal to 1, so it returns 1, causing
    fact(2) to return $2 \times 1 = 2$, causing
fact(3) to return $3 \times 2 = 6$.

Notice how the unfinished calls of fact "pile up" until fact is finally passed 1. At that point, the old calls of fact begin to "unwind" one by one, until the original call—fact(3)—finally returns with the answer, 6.

Here's another example of recursion: a function that computes x^n, using the formula $x^n = x \times x^{n-1}$.

```
int power(int x, int n)
{
  if (n == 0)
    return 1;
  else
    return x * power(x, n-1);
}
```

The call power(5, 3) would be executed as follows:

power(5, 3) finds that 3 is not equal to 0, so it calls
  power(5, 2), which finds that 2 is not equal to 0, so it calls
    power(5, 1), which finds that 1 is not equal to 0, so it calls
      power(5, 0), which finds that 0 *is* equal to 0, so it returns 1, causing
    power(5, 1) to return $5 \times 1 = 5$, causing
  power(5, 2) to return $5 \times 5 = 25$, causing
power(5, 3) to return $5 \times 25 = 125$.

Incidentally, we can condense the `power` function a bit by putting a conditional expression in the `return` statement:

```
int power(int x, int n)
{
  return n == 0 ? 1 : x * power(x, n-1);
}
```

Both `fact` and `power` are careful to test a "termination condition" as soon as they're called. When `fact` is called, it immediately checks whether its parameter is less than or equal to 1. When `power` is called, it first checks whether its second parameter is equal to 0. All recursive functions need some kind of termination condition in order to prevent infinite recursion.

The Quicksort Algorithm

At this point, you may wonder why we're bothering with recursion; after all, neither `fact` nor `power` really needs it. Well, you've got a point. Neither function makes much of a case for recursion, because each calls itself just once. Recursion is much more helpful for sophisticated algorithms that require a function to call itself two or more times.

In practice, recursion often arises naturally as a result of an algorithm design technique known as **divide-and-conquer**, in which a large problem is divided into smaller pieces that are then tackled by the same algorithm. A classic example of the divide-and-conquer strategy can be found in the popular sorting algorithm known as **Quicksort**. The Quicksort algorithm goes as follows (for simplicity, we'll assume that the array being sorted is indexed from 1 to n):

1. Choose an array element e (the "partitioning element"), then rearrange the array so that elements $1, \ldots, i - 1$ are less than or equal to e, element i contains e, and elements $i + 1, \ldots, n$ are greater than or equal to e.
2. Sort elements $1, \ldots, i - 1$ by using Quicksort recursively.
3. Sort elements $i + 1, \ldots, n$ by using Quicksort recursively.

After step 1, the element e is in its proper location. Since the elements to the left of e are all less than or equal to it, they'll be in their proper places once they've been sorted in step 2; similar reasoning applies to the elements to the right of e.

Step 1 of the Quicksort algorithm is obviously critical. There are various methods to partition an array, some much better than others. We'll use a technique that's easy to understand but not particularly efficient. We'll first describe the partitioning algorithm informally; later, we'll translate it into C code.

The algorithm relies on two "markers" named *low* and *high*, which keep track of positions within the array. Initially, *low* points to the first element of the array and *high* points to the last element. We start by copying the first element (the partitioning element) into a temporary location elsewhere, leaving a "hole" in the array. Next, we move *high* across the array from right to left until it points to a number that's smaller than the partitioning element. We then copy the number into the hole that *low* points to, which creates a a new hole (pointed to by *high*). We now move *low* from left to right, looking for an element that's larger than the partitioning element. When we find one, we copy it into the hole that *high* points to. The process repeats, with *low* and *high* taking turns, until they meet somewhere in the middle of the array. At that time, both will point to a hole; all we need do is copy the partitioning element into the hole. The following diagrams illustrate the process:

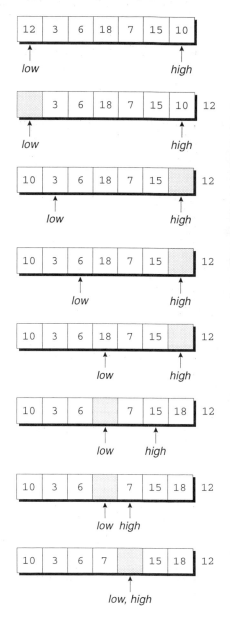

Let's start with an array containing seven elements. *low* points to the first element; *high* points to the last one.

The first element, 12, is the partitioning element. Copying it somewhere else leaves a hole at the beginning of the array.

We now compare the element pointed to by *high* with 12. Since 10 is smaller than 12, it's on the wrong side of the array, so we move it to the hole and shift *low* to the right.

low points to the number 3, which is less than 12 and therefore doesn't need to be moved. We shift *low* to the right instead.

Since 6 is also less than 12, we shift *low* again.

low now points to 18, which is larger than 12 and therefore out of position. After moving 18 to the hole, we shift *high* to the left.

high points to 15, which is greater than 12 and thus doesn't need to be moved. We shift *high* to the left and continue.

high points to 7, which is out of position. After moving 7 to the hole, we shift *low* to the right.

low and *high* are now equal, so we move
the partitioning element to the hole.

10	3	6	7	12	15	18

At this point, we've accomplished our objective: all elements to the left of the partitioning element are less than or equal to 12, and all elements to the right are greater than or equal to 12. Now that the array has been partitioned, we can use Quicksort recursively to sort the first four elements of the array (10, 3, 6, and 7) and the last two (15 and 18).

PROGRAM **Quicksort**

Let's develop a recursive function named quicksort that uses the Quicksort algorithm to sort the elements of an array. To test the function, we'll have main read 10 numbers into an array, call quicksort to sort the array, then print the elements in the array:

```
Enter 10 numbers to be sorted: 9 16 47 82 4 66 12 3 25 51
In sorted order: 3 4 9 12 16 25 47 51 66 82
```

Since the code for partitioning the array is a bit lengthy, we'll put it in a separate function named split.

qsort.c
```c
/* Sorts an array of integers using Quicksort algorithm */

#include <stdio.h>

#define N 10

void quicksort(int a[], int low, int high);
int split(int a[], int low, int high);

main()
{
  int a[N], i;

  printf("Enter %d numbers to be sorted: ", N);
  for (i = 0; i < N; i++)
    scanf("%d", &a[i]);

  quicksort(a, 0, N - 1);

  printf("In sorted order: ");
  for (i = 0; i < N; i++)
    printf("%d ", a[i]);
  printf("\n");

  return 0;
}
```

```
void quicksort(int a[], int low, int high)
{
  int middle;

  if (low >= high) return;
  middle = split(a, low, high);
  quicksort(a, low, middle - 1);
  quicksort(a, middle + 1, high);
}

int split(int a[], int low, int high)
{
  int part_element = a[low];

  for (;;) {
    while (low < high && part_element <= a[high])
      high--;
    if (low >= high) break;
    a[low++] = a[high];

    while (low < high && a[low] <= part_element)
      low++;
    if (low >= high) break;
    a[high--] = a[low];
  }

  a[high] = part_element;
  return high;
}
```

Although this version of Quicksort works, it's not the best. There are numerous ways to improve the program's performance, including:

- **Improving the partitioning algorithm.** Our method isn't the most efficient. Instead of choosing the first element in the array as the partitioning element, it's better to take the median of the first element, the middle element, and the last element. The partitioning process itself can also be sped up. In particular, it's possible to avoid the low < high tests in the two while loops.

- **Using a different method to sort small arrays.** Instead of using Quicksort recursively all the way down to arrays with one element, it's better to use a simpler method for small arrays (those with fewer than, say, 25 elements).

- **Making Quicksort nonrecursive.** Although Quicksort is a recursive algorithm by nature—and is easiest to understand in recursive form—it's actually more efficient if the recursion is removed.

For details about improving Quicksort, consult a book on algorithm design, such as Robert Sedgewick's *Algorithms in C* (Reading, Mass.: Addison-Wesley, 1990).

Q & A

Q: **Some C books appear to use terms other than *parameter* and *argument*. Is there any standard terminology? [p. 156]**

A: As with many other aspects of C, there's no general agreement on terminology, although the C standard uses *parameter* and *argument*. The following table should help you translate:

This book:	*Other books:*
parameter	formal argument, formal parameter
argument	actual argument, actual parameter

Keep in mind that—when no confusion would result—I sometimes deliberately blur the distinction between the two terms, using *argument* to mean either.

Q: **I've seen programs in which parameter types are specified in separate declarations, just after the parameter list:**

```
float average(a, b)
float a, b;
{
  return (a + b) / 2;
}
```

Is this practice legal? [p. 160]

A: This method of defining functions comes from Classic C, so you may encounter it in older books and programs. Standard C supports this style so that older programs will still compile. I'd avoid using it in new programs, however, for a couple of reasons.

First, functions that are defined in the Classic way aren't subject to the same degree of error-checking as the new-style functions. When a function is defined in the Classic way—and no prototype is present—the compiler won't check that the function is called with the right number of arguments, nor will it check that the arguments have the proper types. Instead, it will perform the default argument pro-

default argument promotions ➤*9.3*   motions.

Second, the C standard says that the Classic style is "obsolescent," meaning that its use is discouraged and that it may be dropped from C eventually.

Q: **Some programming languages allow procedures and functions to be nested within each other. Does C allow function definitions to be nested?**

A: No. C does not permit the definition of one function to appear in the body of another. Among other things, this restriction simplifies the compiler.

*Q: **Why does the compiler permit function names that aren't followed by parentheses? [p. 161]**

A: We'll see in a later chapter that the compiler treats a function name not followed by parentheses as a *pointer* to the function. Pointers to functions have legitimate uses, so the compiler can't automatically assume that a function name without parentheses is an error.

*Q: Something's bothering me. In the function call f(a, b), how does the compiler know whether the comma is punctuation or whether it's an operator?

A: It turns out that the arguments in a function call can't be arbitrary expressions. Instead, they must be "assignment expressions," which can't have commas used as operators unless they're enclosed in parentheses. In other words, in the call f(a, b) the comma is punctuation; in the call f((a, b)) it's an operator.

Q: Do the names of parameters in a function prototype have to match the names given later in the function's definition? [p. 164]

A: No. Some programmers take advantage of this capability by giving long names to parameters in the prototype, then using shorter names in the actual definition. Or a French-speaking programmer might use English names in prototypes, then switch to more familiar French names in function definitions.

Q: I still don't understand why we bother with function prototypes. If we just put definitions of all the functions before main, we're covered, right?

A: Wrong. First, you're assuming that only main calls the other functions, which is unrealistic. In practice, some of the functions will call each other. If we put all function definitions above main, we'll have to watch their order carefully. Calling a function that hasn't been defined yet can lead to big problems.

But that's not all. Suppose that two functions call each other (which isn't as far-fetched as it may sound). No matter which function we define first, it will end up calling a function that hasn't been defined yet.

But there's still more! Once programs reach a certain size, it won't be feasible to put all the functions in one file anymore. When we reach that point, we'll need prototypes to tell the compiler about functions in other files.

Q: I've seen function declarations that omit all information about parameters:

```
float average();
```

Is this practice legal? [p. 165]

A: Yes. This declaration informs the compiler that average returns a float value but provides no information about the number and types of its parameters. (Leaving the parentheses empty doesn't necessarily mean that average has no parameters.)

In Classic C, this form of function declaration is the only one allowed; the form that we've been using—the function prototype, in which parameter information *is* included—is a new feature of Standard C. The older kind of function declaration is now obsolescent, although still allowed. In this book, I'll use function prototypes exclusively.

Q: **Is it legal to put a function declaration inside the body of another function?**

A: Yes. Here's an example:

```
main()
{
  float average(float a, float b);
  ...
}
```

This declaration of `average` is valid only for the body of `main`; if other functions need to call `average`, they'll each have to declare it.

   The advantage of this practice is that it's clearer to the reader which functions call which other functions. (In this example, we see that `main` will be calling `average`.) On the other hand, it can be a nuisance if several functions need to call the same function. Even worse, trying to add and remove declarations during program modification can be a real pain. For these reasons, I'll always put function declarations outside function bodies.

Q: **If several functions have the same return type, can their declarations be combined? For example, since both `print_pun` and `print_count` have `void` as their return type, is the following declaration legal?**

```
void print_pun(void), print_count(int n);
```

A: Yes. In fact, C even allows us to combine function declarations with variable declarations:

```
float x, y, average(float a, float b);
```

Combining declarations in this way usually isn't a good idea, though; it can make programs a bit confusing.

Q: **What happens if I specify a length for a one-dimensional array parameter? [p. 167]**

A: The compiler ignores it. Consider the following example:

```
float inner_product(float v[3], float w[3]);
```

Other than documenting that `inner_product`'s arguments are supposed to be arrays of length 3, specifying a length doesn't buy you much. The compiler won't check that the arguments actually have length 3, so there's no added security. In fact, the practice is misleading in that it suggests that `inner_product` can only be passed arrays of length 3, when in fact we can pass arrays of arbitrary length.

*Q: **Why can the first dimension in an array parameter be left unspecified, but not the other dimensions? [p. 169]**

A: First, you need to know how arrays are passed in C. As Section 12.2 explains, when an array is passed to a function, the function is given a *pointer* to the first element in the array.

Next, you need to know how the subscripting operator works. Suppose that a is a one-dimensional array passed to a function. When we write

```
a[i] = 0;
```

the compiler computes the address of a[i] by multiplying i by the size of each array element and adding the result to the address that a represents (the pointer passed to the function). This calculation doesn't depend on the length of a, which explains why we can omit it when defining the function.

What about multidimensional arrays? Recall that C stores arrays in row-major order, with the elements in row 0 stored first, then the elements in row 1, and so forth. Suppose that a is a two-dimensional array parameter and we write

```
a[i][j] = 0;
```

The compiler generates instructions to do the following: (1) multiply i by the size of each row in a; (2) add this result to the address that a represents; (3) multiply j by the size of each array element; and (4) add this result to the address computed in step 2. To generate these instructions, the compiler must know the size of each row in the array, which is determined by the number of columns. The bottom line: the programmer must declare how many columns a has.

Q: Why do some programmers put parentheses around the expression in a `return` statement?

A: The examples in the first edition of Kernighan and Ritchie's *The C Programming Language* always have parentheses in `return` statements, even though they aren't required. Programmers (and authors of subsequent books) picked up the habit from K&R. I don't use these parentheses, since they're unnecessary and contribute nothing to readability. (Kernighan and Ritchie apparently agree: the `return` statements in the second edition of *The C Programming Language* lack parentheses.)

Q: How can I test `main`'s return value to see if a program has terminated normally? [p. 171]

A: That depends on your operating system. Many operating systems allow this value to be tested within a "batch" or "shell" file that contains commands to run several programs. For example, the line

```
if errorlevel 1 …
```

in a DOS batch file tests whether the last program terminated with a status code greater than or equal to 1.

In UNIX, each shell has its own method for testing the status code. In the Bourne shell, the variable $? contains the status of the last program run. The C shell has a similar variable, but its name is $status.

Q: Why does my compiler produce a *"Function should return a value"* warning when it compiles `main`?

A: The compiler has noticed that main, despite having int as its return type, doesn't have a return statement. Putting the statement

```
return 0;
```

at the end of main will keep the compiler happy. Incidentally, this is good practice even if your compiler doesn't object to the lack of a return statement.

Q: **With regard to the previous question: Why not just define main's return type to be void?**

A: Although this practice is fairly common, it's illegal according to the C standard. Even if it weren't illegal, it wouldn't be a good idea, since it presumes that no one will ever test the program's status upon termination.

Q: **Is it legal for a function f1 to call a function f2, which then calls f1?**

A: Yes. This is just an indirect form of recursion in which one call of f1 leads to another. (But make sure that either f1 or f2 eventually terminates!)

Exercises

Section 9.1

1. The following function, which computes the area of a triangle, contains two errors. Locate the errors and show how to fix them. (*Hint:* There are no errors in the formula.)

```
float triangle_area(float base, height)
float product;
{
  product = base * height;
  return (product / 2);
}
```

2. Write a function check(x, y, n) that returns 1 if both x and y fall between 0 and n − 1, inclusive. The function should return 0 otherwise. Assume that x, y, and n are all of type int.

3. Write a function gcd(m, n) that calculates the greatest common divisor of the integers m and n. (Exercise 2 in Chapter 6 describes Euclid's algorithm for computing the GCD.)

4. Write a function day_of_year(month, day, year) that returns the day of the year (an integer between 1 and 366) specified by the three arguments.

5. Write a function num_digits(n) that returns the number of digits in a positive integer n. *Hint:* To determine the number of digits in a number *n*, divide it by 10 repeatedly. When *n* reaches 0, the number of divisions indicates how many digits *n* originally had.

6. Write a function digit(n, k) that returns the kth digit (from the right) in the positive integer n. For example, digit(829, 1) returns 9, digit(829, 2) returns 2, and digit(829, 3) returns 8. If k is greater than the number of digits in n, have the function return −1.

7. Suppose that the function f has the following definition:

```
int f(int a, int b) { ... }
```

Which of the following statements are legal? (Assume that i has type int and x has type float.)

(a) `i = f(83, 12);`
(b) `x = f(83, 12);`
(c) `i = f(3.15, 9.28);`
(d) `x = f(3.15, 9.28);`
(e) `f(83, 12);`

Section 9.2

8. Which of the following would be valid prototypes for a function that returns nothing and has one float parameter?

(a) `void f(float x);`
(b) `void f(float);`
(c) `void f(x);`
(d) `f(float x);`

Section 9.3

*9. What will be the output of the following program?

```
#include <stdio.h>

void swap(int a, int b);

main()
{
  int x = 1, y = 2;

  swap(x, y);
  printf("x = %d, y = %d\n", x, y);
  return 0;
}

void swap(int a, int b)
{
  int temp;

  temp = a;
  a = b;
  b = temp;
}
```

10. Write functions that return the following values. (Assume that a and n are parameters, where a is an array of int values and n is the length of the array.)

(a) The largest element in a.
(b) The average of all elements in a.
(c) The number of positive elements in a.

Section 9.4

11. The following function is supposed to return TRUE if any element of the array a has the value 0 and FALSE if all elements are nonzero. Sadly, it contains an error. Find the error and show how to fix it:

```
Bool has_zero(int a[], int n)
{
  int i;

  for (i = 0; i < n; i++)
    if (a[i] == 0)
      return TRUE;
    else
      return FALSE;
}
```

12. The following (rather confusing) function finds the median of three numbers. Rewrite the function so that it has just one `return` statement.

```
float median(float x, float y, float z)
{
  if (x <= y)
    if (y <= z) return y;
    else if (x <= z) return z;
    else return x;
  if (z <= y) return y;
  if (x <= z) return x;
  return z;
}
```

Section 9.6

13. Condense the `fact` function in same way we condensed `power`.

14. Rewrite the `fact` function so that it's no longer recursive.

15. Write a recursive version of the gcd function (see Exercise 3). Here's the strategy to use for computing gcd(m, n): If n is 0, return m. Otherwise, call gcd recursively, passing n as the first argument and m % n as the second.

*16. Consider the following "mystery" function:

```
void pb(int n)
{
  if (n != 0) {
    pb(n / 2);
    putchar('0' + n % 2);
  }
}
```

Trace the execution of the function by hand. Then write a program that calls the function, passing it a number entered by the user. What does the function do?

17. Write a program that asks the user to enter a series of integers (which it stores in an array), then sorts the integers by calling the function `selection_sort`. When given an array with *n* elements, `selection_sort` must do the following:

1. Search the array to find the largest element, then move it to the last position in the array.

2. Call itself recursively to sort the first *n* – 1 elements of the array.

10 Program Organization

*As Will Rogers would have said, "There
is no such thing as a free variable."*

Having covered functions in Chapter 9, we're ready to confront several issues that arise when a program contains more than one function. The first two sections discuss the differences between *local variables* and *external variables.* Section 10.3 then considers *blocks* (compound statements containing declarations). Section 10.4 tackles the scope rules that apply to local names, external names, and names declared in blocks. Finally, Section 10.5 suggests a method of organizing prototypes, function definitions, variable declarations, and other parts of a C program.

10.1 Local Variables

A variable declared in the body of a function is said to be *local* to the function. In the following function, log is a local variable:

```
int log2(int n)
{
  int log = 0;   /* local variable */

  while (n > 1) {
    n /= 2;
    log++;
  }
  return log;
}
```

By default, local variables have the following properties:

■ *Automatic storage duration.* The *storage duration* (or *extent*) of a variable is the portion of program execution during which storage for the variable exists.

Storage for a local variable is "automatically" allocated when the enclosing function is called and deallocated when the function returns, so the variable is said to have **automatic** storage duration. A local variable doesn't retain its value when its enclosing function returns. When the function is called again, there's no guarantee that the variable will still have its old value.

- **Block scope.** The *scope* of a variable is the portion of the program text in which the variable can be referenced. A local variable has **block scope:** it is visible from its point of declaration to the end of the enclosing function body. Since the scope of a local variable doesn't extend beyond the function to which it belongs, other functions can use the same name for other purposes.

Section 18.2 covers these and other related concepts in more detail.

Putting the word `static` in the declaration of a local variable causes it to have *static* storage duration instead of automatic storage duration. A variable with static storage duration has a permanent storage location, so it retains its value throughout the execution of the program. Consider the following function:

```
void f(void)
{
  static int i;
  ...
}
```

Q&A

Since the local variable `i` has been declared `static`, it occupies the same memory location throughout the execution of the program. When `f` returns, `i` won't lose its value.

A static local variable still has block scope, so it's not visible to other functions. In a nutshell, a static variable is a place to hide data from other functions but retain it for future calls of the same function.

Parameters

Parameters have the same properties—automatic storage duration and block scope—as local variables. In fact, the only real difference between parameters and local variables is that parameters are initialized automatically each time the function is called (by being assigned the values of the arguments in the call).

10.2   External Variables

Passing arguments is one way to transmit information to a function. Functions can also communicate through *external variables*—variables that are declared outside the body of any function.

The properties of external variables (or *global* variables, as they're sometimes called) are different from those of local variables:

■ *Static storage duration.* External variables have static storage duration, just like local variables that have been declared `static`. A value stored in an external variable will stay there indefinitely.

■ *File scope.* An external variable has *file scope:* it is visible from its point of declaration to the end of the enclosing file. As a result, an external variable can be accessed by all functions that follow its declaration.

Example: Using External Variables to Implement a Stack

To illustrate how external variables might be used, let's look at a data structure known as a *stack*. (Stacks are an abstraction, not a C feature; they can be implemented in most programming languages.) A stack, like an array, can store multiple data items of the same type. However, the operations on the items in a stack are quite restricted: we can *push* an item onto the stack (add it to one end—the "stack top") or *pop* it from the stack (remove it from the same end). For obvious reasons, a stack is often said to be a *LIFO* (last-in, first-out) data structure. Examining or modifying an item that's not at the top of the stack is forbidden.

One way to implement a stack in C is to store its elements in an array, which we'll call `contents`. A separate integer variable named `top` marks the position of the stack top. When the stack is empty, `top` has the value 0. To push an item on the stack, we simply store the item in `contents` at the position marked by `top`, then increment `top`. Popping an item requires decrementing `top`, then using it as an index into `contents` to fetch the item that's being popped.

Based on this outline, here's a code fragment (not a complete program) that sets aside variables for a stack and provides a set of functions that represent operations on the stack. All five functions need access to the `top` variable, and two functions need access to `contents`, so we'll make `contents` and `top` external.

```
#define STACK_SIZE 100
#define TRUE 1
#define FALSE 0

typedef int Bool;

int contents[STACK_SIZE];    /* external */
int top = 0;                 /* external */

void make_empty(void)
{
  top = 0;
}

Bool is_empty(void)
{
  return top == 0;
}
```

```
Bool is_full(void)
{
  return top == STACK_SIZE;
}

void push(int i)
{
  if (is_full())
    stack_overflow();
  else
    contents[top++] = i;
}

int pop(void)
{
  if (is_empty())
    stack_underflow();
  else
    return contents[--top];
}
```

Pros and Cons of External Variables

External variables are convenient when many functions must share a variable or when a few functions share a large number of variables. In most cases, however, it's better for functions to communicate through parameters rather than by sharing variables. Here's why:

- If we change an external variable during program modification (by altering its type, say), we'll need to check every function in the same file to see how the change affects it.

- If an external variable is assigned an incorrect value, it may be difficult to identify the guilty function. It's like trying to solve a murder committed at a crowded party—there's no easy way to narrow the list of suspects.

- Functions that rely on external variables are hard to reuse in other programs. A function that depends on external variables isn't "self-contained"; to use the function in another program, we'll have to drag along any external variables that it needs.

Many C programmers rely far too much on external variables. One common abuse: using the same external variable for different purposes in different functions. Suppose that several functions need a variable (i, say) to control a for statement. Instead of declaring i in each function that uses it, some programmers declare it at the top of the program, thereby making the variable visible to all functions. This practice is poor not only for the reasons listed earlier, but also because it's misleading; someone reading the program later may think that the uses of the variable are related, when in fact they're not.

When you use external variables, make sure they have meaningful names. (Local variables don't always need meaningful names: it's often hard to think of a good name for the control variable in a `for` loop.) If you find yourself using names like `i` and `temp` for external variables, that's a clue that perhaps they should really be local variables.

 Making variables external when they should be local can lead to some rather frustrating bugs. Consider the following example, which is supposed to display a 10×10 arrangement of asterisks:

```
int i;

void print_row(void)
{
  for (i = 1; i <= 10; i++)
    printf("*");
}

void print_matrix(void)
{
  for (i = 1; i <= 10; i++) {
    print_row();
    printf("\n");
  }
}
```

Instead of printing ten rows, `print_matrix` prints only one row. When `print_row` returns after being called the first time, `i` will have the value 11. The `for` statement in `print_matrix` then increments `i` and compares it with 10, causing the loop to terminate and `print_matrix` to return.

PROGRAM **Guessing a Number**

To get more experience with external variables, we'll write a simple game-playing program. The program generates a random number between 1 and 100, which the user attempts to guess in as few tries as possible. Here's what the user will see when the program is run:

```
Guess the secret number between 1 and 100.

A new number has been chosen.
Enter guess: 55
Too low; try again.
Enter guess: 65
Too high; try again.
Enter guess: 60
Too high; try again.
Enter guess: 58
You won in 4 guesses!

Play again? (Y/N) y
```

```
A new number has been chosen.
Enter guess: 78
Too high; try again.
Enter guess: 34
You won in 2 guesses!

Play again? (Y/N) n
```

This program will need to carry out several different tasks: initializing the random number generator, choosing a secret number, and interacting with the user until the correct number is picked. If we write a separate function to handle each task, we might end up with the following program.

guess.c
```c
/* Asks user to guess a hidden number */

#include <stdio.h>
#include <stdlib.h>
#include <time.h>

#define MAX_NUMBER 100

int secret_number;

void initialize_number_generator(void);
void choose_new_secret_number(void);
void read_guesses(void);

main()
{
  char command;

  printf("Guess the secret number between 1 and %d.\n\n",
         MAX_NUMBER);
  initialize_number_generator();
  do {
    choose_new_secret_number();
    printf("A new number has been chosen.\n");
    read_guesses();
    printf("Play again? (Y/N) ");
    scanf(" %c", &command);
    printf("\n");
  } while (command == 'y' || command == 'Y');
  return 0;
}

/*************************************************************
 * initialize_number_generator: Initializes the random      *
 *                              number generator using      *
 *                              the time of day.            *
 *************************************************************/
void initialize_number_generator(void)
{
  srand((unsigned) time(NULL));
}
```

```
/***********************************************************
 * choose_new_secret_number: Randomly selects a number     *
 *                           between 1 and MAX_NUMBER and  *
 *                           stores it in secret_number.   *
 ***********************************************************/
void choose_new_secret_number(void)
{
  secret_number = rand() % MAX_NUMBER + 1;
}


/***********************************************************
 * read_guesses: Repeatedly reads user guesses and tells   *
 *               the user whether each guess is too low,   *
 *               too high, or correct.  When the guess is  *
 *               correct, prints the total number of       *
 *               guesses and returns.                      *
 ***********************************************************/
void read_guesses(void)
{
  int guess, num_guesses = 0;

  for (;;) {
    num_guesses++;
    printf("Enter guess: ");
    scanf("%d", &guess);
    if (guess == secret_number) {
      printf("You won in %d guesses!\n\n", num_guesses);
      return;
    } else if (guess < secret_number)
      printf("Too low; try again.\n");
    else
      printf("Too high; try again.\n");
  }
}
```

time function ➤26.3
srand function ➤26.2
rand function ➤26.2

For random number generation, the guess.c program relies on the time, srand, and rand functions, which we first used in deal.c (Section 8.2). This time, we're scaling the return value of rand so that it falls between 1 and MAX_NUMBER.

Although guess.c works fine, it relies on an external variable. We made secret_number external so that both choose_new_secret_number and read_guesses could access it. If we alter choose_new_secret_number and read_guesses just a little, we should be able to move secret_number into the main function. We'll modify choose_new_secret_number so that it returns the new number, and we'll rewrite read_guesses so that secret_number can be passed to it as an argument.

Here's our new program, with changes in **bold**:

guess2.c
```
/* Asks user to guess a hidden number */

#include <stdio.h>
#include <stdlib.h>
```

```c
#include <time.h>

#define MAX_NUMBER 100

void initialize_number_generator(void);
int new_secret_number(void);
void read_guesses(int secret_number);

main()
{
  char command;
  int secret_number;

  printf("Guess the secret number between 1 and %d.\n\n",
         MAX_NUMBER);
  initialize_number_generator();
  do {
    secret_number = new_secret_number();
    printf("A new number has been chosen.\n");
    read_guesses(secret_number);
    printf("Play again? (Y/N) ");
    scanf(" %c", &command);
    printf("\n");
  } while (command == 'y' || command == 'Y');
  return 0;
}

/**********************************************************
 * initialize_number_generator: Initializes the random   *
 *                              number generator using    *
 *                              the time of day.          *
 **********************************************************/
void initialize_number_generator(void)
{
  srand((unsigned) time(NULL));
}

/**********************************************************
 * new_secret_number: Returns a randomly chosen number    *
 *                    between 1 and MAX_NUMBER.            *
 **********************************************************/

int new_secret_number(void)
{
  return rand() % MAX_NUMBER + 1;
}

/**********************************************************
 * read_guesses: Repeatedly reads user guesses and tells  *
 *               the user whether each guess is too low,   *
 *               too high, or correct.  When the guess is  *
 *               correct, prints the total number of       *
 *               guesses and returns.                      *
 **********************************************************/
```

```
void read_guesses(int secret_number)
{
  int guess, num_guesses = 0;

  for (;;) {
    num_guesses++;
    printf("Enter guess: ");
    scanf("%d", &guess);
    if (guess == secret_number) {
      printf("You won in %d guesses!\n\n", num_guesses);
      return;
    } else if (guess < secret_number)
      printf("Too low; try again.\n");
    else
      printf("Too high; try again.\n");
  }
}
```

10.3 Blocks

In Section 5.2, we encountered compound statements of the form

{ *statements* }

It turns out that C allows compound statements to contain declarations as well:

block

{ *declarations* *statements* }

I'll use the term *block* to describe such a compound statement. Here's an example
of a block:

```
if (i > j) {
  int temp;

  temp = i;    /* swaps values of i and j */
  i = j;
  j = temp;
}
```

By default, the storage duration of a variable declared in a block is automatic: storage for the variable is allocated when the block is entered and deallocated when
the block is exited. The variable has block scope; it can't be referenced outside the
block.

The body of a function is a block. Blocks are also useful inside a function
body when we need variables for temporary use. In our last example, we needed a
variable temporarily so that we could exchange the values of i and j. Putting temporary variables in blocks has two advantages: (1) It avoids cluttering the declarations at the beginning of the function body with variables that are used only briefly.

(2) It reduces name conflicts. In our example, the name `temp` can be used elsewhere in the same function for different purposes—the variable `temp` declared in the block is strictly local to the block.

10.4 Scope

In a C program, the same identifier may have several different meanings. C's scope rules enable the programmer (and the compiler) to determine which meaning is relevant at a given point in the program.

Here's the most important scope rule: When a declaration inside a block names an identifier that's already visible (because it has file scope or because it's declared in an enclosing block), the new declaration temporarily "hides" the old one, and the identifier takes on a new meaning. At the end of the block, the identifier regains its old meaning.

Consider the following (somewhat extreme) example, in which the identifier `i` has four different meanings:

```
int i ;              /* Declaration 1 */

void f(int i )       /* Declaration 2 */
{
   i = 1;
}

void g(void)
{
   int i = 2;        /* Declaration 3 */

   if (i > 0) {
      int i ;        /* Declaration 4 */

      i = 3;
   }

   i = 4;
}

void h(void)
{
   i = 5;
}
```

- In Declaration 1, `i` is a variable with static storage duration and file scope.
- In Declaration 2, `i` is a parameter with block scope.
- In Declaration 3, `i` is an automatic variable with block scope.
- In Declaration 4, `i` is also automatic and has block scope.

i is used five times. C's scope rules allow us to determine the meaning of i in each case:

- The i = 1 assignment refers to the parameter in Declaration 2, not the variable in Declaration 1, since Declaration 2 hides Declaration 1.
- The i > 0 test refers to the variable in Declaration 3, since Declaration 3 hides Declaration 1 and Declaration 2 is out of scope.
- The i = 3 assignment refers to the variable in Declaration 4, which hides Declaration 3.
- The i = 4 assignment refers to the variable in Declaration 3. It can't refer to Declaration 4, which is out of scope.
- The i = 5 assignment refers to the variable in Declaration 1.

10.5 Organizing a C Program

Now that we've seen the major elements that make up a C program, it's time to develop a strategy for their arrangement. For now, we'll assume that a program always fits into a single file. Chapter 15 shows how to organize a program that is split over several files.

So far, we've seen that a program may contain

Preprocessor directives such as #include and #define
Type definitions
Declarations of functions and external variables
Function definitions

C imposes only a few rules on the order of these items: A preprocessor directive doesn't take effect until the line at which it appears. A type name can't be used until it's been defined. A variable can't be used until it's declared. Although C isn't as picky about functions, I strongly recommend that every function be defined or declared prior to its first call.

There are several ways to organize a program so that these rules are obeyed. Here's one possible ordering:

#include directives
#define directives
Type definitions
Declarations of external variables
Prototypes for functions other than main
Definition of main
Definitions of other functions

It makes sense to put #include directives first, since they bring in information that will likely be needed in several places within the program. #define directives create macros, which are generally used throughout the program. Putting type definitions above the declarations of external variables is logical, since the declarations of these variables may refer to the type names just defined. Declaring external variables next makes them available to all the functions that follow. Declaring all functions except for `main` avoids the problems that arise when a function is called before the compiler has seen its prototype. This practice also makes it possible to arrange the function definitions in any order whatsoever: alphabetically by function name or with related functions grouped together, for example. Defining `main` before the other functions makes it easier for the reader to locate the program's starting point.

A final suggestion: Precede each function definition by a boxed comment that gives the name of the function, describes its purpose, discusses the meaning of each parameter, describes the return value, and lists any side effects.

PROGRAM   Classifying a Poker Hand

To show how a C program might be organized, let's attempt a program that's a little more complex than our previous examples. The program will read and classify a poker hand. Each card in the hand will have both a *suit* (clubs, diamonds, hearts, or spades) and a *rank* (two, three, four, five, six, seven, eight, nine, ten, jack, queen, king, or ace). We won't allow the use of jokers, and we'll assume that aces are high. The program will read a hand of five cards, then classify the hand into one of the following categories (listed in order from best to worst):

> straight flush (both a straight and a flush)
> four-of-a-kind (four cards of the same rank)
> full house (a three-of-a-kind and a pair)
> flush (five cards of the same suit)
> straight (five cards with consecutive ranks)
> three-of-a-kind (three cards of the same rank)
> two pairs
> pair (two cards of the same rank)
> high card (any other hand)

If a hand falls into two or more categories, the program will choose the best one.

For input purposes, we'll abbreviate ranks and suits as follows (letters may be either upper- or lower-case):

> Ranks: `2 3 4 5 6 7 8 9 t j q k a`
> Suits: `c d h s`

If the user enters an illegal card or tries to enter the same card twice, the program will ignore the card, issue an error message, and then request another card. Entering the number 0 instead of a card will cause the program to terminate.

A session with the program will have the following appearance:

```
Enter a card: 2s
Enter a card: 5s
```

```
Enter a card: 4s
Enter a card: 3s
Enter a card: 6s
Straight flush

Enter a card: 8c
Enter a card: as
Enter a card: 8c
Duplicate card; ignored.
Enter a card: 7c
Enter a card: ad
Enter a card: 3h
Pair

Enter a card: 6s
Enter a card: d2
Bad card; ignored.
Enter a card: 2d
Enter a card: 9c
Enter a card: 4h
Enter a card: ts
High card

Enter a card: 0
```

From this description of the program, we see that it has three tasks:

Read a hand of five cards.
Analyze the hand for pairs, straights, and so forth.
Print the classification of the hand.

We'll divide the program into three functions—read_cards, analyze_hand, and print_result—that perform these three tasks. main does nothing but call these functions inside an endless loop. The functions will need to share a fairly large amount of information, so we'll have them communicate through external variables. read_cards will store information about the hand into several external variables. analyze_hand will then examine these variables, storing its findings into other external variables for the benefit of print_result.

Based on this preliminary design, we can begin to sketch an outline of the program:

```
/* #include directives */

/* #define directives */

/* declarations of external variables */

void read_cards(void);
void analyze_hand(void);
void print_result(void);
```

```
/**************************************************************
 * main: Calls read_cards, analyze_hand, and print_result   *
 *       repeatedly.                                         *
 **************************************************************/
main()
{
  for (;;) {              /* infinite loop */
    read_cards();
    analyze_hand();
    print_result();
  }
}

/**************************************************************
 * read_cards:  Reads the cards into external variables;    *
 *              checks for bad cards and duplicate cards.    *
 **************************************************************/
void read_cards(void)
{
  ...
}

/**************************************************************
 * analyze_hand: Determines whether the hand contains a     *
 *               straight, a flush, four-of-a-kind,         *
 *               and/or a three-of-a-kind; determines the   *
 *               number of pairs; stores the results into   *
 *               external variables.                        *
 **************************************************************/
void analyze_hand(void)
{
  ...
}

/**************************************************************
 * print_result: Notifies the user of the result, using    *
 *               the external variables set by             *
 *               analyze_hand.                              *
 **************************************************************/
void print_result(void)
{
  ...
}
```

The most pressing question that remains is how to represent the hand of cards. Let's see what operations read_cards and analyze_hand will perform on the hand. During the analysis of the hand, analyze_hand will need to know how many cards are in each rank and each suit. This suggests that we use two arrays, num_in_rank and num_in_suit. The value of num_in_rank[r] will be the number of cards with rank r, and the value of num_in_suit[s] will be the number of cards with suit s. (We'll encode ranks as numbers between 0 and 12, suits as numbers between 0 and 3.) We'll also need a third array, card_exists, so that read_cards can detect duplicate cards. Each time read_cards reads a card with rank r and suit s, it checks whether the value of card_exists[r][s] is TRUE. If so, the card was previously entered; if not, read_cards assigns TRUE to card_exists[r][s].

Both read_cards and analyze_hand need access to the num_in_rank and num_in_suit arrays, so they must be external variables. The card_exists array, however, is used only by read_cards, so we'll make it local to that function. As a rule, variables should be made external only if necessary.

Having decided on the major data structures, we can now finish the program:

poker.c

```
/* Classifies a poker hand */

#include <stdio.h>
#include <stdlib.h>

#define NUM_RANKS 13
#define NUM_SUITS 4
#define NUM_CARDS 5
#define TRUE 1
#define FALSE 0

typedef int Bool;

int num_in_rank[NUM_RANKS];
int num_in_suit[NUM_SUITS];
Bool straight, flush, four, three;
int pairs;   /* can be 0, 1, or 2 */

void read_cards(void);
void analyze_hand(void);
void print_result(void);

/************************************************************
 * main: Calls read_cards, analyze_hand, and print_result  *
 *       repeatedly.                                        *
 ************************************************************/
main()
{
  for (;;) {            /* infinite loop */
    read_cards();
    analyze_hand();
    print_result();
  }
}

/************************************************************
 * read_cards: Reads the cards into the external           *
 *             variables num_in_rank and num_in_suit;      *
 *             checks for bad cards and duplicate cards.    *
 ************************************************************/
```

```
void read_cards(void)
{
  Bool card_exists[NUM_RANKS][NUM_SUITS];
  char ch, rank_ch, suit_ch;
  int rank, suit;
  Bool bad_card;
  int cards_read = 0;

  for (rank = 0; rank < NUM_RANKS; rank++) {
    num_in_rank[rank] = 0;
    for (suit = 0; suit < NUM_SUITS; suit++)
      card_exists[rank][suit] = FALSE;
  }

  for (suit = 0; suit < NUM_SUITS; suit++)
    num_in_suit[suit] = 0;

  while (cards_read < NUM_CARDS) {

    bad_card = FALSE;

    printf("Enter a card: ");

    rank_ch = getchar();
    switch (rank_ch) {
      case '0':            exit(EXIT_SUCCESS);
      case '2':            rank = 0; break;
      case '3':            rank = 1; break;
      case '4':            rank = 2; break;
      case '5':            rank = 3; break;
      case '6':            rank = 4; break;
      case '7':            rank = 5; break;
      case '8':            rank = 6; break;
      case '9':            rank = 7; break;
      case 't': case 'T': rank = 8; break;
      case 'j': case 'J': rank = 9; break;
      case 'q': case 'Q': rank = 10; break;
      case 'k': case 'K': rank = 11; break;
      case 'a': case 'A': rank = 12; break;
      default:             bad_card = TRUE;
    }

    suit_ch = getchar();
    switch (suit_ch) {
      case 'c': case 'C': suit = 0; break;
      case 'd': case 'D': suit = 1; break;
      case 'h': case 'H': suit = 2; break;
      case 's': case 'S': suit = 3; break;
      default:             bad_card = TRUE;
    }

    while ((ch = getchar()) != '\n')
      if (ch != ' ') bad_card = TRUE;
```

```
      if (bad_card)
        printf("Bad card; ignored.\n");
      else if (card_exists[rank][suit])
        printf("Duplicate card; ignored.\n");
      else {
        num_in_rank[rank]++;
        num_in_suit[suit]++;
        card_exists[rank][suit] = TRUE;
        cards_read++;
      }
    }
  }
}

/**********************************************************
 * analyze_hand: Determines whether the hand contains a    *
 *               straight, a flush, four-of-a-kind,        *
 *               and/or a three-of-a-kind; determines the  *
 *               number of pairs; stores the results into  *
 *               the external variables straight, flush,   *
 *               four, three, and pairs.                   *
 **********************************************************/
void analyze_hand(void)
{
  int num_consec = 0;
  int rank, suit;

  straight = FALSE;
  flush = FALSE;
  four = FALSE;
  three = FALSE;
  pairs = 0;

  /* check for flush */
  for (suit = 0; suit < NUM_SUITS; suit++)
    if (num_in_suit[suit] == NUM_CARDS)
      flush = TRUE;

  /* check for straight */
  rank = 0;
  while (num_in_rank[rank] == 0) rank++;
  for (; rank < NUM_RANKS && num_in_rank[rank]; rank++)
    num_consec++;
  if (num_consec == NUM_CARDS) {
    straight = TRUE;
    return;
  }

  /* check for 4-of-a-kind, 3-of-a-kind, and pairs */
  for (rank = 0; rank < NUM_RANKS; rank++) {
    if (num_in_rank[rank] == 4) four = TRUE;
    if (num_in_rank[rank] == 3) three = TRUE;
    if (num_in_rank[rank] == 2) pairs++;
  }
}
```

```
/**************************************************************
 * print_result: Notifies the user of the result, using     *
 *               the external variables straight, flush,     *
 *               four, three, and pairs.                     *
 **************************************************************/
void print_result(void)
{
  if (straight && flush) printf("Straight flush\n\n");
  else if (four)         printf("Four of a kind\n\n");
  else if (three &&
             pairs == 1)  printf("Full house\n\n");
  else if (flush)        printf("Flush\n\n");
  else if (straight)     printf("Straight\n\n");
  else if (three)        printf("Three of a kind\n\n");
  else if (pairs == 2)   printf("Two pairs\n\n");
  else if (pairs == 1)   printf("Pair\n\n");
  else                   printf("High card\n\n");
}
```

Notice the use of the `exit` function in `read_cards`. `exit` is convenient for this program because of its ability to terminate program execution from any function.

Q & A

*Q: If local variables have static storage duration, what impact does this have on recursive functions? [p. 186]

A: When a function is recursive, fresh copies are made of its automatic variables each time it's called. This doesn't occur for static variables, though. Instead, all calls of the function share the *same* static variables.

Q: In the following example, `j` is initialized to the same value as `i`, but there are two variables named `i`:

```
int i = 1;

void f(void)
{
  int j = i;
  int i = 2;
}
```

Is this code legal? If so, what is `j`'s initial value, 1 or 2?

A: The scope of a local variable doesn't begin until its declaration. Therefore, the declaration of `j` refers to the external variable named `i`. The initial value of `j` will be 1.

Exercises

Section 10.2

1. Modify the stack example so that it stores characters instead of integers. Next, add a `main` function that asks the user to enter a series of parentheses and/or braces, then indicates whether or not they're properly nested:

   ```
   Enter parentheses and/or braces: ((){}{()})
   Parentheses/braces are nested properly
   ```

   Hint: As the program reads characters, have it push each left parenthesis or left brace. When it reads a right parenthesis or brace, have it pop the stack and check that the item popped is a matching parenthesis or brace. (If not, the parentheses/braces aren't nested properly.) When the program reads the new-line character, have it check whether the stack is empty; if so, the parentheses/braces are matched. If the stack *isn't* empty (or if `stack_underflow` is ever called), the parentheses/braces aren't matched. If `stack_overflow` is called, have the program print the message `Stack overflow` and terminate immediately.

Section 10.4

2. The following program outline shows only function definitions and variable declarations.

   ```
   int a;

   void f(int b)
   {
     int c;
   }

   void g(void)
   {
     int d;
     {
       int e;
     }
   }

   main()
   {
     int f;
   }
   ```

   For each of the following scopes, list all variable and parameter names visible in that scope:

   (a) The f function.
   (b) The g function.
   (c) The block in which e is declared.
   (d) The `main` function.

Section 10.5

3. Modify the `poker.c` program by moving the `num_in_rank` and `num_in_suit` arrays into `main`, which will pass them as arguments to `read_cards` and `analyze_hand`.

4. Remove the `num_in_rank`, `num_in_suit`, and `card_exists` arrays from the `poker.c` program. Have the program store the cards in a 5×2 array instead.

5. Modify the `poker.c` program by having it recognize an additional category, "royal flush" (ace, king, queen, jack, ten of the same suit). A royal flush ranks higher than all other hands.

6. Modify the `poker.c` program by allowing "ace-low" straights (ace, two, three, four, five).

11 Pointers

Pointers are one of C's most important—and most often misunderstood—features. Because of their importance, we'll devote three chapters to pointers. In this chapter, we'll concentrate on the basics; Chapters 12 and 17 cover more advanced uses of pointers.

We'll start with a discussion of machine addresses and their relationship to pointer variables (Section 11.1). Section 11.2 then introduces the address and indirection operators. Section 11.3 covers pointer assignment. Section 11.4 explains how to pass pointers to functions, while Section 11.5 discusses returning pointers from functions.

11.1 Pointer Variables

The first step in understanding pointers is visualizing what they represent at the machine level. In most modern computers, main memory is divided into *bytes*, with each byte capable of storing eight bits of information:

A machine with 16 megabytes of main memory has 16,777,216 of these bytes. Each byte has a unique *address* to distinguish it from the other bytes in memory. If there are *n* bytes in memory, we can think of addresses as numbers that range from 0 to *n* − 1 (see the figure at the top of the next page).

An executable program consists of both code (machine instructions corresponding to statements in the original C program) and data (variables in the origi-

Address   Contents

0	01010011
1	01110101
2	01110011
3	01100001
4	01101110
⋮	⋮
n–1	01000011

nal program). Each variable in the program occupies one or more bytes of memory; the address of the first byte is said to be the address of the variable. In the following figure, the variable i occupies the bytes at addresses 2000 and 2001, so i's address is 2000:

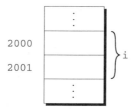

Here's where pointers come in. Although addresses are represented by numbers, their range of values may differ from that of integers, so we can't necessarily store them in ordinary integer variables. We can, however, store them in special *pointer variables*. When we store the address of a variable i in the pointer variable p, we say that p "points to" i. In other words, a *pointer* is nothing more than an address, and a pointer variable is just a variable that can store an address.

Q&A

Instead of showing addresses as numbers in our examples, I'll use a simpler notation. To indicate that a pointer variable p stores the address of a variable i, I'll show the contents of p as an arrow directed toward i:

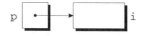

Declaring Pointer Variables

A pointer variable is declared in much the same way as an ordinary variable. The only difference is that the name of a pointer variable must be preceded by an asterisk:

```
int *p;
```

This declaration states that p is a pointer variable capable of pointing to **objects** of type int. We're using the term *object* instead of *variable* since—as we'll see in Chapter 17—p might point to an area of memory that's not used as a variable. (Be aware that "object" will have a different meaning when we discuss program design later.)

abstract objects ➤ 19.1

     Pointer variables can appear in declarations along with other variables:

```
int i, j, a[10], b[20], *p, *q;
```

In this example, i and j are ordinary integer variables, a and b are arrays of integers, and p and q are pointers to integer objects.

     C requires that every pointer variable point only to objects of a particular type (the **referenced type**):

```
int *p;      /* points only to integers    */
float *q;    /* points only to floats      */
char *r;     /* points only to characters */
```

There are no restrictions on what the referenced type may be. (A pointer variable can even point to another pointer.)

pointers to pointers ➤ 17.6

11.2   The Address and Indirection Operators

C provides a pair of operators designed specifically for use with pointers. To find the address of a variable, we use the & (**address**) operator. If x is a variable, then &x is the address of x in memory. To gain access to the object that a pointer points to, we use the * (**indirection**) operator. If p is a pointer, then *p represents the object to which p currently points.

The Address Operator

Declaring a pointer variable sets aside space for a pointer but doesn't make it point to an object:

```
int *p;    /* points nowhere in particular */
```

(In this respect, pointers are no different than other variables.) It is crucial to initialize p before we use it. One way to initialize a pointer variable is to assign it the address of some variable—or, more generally, lvalue—using the & operator:

lvalues ➤ 4.2

```
int i, *p;
```

```
p = &i;
```

By assigning the address of i to the variable p, this statement makes p point to i:

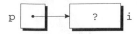

The assignment of &i to p doesn't affect the value of i, by the way.

The address operator can appear in declarations, so it's possible to initialize a pointer at the time we declare it:

```
int i;
int *p = &i;
```

We can even combine the declaration of i with the declaration of p, provided that i comes first:

```
int i, *p = &i;
```

The Indirection Operator

Once a pointer variable points to an object, we can use the * (indirection) operator to access what's stored in the object. If p points to i, for example, we can print the value of i as follows:

```
printf("%d\n", *p);
```

`printf` will display the *value* of i, not the *address* of i.

The mathematically inclined reader may wish to think of * as the inverse of &. Applying & to a variable produces a pointer to the variable; applying * to the pointer takes us back to the original variable:

```
j = *&i;   /* same as j = i; */
```

As long as p points to i, *p is an **alias** for i. Not only does *p have the same value as i, but changing the value of *p also changes the value of i. (*p is an lvalue, so assignment to it is legal.) The following example illustrates the equivalence of *p and i; diagrams show the values of p and i at various points in the computation.

```
p = &i;
```

i = 1;

```
printf("%d\n", i);    /* prints 1 */
printf("%d\n", *p);   /* prints 1 */
*p = 2;
```

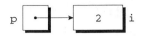

```
printf("%d\n", i);    /* prints 2 */
printf("%d\n", *p);   /* prints 2 */
```

 Never apply the indirection operator to an uninitialized pointer variable. If a pointer variable p hasn't been initialized, the value of *p is undefined:

```
int *p;

printf("%d", *p);    /* prints garbage */
```

Assigning a value to *p is even worse; p might point anywhere in memory, so the assignment modifies some unknown memory location:

```
int *p;

*p = 1;    /*** WRONG ***/
```

The location modified by this assignment might belong to the program (perhaps causing it to behave erratically) or to the operating system (possibly causing a system crash).

11.3 Pointer Assignment

C allows the use of the assignment operator to copy pointers, provided that they have the same type. Suppose that i, j, p, and q have been declared as follows:

```
int i, j, *p, *q;
```

The statement

```
p = &i;
```

is an example of pointer assignment; the address of i is copied into p. Here's another example of pointer assignment:

```
q = p;
```

This statement copies the contents of p (the address of i) into q, in effect making q point to the same place as p:

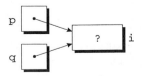

Both p and q now point to i, so we can change i by assigning a new value to either *p or *q:

```
*p = 1;
```

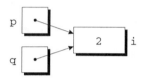

```
*q = 2;
```

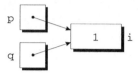

Any number of pointer variables may point to the same object.

Be careful not to confuse

```
q = p;
```

with

```
*q = *p;
```

The first statement is a pointer assignment; the second isn't, as the following example shows:

```
p = &i;
q = &j;
i = 1;
```

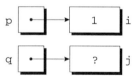

```
*q = *p;
```

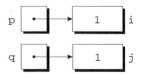

The assignment *q = *p copies the value that p points to (the value of i) into the location that q points to (the variable j).

11.4 Pointers as Arguments

So far, we've managed to avoid a rather important question: What are pointers good for? There's no single answer to that question, since pointers have several distinct uses in C. In this section, we'll look at just one application: by passing a pointer to a variable when calling a function, it becomes possible for the function to change the variable's value.

We saw in Section 9.3 that a variable supplied as an argument in a function call is protected against change, because C passes arguments by value. This property of C can be a nuisance if we want the function to be able to modify the variable. In Section 9.3, we were unable to write a decompose function that could modify two of its arguments.

Pointers offer a solution to this problem: instead of passing a variable x as the argument to a function, we'll supply &x, a pointer to x. We'll declare the corresponding parameter p to be a pointer. When the function is called, p will have the value &x, hence *p (the object that p points to) will be an alias for x. Each appearance of *p in the body of the function will be an indirect reference to x, allowing the function both to read x and to modify it.

To see this method in action, let's modify the decompose function by declaring the parameters int_part and frac_part to be pointers. The definition of decompose will now look like this:

```
void decompose(float x, int *int_part, float *frac_part)
{
  *int_part = (int) x;
  *frac_part = x - *int_part;
}
```

The prototype for decompose could be either

```
void decompose(float x, int *int_part, float *frac_part);
```

or

```
void decompose(float, int *, float *);
```

We'll call decompose in the following way:

```
decompose(3.14159, &i, &f);
```

Because of the & operator in front of i and f, the arguments to decompose are *pointers* to i and f, not the *values* of i and f. When decompose is called, the value 3.14159 is copied into x, a pointer to i is stored in int_part, and a pointer to f is stored in frac_part:

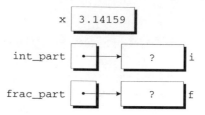

The first assignment in the body of decompose converts the value of x to type int and stores it into the location pointed to by int_part. Since int_part points to i, the assignment puts the value 3 in i:

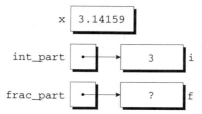

The second assignment fetches the value that int_part points to (the value of i), which is 3. This value is converted to type float and subtracted from x, giving .14159, which is then stored in the location that frac_part points to:

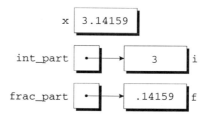

When decompose returns, i and f will have the values 3 and .14159, just as we originally wanted.

Using pointers as arguments to functions is actually nothing new; we've been doing it in calls of scanf since Chapter 2. Consider the following example:

```
int i;

scanf("%d", &i);
```

We must put the & operator in front of i so that scanf is given a *pointer* to i; that pointer tells scanf where to put the value that it reads. Without the &, scanf would be supplied with the *value* of i.

Although scanf's arguments need to be pointers, it's not always true that every argument needs the & operator. In the following example, scanf is passed a pointer variable:

```
int i, *p;

p = &i;
scanf("%d", p);
```

Since p contains the address of i, scanf will read an integer and store it in i. Using the & operator in the call would be wrong:

```
scanf("%d", &p);    /*** WRONG ***/
```

scanf would read an integer and store it in p instead of in i.

Failing to pass a pointer to a function when one is expected can have disastrous results. Suppose that we call decompose without the & operator in front of i and f:

```
decompose(3.14159, i, f);
```

decompose is expecting pointers as its second and third arguments, but it's been given the *values* of i and f instead. decompose has no way to tell the difference, so it will use the values of i and f as though they were pointers. When decompose stores values into *int_part and *frac_part, it will write to unknown memory locations instead of modifying i and f.

If we've provided a prototype for decompose (as we should always do, of course), the compiler will let us know that we're attempting to pass the wrong type of arguments. In the case of scanf, however, failing to pass pointers usually goes undetected by the compiler, making scanf an especially error-prone function.

C++ provides a way for functions to modify arguments without the need to pass pointers. Section 19.4 gives details.

PROGRAM **Finding the Largest and Smallest Elements in an Array**

To illustrate how pointers are passed to functions, let's look at a function named max_min that finds the largest and smallest elements in an array. When we call max_min, we'll pass it pointers to two variables; max_min will then store its answers in these variables. max_min has the following prototype:

```
void max_min(int a[], int n, int *max, int *min);
```

A call of max_min might have the following appearance:

```
max_min(b, N, &big, &small);
```

b is an array of integers, and N is the number of elements in b. big and small are ordinary integer variables. When max_min finds the largest element in b, it stores the value in big by assigning it to *max. (Since max points to big, an assignment to *max will modify the value of big.) max_min stores the smallest element of b in small by assigning it to *min.

To test max_min, we'll write a program that reads ten numbers into an array, passes the array to max_min, and prints the results:

```
Enter 10 numbers: 34 82 49 102 7 94 23 11 50 31
Largest: 102
Smallest: 7
```

Here's the complete program:

maxmin.c
```
/* Finds the largest and smallest elements in an array */

#include <stdio.h>

#define N 10

void max_min(int a[], int n, int *max, int *min);

main()
{
  int b[N], i, big, small;

  printf("Enter %d numbers: ", N);
  for (i = 0; i < N; i++)
    scanf("%d", &b[i]);

  max_min(b, N, &big, &small);

  printf("Largest: %d\n", big);
  printf("Smallest: %d\n", small);

  return 0;
}

void max_min(int a[], int n, int *max, int *min)
{
  int i;

  *max = *min = a[0];
  for (i = 1; i < n; i++) {
    if (a[i] > *max)
      *max = a[i];
    else if (a[i] < *min)
      *min = a[i];
  }
}
```

Using const to Protect Arguments

When we call a function and pass it a pointer to a variable, we normally assume that the function will modify the variable (otherwise, why would the function require a pointer?). For example, if we see a statement like

```
f(&x);
```

in a program, we'd probably expect f to change the value of x. It's possible, though, that f merely needs to examine the value of x, not change it. The reason for the pointer might be efficiency: passing the value of a variable can waste time and space if the variable requires a large amount of storage. (Section 12.3 covers this point in more detail.)

We can use the word const to document that a function won't change an object whose pointer is passed to the function. To allow f to examine—but not change—an argument whose pointer has been passed, we'd put const in the parameter's declaration, just before the specification of its type:

```
void f(const int *p)
{
   *p = 0;    /*** WRONG ***/
}
```

This use of const indicates that p is a pointer to a "constant integer." Attempting to change *p will provoke a message from the compiler.

11.5 Pointers as Return Values

We can not only pass pointers to functions, but also write functions that *return* pointers. For example, we may want a function to return the location of an answer instead of returning its value. Functions that return pointers are relatively common; in Chapter 13, we'll encounter several.

The following function, when given pointers to two integers, returns a pointer to whichever integer is larger:

```
int *max(int *a, int *b)
{
   if (*a > *b)
     return a;
   else
     return b;
}
```

When we call max, we'll pass pointers to two int variables and store the result in a pointer variable:

```
int *p, x, y;

p = max(&x, &y);
```

During the call of max, *a is an alias for x, while *b is an alias for y. If x has a larger value than y, max returns the address of x; otherwise, it returns the address of y. After the call, p points to either x or y.

Although the max function returns one of the pointers passed to it as an argument, that's not the only thing a function can return. Some functions return a pointer to one element of an array passed as an argument. Another possibility is to return a pointer to an external variable or to a local variable that's been declared `static`.

 Never return a pointer to an *automatic* local variable:

```
int *f(void)
{
  int i;
  ...
  return &i;
}
```

The variable `i` doesn't exist once `f` returns, so the pointer to it will be invalid.

Q & A

*Q: Is a pointer always the same as an address? [p. 206]

A: Usually, but not always. Consider a computer whose main memory is divided into *words* rather than bytes. A word might contain 36 bits, 60 bits, or some other number. If we assume 36-bit words, memory will have the following appearance:

Address	Contents
0	001010011001010011001010011001010011
1	001110101001110101001110101001110101
2	001110011001110011001110011001110011
3	001100001001100001001100001001100001
4	001101110001101110001101110001101110
⋮	⋮
n-1	001000011001000011001000011001000011

When memory is divided into words, each word has an address. An integer usually occupies one word, so a pointer to an integer can just be an address. However, a word can store more than one character. For example, a 36-bit word could store six 6-bit characters:

| 010011 | 110101 | 110011 | 100001 | 101110 | 000011 |

or four 9-bit characters:

| 001010011 | 001110101 | 001110011 | 001100001 |

For this reason, a pointer to a character may need to be stored in a different form than other pointers. A pointer to a character might consist of an address (the word in which the character is stored) plus a small integer (the position of the character within the word).

On some computers, pointers may be "offsets" rather than complete addresses. For example, Intel microprocessors (used in IBM PCs and their clones) have a complicated scheme in which addresses are sometimes represented by a single 16-bit number (an *offset*) and sometimes by two 16-bit numbers (a *segment:offset pair*). An offset isn't a true memory address; the CPU must combine it with a segment value stored in a special register.

C compilers for the IBM PC family deal with Intel's segmented architecture by providing two kinds of pointers: *near* pointers (16-bit offsets) and *far* pointers (32-bit segment:offset pairs). For this reason, PC compilers usually reserve the words `near` and `far` for use in declaring pointer variables.

*Q: If a pointer can point to *data* in a program, is it possible to have a pointer to program *code*?

A: Yes. We'll cover pointers to functions in Section 17.7.

Q: Is there some way to print the value of a pointer?

A: Call `printf`, using the `%p` conversion in the format string; see Section 22.3 for details.

Q: The following declaration is confusing:

```
void f(const int *p);
```

Does this say that we can't modify p?

A: No. It says that we can't change the integer that p *points to*; it doesn't prevent us from changing p itself.

```
void f(const int *p)
{
  int j;

  p = &j;    /* legal */
}
```

Since arguments are passed by value, assigning p a new value—by making it point somewhere else—won't have any effect outside the function.

*Q: When declaring a parameter of a pointer type, is it legal to put the word `const` in front of the parameter name, as in the following example? [p. 215]

```
void f(int * const p);
```

A: Yes, although the effect isn't the same as if const precedes p's type. We saw in Section 11.4 that putting const *before* p's type protects the object that p points to. Putting const *after* p's type protects p itself:

```
void f(int * const p)
{
  int j;

  *p = 0;    /* legal */
  p = &j;    /*** WRONG ***/
}
```

This feature isn't used very often. Since p is merely a copy of another pointer (the argument when the function is called), there's rarely any reason to protect it.

An even greater rarity is the need to protect both p *and* the object it points to, which can be done by putting const both before and after p's type:

```
void f(const int * const p)
{
  int j;

  *p = 0;    /*** WRONG ***/
  p = &j;    /*** WRONG ***/
}
```

Exercises

Section 11.2   1.   If i is a variable and p points to i, which of the following expressions are aliases for i?

(a) *p   (c) *&p   (e) *i   (g) *&i
(b) &p   (d) &*p   (f) &i   (h) &*i

Section 11.3   2.   If i is an int variable and p and q are pointers to int, which of the following assignments are legal?

(a) p = i;   (d) p = &q;   (g) p = *q;
(b) *p = &i;   (e) p = *&q;   (h) *p = q;
(c) &p = q;   (f) p = q;   (i) *p = *q;

Section 11.4   3.   The following function supposedly computes the sum and average of the numbers in the array a, which has length n. avg and sum point to variables that the function should modify. Unfortunately, the function contains several errors; find and correct them.

```
void avg_sum(float a[], int n, float *avg, float *sum)
{
  int i;

  sum = 0.0;
  for (i = 0; i < n; i++)
    sum += a[i];
  avg = sum / n;
}
```

4. Write the following function:

   ```
   void swap(int *p, int *q);
   ```

   When passed the addresses of two variables, swap should exchange their values:

   ```
   swap(&x, &y);    /* exchanges values of x and y */
   ```

   Using this function, modify the program in Exercise 9 of Chapter 9 so that it works.

5. Write the following function:

   ```
   void split_time(long int total_sec,
                   int *hr, int *min, int *sec);
   ```

   total_sec is a time measured in number of seconds since midnight. hr, min, and sec are pointers to variables into which the function will store the equivalent time in hours (0–23), minutes (0–59), and seconds (0–59), respectively.

6. Write the following function:

   ```
   void find_two_largest(int a[], int n, int *largest,
                         int *second_largest);
   ```

   When passed an array a of length n, the function will search a for its largest and second-largest elements, storing them in the variables pointed to by largest and second_largest, respectively.

Section 11.5

7. Write the following function:

   ```
   int *find_middle(int a[], int n);
   ```

   When passed an array a of length n, the function will return a pointer to the array's middle element. (If n is even, choose the middle element with the larger index; for example, if n = 4, the middle element is a[2], not a[1].)

12 Pointers and Arrays

Optimization hinders evolution.

Chapter 11 introduced pointers and showed how they're used as function arguments and as values returned by functions. This chapter covers another application for pointers. When pointers point to array elements, C allows us to perform arithmetic—addition and subtraction—on the pointers, which leads to an alternative way of processing arrays in which pointers take the place of array subscripts.

The relationship between pointers and arrays in C is a close one, as we'll see in this chapter. We'll exploit this relationship in subsequent chapters, including Chapter 13 (Strings) and Chapter 17 (Advanced Uses of Pointers). Understanding the connection between pointers and arrays is critical for mastering C: it will give you insight into how C was designed and help you understand existing programs. Be aware, however, that one of the primary reasons for using pointers to process arrays—efficiency—is no longer as important as it once was, thanks to improved compilers.

Section 12.1 discusses pointer arithmetic and shows how pointers can be compared using the relational and equality operators. Section 12.2 then demonstrates how we can use pointer arithmetic for processing array elements. Section 12.3 reveals a key fact about arrays—an array name can serve as a pointer to the array's first element—and uses it to show how array arguments really work. To wrap up the chapter, Section 12.4 shows how the topics of the first three sections apply to multidimensional arrays.

12.1 Pointer Arithmetic

Pointers can point to array elements, not just ordinary variables. For example, suppose that a and p have been declared as follows:

```
int a[10], *p;
```

We can make p point to a[0] by writing

```
p = &a[0];
```

Graphically, here's what we've just done:

We can now access a[0] through p; for example, we can store the value 5 in a[0] by writing

```
*p = 5;
```

Here's our picture now:

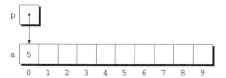

Making a pointer p point to an element of an array a isn't particularly exciting. However, by performing *pointer arithmetic* (or *address arithmetic*) on p, we can access the other elements of a. C supports three (and only three) forms of pointer arithmetic:

> adding an integer to a pointer
> subtracting an integer from a pointer
> subtracting two pointers

Let's take a close look at each of these operations. Our examples assume the following declarations:

```
int a[10], *p, *q, i;
```

Adding an Integer to a Pointer

Adding an integer j to a pointer p yields a pointer to the element that is j places after the one that p points to. More precisely, if p points to the array element a[i], then p + j points to a[i+j] (provided, of course, that a[i+j] exists).

The following example illustrates pointer addition; diagrams show the values of p and q at various points in the computation.

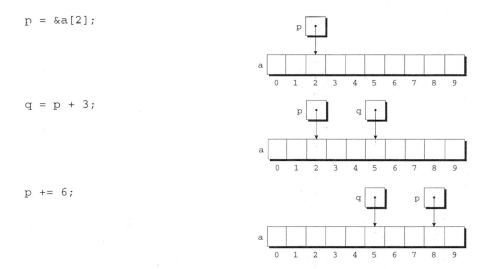

```
p = &a[2];
```

```
q = p + 3;
```

```
p += 6;
```

Subtracting an Integer from a Pointer

If p points to the array element a[i], then p - j points to a[i-j]. For example:

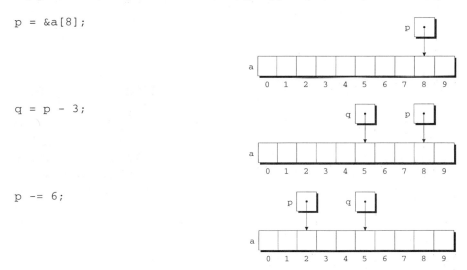

```
p = &a[8];
```

```
q = p - 3;
```

```
p -= 6;
```

Subtracting Pointers

When two pointers are subtracted, the result is the distance (measured in array elements) between the pointers. Thus, if p points to a[i] and q points to a[j], then p - q is equal to i - j. For example:

```
p = &a[5];
q = &a[1];
```

```
i = p - q;    /* i is 4 */
i = q - p;    /* i is -4 */
```

Note: Performing arithmetic on a pointer p gives a meaningful result only when p points to an array element. Furthermore, subtracting two pointers is meaningful only when both point to elements of the *same* array.

Comparing Pointers

We can compare pointers using the relational operators (<, <=, >, >=) and the equality operators (== and !=). Using the relational operators to compare two pointers is meaningful only when both point to elements of the same array. The outcome of the comparison depends on the relative position of the two elements in the array. For example, after the assignments

```
p = &a[5];
q = &a[1];
```

the value of p <= q is 0 and the value of p >= q is 1.

12.2 Using Pointers for Array Processing

Pointer arithmetic allows us to visit the elements of an array by repeatedly incrementing a pointer variable. The following program fragment, which sums the elements of an array a, illustrates the technique. In this example, the pointer variable p initially points to a[0]. Each time through the loop, p is incremented; as a result, it points to a[1], then a[2], and so forth. The loop terminates when p steps past the last element of a.

```
#define N 10

int a[N], sum, *p;

sum = 0;
for (p = &a[0]; p < &a[N]; p++)
  sum += *p;
```

The following figures show the contents of a, sum, and p at the end of the first three loop iterations (before p has been incremented).

At the end of the first iteration:

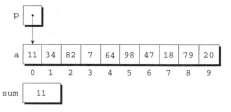

At the end of the second iteration:

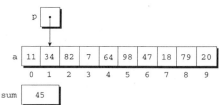

At the end of the third iteration:

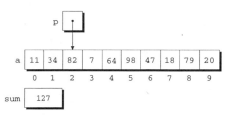

The condition p < &a[N] in the for statement deserves special mention. In Standard C, it's legal to apply the address operator to a[N], even though this element doesn't exist (a is indexed from 0 to N   1). Using a[N] in this fashion is perfectly safe, since the loop doesn't attempt to examine its value. The body of the loop will be executed with p equal to &a[0], &a[1], ..., &a[N-1], but when p is equal to &a[N], the loop terminates.

We could just as easily have written the loop without pointers, of course, using subscripting instead. The argument most often cited in support of pointer arithmetic is that it can save execution time. However, that depends on the implementation—some C compilers actually produce better code for loops that rely on subscripting.

Q&A

Combining the * and ++ Operators

C programmers often combine the * (indirection) and ++ operators in statements that process array elements. Consider the simple case of storing a value into an array element, then advancing to the next element. Using array subscripting, we might write

```
a[i++] = j;
```

If p is pointing to an array element, the corresponding statement would be

```
*p++ = j;
```

Because the postfix version of ++ takes precedence over *, the compiler sees this as

```
*(p++) = j;
```

The value of p++ is p. (Since we're using the postfix version of ++, p won't be incremented until after the expression has been evaluated.) Thus, the value of *(p++) will be *p—the object to which p is pointing.

Of course, *p++ isn't the only legal combination of * and ++. We could write (*p)++, for example, which returns the value of the object that p points to, then increments that object (p itself is unchanged). If you find this confusing, the following table may help:

Expression	*Meaning*
*p++ or * (p++)	Value of expression is *p before increment; increment p later
(*p)++	Value of expression is *p before increment; increment *p later
*++p or * (++p)	Increment p first; value of expression is *p after increment
++*p or ++(*p)	Increment *p first; value of expression is *p after increment

All four combinations appear in programs, although some are far more common than others. The one we'll see most frequently is *p++, which is handy in loops. Instead of writing

```
for (p = &a[0]; p < &a[N]; p++)
  sum += *p;
```

to sum the elements of the array a, we could write

```
p = &a[0];
while (p < &a[N])
  sum += *p++;
```

The * and -- operators mix in the same way as * and ++. For an application that combines * and --, let's return to the stack example of Section 10.2. The original version of the stack relied on an integer variable named top to keep track of the "top-of-stack" position in the contents array. Let's replace top by a pointer variable that points initially to element 0 of the contents array:

```
int *top_ptr = &contents[0];
```

Here are the new push and pop functions (updating the other stack functions is left as an exercise):

```
void push(int i)
{
  if (is_full())
    stack_overflow();
  else
    *top_ptr++ = i;
}
```

```
int pop(void)
{
  if (is_empty())
    stack_underflow();
  else
    return *--top_ptr;
}
```

Note that I've written *--top_ptr, not *top_ptr--, since I want pop to decrement top_ptr *before* fetching the value to which it points.

12.3   Using an Array Name as a Pointer

Pointer arithmetic is one way in which arrays and pointers are related, but it's not the only connection between the two. Here's another key relationship: *The name of an array can be used as a pointer to the first element in the array.* This relationship simplifies pointer arithmetic and makes both arrays and pointers more versatile.

For example, suppose that a is declared as follows:

```
int a[10];
```

Using a as a pointer to the first element in the array, we can modify a[0]:

```
*a = 7;    /* stores 7 in a[0] */
```

We can modify a[1] through the pointer a + 1:

```
*(a+1) = 12;    /* stores 12 in a[1] */
```

In general, a + i is the same as &a[i] (both represent a pointer to element i of a) and *(a+i) is equivalent to a[i] (both represent element i itself). In other words, array subscripting can be viewed as a form of pointer arithmetic.

The fact that an array name can serve as a pointer makes it easier to write loops that step through an array. Consider the following loop from Section 12.2:

```
for (p = &a[0]; p < &a[N]; p++)
  sum += *p;
```

To simplify the loop, we can replace &a[0] by a and &a[N] by a + N:

idiom
```
for (p = a; p < a + N; p++)
  sum += *p;
```

Although an array name can be used as a pointer, it's not possible to assign it a new value. Attempting to make it point elsewhere is an error:

```
while (*a != 0)
  a++;                /*** WRONG ***/
```

This is no great loss; we can always copy a into a pointer variable, then change the pointer variable:

```
p = a;
while (*p != 0)
  p++;
```

PROGRAM   **Reversing a Series of Numbers (Revisited)**

The reverse.c program of Section 8.1 reads ten numbers, then writes the numbers in reverse order. As the program reads the numbers, it stores them in an array. Once all the numbers are read, the program steps through the array backwards as it prints the numbers.

The original program used subscripting to access elements of the array. Here's a new version in which I've replaced subscripting with pointer arithmetic.

reverse2.c

```
/* Reverses a series of numbers (pointer version) */

#include <stdio.h>

#define N 10

main()
{
  int a[N], *p;

  printf("Enter %d numbers: ", N);
  for (p = a; p < a + N; p++)
    scanf("%d", p);

  printf("In reverse order:");
  for (p = a + N - 1; p >= a; p--)
    printf(" %d", *p);
  printf("\n");

  return 0;
}
```

In the original program, an integer variable i kept track of the current position within the array. Our new version replaces i with p, a pointer variable. The numbers are still stored in an array; we're simply using a different technique to keep track of where we are in the array.

Note that the second argument to scanf is p, not &p. Since p points to an array element, it's a satisfactory argument for scanf; &p, on the other hand, would be a pointer to a pointer to an array element.

Array Arguments (Revisited)

When passed to a function, an array name is always treated as a pointer. Consider the following function, which returns the largest element in an array of integers:

```
int find_largest(int a[], int n)
{
  int i, max;

  max = a[0];
  for (i = 1; i < n; i++)
    if (a[i] > max)
      max = a[i];
  return max;
}
```

Suppose that we call `find_largest` as follows:

```
largest = find_largest(b, N);
```

This call causes a pointer to the first element of b to be assigned to a; the array itself isn't copied.

The fact that an array parameter is treated as a pointer has some important consequences:

- When an ordinary variable is passed to a function, its value is copied; any changes to the corresponding parameter don't affect the variable. In contrast, an array used as an argument isn't protected against change, since no copy is made of the array itself. For example, the following function modifies an array by storing zero into each of its elements:

  ```
  void store_zeros(int a[], int n)
  {
    int i;

    for (i = 0; i < n; i++)
      a[i] = 0;
  }
  ```

  To indicate that an array parameter won't be changed, we can include the word `const` in its declaration:

  ```
  int find_largest(const int a[], int n)
  {
    ...
  }
  ```

  If `const` is present, the compiler will check that no assignment to an element of a appears in the body of `find_largest`.

- The time required to pass an array to a function doesn't depend on the size of the array. There's no penalty for passing a large array, since no copy of the array is made.

■ An array parameter can be declared as a pointer if desired. For example, `find_largest` could be defined as follows:

```
int find_largest(int *a, int n)
{
  ...
}
```

Declaring `a` to be a pointer is equivalent to declaring it to be an array; the compiler treats the declarations as though they were identical.

Although declaring a *parameter* to be an array is the same as declaring it to be a pointer, the same is not true for a *variable*. The declaration

```
int a[10];
```

causes the compiler to set aside space for ten integers. In contrast, the declaration

```
int *a;
```

causes the compiler to allocate space for a pointer variable. In the latter case, `a` is not an array; attempting to use it as an array can have disastrous results. For example, the assignment

```
*a = 0;    /*** WRONG ***/
```

will store 0 where `a` is pointing. Since we don't know where `a` is pointing, the effect on the program is unpredictable.

■ A function with an array parameter can be passed an array "slice"—a sequence of consecutive elements. Suppose that we want `find_largest` to locate the largest element in some portion of an array `b`, say elements `b[5]`, ..., `b[14]`. When we call `find_largest`, we'll pass it the address of `b[5]` and the number 10, indicating that we want `find_largest` to examine ten array elements, starting at `b[5]`:

```
largest = find_largest(&b[5], 10);
```

Using a Pointer as an Array Name

If we can use an array name as a pointer, will C allow us to subscript a pointer as though it were an array name? By now, you'd probably expect the answer to be yes, and you'd be right. Here's an example:

```
#define N 100

int a[N], i, sum = 0, *p = a;

for (i = 0; i < N; i++)
  sum += p[i];
```

The compiler treats `p[i]` as `*(p+i)`, which is a perfectly legal use of pointer arithmetic. Although the ability to subscript a pointer may seem to be little more than a curiosity, we'll see in Section 17.3 that it's actually quite useful.

12.4 Pointers and Multidimensional Arrays

Just as pointers can point to elements of one-dimensional arrays, they can also point to elements of multidimensional arrays. In this section, we'll explore common techniques for using pointers to process the elements of multidimensional arrays. For simplicity, we'll stick to two-dimensional arrays, but everything we'll do applies equally to higher-dimensional arrays.

Processing the Elements of a Multidimensional Array

We saw in Section 8.2 that C always stores two-dimensional arrays in row-major order; in other words, the elements of row 0 come first, followed by the elements of row 1, and so forth. An array with *r* rows would have the following appearance:

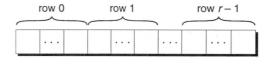

We can take advantage of this layout when working with pointers. If we make a pointer p point to the first element in a two-dimensional array (the element in row 0, column 0), we can visit every element in the array by incrementing p repeatedly.

As an example, let's look at the problem of initializing all elements of a two-dimensional array to zero. Suppose that the array has been declared as follows:

```
int a[NUM_ROWS][NUM_COLS];
```

The obvious technique would be to use nested `for` loops:

```
int row, col;

for (row = 0; row < NUM_ROWS; row++)
  for (col = 0; col < NUM_COLS; col++)
    a[row][col] = 0;
```

But if we view a as a one-dimensional array of integers (which is how it's stored), we can replace the pair of loops by a single loop:

```
int *p;

for (p = &a[0][0]; p <= &a[NUM_ROWS-1][NUM_COLS-1]; p++)
  *p = 0;
```

The loop begins with p pointing to a[0][0]. Successive increments of p make it point to a[0][1], a[0][2], and so on. When p reaches a[0][NUM_COLS-1] (the last element in row 0), incrementing it again makes p point to a[1][0], the first element in row 1. The process continues until p goes past a[NUM_ROWS-1][NUM_COLS-1], the last element in the array.

Although treating a two-dimensional array as one-dimensional may seem like cheating, it's perfectly legal in C. Whether it's a good idea to do so is another matter. Techniques like this one definitely hurt program readability, but—at least with some older compilers—produce a compensating increase in efficiency. With many modern compilers, though, there's often little or no speed advantage.

Processing the Rows of a Multidimensional Array

What about processing the elements in just one *row* of a two-dimensional array? Again, we have the option of using a pointer variable p. To visit the elements of row i, we'd initialize p to point to element 0 in row i in the array a:

```
p = &a[i][0];
```

Or we could simply write

```
p = a[i];
```

since, for any two-dimensional array a, the expression a[i] is a pointer to the first element in row i. To see why this works, recall the magic formula that relates array subscripting to pointer arithmetic: for any array a, the expression a[i] is equivalent to *(a + i). Thus, &a[i][0] is the same as &(*(a[i] + 0)), which is equivalent to &*a[i], which is the same as a[i], since the & and * operators cancel. We'll use this simplification in the following loop, which clears row i of the array a:

```
int a[NUM_ROWS][NUM_COLS], *p, i;
...
for (p = a[i]; p < a[i] + NUM_COLS; p++)
  *p = 0;
```

Since a[i] is a pointer to row i of the array a, we can pass a[i] to a function that's expecting a one-dimensional array as its argument. In other words, a function that's designed to work with one-dimensional arrays will also work with a row belonging to a two-dimensional array. As a result, functions such as find_largest and store_zeros are more versatile than you might expect. Consider find_largest, which we originally designed to find the largest element of a one-dimensional array. We can just as easily use find_largest to determine the largest element in one row of a two-dimensional array:

```
largest = find_largest(a[i], NUM_COLS);
```

Using the Name of a Multidimensional Array as a Pointer

Just as the name of a one-dimensional array can be used as a pointer, so can the name of *any* array, regardless of how many dimensions it has. Some care is required, though. Consider the following arrays:

```
int a[10], b[10][10];
```

Although we can use a as a pointer to the element a[0], it's not the case that b is a pointer to b[0][0]; instead, it's a pointer to b[0]. This makes more sense if we look at it from the standpoint of C, which regards b not as a two-dimensional array but as a one-dimensional array whose elements are one-dimensional arrays. In terms of types, a can be used as a pointer of type int *, whereas b—when used as a pointer—has type int ** (pointer to pointer to int).

For example, consider how we might use find_largest to find the largest element in the following two-dimensional array:

```
int a[NUM_ROWS][NUM_COLS];
```

Our plan is to trick find_largest into thinking that a is one-dimensional. As the first argument to find_largest, we'll try passing a (the address of the array); as the second, we'll pass NUM_ROWS * NUM_COLS (the total number of elements in a):

```
largest = find_largest(a, NUM_ROWS * NUM_COLS); /* WRONG */
```

This statement won't compile, because a has type int ** and find_largest is expecting an argument of type int *. The correct call is

```
largest = find_largest(a[0], NUM_ROWS * NUM_COLS);
```

a[0] points to element 0 in row 0, and it has type int *, so the call will work correctly.

Q&A

Q & A

Q: **I don't understand pointer arithmetic. If a pointer is an address, does that mean that an expression like p + j adds j to the address stored in p? [p. 222]**

A: No. Integers used in pointer arithmetic are scaled depending on the type of the pointer. If p is of type int *, for example, then p + j typically adds either $2 \times j$ or $4 \times j$ to p, depending on whether int values require 2 bytes or 4 bytes. But if p has type double *, then p + j will probably add $8 \times j$ to p, since double values are usually 8 bytes long.

Q: **What do you mean when you say that pointer arithmetic is meaningful only for pointers to array elements? [p. 224]**

A: Performing arithmetic on a pointer that doesn't point to an array element is "undefined," according to the C standard. That doesn't mean you can't do it; it just means that there's no guarantee about what will happen.

Q: **When writing a loop to process an array, is it better to use array subscripting or pointer arithmetic? [p. 225]**

A: There's no easy answer to this question, since it depends on the machine you're using and the compiler itself. In the early days of C on the PDP-11, pointer arithmetic yielded a faster program. On today's machines, using today's compilers, array subscripting is often just as good, and sometimes even better. The bottom line: Learn both ways and then use whichever is more natural for the kind of program you're writing.

*Q: **I read somewhere that i[a] is the same as a[i]. Is this true?**

A: Yes, it is, oddly enough. The compiler treats i[a] as *(i + a), which is the same as *(a + i). (Pointer addition, like ordinary addition, is commutative.) But *(a + i) is equivalent to a[i]. Q.E.D. But please don't use i[a] in programs unless you're planning to enter the next Obfuscated C contest.

Q: **Why is *a the same as a[] in a parameter declaration? [p. 230]**

A: Both indicate that the argument is expected to be a pointer. The same operations on a are possible in both cases (pointer arithmetic and array subscripting, in particular). And, in both cases, a itself can be assigned a new value within the function. (Although C allows us to use the name of an array *variable* only as a "constant pointer," there's no such restriction on the name of an array *parameter*.)

Q: **When a function has an array parameter a, is it better style to declare the parameter as *a or a[]?**

A: That's a tough one. From one standpoint, a[] is the obvious choice, since *a is ambiguous (does the function want an array of objects or a pointer to a single object?). On the other hand, many programmers argue that declaring the parameter as *a is more accurate, since it reminds us that only a pointer is passed, not a copy of the array. Others switch between *a and a[], depending on whether the function uses pointer arithmetic or subscripting to access the elements of the array. (That's the approach I'll use.) In practice, *a is more common than a[], so you'd better get used to it. For what it's worth, Dennis Ritchie now refers to the a[] notation as "a living fossil" that "serves as much to confuse the learner as to alert the reader."

Q: **We've seen that arrays and pointers are closely related in C. Would it be accurate to say that they're interchangeable?**

A: No. It's true that array *parameters* are interchangeable with pointer parameters, but array *variables* are not the same as pointer variables. Technically, the name of an array is not a pointer; rather, the C compiler *converts* it to a pointer when necessary. To see this difference more clearly, consider what happens when we apply the sizeof operator to an array a. The value of sizeof(a) is the total number of bytes in the array—the size of each element multiplied by the number of elements. But if p is a pointer variable, sizeof(p) is the number of bytes required to store a pointer value.

*Q: **You showed how to use a pointer to process the elements in a row of a two-dimensional array. Is it possible to use a similar technique to process the elements in a *column?***

A: Yes, but it's not as easy, since arrays are stored by row, not by column. Here's a loop that clears the elements of column i in the array a:

```
int a[NUM_ROWS][NUM_COLS], i, (*p)[NUM_COLS];

for (p = a; p <= &a[NUM_ROWS-1]; p++)
  (*p)[i] = 0;
```

I've declared p to be a pointer to an array of length NUM_COLS whose elements are integers. The parentheses around *p in (*p)[NUM_COLS] are required; without them, the compiler would treat p as an array of pointers instead of a pointer to an array. The expression p++ advances p to the beginning of the next row. In the expression (*p)[i], *p represents an entire row of a, so (*p)[i] selects the element in column i of that row. The parentheses in (*p)[i] are essential, since the compiler would interpret *p[i] as *(p[i]).

Q: **If a is a two-dimensional array, why can we pass a[0]—but not a itself—to find_largest? Don't both a and a[0] point to the same place (the beginning of the array)? [p. 233]**

A: They do, as a matter of fact—both point to element a[0][0]. However, the compiler notices that a has type int ** (not what find_largest was expecting) but a[0] has type int *. This concern about types is actually good; if C weren't so picky, we could make all kinds of horrible pointer mistakes without the compiler noticing.

Exercises

Section 12.1

1. Suppose that the following declarations are in effect:

```
int a[] = {5, 15, 34, 54, 14, 2, 52, 72};
int *p = &a[1], *q = &a[5];
```

(a) What is the value of *(p+3)?
(b) What is the value of *(q-3)?
(c) What is the value of q – p?
(d) Is the condition p < q true or false?
(e) Is the condition *p < *q true or false?

*2. Suppose that high, low, and middle are all pointers of the same type, and that low and high point to elements of an array. Why is the following statement illegal, and how could it be fixed?

```
middle = (low + high) / 2;
```

Section 12.2

3. What will be the contents of the a array after the following statements are executed?

```
#define N 10

int a[N] = {1, 2, 3, 4, 5, 6, 7, 8, 9, 10};
int *p = &a[0], *q = &a[N-1], temp;

while (p < q) {
  temp = *p;
  *p++ = *q;
  *q-- = temp;
}
```

4. (a) Write a program that reads a message, then prints the reversal of the message. The output of the program should look like this:

Enter a message: <u>Don't get mad, get even.</u>
Reversal is: .neve teg ,dam teg t'noD

Hint: Read the message one character at a time (using getchar) and store the characters in an array. Stop reading when the array is full or the character read is '\n'.

(b) Revise the program to use a pointer instead of an integer to keep track of the current position in the array.

5. (a) Write a program that reads a message, then checks whether it's a palindrome (the letters in the message are the same from left to right as from right to left):

Enter a message: <u>He lived as a devil, eh?</u>
Palindrome

Enter a message: <u>Madam, I am Adam.</u>
Not a palindrome

Ignore all characters that aren't letters. Use integer variables to keep track of positions within the array.

(b) Revise the program to use pointers instead of integers to keep track of positions in the array.

6. Rewrite the stack functions make_empty, is_empty, and is_full (Section 10.2) to use the pointer variable top_ptr instead of the integer variable top.

Section 12.3

7. Suppose that a is a one-dimensional array and p is a pointer variable. Assuming that the assignment p = a has just been performed, which of the following expressions are illegal because of mismatched types? Of the remaining expressions, which are true (have a nonzero value)?

(a) p == a[0]
(b) p == &a[0]
(c) *p == a[0]
(d) p[0] == a[0]

8. Simplify the program of Exercise 4(b) by taking advantage of the fact that an array name can be used as a pointer.

9. Simplify the program of Exercise 5(b) by taking advantage of the fact that an array name can be used as a pointer.

10. Rewrite the following function to use pointer arithmetic instead of array subscripting. (In other words, eliminate the variable i and all uses of the [] operator.) Make as few changes as possible.

```
int sum_array(int a[], int n)
{
  int i, sum;

  sum = 0;
  for (i = 0; i < n; i++)
    sum += a[i];
  return sum;
}
```

11. Write the following function:

```
Bool search(int a[], int n, int key);
```

a is an array to be searched, n is the number of elements in the array, and key is the search key. search should return TRUE if key matches some element of a, FALSE if it doesn't. Use pointer arithmetic—not subscripting—to visit array elements.

Section 12.4

12. Section 8.2 had a code fragment in which two nested for loops initialized the array ident for use as an identity matrix. Rewrite this code, using a single pointer to step through the array one element at a time. *Hint:* Since we won't be using row and col index variables, it won't be easy to tell where to store 1. Instead, we can use the fact that the first element of the array should be 1, the next N elements should be 0, the next element should be 1, and so forth. Use a variable that keeps track of how many consecutive 0s have been stored; when the count reaches N, it's time to store 1.

13. Assume that the following array contains a week's worth of hourly temperature readings, with each row containing the readings for one day:

```
int temperatures[7][24];
```

Write a statement that uses the search function (Exercise 11) to search the entire temperatures array for the value 32.

14. Write a loop that prints all temperature readings stored in row i of the temperatures array (Exercise 13). Use a pointer to visit each element of the row.

15. Write a loop that prints the highest temperature in the temperatures array (Exercise 13) for each day of the week. The loop body should call the find_largest function, passing it one row of the array at a time.

13 Strings

It's difficult to extract sense from strings, but
they're the only communication coin we can count on.

Although we've used `char` variables and arrays of `char` values in previous chapters, we still lack any convenient way to process a series of characters (or **string,** in C terminology). We'll remedy that defect in this chapter, which covers both string *constants* (or **literals,** as they're called in the C standard) and string *variables,* which can change during the execution of a program.

Section 13.1 explains the rules that govern string literals, including the rules for embedding escape sequences in string literals and for breaking long string literals. Section 13.2 then shows how to declare string variables, which are little more than arrays of characters in which a special character—the **null character**—marks the end of a string. Section 13.3 describes ways to read and write strings. Section 13.4 discusses ways to write functions that process strings, and Section 13.5 covers some of the string-handling functions in the C library. Section 13.6 presents idioms that are often used when working with strings. Finally, Section 13.7 describes how to set up arrays whose elements are pointers to strings of different lengths. This section also explains how C uses such an array to supply command-line information to programs.

13.1 String Literals

A **string literal** is a sequence of characters enclosed within double quotes:

```
"Put a disk in drive A, then press any key to continue\n"
```

We first encountered string literals in Chapter 2; they often appear as format strings in calls of `printf` and `scanf`.

Escape Sequences in String Literals

escape sequences ➤ 7.3 String literals may contain the same escape sequences as character constants. We've used character escapes in `printf` and `scanf` format strings for some time. For example, we've seen that each `\n` character in the string

```
"Candy\nIs dandy\nBut liquor\nIs quicker.\n  --Ogden Nash\n"
```

causes the cursor to advance to the next line:

```
Candy
Is dandy
But liquor
Is quicker.
  --Ogden Nash
```

Although octal and hexadecimal escapes are also legal in string literals, they're not as common as character escapes.

Be careful when using octal and hexadecimal escape sequences in string literals. An octal escape ends after three digits or with the first non-octal character. For example, the string `"\1234"` contains two characters (`\123` and `4`), and the string `"\189"` contains three characters (`\1`, `8`, and `9`). A hexadecimal escape, on the other hand, isn't limited to three digits; it doesn't end until the first non-hex character. Consider what happens if a string contains the escape `\x81`, which represents the character *ü* on IBM-compatible personal computers. The string `"Z\x81rich"` ("Zürich") has six characters (`Z`, `\x81`, `r`, `i`, `c`, and `h`), but the string `"\x81ber"` (a failed attempt at "über") has only two (`\x81be` and `r`). Most compilers will reject the latter string, since computers normally limit hex escapes to the range `\x0–\x7f` (or possibly `\x0–\xff`).

Continuing a String Literal

If we find that a string literal is too long to fit conveniently on a single line, C allows us to continue it on the next line, provided that we end the first line with a `\` character. No other characters may follow `\` on the same line, other than the (invisible) new-line character at the end:

```
printf("Put a disk in drive A, then \
press any key to continue\n");
```

Incidentally, the `\` character can be used to break any long symbol, not just strings (although that's how it's normally used).

The `\` technique has one drawback: the string must continue at the beginning of the next line, thereby wrecking the program's indented structure. A better way to deal with long string literals was added to C when the language was standardized. According to the C standard, when two or more string literals are adjacent (separated only by white space), the compiler must join them into a single string. This rule allows us to split a string literal over two or more lines:

```
printf("Put a disk in drive A, then "
       "press any key to continue\n");
```

How String Literals Are Stored

We've used string literals often in calls of `printf` and `scanf`. But when we call `printf` and supply a string literal as an argument, what are we actually passing? To answer this question, we need to know how string literals are stored.

In essence, C treats string literals as character arrays. When a C compiler encounters a string literal of length *n* in a program, it sets aside *n* + 1 characters of memory for the string. This area of memory will contain the characters in the string, plus one extra character—the ***null character***—to mark the end of the string. ASCII character set ➤ *Appendix E* The null character is the very first character in the ASCII character set, so it's represented by the \0 escape sequence.

 Don't confuse the null character (`'\0'`) with the zero character (`'0'`). The null character has the ASCII code 0; the zero character has the code 48.

For example, the string literal `"abc"` is stored as an array of four characters (a, b, c, and \0):

String literals may be empty; the string `""` is stored as a single null character:

Since a string literal is stored as an array, the compiler treats it as a pointer of type `char *`. Both `printf` and `scanf`, for example, expect a value of type `char *` as their first argument. Consider the following example:

```
printf("abc");
```

When `printf` is called, it is passed the address of `"abc"` (a pointer to where the letter a is stored in memory).

Operations on String Literals

In general, we can use a string literal wherever C allows a `char *` pointer. For example, a string literal can appear on the right side of an assignment:

```
char *p;

p = "abc";
```

This assignment doesn't copy the characters in "abc"; it merely makes p point to the first character of the string.

C allows pointers to be subscripted, so we can subscript string literals:

```
char ch;

ch = "abc"[1];
```

The new value of ch will be the letter b. The other possible subscripts are 0 (which would select the letter a), 2 (the letter c), and 3 (the null character). This property of string literals isn't used that much, but occasionally we'll find it useful. Consider the following function, which converts a number between 0 and 15 into the character form of the equivalent hex digit:

```
char digit_to_hex_char(int digit)
{
  return "0123456789ABCDEF"[digit];
}
```

Changing the characters in a string literal is possible, but not recommended:

```
char *p = "abc";

*p = 'b';    /* string literal is now "bbc" */
```

With some compilers, changing a string literal may cause programs to behave erratically.

String Literals versus Character Constants

A string literal containing a single character isn't the same as a character constant. The string literal "a" is represented by a *pointer* to a memory location that contains the character a (followed by a null character). The character constant 'a' is represented by an *integer* (the ASCII code for the character).

Don't ever use a character when a string is required (or vice versa). The call

```
printf("\n");
```

is legal, because printf expects a pointer as its first argument. The following call isn't legal, however:

```
printf('\n');    /*** WRONG ***/
```

13.2 String Variables

Some programming languages provide a special `string` type for declaring string variables. C takes a different tack: any one-dimensional array of characters can be used to store a string, with the understanding that the string is terminated by a null character. This approach is simple, but has significant difficulties. It's sometimes hard to tell whether an array of characters is being used as a string. If we write our own string-handling functions, we've got to be careful that they deal properly with the null character. Also, there's no faster way to determine the length of a string than a character-by-character search for the null character.

Let's say that we need a variable capable of storing a string of up to 80 characters. Since the string will need a null character at the end, we'll declare the variable to be an array of 81 characters:

```
#define STR_LEN 80
```

idiom
```
char str[STR_LEN+1];
```

Notice that we defined `STR_LEN` to be `80` rather than `81`, thus emphasizing the fact that `str` can store strings of no more than 80 characters. Adding 1 to the macro in this way is a common practice among C programmers.

 When declaring an array of characters that will be used to hold a string, always make the array one character longer than the string, because of the C convention that every string is terminated by a null character. Failing to leave room for the null character may cause unpredictable results when the program is executed, since functions in the C library assume that strings are null-terminated.

Declaring a character array to have length STR_LEN + 1 doesn't mean that it will always contain a string of STR_LEN characters. The length of a string depends on the position of the terminating null character, not on the length of the array in which the string is stored. An array of STR_LEN + 1 characters can hold strings of various lengths, ranging from the empty string to strings of length STR_LEN.

Initializing a String Variable

A string variable can be initialized at the point of declaration:

```
char date1[8] = "June 14";
```

The compiler will copy the characters from `"June 14"` into the `date1` array, then add a null character so that `date1` can be used as a string. Here's what `date1` will look like:

Although `"June 14"` appears to be a string literal, it's not. Instead, C views it as an abbreviation for an array initializer. In fact, we could have written

```
char date1[8] = {'J', 'u', 'n', 'e', ' ', '1', '4', '\0'};
```

I think you'll agree that the original version is easier to read.

What if the initializer is too short to fill the string variable? In that case, the compiler adds extra null characters. Thus, after the declaration

```
char date2[9] = "June 14";
```

date2 will have the following appearance:

array initializers ➤8.1 This behavior is consistent with C's treatment of array initializers in general. When an array initializer is shorter than the array itself, the remaining elements are initialized to 0. By initializing the extra elements of a character array to `\0`, the compiler is following the same rule.

What if the initializer is longer than the string variable? That's illegal for strings, just as it's illegal for other arrays. However, C does allow the initializer (not counting the null character) to have exactly the same length as the variable:

```
char date3[7] = "June 14";
```

The compiler simply copies the characters from the initializer into date3:

There's no room for the null character, so the compiler makes no attempt to store one.

If you're planning to initialize a character array to contain a string, be sure that the length of the array is longer than the length of the initializer. Otherwise, the compiler will quietly omit the null character, making the array unusable as a string.

The declaration of a string variable may omit its length, in which case the compiler computes it:

```
char date4[] = "June 14";
```

The compiler sets aside eight characters for date4, enough to store the characters in `"June 14"` plus a null character. (The fact that the length of date4 isn't specified doesn't mean that the array can change its length later. Once the program is compiled, the length of date4 is fixed at eight.) Omitting the length of a string variable is especially useful if the initializer is long, since computing the length by hand can be error-prone.

Character Arrays versus Character Pointers

Let's compare the declaration

```
char date[] = "June 14";
```

which declares date to be an *array* of characters, with the similar-looking

```
char *date = "June 14";
```

which declares date to be a *pointer* to a string literal. Thanks to the close relationship between arrays and pointers, we can use either version of date as a string. In particular, any function expecting to be passed a character array or character pointer will accept either version of date as an argument.

However, we must be careful not to make the mistake of thinking that the two versions of date are interchangeable. There are significant differences between the two:

- In the array version, the characters stored in date can be modified, like the elements of any array. In the pointer version, date points to a string literal, and we saw in Section 13.1 that string literals shouldn't be modified.
- In the array version, date is an array name. In the pointer version, date is a variable that can be made to point to other strings during program execution.

If we need a string that can be modified, it's our responsibility to set up an array of characters in which to store the string; declaring a pointer variable isn't enough. The declaration

```
char *p;
```

causes the compiler to set aside enough memory for a pointer variable; unfortunately, it doesn't allocate space for a string. (And how could it? We haven't indicated how long the string would be.) Before we can use p as a string, it must point to an array of characters. One possibility is to make p point to a string variable that already exists:

```
char str[STR_LEN+1], *p;

p = str;
```

p now points to the first character of str, so we can use p as a string.

Using an uninitialized pointer variable as a string is a serious error. Consider the following example, which attempts to build the string "abc":

```
char *p;

p[0] = 'a';      /*** WRONG ***/
p[1] = 'b';      /*** WRONG ***/
p[2] = 'c';      /*** WRONG ***/
p[3] = '\0';     /*** WRONG ***/
```

Since p hasn't been initialized, we don't know where it's pointing. Writing the characters a, b, c, and \0 into memory at that location will have an unknown effect on the program. The program may continue without problems, or it may crash or behave erratically.

13.3 Reading and Writing Strings

Writing a string is easy using either the printf or puts functions. Reading a string is a bit harder, primarily because of the possibility that the input string may be longer than the string variable into which it's being stored. To read a string in a single step, we can use either scanf or gets. As an alternative, we can read strings one character at a time.

Writing Strings Using printf and puts

The %s conversion specification allows printf to write a string. Consider the following example:

```
char str[] = "Are we having fun yet?";

printf("Value of str: %s\n", str);
```

The output will be

```
Value of str: Are we having fun yet?
```

printf writes the characters in a string one by one until it encounters a null character. (If the null character is missing, printf continues past the end of the string until—eventually—it finds a null character somewhere in memory.)

To print just part of a string, we can use the conversion specification %.ps, where p is the number of characters to be displayed. The statement

```
printf("%.6s\n", str);
```

will print

```
Are we
```

A string, like a number, can be printed within a field. The %ms conversion will display a string in a field of size m. (A string with more than m characters will be printed in full, not truncated.) If the string has fewer than *m* characters, it will be right-justified within the field. To force left justification instead, we can make put a minus sign in front of *m*. The *m* and *p* values can be used in combination: a conversion specification of the form %*m.ps* causes the first *p* characters of a string to be displayed in a field of size *m*.

printf isn't the only function that can write strings. The C library also provides puts, which is used in the following way:

```
puts(str);
```

puts has only one argument, the string to be printed; there is no format string. After writing a string, puts always writes an additional new-line character, thus advancing to the beginning of the next output line.

Reading Strings Using scanf and gets

The %s conversion specification allows scanf to read a string:

```
scanf("%s", str);
```

There's no need to put the & operator in front of str in the call of scanf; since str is an array name, it's treated as a pointer automatically.

When scanf is called, it skips white space, then reads characters and stores them into str until it encounters a white-space character. scanf always stores a null character at the end of the string.

A string read using scanf will never contain white space. Consequently, scanf won't usually read a full line of input; a new-line character will cause scanf to stop reading, but so will a space or tab character. To read an entire line of input at a time, we can use gets. Like scanf, the gets function reads input characters into an array, then stores a null character. In other respects, however, gets is somewhat different from scanf:

- gets doesn't skip white space before starting to read the string (scanf does).
- gets reads until it finds a new-line character (scanf stops at any white-space character). Incidentally, gets discards the new-line character instead of storing it in the array; the null character takes the place of the new-line character.

To see the difference between scanf and gets, consider the following program fragment:

```
char sentence[SENT_LEN+1];

printf("Enter a sentence:\n");
scanf("%s", sentence);
```

Suppose that after the prompt

```
Enter a sentence:
```

the user enters the line

```
To C, or not to C: that is the question.
```

`scanf` will store the string `"To"` into `sentence`. The next call of `scanf` will resume reading the line at the space after the word `To`.

Now suppose that we replace `scanf` by `gets`:

```
gets(sentence);
```

When the user enters the same input as before, `gets` will store the string

```
"  To C, or not to C: that is the question."
```

into `sentence`.

---

fgets function ➤ 22.5

As they read characters into an array, `scanf` and `gets` have no way to detect when they've filled the array. Consequently, they may store characters past the end of the array, causing the program to behave erratically. `scanf` can be made safer by using the conversion specification %*n*s instead of %s, where *n* is a number indicating the maximum number of characters to be stored. `gets`, unfortunately, is inherently unsafe; `fgets` is a safer alternative.

A final note about `gets` and `puts`: Since these functions are simpler than `scanf` and `printf`, they're usually faster as well.

Reading Strings Character by Character

Since both `scanf` and `gets` are risky and insufficiently flexible for many applications, C programmers often write their own input functions. By reading strings one character at a time, these functions provide a greater degree of control than the standard input functions.

If we decide to design our own input function, we'll need to consider the following issues:

- Should the function skip white space before beginning to store the string?
- What character causes the function to stop reading: a new-line character, any white-space character, or some other character? Is this character stored in the string or discarded?
- What should the function do if the input string is too long to store: discard the extra characters or leave them for the next input operation?

Suppose we need a function that doesn't skip white-space characters, stops reading at the first new-line character (which isn't stored in the string), and discards extra characters. The function will have the following prototype:

```
int read_line(char str[], int n);
```

`str` represents the array into which we'll store the input, and n is the maximum number of characters to be read. If the input line contains more than n characters, `read_line` will discard the additional characters. We'll have `read_line` return the number of characters it actually stores into `str` (a number anywhere from 0 to n). We may not always need `read_line`'s return value, but it doesn't hurt to have it available.

`read_line` consists primarily of a loop that reads characters one by one and stores them, provided that there's room left in `str`. The loop terminates when the new-line character is read. (Strictly speaking, we should also have the loop terminate if `getchar` should fail to read a character, but we'll ignore that complication for now.) Here's the complete definition of `read_line`:

Q&A

```c
int read_line(char str[], int n)
{
  char ch;
  int i = 0;

  while ((ch = getchar()) != '\n')
    if (i < n)
      str[i++] = ch;

  str[i] = '\0';          /* terminates string */
  return i;               /* number of characters stored */
}
```

Before returning, `read_line` puts a null character at the end of the string. Standard functions such as `scanf` and `gets` automatically put a null character at the end of an input string; if we're writing our own input function, however, we must take on that responsibility.

13.4   Accessing the Characters in a String

Since strings are stored as arrays, we can use subscripting to access the characters in a string. To process every character in a string s, for example, we can set up a loop that increments a counter i and selects characters via the expression s[i].

Suppose that we need a function that counts the number of spaces in a string. Using array subscripting, we might write the function in the following way:

```c
int count_spaces(const char s[])
{
  int count = 0, i;

  for (i = 0; s[i] != '\0'; i++)
    if (s[i] == ' ')
      count++;
  return count;
}
```

I've included const in the declaration of s to indicate that count_spaces doesn't change the array. If s were not a string, count_spaces would need a second argument specifying the length of the array. Since s is a string, however, count_spaces can locate the end of s by testing for the null character.

Many C programmers wouldn't write count_spaces as we have. Instead, they'd use a pointer to keep track of the current position within the string. As we saw in Section 12.2, this technique is always available for processing arrays, but it proves to be especially convenient for working with strings.

Let's rewrite the count_spaces function using pointer arithmetic instead of array subscripting. We'll eliminate the variable i and use s itself to keep track of our position in the string. By incrementing s repeatedly, count_spaces can step through each character in the string. Here's our new version of count_spaces:

```
int count_spaces(const char *s)
{
  int count = 0;

  for (; *s != '\0'; s++)
    if (*s == ' ')
      count++;
  return count;
}
```

Note that const doesn't prevent count_spaces from modifying s; it's there to prevent the function from modifying what s points to. And since s is a copy of the argument that's passed to count_spaces, incrementing s doesn't affect that argument.

The count_spaces function raises some questions about how to write string functions:

- ***Is it better to use array operations or pointer operations to access the characters in a string?*** We're free to use whichever is more convenient; we can even mix the two. In the second version of count_spaces, treating s as a pointer simplifies the function slightly by removing the need for the variable i. Traditionally, C programmers lean toward using pointer operations for processing strings.

- ***Should a string parameter be declared as an array or as a pointer?*** The two versions of count_spaces illustrate the options: the first version of count_spaces declares s to be an array; the second version declares s to be a pointer. Actually, there's no difference between the two declarations—recall from Section 12.3 that the compiler treats an array parameter as though it had been declared as a pointer.

- ***Does the form of the parameter (s[] or *s) affect what can be supplied as an argument?*** No. When count_spaces is called, the argument could be an array name, a pointer variable, or a string literal—count_spaces can't tell the difference.

13.5   Using the C String Library

Some programming languages provide operators that can copy strings, compare strings, concatenate strings, select substrings, and the like. C's operators, in contrast, are essentially useless for working with strings. Strings are treated as arrays in C, so they're restricted in the same ways as arrays—in particular, they can't be copied or compared using C's operators.

 Direct attempts to copy or compare strings will fail. For example, suppose that str1 and str2 have been declared as follows:

```
char str1[10], str2[10];
```

Copying a string into a character array using the = operator is not possible:

```
str1 = "abc";   /*** WRONG ***/
str2 = str1;    /*** WRONG ***/
```

C interprets these statements as (illegal) assignments of one pointer to another. *Initializing* a character array using = is legal, though:

```
char str1[10] = "abc";
```

In the context of a declaration, = is not the assignment operator.

Attempting to compare strings using a relational or equality operator is legal, but won't produce the desired result:

```
if (str1 == str2) …   /*** WRONG ***/
```

This statement compares str1 and str2 as *pointers*; it doesn't compare the contents of the two arrays. Since str1 and str2 have different addresses, the expression str1 == str2 must have the value 0.

Fortunately, all is not lost: the C library provides a rich set of functions for performing operations on strings. Prototypes for these functions reside in the header <string.h>, so programs that need string operations should contain the following line:

<string.h> header ➤23.5

```
#include <string.h>
```

Each function declared in <string.h> requires at least one string as an argument. String parameters are declared to have type char *, allowing the argument to be a character array, a variable of type char *, or a string literal—all are suitable as strings. Watch out for string parameters that aren't declared const, however. Such a parameter will be modified when the function is called, so the corresponding argument shouldn't be a string literal.

There are many functions in `<string.h>`; I'll cover four of the more widely used. In subsequent examples, assume that `str1` and `str2` are character arrays used as strings.

The `strcpy` (String Copy) Function

The `strcpy` function has the following prototype in `<string.h>`:

```
char *strcpy(char *s1, const char *s2);
```

`strcpy` copies the string `s2` into the string `s1`. (To be precise, we should say "`strcpy` copies the string pointed to by `s2` into the array pointed to by `s1`," but that's a bit long-winded.) That is, `strcpy` copies characters from `s2` to `s1` up to (and including) the first null character in `s2`. `strcpy` returns `s1` (a pointer to the destination string). The string pointed to by `s2` isn't modified, so it's declared `const`.

The existence of `strcpy` compensates for the fact that we can't use the assignment operator to copy strings. For example, suppose that we want to store the string `"abcd"` in `str1`. We can't use the assignment

```
str1 = "abcd";               /*** WRONG ***/
```

because `str1` is an array name and can't appear on the left side of an assignment. Instead, we can call `strcpy`:

```
strcpy(str1, "abcd");   /* str1 now contains "abcd" */
```

Similarly, we can't assign `str1` to `str2` directly, but we can call `strcpy`:

```
strcpy(str2, str1);     /* str2 now contains "abcd" */
```

In the call `strcpy(str2, str1)`, `strcpy` has no way to check that the string pointed to by `str1` will actually fit in the array pointed to by `str2`. Suppose that `str2` points to an array of length *n*. If the string that `str1` points to has no more than *n* − 1 characters, then the copy will succeed. But if `str1` points to a longer string, the result is unpredictable. (Since `strcpy` always copies up to the first null character, it will continue copying past the end of the array that `str2` points to. Whatever was previously stored in memory after that array will be overwritten.)

strncpy function ▶23.5 Calling the `strncpy` function is a safer, albeit slower, way to copy a string.

Most of the time, we'll discard `strcpy`'s return value. On occasion, though, it can be useful to call `strcpy` as part of a larger expression in order to use its return value. For example, we could chain together a series of `strcpy` calls to get the same effect as a multiple assignment:

```
strcpy(str2, strcpy(str1, "abcd"));
  /* both str1 and str2 now contain "abcd" */
```

The `strcat` (String Concatenate) Function

The `strcat` function has the following prototype:

```
char *strcat(char *s1, const char *s2);
```

`strcat` appends the contents of the string `s2` to the end of the string `s1`; it returns `s1` (a pointer to the resulting string).

Here are some examples of `strcat` in action:

```
strcpy(str1, "abc");
strcat(str1, "def");    /* str1 now contains "abcdef" */

strcpy(str1, "abc");
strcpy(str2, "def");
strcat(str1, str2);     /* str1 now contains "abcdef" */
```

As with `strcpy`, the value returned by `strcat` is normally discarded. The following example shows how the return value might be used:

```
strcpy(str1, "abc");
strcpy(str2, "def");
strcat(str1, strcat(str2, "ghi"));
 /* str1 now contains "abcdefghi"; str2 contains "defghi" */
```

The effect of the call `strcat(str1, str2)` is unpredictable if the array pointed to by `str1` isn't long enough to accommodate the characters in the string pointed to by `str2`. Consider the following example:

```
char str1[6] = "abc";

strcat(str1, "def");    /*** WRONG ***/
```

`strcat` will attempt to add the characters `d`, `e`, `f`, and `\0` to the end of the string already stored in `str1`. Unfortunately, `str1` is limited to six characters, causing `strcat` to write past the end of the array.

The `strcmp` (String Compare) Function

The `strcmp` function has the following prototype:

```
int strcmp(const char *s1, const char *s2);
```

Q&A

`strcmp` compares the strings `s1` and `s2`, returning a value less than, equal to, or greater than 0, depending on whether `s1` is less than, equal to, or greater than `s2`. For example, to see if `str1` is less than `str2`, we'd write

```
if (strcmp(str1, str2) < 0)    /* is str1 < str2? */
  ...
```

To test whether `str1` is less than or equal to `str2`, we'd write

```
if (strcmp(str1, str2) <= 0)    /* is str1 <= str2? */
    ...
```

By choosing the proper relational operator (<, <=, >, >=) or equality operator (==, !=), we can test any possible relationship between `str1` and `str2`.

strcmp compares strings using lexicographic ordering, which resembles the way words are arranged in a dictionary. More precisely, `strcmp` considers s1 to be less than s2 if either one of the following conditions is satisfied:

- The first i characters of s1 and s2 match, but the $(i+1)$st character of s1 is less than the $(i+1)$st character of s2. For example, `"abc"` is less than `"bcd"`, and `"abd"` is less than `"abe"`.

- All characters of s1 match s2, but s1 is shorter than s2. For example, `"abc"` is less than `"abcd"`.

As it compares characters from two strings, `strcmp` looks at the numerical codes that represent the characters. Some knowledge of the underlying character set is helpful in order to predict what `strcmp` will do. Assuming that our machine uses the ASCII character set, here are some of the rules that `strcmp` will follow:

ASCII character set ➤ *Appendix E*

- All upper-case letters are less than all lower-case letters. (In ASCII, codes between 65 and 90 represent upper-case letters; codes between 97 and 122 represent lower-case letters.)

- Digits are less than letters. (Codes between 48 and 57 represent digits.)

- Spaces are less than all printing characters. (The space character has the value 32 in ASCII.)

The **strlen** (String Length) Function

The `strlen` function has the following prototype:

```
size_t strlen(const char *s);
```

size_t type ➤ *21.3*

`size_t`, which is defined in the C library, is an unsigned integer type (usually `unsigned int` or `unsigned long int`). Unless we're dealing with extremely long strings, this technicality need not concern us—we simply treat the return value of `strlen` as an integer.

`strlen` returns the length of a string s. More precisely, `strlen` returns the number of characters in s up to, but not including, the first null character. For example:

```
int len;

len = strlen("abc");    /* len is now 3 */
len = strlen("");       /* len is now 0 */
strcpy(str1, "abc");
len = strlen(str1);     /* len is now 3 */
```

The last example illustrates an important point: When given an array as its argument, `strlen` doesn't measure the length of the array itself; instead, it returns the length of the string stored in the array.

PROGRAM   **Printing a One-Month Reminder List**

To illustrate the use of the C string library, we'll now look at a program that prints a one-month list of daily reminders. The user will enter a series of reminders, with each prefixed by a day of the month. When the user enters 0 instead of a valid day, the program will print a list of all reminders entered, sorted by day. Here's what a session with the program will look like:

```
Enter day and reminder: 24 Susan's birthday
Enter day and reminder: 5 6:00 - Dinner with Marge and Russ
Enter day and reminder: 26 Movie - "Chinatown"
Enter day and reminder: 7 10:30 - Dental appointment
Enter day and reminder: 12 Movie - "Dazed and Confused"
Enter day and reminder: 5 Saturday class
Enter day and reminder: 12 Saturday class
Enter day and reminder: 0

Day Reminder
  5 Saturday class
  5 6:00 - Dinner with Marge and Russ
  7 10:30 - Dental appointment
 12 Saturday class
 12 Movie - "Dazed and Confused"
 24 Susan's birthday
 26 Movie - "Chinatown"
```

The overall strategy isn't very complicated: we'll have the program read a series of day-and-reminder combinations, storing them in order (sorted by day), and then display them. To read the days, we'll use `scanf`; to read the reminders, we'll use the `read_line` function (Section 13.3).

We'll store the strings in a two-dimensional array of characters, with each row of the array containing one string. After the program reads a day and its associated reminder, it will search the array to determine where the day belongs, using `strcmp` to do comparisons. It will then use `strcpy` to move all strings *below* that point down one position. Finally, the program will copy the day into the array and call `strcat` to append the reminder to the day. (The day and the reminder have been kept separate up to this point.).

Of course, there are always a few minor complications. For example, we want the days to be right-justified in a two-character field, so that their ones digits will line up. There are many ways to handle the problem. I've chosen to have the program use `scanf` to read the day into an integer variable, then call `sprintf` to convert the day back into string form. `sprintf` is a library function that's similar to `printf`, except that it writes output into a string. The call

sprintf function ▶ 22.8

```
sprintf(day_str, "%2d", day);
```

writes the value of day into day_str. Since sprintf automatically adds a null character when it's through writing, day_str will contain a properly null-terminated string.

Another complication is making sure that the user doesn't enter more than two digits. We'll use the following call of scanf for this purpose:

```
scanf("%2d", &day);
```

The number 2 between % and d tells scanf to stop reading after two digits, even if the input has more digits.

With those details out of the way, here's the program:

remind.c

```
/* Prints a one-month reminder list */

#include <stdio.h>
#include <string.h>

#define MAX_REMIND 50
#define MSG_LEN 60

int read_line(char str[], int n);

main()
{
  char reminders[MAX_REMIND][MSG_LEN+3];
  char day_str[3], msg_str[MSG_LEN+1];
  int day, i, j, num_remind = 0;

  for (;;) {
    if (num_remind == MAX_REMIND) {
      printf("-- No space left --\n");
      break;
    }

    printf("Enter day and reminder: ");
    scanf("%2d", &day);
    if (day == 0)
      break;
    sprintf(day_str, "%2d", day);
    read_line(msg_str, MSG_LEN);

    for (i = 0; i < num_remind; i++)
      if (strcmp(day_str, reminders[i]) < 0)
        break;
    for (j = num_remind; j > i; j--)
      strcpy(reminders[j], reminders[j-1]);

    strcpy(reminders[i], day_str);
    strcat(reminders[i], msg_str);

    num_remind++;
  }
```

```
      printf("\nDay Reminder\n");
      for (i = 0; i < num_remind; i++)
        printf(" %s\n", reminders[i]);

      return 0;
    }

    int read_line(char str[], int n)
    {
      char ch;
      int i = 0;

      while ((ch = getchar()) != '\n')
        if (i < n)
          str[i++] = ch;

      str[i] = '\0';
      return i;
    }
```

Although the `remind.c` program is a good illustration of the `strcpy`, `strcat`, and `strcmp` functions, it lacks something as a practical reminder program. There are obviously a number of improvements needed, ranging from minor tweaks to major enhancements (such as saving the database in a file when the program terminates). We'll discuss some of these improvements in the exercises at the end of this chapter and in later chapters.

13.6   String Idioms

Functions that manipulate strings are a particularly rich source of idioms. In this section, we'll explore two of the most famous idioms by using them to write the `strlen` and `strcat` functions. (You'll never have to write these functions, of course, since they're part of the standard library. But you may have to write functions that are similar.)

The concise style I'll use in this section is popular with many C programmers. You should master this style even if you don't plan to use it in your own programs, since you're likely to encounter it in programs written by others.

Searching for the End of a String

Many string operations require searching for the end of a string. The `strlen` function is a prime example. The following version of `strlen` searches its string argument to find the end, using a variable to keep track of the string's length:

```
size_t strlen(const char *s)
{
  size_t n;

  for (n = 0; *s != '\0'; s++)
    n++;
  return n;
}
```

As the pointer s moves across the string from left to right, the variable n keeps track of how many characters have been seen so far. When s finally points to a null character, n contains the length of the string.

Let's see if we can condense the definition of strlen. First, we'll move the initialization of n to its declaration:

```
size_t strlen(const char *s)
{
  size_t n = 0;

  for (; *s != '\0'; s++)
    n++;
  return n;
}
```

Next, we notice that the condition *s != '\0' is the same as *s != 0, because the ASCII code for the null character is 0. But testing *s != 0 is the same as testing *s; both are true if *s isn't equal to 0. These observations lead to our next version of strlen:

```
size_t strlen(const char *s)
{
  size_t n = 0;

  for (; *s; s++)
    n++;
  return n;
}
```

But, as we saw in Section 12.2, it's possible to increment s and test *s in the same expression:

```
size_t strlen(const char *s)
{
  size_t n = 0;

  for (; *s++;)
    n++;
  return n;
}
```

Replacing the for statement by a while statement, we arrive at the following version of strlen:

```
size_t strlen(const char *s)
{
  size_t n = 0;

  while (*s++)
    n++;
  return n;
}
```

Although we've condensed `strlen` quite a bit, it's likely that we haven't increased its speed. Here's a version that *does* run faster, at least with some compilers:

```
size_t strlen(const char *s)
{
  const char *p = s;

  while (*s)
    s++;
  return s - p;
}
```

This version of `strlen` computes the length of the string by locating the position of the null character, then subtracting from it the position of the first character in the string. The improvement in speed comes from not having to increment n inside the `while` loop. Note the appearance of the word `const` in the declaration of p, by the way; without it, the compiler would notice that assigning s to p places the string that s points to at risk.

The statement

idiom
```
while (*s)
  s++;
```

and the related

idiom
```
while (*s++)
  ;
```

are idioms meaning "search for the null character at the end of a string." The first version leaves s pointing to the null character. The second version is more concise, but leaves s pointing just past the null character.

Copying a String

Copying a string is another common operation. To introduce C's "string copy" idiom, we'll develop a version of the `strcat` function. Let's start with a straightforward but somewhat lengthy version of `strcat`:

```
char *strcat(char *s1, const char *s2)
{
  char *p;

  p = s1;
  while (*p != '\0')
    p++;
  while (*s2 != '\0') {
    *p = *s2;
    p++;
    s2++;
  }
  *p = '\0';
  return s1;
}
```

This version of strcat uses a two-step algorithm: (1) Locate the null character at the end of the string s1 and make p point to it. (2) Copy characters one by one from s2 to where p is pointing.

The first while statement in the function implements step (1). p is set to point to the first character in s1. Assuming that s1 points to the string "abc", we have the following picture:

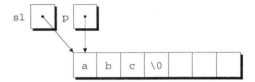

p is then incremented as long as it doesn't point to a null character. When the loop terminates, p must be pointing to the null character:

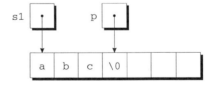

The second while statement implements step (2). The loop body copies one character from where s2 points to where p points, then increments both p and s2. If s2 originally points to the string "def", here's what the strings will look like after the first loop iteration:

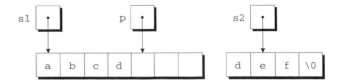

The loop terminates when s2 points to the null character:

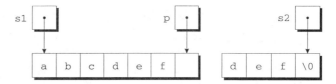

After putting a null character where p is pointing, strcat returns.

By a process similar to the one we used for strlen, we can condense the definition of strcat, arriving at the following version:

```
char *strcat(char *s1, const char *s2)
{
  char *p = s1;

  while (*p)
    p++;
  while (*p++ = *s2++)
    ;
  return s1;
}
```

The heart of our streamlined strcat function is the "string copy" idiom:

idiom
```
while (*p++ = *s2++)
  ;
```

If we ignore the two ++ operators, the expression inside the parentheses simplifies to an ordinary assignment:

```
*p = *s2
```

This expression copies a character from where s2 points to where p points. After the assignment, both p and s2 are incremented, thanks to the two ++ operators. Repeatedly executing this expression has the effect of copying a series of characters from where s2 points to where p points.

But what causes the loop to terminate? Since the primary operator inside the parentheses is assignment, the while statement tests the value of the assignment—the character that was copied. All characters except the null character test true, so the loop won't terminate until the null character has been copied. And since the loop terminates *after* the assignment, we don't need a separate statement to put a null character at the end of the new string.

13.7 Arrays of Strings

Let's now turn to a common problem that we'll encounter when working with strings: What's the best way to store an array of strings? The obvious solution is to create a two-dimensional array of characters, then store the strings in the array, one per row. Consider the following example:

```
char planets[][8] = {"Mercury", "Venus", "Earth",
                     "Mars", "Jupiter", "Saturn",
                     "Uranus", "Neptune", "Pluto"};
```

Although we're allowed to omit the number of rows in the `planets` array (since that's obvious from the number of elements in the initializer), C requires that we specify the number of columns. Here's what the array would look like:

	0	1	2	3	4	5	6	7
0	M	e	r	c	u	r	y	\0
1	V	e	n	u	s	\0	\0	\0
2	E	a	r	t	h	\0	\0	\0
3	M	a	r	s	\0	\0	\0	\0
4	J	u	p	i	t	e	r	\0
5	S	a	t	u	r	n	\0	\0
6	U	r	a	n	u	s	\0	\0
7	N	e	p	t	u	n	e	\0
8	P	l	u	t	o	\0	\0	\0

Not all our strings were long enough to fill an entire row of the array, so C padded them with null characters. There's a bit of wasted space in this array, since only three planets have names long enough to require eight characters (including the terminating null character). The `remind.c` program (Section 13.5) is a glaring example of this kind of waste. It stores reminders in rows of a two-dimensional character array, with 60 characters set aside for each reminder. In our example, the reminders ranged from 14 to 33 characters in length, so the amount of wasted space was considerable.

The inefficiency that's apparent in these examples is common when working with strings, since most collections of strings will have a mixture of long strings and short strings. What we need is a ***ragged array:*** an array whose rows can have different lengths. C doesn't provide a "ragged array type," but it does give us the tools to simulate one. The secret is to create an array whose elements are *pointers* to strings.

Here's the `planets` array again, this time as an array of pointers to strings:

```
char *planets[] = {"Mercury", "Venus", "Earth",
                   "Mars", "Jupiter", "Saturn",
                   "Uranus", "Neptune", "Pluto"};
```

Not much of a change, eh? We simply removed one pair of brackets and put an asterisk in front of `planets`. The effect on how `planets` is stored is dramatic, though:

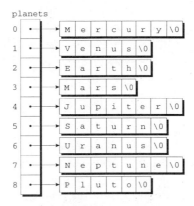

Each element of `planets` is a pointer to a null-terminated string. There are no longer any wasted characters in the strings, although we've had to allocate space for the pointers in the `planets` array.

To access one of the planet names, all we need do is subscript the `planets` array. Accessing a character in a planet name is done in the same way as accessing an element of a two-dimensional array, thanks to the close relationship between pointers and arrays. To search the `planets` array for strings beginning with the letter M, for example, we might use the following loop:

```
for (i = 0; i < 9; i++)
  if (planets[i][0] == 'M')
    printf("%s begins with M\n", planets[i]);
```

Command-Line Arguments

When we run a program, we'll often need to supply it with information—a file name, perhaps, or a switch that modifies the program's behavior. Consider the UNIX `ls` command. If we run `ls` by typing

```
ls
```

it will display the names of the files in the current directory. (The corresponding DOS command is `dir`.) But if we instead type

```
ls -l
```

then `ls` will display a "long" (detailed) listing of files, showing the size of each file, the file's owner, the date and time the file was last modified, and so forth. To modify the behavior of `ls` further, we can specify that it show details for just one file:

```
ls -l remind.c
```

`ls` will display detailed information about the file named `remind.c`.

Q&A

Q&A

Command-line information is available to all programs, not just operating system commands. To obtain access to these *command-line arguments* (called *program parameters* in the standard), we must define main as a function with two parameters, which are customarily named argc and argv:

```
main(int argc, char *argv[])
{
    ...
}
```

argc ("argument count") is the number of command-line arguments (including the name of the program itself). argv ("argument vector") is an array of pointers to the command-line arguments, which are stored in string form. argv[0] points to the name of the program, while argv[1] through argv[argc-1] point to the remaining command-line arguments.

argv has one additional element, argv[argc], which is always a *null pointer*—a special pointer that points to nothing. We'll discuss null pointers in a later chapter; for now, all we need to know is that the macro NULL represents the null pointer.

null pointers ➤ 17.1

If the user enters the command line

```
ls -l remind.c
```

then argc will be 3, argv[0] will point to a string containing the program name, argv[1] will point to the string "-l", argv[2] will point to the string "remind.c", and argv[3] will be a null pointer:

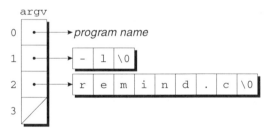

This figure doesn't show the program name in detail, since it may include a path or other information that depends on the operating system. If the program name isn't available, argv[0] points to an empty string.

Since argv is an array of pointers, we already know how to access command-line arguments. Typically, a program that expects command-line arguments will set up a loop that examines each argument in turn. One way to set up such a loop is to use an integer variable as an index into the argv array. For example, the following loop prints the command-line arguments, one per line:

```
int i;

for (i = 1; i < argc; i++)
  printf("%s\n", argv[i]);
```

Another technique is to set up a pointer to `argv[1]`, then increment the pointer repeatedly to step through the rest of the array. Since the last element of `argv` is always a null pointer, the loop can terminate when it finds a null pointer in the array:

```
char **p;

for (p = &argv[1]; *p != NULL; p++)
  printf("%s\n", *p);
```

Since p is a *pointer* to a *pointer* to a character, we've got to use it carefully. Setting p equal to `&argv[1]` makes sense; `argv[1]` is a pointer to a character, so `&argv[1]` will be a pointer to a pointer. The test `*p != NULL` is OK, since `*p` and NULL are both pointers. Incrementing p looks good; p points to an array element, so incrementing it will advance it to the next element. Printing `*p` is fine, since `*p` is a pointer to a character.

PROGRAM   **Checking Planet Names**

Our next program, `planet.c`, illustrates how to access command-line arguments. The program is designed to check a series of strings to see which ones are names of planets. When the program is run, the user will put the strings to be tested on the command line:

```
planet Jupiter venus Earth fred
```

The program will indicate whether or not each string is a planet name; if it is, the program will also display the planet's number (with planet 1 being the one closest to the sun):

```
Jupiter is planet 5
venus is not a planet
Earth is planet 3
fred is not a planet
```

Notice that the program doesn't recognize a string as a planet name unless its first letter is upper-case and its remaining letters are lower-case.

planet.c
```
/* Checks planet names */

#include <stdio.h>
#include <string.h>

#define NUM_PLANETS 9

main(int argc, char *argv[])
{
  char *planets[] = {"Mercury", "Venus", "Earth",
                     "Mars", "Jupiter", "Saturn",
                     "Uranus", "Neptune", "Pluto"};
  int i, j;
```

```
      for (i = 1; i < argc; i++) {
        for (j = 0; j < NUM_PLANETS; j++)
          if (strcmp(argv[i], planets[j]) == 0) {
            printf("%s is planet %d\n", argv[i], j+1);
            break;
          }
        if (j == NUM_PLANETS)
          printf("%s is not a planet\n", argv[i]);
      }

      return 0;
    }
```

The program visits each command-line argument in turn, comparing it with the strings in the `planets` array until it finds a match or reaches the end of the array. The most interesting part of the program is the call of `strcmp`, in which the arguments are `argv[i]` (a pointer to a command-line argument) and `planets[j]` (a pointer to a planet name).

Q & A

Q: **How long can a string literal be?**

A: According to the C standard, compilers must allow string literals to be at least 509 characters long. (Yes, you read that right—509. Don't ask.) Many compilers will allow string literals of much greater length.

Q: **Why aren't string literals called "string constants"?**

A: Because they're not necessarily constant. Since string literals are accessed through pointers, there's nothing to prevent a program from modifying the characters in a string literal.

Q: **Changing a string literal seems harmless enough. Why does Standard C discourage this practice? [p. 242]**

A: Some compilers try to reduce memory requirements by storing single copies of identical string literals. Consider the following example:

```
char *p = "abc", *q = "abc";
```

Some compilers will store `"abc"` just once, making both `p` and `q` point to it. If we were to change `"abc"` through the pointer `p`, the string that `q` points to would also be affected. Needless to say, this could lead to some annoying bugs.

Despite Standard C's injunction against modifying string literals, some programmers do so anyway, knowing that their compiler stores string literals uniquely. I recommend avoiding this practice, however, since it reduces the portability of the program.

Q: **Should every array of characters include room for a null character?**

A: Not necessarily, since not every array of characters is used as a string. Including room for the null character (and actually putting one into the array) is necessary only if you're planning to call a function that requires a null-terminated string.

You do *not* need a null character if you'll only be performing operations on individual characters. For example, we might have an array of characters that we'll use as a translation table:

```
char translation_table[128];
```

The only operation we'll perform on this array is subscripting. We don't view `translation_table` as a string, and we won't perform any string operations on it.

Q: **If `printf` and `scanf` expect their first argument to be of type `char *`, does that mean that the argument can be a string *variable* instead of a string *literal*?**

A: Yes, as the following example shows:

```
char fmt[] = "%d\n";
int i;

printf(fmt, i);
```

This ability opens the door to some intriguing possibilities—reading a format string as input, for example.

Q: **If I want `printf` to write a string `str`, can't I just supply `str` as the format string, as in the following example?**

```
printf(str);
```

A: Yes, but it's risky. If `str` contains the `%` character, you won't get the desired result, since `printf` will assume the `%` is the beginning of a conversion specification.

*Q: **How can `read_line` detect whether `getchar` has failed to read a character? [p. 249]**

A: If it can't read a character, either because of an error or because of end-of-file, `getchar` returns the value EOF, which has type `int`. Here's a revised version of `read_line` that tests the return value of `getchar` for EOF. Changes are marked in **bold**:

EOF macro ➤22.4

```
int read_line(char str[], int n)
{
  int ch;
  int i = 0;

  while ((ch = getchar()) != '\n' && ch != EOF)
    if (i < n)
      str[i++] = ch;
```

```
        str[i] = '\0';
        return i;
}
```

Q: **Why does `strcmp` return a number that's less than, equal to, or greater than zero? Does the return value have any significance? [p. 253]**

A: `strcmp`'s return value probably stems from the way the function is traditionally written. Consider the version in Kernighan and Ritchie's *The C Programming Language:*

```
int strcmp(char *s, char *t)
{
    int i;

    for (i = 0; s[i] == t[i]; i++)
        if (s[i] == '\0')
            return 0;
    return s[i] - t[i];
}
```

The return value is the difference between the first "mismatched" characters in the s and t strings, which will be negative if s points to a "smaller" string than t and positive if s points to a "larger" string. There's no guarantee that `strcmp` is actually written this way, though, so it's best not to assume that the magnitude of its return value has any particular meaning.

Q: **My compiler gives the warning *"Possibly incorrect assignment"* when I try to compile the `while` statement in the `strcat` function:**

```
while (*p++ = *s2++)
    ;
```

What am I doing wrong?

A: Nothing. Many compilers—but not all, by any means—issue a warning if you use = where == is normally expected. This warning is valid at least 95% of the time, and it will save you a lot of debugging if you heed it. Unfortunately, the warning isn't relevant in this particular example; we actually *do* mean to use =, not ==. To get rid of the warning, rewrite the `while` loop as follows:

```
while ((*p++ = *s2++) != 0)
    ;
```

Since the `while` statement normally tests whether `*p++ = *s2++` is not 0, we haven't changed the meaning of the `while` statement. The warning goes away, however, since the statement now tests a condition, not an assignment.

Q: **Are the `strlen` and `strcat` functions actually written as shown in Section 13.6?**

A: Possibly, although it's common practice for compiler vendors to write these functions—and many other string functions—in assembly language instead of C. The string functions need to be as fast as possible, since they're used often and have to deal with strings of arbitrary length. Writing these functions in assembly language makes it possible to achieve great efficiency by taking advantage of any special string-handling instructions that the CPU may provide.

Q: Why does the C standard use the term "program parameters" instead of "command-line arguments"? [p. 264]

A: Programs aren't always run from a command line. In a windowing environment, for example, programs are launched with a mouse click. In such an environment, there's no traditional command line, although there may be other ways of passing information to a program; the term "program parameters" leaves the door open for these alternatives.

Q: Do I have to use the names `argc` and `argv` for `main`'s parameters? [p. 264]

A: No. Using the names `argc` and `argv` is merely a convention, not a language requirement.

Q: I've seen `argv` declared as `**argv` instead of `*argv[]`. Is this legal?

A: Certainly. When declaring a parameter, writing `*a` is always the same as writing `a[]`, regardless of the type of `a`'s elements.

Q: We've seen how to set up an array whose elements are pointers to string literals. Are there any other applications for arrays of pointers?

A: Yes. Although we've focused on arrays of pointers to character strings, that's not the only application of arrays of pointers. We could just as easily have an array whose elements point to any type of data, whether in array form or not. Arrays of pointers are particularly useful in conjunction with dynamic storage allocation.

dynamic storage allocation ➤*17.1*

Exercises

Section 13.3

1. The following function calls supposedly write a single new-line character, but some are incorrect. Identify which calls don't work and explain why.

(a) `printf("%c", '\n');`   (g) `putchar('\n');`
(b) `printf("%c", "\n");`   (h) `putchar("\n");`
(c) `printf("%s", '\n');`   (i) `puts('\n');`
(d) `printf("%s", "\n");`   (j) `puts("\n");`
(e) `printf('\n');`   (k) `puts("");`
(f) `printf("\n");`

2. Suppose that p is defined as follows:

`char *p = "abc";`

Which of the following function calls are legal? Show the output produced by each legal call, and explain why the others are illegal.

(a) `putchar(p);`
(b) `putchar(*p);`
(c) `puts(p);`
(d) `puts(*p);`

*3. Suppose that we call `scanf` as follows:

```
scanf("%d%s%d", &i, s, &j);
```

If the user enters `12abc34 56def78`, what will the values of `i`, `s`, and `j` be after the call? (Assume that `i` and `j` are `int` variables and `s` is an array of characters.)

4. Write each of the following variations on the `read_line` function:

(a) Have it skip white space before beginning to store input characters.
(b) Have it stop reading at the first white-space character. *Hint:* To determine whether or not a character is white space, call the `isspace` function.

isspace function ➤*23.4*

(c) Have it stop reading at the first new-line character, then store the new-line character in the string.
(d) Have it leave behind characters that it doesn't have room to store.

Section 13.4

5. (a) Write a function named `strcap` that capitalizes all letters in its argument. The argument will be a null-terminated string containing any ASCII characters, not just letters. Use array subscripting to access the characters in the string. *Hint:* Use the `toupper` function to convert each character to upper-case.

toupper function ➤*23.4*

(b) Rewrite the `strcap` function, this time using pointer arithmetic to access the characters in the string.

6. Write a function named `censor` that modifies a string by replacing every occurrence of the letters `foo` by `xxx`. For example, the string `"food fool"` would become `"xxxd xxxl"`. Make the function as short as possible without sacrificing clarity.

*7. What does the following program print?

```
#include <stdio.h>

main()
{
  char s[] = "Hsjodi", *p;

  for (p = &s[5]; p >= s; p--) --*p;
  puts(s);
  return 0;
}
```

*8. Let f be the following function:

```
int f(char *s, char *t)
{
  char *p1, *p2;

  for (p1 = s; *p1; p1++) {
    for (p2 = t; *p2; p2++)
      if (*p1 == *p2) break;
    if (*p2 == '\0') break;
  }
  return p1 - s;
}
```

(a) What is the value of f("abcd", "babc")?

(b) What is the value of f("abcd", "bcd")?

(c) In general, what value does f return when passed two strings s and t?

Section 13.5   9.   Suppose that str is an array of characters. Which one of the following statements is not equivalent to the other three?

(a) `*str = 0;`

(b) `str[0] = '\0';`

(c) `strcpy(str, "");`

(d) `strcat(str, "");`

*10.   What will be the value of the string str after the following statements have been executed?

```
strcpy(str, "tire-bouchon");
strcpy(&str[4], "d-or-wi");
strcat(str, "red?");
```

11.   What will be the values of the strings s1 and s2 after the following statements have been executed?

```
strcpy(s1, "computer");
strcpy(s2, "science");
if (strcmp(s1, s2) < 0)
  strcat(s1, s2);
else
  strcat(s2, s1);
s2[strlen(s2)-6] = '\0';
```

12.   The following function supposedly creates an identical copy of a string. What's wrong with the function?

```
char *strdup(const char *p)
{
  char *q;

  strcpy(q, p);
  return q;
}
```

13.   The Q&A section at the end of this chapter shows how the strcmp function might be written using array subscripting. Modify the function to use pointer arithmetic instead.

14.   Write a program that finds the "smallest" and "largest" in a series of words. After the user enters the words, the program will determine which words would come first and last if the words were listed in dictionary order. The program must stop accepting input when the user enters a four-letter word. Assume that no word is more than 20 letters long. An interactive session with the program might look like this:

```
Enter word: dog
Enter word: zebra
Enter word: rabbit
Enter word: catfish
Enter word: walrus
Enter word: cat
Enter word: fish
```

```
Smallest word: cat
Largest word: zebra
```

Hint: Use two strings named smallest_word and largest_word to keep track of the "smallest" and "largest" words entered so far. Each time the user enters a new word, use strcmp to compare it with smallest_word; if the new word is "smaller," use strcpy to save it in smallest_word. Do a similar comparison with largest_word. Use strlen to determine when the user has entered a four-letter word.

15. Improve the remind.c program in the following ways:

(a) Have the program print an error message and ignore a reminder if the corresponding day is negative or larger than 31. *Hint:* Use the continue statement.

(b) Allow the user to enter a day, a 24-hour time (possibly blank), and a reminder. The printed reminder list should be sorted first by day, then by time. (The original remind.c program allows the user to enter a time, but it's treated as part of the reminder.)

(c) Have the program print a one-*year* reminder list. Require the user to enter days in the form *month/day*.

Section 13.6

16. Use the techniques of Section 13.6 to condense the count_spaces function (Section 13.4). In particular, replace the for statement by a while loop.

Section 13.7

17. Modify the deal.c program of Section 8.2 so that it prints the full names of the cards it deals:

```
Enter number of cards in hand: 5
Your hand:
Seven of clubs
Two of spades
Five of diamonds
Ace of spades
Two of hearts
```

Hint: Replace the rank_code and suit_code arrays by arrays containing pointers to strings.

18. Write a program named reverse.c that echoes its command-line arguments in reverse order. Running the program by typing

```
reverse void and null
```

should produce the following output:

```
null and void
```

19. Write a program named sum.c that adds up its command-line arguments, which are assumed to be integers. Running the program by typing

```
sum 8 24 62
```

should produce the following output:

```
Total: 94
```

atoi function ➤*26.2*   *Hint:* Use the atoi function to convert each command-line argument from string form to integer form.

20. Improve the planet.c program by having it ignore case when comparing command-line arguments with strings in the planets array.

14 The Preprocessor

*There will always be things we wish to say in our programs
that in all known languages can only be said poorly.*

In previous chapters, I've used the `#define` and `#include` directives without going into detail about what they do. These directives—and others that we haven't yet covered—are handled by the *preprocessor*, a piece of software that edits C programs just prior to compilation. Its reliance on a preprocessor makes C (along with C++) unique among major programming languages.

The preprocessor is a powerful tool, but it also can be a source of hard-to-find bugs. Moreover, the preprocessor can easily be misused to create programs that are almost impossible to understand. Although some C programmers depend heavily on the preprocessor, I recommend that it—like so many other things in life—be used in moderation. Modern C programming style calls for decreased reliance on the preprocessor. In C++, language changes make it possible to limit use of the preprocessor to an even greater degree.

This chapter begins by describing how the preprocessor works (Section 14.1) and giving some general rules that affect all preprocessor directives (Section 14.2). Sections 14.3 and 14.4 cover two of the preprocessor's major capabilities: macro definition and conditional compilation. (I'll defer detailed coverage of file inclusion, the other major capability, until Chapter 15.) Section 14.5 discusses the preprocessor's lesser-used directives: `#error`, `#line`, and `#pragma`.

14.1 How the Preprocessor Works

The behavior of the preprocessor is controlled by *directives:* commands that begin with a # character. We've encountered two of these directives, `#define` and `#include`, in previous chapters.

The #define directive defines a *macro*—a name that represents something else, typically a constant of some kind. The preprocessor responds to a #define directive by storing the name of the macro together with its definition. When the macro is used later in the program, the preprocessor "expands" the macro, replacing it by its defined value.

The #include directive tells the preprocessor to open a particular file and "include" its contents as part of the file being compiled. For example, the line

```
#include <stdio.h>
```

instructs the preprocessor to open the file named stdio.h and bring its contents into the program. (Among other things, stdio.h contains prototypes for C's standard input/output functions.)

The following diagram shows the preprocessor's role in the compilation process:

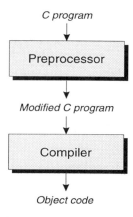

The input to the preprocessor is a C program, possibly containing directives. The preprocessor executes these directives, removing them in the process. The output of the preprocessor is another C program: an edited version of the original program, containing no directives. The preprocessor's output goes directly into the compiler, which checks the program for errors and translates it to object code (machine instructions).

To see what the preprocessor does, let's apply it to the celsius.c program from Section 2.6. Here's the original program:

```
/* Converts a Fahrenheit temperature to Celsius */

#include <stdio.h>

#define FREEZING_PT 32.0
#define SCALE_FACTOR (5.0 / 9.0)

main()
{
  float fahrenheit, celsius;
```

```
      printf("Enter Fahrenheit temperature: ");
      scanf("%f", &fahrenheit);

      celsius = (fahrenheit - FREEZING_PT) * SCALE_FACTOR;

      printf("Celsius equivalent is: %.1f\n", celsius);

      return 0;
}
```

After preprocessing, the program will have the following appearance:

Blank line
Blank line
Lines brought in from stdio.h
Blank line
Blank line
Blank line
Blank line
```
main()
{
   float fahrenheit, celsius;

   printf("Enter Fahrenheit temperature: ");
   scanf("%f", &fahrenheit);

   celsius = (fahrenheit - 32.0) * (5.0 / 9.0);

   printf("Celsius equivalent is: %.1f\n", celsius);

   return 0;
}
```

The preprocessor responded to the #include directive by bringing in the contents of stdio.h, which is not shown here because of its length. The preprocessor also removed the #define directives and replaced FREEZING_PT and SCALE_FACTOR wherever they appeared later in the file. Notice that the preprocessor doesn't remove lines containing directives; instead, it simply makes them empty.

As this example shows, the preprocessor does a bit more than just execute directives. In particular, it replaces each comment with a single space character. Some preprocessors go further and remove unnecessary white-space characters, including spaces and tabs at the beginning of indented lines.

In the early days of C, the preprocessor was a separate program that fed its output into the compiler. Nowadays, the preprocessor is often integrated with the compiler (to improve compilation speed); nevertheless, we still think of the two as separate programs. In fact, most C compilers provide a way to view the output of the preprocessor. Some compilers generate preprocessor output when a certain option is specified (usually –P under UNIX). Others come with a stand-alone program that behaves just like the integrated preprocessor. Check your compiler's documentation for more information.

A word of caution: The preprocessor has only a limited knowledge of C. As a result, it's quite capable of creating illegal programs as it executes directives. Often the original program looks fine, making errors harder to find. In complicated programs, examining the output of the preprocessor may prove useful for locating this kind of error.

14.2   Preprocessor Directives

Most preprocessor directives fall into one of three categories:

- *Macro definition.* The #define directive defines a macro; the #undef directive removes a macro definition.
- *File inclusion.* The #include directive causes the contents of a specified file to be included in a program.
- *Conditional compilation.* The #if, #ifdef, #ifndef, #elif, #else, and #endif directives allow blocks of text to be either included in or excluded from a program, depending on conditions that can be tested by the preprocessor.

The remaining directives—#error, #line, and #pragma—are more specialized and therefore used less often. We'll devote the rest of this chapter to an in-depth examination of preprocessor directives. The only directive we won't discuss in detail is #include, since it's covered in Section 15.2.

Before we go further, though, let's look at a few rules that apply to all directives:

- *Directives always begin with the # symbol.* The # symbol need not be at the beginning of a line, as long as only white space precedes it. After the # comes the name of the directive, followed by any other information the directive requires.
- *Any number of spaces and horizontal tab characters may separate the tokens in a directive.* For example, the following directive is legal:

```
#     define     N     100
```

- *Directives always end at the first new-line character, unless explicitly continued.* To continue a directive to the next line, we must end the current line with a \ character. For example, the following directive defines a macro that represents the capacity of a hard disk, measured in bytes:

```
#define DISK_CAPACITY (SIDES *               \
                       TRACKS_PER_SIDE *    \
                       SECTORS_PER_TRACK *  \
                       BYTES_PER_SECTOR)
```

- *Directives can appear anywhere in a program.* Although we usually put #define and #include directives at the beginning of a file, other directives are more likely to show up later, even in the middle of function definitions.
- *Comments may appear on the same line as a directive.* In fact, it's good practice to put a comment at the end of a macro definition to explain the macro's significance:

```
#define FREEZING_PT 32.0    /* Freezing point of water */
```

14.3 Macro Definition

The macros that we've been using since Chapter 2 are known as *simple macros:* they have no parameters. The preprocessor also supports *parameterized macros.* We'll look first at simple macros, then at parameterized macros. After covering them separately, we'll examine properties shared by both.

Simple Macros

The definition of a simple macro has the form

#define directive (simple macro)

> #define *identifier replacement-list*

replacement-list is any sequence of C tokens; it may include identifiers, keywords, numbers, character constants, string literals, operators, and punctuation. When it encounters a macro definition, the preprocessor makes a note that *identifier* represents *replacement-list*; wherever *identifier* appears later in the file, the preprocessor substitutes *replacement-list*.

Don't put any extra symbols in a macro definition—they'll become part of the replacement list. Putting the = symbol in a macro definition is a common error:

```
#define N = 100    /*** WRONG ***/

int a[N];          /* becomes int a[= 100]; */
```

In this example, we've (incorrectly) defined N to be a pair of tokens (= and 100). Ending a macro definition with a semicolon is another popular mistake:

```
#define N 100;    /*** WRONG ***/

int a[N];          /* becomes int a[100;]; */
```

Here N is defined to be the tokens 100 and ;.

The compiler will detect most errors caused by extra symbols in a macro definition. Unfortunately, the compiler will flag each use of the macro as incorrect, rather than identifying the actual culprit—the macro's definition—which will have been removed by the preprocessor.

Q&A

Simple macros are primarily used for defining what Kernighan and Ritchie call "manifest constants." Using macros, we can give names to numeric, character, and string values:

```
#define STR_LEN 80
#define TRUE    1
#define FALSE   0
#define PI      3.14159
#define CR      '\r'
#define EOS     '\0'
#define MEM_ERR "Error: not enough memory"
```

Using #define to create names for constants has several significant advantages:

- *It makes programs easier to read.* The name of the macro—if well-chosen—helps the reader understand the meaning of the constant. The alternative is a program full of "magic numbers" that can easily mystify the reader.

- *It makes programs easier to modify.* We can change the value of a constant throughout a program by modifying a single macro definition. "Hard-coded" constants are much harder to change, especially since they sometimes appear in a slightly altered form. (For example, a program with an array of length 100 may have a loop that goes from 0 to 99. If we merely try to locate occurrences of 100 in the program, we'll miss the 99.)

- *It helps avoid inconsistencies and typographical errors.* If a numerical constant like 3.14159 appears many times in a program, chances are it will occasionally be written 3.1416 or 3.14195 by accident.

Although simple macros are most often used to define names for constants, they do have other applications:

- *Making minor changes to the syntax of C.* We can—in effect—alter the syntax of C by defining macros that serve as alternate names for C symbols. For example, programmers who prefer Pascal's begin and end to C's { and } can define the following macros:

```
#define BEGIN {
#define END   }
```

We could go so far as to invent our own language. For example, we might create a LOOP "statement" that establishes an infinite loop:

```
#define LOOP for (;;)
```

Changing the syntax of C usually isn't a good idea, though, since it can make programs harder for others to understand.

- **Renaming types.** In Section 5.2, we created a Boolean type by renaming `int`:

```
#define BOOL int
```

type definitions ➤ 7.6 Although some programmers use macros for this purpose, type definitions are a superior way to define new types.

- **Controlling conditional compilation.** Macros play an important role in controlling conditional compilation, as we'll see in Section 14.4. For example, the presence of the following line in a program might indicate that it's to be compiled in "debugging mode," with extra statements included to produce debugging output:

```
#define DEBUG
```

Incidentally, it's legal for a macro's replacement list to be empty, as this example shows.

When macros are used as constants, C programmers customarily use only upper-case letters in their names. However, there's no consensus as to how to capitalize macros used for other purposes. Since macros (especially parameterized macros) can be a source of bugs, some programmers like to draw attention to them by writing their names in upper-case letters. Others prefer lower-case, following the style of Kernighan and Ritchie's *The C Programming Language*.

Parameterized Macros

The definition of a parameterized macro has the form

**#define directive
(parameterized macro)**

> #define *identifier*(x_1 , x_2 , ... , x_n) *replacement-list*

where x_1, x_2, ..., x_n are identifiers (the macro's **parameters**). The parameters may appear as many times as desired in the replacement list.

There must be *no space* between the macro name and the left parenthesis. If space is left, the preprocessor will assume that we're defining a simple macro, with $(x_1, x_2, ..., x_n)$ part of *replacement-list*.

When the preprocessor encounters the definition of a parameterized macro, it stores the definition away for later use. Wherever a macro **invocation** of the form *identifier*(y_1, y_2, ..., y_n) appears later in the program (where y_1, y_2, ..., y_n are sequences of tokens), the preprocessor replaces it with *replacement-list*, substituting y_1 for x_1, y_2 for x_2, and so forth.

For example, suppose that we've defined the following macros:

```
#define MAX(x,y)    ((x)>(y)?(x):(y))
#define IS_EVEN(n)  ((n)%2==0)
```

Now suppose that the following statements appear later in the program:

```
i = MAX(j+k, m-n);
if (IS_EVEN(i)) i++;
```

The preprocessor will replace these lines by

```
i = ((j+k)>(m-n)?(j+k):(m-n));
if (((i)%2==0)) i++;
```

As this example shows, parameterized macros often serve as simple functions. MAX behaves like a function that computes the larger of two values. IS_EVEN behaves like a function that returns 1 if its argument is an even number and 0 otherwise.

Here's a more complicated macro that behaves like a function:

```
#define TOUPPER(c) ('a'<=(c)&&(c)<='z'?(c)-'a'+'A':(c))
```

This macro tests whether the character c is between 'a' and 'z'. If so, it produces the upper-case version of c by subtracting 'a' and adding 'A'. If not, it leaves c unchanged. Character-handling macros like this one are so useful that the C library provides a collection of them in <ctype.h>; one of them, toupper, behaves the same as our TOUPPER example (but is more efficient and more portable).

<ctype.h> header ➤23.4

A parameterized macro may have an empty parameter list. Here's an example:

```
#define getchar() getc(stdin)
```

The empty parameter list isn't really needed, but it makes getchar resemble a function. (Yes, this is the same getchar that belongs to <stdio.h>. And yes, getchar is really a macro, not a function, although it behaves like a function.)

Using a parameterized macro instead of a true function has a couple of advantages:

- ■ *The program may be slightly faster.* A function call usually requires some overhead during program execution—context information must be saved, arguments copied, and so forth. A macro invocation, on the other hand, requires no run-time overhead.

- ■ *Macros are "generic."* Macro parameters, unlike function parameters, have no particular type. As a result, a macro can accept arguments of any type, provided that the resulting program—after preprocessing—is valid. For example, we could use the MAX macro to find the larger of two values of type int, long int, float, double, and so forth.

But parameterized macros have their disadvantages:

- ■ *The compiled code will often be larger.* Each macro invocation causes the insertion of the macro's replacement list, thereby increasing the size of the source program (and hence the compiled code). The more often the macro is used, the more pronounced this effect is. The problem is compounded when macro invocations are nested. Consider what happens when we use MAX to find the largest of three numbers:

```
n = MAX(i, MAX(j, k));
```

Here's the same statement after preprocessing:

```
n = ((i)>(((j)>(k)?(j):(k)))?(i):(((j)>(k)?(j):(k))));
```

- **Arguments aren't type-checked.** When a function is called, the compiler checks each argument to see if it has the appropriate type. If not, either the argument is converted to the proper type or the compiler produces an error message. Macro arguments aren't checked by the preprocessor, nor are they converted.

- **It's not possible to have a pointer to a macro.** As we'll see in Section 17.7, C allows pointers to functions, a concept that's quite useful in certain programming situations. Macros are removed during preprocessing, so there's no corresponding notion of "pointer to a macro"; as a result, macros can't be used in these situations.

- **A macro may evaluate its arguments more than once.** A function evaluates its arguments only once; a macro may evaluate its arguments two or more times. Evaluating an argument more than once can cause unexpected behavior if the argument has side effects. Consider what happens if one of MAX's arguments has a side effect:

```
n = MAX(i++, j);
```

Here's the same line after preprocessing:

```
n = ((i++)>(j)?(i++):(j));
```

If i is larger than j, then i will be (incorrectly) incremented twice, and n may be assigned the wrong value.

 Errors caused by evaluating a macro argument more than once can be difficult to find, because a macro invocation looks the same as a function call. To make matters worse, a macro may work properly most of the time, failing only when certain arguments have side effects. For self-protection, it's a good idea to avoid side effects in arguments.

Parameterized macros are good for more than just simulating functions. In particular, they're often used as patterns for segments of code that we find ourselves repeating. Suppose that we grow tired of writing

```
printf("%d\n", x);
```

every time we need to print an integer x. We might define the following macro, which makes it easier to display integers:

```
#define PRINT_INT(x) printf("%d\n", x)
```

Once `PRINT_INT` has been defined, the preprocessor will turn the line

```
PRINT_INT(i/j);
```

into

```
printf("%d\n", i/j);
```

The # Operator

Macro definitions may contain two special operators, # and ##. Neither operator is recognized by the compiler; instead, they're executed during preprocessing.

Q&A　　The # operator converts a macro argument into a string literal; it can appear only in the replacement list of a parameterized macro. (Some C programmers refer to the # operation as "stringization"; others feel that this term is too great an abuse of the English language.)

There are a number of uses for #; let's consider just one. Suppose that we decide to use the `PRINT_INT` macro during debugging as a convenient way to print the values of integer variables and expressions. The # operator makes it possible for `PRINT_INT` to label each value that it prints. Here's an improved version of `PRINT_INT`:

```
#define PRINT_INT(x) printf(#x " = %d\n", x)
```

The # operator in front of x instructs the preprocessor to create a string literal from `PRINT_INT`'s argument. Thus, the invocation

```
PRINT_INT(i/j);
```

will become

```
printf("i/j" " = %d\n", i/j);
```

Adjacent string literals are concatenated in C, so this statement is equivalent to

```
printf("i/j = %d\n", i/j);
```

When the program is executed, `printf` will display both the expression i/j and its value. If i is 11 and j is 2, for example, the output will be

```
i/j = 5
```

The ## Operator

The ## operator can "paste" two tokens (identifiers, for example) together to form a single token. (Not surprisingly, the ## operation is known as "token-pasting.") If one of the operands is a macro parameter, pasting occurs after the parameter has been replaced by the corresponding argument. Consider the following macro:

```
#define MK_ID(n) i##n
```

When `MK_ID` is invoked (as `MK_ID(1)`, say), the preprocessor first replaces the parameter n by the argument (1 in this case). Next, the preprocessor joins i and 1 to make a single token (i1). The following declaration uses `MK_ID` to create three identifiers:

```
int MK_ID(1), MK_ID(2), MK_ID(3);
```

After preprocessing, this declaration becomes

```
int i1, i2, i3;
```

The `##` operator isn't one of the most frequently used features of the preprocessor; in fact, it's hard to think of many situations that require it. To find a realistic application of `##`, let's reconsider the `MAX` macro described earlier in this section. As we observed then, `MAX` doesn't behave properly if its arguments have side effects. The alternative to using the `MAX` macro is to write a `max` function. Unfortunately, one `max` function usually isn't enough; we may need a `max` function whose arguments are `int` values, one whose arguments are `float` values, and so on. All these versions of `max` would be identical except for the types of the arguments and the return type, so it seems a shame to define each one from scratch.

The solution is to write a macro that expands into the definition of a `max` function. The macro will have a single parameter, `type`, which represents the type of the arguments and the return value. There's just one snag: if we use the macro to create more than one `max` function, the program won't compile. (C doesn't allow two functions to have the same name if both are defined in the same file.) To solve this problem, we'll use the `##` operator to create a different name for each version of `max`. Here's what the macro will look like:

```
#define GENERIC_MAX(type)           \
type type##_max(type x, type y) \
{                                   \
  return x > y ? x : y;             \
}
```

Notice how `type` is joined with `_max` to form the name of the new function.

Now, let's say that we need a `max` function that works with `float` values. Here's how we'd use `GENERIC_MAX` to define the function:

```
GENERIC_MAX(float)
```

The preprocessor expands this line into the following code:

```
float float_max(float x, float y) { return x > y ? x : y; }
```

General Properties of Macros

Now that we've discussed both simple and parameterized macros, let's look at some rules that apply to both:

■ *A macro's replacement list may contain invocations of other macros.* For example, we could define the macro `TWO_PI` in terms of the macro `PI`:

```
#define PI      3.14159
#define TWO_PI (2*PI)
```

When the preprocessor encounters `TWO_PI` later in the program, it replaces it by `(2*PI)`. The preprocessor then ***rescans*** the replacement list to see if it contains invocations of other macros (`PI` in this case). The preprocessor will rescan the replacement list as many times as necessary to eliminate all macro names.

Q&A

■ *The preprocessor replaces only entire tokens, not portions of tokens.* As a result, the preprocessor ignores macro names that are embedded in identifiers, character constants, and string literals. For example, suppose that a program contains the following lines:

```
#define SIZE 256

int BUFFER_SIZE;

if (BUFFER_SIZE > SIZE)
  puts("Error: SIZE exceeded");
```

After preprocessing, these lines will have the following appearance:

```
int BUFFER_SIZE;

if (BUFFER_SIZE > 256)
  puts("Error: SIZE exceeded");
```

The identifier `BUFFER_SIZE` and the string `"Error: SIZE exceeded"` weren't affected by preprocessing, even though both contain the word `SIZE`.

■ *A macro definition normally remains in effect until the end of the file in which it appears.* Since macros are handled by the preprocessor, they don't obey normal scope rules. A macro defined inside a function definition isn't local to that function; it remains defined until the end of the file.

■ *A macro may not be defined twice unless the new definition is identical to the old one.* Minor differences in spacing are allowed, but the tokens in the macro's replacement list (and the parameters, if any) must be the same.

■ *Macros may be "undefined" by the **#undef** directive.* The #undef directive has the form

#undef directive

```
#undef identifier
```

where *identifier* is a macro name. For example, the directive

```
#undef N
```

removes the current definition of the macro N. (If N hasn't been defined as a macro, the #undef directive has no effect.) One use of #undef is to remove the existing definition of a macro so that it can be given a new definition.

Parentheses in Macro Definitions

The replacement lists in our macro definitions have been full of parentheses. Is it really necessary to have so many? The answer is an emphatic yes; if we use fewer parentheses, the macros will sometimes give unexpected—and undesirable—results.

There are two rules to follow when deciding where to put parentheses in a macro definition. First, if the macro's replacement list contains an operator, always enclose the replacement list in parentheses:

```
#define TWO_PI (2*3.14159)
```

Second, if the macro has parameters, put parentheses around each parameter every time it appears in the replacement list:

```
#define SCALE(x) ((x)*10)
```

Without the parentheses, we can't guarantee that the compiler will treat replacement lists and arguments as whole expressions. The compiler may apply the rules of operator precedence and associativity in ways that we didn't anticipate.

To illustrate the importance of putting parentheses around the replacement list, consider the following macro definition, in which the parentheses are missing:

```
#define TWO_PI 2*3.14159
  /* needs parentheses around replacement list */
```

During preprocessing, the statement

```
conversion_factor = 360/TWO_PI;
```

becomes

```
conversion_factor = 360/2*3.14159;
```

The division will be performed before the multiplication, yielding a result different from the one intended.

Putting parentheses around the replacement list isn't enough if the macro has parameters—each occurrence of a parameter needs parentheses as well. For example, suppose that SCALE is defined as follows:

```
#define SCALE(x) (x*10)    /* needs parentheses around x */
```

During preprocessing, the statement

```
j = SCALE(i+1);
```

becomes

```
j = (i+1*10);
```

Since multiplication takes precedence over addition, this statement is equivalent to

```
j = i+10;
```

Of course, what we wanted was

```
j = (i+1)*10;
```

 A shortage of parentheses in a macro definition can cause some of C's most frustrating errors. The program will usually compile and the macro will appear to work, failing only at the least convenient times.

Creating Longer Macros

The comma operator can be useful for creating more sophisticated macros. In particular, we can use the comma operator to make the replacement list a series of expressions. For example, the following macro will read a string and then print it:

```
#define ECHO(s) (gets(s), puts(s))
```

Calls of `gets` and `puts` are expressions, so it's perfectly legal to combine them using the comma operator. We can use ECHO as though it were a function:

```
ECHO(str);    /* becomes (gets(str), puts(str)); */
```

Instead of using the comma operator, we could have enclosed the calls of `gets` and `puts` in braces to form a compound statement:

```
#define ECHO(s) { gets(s); puts(s); }
```

Unfortunately, this method doesn't work as well. Suppose that we use ECHO in an `if` statement:

```
if (echo_flag)
  ECHO(str);
else
  gets(str);
```

Replacing ECHO gives the following result:

```
if (echo_flag)
  { gets(str); puts(str); };
else
  gets(str);
```

The compiler treats the first two lines as a complete `if` statement:

```
if (echo_flag)
  { gets(str); puts(str); }
```

It treats the semicolon that follows as a null statement and produces an error message for the `else` clause, since it doesn't belong to any `if`. We could solve the problem by remembering not to put a semicolon after each invocation of ECHO, but then the program would look odd.

The comma operator solves this problem for ECHO, but not for all macros. Suppose that a macro needs to contain a series of *statements*, not just a series of *expressions*. The comma operator is of no help; it can glue together expressions, but not statements. The solution is to wrap the statements in a `do` loop whose condition is false:

```
do { … } while (0)
```

A `do` loop must always be followed by a semicolon, so we won't run into problems when using the macro in `if` statements. To see this trick (ahem, technique) in action, let's incorporate it into our ECHO macro:

```
#define ECHO(s)      \
        do {         \
          gets(s);   \
          puts(s);   \
        } while (0)
```

When ECHO is used, it must be followed by a semicolon:

```
ECHO(str);
  /* becomes do { gets(str); puts(str); } while (0); */
```

Predefined Macros

Several handy macros are predefined in C. As Table 14.1 shows, these macros primarily provide information about the current compilation. The __LINE__ and __STDC__ macros represent integer constants, while the other three macros represent string literals. We'll encounter uses for __STDC__ later in the chapter, so let's focus on the other macros for now.

Table 14.1
Predefined Macros

Name	Description
__LINE__	Line number of file being compiled
__FILE__	Name of file being compiled
__DATE__	Date of compilation (in the form `"Mmm dd yyyy"`)
__TIME__	Time of compilation (in the form `"hh:mm:ss"`)
__STDC__	1 if the compiler accepts Standard C

The __DATE__ and __TIME__ macros identify when a program was compiled. For example, suppose that a program begins with the following statements:

```
printf("Wacky Windows (c) 1996 Wacky Software, Inc.\n");
printf("Compiled on %s at %s\n", __DATE__, __TIME__);
```

Each time it begins to execute, the program will print two lines of the form

```
Wacky Windows (c) 1996 Wacky Software, Inc.
Compiled on Dec 23 1996 at 22:18:48
```

This information can be helpful for distinguishing among different versions of the same program.

We can use the __LINE__ and __FILE__ macros to help locate errors. Consider the problem of detecting the location of a division by zero. When a C program terminates prematurely because of a division by zero, there's usually no indication of which division caused the problem. The following macro can help us pinpoint the source of the error:

```
#define CHECK_ZERO(divisor) \
  if (divisor == 0) \
    printf("*** Attempt to divide by zero on line %d " \
           "of file %s ***\n", __LINE__, __FILE__)
```

The CHECK_ZERO macro would be invoked prior to a division:

```
CHECK_ZERO(j);
k = i / j;
```

If j happens to be zero, a message of the following form will be printed:

```
*** Attempt to divide by zero on line 9 of file FOO.C ***
```

assert macro ➤24.1

Error-detecting macros like this one are quite useful. In fact, the C library provides a general-purpose error-detecting macro named assert.

14.4 Conditional Compilation

The C preprocessor recognizes a number of directives that support *conditional compilation*—the inclusion or exclusion of a section of program text depending on the outcome of a test performed by the preprocessor.

The #if and #endif Directives

Suppose we're in the process of debugging a program. We'd like the program to print the values of certain variables, so we put calls of printf in critical parts of the program. Once we've located the bugs, it's often a good idea to let the printf calls remain, just in case we need them later. Conditional compilation allows us to leave the calls in place, but have the compiler ignore them.

Here's how we'll proceed. We'll first define a macro and give it a nonzero value:

```
#define DEBUG 1
```

The name of the macro doesn't matter. Next, we'll surround each group of printf calls by an #if-#endif pair:

```
#if DEBUG
printf("Value of i: %d\n", i);
printf("Value of j: %d\n", j);
#endif
```

During preprocessing, the #if directive will test the value of DEBUG. Since its value isn't zero, the preprocessor will leave the two calls of printf in the program (the #if and #endif lines will disappear, though). If we change the value of DEBUG to zero and recompile the program, the preprocessor will remove all four lines from the program. The compiler won't see the calls of printf, so they won't occupy any space in the object code and won't cost any time when the program is run. We can leave the #if-#endif blocks in the final program, allowing diagnostic information to be produced later (by recompiling with DEBUG set to 1) if errors should arise during the operation of the program.

In general, the #if directive has the form

#if directive

$$\text{\#if } \textit{constant-expression}$$

The #endif directive is even simpler:

#endif directive

$$\text{\#endif}$$

When the preprocessor encounters the #if directive, it evaluates the constant expression. If the value of the expression is zero, the lines between #if and #endif will be removed from the program during preprocessing. Otherwise, the lines between #if and #endif will remain in the program to be processed by the compiler—the #if and #endif will have had no effect on the program.

It's worth noting that the #if directive treats undefined identifiers as macros that have the value 0. Thus, if we neglect to define DEBUG, the test

```
#if DEBUG
```

will fail (but not generate an error message), while the test

```
#if !DEBUG
```

will succeed.

The defined Operator

We encountered the # and ## operators in Section 14.3. There's just one other operator, defined, that's specific to the preprocessor. When applied to an identifier, defined produces the value 1 if the identifier is a currently defined macro; it produces 0 otherwise. The defined operator is normally used in conjunction with the #if directive; it allows us to write

```
#if defined(DEBUG)
...
#endif
```

The lines between the `#if` and `#endif` directives will be included in the program only if DEBUG is defined as a macro. The parentheses around DEBUG aren't required; we could simply write

```
#if defined DEBUG
```

Since `defined` tests only whether DEBUG is defined or not, it's not necessary to give DEBUG a value:

```
#define DEBUG
```

The `#ifdef` and `#ifndef` Directives

The `#ifdef` directive tests whether an identifier is currently defined as a macro:

`#ifdef` directive

<code>#ifdef</code> identifier

Using `#ifdef` is similar to using `#if`:

```
#ifdef identifier
lines to be included if identifier is defined as a macro
#endif
```

Strictly speaking, there's no need for `#ifdef`, since we can combine the `#if` directive with the `defined` operator to get the same effect. In other words, the directive

```
#ifdef identifier
```

is equivalent to

```
#if defined(identifier)
```

The `#ifndef` directive is similar to `#ifdef`, but tests whether an identifier is *not* defined as a macro:

`#ifndef` directive

<code>#ifndef</code> identifier

Writing

```
#ifndef identifier
```

is the same as writing

```
#if !defined(identifier)
```

The #elif and #else Directives

#if, #ifdef, and #ifndef blocks can be nested just like ordinary if statements. When nesting occurs, it's a good idea to use an increasing amount of indentation as the level of nesting grows. Some programmers put a comment on each closing #endif to indicate what condition the matching #if tests:

```
#if DEBUG
...
#endif /* DEBUG */
```

This technique makes it easier for the reader to find the beginning of the #if block.

For additional convenience, the preprocessor provides the #elif and #else directives:

#elif directive

```
#elif expr
```

#else directive

```
#else
```

#elif and #else can be used in conjunction with #if, #ifdef, or #ifndef to test a series of conditions:

```
#if expr1
lines to be included if expr1 is nonzero
#elif expr2
lines to be included if expr1 is zero but expr2 is nonzero
#else
lines to be included otherwise
#endif
```

Although the #if directive is shown above, the #ifdef or #ifndef directive can be used instead. Any number of #elif directives—but at most one #else—may appear between #if and #endif.

Uses of Conditional Compilation

Conditional compilation is certainly handy for debugging, but its uses don't stop there. Here are a few other common applications:

- *Writing programs that are portable to several machines or operating systems.* The following example includes one of three groups of lines depending on whether WINDOWS, DOS, or OS2 is defined as a macro:

```
#if defined(WINDOWS)
...
#elif defined(DOS)
...
```

```
#elif defined(OS2)
...
#endif
```

A program might contain many of these #if blocks. At the beginning of the program, one (and only one) of the macros will be defined, thereby selecting a particular operating system. For example, defining the OS2 macro might indicate that the program is to run under the OS/2 operating system.

■ *Writing programs that can be compiled with different compilers.* Different compilers often recognize somewhat different versions of C. Some accept Standard C, some don't. Some provide machine-specific language extensions; some don't, or provide a different set of extensions. Conditional compilation can allow a program to adjust to different compilers. Consider the problem of writing a program that may or may not be compiled using a Standard C compiler. The __STDC__ macro allows the preprocessor to detect whether a compiler recognizes Standard C; if it doesn't, we may have to change certain aspects of a program. In particular, we may have to use Classic C function declarations instead of Standard C's function prototypes. At each point where functions are declared, we can put the following lines:

```
#if __STDC__
```
Standard C function prototypes
```
#else
```
Classic C function declarations
```
#endif
```

■ *Providing a default definition for a macro.* Conditional compilation allows us to check whether a macro is currently defined and, if not, give it a default definition. For example, the following lines will define the macro BUFFER_SIZE if it wasn't previously defined:

```
#ifndef BUFFER_SIZE
#define BUFFER_SIZE 256
#endif
```

■ *Temporarily disabling code that contains comments.* Since comments can't be nested in Standard C, it's not possible to "comment out" code that contains comments. Instead, we can use an #if directive:

```
#if 0
```
lines containing comments
```
#endif
```

Q&A   Disabling code in this way is often called "conditioning out."

Section 15.2 discusses another common use of conditional compilation: protecting header files against multiple inclusion.

14.5 Miscellaneous Directives

To end the chapter, we'll take a brief look at the #error, #line, and #pragma directives. These directives have one thing in common: they're not used much by beginning C programmers. In fact, none of the programs in this book use these directives, so you can safely skip this section for now. Later, when you're ready to become a C wizard, you'll need to become familiar with these directives.

The #error Directive

The #error directive has the form

#error directive

> #error *message*

where *message* is any sequence of C tokens. If the preprocessor encounters an #error directive, it prints an error message which must include *message*. The exact form of the error message can vary from one compiler to another; here's a typical example:

Error directive: *message*

Encountering an #error directive is indicative of a serious flaw in the program; most compilers immediately terminate compilation without attempting to find other errors.

#error directives are often used in conjunction with conditional compilation to check for situations that shouldn't arise during a normal compilation. For example, suppose that we want to ensure that a program can't be compiled on a machine whose int type isn't capable of storing numbers up to 100,000. The largest possible int value is represented by the INT_MAX macro, so all we need do is invoke an #error directive if INT_MAX isn't at least 100,000:

INT_MAX macro ➤ *23.2*

```
#if INT_MAX < 100000
#error int type is too small
#endif
```

Attempting to compile the program on a machine whose integers are stored in 16 bits will produce a message such as

Error directive: int type is too small

The #error directive is often found in the #else part of an #if-#elif-#else series:

```
#if defined(WINDOWS)
...
```

```
#elif defined(DOS)
...
#elif defined(OS2)
...
#else
#error No operating system specified
#endif
```

The #line Directive

The #line directive is used to alter the way program lines are numbered. (Lines are usually numbered 1, 2, 3, as you'd expect.) We can also use this directive to make the compiler think that it's reading the program from a file with a different name.

The #line directive has two forms. In one form, we specify a line number:

#line directive
(form 1)

> #line *n*

n must be an integer between 1 and 32,767. This directive causes subsequent lines in the program to be numbered *n*, *n* + 1, *n* + 2, and so forth.

In the second form of the #line directive, both a line number and a file name are specified:

#line directive
(form 2)

> #line *n* "*file*"

The lines that follow this directive are assumed to come from *file*, with line numbers starting at *n*.

One effect of the #line directive is to change the values of the __LINE__ macro (and possibly the __FILE__ macro). More importantly, most compilers will use the information from the #line directive when generating error messages. For example, suppose that the following directive appears at the beginning of the file foo.c:

```
#line 10 "bar.c"
```

Now, let's say that the compiler detects an error on line 5 of foo.c. The error message will refer to line 13 of file bar.c, not line 5 of file foo.c. (Why line 13? The directive occupies line 1 of foo.c, so the renumbering of foo.c begins at line 2, which is treated as line 10 of bar.c.)

At first glance, the #line directive is mystifying. Why would we want error messages to refer to a different line and possibly a different file? Wouldn't this make programs harder to debug?

In fact, the #line directive isn't used very often by programmers. Instead, it's used primarily by programs that generate C code as output. The most famous example of such a program is yacc (Yet Another Compiler-Compiler), a UNIX utility that automatically generates part of a compiler. Before using yacc, the programmer prepares a file that contains information for `yacc` as well as fragments of C code. From this file, `yacc` generates a C program, `y.tab.c`, incorporating the code supplied by the programmer. The programmer then compiles `y.tab.c` in the normal way. By inserting `#line` directives in `y.tab.c`, `yacc` tricks the compiler into believing that the code comes from the original file—the one written by the programmer. As a result, any error messages produced during the compilation of `y.tab.c` will refer to lines in the original file, not lines in `y.tab.c`. The net result: debugging is easier, because error messages refer to the file written by the programmer, not the (more complicated) file generated by `yacc`.

The #pragma Directive

The `#pragma` directive provides a way to request special behavior from the compiler. This directive is most useful for programs that are unusually large or that need to take advantage of the capabilities of a particular compiler.

The `#pragma` directive has the form

#pragma directive

> `#pragma` *tokens*

where *tokens* are normal C tokens. `#pragma` is usually followed by a single token, which represents a command for the compiler to obey.

Some compilers allow `#pragma` directives to contain more than just simple commands. In particular, some allow `#pragma` directives to have arguments:

```
#pragma data(heap_size => 1000, stack_size => 2000)
```

Not surprisingly, the set of commands that can appear in `#pragma` directives is different for each compiler; you'll have to consult the documentation for your compiler to see which commands it allows and what those commands do. Incidentally, the preprocessor must ignore any `#pragma` directive that contains an unrecognized command; it's not permitted to give an error message.

Q & A

Q: **I've seen programs that contain a # on a line by itself. Is this legal?**

A: Yes. This is the *null directive;* it has no effect. Some programmers use null directives for spacing within conditional compilation blocks:

```
#if INT_MAX < 100000
#
#error int type is too small
#
#endif
```

Blank lines would also work, of course, but the # helps the reader see the extent of the block.

Q: **I'm not sure which constants in a program need to be defined as macros. Are there any guidelines to follow? [p. 278]**

A: One rule of thumb says that every numeric constant, other than 0 or 1, should be a macro. Character and string constants are problematic, since replacing a character or string constant by a macro doesn't always improve readability. I recommend using a macro instead of a character constant or string literal provided that (1) the constant is used more than once and (2) the possibility exists that the constant might someday be modified. Because of rule (2), I don't use macros such as

```
#define NUL '\0'
```

although some programmers do.

*Q: **What does the # operator do if the argument that it's supposed to "stringize" contains a " or \ character? [p. 282]**

A: It converts " to \" and \ to \\. Consider the following macro:

```
#define STRINGIZE(x) #x
```

The preprocessor will replace STRINGIZE("foo") by "\"foo\"".

*Q: **I can't get the following macro to work properly:**

```
#define CONCAT(x,y) x##y
```

CONCAT(a,b) gives ab, as expected, but CONCAT(a,CONCAT(b,c)) gives an odd result. What's going on?

A: Thanks to rules that even Kernighan and Ritchie admit are "bizarre," macros whose replacement lists depend on ## usually can't be called in a nested fashion. The problem is that CONCAT(a,CONCAT(b,c)) isn't expanded in a "normal" fashion, with CONCAT(b,c) yielding bc, then CONCAT(a,bc) giving abc. The C standard specifies that macro parameters that are preceded or followed by ## in a replacement list aren't expanded at the time of substitution. As a result, CONCAT(a,CONCAT(b,c)) expands to aCONCAT(b,c), which can't be expanded further, since there's no macro named aCONCAT.

There's a way to solve the problem, but it's not pretty. The trick is to define a second macro that simply calls the first one:

```
#define CONCAT2(x,y) CONCAT(x,y)
```

Writing CONCAT2(a,CONCAT2(b,c)) gives us the desired result. As it expands the outer call of CONCAT2, the preprocessor will expand CONCAT2(b,c) as well; the difference is that CONCAT2's replacement list doesn't contain ##. If none of this makes any sense, don't worry; it's not a problem that arises often.

The # operator has a similar difficulty, by the way. If #x appears in a replacement list, where x is a macro parameter, the corresponding argument is not expanded. Thus, if N is a macro representing 10, and STR(x) has the replacement list #x, expanding STR(N) yields "N", not "10". The solution is similar to the one we used with CONCAT: defining a second macro whose job is to call STR.

*Q: **Suppose that the preprocessor encounters the original macro name during rescanning, as in the following example:**

```
#define N (2*M)
#define M (N+1)

i = N;    /* infinite loop? */
```

The preprocessor will replace N by (2*M), then replace M by (N+1). Will the preprocessor replace N again, thus going into an infinite loop? [p. 284]

A: Some older preprocessors will indeed go into an infinite loop, but preprocessors that conform to Standard C shouldn't. According to the standard, if the original macro name reappears during the expansion of a macro, the name is not replaced again. Here's how the assignment to i will look after preprocessing:

```
i = (2*(N+1));
```

Some enterprising programmers take advantage of this behavior by writing macros whose names match reserved words or functions in the standard library. Consider the sqrt library function. sqrt computes the square root of its argument, returning an implementation-defined value if the argument is negative. Perhaps we want sqrt to return 0 if its argument is negative. Since sqrt is part of the standard library, we can't easily change it. We can, however, define a sqrt *macro* that evaluates to 0 when given a negative argument:

sqrt function ►23.3

```
#define sqrt(x) ((x)>=0 ? sqrt(x) : 0)
```

A call of sqrt will be intercepted by the preprocessor, which expands it into the conditional expression shown here. The call of sqrt inside the conditional expression won't be replaced during rescanning, so it will remain for the compiler to handle.

Q: **I thought the preprocessor was just an editor. How can it evaluate constant expressions? [p. 289]**

A: The preprocessor is more sophisticated than you might expect; it knows enough about C to be able to evaluate constant expressions, although it doesn't do so in quite the same way as the compiler. (For one thing, the preprocessor treats any undefined name as having the value 0. The other differences are too esoteric to go into here.) In practice, the operands in a preprocessor constant expression are usually constants, macros that represent constants, and applications of the defined operator.

Q: **Why does C provide the `#ifdef` and `#ifndef` directives, since we can get the same effect using the `#if` directive and the `defined` operator? [p. 290]**

A: The `#ifdef` and `#ifndef` directives have been a part of C since the 1970s. The `defined` operator, on the other hand, was added to C in the 1980s during standardization. So the real question is: Why was `defined` added to the language? The answer is that `defined` adds flexibility. Instead of just being able to test the existence of a single macro using `#ifdef` or `#ifndef`, we can now test any number of macros using `#if` together with `defined`. For example, the following directive checks whether FOO and BAR are defined but BAZ is not defined:

```
#if defined(FOO) && defined(BAR) && !defined(BAZ)
```

Q: **I wanted to compile a program that I hadn't finished writing, so I "conditioned out" the unfinished part. I put a message at the beginning as a reminder to complete the program later:**

```
#if 0
Haven't finished this part yet.
...
#endif
```

Why did I get an error message during compilation? Doesn't the preprocessor just ignore all lines between `#if` and `#endif`? [p. 292]

A: The lines between `#if` and `#endif` must consist of *preprocessing tokens,* which are similar to ordinary C tokens (identifiers, operators, numbers, and the like). As it tried to break the first line into tokens, the preprocessor encountered Haven (a legal identifier), followed by 't (an illegal character constant). Some preprocessors skip all lines between `#if` and `#endif` without attempting to check for preprocessing tokens, but they're not enforcing the rules of the C standard.

preprocessing tokens ➤ *Appendix A*

Exercises

Section 14.3

1. Write macros that compute the following values.

    (a) The cube of x.
    (b) The remainder when x is divided by 4.
    (c) 1 if the product of x and y is less than 100, 0 otherwise.

    Do your macros always work? If not, describe what arguments would make them fail.

2. Write a macro NELEMS(a) that computes the number of elements in a one-dimensional array a. *Hint:* Use the `sizeof` operator.

3. Let DOUBLE be the following macro:

    ```
    #define DOUBLE(x) 2*x
    ```

    (a) What is the value of DOUBLE(1+2)?
    (b) What is the value of 4/DOUBLE(2)?
    (c) Fix the definition of DOUBLE.

4. For each of the following macros, give an example that illustrates a problem with the macro and show how to fix it.

   (a) `#define AVG(x,y)  (x+y)/2`
   (b) `#define AREA(x,y) (x)*(y)`

*5. The following macro definition has a subtle problem:

   `#define ABS(a)  ((a)<0?-(a):a)`

   Give an example that shows why `ABS` doesn't work, and show how to fix the problem. You may assume that the argument to `ABS` doesn't have a side effect.

6. Let `TOUPPER` be the following macro:

   `#define TOUPPER(c)  ('a'<=(c)&&(c)<='z'?(c)-'a'+'A':(c))`

   Let `s` be a string and let `i` be an `int` variable. Show the output produced by each of the following code fragments.

   (a) `strcpy(s, "abcd");`
       `i = 0;`
       `putchar(TOUPPER(s[++i]));`
   (b) `strcpy(s, "0123");`
       `i = 0;`
       `putchar(TOUPPER(s[++i]));`

7. (a) Write a macro `DISP(f,x)` that expands into a call of `printf` that displays the value of the function `f` when called with argument `x`. For example

   `DISP(sqrt, 3.0);`

   should expand into

   `printf("sqrt(%g) = %g\n", 3.0, sqrt(3.0));`

   (b) Write a macro `DISP2(f,x,y)` that's similar to `DISP` but works for functions with two arguments.

*8. Let GENERIC_MAX be the following macro:

   ```
   #define GENERIC_MAX(type)          \
   type type##_max(type x, type y) \
   {                                  \
     return x > y ? x : y;            \
   }
   ```

   (a) Show the preprocessor's expansion of `GENERIC_MAX(long)`.
   (b) Explain why GENERIC_MAX doesn't work for basic types such as `unsigned long`.
   (c) How could we make GENERIC_MAX work with any basic type? *Hint:* Don't change the definition of GENERIC_MAX.

*9. Suppose we want a macro that expands into a string containing the current line number and file name. In other words, we'd like to write

   `const char *str = LINE_FILE;`

   and have it expand into

   `const char *str = "Line 10 of file foo.c";`

   where `foo.c` is the file containing the program and 10 is the line on which the invocation of `LINE_FILE` appears. *Warning:* This exercise is for experts only. Be sure to read the Q&A section carefully before attempting!

10.   Suppose that the macro M has been defined as follows:

```
#define M 10
```

Which of the following tests will fail?

(a) `#if M`
(b) `#ifdef M`
(c) `#ifndef M`
(d) `#if defined(M)`
(e) `#if !defined(M)`

11.   (a) Show what the following program will look like after preprocessing.

```
#define N 100

void f(void);

main()
{
   f();
#ifdef N
#undef N
#endif
   return 0;
}

void f(void)
{
#if defined(N)
   printf("N is %d\n", N);
#else
   printf("N is undefined\n");
#endif
}
```

(b) What will be the output of this program?

*12.   Show what the following program will look like after preprocessing. Some lines of the program may cause compilation errors; find all such errors.

```
#define N = 10
#define INC(x) x+1
#define SUB (x,y) x - y
#define SQR(x) ((x)*(x))
#define CUBE(x) (SQR(x)*(x))
#define M1(x,y) x##y
#define M2(x,y) #x #y

main()
{
   int a[N], i, j, k, m;

#ifdef N
   i = j;
#else
   j = i;
#endif
```

```
      i = 10 * INC(j);
      i = SUB(j, k);
      i = SQR(SQR(j++));
      i = CUBE(j);
      i = M1(j, k);
      puts(M2(i, j));

#undef SQR
      i = SQR(j);
#define SQR
      i = SQR(j);

      return 0;
}
```

15 Writing Large Programs

Around computers it is difficult to find the correct unit of time to measure progress. Some cathedrals took a century to complete. Can you imagine the grandeur and scope of a program that would take as long?

Although some C programs are small enough to be put in a single file, most aren't. Programs that consist of more than one file are the rule rather than the exception. In this chapter, we'll see that a typical program consists of several *source files* and usually some *header files* as well. Source files contain definitions of functions and external variables; header files contain information to be shared among source files. Section 15.1 discusses source files, while Section 15.2 covers header files in detail. Section 15.3 describes how to divide a program into source files and header files. Section 15.4 then shows how to "build" (compile and link) a program that consists of more than one file, and how to "rebuild" a program after part of it has been changed.

15.1 Source Files

Up to this point, we've assumed that a C program consists of a single file. In fact, a program may be divided among any number of *source files*. By convention, source files have the extension `.c`. Each source file contains part of the program, primarily definitions of functions and variables. One source file must contain a function named `main`, which serves as the starting point for the program.

For example, suppose that we want to write a simple calculator program that evaluates integer expressions entered in Reverse Polish notation (RPN), in which operators follow operands. If the user enters an expression such as

```
30 5 - 7 *
```

we want the program to print its value (175, in this case). Evaluating an RPN expression is easy if we have the program read the operands and operators, one by one, using a stack to keep track of intermediate results. If the program reads a number, we'll have it push the number onto the stack. If it reads an operator, we'll have it pop two numbers from the stack, perform the operation, then push the result back onto the stack. When the program reaches the end of the user's input, the value of the expression will be on the stack. For example, the program will evaluate the expression 30 5 - 7 * in the following way:

1. Push 30 onto the stack.
2. Push 5 onto the stack.
3. Pop the top two numbers from the stack, subtract 5 from 30, giving 25, and then push the result back onto the stack.
4. Push 7 onto the stack.
5. Pop the top two numbers from the stack, multiply them, and then push the result back onto the stack.

After these steps, the stack will contain the value of the expression (175).

Turning this strategy into a program isn't hard. The program's main function will contain a loop that performs the following actions:

Read a "token" (a number or an operator).
If the token is a number, push it on a stack.
If the token is an operator, pop its operands from the stack, perform the operation, and push the result back onto the stack.

When dividing a program like this one into files, it makes sense to put related functions and variables into the same file. The function that reads tokens could go into one source file (token.c, say), together with any functions that have to do with tokens. Stack-related functions such as push, pop, make_empty, is_empty, and is_full could go into a different file, stack.c. The variables that represent the stack would also go into stack.c. The main function would go into yet another file, calc.c.

Splitting a program into multiple source files has significant advantages:

- Grouping related functions and variables into a single file helps clarify the structure of the program.
- Each source file can be compiled separately—a great time-saver if the program is large and must be changed frequently (which is common during program development).
- Functions are more easily reused in other programs when grouped in separate source files. In our example, splitting off stack.c and token.c from the main function makes it simpler to reuse the stack functions and token functions in the future.

15.2   Header Files

When we divide a program into several source files, problems arise: How can a function in one file call a function that's defined in another file? How can a function access an external variable in another file? How can two files share the same macro definition or type definition? The answer lies with the `#include` directive, which makes it possible to share information—function prototypes, macro definitions, type definitions, and more—among any number of source files.

The `#include` directive tells the preprocessor to open a specified file and insert its contents into the current file. Thus, if we want several source files to have access to the same information, we'll put that information in a file and then use `#include` to bring the file's contents into each of the source files. Files that are included in this fashion are called ***header files*** (or sometimes ***include files***); I'll discuss them in more detail later in this section. By convention, header files have the extension `.h`.

Note: The C standard uses the term "source file" to refer to all files written by the programmer, including both `.c` and `.h` files. I'll use "source file" to refer to `.c` files only.

The `#include` Directive

The `#include` directive has two forms. The first form is used for header files that belong to C's own library:

`#include` directive (form 1)

> `#include <`*filename*`>`

The second form is used for all other header files, including any that we write:

`#include` directive (form 2)

> `#include "`*filename*`"`

 The difference between the two is a subtle one having to do with how the compiler locates the header file. Here are the rules that most compilers follow:

- `#include <`*filename*`>`: Search the directory (or directories) in which system header files reside. (On UNIX systems, for example, system header files are usually kept in the directory `/usr/include`.)
- `#include "`*filename*`"`: Search the current directory, then search the directory (or directories) in which system header files reside.

The places to be searched for header files can usually be altered, often by a command-line option such as `-I`*path*.

Don't use brackets when including header files that you have written:

```
#include <myheader.h>    /*** WRONG ***/
```

The preprocessor will probably look for myheader.h where the system header files are kept (and, of course, won't find it).

The file name in an #include directive may include information that helps locate the file, such as a directory path or drive specifier:

```
#include "c:\cprogs\utils.h"   /* DOS path */

#include "/cprogs/utils.h"     /* UNIX path */
```

Although the quotation marks in the #include directive make file names look like string literals, the preprocessor doesn't treat them that way. (That's fortunate, since \c and \u—which appear in the DOS example—would be treated as escape sequences in a string literal.)

portability tip   *It's usually best not to include path or drive information in* #include *directives. Such information makes it difficult to compile a program when it's transported to another machine or, worse, another operating system.*

For example, the following #include directives specify drive and/or path information that may not always be valid:

```
#include "d:utils.h"
#include "\cprogs\utils.h"
#include "d:\cprogs\utils.h"
```

The following directives are better; they're not restricted to a particular drive, and directories are specified relative to the current directory:

```
#include <sys\stat.h>
#include "utils.h"
#include "..\include\utils.h"
```

Sharing Macro Definitions and Type Definitions

Most large programs contain macro definitions and type definitions that need to be shared by several source files (or, in the most extreme case, by *all* source files). These definitions should go into header files.

For example, suppose that we're writing a program that uses macros named BOOL, TRUE, and FALSE. Instead of repeating the definitions of these macros in each source file that needs them, it makes more sense to put the definitions in a header file with a name like boolean.h:

```
#define BOOL int
#define TRUE 1
#define FALSE 0
```

Any source file that requires these macros will simply contain the line

```
#include "boolean.h"
```

In the following figure, two files include `boolean.h`:

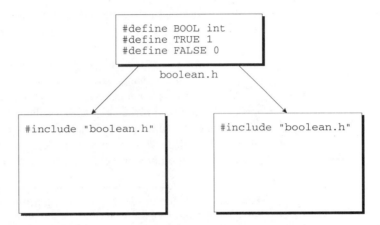

boolean.h

Type definitions are also common in header files. For example, instead of defining a BOOL macro, we might use `typedef` to create a `Bool` type. If we do, the `boolean.h` file will have the following appearance:

```
#define TRUE 1
#define FALSE 0
typedef int Bool;
```

Putting definitions of macros and types in header files has some obvious advantages. First, we save time by not having to copy the definitions into the source files where they're needed. Second, the program becomes easier to modify. Changing the definition of a macro or type requires only that we edit a single header file; we don't have to modify the many source files in which the macro or type is used. Third, we don't have to worry about inconsistencies caused by source files containing different definitions of the same macro or type.

Sharing Function Prototypes

Suppose that a source file contains a call of a function f that's defined in another file, `foo.c`. Calling f without declaring it first is risky. Without a prototype to rely on, the compiler is forced to assume that f's return type is `int` and that the number of parameters matches the number of arguments in the call of f. The arguments themselves are converted automatically to a kind of "standard form" by the default argument promotions. The compiler's assumptions may well be wrong, but

default argument promotions ➤9.3

it has no way to check them, since it compiles only one file at a time. If the assumptions are incorrect, the program probably won't work, and there won't be any clues as to the reason.

When calling a function f that's defined in another file, always make sure that the compiler has seen a prototype for f prior to the call.

Our first impulse is to declare f in the file where it's called. That solves the problem but can create a maintenance nightmare. Suppose that the function is called in fifty different source files. How can we ensure that f's prototypes are the same in all the files? How can we guarantee that they match the definition of f in foo.c? If f should change later, how can we find all the files where it's used?

The solution is obvious: put f's prototype in a header file, then include the header file in all the places where f is called. Since f is defined in foo.c, let's name the header file foo.h. In addition to including foo.h in the source files where f is called, we'll need to include it in foo.c, enabling the compiler to check that f's prototype in foo.h matches its definition in foo.c.

Always include the header file declaring a function f in the source file that contains f's definition. Failure to do so can cause hard-to-find bugs, since calls of f elsewhere in the program may not match f's definition.

If foo.c contains other functions, most of them should be declared in the same header file as f. After all, the other functions in foo.c are presumably related to f; any file that contains a call of f probably needs some of the other functions in foo.c. Functions that are intended for use only within foo.c shouldn't be declared in a header file, however; to do so would be misleading.

To illustrate the use of function prototypes in header files, let's return to the RPN calculator of Section 15.1. The file stack.c will contain definitions of the make_empty, is_empty, is_full, push, and pop functions. Prototypes for these functions should go in the header file stack.h:

```
void make_empty(void);
int is_empty(void);
int is_full(void);
void push(int i);
int pop(void);
```

(To avoid complicating the example, is_empty and is_full will return int values instead of Bool values.) We'll include stack.h in calc.c so that the compiler will know each function's return type and the number and type of its parameters. We'll also include stack.h in stack.c so the compiler can check that the prototypes in stack.h match the definitions in stack.c. The following figure shows stack.h, stack.c, and calc.c:

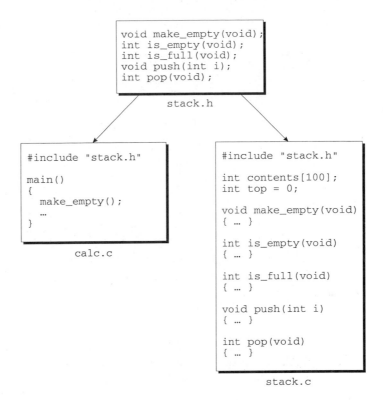

Sharing Variable Declarations

Variables can be shared among files in much the same way functions are. To share a function, we put its *definition* in one source file, then put *declarations* in other files that need to call the function. Sharing a variable is done in much the same way.

Up to this point, we haven't needed to distinguish between a variable's declaration and its definition. To declare a variable `i`, we've written

```
int i;          /* declares i and defines it as well */
```

which not only declares `i` to be a variable of type `int`, but defines `i` as well, by causing the compiler to set aside space for `i`. To declare `i` without defining it, we must put the keyword `extern` at the beginning of its declaration:

```
extern int i;   /* declares i without defining it */
```

`extern` informs the compiler that `i` is defined elsewhere in the program (most likely in a different source file), so there's no need to allocate space for it.

`extern` works with variables of all types, by the way. When we use it in the declaration of an array, we can omit the length of the array:

```
extern int a[];
```

Since the compiler doesn't allocate space for a at this time, there's no need for it to know a's length.

To share a variable i among several source files, we first put a definition of i in one file:

```
int i;
```

If i needs to be initialized, the initializer would go here. When this file is compiled, the compiler will allocate storage for i. The other files will contain declarations of i:

```
extern int i;
```

By declaring i in each file, it becomes possible to access and/or modify i within those files. Because of the word extern, however, the compiler doesn't allocate additional storage for i each time one of the files is compiled.

When a variable is shared among files, we'll face a challenge similar to one that we had with shared functions: ensuring that all declarations of a variable agree with the definition of the variable.

When declarations of the same variable appear in different files, the compiler can't check that the declarations match the variable's definition. For example, one file may contain the definition

```
int i;
```

while another file contains the declaration

```
extern long int i;
```

An error of this kind can cause the program to behave unpredictably.

To avoid inconsistency, declarations of shared variables are usually put in header files. A source file that needs access to a particular variable can then include the appropriate header file. In addition, each header file that contains a variable declaration is included in the source file that contains the variable's definition, enabling the compiler to check that the two match.

Although sharing variables among files is a long-standing practice in the C world, it has significant disadvantages. In Section 19.2, we'll see what the problems are and learn how to design programs that don't need shared variables.

Nested Includes

A header file may itself contain #include directives. Although this practice may seem a bit odd, it can be quite useful in practice. Consider the stack.h file, which contains the following prototypes:

```
int is_empty(void);
int is_full(void);
```

Since these functions return only 0 or 1, it's a good idea to declare their return type to be `Bool` instead of `int`:

```
Bool is_empty(void);
Bool is_full(void);
```

Of course, we'll need to include the file `boolean.h` in `stack.h` so that the definition of `Bool` is available when `stack.h` is compiled.

Traditionally, C programmers shun nested includes. (Early versions of C didn't allow them at all.) However, the bias against nested includes is gradually fading away. One reason is that nested includes are common practice in C++.

C++

Protecting Header Files

If a source file includes the same header file twice, compilation errors may result. This problem is common when header files include other header files. For example, suppose that `file1.h` includes `file3.h`, `file2.h` includes `file3.h`, and `prog.c` includes both `file1.h` and `file2.h`:

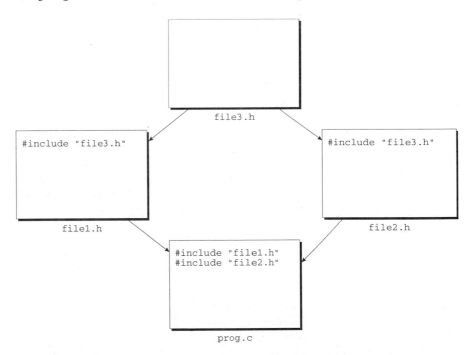

When `prog.c` is compiled, `file3.h` will be compiled twice.

Including the same header file twice doesn't always cause a compilation error. If the file contains only macro definitions, function prototypes, and/or variable declarations, there won't be any difficulty. If the file contains a type definition, however, we'll get a compilation error.

Just to be safe, it's probably a good idea to protect all header files; that way, we can add type definitions to a file later without the risk that we might forget to protect the file. In addition, we might save some time during program development by avoiding unnecessary recompilation of the same header file.

To protect a header file against multiple inclusion, we'll enclose the contents of the file in an #ifndef-#endif pair. For example, the boolean.h file could be protected in the following way:

```
#ifndef BOOLEAN_H
#define BOOLEAN_H

#define TRUE 1
#define FALSE 0
typedef int Bool;

#endif
```

When this file is included the first time, the BOOLEAN_H macro won't be defined, so the preprocessor will allow the lines between #ifndef and #endif to stay. But if the file should be included a second time, the preprocessor will remove the lines between #ifndef and #endif.

The name of the macro (BOOLEAN_H) doesn't really matter. However, making it resemble the name of the header file is a good way to avoid conflicts with other macros. Since we can't name the macro BOOLEAN.H (identifiers can't contain periods), a name such as BOOLEAN_H is a good alternative.

#error Directives in Header Files

#error directives ➤14.5
#error directives are often put in header files to check for conditions under which the header file shouldn't be included. For example, suppose that a header file contains prototypes for graphics functions that work properly only in DOS programs. To guarantee that it is included only in DOS programs, the header file could contain an #ifdef (or #if) directive to test for a macro indicating that DOS is the operating system:

```
#ifndef DOS
#error Graphics supported only under DOS
#endif
```

If a non-DOS program attempted to include this header file, compilation would halt at the #error directive.

15.3 Dividing a Program into Files

Let's now use what we know about header files and source files to develop a simple technique for dividing a program into files. We'll concentrate on functions, but the same principles apply to external variables as well. We'll assume that the program has already been designed; that is, we've decided what functions the program will need and how to arrange the functions into logically related groups. (Program design is an entire topic in itself; we'll discuss it in Chapter 19.)

Here's how we'll proceed. Each set of functions will go into a separate source file (let's use the name `foo.c` for one such file). In addition, we'll create a header file with the same name as the source file, but with the extension `.h` (`foo.h`, in our case). Into `foo.h`, we'll put prototypes for the functions defined in `foo.c`. (Functions that are designed for use only within `foo.c` need not—and should not—be declared in `foo.h`.) We'll include `foo.h` in each source file that needs to call a function defined in `foo.c`. Moreover, we'll include `foo.h` in `foo.c` so that the compiler can check that the function prototypes in `foo.h` are consistent with the definitions in `foo.c`.

The `main` function will go in a file whose name matches the name of the program—if we want the program to be known as `bar`, then `main` should be in the file `bar.c`. It's possible that there are other functions in the same file as `main`, so long as they're not called from other files in the program.

PROGRAM **Text Formatting**

To illustrate the technique that we've just discussed, let's apply it to a small text-formatting program. We'll name the program `fmt`, since some operating systems already have a program named `format`. As sample input to `fmt`, we'll use the file `quote`, which we'll assume contains the following (poorly formatted) quotation from "The Development of the C Language" by Dennis M. Ritchie (*ACM SIGPLAN Notices* (March 1993): 207):

```
   C     is quirky,  flawed,    and  an
enormous   success.       While accidents of   history
 surely  helped,   it evidently    satisfied   a    need

   for   a   system  implementation   language    efficient
 enough   to  displace        assembly  language,
   yet sufficiently   abstract  and fluent   to describe
  algorithms   and       interactions   in a   wide   variety
of   environments.
                  --        Dennis    M.        Ritchie
```

To run the program from a UNIX or DOS prompt, we'd enter the command

```
fmt <quote
```

input redirection ➤22.1
The < symbol informs the operating system that `fmt` will read from the file `quote` instead of accepting input from the keyboard. This feature, supported by UNIX, DOS, and other operating systems, is called ***input redirection***. When given the `quote` file as input, the `fmt` program will produce the following output:

```
C  is  quirky,  flawed,  and  an  enormous  success.    While
accidents of history surely helped, it evidently satisfied a
need  for  a  system  implementation  language   efficient   enough
to  displace  assembly  language,  yet  sufficiently  abstract  and
fluent  to  describe  algorithms  and   interactions   in  a  wide
variety of environments. -- Dennis M. Ritchie
```

output redirection ➤22.1
The output of `fmt` will normally appear on the screen, but we can save it in a file by using ***output redirection***:

```
fmt <quote >newquote
```

The output of `fmt` will go into the file `newquote`.

In general, `fmt`'s output should be identical to its input, except that extra spaces and blank lines are deleted, and lines are filled and justified. "Filling" a line means adding words until one more word would cause the line to overflow. "Justifying" a line means adding extra spaces between words so that each line has exactly the same length (60 characters). Justification must be done so that the space between words in a line is equal (or as nearly equal as possible). The last line of the output won't be justified.

We'll assume that no word is longer than 20 characters. (A punctuation mark is considered part of the word to which it is adjacent.) That's a bit restrictive, of course, but once the program is written and debugged we can easily increase this limit to the point that it would virtually never be exceeded. If the program encounters a longer word, it must ignore all characters after the first 20, replacing them with a single asterisk. For example, the word

```
antidisestablishmentarianism
```

would be printed as

```
antidisestablishment*
```

Now that we understand what the program should do, it's time to think about a design. We'll start by observing that the program can't write the words one by one as they're read. Instead, it will have to store them in a "line buffer" until there are enough to fill a line. After further reflection, we decide that the heart of the program will be a loop that goes something like this:

```
for (;;) {
  read word;
  if (can't read word) {
      write contents of line buffer without justification;
      terminate program;
  }
```

```
if  (word doesn't fit in line buffer)  {
   write contents of line buffer with justification;
   clear line buffer;
}
add word to line buffer;
}
```

Since we'll need functions that deal with words and functions that deal with the line buffer, let's split the program into three source files, putting all functions related to words in one file (`word.c`) and all functions related to the line buffer in another file (`line.c`). A third file (`fmt.c`) will contain the `main` function. In addition to these files, we'll need two header files, `word.h` and `line.h`. The `word.h` file will contain prototypes for the functions in `word.c`; `line.h` will play a similar role for `line.c`.

By examining the main loop, we see that the only word-related function that we'll need is a `read_word` function. (If `read_word` can't read a word because it's reached the end of the input file, we'll have it signal the main loop by pretending to read an "empty" word.) Consequently, the `word.h` file is a small one:

word.h
```c
#ifndef WORD_H
#define WORD_H

/**************************************************************
 * read_word: Reads the next word from the input and         *
 *            stores it in word. Makes word empty if no       *
 *            word could be read because of end-of-file.      *
 *            Truncates the word if its length exceeds        *
 *            len.                                            *
 **************************************************************/
void read_word(char *word, int len);

#endif
```

Notice how the `WORD_H` macro protects `word.h` from being included more than once. Although `word.h` doesn't really need it, it's good practice to protect all header files in this way.

The `line.h` file won't be as short as `word.h`. Our outline of the main loop reveals the need for functions that perform the following operations:

Write contents of line buffer without justification
Check whether word fits in line buffer
Write contents of line buffer with justification
Clear line buffer
Add word to line buffer

We'll call these functions `flush_line`, `space_remaining`, `write_line`, `clear_line`, and `add_word`. Here's the `line.h` header file:

line.h
```
#ifndef LINE_H
#define LINE_H

/***********************************************************
 * clear_line: Clears the current line.                    *
 ***********************************************************/
void clear_line(void);

/***********************************************************
 * add_word: Adds word to the end of the current line.     *
 *           If this is not the first word on the line,    *
 *           puts one space before word.                   *
 ***********************************************************/
void add_word(const char *word);

/***********************************************************
 * space_remaining: Returns the number of characters left  *
 *                  in the current line.                   *
 ***********************************************************/
int space_remaining(void);

/***********************************************************
 * write_line: Writes the current line with                *
 *             justification.                              *
 ***********************************************************/
void write_line(void);

/***********************************************************
 * flush_line: Writes the current line without             *
 *             justification. If the line is empty, does   *
 *             nothing.                                    *
 ***********************************************************/
void flush_line(void);

#endif
```

Before we write the word.c and line.c files, we can use the functions declared in word.h and line.h to write fmt.c, the main program. Writing this file is mostly a matter of translating our original loop design into C.

fmt.c
```
/* Formats a file of text */

#include <string.h>
#include "line.h"
#include "word.h"

#define MAX_WORD_LEN 20

main()
{
  char word[MAX_WORD_LEN+2];
  int word_len;
```

```
    clear_line();
    for (;;) {
      read_word(word, MAX_WORD_LEN+1);
      word_len = strlen(word);
      if (word_len == 0) {
        flush_line();
        return 0;
      }
      if (word_len > MAX_WORD_LEN)
        word[MAX_WORD_LEN] = '*';
      if (word_len + 1 > space_remaining()) {
        write_line();
        clear_line();
      }
      add_word(word);
    }
  }
}
```

Including both line.h and word.h gives the compiler access to the function prototypes in both files as it compiles fmt.c.

main uses a trick to handle words that exceed 20 characters. When it calls read_word, main tells it to truncate any word that exceeds 21 characters. After read_word returns, main checks whether word contains a string that's longer than 20 characters. If so, the word that was read must have been at least 21 characters long (before truncation), so main replaces the word's 21st character by an asterisk.

Now it's time to write word.c. Although the word.h header file has a prototype for only one function, read_word, we can put additional functions in word.c if we need to. As it turns out, read_word is easier to write if we add a small "helper" function, read_char. read_char's job is to read a single character and, if it's a new-line character or tab, convert it to a space. By calling read_char instead of getchar, read_word will automatically treat new-line characters and tabs as spaces.

Here's the word.c file:

word.c
```
#include <stdio.h>
#include "word.h"

int read_char(void)
{
  int ch = getchar();

  if (ch == '\n' || ch == '\t')
    return ' ';

  return ch;
}

void read_word(char *word, int len)
{
  int ch, pos = 0;
```

```
        while ((ch = read_char()) == ' ')
          ;

        while (ch != ' ' && ch != EOF) {
          if (pos < len)
            word[pos++] = ch;
          ch = read_char();
        }

        word[pos] = '\0';
      }
```

Before we discuss read_word, a couple of comments are in order concerning getchar. First, getchar actually returns an int value instead of a char value; that's why the variable ch in read_char is declared to have type int.

EOF macro ➤22.4 Also, getchar returns the value EOF when it's unable to continue reading (usually because it has reached the end of the input file).

read_word consists of two loops. The first loop skips over spaces, stopping at the first nonblank character. (EOF isn't a blank, so the loop stops if it reaches the end of the input file.) The second loop reads characters until encountering a space or EOF. The body of the loop stores the characters into word until reaching the len limit. After that, the loop continues reading characters but doesn't store them. The final statement in read_word ends the word with a null character, thereby making it a string. If read_word encounters EOF before finding a nonblank character, pos will be 0 at the end, making word an empty string.

The only file left is line.c, which supplies definitions of the functions declared in the line.h file. line.c will also need variables to keep track of the state of the line buffer. One variable, line, will store the characters in the current line. Strictly speaking, line is the only variable we need. For speed and convenience, however, we'll use two other variables: line_len (the number of characters in the current line) and num_words (the number of words in the current line).

Here's the line.c file:

line.c
```
#include <stdio.h>
#include <string.h>
#include "line.h"

#define MAX_LINE_LEN 60

char line[MAX_LINE_LEN+1];
int line_len = 0;
int num_words = 0;

void clear_line(void)
{
  line[0] = '\0';
  line_len = 0;
  num_words = 0;
}
```

```
void add_word(const char *word)
{
  if (num_words > 0) {
    line[line_len] = ' ';
    line[line_len+1] = '\0';
    line_len++;
  }
  strcat(line, word);
  line_len += strlen(word);
  num_words++;
}

int space_remaining(void)
{
  return MAX_LINE_LEN - line_len;
}

void write_line(void)
{
  int extra_spaces, spaces_to_insert, i, j;

  extra_spaces = MAX_LINE_LEN - line_len;
  for (i = 0; i < line_len; i++) {
    if (line[i] != ' ')
      putchar(line[i]);
    else {
      spaces_to_insert = extra_spaces / (num_words - 1);
      for (j = 1; j <= spaces_to_insert + 1; j++)
        putchar(' ');
      extra_spaces -= spaces_to_insert;
      num_words--;
    }
  }
  putchar('\n');
}

void flush_line(void)
{
  if (line_len > 0)
    puts(line);
}
```

Most of the functions in line.c are easy to write. The only tricky one is
write_line, which writes a line with justification. write_line writes the
characters in line one by one, pausing at the space between each pair of words to
write additional spaces if needed. The number of additional spaces is stored in
spaces_to_insert, which has the value extra_spaces / (num_words
- 1), where extra_spaces is initially the difference between the maximum
line length and the actual line length. Since extra_spaces and num_words
change after each word is printed, spaces_to_insert will change as well. If
extra_spaces is 10 initially and num_words is 5, then the first word will be
followed by 2 extra spaces, the second by 2, the third by 3, and the fourth by 3.

15.4   Building a Multiple-File Program

In Section 2.1, we examined the process of compiling and linking a program that fits into a single file. Let's expand that discussion to cover multiple-file programs. Building a large program requires the same basic steps as building a small one:

- *Compiling.* Each source file in the program must be compiled separately. (Header files don't need to be compiled; a header file is automatically compiled whenever a source file that includes it is compiled.) The compiler generates a file containing object code from each source file. These files—known as *object files*—have the extension .o in UNIX and .obj in DOS.

- *Linking.* The linker combines the object files created in the previous step—along with code for library functions—to produce an executable program. Among other duties, the linker is responsible for resolving external references left behind by the compiler. (An external reference occurs when a function in one file calls a function defined in another file or accesses a variable defined in another file.)

Most compilers allow us to build a program in a single step. With the UNIX cc compiler, for example, we'd use the following command line to build the fmt program from Section 15.3:

```
% cc -o fmt fmt.c line.c word.c
```

(The % character is the UNIX prompt.) The three source files are first compiled into object code and stored in files named fmt.o, line.o, and word.o. The object files are then automatically passed to the linker, which combines them into a single file. The -o option tells the compiler that we want the executable file to be named fmt.

Makefiles

Putting the names of all the source files on the command line quickly gets tedious. Worse still, we could waste a lot of time when rebuilding a program if we recompile all source files, not just the ones that were affected by our most recent changes.

To make it easier to build large programs, UNIX originated the concept of the *makefile,* a file containing the information necessary to build a program. A makefile not only lists the files that are part of the program, but also describes *dependencies* among the files. Suppose that the file foo.c includes the file bar.h. We say that foo.c "depends" on bar.h, because a change to bar.h will require us to recompile foo.c.

Here's a UNIX makefile for the fmt program:

```
fmt: fmt.o word.o linc.o
        cc -o fmt fmt.o word.o line.o

fmt.o: fmt.c word.h line.h
        cc -c fmt.c

word.o: word.c word.h
        cc -c word.c

line.o: line.c line.h
        cc -c line.c
```

There are four groups of lines. The first line in each group gives a ***target*** file, followed by the files on which it depends. The second line is a command to be executed if the target should need to be rebuilt because of a change to one of its dependent files. Let's look at the first two groups; the last two are similar.

In the first group, fmt (the executable program) is the target:

```
fmt: fmt.o word.o line.o
        cc -o fmt fmt.o word.o line.o
```

The first line states that fmt depends on the files fmt.o, word.o, and line.o; if any one of these three files has changed since the program was last built, then fmt needs to be rebuilt. The command on the following line shows how the rebuilding is to be done (by using cc to link the three object files).

In the second group, fmt.o is the target:

```
fmt.o: fmt.c word.h line.h
        cc -c fmt.c
```

The first line indicates that fmt.o needs to be rebuilt if there's been a change to fmt.c, word.h, or line.h. (The reason for mentioning word.h and line.h is that fmt.c includes both these files, so it's potentially affected by a change to either one.) The next line shows how to update fmt.o (by recompiling fmt.c). The −c option tells the compiler to compile fmt.c, but not attempt to link it, since it's not a complete program.

Makefiles for other operating systems are similar, although not identical. If we were using Borland's bcc compiler, for example, we'd use a slightly different makefile:

```
fmt.exe: fmt.obj word.obj line.obj
        bcc fmt.obj word.obj line.obj

fmt.obj: fmt.c word.h line.h
        bcc -c fmt.c

word.obj: word.c word.h
        bcc -c word.c

line.obj: line.c line.h
        bcc -c line.c
```

The compiler is `bcc` instead of `cc`, the object files have the extension `.obj` instead of `.o`, and the executable file is `fmt.exe` instead of `fmt`. Also, we don't need the `-o` option, because the name of the first object file—`fmt.obj`—determines the name of the executable file.

Once we've created a makefile for a program, we can use the `make` utility to build (or rebuild) the program. By checking the time and date associated with each file in the program, `make` can determine which files are out of date. It then automatically invokes the compiler and linker as needed to rebuild the program.

`make` is complicated enough to warrant a book of its own (Tondo, Nathanson, and Yount, *Mastering MAKE*, second edition, Prentice-Hall, 1994), so we won't attempt to delve any further into its intricacies. Let's just say that real makefiles aren't usually as easy to understand as the examples shown here. There are numerous techniques that reduce the amount of redundancy in makefiles and make them easier to modify; at the same time, though, these techniques greatly reduce their readability.

Not everyone uses makefiles, by the way. Other program maintenance tools are becoming popular, including the "project files" supported by some integrated development environments. Check the documentation for your system to see whether it supports makefiles, project files, or both.

Errors During Linking

Some errors that can't be detected during compilation will be found during linking. In particular, if the definition of a function or variable is missing from a program, the linker will be unable to resolve external references to it, causing a message such as *"Undefined symbol"* or *"Unresolved external reference."*

Errors detected by the linker are usually easy to fix. Here are some of the most common causes:

- *Misspellings.* If the name of a variable or function is misspelled, the linker will report it as missing. For example, if the function `read_char` is defined in the program but called as `read_cahr`, the linker will report that `read_cahr` is missing.
- *Missing files.* If the linker can't find the functions that are in file `foo.c`, it may not know about the file. Check the makefile or project file to make sure that `foo.c` is listed there.
- *Missing libraries.* The linker may not be able to find all library functions used in the program. A classic example occurs in UNIX, where the math library won't be searched during linking unless the `-lm` option is present. Check the documentation for your system to see what options are available for the linker.

Rebuilding a Program

During the development of a program, it's rare that we'll need to compile all its files. Most of the time, we'll test the program, make a change, then build the program again. To save time, the rebuilding process should recompile only those files that might be affected by the latest change.

Let's assume that we've designed our program in the way outlined in Section 15.3, with a header file for each source file. To see how many files will need to be recompiled after a change, we need to consider two possibilities.

The first possibility is that the change affects a single source file. In that case, only that file must be recompiled. (After that, the entire program will need to be relinked, of course.) Consider the `fmt` program. Suppose that we decide to condense the `read_char` function in `word.c` (changes are marked in **bold**):

```
int read_char(void)
{
  int ch = getchar();

  return (ch == '\n' || ch == '\t' ? ' ' : ch);
}
```

This modification doesn't affect the way `read_char` is called, so there's no need to modify `word.h`. After making the change, we need only recompile `word.c` and relink the program.

The second possibility is that the change affects a header file. In that case, we should recompile all files that include the header file, since they could potentially be affected by the change. (Some of them might not be, but it pays to be conservative.)

As an example, consider the `read_word` function in the `fmt` program. Notice that `main` calls `strlen` immediately after calling `read_word`, in order to determine the length of the word that was just read. Since `read_word` already knows the length of the word (`read_word`'s `pos` variable keeps track of the length), it seems silly to use `strlen`. Modifying `read_word` to return the word's length is easy. First, we change the prototype of `read_word` in `word.h`:

```
/************************************************************
 * read_word: Reads the next word from the input and       *
 *            stores it in word. Makes word empty if no     *
 *            word could be read because of end-of-file.    *
 *            Truncates the word if its length exceeds      *
 *            len. Returns the number of characters         *
 *            stored.                                       *
 ************************************************************/
int read_word(char *word, int len);
```

Of course, we're careful to change the comment that accompanies `read_word`. Next, we change the definition of `read_word` in `word.c`:

```
int read_word(char *word, int len)
{
  int ch, pos = 0;

  while ((ch = read_char()) == ' ')
    ;
```

```
    while (ch != ' ' && ch != EOF) {
      if (pos < len)
        word[pos++] = ch;
      ch = read_char();
    }

    word[pos] = '\0';
    return pos;
  }
```

Finally, we modify fmt.c by removing the include of <string.h> and changing main as follows:

```
main()
{
  char word[MAX_WORD_LEN+2];
  int word_len;

  clear_line();
  for (;;) {
    word_len = read_word(word, MAX_WORD_LEN+1);
    if (word_len == 0) {
      flush_line();
      return 0;
    }
    if (word_len > MAX_WORD_LEN)
      word[MAX_WORD_LEN] = '*';
    if (word_len + 1 > space_remaining()) {
      write_line();
      clear_line();
    }
    add_word(word);
  }
}
```

Once we've made these changes, we'll rebuild the fmt program by recompiling word.c and fmt.c and then relinking. There's no need to recompile line.c, which didn't include word.h and therefore won't be affected by changes to it. In UNIX, we could use the following command to rebuild the program:

```
% cc -o fmt fmt.c word.c line.o
```

Note the mention of line.o instead of line.c.

One of the advantages of using makefiles is that rebuilding is handled automatically. By examining the date of each file, the make utility can determine which files have changed since the program was last built. It then recompiles these files, together with all files that depend on them, either directly or indirectly.

Defining Macros Outside a Program

C compilers usually provide some method of specifying the value of a macro at the time a program is compiled. This ability makes it easy to change the value of a macro without editing any of the program's files. It's especially valuable when programs are built automatically using makefiles.

Most UNIX compilers (and some non-UNIX compilers) support the −D option, which allows the value of a macro to be specified on the command line:

```
% cc -DDEBUG=1 foo.c
```

In this example, the DEBUG macro is defined to have the value 1 in the program foo.c, just as if the line

```
#define DEBUG 1
```

appeared at the beginning of foo.c. If the −D option names a macro without specifying its value, the value is taken to be 1.

Many compilers also support the −U option, which "undefines" a macro as if by using #undef:

```
% cc -UDEBUG foo.c
```

Q & A

Q: **You don't have any examples that use the #include directive to include a source file. What would happen if we were to do this?**

A: That's not a good practice, although it's not illegal. Here's an example of the kind of trouble you can get into. Suppose that foo.c defines a function f that we'll need in bar.c and baz.c, so we put the directive

```
#include "foo.c"
```

in both bar.c and baz.c. Each of these files will compile nicely. The problem comes later, when the linker discovers two copies of the object code for f. Of course, we would have gotten away with including foo.c if only bar.c had included it, not baz.c as well. To avoid problems, it's best to use #include only with header files, not source files.

Q: **What are the exact search rules for the #include directive? [p. 305]**

A: That depends on your compiler. The C standard is deliberately vague in its description of #include. If the file name is enclosed in *brackets*, the preprocessor looks in a "sequence of implementation-defined places," as the standard obliquely puts it. If the file name is enclosed in *quotation marks*, the file "is searched for in an implementation-defined manner" and, if not found, then searched as if its name had been enclosed in brackets. The reason for this waffling is simple: unlike DOS and UNIX, not all operating systems have hierarchical (tree-like) file systems.

To make matters even more interesting, the standard doesn't require that names enclosed in brackets be file names at all, leaving open the possibility that #include directives using <> are handled entirely within the compiler.

Q: **I don't understand why each source file needs its own header file. Why not have one big header file containing macro definitions, type definitions, and function prototypes? By including this file, each source file would have access to all the shared information it needs. [p. 308]**

A: The "one big header file" approach certainly works; a number of programmers use it. And it has one advantage: with only one header file, there are fewer files to manage. For large programs, however, the disadvantages of this approach tend to outweigh its advantages.

Using a single header file provides no useful information to someone reading the program later. With multiple header files, the reader can quickly see what other parts of the program are used by a particular source file.

But that's not all. Since each source file depends on the big header file, changing it will cause all source files to be recompiled—a significant drawback in a large program. To make matters worse, the header file will probably change frequently because of the large amount of information it contains.

Q: **The chapter says that a shared array should be declared as follows:**

```
extern int a[];
```

Since arrays and pointers are closely related, would it be legal to write

```
extern int *a;
```

instead? [p. 310]

A: No. When used in *expressions*, arrays "decay" into pointers. (We've noticed this behavior when an array name is used as an argument in a function call.) In variable declarations, arrays and pointers are distinct types.

Q: **Does it hurt if a source file includes headers that it doesn't really need?**

A: Not unless the header has a declaration or definition that conflicts with one in the source file. Otherwise, the worst that can happen is a minor increase in the time it takes to compile the source file.

Q: **I needed to call a function in the file foo.c, so I included the matching header file, foo.h. My program compiled, but it won't link. Why?**

A: Compilation and linking are completely separate in C. Header files exist to provide information to the compiler, not the linker. If you want to call a function in foo.c, then you have to make sure that foo.c is compiled and that the linker is aware that it must search the object file for foo.c to find the function. Usually this means naming foo.c in the program's makefile or project file.

Q: **If my program calls a function in <stdio.h>, does that mean that all functions in <stdio.h> will be linked with the program?**

A: No. Including <stdio.h> (or any other header) has no effect on linking. In any event, most linkers will link only functions that your program actually needs.

Exercises

Section 15.1   1. Section 15.1 listed several advantages of dividing a program into multiple source files.

(a) Describe several other advantages.

(b) Describe some disadvantages.

Section 15.2   2. Which of the following should *not* be put in a header file? Why not?

(a) function prototypes

(b) function definitions

(c) macro definitions

(d) type definitions

3. We saw that writing #include *<file>* instead of #include "*file*" may not work if *file* is one that we've written. Would there be any problem with writing #include "*file*" instead of #include *<file>* if *file* is a system header?

4. Suppose that the file foo.c defines the external variable i as

        int i;

    and the file bar.c declares it as

        extern long int i;

(a) Explain what happens if one of the functions in bar.c assigns i the value 0, assuming that sizeof(int) is the same as sizeof(long int).

(b) Repeat part (a), assuming that sizeof(int) is less than sizeof(long int).

Section 15.3   5. The fmt program justifies lines by inserting extra spaces between words. The way the write_line function is currently written, the words closer to the end of a line tend to have slightly wider gaps between them than the words at the beginning. (For example, the words closer to the end might have three spaces between them, while the words closer to the beginning might be separated by only two spaces.) Improve the program by having write_line alternate between putting the larger gaps at the end of the line and putting them at the beginning of the line.

6. Write the RPN calculator program, using the design of Section 15.2. Implement the binary operators +, -, *, and /, assuming that they have the same meanings as in C.

Section 15.4   7. Suppose that a program consists of three source files—main.c, f1.c, and f2.c—plus two header files, f1.h and f2.h. All three source files include f1.h, but only f1.c and f2.c include f2.h. Write a UNIX makefile for this program, assuming that we want the executable file to be named demo.

8. The following questions refer to the program described in Exercise 7.

(a) Which files need to be compiled when the program is built for the first time?

(b) If f1.c is changed after the program has been built, which file(s) needs to be recompiled?

(c) If f1.h is changed after the program has been built, which file(s) needs to be recompiled?

(d) If f2.h is changed after the program has been built, which file(s) needs to be recompiled?

9. (a) Modify the fmt program by having the read_word function (instead of main) store the * character at the end of a word that's been truncated.

    (b) If we make the change described in part (a), which file(s) will need to be recompiled?

16 Structures, Unions, and Enumerations

Functions delay binding: data structures induce binding.
Moral: Structure data late in the programming process.

This chapter introduces three new types: structures, unions, and enumerations. A *structure* is a collection of values (*members*), possibly of different types. A *union* is similar to a structure, except that its members share the same storage; as a result, a union can store one member at a time, but not all members simultaneously. An *enumeration* is an integer type whose values are named by the programmer.

Of these three types, structures are by far the most important, so I'll devote most of the chapter to them. Section 16.1 shows how to declare structure variables and perform basic operations on them. Section 16.2 then explains how to define structure types, which, among other things, enable us to write functions that accept structure arguments or return structures. Section 16.3 explores how arrays and structures can be nested. The last two sections are devoted to unions (Section 16.4) and enumerations (Section 16.5).

16.1 Structure Variables

The only data structure we've covered so far is the array. Arrays have two important properties. First, all elements of an array have the same type. Second, to select an array element, we specify its position (as an integer subscript).

A *structure* has properties quite different from an array's. The elements of a structure (its *members*, in C parlance) may have *different* types. Furthermore, each member of a structure has a name; to select a particular member, we specify its *name*, not its position.

Structures may sound familiar, since most programming languages provide a similar feature. In other languages, structures are often called *records*; members of structures are known as *fields*.

Declaring Structure Variables

When we need to store a collection of related data items, a structure is a logical choice. For example, suppose that we need to keep track of parts stored in a warehouse. The information that we'll need to store for each part might include a part number (an integer), a part name (a string of characters), and the number of parts on hand (an integer). To create variables that can store all three items of data, we might use a declaration such as the following:

```
struct {
  int number;
  char name[NAME_LEN+1];
  int on_hand;
} part1, part2;
```

Each structure variable has three members: `number` (the part number), `name` (the name of the part), and `on_hand` (the quantity on hand). Notice that this declaration has the same form as other variable declarations in C; `struct { ... }` specifies a type, while `part1` and `part2` are variables of that type.

The members of a structure are stored in memory in the order in which they're declared. In order to show what the `part1` variable looks like when it's stored in memory, let's assume that (1) `part1` is stored at address 2000, (2) integers occupy two bytes, (3) NAME_LEN has the value 25, and (4) there are no gaps between the members. With these assumptions, `part1` will have the following appearance in memory:

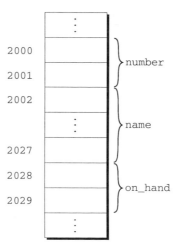

Usually it's not necessary to draw structures in such detail. I'll normally show them more abstractly, as a series of boxes:

I may sometimes draw the boxes horizontally instead of vertically:

Member values will go in the boxes later; for now, I've left them empty.

Each structure represents a new scope; any names declared in that scope won't conflict with other names in a program. (In C terminology, we say that each structure has a separate *name space* for its members.) For example, the following declarations can appear in the same program:

```
struct {
  int number;
  char name[NAME_LEN+1];
  int on_hand;
} part1, part2;

struct {
  char name[NAME_LEN+1];
  int number;
  char sex;
} employee1, employee2;
```

The `number` and `name` members in the `part1` and `part2` structures don't conflict with the `number` and `name` members in `employee1` and `employee2`.

Initializing Structure Variables

Like an array, a structure variable may be initialized at the time it's declared. To initialize a structure, we prepare a list of values to be stored in the structure and enclose it in braces:

```
struct {
  int number;
  char name[NAME_LEN+1];
  int on_hand;
} part1 = {528, "Disk drive", 10},
  part2 = {914, "Printer cable", 5};
```

The values in the initializer must appear in the same order as the members of the structure. In our example, the `number` member of `part1` will be 528, the `name` member will be `"Disk drive"`, and so on. Here's how `part1` will look after initialization:

number	528
name	Disk drive
on_hand	10

Structure initializers follow rules similar to those for array initializers. Expressions used in a structure initializer must be constant; for example, we couldn't have used a variable to initialize part1's on_hand member. An initializer can be shorter than the structure it's initializing; as with arrays, any "leftover" members are given 0 as their initial value.

Operations on Structures

Since the most common array operation is subscripting—selecting an element by position—it's not surprising that the most common operation on a structure is selecting one of its members. Structure members are accessed by name, though, not by position.

To access a member within a structure, we write the name of the structure first, then a period, then the name of the member. For example, the following statements will display the values of part1's members:

```
printf("Part number: %d\n", part1.number);
printf("Part name: %s\n", part1.name);
printf("Quantity on hand: %d\n", part1.on_hand);
```

lvalues ➤4.2   The members of a structure are lvalues, so they can appear on the left side of an assignment, or as the operand in an increment or decrement expression:

```
part1.number = 258;        /* changes part1's part number */
part1.on_hand++;   /* increments part1's quantity on hand */
```

table of operators ➤Appendix B   The period that we use to access a structure member is actually a C operator. It has the same precedence as the postfix ++ and -- operators, so it takes precedence over nearly all other operators. Consider the following example:

```
scanf("%d", &part1.on_hand);
```

The expression &part1.on_hand contains two operators (& and .). The . operator takes precedence over the & operator, so & computes the address of part1.on_hand, as we wished.

The other major structure operation is assignment:

```
part2 = part1;
```

part2.number will now contain the same value as part1.number, part2.name will be the same as part1.name, and so on.

Since arrays can't be copied using =, it comes as something of a surprise to discover that structures can. It's even more surprising when you consider that an array embedded within a structure is copied when the enclosing structure is copied. Some programmers exploit this property by creating "dummy" structures to enclose arrays that will be copied later:

```
struct { int a[10]; } a1, a2;

a1 = a2;   /* legal, since a1 and a2 are structures */
```

The = operator can be used only with structures of compatible types. Two structures declared at the same time (as part1 and part2 were) are compatible. As we'll see in the next section, structures declared using the same "structure tag" or the same type name are also compatible.

Other than assignment, C provides no operations on entire structures. In particular, we can't use the == and != operators to test whether two structures are equal or not equal.

Q&A

16.2 Structure Types

Although the previous section showed how to declare structure *variables,* it failed to discuss an important issue: naming structure *types.* Suppose a program needs to declare several structure variables with identical members. If all the variables can be declared at one time, there's no problem. But if we need to declare the variables at different points in the program, then life becomes more difficult. If we write

```
struct {
  int number;
  char name[NAME_LEN+1];
  int on_hand;
} part1;
```

in one place and

```
struct {
  int number;
  char name[NAME_LEN+1];
  int on_hand;
} part2;
```

in another, we'll quickly run into problems. Repeating the structure information will bloat the program. Changing the program later will be risky, since we can't easily guarantee that the declarations will remain consistent.

But those aren't the biggest problems. According to the rules of C, part1 and part2 don't have compatible types. As a result, part1 can't be assigned to part2, and vice versa. Also, since we don't have a name for the type of part1 or part2, we can't use them as arguments in function calls.

To avoid these difficulties, we need to be able to define a name that represents a *type* of structure, not a particular structure *variable.* As it turns out, C provides

type definitions ➤7.6

two ways to name structures: we can either declare a "structure tag" or use `typedef` to define a type name.

Declaring a Structure Tag

A *structure tag* is a name used to identify a particular kind of structure. The following example declares a structure tag named `part`:

```
struct part {
  int number;
  char name[NAME_LEN+1];
  int on_hand;
};
```

Notice the semicolon that follows the right brace—it must be present to terminate the declaration.

Accidentally omitting the semicolon at the end of a structure declaration can lead to unexpected results. Consider the following example:

```
struct part {
  int number;
  char name[NAME_LEN+1];
  int on_hand;
}                       /*** WRONG--semicolon missing ***/

f(void)
{
  …
  return 0;        /* error detected at this line */
}
```

Since the return type of the function `f` is missing, it would normally be `int` by default. In this case, however, the compiler assumes a return type of `struct part` because the preceding structure declaration hasn't been terminated properly. The compiler doesn't detect the error until it reaches the first `return` statement in the function. The result: a cryptic error message.

Once we've created the `part` tag, we can use it to declare variables:

```
struct part part1, part2;
```

Unfortunately, we can't abbreviate this declaration by dropping the word `struct`:

```
part part1, part2;    /*** WRONG ***/
```

`part` isn't a type name; without the word `struct`, it is meaningless.

Since structure tags are meaningless unless preceded by the word `struct`, they don't conflict with other names used in a program. It would be perfectly legal (although more than a little confusing) to have a variable named `part`.

Incidentally, the declaration of a structure *tag* can be combined with the declaration of structure *variables*:

```
struct part {
  int number;
  char name[NAME_LEN+1];
  int on_hand;
} part1, part2;
```

Here, we've not only declared `part` as a structure tag (making it possible to use `part` later to declare more variables) but also declared the variables `part1` and `part2`.

All structures declared to have type `struct part` are compatible with one another:

```
struct part part1 = {528, "Disk drive", 10};
struct part part2;

part2 = part1;    /* legal; both parts have the same type */
```

Defining a Structure Type

As an alternative to declaring a structure tag, we can use `typedef` to define a genuine type name. For example, we could define a type named `Part` in the following way:

```
typedef struct {
  int number;
  char name[NAME_LEN+1];
  int on_hand;
} Part;
```

Note that the name of the type, `Part`, must come at the end of the definition, not after the word `struct`.

We can use `Part` in the same way as the built-in types. For example, we might use it to declare variables:

```
Part part1, part2;
```

Since `Part` is a `typedef` name, we're not allowed to write `struct Part`. All `Part` variables, regardless of where they're declared, are compatible.

When it comes time to name a structure, we can usually choose either to declare a structure tag or to use `typedef`. However, as we'll see later, declaring a structure tag is mandatory when the structure is to be used in a linked list.

linked lists ➤ 17.5

Structures as Arguments and Return Values

Functions may have structures as arguments and return values. Let's look at two examples. Our first function, when given a `part` structure as its argument, prints the structure's members:

```
void print_part(struct part p)
{
  printf("Part number: %d\n", p.number);
  printf("Part name: %s\n", p.name);
  printf("Quantity on hand: %d\n", p.on_hand);
}
```

Here's how print_part might be called:

```
print_part(part1);
```

Our second function returns a part structure that it constructs from its arguments:

```
struct part build_part(int number, const char* name,
                       int on_hand)
{
  struct part p;

  p.number = number;
  strcpy(p.name, name);
  p.on_hand = on_hand;
  return p;
}
```

Notice that it's legal for build_part's parameters to have names that match the members of the part structure, since the structure has its own name space. Here's how build_part might be called:

```
part1 = build_part(528, "Disk drive", 10);
```

Passing a structure to a function and returning a structure from a function both require making a copy of all members in the structure. As a result, these operations impose a fair amount of overhead on a program, especially if the structure is large. To avoid this overhead, it's sometimes advisable to pass a *pointer* to a structure instead of passing the structure itself. Similarly, we might have a function return a pointer to a structure instead of returning an actual structure.

On occasion, we may want to initialize a structure variable inside a function to match another structure, possibly supplied as a parameter to the function. In the following example, the initializer for part2 is the parameter passed to the f function:

```
void f(struct part part1)
{
  struct part part2 = part1;
  ...
}
```

C permits initializers of this kind, provided that the structure we're initializing (part2, in this case) has automatic storage duration (it's local to a function and hasn't been declared static). The initializer can be *any* expression of the proper type, including a function call that returns a structure.

16.3 Nested Arrays and Structures

Structures and arrays can be combined without restriction. Arrays may have structures as their elements, and structures may contain arrays and structures as members. We've already seen an example of an array nested inside a structure (the `name` member of the `part` structure). Let's explore the other possibilities: structures whose members are structures and arrays whose elements are structures.

Nested Structures

Nesting one kind of structure inside another is often useful. For example, suppose that we've declared the following structure, which can store a person's first name, middle initial, and last name:

```
struct person_name {
  char first[FIRST_NAME_LEN+1];
  char middle_initial;
  char last[LAST_NAME_LEN+1];
};
```

We can use the `person_name` structure as part of a larger structure:

```
struct student {
  struct person_name name;
  int id, age;
  char sex;
} student1, student2;
```

Accessing `student1`'s first name, middle initial, or last name requires two applications of the `.` operator:

```
strcpy(student1.name.first, "Fred");
```

One advantage of making `name` a structure (instead of having `first`, `middle_initial`, and `last` be members of the `student` structure) is that we can more easily treat names as units of data. For example, if we were to write a function that displays a name, we could pass it just one argument—a `person_name` structure—instead of three arguments:

```
display_name(student1.name);
```

Likewise, copying the information from a `person_name` structure to the `name` member of a `student` structure would take one assignment instead of three:

```
struct person_name new_name;
...
student1.name = new_name;
```

Arrays of Structures

One of the most common combinations of arrays and structures is an array whose elements are structures. An array of this kind can serve as a simple database. For example, the following array of `part` structures is capable of storing information about 100 parts:

```
struct part inventory[100];
```

To access one of the parts in the array, we'd use subscripting. To print the part stored in position `i`, for example, we could write

```
print_part(inventory[i]);
```

Accessing a member within a `part` structure requires a combination of subscripting and member selection. To assign 883 to the `number` member of `inventory[i]`, we could write

```
inventory[i].number = 883;
```

Accessing a single character in a part name requires subscripting (to select a particular part), followed by selection (to select the `name` member), followed by subscripting (to select a character within the part name). To change the name stored in `inventory[i]` to an empty string, we could write

```
inventory[i].name[0] = '\0';
```

Initializing an Array of Structures

Initializing an array of structures is done in much the same way as initializing a multidimensional array. Each structure has its own brace-enclosed initializer; the initializer for the array simply wraps another set of braces around the structure initializers.

One reason for initializing an array of structures is that we're planning to treat it as a database of information that won't change during program execution. For example, suppose that we're working on a program that will need access to the country codes used when making international telephone calls. First, we'll set up a structure that can store the name of a country along with its code:

```
struct dialing_code {
  char *country;
  int code;
};
```

Note that `country` is a pointer, not an array of characters. That could be a problem if we were planning to use `dialing_code` structures as variables, but we're not. When we initialize a `dialing_code` structure, `country` will end up pointing to a string literal.

Next, we'll declare an array of these structures and initialize it to contain the codes for some of the world's most populous nations:

```
const struct dialing_code country_codes[] =
    {{"Argentina",              54}, {"Bangladesh",   880},
     {"Brazil",                 55}, {"China",         86},
     {"Colombia",               57}, {"Egypt",         20},
     {"Ethiopia",              251}, {"France",        33},
     {"Germany",                49}, {"India",         91},
     {"Indonesia",              62}, {"Iran",          98},
     {"Italy",                  39}, {"Japan",         81},
     {"Korea, Republic of",     82}, {"Mexico",        52},
     {"Nigeria",               234}, {"Pakistan",      92},
     {"Philippines",            63}, {"Poland",        48},
     {"Russia",                  7}, {"South Africa",  27},
     {"Spain",                  34}, {"Thailand",      66},
     {"Turkey",                 90}, {"Ukraine",        7},
     {"United Kingdom",         44}, {"Vietnam",       84},
     {"Zaire",                 243}};
```

The inner braces around each structure value are optional. As a matter of style, however, I prefer not to omit them.

PROGRAM **Maintaining a Parts Database**

To illustrate how nested arrays and structures are used in practice, we'll now develop a fairly long program that maintains a database of information about parts stored in a warehouse. The program is built around an array of structures, with each structure containing information—part number, name, and quantity—about one part. Our program will support the following operations:

- *Add a new part number, part name, and initial quantity on hand.* The program must print an error message if the part is already in the database or if the database is full.

- *Given a part number, print the name of the part and the current quantity on hand.* The program must print an error message if the part number isn't in the database.

- *Given a part number, change the quantity on hand.* The program must print an error message if the part number isn't in the database.

- *Print a table showing all information in the database.* Parts must be displayed in the order in which they were entered.

- *Terminate program execution.*

We'll use the codes i (insert), s (search), u (update), p (print), and q (quit) to represent these operations. A session with the program might look like this:

```
Enter operation code: i
Enter part number: 528
Enter part name: Disk drive
Enter quantity on hand: 10
```

```
Enter operation code: s
Enter part number: 528
Part name: Disk drive
Quantity on hand: 10

Enter operation code: s
Enter part number: 914
Part not found.

Enter operation code: i
Enter part number: 914
Enter part name: Printer cable
Enter quantity on hand: 5

Enter operation code: u
Enter part number: 528
Enter change in quantity on hand: -2

Enter operation code: s
Enter part number: 528
Part name: Disk drive
Quantity on hand: 8

Enter operation code: p
Part Number    Part Name                     Quantity on Hand
    528        Disk drive                           8
    914        Printer cable                        5

Enter operation code: q
```

The program will store information about each part in a structure. We'll limit the size of the database to 100 parts, making it possible to store the structures in an array, which we'll call inventory. (If this limit proves to be too small, we can always change it later.) To keep track of the number of parts currently stored in the array, we'll use a variable named num_parts.

Since this program is menu-driven, it's fairly easy to sketch the main loop:

```
for (;;) {
  prompt user to enter operation code;
  read code;
  switch (code) {
    case 'i': perform insert operation; break;
    case 's': perform search operation; break;
    case 'u': perform update operation; break;
    case 'p': perform print operation; break;
    case 'q': terminate program;
    default:  print error message;
  }
}
```

For convenience, we'll have separate functions perform the insert, search, update, and print operations. Since these functions will all need access to inventory and num_parts, we might want to make these variables external.

Or we could hide the variables inside `main`, and then pass them to the functions as arguments. From a design standpoint, it's usually better to make variables local to a function rather than making them external (see Section 10.2 if you've forgotten why). In this program, however, hiding `inventory` and `num_parts` inside `main` would merely complicate the program.

For reasons that I'll explain later, I've decided to split the program into three files: `invent.c`, which contains the bulk of the program; `readline.h`, which contains the prototype for the `read_line` function; and `readline.c`, which contains the definition of `read_line`. We'll discuss the latter two files later in this section. For now, let's concentrate on `invent.c`.

invent.c

```
/* Maintains a parts database (array version) */

#include <stdio.h>
#include "readline.h"

#define NAME_LEN 25
#define MAX_PARTS 100

struct part {
  int number;
  char name[NAME_LEN+1];
  int on_hand;
} inventory[MAX_PARTS];

int num_parts = 0;    /* number of parts currently stored */

int find_part(int number);
void insert(void);
void search(void);
void update(void);
void print(void);

/************************************************************
 * main: Prompts the user to enter an operation code,      *
 *       then calls a function to perform the requested    *
 *       action. Repeats until the user enters the         *
 *       command 'q'. Prints an error message if the user  *
 *       enters an illegal code.                            *
 ************************************************************/
main()
{
  char code;

  for (;;) {
    printf("Enter operation code: ");
    scanf(" %c", &code);
    while (getchar() != '\n')   /* skips to end of line */
      ;
    switch (code) {
      case 'i': insert();
                break;
```

```
            case 's': search();
                      break;
            case 'u': update();
                      break;
            case 'p': print();
                      break;
            case 'q': return 0;
            default:  printf("Illegal code\n");
      }
    printf("\n");
  }
}

/************************************************************
 * find_part: Looks up a part number in the inventory      *
 *            array. Returns the array index if the part    *
 *            number is found; otherwise, returns -1.       *
 ************************************************************/
int find_part(int number)
{
  int i;

  for (i = 0; i < num_parts; i++)
    if (inventory[i].number == number)
      return i;
  return -1;
}

/************************************************************
 * insert: Prompts the user for information about a new    *
 *         part and then inserts the part into the          *
 *         database. Prints an error message and returns    *
 *         prematurely if the part already exists or the    *
 *         database is full.                                *
 ************************************************************/
void insert(void)
{
  int part_number;

  if (num_parts == MAX_PARTS) {
    printf("Database is full; can't add more parts.\n");
    return;
  }

  printf("Enter part number: ");
  scanf("%d", &part_number);
  if (find_part(part_number) >= 0) {
    printf("Part already exists.\n");
    return;
  }

  inventory[num_parts].number = part_number;
  printf("Enter part name: ");
  read_line(inventory[num_parts].name, NAME_LEN);
```

```
    printf("Enter quantity on hand: ");
    scanf("%d", &inventory[num_parts].on_hand);
    num_parts++;
}

/**************************************************************
 * search: Prompts the user to enter a part number, then     *
 *         looks up the part in the database. If the part     *
 *         exists, prints the name and quantity on hand;      *
 *         if not, prints an error message.                   *
 **************************************************************/
void search(void)
{
    int i, number;

    printf("Enter part number: ");
    scanf("%d", &number);
    i = find_part(number);
    if (i >= 0) {
        printf("Part name: %s\n", inventory[i].name);
        printf("Quantity on hand: %d\n", inventory[i].on_hand);
    } else
        printf("Part not found.\n");
}

/**************************************************************
 * update: Prompts the user to enter a part number.          *
 *         Prints an error message if the part doesn't        *
 *         exist; otherwise, prompts the user to enter        *
 *         change in quantity on hand and updates the         *
 *         database.                                          *
 **************************************************************/
void update(void)
{
    int i, number, change;

    printf("Enter part number: ");
    scanf("%d", &number);
    i = find_part(number);
    if (i >= 0) {
        printf("Enter change in quantity on hand: ");
        scanf("%d", &change);
        inventory[i].on_hand += change;
    } else
        printf("Part not found.\n");
}

/**************************************************************
 * print: Prints a listing of all parts in the database,     *
 *        showing the part number, part name, and            *
 *        quantity on hand. Parts are printed in the          *
 *        order in which they were entered into the          *
 *        database.                                          *
 **************************************************************/
```

```
void print(void)
{
  int i;

  printf("Part Number    Part Name                      "
         "Quantity on Hand\n");
  for (i = 0; i < num_parts; i++)
    printf("%7d        %-25s%11d\n", inventory[i].number,
           inventory[i].name, inventory[i].on_hand);
}
```

In main, the format string " %c" allows scanf to skip over white space before reading the operation code. The space in the format string is crucial; without it, scanf would sometimes read the new-line character that terminated a previous line of input.

The program contains one function, find_part, that isn't called from main. This "auxiliary" function helps us avoid redundant code and simplify the more important functions. By calling find_part, the insert, search, and update functions can locate a part in the database (or simply determine if the part exists).

There's just one detail left: the read_line function, which we've used to read the part name. Section 13.3 discussed the issues that are involved in writing such a function. Unfortunately, the version of read_line we developed in that section won't work properly in the current program. Consider what happens when the user inserts a part:

```
Enter part number: 528
Enter part name: Disk drive
```

The user presses the Enter (or Return) key after entering the part number and again after entering the part name, each time leaving an invisible new-line character that the program must read. For the sake of discussion, let's pretend that these characters are visible:

```
Enter part number: 528¤
Enter part name: Disk drive¤
```

When we call scanf to read the part number, it consumes the 5, 2, and 8, but leaves the ¤ character unread. If we try to read the part name using our original read_line function, it will encounter the ¤ character immediately and stop reading. This problem is common when numerical input is followed by character input. Our solution will be to write a version of read_line that skips white-space characters before it begins storing characters into the string. Not only will this solve the new-line problem, but it also enables us to avoid storing any blanks that the user may enter at the beginning of the part name.

Since read_line is unrelated to the other functions in invent.c, and since it's potentially reusable in other programs, I've decided to separate it from invent.c. The prototype for read_line will go in the readline.h header file:

readline.h
```
#ifndef READLINE_H
#define READLINE_H

/***********************************************************
 * read_line: Skips leading white-space characters, then   *
 *            reads the remainder of the input line and    *
 *            stores it in str. Truncates the line if its  *
 *            length exceeds n. Returns the number of      *
 *            characters stored.                           *
 ***********************************************************/
int read_line(char str[], int n);

#endif
```

We'll put the definition of read_line in the readline.c file:

readline.c
```
#include <ctype.h>
#include <stdio.h>
#include "readline.h"

int read_line(char str[], int n)
{
  int ch, i = 0;

  while (isspace(ch = getchar()))
    ;

  while (ch != '\n' && ch != EOF) {
    if (i < n)
      str[i++] = ch;
    ch = getchar();
  }

  str[i] = '\0';
  return i;
}
```

isspace function ➤ *23.4*   The isspace function tests whether its argument is a white-space character. Section 15.3 explains why ch has type int instead of char, and why it's good to test for EOF.

16.4 Unions

A *union*, like a structure, consists of one or more members, which may be of different types. However, the compiler allocates only enough space for the largest of the members in a union. The members of the union overlay each other within this space. As a result, assigning a new value to one member alters the values of all the other members as well.

To illustrate the basic properties of unions, let's declare a union variable, u, with two members:

```
union {
  int i;
  float f;
} u;
```

Notice how the declaration of a union closely resembles a structure declaration:

```
struct {
  int i;
  float f;
} s;
```

In fact, the structure s and the union u differ in just one way: the members of s are stored at *different* addresses in memory, while the members of u are stored at the *same* address. Here's what s and u will look like in memory (assuming that int values require two bytes and float values take four bytes):

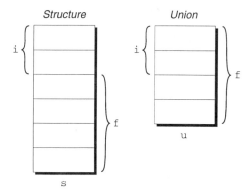

In the s structure, i and f occupy different memory locations; the total size of s is six bytes. In the u union, i and f overlap (i is really the first two bytes of f), so u occupies only four bytes. As the figure shows, u.i and u.f have the same address.

Members of a union are accessed in the same way as members of a structure. To store the number 82 in the i member of u, we would write

```
u.i = 82;
```

To store the value 74.8 in the f member, we would write

```
u.f = 74.8;
```

Since the compiler overlays storage for the members of a union, changing one member alters any value previously stored in any of the other members. Thus, if we store a value into u.f, any value previously stored in u.i will be lost. (If we examine the value of u.i, it will appear to be meaningless.) Similarly, changing u.i corrupts u.f. Because of this property, we can think of u as a place to store either i *or* f, not both. (The structure s allows us to store i *and* f.)

The properties of unions are almost identical to the properties of structures. We can declare union tags and union types in the same way we declare structure tags and types. Like structures, unions can be copied using the = operator, passed to functions, and returned by functions.

Unions can even be initialized in a manner similar to structures. However, only the first member of a union can be given an initial value. For example, we can initialize the i member of u to 0 in the following way:

```
union {
   int i;
   float f;
} u = {0};
```

Notice the presence of the braces, even though the initializer is a single expression. The expression inside the braces must be constant.

There are several important applications for unions. We'll discuss two of these now. Another application—viewing storage in different ways—is highly machine-dependent, so we'll postpone it until Section 20.3.

Using Unions to Save Space

We'll often use unions as a way to save space in structures. Suppose that we're designing a structure that will contain information about an item that's sold through a gift catalog. The catalog carries only three kinds of merchandise: books, mugs, and shirts. Each item has a stock number and a price, as well as other information that depends on the type of the item:

> *Books:* Title, author, number of pages
> *Mugs:* Design
> *Shirts:* Design, colors available, sizes available

Our first design attempt might result in the following structure:

```
struct catalog_item {
   int stock_number;
   float price;
   int item_type;
   char title[TITLE_LEN+1];
   char author[AUTHOR_LEN+1];
   int num_pages;
   char design[DESIGN_LEN+1];
   int colors;
   int sizes;
};
```

The item_type member would have one of the values BOOK, MUG, or SHIRT. The colors and sizes members would store encoded combinations of colors and sizes.

Although this structure is perfectly usable, it wastes space, since only part of the information in the structure is common to all items in the catalog. If an item is a book, for example, there's no need to store `design`, `colors`, and `sizes`. By putting a union inside the `catalog_item` structure, we can reduce the space required by the structure. The members of the union will be structures, each containing the data that's needed for a particular kind of catalog item:

```
struct catalog_item {
  int stock_number;
  float price;
  int item_type;
  union {
    struct {
      char title[TITLE_LEN+1];
      char author[AUTHOR_LEN+1];
      int num_pages;
    } book;
    struct {
      char design[DESIGN_LEN+1];
    } mug;
    struct {
      char design[DESIGN_LEN+1];
      int colors;
      int sizes;
    } shirt;
  } item;
};
```

Notice that the union (named `item`) is a member of the `catalog_item` structure, and the `book`, `mug`, and `shirt` structures are members of `item`. If `c` is a `catalog_item` structure that represents a book, we can print the book's title in the following way:

```
printf("%s", c.item.book.title);
```

C++   As this example shows, accessing a union that's nested inside a structure can be awkward: to locate a book title, we had to specify the name of a structure (`c`), the name of the union member of the structure (`item`), the name of a structure member of the union (`book`), and then the name of a member of that structure (`title`). C++ makes unions a little easier to use by allowing them to be ***anonymous***. In C++, we could have omitted the name `item` when creating the structure, then written `c.book.title` instead of `c.item.book.title`.

Using Unions to Build Mixed Data Structures

Unions have another important application: creating data structures that contain a mixture of data of different types. Let's say that we need an array whose elements are a mixture of `int` and `float` values. Since the elements of an array must be of the same type, it seems impossible to create such an array. Using unions, though, it's relatively easy. First, we define a union type whose members represent the different kinds of data to be stored in the array:

```
typedef union {
  int i;
  float f;
} Number;
```

Next, we create an array whose elements are Number values:

```
Number number_array[1000];
```

Each element of number_array is a Number union. A Number union can store either an int value or a float value, making it possible to store a mixture of int and float values in number_array. For example, suppose that we want element 0 of number_array to store 5, while element 1 stores 8.395. The following assignments will have the desired effect:

```
number_array[0].i = 5;
number_array[1].f = 8.395;
```

Adding a "Tag Field" to a Union

Unions suffer from a major problem: there's no easy way to tell which member of a union was last changed and therefore contains a meaningful value. Consider the problem of writing a function that displays the value currently stored in a Number union. This function might have the following outline:

```
void print_number(Number n)
{
  if (n contains an integer)
    printf("%d", n.i);
  else
    printf("%g", n.f);
}
```

Unfortunately, there's no way for print_number to determine whether n contains an integer or a floating-point number.

In order to keep track of this information, we can embed the union within a structure that has one other member: a "tag field" or "discriminant" whose purpose is to remind us what's currently stored in the union. In the catalog_item structure discussed earlier in this section, item_type served this purpose.

Let's convert the Number type into a structure with an embedded union:

```
#define INT_KIND   0
#define FLOAT_KIND 1

typedef struct {
  int kind;    /* tag field */
  union {
    int i;
    float f;
  } u;
} Number;
```

Number has two members, kind and u. kind has two possible values,
INT_KIND and FLOAT_KIND.

Each time we assign a value to a member of u, we'll also change kind to
remind us which member of u we modified. For example, if n is a Number variable, an assignment to the i member of u would have the following appearance:

```
n.kind = INT_KIND;
n.u.i = 82;
```

Notice that assigning to i requires that we first select the u member of n, then the
i member of u.

When we need to retrieve the number stored in a Number variable, kind will
tell us which member of the union was the last to be assigned a value. The
print_number function can take advantage of this capability:

```
void print_number(Number n)
{
  if (n.kind == INT_KIND)
    printf("%d", n.u.i);
  else
    printf("%g", n.u.f);
}
```

It's the program's responsibility to change the tag field each time an assignment is
made to a member of the union. Failing to keep the tag field up to date can result in
bizarre errors. Some programming languages treat tag fields in a more secure way,
but C makes no attempt.

16.5 Enumerations

In many programs, we'll need variables that have only a small set of meaningful
values. A "Boolean" variable, for example, should have only two possible values:
"true" and "false." A variable that stores the suit of a playing card should have
only four potential values: "clubs," "diamonds," "hearts," or "spades." The obvious way to deal with such a variable is to declare it as an integer, and have a set of
codes that represent the possible values of the variable:

```
int s;    /* s will store a suit     */

s = 2;    /* 2 represents "hearts"    */
```

Although this technique works, it leaves much to be desired. Someone reading the
program may not realize that suit isn't an ordinary integer variable, and the significance of 2 isn't immediately apparent.

Using macros to define a suit "type" and names for the various suits is a step in the right direction:

```
#define SUIT     int
#define CLUBS    0
#define DIAMONDS 1
#define HEARTS   2
#define SPADES   3
```

Our previous example now becomes easier to read:

```
SUIT s;

s = HEARTS;
```

This technique is an improvement, but it's still not the best solution. There's no indication to someone reading the program that the macros represent values of the same "type." If the number of possible values is more than a few, defining a separate macro for each will be tedious. Moreover, the names we've defined—CLUBS, DIAMONDS, HEARTS, and SPADES—will be removed by the preprocessor, so they won't be available during debugging.

C provides a special kind of type designed specifically for variables that have a small number of possible values. An ***enumeration*** is a type whose values are listed ("enumerated") by the programmer, who must create a name (an ***enumeration constant***) for each of the values. The following example enumerates the values (CLUBS, DIAMONDS, HEARTS, and SPADES) that can be assigned to the variables s1 and s2:

```
enum {CLUBS, DIAMONDS, HEARTS, SPADES} s1, s2;
```

Although enumerations have little in common with structures and unions, they're declared in a similar way. Unlike the members of a structure or union, however, the names of enumeration constants must be different from other identifiers declared in the enclosing scope.

Enumeration constants are similar to constants created with the #define directive, but they're not equivalent. In particular, enumeration constants are subject to C's scope rules: if an enumeration is declared inside a function, its constants won't be visible outside the function.

Enumeration Tags and Types

We'll often need to create names for enumerations, for the same reasons that we name structures and unions. As with structures and unions, there are two ways to name an enumeration: by declaring a tag or by using typedef to create a genuine type name.

Enumeration tags resemble structure and union tags. To define the tag suit, for example, we could write

```
enum suit {CLUBS, DIAMONDS, HEARTS, SPADES};
```

`suit` variables would be declared in the following way:

```
enum suit s1, s2;
```

As an alternative, we could use `typedef` to make `Suit` a type name:

```
typedef enum {CLUBS, DIAMONDS, HEARTS, SPADES} Suit;
Suit s1, s2;
```

Using `typedef` is an excellent way to create a Boolean type, by the way:

```
typedef enum {FALSE, TRUE} Bool;
```

Enumerations as Integers

Behind the scenes, C treats enumeration variables and constants as integers. In our `suit` enumeration, for example, CLUBS, DIAMONDS, HEARTS, and SPADES represent the numbers 0, 1, 2, and 3, respectively.

We're free to choose different values for enumeration constants. Let's say that we want CLUBS, DIAMONDS, HEARTS, and SPADES to stand for 1, 2, 3, and 4. We can specify these numbers when declaring the enumeration:

```
enum suit {CLUBS = 1, DIAMONDS = 2, HEARTS = 3, SPADES = 4};
```

The values of enumeration constants may be arbitrary integers, listed in no particular order:

```
enum dept {RESEARCH = 20, PRODUCTION = 10, SALES = 25};
```

It's even legal for two or more enumeration constants to have the same value.

When no value is specified for an enumeration constant, its value is one greater than the value of the previous constant. (The first enumeration constant has the value 0 by default.) In the following enumeration, BLACK has the value 0, LT_GRAY is 7, DK_GRAY is 8, and WHITE is 15:

```
enum EGA_colors {BLACK, LT_GRAY = 7, DK_GRAY, WHITE = 15};
```

Since enumeration values are nothing but thinly disguised integers, C allows us to mix them with ordinary integers:

```
int i;
enum {CLUBS, DIAMONDS, HEARTS, SPADES} s;

i = DIAMONDS;    /* i is now 1              */
s = 0;           /* s is now 0 (CLUBS)      */
s++;             /* s is now 1 (DIAMONDS)   */
i = s + 2;       /* i is now 3              */
```

The compiler treats s as an integer variable; the names CLUBS, DIAMONDS, HEARTS, and SPADES are just synonyms for the numbers 0, 1, 2, and 3.

C++   Although it's convenient to be able to use an enumeration value as an integer, it's dangerous to use an integer as an enumeration value (we might store the number 1 into s, for example). C++ is stricter than C in this respect—it doesn't allow an integer to be used as an enumeration value without a cast.

Using Enumerations to Declare "Tag Fields"

Enumerations are perfect for solving a problem that we encountered in Section 16.4: determining which member of a union was the last to be assigned a value. In the Number structure, for example, we can make the kind member an enumeration instead of an int:

```
typedef struct {
  enum {INT_KIND, FLOAT_KIND} kind;
  union {
    int i;
    float f;
  } u;
} Number;
```

The new structure is used in exactly the same way as the old one. The advantages are that we've done away with the INT_KIND and FLOAT_KIND macros (they're now enumeration constants), and we've clarified the meaning of kind—it's now obvious that kind should have only two possible values: INT_KIND and FLOAT_KIND.

Q & A

Q: **When I tried using `sizeof` to determine the number of bytes in a structure, I got a number that was larger than the sizes of the members added together. How can this be?**

A: Let's look at the following example:

```
struct {
  char a;
  int b;
} s;
```

If char values occupy one byte and int values occupy four bytes, how large is s? The obvious answer—five bytes—may not be the correct one. Some computers require that data items begin on a multiple of some number of bytes (typically four). To satisfy the computer's requirements, a compiler will "align" the members of a structure by leaving "holes" (unused bytes) between adjacent members. If we assume that data items must begin on a multiple of four bytes, the a member of the s structure will be followed by a three-byte hole. As a result, sizeof(s) will be 8.

By the way, a structure can have a hole at the end, as well as holes between members. For example, the structure

```
struct {
  int a;
  char b;
} s;
```

might have a three-byte hole after the b member.

Q: Can there be a "hole" at the beginning of a structure?

A: No. The C standard specifies that holes are allowed only *between* members or *after* the last member. One consequence is that the address of the first member of a structure is guaranteed to be the same as the address of the entire structure. (Note, however, that the two pointers won't have the same type.)

Q: Why isn't it legal to use == to test whether two structures are equal? [p. 333]

A: This operation was left out of C because there's no way to implement it that would be consistent with the language's philosophy. Comparing structure members one by one would be too inefficient. Comparing all bytes in the structures would be better (many computers have special instructions that can perform such a comparison rapidly). If the structures contain holes, however, comparing bytes could yield an incorrect answer; even if corresponding members have identical values, garbage present in the holes might be different. The problem could be solved by having the compiler ensure that holes always contain the same value (zero, say). Initializing holes would impose a performance penalty on all programs that use structures, however, so it's not feasible.

Q: Why does C provide two ways to name structure types (tags and typedef names)? [p. 334]

A: C originally lacked typedef, so tags were the only technique available for naming structure types. When typedef was added, it was too late to remove tags. Besides, a tag is still necessary when a member of a structure is a pointer to the structure itself.

Q: Can a structure have both a tag *and* a type name? [p. 335]

A: Yes. In fact, the tag and the type name can even be the same, although that's not required:

```
typedef struct part {
  int number;
  char name[NAME_LEN+1];
  int on_hand;
} part;
```

C++   In C++, all tags are type names as well; declaring part as a tag automatically makes part a type name also, without the need for a type definition.

Q: **How can I share a structure type among several files in a program?**

A: Put a declaration of the structure tag (or a `typedef`, if you prefer) in a header file, then include the header file where the structure is needed. To share the `part` structure, for example, we'd put the following lines in a header file:

```
struct part {
   int number;
   char name[NAME_LEN+1];
   int on_hand;
};
```

Notice that we're declaring only the structure *tag*, not variables of this type.

protecting header files ➤ 15.2   Incidentally, a header file that contains a declaration of a structure tag or structure type may need protection against multiple inclusion. Declaring a tag or type twice in the same file is an error. Similar remarks apply to unions and enumerations.

Q: **If I include the declaration of the `part` structure into two different files, will `part` variables in one file be of the same type as `part` variables in the other file?**

A: Technically, no. However, the C standard says that the `part` variables in one file have a type that's compatible with the type of the `part` variables in the other file. Variables with compatible types can be assigned to each other, so there's little practical difference between types being "compatible" and being "the same."

Exercises

Section 16.1

1. In the following declarations, the x and y structures have members named x and y:

```
struct { int x, y; } x;
struct { int x, y; } y;
```

Are these declarations legal on an individual basis? Could both declarations appear as shown in a program? Justify your answer.

2. (a) Declare structure variables named c1, c2, and c3, each with members re and im of type `double`.

(b) Modify the declaration in part (a) so that c1's members initially have the values 0.0 and 1.0, while c2's members are 1.0 and 0.0 initially. (c3 is not initialized.)

(c) Write statements that copy the members of c2 into c1. Can this be done in one statement, or does it require two?

(d) Write statements that add the corresponding members of c1 and c2, storing the result in c3.

Section 16.2

3. (a) Show how to declare a tag named `complex` for a structure with two members, re and im, of type `double`.

(b) Use the `complex` tag to declare variables named c1, c2, and c3.

(c) Write a function named `make_complex` that stores its two arguments (both of type `double`) into a `complex` structure, then returns the structure.

(d) Write a function named `add_complex` that adds the corresponding members of its arguments (both `complex` structures), then returns the result (another `complex` structure).

4.   Repeat Exercise 3, but this time using a *type* named `Complex`.

Section 16.3

5.   The following structures are designed to store information about objects on a graphics screen. A `point` structure stores the *x* and *y* coordinates of a point on the screen. A `rectangle` structure stores the coordinates of the upper left and lower right corners of a rectangle.

```
struct point { int x, y; };
struct rectangle { struct point upper_left, lower_right; };
```

Write functions that perform the following operations on a `rectangle` structure r passed as an argument:

(a) Compute the area of r.
(b) Compute the center of r, returning it as a `point` value.
(c) Move r by x units in the *x* direction and y units in the *y* direction, returning the modified version of r. (x and y are additional arguments to the function.)
(d) Determine whether a point p lies within r, returning TRUE or FALSE. (p is an additional argument of type `struct point`.)

6.   Write a program that asks the user for a country name and looks it up in the `country_codes` array. If it finds the country name, the program should display the corresponding dialing code; if not, the program should print an error message.

7.   Modify `invent.c` so that the p (print) operation displays the parts sorted by part number.

8.   Modify `invent.c` by making `inventory` and `num_parts` local to the `main` function.

9.   Modify `invent.c` by adding a `price` member to the `part` structure. The `insert` function should ask the user for the price of a new item. The `search` and `print` functions should display the price. Add a new command that allows the user to change the price of a part.

Section 16.4

10.   Suppose that s is the following structure:

```
struct {
  float a;
  union {
    char b[4];
    float c;
    int d;
  } e;
  char f[4];
} s;
```

If `char` values occupy 1 byte, `int` values occupy 2 bytes, and `float` values occupy 4 bytes, how much space will a C compiler allocate for s? (Assume that the compiler leaves no "holes" between members.)

11. Suppose that s is the following structure (point is a structure tag declared in Exercise 5):

```
struct shape {
  int shape_kind;        /* RECTANGLE or CIRCLE */
  struct point center;   /* coordinates of center */
  union {
    struct {
      int length, width;
    } rectangle;
    struct {
      int radius;
    } circle;
  } u;
} s;
```

Indicate which of the following statements are legal, and show how to repair the ones that aren't:

(a) `s.shape_kind = RECTANGLE;`
(b) `s.center.x = 10;`
(c) `s.length = 25;`
(d) `s.u.rectangle.width = 8;`
(e) `s.u.circle = 5;`
(f) `s.u.radius = 5;`

12. Let shape be the structure tag declared in Exercise 11. Write functions that perform the following operations on a shape structure s passed as an argument:

(a) Compute the area of s.
(b) Compute the center of s, returning it as a point value.
(c) Move s by x units in the x direction and y units in the y direction, returning the modified version of s. (x and y are additional arguments to the function.)
(d) Determine whether a point p lies within s, returning TRUE or FALSE. (p is an additional argument of type struct point.)

13. Write a program similar to invent.c that uses the catalog_item structure to store information about items in a catalog.

Section 16.5

14. (a) Declare a tag for an enumeration whose values represent the seven days of the week.

(b) Use typedef to define a name for the enumeration of part (a).

15. Which of the following statements about enumeration constants are true?

(a) An enumeration constant may represent any integer specified by the programmer.
(b) Enumeration constants have exactly the same properties as constants created using #define.
(c) Enumeration constants have the values 0, 1, 2, ... by default.
(d) All constants in an enumeration must have different values.
(e) Enumeration constants may be used as integers in expressions.

16. Suppose that b and i are declared as follows:

```
enum {FALSE, TRUE} b;
int i;
```

Which of the following statements are legal? Which ones are "safe" (always yield a meaningful result)?

(a) `b = FALSE;`

(b) `b = i;`

(c) `b++;`

(d) `i = b;`

(e) `i = 2 * b + 1;`

17.   (a) Each square of a chessboard can hold one piece—a pawn, knight, bishop, rook, queen, or king—or it may be empty. Each piece is either black or white. Define two enumeration types: `Piece`, which has seven possible values (one of which is "empty"), and `Color`, which has two.

(b) Using the types from part (a), define a structure type named `Square` that can store both the type of a piece and its color.

(c) Using the `Square` type from part (b), declare an 8 × 8 array named `board` that can store the entire contents of a chessboard.

(d) Add an initializer to the declaration in part (c) so that `board`'s initial value corresponds to the usual arrangement of pieces at the start of a chess game.

17 Advanced Uses of Pointers

One can only display complex information in the mind.
Like seeing, movement or flow or alteration of view is more
important than the static picture, no matter how lovely.

Previous chapters described two important uses of pointers. Chapter 11 showed how using a pointer to a variable as a function argument allows the function to modify the variable. Chapter 12 showed how to process arrays by performing arithmetic on pointers to array elements. This chapter completes our coverage of pointers by examining two additional applications: *dynamic storage allocation* and pointers to functions.

Using dynamic storage allocation, a program can obtain blocks of memory as needed during execution. Section 17.1 explains the basics of dynamic storage allocation. Section 17.2 discusses dynamically allocated strings, which are more flexible than C's usual fixed-length character arrays. Section 17.3 covers dynamic storage allocation for arrays in general. Section 17.4 deals with the issue of storage deallocation—releasing blocks of dynamically allocated memory when they're no longer needed.

Dynamically allocated structures play a big role in C programming, since they can be linked together to form lists, trees, and other highly flexible data structures. Section 17.5 focuses on *linked lists,* the most fundamental linked data structure. Section 17.6 covers pointers to pointers, a topic that arises in Section 17.5.

Section 17.7 introduces pointers to functions, a surprisingly useful concept. Some of C's most powerful library functions expect function pointers as arguments. We'll examine one of these functions, qsort, which can sort any array.

17.1 Dynamic Storage Allocation

C's data structures are normally fixed in size; an array, for example, has a fixed number of elements, and each element has a fixed size. Fixed-size data structures

359

can be a problem, since we're forced to choose their sizes when writing a program; we can't change the sizes without modifying the program and compiling it again.

Consider the `invent` program of Section 16.3, which allows the user to add parts to a database. The database is stored in an array of length 100. To enlarge the capacity of the database, we can increase the size of the array and recompile the program. But no matter how large we make the array, there's always the possibility that it will fill up. Fortunately, all is not lost. C supports ***dynamic storage allocation:*** the ability to allocate storage during program execution. Using dynamic storage allocation, we can design data structures that grow (and shrink) as needed.

Although it's available for all types of data, dynamic storage allocation is used most often for strings, arrays, and structures. Dynamically allocated structures are of particular interest, since we can link them together to form lists, trees, and other data structures.

Memory Allocation Functions

To allocate storage dynamically, we'll need to call one of the three memory allocation functions declared in the `<stdlib.h>` header:

- `malloc`—Allocates a block of memory, but doesn't initialize it.
- `calloc`—Allocates a block of memory and clears it.
- `realloc`—Resizes a previously allocated block of memory.

Of the three, `malloc` is probably the most used. It's more efficient than `calloc`, since it doesn't have to clear the memory block that it allocates.

When we call a memory allocation function to request a block of memory, the function has no idea what type of data we're planning to store in the block, so it can't return an ordinary `int` pointer or `char` pointer or whatever. Instead, the function returns a value of type `void *`. A `void *` value is a "generic" pointer—essentially, just a memory address.

Null Pointers

When we call a memory allocation function, there's always a possibility that it won't be able to locate a block of memory large enough to satisfy our request. If that should happen, the function will return a ***null pointer.*** A null pointer is a "pointer to nothing"—a special value that can be distinguished from all valid pointers. After we've stored the return value in a pointer variable p, we must test p to see if it's a null pointer.

It's the programmer's responsibility to test the return value of any memory allocation function and take appropriate action if it's a null pointer. The effect of attempting to access memory through a null pointer is undefined; the program may crash or behave unpredictably.

Q&A   The null pointer is represented by a macro named NULL, so we can test `malloc`'s return value in the following way:

```
p = malloc(10000);
if (p == NULL) {
  /* allocation failed; take appropriate action */
}
```

Some programmers combine the call of `malloc` with the NULL test:

```
if ((p = malloc(10000)) == NULL) {
  /* allocation failed; take appropriate action */
}
```

The NULL macro is defined in six headers: `<locale.h>`, `<stddef.h>`, `<stdio.h>`, `<stdlib.h>`, `<string.h>`, and `<time.h>`. As long as one of these headers is included in a program, the compiler will recognize NULL. A program that uses any of the memory allocation functions will include `<stdlib.h>`, of course, making NULL available.

In C, pointers test true or false in the same way as numbers. All non-null pointers test true; only null pointers are false. Thus, instead of writing

```
if (p == NULL) …
```

we could write

```
if (!p) …
```

and instead of writing

```
if (p != NULL) …
```

we could write

```
if (p) …
```

As a matter of style, I prefer the explicit comparison with NULL.

17.2   Dynamically Allocated Strings

Dynamic storage allocation is often useful for working with strings. Strings are always stored in fixed-size arrays, and it can be hard to anticipate how long these arrays need to be. By allocating strings dynamically, we can postpone the decision until the program is running.

Using **malloc** to Allocate Memory for a String

The `malloc` function has the following prototype:

```
void *malloc(size_t size);
```

size_t type ►*21.3*

`malloc` allocates a block of `size` bytes and returns a pointer to it. Note that `size` has type `size_t`, an unsigned integer type defined in the C library. Unless we're allocating a very large block of memory, we can just think of `size` as an ordinary integer.

Using `malloc` to allocate memory for a string is easy, because C guarantees that a `char` value requires exactly one byte of storage (`sizeof(char)` is 1, in other words). To allocate space for a string of n characters, we'd write

```
p = malloc(n+1);
```

where p is a `char *` variable. The generic pointer that `malloc` returns will be converted to `char *` when the assignment is performed; no cast is necessary. (In general, we can assign a `void *` value to a variable of any pointer type and vice versa.) Nevertheless, some programmers prefer to cast `malloc`'s return value:

Q&A

```
p = (char *) malloc(n+1);
```

 When using `malloc` to allocate space for a string, don't forget to include room for the null character.

Memory allocated using `malloc` isn't cleared or initialized in any way, so p points to an uninitialized array of n + 1 characters:

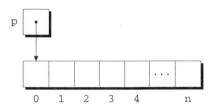

Calling `strcpy` is one way to initialize this array:

```
strcpy(p, "abc");
```

The first four characters in the array will now be a, b, c, and \0:

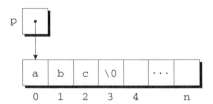

Using Dynamic Storage Allocation in String Functions

Dynamic storage allocation makes it possible to write functions that return a pointer to a "new" string—a string that didn't exist before the function was called.

Consider the problem of writing a function that concatenates two strings without changing either one. C's standard library doesn't include such a function (`strcat` isn't quite what we want, since it modifies one of the strings passed to it), but we can easily write our own.

Our function will measure the lengths of the two strings to be concatenated, then call `malloc` to allocate just the right amount of space for the result. The function next copies the first string into the new space and calls `strcat` to concatenate the second string.

```c
char *concat(const char *s1, const char *s2)
{
  char *result;

  result = malloc(strlen(s1) + strlen(s2) + 1);
  if (result == NULL) {
    printf("Error: malloc failed in concat\n");
    exit(EXIT_FAILURE);
  }
  strcpy(result, s1);
  strcat(result, s2);
  return result;
}
```

If `malloc` returns a null pointer, `concat` prints an error message and terminates the program. That's not always the right action to take; some programs need to recover from memory allocation failures and continue running.

Here's how the `concat` function might be called:

```c
p = concat("abc", "def");
```

After the call, p will point to the string `"abcdef"`, which is stored in a dynamically allocated array. The array is seven characters long, including the null character at the end.

 Functions like `concat` that dynamically allocate storage must be used with care. When the string that `concat` returns is no longer needed, we'll need to call `free` to release the space that it occupies. If we don't, the program may run out of memory prematurely.

Arrays of Dynamically Allocated Strings

In Section 13.7, we tackled the problem of storing strings in an array. We found that storing strings as rows in a two-dimensional array of characters can waste space, so we tried setting up an array of pointers to string literals. The techniques of Section 13.7 work just as well if the elements of an array are pointers to dynamically allocated strings. To illustrate this point, let's rewrite the `remind.c` program of Section 13.5, which printed a one-month list of daily reminders.

PROGRAM   **Printing a One-Month Reminder List (Revisited)**

The original `remind.c` program stores the reminder strings in a two-dimensional array of characters, with each row of the array containing one string. After the program reads a day and its associated reminder, it searches the array to determine where the day belongs, using `strcmp` to do comparisons. It then uses `strcpy` to move all strings below that point down one position. Finally, the program copies the day into the array and calls `strcat` to append the reminder to the day.

In the new program (`remind2.c`), the array will be one-dimensional; its elements will be pointers to dynamically allocated strings. Switching to dynamically allocated strings in this program will have two primary advantages. First, we can use space more efficiently by allocating the exact number of characters needed to store a reminder, rather than storing the reminder in a fixed number of characters (as the original program does). Second, we won't need to call `strcpy` to move strings "down" in order to make room for a new reminder. Instead, we'll merely move *pointers* to strings.

Here's the new program, with changes in **bold.** Switching from a two-dimensional array to an array of pointers turns out to be remarkably easy: we'll only need to change eight lines of the program.

remind2.c

```
/* Prints a one-month reminder list */

#include <stdio.h>
#include <stdlib.h>
#include <string.h>

#define MAX_REMIND 50
#define MSG_LEN 60

int read_line(char str[], int n);

main()
{
  char *reminders[MAX_REMIND];
  char day_str[3], msg_str[MSG_LEN+1];
  int day, i, j, num_remind = 0;

  for (;;) {
    if (num_remind == MAX_REMIND) {
      printf("-- No space left --\n");
      break;
    }

    printf("Enter day and reminder: ");
    scanf("%2d", &day);
    if (day == 0)
      break;
    sprintf(day_str, "%2d", day);
    read_line(msg_str, MSG_LEN);
```

```
      for (i = 0; i < num_rcmind; i++)
        if (strcmp(day_str, reminders[i]) < 0)
          break;
      for (j = num_remind; j > i; j--)
        reminders[j] = reminders[j-1];

      reminders[i] = malloc(2 + strlen(msg_str) + 1);
      if (reminders[i] == NULL) {
        printf("-- No space left --\n");
        break;
      }

      strcpy(reminders[i], day_str);
      strcat(reminders[i], msg_str);

      num_remind++;
    }

    printf("\nDay Reminder\n");
    for (i = 0; i < num_remind; i++)
      printf(" %s\n", reminders[i]);

    return 0;
  }

  int read_line(char str[], int n)
  {
    char ch;
    int i = 0;

    while ((ch = getchar()) != '\n')
      if (i < n)
        str[i++] = ch;

    str[i] = '\0';
    return i;
  }
```

17.3 Dynamically Allocated Arrays

Dynamically allocated arrays have the same advantages as dynamically allocated strings (not surprisingly, since strings *are* arrays). When we're writing a program, it's often difficult to estimate the proper size for an array; it would be more convenient to wait until the program is run to decide how large the array should be. C solves this problem by allowing a program to allocate space for an array during execution, then access the array through a pointer to its first element. The close relationship between arrays and pointers, which we explored in Chapter 12, makes a dynamically allocated array just as easy to use as an ordinary array.

Although `malloc` can allocate space for an array, the `calloc` function is often used as an alternative, since it initializes the memory that it allocates. The `realloc` function allows us to make an array "grow" or "shrink" as needed.

Using `malloc` to Allocate Storage for an Array

We can use `malloc` to allocate space for an array in much the same way we used it to allocate space for a string. The primary difference is that the elements of an arbitrary array won't necessarily be one byte long, as they are in a string. As a result, we'll need to use the `sizeof` operator to calculate the amount of space required for each element.

sizeof operator ➤ 7.4

Suppose we're writing a program that needs an array of n integers, where n is to be computed during the execution of the program. We'll first declare a pointer variable:

```
int *a;
```

Once the value of n is known, we'll have the program call `malloc` to allocate space for the array:

```
a = malloc(n * sizeof(int));
```

Always use `sizeof` when calculating how much space is needed for an array. Failing to allocate enough memory can have severe consequences. Consider the following attempt to allocate space for an array of n integers:

```
a = malloc(n * 2);
```

If `int` values are larger than two bytes (as they are on many computers), `malloc` won't allocate a large enough block of memory. When we later store values into the array, the program may crash or behave erratically.

Once it points to a dynamically allocated block of memory, we can ignore the fact that a is a pointer and use it instead as an array name, thanks to the relationship between arrays and pointers in C. For example, we could use the following loop to initialize the array that a points to:

```
for (i = 0; i < n; i++)
  a[i] = 0;
```

Of course, we have the option of using pointer arithmetic instead of subscripting to access the elements of the array.

The `calloc` Function

Although the `malloc` function can be used to allocate memory for an array, C provides an alternative—the `calloc` function—that's sometimes better. `calloc` has the following prototype in `<stdlib.h>`:

```
void *calloc(size_t nmemb, size_t size);
```

`calloc` allocates space for an array with `nmemb` elements, each of which is `size` bytes long; it returns a null pointer if the requested space isn't available. After locating the memory, `calloc` initializes it by setting all bits to 0. For example, the following call of `calloc` allocates space for an array of n integers, which are all guaranteed to be zero initially:

```
a = calloc(n, sizeof(int));
```

Since `calloc` clears the memory that it allocates but `malloc` doesn't, we may occasionally want to use `calloc` to allocate space for a non-array. By calling `calloc` with 1 as its first argument, we can allocate space for a data item of any type:

```
struct point { int x, y; } *p;

p = calloc(1, sizeof(struct point));
```

After this statement has been executed, p will point to a structure whose x and y members have been set to zero.

The `realloc` Function

Once we've allocated memory for an array, we may later find that it's too large or too small. The `realloc` function can resize the array to better suit our needs. The following prototype for `realloc` appears in `<stdlib.h>`:

```
void *realloc(void *ptr, size_t size);
```

When `realloc` is called, `ptr` must point to a memory block obtained by a previous call of `malloc`, `calloc`, or `realloc`. `size` represents the new size of the block, which may be larger or smaller than the original size. Although `realloc` doesn't require that `ptr` point to memory that's being used as an array, in practice it usually does.

 Be sure that a pointer passed to `realloc` came from a previous call of `malloc`, `calloc`, or `realloc`. If it didn't, the program may behave erratically.

The C standard spells out a number of rules concerning the behavior of `realloc`:

- When it expands a memory block, `realloc` doesn't initialize the bytes that are added to the block.
- If `realloc` can't enlarge the memory block as requested, it returns a null pointer; the data in the old memory block is unchanged.
- If `realloc` is called with a null pointer as its first argument, it behaves like `malloc`.

■ If `realloc` is called with 0 as its second argument, it frees the memory block.

The C standard stops short of specifying exactly how `realloc` works. Still, we expect it to be reasonably efficient. When asked to reduce the size of a memory block, `realloc` should shrink the block "in place," without moving the data stored in the block. By the same token, `realloc` should always attempt to expand a memory block without moving it. If it's unable to enlarge the block (because the bytes following the block are already in use for some other purpose), `realloc` will allocate a new block elsewhere, then copy the contents of the old block into the new one.

Once `realloc` has returned, be sure to update all pointers to the memory block, since it's possible that `realloc` has moved the block elsewhere.

17.4 Deallocating Storage

`malloc` and the other memory allocation functions obtain memory blocks from a storage pool known as the **heap.** Calling these functions often—or asking them for large blocks of memory—can exhaust the heap, causing the functions to return a null pointer.

To make matters worse, a program may allocate blocks of memory and then lose track of them, thereby wasting space. Consider the following example:

```
p = malloc(…);
q = malloc(…);
p = q;
```

After the first two statements have been executed, `p` points to one memory block, while `q` points to another:

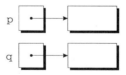

After `q` is assigned to `p`, both pointers now point to the second memory block:

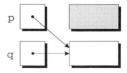

There are no pointers to the first block (shaded), so we'll never be able to use it again.

A block of memory that's no longer accessible to a program is said to be ***garbage.*** A program that leaves garbage behind has a ***memory leak.*** Some languages provide a ***garbage collector*** that automatically locates and recycles garbage, but C doesn't. Instead, each C program is responsible for recycling its own garbage by calling the `free` function to release unneeded memory.

The `free` Function

The `free` function has the following prototype in `<stdlib.h>`:

```
void free(void *ptr);
```

Using `free` is easy; we simply pass it a pointer to a memory block that we no longer need:

```
p = malloc(…);
q = malloc(…);
free(p);
p = q;
```

Calling `free` releases the block of memory that p points to. This block is returned to the heap, where it becomes available for reuse in subsequent calls of `malloc` or other memory allocation functions.

 The argument to `free` must be a pointer that was previously returned by a memory allocation function. Calling `free` with any other argument (a pointer to a variable or array element, for example) can cause unpredictable behavior.

The "Dangling Pointer" Problem

Although the `free` function allows us to reclaim memory that's no longer needed, using it leads to a new problem: ***dangling pointers.*** The call `free(p)` deallocates the memory block that p points to, but doesn't change p itself. If we forget that p no longer points to a valid memory block, chaos may ensue:

```
char *p = malloc(4);
…
free(p);
…
strcpy(p, "abc");    /*** WRONG ***/
```

Modifying the memory that p points to is a serious error, since our program no longer has control of that memory.

Attempting to modify a deallocated memory block can have disastrous consequences, including a program crash.

Dangling pointers can be hard to spot, since several pointers may point to the same block of memory. When the block is freed, all the pointers are left dangling.

17.5   Linked Lists

Dynamic storage allocation is especially useful for building lists, trees, graphs, and other linked data structures. We'll look at linked lists in this section; a discussion of other linked data structures is beyond the scope of this book. For more information, consult a book such as Horowitz, Sahni, and Anderson-Freed, *Fundamentals of Data Structures in C* (New York: Computer Science Press, 1993).

A *linked list* consists of a chain of structures (called *nodes*), with each node containing a pointer to the next node in the chain:

The last node in the list contains a null pointer, shown here as a diagonal line.

In previous chapters, we've used an array whenever we've needed to store a collection of data items; linked lists give us an alternative. A linked list is more flexible than an array; we can easily insert and delete nodes in a linked list, allowing the list to grow and shrink as needed. On the other hand, we lose the "random access" capability of an array. Any element of an array can be accessed in the same amount of time; accessing a node in a linked list is fast if the node is close to the beginning of the list, slow if it's near the end.

This section describes how to set up a linked list in C. It also shows how to perform several common operations on linked lists: inserting a node at the beginning of a list, searching for a node, and deleting a node.

Declaring a Node Type

To set up a linked list, the first thing we'll need is a structure that represents a single node in the list. For simplicity, let's assume that a node contains nothing but an integer (the node's data) plus a pointer to the next node in the list. Here's what our node structure will look like:

```
struct node {
  int value;            /* data stored in the node  */
  struct node *next;    /* pointer to the next node */
};
```

Notice that the `next` member has type `struct node *`, which means that it can store a pointer to a `node` structure. There's nothing special about the name `node`, by the way; it's just an ordinary structure tag.

One aspect of the `node` structure deserves special mention. As Section 16.2 explained, we normally have the option of using either a tag or a `typedef` name to define a name for a particular kind of structure. However, when a structure has a member that points to the same kind of structure, as `node` does, we're required to use a structure tag. Without the `node` tag, we'd have no way to declare the type of `next`.

Q&A

Now that we have the `node` structure declared, we'll need a way to keep track of where the list begins. In other words, we'll need a variable that always points to the first node in the list. Let's name the variable `first`:

```
struct node *first = NULL;
```

We've initialized `first` to NULL to indicate that the list is initially empty.

Creating Nodes

As we construct a linked list, we'll need to create nodes one by one, adding each to the list. Creating a node involves three steps:

1. allocating memory for the node,
2. storing data into the node, and
3. inserting the node into the list.

We'll concentrate on the first two steps for now.

In order to create a node, we'll need a variable that can point to the node temporarily, until it's been inserted into the list. Let's call this variable `new_node`:

```
struct node *new_node;
```

We'll use `malloc` to allocate memory for the new node, saving the return value in `new_node`:

```
new_node = malloc(sizeof(struct node));
```

`new_node` now points to a block of memory just large enough to hold a `node` structure:

Be careful to give `sizeof` the name of the *type* to be allocated, not the name of a *pointer* to that type:

```
new_node = malloc(sizeof(new_node));    /*** WRONG ***/
```

The program will still compile, but `malloc` will allocate only enough memory for a pointer to a `node` structure, not the structure itself. The likely result is a crash later, when the program attempts to store data in the node that `new_node` is presumably pointing to.

Next, we'll store data into the `value` member of the new node:

```
(*new_node).value = 10;
```

Here's how the picture will look after this assignment:

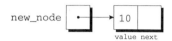

To access the `value` member of the node, we've applied the indirection operator `*` (to reference the structure to which `new_node` points), then the selection operator `.` (to select a member within this structure). The parentheses around `*new_node` are mandatory because the `.` operator would otherwise take prece-

table of operators ➤Appendix B   dence over the `*` operator.

The -> Operator

Before we go on to the next step, inserting a new node into a list, let's take a moment to discuss a useful shortcut. Accessing a member of a structure using a pointer is so common that C provides a special operator just for this purpose. This operator, known as **right arrow selection,** is a minus sign followed by `>`. Using the `->` operator, we can write

```
new_node->value = 10;
```

instead of

```
(*new_node).value = 10;
```

The `->` operator is a combination of the `*` and `.` operators; it performs indirection on `new_node` to locate the structure that it points to, then selects the `value` member of the structure.

lvalues ➤4.2   The `->` operator produces an lvalue, so we can use it wherever an ordinary variable would be allowed. We've just seen an example in which `new_node->value` appears on the left side of an assignment. It could just as easily appear in a call of `scanf`:

```
scanf("%d", &new_node->value);
```

Notice that the `&` operator is still required, even though `new_node` is a pointer. Without the `&`, we'd be passing `scanf` the *value* of `new_node->value`, which has type `int`.

Inserting a Node at the Beginning of a Linked List

We're now ready to insert a new node into a linked list. One of the advantages of a linked list is that nodes can be added at any point in the list: at the beginning, at the end, or anywhere in the middle. The beginning of a list is the easiest place to insert a node, however, so let's focus on that case.

If new_node is pointing to the node to be inserted, and first is pointing to the first node in the linked list, then we'll need two statements to insert the node into the list. First, we'll modify the new node's next member to point to the node that was previously at the beginning of the list:

```
new_node->next = first;
```

Second, we'll make first point to the new node:

```
first = new_node;
```

Will these statements work if the list is empty when we insert a node? Yes, fortunately. To make sure this is true, let's trace the process of inserting two nodes into an empty list. We'll insert a node containing the number 10 first, followed by a node containing 20. In the figures that follow, null pointers are shown as diagonal lines.

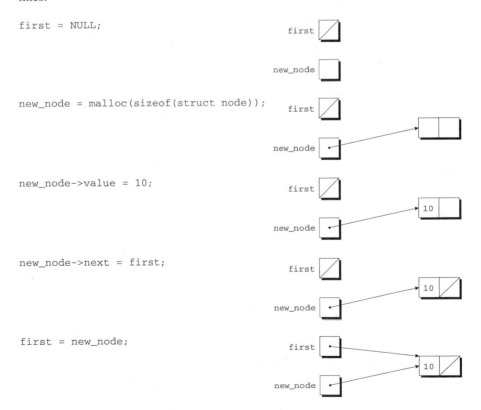

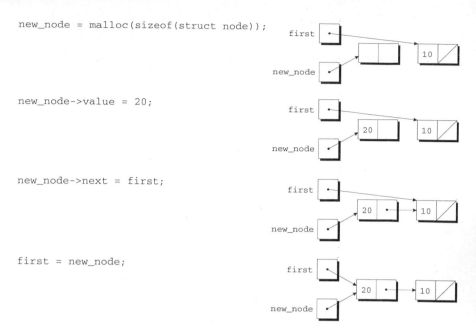

```
new_node = malloc(sizeof(struct node));
```

```
new_node->value = 20;
```

```
new_node->next = first;
```

```
first = new_node;
```

Inserting a node into a linked list is such a common operation that we'll probably want to write a function for that purpose. Let's name the function add_to_list. It will have two parameters: list (a pointer to the first node in the old list) and n (the integer to be stored in the new node).

```
struct node *add_to_list(struct node *list, int n)
{
  struct node *new_node;

  new_node = malloc(sizeof(struct node));
  if (new_node == NULL) {
    printf("Error: malloc failed in add_to_list\n");
    exit(EXIT_FAILURE);
  }
  new_node->value = n;
  new_node->next = list;
  return new_node;
}
```

Note that add_to_list doesn't modify the list pointer. Instead, it returns a pointer to the newly created node (now at the beginning of the list). When we call add_to_list, we'll need to store its return value into first:

```
first = add_to_list(first, 10);
first = add_to_list(first, 20);
```

These statements add nodes containing 10 and 20 to the list pointed to by first. Getting add_to_list to update first directly, rather than return a new value for first, turns out to be tricky. We'll come back to this issue in Section 17.6.

The following function uses `add_to_list` to create a linked list containing numbers entered by the user:

```
struct node *read_numbers(void)
{
  struct node *first = NULL;
  int n;

  printf("Enter a series of integers (0 to terminate): ");
  for (;;) {
    scanf("%d", &n);
    if (n == 0)
      return first;
    first = add_to_list(first, n);
  }
}
```

The numbers will be in reverse order within the list, since `first` always points to the node containing the last number entered.

Searching a Linked List

Once we've created a linked list, we may need to search it for a particular piece of data. Although a `while` loop can be used to search a list, the `for` statement is often superior. We're accustomed to using the `for` statement when writing loops that involve counting, but its flexibility makes the `for` statement suitable for other tasks as well, including operations on linked lists. Here's the customary way to search a linked list, using a pointer variable p to keep track of the "current" node:

idiom
```
for (p = first; p != NULL; p = p->next)
  ...
```

The assignment

```
p = p->next
```

advances the p pointer from one node to the next. An assignment of this form is invariably used in C when writing a loop that traverses a linked list.

Let's write a function named `search_list` that searches a list (pointed to by the parameter `list`) for an integer n. If it finds n, `search_list` will return a pointer to the node containing n; otherwise, it will return a null pointer. Our first version of `search_list` relies on the usual "list-searching" idiom:

```
struct node *search_list(struct node *list, int n)
{
  struct node *p;

  for (p = list; p != NULL; p = p->next)
    if (p->value == n)
      return p;
  return NULL;
}
```

Of course, there are many other ways to write `search_list`. One alternative would be to eliminate the `p` variable, instead using `list` itself to keep track of the current node:

```
struct node *search_list(struct node *list, int n)
{
  for (; list != NULL; list = list->next)
    if (list->value == n)
      return list;
  return NULL;
}
```

Since `list` is a copy of the original list pointer, there's no harm in changing it within the function.

Another alternative is to combine the `list->value == n` test with the `list != NULL` test:

```
struct node *search_list(struct node *list, int n)
{
  for (; list != NULL && list->value != n;
         list = list->next)
    ;
  return list;
}
```

Since `list` is NULL if we reach the end of the list, returning `list` is correct even if we don't find n. This version of `search_list` might be a bit clearer if we used a `while` statement:

```
struct node *search_list(struct node *list, int n)
{
  while (list != NULL && list->value != n)
    list = list->next;
  return list;
}
```

Deleting a Node from a Linked List

A big advantage of storing data in a linked list is that we can easily delete nodes that we no longer need. Deleting a node, like creating a node, involves three steps:

1. locating the node to be deleted,
2. altering the previous node so that it "bypasses" the deleted node, and
3. calling `free` to reclaim the space occupied by the deleted node.

Step 1 is harder than it looks. If we search the list in the obvious way, we'll end up with a pointer to the node to be deleted. Unfortunately, we won't be able to perform step 2, which requires changing the *previous* node.

There are various solutions to this problem. We'll use the "trailing pointer" technique: as we search the list in step 1, we'll keep a pointer to the previous node (`prev`) as well as a pointer to the current node (`cur`). If `list` points to the list to be searched and n is the integer to be deleted, the following loop implements step 1:

```
for (cur = list, prev = NULL;
     cur != NULL && cur->value != n;
     prev = cur, cur = cur->next)
  ;
```

Here we see the power of C's for statement. This rather exotic example, with its empty body and liberal use of the comma operator, performs all the actions needed to search for n. When the loop terminates, cur points to the node to be deleted, while prev points to the previous node (if there is one).

To see how this loop works, let's assume that list points to a list containing 30, 40, 20, and 10, in that order:

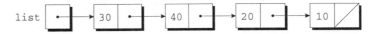

Let's say that n is 20, so our goal is to delete the third node in the list. After cur = list, prev = NULL has been executed, cur points to the first node in the list:

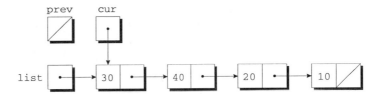

The test cur != NULL && cur->value != n is true, since cur is pointing to a node and the node doesn't contain 20. After prev = cur, cur = cur->next has been executed, we begin to see how the prev pointer will trail behind cur:

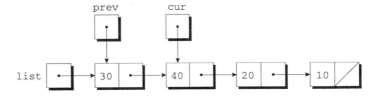

Again, the test cur != NULL && cur->value != n is true, so prev = cur, cur = cur->next is executed once more:

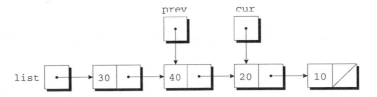

Since cur now points to the node containing 20, the condition cur->value !=
n is false and the loop terminates.

Next, we'll perform the bypass required by step 2. The statement

```
prev->next = cur->next;
```

makes the pointer in the previous node point to the node *after* the current node:

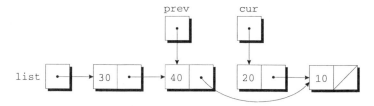

We're now ready for step 3, releasing the memory occupied by the current node:

```
free(cur);
```

The following function uses the strategy that we've just outlined. When given
a list and an integer n, delete_from_list deletes the first node containing n.
If no node contains n, the function does nothing. In either case, the function
returns a pointer to the list.

```
struct node *delete_from_list(struct node *list, int n)
{
  struct node *cur, *prev;

  for (cur = list, prev = NULL;
       cur != NULL && cur->value != n;
       prev = cur, cur = cur->next)
    ;

  if (cur == NULL)
    return list;                    /* n was not found */
  if (prev == NULL)
    list = list->next;              /* n is in the first node */
  else
    prev->next = cur->next;    /* n is in some other node */
  free(cur);
  return list;
}
```

Deleting the first node in the list is a special case. The prev == NULL test checks
for this case, which requires a different bypass step.

Ordered Lists

When the nodes of a list are kept in order—sorted by the data stored inside the
nodes—we say that the list is **ordered.** Working with an ordered list is similar to

working with one that's not ordered. Inserting a node into an ordered list is more difficult, though (the node won't always be put at the beginning of the list), but searching is faster (we can stop looking after reaching the point at which the desired node would have been located). The following program illustrates both the increased difficulty of inserting a node and the faster search.

PROGRAM   **Maintaining a Parts Database (Revisited)**

Let's redo the parts database program of Section 16.3, this time storing the database in a linked list. Using a linked list instead of an array has two major advantages: (1) We don't need to put a preset limit on the size of the database; it can grow until there's no more memory to store parts. (2) We can easily keep the database sorted by part number—when a new part is added to the database, we simply insert it in its proper place in the list. In the original program, the database wasn't sorted.

In the new program, the part structure will contain an additional member (a pointer to the next node in the linked list), and the variable inventory will be a pointer to the first node in the list:

```
struct part {
  int number;
  char name[NAME_LEN+1];
  int on_hand;
  struct part *next;
};

struct part *inventory = NULL;   /* points to first part */
```

Most of the functions in the new program will closely resemble their counterparts in the original program. The find_part and insert functions have become more complex, however, since we're keeping the nodes in the inventory list sorted by part number.

In the original program, find_part returns an index into the inventory array. In the new program, find_part will return a pointer to the node that contains the desired part number. If it doesn't find the part number, find_part will return a null pointer. Since the inventory list is sorted by part number, the new version of find_part can save time by stopping its search when it finds a node containing a part number that's greater than or equal to the desired part number. find_part's search loop will have the form

```
for (p = inventory;
     p != NULL && number > p->number;
     p = p->next)
  ;
```

The loop will terminate when p becomes NULL (indicating that the part number wasn't found) or when number > p->number is false (indicating that the part number we're looking for is less than or equal to a number already stored in a node). In the latter case, we still don't know whether or not the desired number is actually in the list, so we'll need another test:

```
if (p != NULL && number == p->number)
  return p;
```

The original version of `insert` stores a new part in the next available array element. The new version must determine where the new part belongs in the list and insert it there. We'll also have `insert` check whether the part number is already present in the list. `insert` can accomplish both tasks by using a loop similar to the one in `find_part`:

```
for (cur = inventory, prev = NULL;
     cur != NULL && new_node->number > cur->number;
     prev = cur, cur = cur->next)
  ;
```

This loop relies on two pointers: `cur`, which points to the current node, and `prev`, which points to the previous node. Once the loop terminates, `insert` will check whether `cur` isn't `NULL` and `new_node->number` equals `cur->number`; if so, the part number is already in the list. Otherwise `insert` will insert a new node between the nodes pointed to by `prev` and `cur`, using a strategy similar to the one we employed for deleting a node. (This strategy works even if the new part number is larger than any in the list; in that case, `cur` will be `NULL` but `prev` will point to the last node in the list.)

Here's the new program. Like the original program, this version requires the `read_line` function described in Section 16.3; I assume that `readline.h` contains a prototype for this function.

invent2.c   `/* Maintains a parts database (linked list version) */`

```
#include <stdio.h>
#include <stdlib.h>
#include "readline.h"

#define NAME_LEN 25

struct part {
  int number;
  char name[NAME_LEN+1];
  int on_hand;
  struct part *next;
};

struct part *inventory = NULL;   /* points to first part */

struct part *find_part(int number);
void insert(void);
void search(void);
void update(void);
void print(void);
```

```
/*********************************************************
 * main: Prompts the user to enter an operation code,   *
 *       then calls a function to perform the requested *
 *       action. Repeats until the user enters the      *
 *       command 'q'. Prints an error message if the user *
 *       enters an illegal code.                        *
 *********************************************************/
main()
{
  char code;

  for (;;) {
    printf("Enter operation code: ");
    scanf(" %c", &code);
    while (getchar() != '\n')   /* skips to end of line */
      ;
    switch (code) {
      case 'i': insert();
                break;
      case 's': search();
                break;
      case 'u': update();
                break;
      case 'p': print();
                break;
      case 'q': return 0;
      default:  printf("Illegal code\n");
    }
    printf("\n");
  }
}

/*********************************************************
 * find_part: Looks up a part number in the inventory   *
 *            list. Returns a pointer to the node        *
 *            containing the part number; if the part    *
 *            number is not found, returns NULL.         *
 *********************************************************/
struct part *find_part(int number)
{
  struct part *p;

  for (p = inventory;
       p != NULL && number > p->number;
       p = p->next)
    ;
  if (p != NULL && number == p->number)
    return p;
  return NULL;
}
```

```
/*********************************************************
 * insert: Prompts the user for information about a new  *
 *         part and then inserts the part into the       *
 *         inventory list; the list remains sorted by    *
 *         part number. Prints an error message and      *
 *         returns prematurely if the part already exists *
 *         or space could not be allocated for the part. *
 *********************************************************/
void insert(void)
{
  struct part *cur, *prev, *new_node;

  new_node = malloc(sizeof(struct part));
  if (new_node == NULL) {
    printf("Database is full; can't add more parts.\n");
    return;
  }

  printf("Enter part number: ");
  scanf("%d", &new_node->number);

  for (cur = inventory, prev = NULL;
       cur != NULL && new_node->number > cur->number;
       prev = cur, cur = cur->next)
    ;
  if (cur != NULL && new_node->number == cur->number) {
    printf("Part already exists.\n");
    free(new_node);
    return;
  }

  printf("Enter part name: ");
  read_line(new_node->name, NAME_LEN);
  printf("Enter quantity on hand: ");
  scanf("%d", &new_node->on_hand);

  new_node->next = cur;
  if (prev == NULL)
    inventory = new_node;
  else
    prev->next = new_node;
}

/*********************************************************
 * search: Prompts the user to enter a part number, then *
 *         looks up the part in the database. If the part *
 *         exists, prints the name and quantity on hand; *
 *         if not, prints an error message.              *
 *********************************************************/
void search(void)
{
  int number;
  struct part *p;
```

```
    printf("Enter part number: ");
    scanf("%d", &number);
    p = find_part(number);
    if (p != NULL) {
      printf("Part name: %s\n", p->name);
      printf("Quantity on hand: %d\n", p->on_hand);
    } else
      printf("Part not found.\n");
}

/**************************************************************
 * update: Prompts the user to enter a part number.         *
 *         Prints an error message if the part doesn't      *
 *         exist; otherwise, prompts the user to enter      *
 *         change in quantity on hand and updates the       *
 *         database.                                        *
 **************************************************************/
void update(void)
{
  int number, change;
  struct part *p;

  printf("Enter part number: ");
  scanf("%d", &number);
  p = find_part(number);
  if (p != NULL) {
    printf("Enter change in quantity on hand: ");
    scanf("%d", &change);
    p->on_hand += change;
  } else
    printf("Part not found.\n");
}

/**************************************************************
 * print: Prints a listing of all parts in the database,    *
 *        showing the part number, part name, and           *
 *        quantity on hand. Part numbers will appear in     *
 *        ascending order.                                  *
 **************************************************************/
void print(void)
{
  struct part *p;

  printf("Part Number    Part Name                    "
         "Quantity on Hand\n");
  for (p = inventory; p != NULL; p = p->next)
    printf("%7d        %-25s%11d\n", p->number,
           p->name, p->on_hand);
}
```

Notice the use of free in the insert function. insert allocates space for a part before checking to see if the part already exists. If it does, insert releases the memory so that the program won't risk running out of space prematurely.

17.6   Pointers to Pointers

In Section 13.7, we came across the notion of a *pointer* to a *pointer*. In that section, we used an array whose elements were of type char *; a pointer to one of the array elements itself had type char **. The concept of "pointers to pointers" also pops up frequently in the context of linked data structures. In particular, when an argument to a function is a pointer variable, we'll sometimes want the function to be able to modify the variable by making it point somewhere else. Doing so requires the use of a pointer to a pointer.

Consider the add_to_list function of Section 17.5, which inserts a node at the beginning of a list. When we call add_to_list, we pass it a pointer to the first node in the list; it then returns a pointer to the new list:

```
struct node *add_to_list(struct node *list, int n)
{
  struct node *new_node;

  new_node = malloc(sizeof(struct node));
  if (new_node == NULL) {
    printf("Error: malloc failed in add_to_list\n");
    exit(EXIT_FAILURE);
  }
  new_node->value = n;
  new_node->next = list;
  return new_node;
}
```

Suppose that we modify the function so that it assigns new_node to list instead of returning new_node. In other words, let's remove the return statement from add_to_list and replace it by

```
list = new_node;
```

Unfortunately, this idea doesn't work. Suppose that we call add_to_list in the following way:

```
add_to_list(first, 10);
```

At the point of the call, first is copied into list. (Pointers, like all other arguments, are passed by value.) The last line in the function changes the value of list, making it point to the new node. This assignment doesn't affect first, however.

Getting add_to_list to modify first is possible, but it requires passing add_to_list a *pointer* to first. Here's the correct version of the function:

```
void add_to_list(struct node **list, int n)
{
  struct node *new_node;
```

```
new_node = malloc(sizeof(struct node));
if (new_node == NULL) {
  printf("Error: malloc failed in add_to_list\n");
  exit(EXIT_FAILURE);
}
new_node->value = n;
new_node->next = *list;
*list = new_node;
}
```

When we call the new version of add_to_list, the first argument will be the address of first:

```
add_to_list(&first, 10);
```

Since list is assigned the address of first, we can use *list as an alias for first. In particular, assigning new_node to *list will modify first.

17.7 Pointers to Functions

So far, we've used pointers to various kinds of data, including variables, array elements, and dynamically allocated blocks of memory. But C doesn't require that pointers point only to *data;* it's also possible to have pointers to *functions*. Pointers to functions aren't as odd as you might think. After all, functions occupy memory locations, so every function has an address, just like each variable has an address.

Function Pointers as Arguments

We can use function pointers in much the same way we use pointers to data. Passing a function pointer as an argument is fairly common in C. Suppose that we're writing a function named integrate that integrates a function f between points a and b. We'd like to make integrate as general as possible by passing it f as an argument. To achieve this effect in C, we'll declare f to be a pointer to a function. Assuming that we want to integrate functions that have a double parameter and return a double result, the prototype for integrate will look like this:

```
double integrate(double (*f)(double), double a, double b);
```

The parentheses around *f indicate that f is a pointer to a function, not a function that returns a pointer. It's also legal to declare f as though it were a function:

```
double integrate(double f(double), double a, double b);
```

From the compiler's standpoint, this prototype is identical to the previous one.

sin function ➤23.3 When we call integrate, we'll supply a function name as the first argument. For example, the following call will integrate the sin (sine) function from 0 to π/2:

```
result = integrate(sin, 0.0, PI/2);
```

Notice that there are no parentheses after `sin`. When a function name isn't followed by parentheses, the C compiler produces a pointer to the function instead of generating code for a function call. In our example, we're not calling `sin`; instead, we're passing `integrate` a pointer to `sin`. If this seems confusing, think of how C handles arrays. If `a` is the name of an array, then `a[i]` represents one element of the array, while `a` by itself serves as a pointer to the array. In a similar way, if `f` is a function, C treats `f(x)` as a *call* of the function but `f` by itself as a *pointer* to the function.

Within the body of `integrate`, we can call the function that `f` points to:

```
sum += (*f)(x);
```

`*f` represents the function that `f` points to; `x` is the argument to the call. Thus, during the execution of `integrate(sin, 0.0, PI/2)`, each call of `*f` is actually a call of `sin`. As an alternative to `(*f)(x)`, C allows us to write `f(x)` to call the function that `f` points to. Although `f(x)` looks more natural, I'll stick with `(*f)(x)` as a reminder that `f` is a *pointer* to a function, not a function name.

The `qsort` Function

Although it might seem that pointers to functions aren't very useful for everyday programming, that couldn't be further from the truth. In fact, some of the most powerful functions in the C library require a function pointer as an argument. One of these is `qsort`, whose prototype can be found in `<stdlib.h>`. `qsort` is a general-purpose function capable of sorting *any* array.

Since the elements of the array may be of any type—even a structure or union type—`qsort` must be told how to determine which of two array elements is "smaller." We'll provide this information to `qsort` by writing a **comparison function.** When given two pointers `p` and `q` to array elements, the comparison function must return a number that is *negative* if `*p` is "less than" `*q`, *zero* if `*p` is "equal to" `*q`, and *positive* if `*p` is "greater than" `*q`. The words "less than," "equal to," and "greater than" are in quotes because it's our responsibility to determine how `*p` and `*q` are compared.

`qsort` has the following prototype:

```
void qsort(void *base, size_t nmemb, size_t size,
           int (*compar)(const void *, const void *));
```

`base` must point to the first element in the array. (If only a portion of the array is to be sorted, we'll make `base` point to the first element in this portion.) In the simplest case, `base` is simply the name of the array. `nmemb` is the number of elements to be sorted (not necessarily the number of elements in the array). `size` is the size of each array element, measured in bytes. `compar` is a pointer to the comparison function. When `qsort` is called, it sorts the array into ascending order, calling the comparison function whenever it needs to compare array elements.

Q&A

To sort the `inventory` array of Section 16.3, we'd use the following call of `qsort`:

```
qsort(inventory, num_parts, sizeof(struct part),
    compare_parts);
```

Notice that the second argument is `num_parts`, not `MAX_PARTS`; we don't want to sort the entire `inventory` array, just the portion in which parts are currently stored.

Writing the `compare_parts` function isn't as easy as you might expect, since `qsort` requires that it have parameters of type `void *`. Unfortunately, we can't access part numbers through `void *` pointers; we need pointers to `part` structures. To solve the problem, we'll have `compare_parts` assign p and q to variables of type `struct part *`, thereby converting them to the desired type. `compare_parts` can now use the new pointers to access the members of the structures that p and q point to. Assuming that we want to sort parts by number, here's how the `compare_parts` function might look:

```
int compare_parts(const void *p, const void *q)
{
  struct part *p1 = p;
  struct part *q1 = q;

  if (p1->number < q1->number)
    return -1;
  else if (p1->number == q1->number)
    return 0;
  else
    return 1;
}
```

Although this version of `compare_parts` works, most C programmers would write the function more concisely. First, notice that we can replace p1 and q1 by cast expressions:

```
int compare_parts(const void *p, const void *q)
{
  if (((struct part *) p)->number <
      ((struct part *) q)->number)
    return -1;
  else if (((struct part *) p)->number ==
           ((struct part *) q)->number)
    return 0;
  else
    return 1;
}
```

The parentheses around `((struct part *) p)` are necessary; without them, the compiler would try to cast `p->number` to type `struct part *`.

We can make `compare_parts` even shorter by removing the `if` statements:

```
int compare_parts(const void *p, const void *q)
{
  return ((struct part *) p)->number -
         ((struct part *) q)->number;
}
```

Subtracting q's part number from p's part number produces a negative result if p has a smaller part number, zero if the part numbers are equal, and a positive result if p has a larger part number.

To sort the inventory array by part name instead of part number, we'd use the following version of compare_parts:

```
int compare_parts(const void *p, const void *q)
{
  return strcmp(((struct part *) p)->name,
                ((struct part *) q)->name);
}
```

All compare_parts has to do is call strcmp, which conveniently returns a negative, zero, or positive result.

Other Uses of Function Pointers

Although I've emphasized the usefulness of function pointers as arguments to other functions, that's not all they're good for. C treats pointers to functions just like pointers to data; we can store function pointers in variables or use them as elements of an array or as members of a structure or union. We can even write functions that return function pointers.

Here's an example of a variable that can store a pointer to a function:

```
void (*pf)(int);
```

pf can point to any function with an int argument and a void return value. If f is such a function, we can make pf point to f in the following way:

```
pf = f;
```

Notice that there's no ampersand preceding f. Since pf now points to f, we can call f by writing either

```
(*pf)(i);
```

or

```
pf(i);
```

Arrays whose elements are function pointers have a surprising number of applications. For example, suppose that we're writing a program that displays a menu of commands for the user to choose from. We can write functions that implement these commands, then store pointers to the functions in an array:

```
void (*file_cmd[])(void) = { new_cmd,
                             open_cmd,
                             close_cmd,
                             close_all_cmd,
                             save_cmd,
                             save_as_cmd,
                             save_all_cmd,
                             print_cmd,
                             exit_cmd
                           };
```

If the user selects command n, where n falls between 0 and 8, we can subscript the
file_cmd array to find out which function to call:

```
(*file_cmd[n])();    /* or file_cmd[n](); */
```

Of course, we could get a similar effect by using a switch statement. Storing the
function pointers in an array gives us more flexibility, however, since the elements
of the array can be changed as the program is running.

PROGRAM **Tabulating the Trigonometric Functions**

The following program prints tables showing the values of cos, sin, and tan
<math.h> header ▶23.3 (all three functions are declared in <math.h>). The program is built around a
function named tabulate that, when passed a function pointer f, prints a table
showing the values of f.

tabulate.c
```
/* Tabulates values of trigonometric functions */

#include <math.h>
#include <stdio.h>

void tabulate(double (*f)(double), double first,
              double last, double incr);

main()
{
  double final, increment, initial;

  printf("Enter initial value: ");
  scanf("%lf", &initial);

  printf("Enter final value: ");
  scanf("%lf", &final);

  printf("Enter increment: ");
  scanf("%lf", &increment);

  printf("\n      x         cos(x)\n"
         "   -------      -------\n");
  tabulate(cos, initial, final, increment);
```

```
      printf("\n        x             sin(x)\n"
             "     -------        -------\n");
      tabulate(sin, initial, final, increment);

      printf("\n        x             tan(x)\n"
             "     -------        -------\n");
      tabulate(tan, initial, final, increment);

      return 0;
    }

    void tabulate(double (*f)(double), double first,
                  double last, double incr)
    {
      double x;
      int i, num_intervals;

      num_intervals = ceil((last - first) / incr);
      for (i = 0; i <= num_intervals; i++) {
        x = first + i * incr;
        printf("%10.5f %10.5f\n", x, (*f)(x));
      }
    }
```

ceil function ➤23.3   `tabulate` uses the `ceil` function, which is part of the standard library. When given an argument x of double type, `ceil` returns the smallest integer that's greater than or equal to x.

Here's what a session with `tabulate.c` might look like:

```
Enter initial value: 0
Enter final value: .5
Enter increment: .1

        x             cos(x)
     -------        -------
    0.00000        1.00000
    0.10000        0.99500
    0.20000        0.98007
    0.30000        0.95534
    0.40000        0.92106
    0.50000        0.87758

        x             sin(x)
     -------        -------
    0.00000        0.00000
    0.10000        0.09983
    0.20000        0.19867
    0.30000        0.29552
    0.40000        0.38942
    0.50000        0.47943
```

```
    x          tan(x)
  -------      -------
  0.00000      0.00000
  0.10000      0.10033
  0.20000      0.20271
  0.30000      0.30934
  0.40000      0.42279
  0.50000      0.54630
```

Q & A

Q: **What does the NULL macro represent? [p. 361]**

A: NULL actually stands for 0. When we use 0 in a context where a pointer would be required, C compilers are required to treat it as a null pointer instead of the integer 0. The NULL macro is provided merely to help avoid confusion. The assignment

```
p = 0;
```

could be assigning the value 0 to a numeric variable or assigning a null pointer to a pointer variable; we can't easily tell which. In contrast, the assignment

```
p = NULL;
```

makes it clear that p is a pointer.

`C++`   In C++, it's common practice to use 0 rather than NULL; the reasons are too technical to discuss here. Some programmers prefer to use 0 rather than NULL in C programs as well.

*Q: **In the header files that come with my compiler, NULL is defined as follows:**

```
#define NULL (void *) 0
```

What's the advantage of casting 0 to void *?

A: This trick, which is legal in Standard C, enables compilers to spot incorrect uses of the null pointer. For example, suppose that we try to assign NULL to an integer variable:

```
i = NULL;
```

If NULL is defined as 0, this assignment is perfectly legal. But if NULL is defined as (void *) 0, the compiler will inform us that assigning a pointer to an integer variable violates Standard C rules.

Defining NULL as (void *) 0 has a second, more important, advantage. Suppose that we call a function with a variable-length argument list and pass NULL as one of the arguments. If NULL is defined as 0, the compiler will incorrectly pass a zero integer value. (In an ordinary function call, NULL works fine because the compiler knows from the function's prototype that it expects a pointer.

variable-length argument lists
➤26.1

When a function has a variable-length argument list, however, the compiler has no such knowledge; it assumes that 0 represents an integer.) If NULL is defined as (void *) 0, the compiler will pass a null pointer.

To make matters even more confusing, some header files define NULL to be 0L (the long int version of 0). This definition, like the definition of NULL as 0, is a holdover from C's earlier years, when pointers and integers were compatible. For most purposes, though, it really doesn't matter how NULL is defined; just think of it as a name for the null pointer.

Q: Since 0 is used to represent the null pointer, I guess a null pointer is just an address with all zero bits, right?

A: Not necessarily. Each C compiler is allowed to represent null pointers in a different way, and not all compilers use a zero address. For example, some compilers use a nonexistent memory address for the null pointer; that way, attempting to access memory through a null pointer can be detected by the hardware.

How the null pointer is stored inside the computer shouldn't concern us; that's a detail for compiler experts to worry about. The important thing is that, when used in a pointer context, 0 is converted to the proper internal form by the compiler.

Q: Is it acceptable to use NULL as a null character?

A: Definitely not. NULL is a macro that represents the null *pointer*, not the null *character*. Using NULL as a null character will work with some compilers, but not with all (since some define NULL as (void *) 0). In any event, using NULL as anything other than a pointer can lead to a great deal of confusion. If you want a name for the null character, define the following macro:

```
#define NUL '\0'
```

Q: When my program terminates, I get the message *"Null pointer assignment."* What does this mean?

A: This message, which is produced by some DOS programs, indicates that the program has stored data into memory using a bad pointer (but not necessarily a null pointer). Unfortunately, the message isn't displayed until the program terminates, so there's no clue as to which statement caused the error. The *"Null pointer assignment"* message can be caused by a missing & in scanf:

```
scanf("%d", i);    /* should have been scanf("%d", &i); */
```

Another possibility is an assignment involving a pointer that's uninitialized or null:

```
*p = i;    /* p is uninitialized or null */
```

Q: Since my program seems to work even when I get the *"Null pointer assignment"* message, can I just ignore the message?

A: Reread the answer to the previous question. If you get a "Null pointer assignment" message, your program has a bug in it, period. Fix it, or else. Although the program may appear to work, there's no guarantee that it will always run correctly; if it uses an uninitialized pointer, the program may work on some occasions and fail on others. And if the program is recompiled with a different compiler or ported to another computer, the chances of it working are slim to none.

*Q: **How does a program know that a "null pointer assignment" has occurred?**

A: The message depends on the fact that, in the small and medium memory models, data is stored in a single segment, with addresses beginning at 0. The compiler leaves a "hole" at the beginning of the data segment—a small block of memory that's initialized to 0 but otherwise is not used by the program. When the program terminates, it checks to see if any data in the "hole" area is nonzero. If so, it must have been altered through a bad pointer.

Q: **Is there any advantage to casting the return value of `malloc` or the other memory allocation functions? [p. 362]**

A: Not really, although many programmers do it anyway. Casting the void * pointer that these functions return is unnecessary in Standard C, since pointers of type void * are automatically converted to any pointer type upon assignment. The habit of casting the return value is a holdover from Classic C, in which the memory allocation functions returned a char * value, making the cast necessary.

In Standard C, there's actually a small advantage to *not* performing the cast. Suppose that we've forgotten to include the <stdlib.h> header in the program. When we call malloc, the compiler will assume that its return type is int (the default return value for any C function). If we don't cast the return value of malloc, a Standard C compiler will produce an error (or at least a warning), since we're trying to assign an integer value to a pointer variable. On the other hand, if we cast the return value to a pointer, the program may compile, but likely won't run properly.

Q: **The `calloc` function initializes a memory block to "zero bits." Does this mean that all data items in the block become zero? [p. 367]**

A: Usually, but not always. Setting an integer to zero bits always makes the integer zero. Setting a floating-point number to zero bits usually makes the number zero, but this isn't guaranteed—it depends on how floating-point numbers are stored. The story is the same for pointers; a pointer whose bits are zero isn't necessary a null pointer.

*Q: **I see how the structure tag mechanism allows a structure to contain a pointer to itself. But what if two structures each have a member that points to the other? [p. 371]**

A: Here's how we'd handle that situation:

```
struct s1;    /* incomplete declaration of s1 */
struct s2 {
  ...
  struct s1 *p;
};
```

```
struct s1 {
  ...
  struct s2 *q;
};
```

The first declaration of the s1 structure is "incomplete," since we haven't speci-fied the members of s1. Incomplete declarations of a structure are permitted in C, provided that a full declaration appears later in the same scope.

Q: **Why isn't the qsort function simply named sort? [p. 386]**

A: The name qsort comes from the Quicksort algorithm published by C. A. R. Hoare in 1962. Ironically, the C standard doesn't require that qsort use the Quicksort algorithm, although many versions of qsort do.

Q: **Isn't it necessary to cast qsort's first argument to type void *, as in the fol-lowing example? [p. 387]**

```
qsort((void *) inventory, num_parts, sizeof(struct part),
      compare_parts);
```

A: No. A pointer of any type can be converted to void * automatically.

*Q: **I want to use qsort to sort an array of integers, but I'm having trouble writ-ing a comparison function. What's the secret?**

A: Here's a version that works:

```
int compare_ints(const void *p, const void *q)
{
  return *(int *)p - *(int *)q;
}
```

Bizarre, eh? The expression (int *)p casts p to type int *, so *(int *)p would be the integer that p points to.

*Q: **I needed to sort an array of strings, so I figured I'd just use strcmp as the comparison function. When I passed it to qsort, however, the compiler gave me an error. I tried to fix the problem by embedding strcmp in a comparison function:**

```
int compare_strings(const void *p, const void *q)
{
  return strcmp(p, q);
}
```

Now my program compiles, but qsort doesn't seem to sort the array. What am I doing wrong?

A: First, you can't pass strcmp itself to qsort, since qsort requires a comparison function with two const void * parameters. Your compare_strings func-tion doesn't work because it incorrectly assumes that p and q are strings (char * pointers). In fact, p and q point to array elements containing char * pointers. To

fix `compare_strings`, we'll cast p and q to type char **, then use the *
operator to remove one level of indirection:

```
int compare_strings(const void *p, const void *q)
{
  return strcmp(*(char **)p, *(char **)q);
}
```

Exercises

Section 17.2

1. Having to check the return value of `malloc` (or any other memory allocation function) each time we call it can be an annoyance. Write a function named `my_malloc` that serves as a "wrapper" for `malloc`. When we call `my_malloc` and ask it to allocate n bytes, it in turn calls `malloc`, tests to make sure that `malloc` doesn't return a null pointer, and then returns the pointer from `malloc`. Have `my_malloc` print an error message and terminate the program if `malloc` returns a null pointer.

2. Write a function named `strdup` that uses dynamic storage allocation to create a copy of a string. For example, the call

   ```
   p = strdup(str);
   ```

   would allocate space for a string of the same length as `str`, copy the contents of `str` into the new string, and return a pointer to it. Have `strdup` return a null pointer if the memory allocation fails.

3. Write a program that prompts the user to enter a series of words, which the program then sorts and displays with duplicates removed. *Hint:* Use an array of pointers to dynamically allocated strings. *Extra credit:* Use the `qsort` function (Section 17.7) to do the sorting.

Section 17.3

4. Modify `invent.c` (Section 16.3) so that the `inventory` array is allocated dynamically and later reallocated when it fills up. Use `malloc` initially to allocate enough space for an array of ten `part` structures. When the array has no more room for new parts, use `realloc` to double its size. Repeat the doubling step each time the array becomes full.

Section 17.5

5. Suppose that the following declarations are in effect:

   ```
   struct point { int x, y; };
   struct rectangle { struct point upper_left, lower_right; };
   struct rectangle *p;
   ```

   Assume that we want p to point to a `rectangle` structure whose upper left corner is at (0,1) and whose lower right corner is at (1,0). Write a series of statements that allocate such a structure and initialize it as indicated.

6. Suppose that f and p are declared as follows:

   ```
   struct {
     union {
       char a, b;
       int c;
     } d;
     int e[5];
   } f, *p = &f;
   ```

Which of the following statements are legal?

(a) `p->b = ' ';`

(b) `p->e[3] = 10;`

(c) `(*p).d.a = '*';`

(d) `p->d->c = 20;`

7. Modify the `delete_from_list` function so that it uses only one pointer variable instead of two (`cur` and `prev`).

8. The following loop is supposed to delete all nodes from a list and release the memory that they occupy. Unfortunately, the loop is incorrect. Explain what's wrong with it and show how to fix the bug.

    ```
    for (p = first; p != NULL; p = p->next)
      free(p);
    ```

9. Modify `invent2.c` by adding an e (erase) command that allows the user to remove a part from the database.

10. Section 15.2 describes a file, `stack.c`, that provides functions for storing integers in a stack. In that section, the stack was implemented as an array. Modify `stack.c` so that a stack is now stored as a linked list. Replace the `contents` and `top` variables by a single variable that points to the first node in the list (the "top" of the stack). Write the functions in `stack.c` so that they use this pointer. Remove the `is_full` function, instead having `push` return either `TRUE` (if memory was available to create a node) or `FALSE` (if not).

Section 17.6   11. Modify the `delete_from_list` function (Section 17.5) so that its first argument is of type `struct node **` (a pointer to a pointer to the first node in a list) and its return type is `void`. `delete_from_list` must modify its first argument to point to the list after the desired node has been deleted.

Section 17.7   12. Show the output of the following program and explain what it does.

```
#include <stdio.h>

int f1(int (*f)(int));
int f2(int i);

main()
{
  printf("Answer: %d\n", f1(f2));
  return 0;
}

int f1(int (*f)(int))
{
  int n = 0;

  while ((*f)(n)) n++;
  return n;
}

int f2(int i)
{
  return i * i + i - 12;
}
```

13. Write the following function. The call sum(g, i, j) should return g(i) + ... + g(j).

    ```
    int sum(int (*f)(int), int start, int end);
    ```

14. Let a be an array of 100 integers. Write a call of qsort that sorts only the *last* 50 elements in a. (You don't need to write the comparison function).

15. Modify the compare_parts function so that parts are sorted with their numbers in *descending* order.

16. Modify invent.c (Section 16.3) so that the p (print) command calls qsort to sort the inventory array before it prints the parts.

17. Write a function that, when given a string as its argument, searches the following array of structures for a matching command name, then calls the function associated with that name:

    ```
    struct {
      char *cmd_name;
      void (*cmd_pointer)(void);
    } file_cmd[] =
      {{"new",        new_cmd},
       {"open",       open_cmd},
       {"close",      close_cmd},
       {"close all",  close_all_cmd},
       {"save",       save_cmd},
       {"save as",    save_as_cmd},
       {"save all",   save_all_cmd},
       {"print",      print_cmd},
       {"exit",       exit_cmd}
      };
    ```

18 Declarations

Making something variable is easy.
Controlling duration of constancy is the trick.

Declarations play a central role in C programming. By declaring variables and functions, we furnish vital information that the compiler will need in order to check a program for potential errors and translate it into object code.

Previous chapters have provided examples of declarations without going into full details; this chapter fills in the gaps. It explores the sophisticated options that can be used in declarations and reveals that variable declarations and function declarations have quite a bit in common. It also provides a firm grounding in the important concepts of storage duration, scope, and linkage.

Section 18.1 examines the syntax of declarations in their most general form, a topic that we've avoided up to this point. We'll then focus on the items that appear in declarations: storage classes (Section 18.2), type qualifiers (Section 18.3), declarators (Section 18.4), and initializers (Section 18.5).

Understanding declarations takes time, but it's a vital skill to have. This chapter probably isn't the most exciting in the book, but you'll need to master it before you consider yourself a C programmer.

18.1 Declaration Syntax

Declarations furnish information to the compiler about the meaning of identifiers. When we write

```
int i;
```

we're informing the compiler that, in the current scope, the name i represents a variable of type int. The declaration

```
float f(float);
```

tells the compiler that `f` is a function that returns a `float` value and has one argument, also of type `float`.

In its most general form, a declaration has the following appearance:

declaration   *declaration-specifiers declarators ;*

Declaration specifiers describe the properties of the items being declared. *Declarators* give the names of the items and may provide additional information about their properties.

Declaration specifiers fall into three categories:

- *Storage classes.* There are four storage classes: `auto`, `static`, `extern`, and `register`. At most one storage class may appear in a declaration; if present, it must come first.
- *Type qualifiers.* There are only two type qualifiers: `const` and `volatile`. A declaration may specify either one, both, or neither.
- *Type specifiers.* The keywords `void`, `char`, `short`, `int`, `long`, `float`, `double`, `signed`, and `unsigned` are all type specifiers. These words may be combined as described in Chapter 7; the order in which they appear doesn't matter (`int unsigned long` is the same as `long unsigned int`). Type specifiers also include specifications of structures, unions, and enumerations (for example, `struct point { int x, y; }`, `struct { int x, y; }`, or `struct point`). Type names created using `typedef` are type specifiers as well.

Type qualifiers and type specifiers must follow the storage class, but there are no other restrictions on their order. As a matter of style, I'll put type qualifiers before type specifiers.

Declarators include identifiers (names of simple variables), identifiers followed by `[ ]` (array names), identifiers preceded by `*` (pointer names), and identifiers followed by `( )` (function names). Declarators are separated by commas. A declarator that represents a variable may be followed by an initializer.

Let's look at a few examples that illustrate these rules. Here's a declaration with a storage class and three declarators:

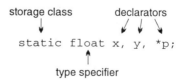

The following declaration has a type qualifier but no storage class. It also has an initializer:

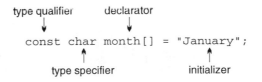

The following declaration has both a storage class and a type qualifier. It also has three type specifiers; their order isn't important:

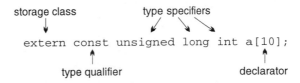

Function declarations, like variable declarations, may have a storage class, type qualifiers, and type specifiers. The following declaration has a storage class and a type specifier:

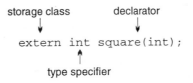

The rest of the chapter covers storage classes, type qualifiers, declarators, and initializers in detail.

18.2   Storage Classes

Storage classes can be specified for variables and—to a lesser extent—functions and parameters. We'll concentrate on variables for now.

For the remainder of this section, I'll use the term **block** to mean either the body of a function (the part enclosed in braces) or a block statement (a compound statement containing declarations).

block statements ➤ *10.3*

Properties of Variables

Every variable in a C program has three properties:

- *Storage duration.* The storage duration of a variable determines when memory is set aside for the variable and when that memory is released. Storage for a variable with *automatic storage duration* is allocated when the surrounding block is executed; storage is deallocated when the block terminates, causing the variable to lose its value. A variable with *static storage duration* stays at the same storage location as long as the program is running, allowing it to retain its value indefinitely.

- *Scope.* The scope of a variable is the portion of the program text in which the variable can be referenced. A variable can have either *block scope* (the variable is visible from its point of declaration to the end of the enclosing block) or *file scope* (the variable is visible from its point of declaration to the end of the enclosing file).

Q&A

- *Linkage.* The linkage of a variable determines the extent to which it can be shared by different parts of a program. A variable with *external linkage* may be shared by several (perhaps all) files in a program. A variable with *internal linkage* is restricted to a single file, but may be shared by the functions in that file. (If a variable with the same name appears in another file, it's treated as a different variable.) A variable with *no linkage* belongs to a single function and can't be shared at all.

The default storage duration, scope, and linkage of a variable depend on where it's declared:

- Variables declared *inside* a block (including a function body) have *automatic* storage duration, *block* scope, and *no* linkage.
- Variables declared *outside* any block, at the outermost level of a program, have *static* storage duration, *file* scope, and *external* linkage.

The following example shows the default properties of the variables i and j:

```
          ___ static storage duration
int i; ======= file scope
          ‾‾‾ external linkage

void f(void)
{
             ___ automatic storage duration
    int j; ======= block scope
             ‾‾‾ no linkage
}
```

For many variables, the default storage duration, scope, and linkage are satisfactory. When they aren't, we can alter these properties by specifying an explicit storage class: auto, static, extern, or register.

The auto Storage Class

The auto storage class is legal only for variables that belong to a block. An auto variable has automatic storage duration (not surprisingly), block scope, and no linkage. The auto storage class is almost never specified explicitly, since it's the default for variables declared inside a block.

The `static` Storage Class

The `static` storage class can be used with all variables, regardless of where they're declared, but it has a different effect on a variable declared outside a block than it does on a variable declared inside a block. When used *outside* a block, the word `static` specifies that a variable has internal linkage. When used *inside* a block, `static` changes the variable's storage duration from automatic to static. The following figure shows the effect of declaring `i` and `j` to be `static`:

```
                           static storage duration
static int i;              file scope
                           internal linkage

void f(void)
{
                           static storage duration
    static int j;          block scope
                           no linkage
}
```

When used in a declaration outside a block, `static` essentially hides a variable within the file in which it's declared; only functions that appear in the same file can see the variable. In the following example, the functions `f1` and `f2` both have access to `i`, but functions in other files don't:

```
static int i;

void f1(void)
{
    /* has access to i */
}

void f2(void)
{
    /* has access to i */
}
```

This use of `static` can help implement a technique known as *information hiding*.

information hiding ➤19.2

A `static` variable declared within a block resides at the same storage location throughout program execution. Unlike automatic variables, which lose their values each time the program leaves the enclosing block, a `static` variable will retain its value indefinitely. `static` variables have some interesting properties:

- A `static` variable in a block is initialized only once, prior to program execution. An `auto` variable is initialized every time it comes into existence (provided, of course, that it has an initializer).

- Each time a function is called recursively, it gets a new set of `auto` variables. If it has a `static` variable, on the other hand, that variable is shared by all calls of the function.

■ Although a function shouldn't return a pointer to an `auto` variable, there's nothing wrong with it returning a pointer to a `static` variable.

Declaring one of its variables to be `static` allows a function to retain information between calls in a "hidden" area that the rest of the program can't access. More often, however, we'll use `static` to make programs more efficient. Consider the following function:

```
char digit_to_hex_char(int digit)
{
  const char hex_chars[16] = "0123456789ABCDEF";

  return hex_chars[digit];
}
```

Each time the `digit_to_hex_char` function is called, the characters `0123456789ABCDEF` will be copied into the `hex_chars` array to initialize it. Now, let's make the array `static`:

```
char digit_to_hex_char(int digit)
{
  static const char hex_chars[16] = "0123456789ABCDEF";

  return hex_chars[digit];
}
```

Since `static` variables are initialized only once, we've improved the speed of `digit_to_hex_char`.

The **extern** Storage Class

The `extern` storage class enables several source files to share the same variable. Section 15.2 covered the essentials of using `extern`, so I won't devote much space to it here. Recall that the declaration

```
extern int i;
```

informs the compiler that `i` is an `int` variable, but doesn't cause it to allocate memory for `i`. In C terminology, this declaration is not a *definition* of `i`; it merely informs the compiler that we need access to a variable that's defined elsewhere (perhaps later in the same file, or—more often—in another file). A variable can have many *declarations* in a program but should have only one *definition*.

There's one exception to the rule that an `extern` declaration of a variable isn't a definition. An `extern` declaration that initializes a variable serves as a definition of the variable. For example, the declaration

```
extern int i = 0;
```

is effectively the same as

```
int i = 0;
```

This rule prevents multiple `extern` declarations from initializing a variable in different ways.

A variable in an `extern` declaration always has static storage duration. The scope of the variable depends on the declaration's placement. If the declaration is inside a block, the variable has block scope; otherwise, it has file scope:

```
                     ┌── static storage duration
extern int i;────── file scope
                     └── ? linkage

void f(void)
{
                        ┌── static storage duration
    extern int j;────── block scope
                        └── ? linkage
}
```

Determining the linkage of an `extern` variable is a bit harder. If the variable was declared `static` earlier in the file (outside of any function definition), then it has internal linkage. Otherwise (the normal case), the variable has external linkage.

The `register` Storage Class

Declaring a variable to have the `register` storage class asks the compiler to store the variable in a register instead of keeping it in main memory like other variables. (A *register* is a storage area located in a computer's CPU. In traditional computer architecture, data stored in a register can be accessed and updated faster than data stored in ordinary memory.) Specifying the storage class of a variable to be `register` is a request, not a command. The compiler is free to store a `register` variable in memory if it chooses.

The `register` storage class is legal only for variables declared in a block. A `register` variable has the same storage duration, scope, and linkage as an `auto` variable. However, a `register` variable lacks one property that an `auto` variable has: since registers don't have addresses, it's illegal to use the `&` operator to take the address of a `register` variable. This restriction applies even if the compiler has elected to store the variable in memory.

`register` is best used for variables that are accessed and/or updated frequently. For example, the loop control variable in a `for` statement is a good candidate for `register` treatment:

```
int sum_array(int a[], int n)
{
  register int i;
  int sum = 0;

  for (i = 0; i < n; i++)
    sum += a[i];
  return sum;
}
```

register isn't nearly as popular among C programmers as it once was. Today's compilers are much more sophisticated than the early C compilers; many can determine automatically which variables would benefit the most from being kept in registers.

The Storage Class of a Function

Function declarations (and definitions), like variable declarations, may include a storage class, but the only options are extern and static. The word extern at the beginning of a function declaration specifies that the function has external linkage, allowing it to be called from other files. static indicates internal linkage—the function may be called only within the file in which it's defined. If no storage class is specified, the function is assumed to have external linkage.

Consider the following function declarations:

```
extern int f(int i);
static int g(int i);
int h(int i);
```

f has external linkage, g has internal linkage, and h (by default) has external linkage.

Declaring functions to be extern is like declaring variables to be auto—it serves no purpose. For that reason, I don't use extern in function declarations. Be aware, however, that some programmers use extern extensively, which certainly does no harm.

Declaring functions to be static, on the other hand, is quite useful. In fact, I recommend using static when declaring any function that isn't intended to be called from other files. The benefits of doing so include:

- *Easier maintenance.* Declaring a function f to be static guarantees that f isn't visible outside the file in which its definition appears. As a result, some-one modifying the program later knows that changes to f won't affect functions in other files. (One exception: a function in another file that's passed a pointer to f might be affected by changes to f. Fortunately, that situation is easy to spot by examining the file in which f is defined, since the function that passes f must also be defined there.)

- *Reduced "name space pollution."* Since functions declared static have internal linkage, their names can be reused in other files. Although we probably wouldn't deliberately reuse a function name for some other purpose, it can be hard to avoid in large programs. An excessive number of names with external linkage can result in what C programmers call "name space pollution": names in different files accidentally conflicting with each other. Using static helps prevent this problem.

Function parameters have the same properties as auto variables: automatic storage duration, block scope, and no linkage. The only storage class that can be specified for parameters is register.

Summary

Now that we've covered the various storage classes, let's summarize what we know. The following code fragment shows all possible ways to include—or omit—storage classes in declarations of variables and parameters.

```
int a;
extern int b;
static int c;

void f(int d, register int e)
{
  auto int g;
  int h;
  static int i;
  extern int j;
  register int k;
}
```

Table 18.1 shows the properties of each variable and parameter in this example.

Table 18.1
Properties of Variables
and Parameters

Name	Storage Duration	Scope	Linkage
a	static	file	external
b	static	file	*
c	static	file	internal
d	automatic	block	none
e	automatic	block	none
g	automatic	block	none
h	automatic	block	none
i	static	block	none
j	static	block	*
k	automatic	block	none

*The definitions of b and j aren't shown, so it's not possible to determine the linkage of these variables. In most cases, the variables will be defined in another file and will have external linkage.

Of the four storage classes, the most important are `static` and `extern`. `auto` has no effect, and modern compilers have made `register` obsolete.

18.3 Type Qualifiers

There are two type qualifiers: `const` and `volatile`. Since `volatile` is used only in low-level programming, we'll postpone discussing it until Section 20.3. `const` is used to declare objects that resemble variables but are "read-only"; a program can access the value of a `const` object, but can't change it. For example, the declaration

```
const int n = 10;
```

creates a `const` object named n whose value is 10. The declaration

```
const int days_per_month[] =
  {31, 28, 31, 30, 31, 30, 31, 31, 30, 31, 30, 31};
```

creates a const array named days_per_month.

Using const to indicate that the value of an object won't change has several advantages:

- const is a form of documentation; declaring an object to be const informs anyone reading the program later that the value of the object won't change.

- The compiler can check that the program doesn't inadvertently attempt to change the value of the object.

- When programs are written for certain types of applications (embedded systems, in particular), the compiler can use the word const to identify data to be stored in ROM (read-only memory).

At first glance, it might appear that const infringes on the #define directive, which we've used in previous chapters to create names for constants. There are significant differences between #define and const, however:

- We can use #define to create a name for a numerical, character, or string constant. const can be used to create read-only objects of *any* type, including constant arrays, pointers, structures, and unions.

- const objects are subject to the same scope rules as variables; constants created using #define aren't. In particular, we can't use #define to create a constant with block scope.

- The value of a const object, unlike the value of a macro, can be viewed in a debugger.

Q&A
- Unlike macros, const objects can't be used in constant expressions. For example, we can't write

```
const int n = 10;
int a[n];              /*** WRONG ***/
```

since array bounds must be constant expressions.

There are no absolute rules that dictate when to use #define and when to use const. I recommend using #define for constants that represent numbers or characters. That way, you'll be able to use the constants as array dimensions, in switch statements, and in other places where constant expressions are required. I use const primarily for protecting constant data stored in arrays.

18.4   Declarators

A declarator consists of an identifier (the name of the variable or function being declared), possibly preceded by the * symbol or followed by [] or (). By combining *, [], and (), we can create declarators of mind-numbing complexity.

Before we look at the more complicated declarators, let's review the declarators that we've seen in previous chapters. In the simplest case, a declarator is just an identifier, like i in the following example:

```
int i;
```

Declarators may also contain the symbols *, [], and ():

- A declarator that begins with * represents a pointer:

```
int *p;
```

- A declarator that ends with [] represents an array:

```
int a[10];
```

The brackets may be left empty if the array is a parameter, if it has an initializer, or if its storage class is extern:

```
extern int a[];
```

Since a is defined elsewhere in the program, the compiler doesn't need to know its length here. (In the case of a multidimensional array, only the first set of brackets can be empty.)

- A declarator that ends with () represents a function:

```
int abs(int i);
void swap(int *a, int *b);
int find_largest(int a[], int n);
```

C allows parameter names to be omitted in a function declaration:

```
int abs(int);
void swap(int *, int *);
int find_largest(int [], int);
```

The parentheses can even be left empty:

```
int abs();
void swap();
int find_largest();
```

These declarations specify the return types of abs, swap, and find_largest, but provide no information about their arguments. Leaving the parentheses empty isn't the same as putting the word void between them, which indicates that there are no arguments. The empty-parentheses style of function declaration, which comes from Classic C, is rapidly disappearing. It's inferior to Standard C's prototype style, since it doesn't allow the compiler to check whether function calls have the right arguments.

If all declarators were as simple as these, C programming would be a snap. Unfortunately, declarators in actual programs often combine the *, [], and () notations. We've seen examples of such combinations already. We know that

```
int *ap[10];
```

declares an array of ten pointers to integers. We know that

```
float *fp(float);
```

declares a function that has a `float` argument and returns a pointer to a `float`. And, in Section 17.7, we learned that

```
void (*pf)(int);
```

declares a pointer to a function with an `int` argument and a `void` return type.

Deciphering Complex Declarations

So far, we haven't had too much trouble understanding declarators. But what about declarators like the following one?

```
int *(*x[10])(void);
```

This declarator combines `*`, `[]`, and `()`, so it's not obvious whether `x` is a pointer, an array, or a function.

Fortunately, there are two simple rules that will allow us to understand any declaration, no matter how convoluted:

- *Always read declarators from the inside out.* In other words, locate the identifier that's being declared, and start deciphering the declaration from there.
- *When there's a choice, always favor* `[]` *and* `()` *over* `*`. If `*` precedes the identifier and `[]` follows it, the identifier represents an array, not a pointer. Likewise, if `*` precedes the identifier and `()` follows it, the identifier represents a function, not a pointer. (Of course, we can always use parentheses to override the normal priority of `[]` and `()` over `*`.)

Let's apply these rules to our simple examples first. In the declaration

```
int *ap[10];
```

the identifier is `ap`. Since `*` precedes `ap` and `[]` follows it, we give preference to `[]`, so `ap` is an *array* of *pointers*. In the declaration

```
float *fp(float);
```

the identifier is `fp`. Since `*` precedes `fp` and `()` follows it, we give preference to `()`, so `fp` is a *function* that returns a *pointer*.

The declaration

```
void (*pf)(int);
```

is a little trickier. Since `*pf` is enclosed in parentheses, `pf` must be a pointer. But `(*pf)` is followed by `(int)`, so `pf` must point to a function with an `int` argument. The word `void` represents the return type of this function.

As the last example shows, understanding a complex declarator often involves zigzagging from one side of the identifier to the other:

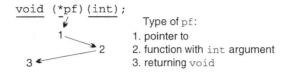

Type of pf:
1. pointer to
2. function with int argument
3. returning void

Let's use this zigzagging technique to decipher the declaration given earlier:

```
int *(*x[10])(void);
```

First, we locate the identifier being declared (x). x is preceded by * and followed by []; since [] have priority over *, we go right (x is an array). Next, we go left to find out the type of the elements in the array (pointers). Next, we go right to find out what kind of data the pointers point to (functions with no arguments). Finally, we go left to see what each function returns (a pointer to an int). Graphically, here's what the process looks like:

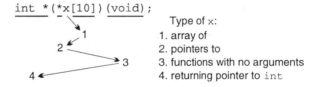

Type of x:
1. array of
2. pointers to
3. functions with no arguments
4. returning pointer to int

Mastering C declarations takes time and practice. The only good news is that there are certain things that can't be declared in C. Functions can't return arrays:

```
int f(int)[];        /*** WRONG ***/
```

Functions can't return functions:

```
int g(int)(int);     /*** WRONG ***/
```

Arrays of functions aren't possible, either:

```
int a[10](int);      /*** WRONG ***/
```

Using Type Definitions to Simplify Declarations

Some programmers use type definitions to help simplify complex declarations. Consider the declaration of x that we examined earlier in this section:

```
int *(*x[10])(void);
```

To make x's type easier to understand, we could use the following series of type definitions:

```
typedef int *Fcn(void);
typedef Fcn *Fcn_ptr;
```

```
typedef Fcn_ptr Fcn_ptr_array[10];
Fcn_ptr_array x;
```

Reading backwards, we see that `x` has type `Fcn_ptr_array`, a `Fcn_ptr_array` is an array of `Fcn_ptr` values, a `Fcn_ptr` is a pointer to type `Fcn`, and a `Fcn` is a function that has no arguments and returns a pointer to an `int` value.

18.5 Initializers

For convenience, C allows us to specify initial values for variables as we're declaring them. To initialize a variable, we write the = symbol after its declarator, then follow that with an initializer. (Don't confuse the = symbol in a declaration with the assignment operator; initialization isn't the same as assignment.)

We've seen various kinds of initializers in previous chapters. The initializer for a simple variable is an expression of the same type as the variable:

```
int i = 5 / 2;    /* i is initially 2 */
```

If the types don't match, C converts the initializer using the same rules as for assignment:

conversion during assignment ➤7.5

```
int j = 5.5;      /* converted to 5 */
```

The initializer for a pointer variable must be a pointer expression of the same type as the variable or of type `void *`:

```
int *p = &i;
```

The initializer for an array, structure, or union is usually a series of values enclosed in braces:

```
int a[5] = {1, 2, 3, 4, 5};
```

To complete our coverage of declarations, let's take a look at some additional rules that govern initializers:

- An initializer for a variable with static storage duration must be constant:

  ```
  #define FIRST 1
  #define LAST 100

  static int i = LAST - FIRST + 1;
  ```

  Since `LAST` and `FIRST` are macros, the compiler can compute the initial value of `i` ($100 - 1 + 1 = 100$). If `LAST` and `FIRST` had been variables, the initializer would be illegal.

- If a variable has automatic storage duration, its initializer need not be constant:

```
int f(int n)
{
  int last = n - 1;
  ...
}
```

- A brace-enclosed initializer for an array, structure, or union must contain only constant expressions, never variables or function calls:

```
#define N 2

int powers[5] = {1, N, N*N, N*N*N, N*N*N*N};
```

Since N is a constant, the initializer for powers is legal; if N were a variable, the program wouldn't compile.

- The initializer for an automatic structure or union can be another structure or union:

```
void g(struct complex c1)
{
  struct complex c2 = c1;
  ...
}
```

The initializer doesn't have to be a variable or parameter name, although it does need to be an expression of the proper type. For example, c2's initializer could be *p, where p is of type struct complex *, or f(c1), where f is a function that returns a complex structure.

Uninitialized Variables

In previous chapters, we've implied that uninitialized variables have undefined values. That's not always true; the initial value of a variable depends on its storage duration:

- Variables with *automatic* storage duration have no default initial value. The initial value of an automatic variable can't be predicted and may change each time the variable comes into existence.
- Variables with *static* storage duration have the value zero by default. Unlike memory allocated by calloc, which is simply set to zero bits, a static variable is correctly initialized based on its type: integer variables are initialized to 0, floating variables are initialized to 0.0, and pointers are initialized to the null pointer.

As a matter of style, it's better to provide initializers for static variables rather than rely on the fact that they're guaranteed to be zero. If a program accesses a variable that hasn't been initialized explicitly, someone reading the program later can't easily determine whether the variable is assumed to be zero or whether it's initialized by an assignment somewhere in the program.

Q & A

Q: What exactly is the difference between "scope" and "linkage"? [p. 402]

A: Scope is for the benefit of the compiler, while linkage is for the benefit of the linker. The compiler uses the scope of an identifier to determine whether or not it's legal to refer to the identifier at a given point in a file. When the compiler translates a source file into object code, it notes which names have external linkage, eventually storing these names in a table inside the object file. Thus, the linker has access to names with external linkage; names with internal linkage or no linkage are invisible to the linker.

Q: I don't understand how a name could have block scope but external linkage. Could you elaborate? [p. 405]

A: Certainly. Suppose that one source file defines a variable i:

```
int i;
```

Let's assume that the definition of i lies outside any function, so i has external linkage by default. In another file, there's a function f that needs to access i, so the body of f declares i as extern:

```
void f(void)
{
  extern int i;
  ...
}
```

In the first file, i has file scope. Within f, however, i has block scope. If other functions besides f need access to i, they'll need to declare it separately. (Or we can simply move the declaration of i outside f so that i has file scope.) What's confusing about this entire business is that each declaration or definition of i establishes a different scope; sometimes it's file scope, and sometimes it's block scope.

*Q: Why can't const objects be used in constant expressions? A constant is a constant, right? [p. 408]

A: Not necessarily. A const object is only guaranteed to stay constant during its *lifetime*, not throughout the execution of the program. Suppose that a const object is declared inside a function:

```
void f(int n)
{
  const int m = n;
}
```

When f is called, m will be initialized to the value of f's argument. m will then stay constant until f returns. When f is called the next time, m will likely be given a different value. That's where the problem arises. Suppose that we use m to specify the length of an array:

```
void f(int n)
{
  const int m = n;
  int a[m];    /*** WRONG ***/
}
```

a's length won't be known until f is called, which violates C's rule that the length of each array be known to the compiler.

That's not the only problem with const, though. const objects declared outside blocks have external linkage and can be shared among files. If C allowed the use of const objects in constant expressions, we could easily find ourselves in the following situation:

```
extern const int n;
int a[n];    /*** WRONG ***/
```

n is probably defined in another file, making it impossible for the compiler to determine a's length.

C++   There's no question that C's restrictions on const objects are annoying. C++ improves matters somewhat by allowing a const object to appear in a constant expression, provided that (a) it's an integer and (b) its initializer is constant:

```
const int n = 10;
int a[n];    /* legal in C++, but not in C */
```

C++ also specifies that const objects have internal linkage by default, making it possible to put their definitions in header files.

Q: **Why is the syntax of declarators so odd?**

A: Declarations are intended to mimic use. A pointer declarator has the form *p, which matches the way the indirection operator will later be applied to p. An array declarator has the form a[...], which matches the way the array will later be subscripted. A function declarator has the form f(...), which matches the syntax of a function call. This reasoning extends to even the most complicated declarators. Consider the file_cmd array of Section 17.7, whose elements were pointers to functions. The declarator for file_cmd has the form

```
(*file_cmd[])(void)
```

and a call of one of the functions has the form

```
(*file_cmd[n])();
```

The parentheses, brackets, and * are in identical positions.

Exercises

Section 18.1

1. For each of the following declarations, identify the storage class, type qualifiers, type specifiers, declarators, and initializers.

   (a) `static char **lookup(int level);`
   (b) `volatile unsigned long io_flags;`
   (c) `extern char *file_name[MAX_FILES], path[];`
   (d) `static const char token_buf[] = "";`

Section 18.2

2. Answer each of the following questions with `auto`, `extern`, `register`, and/or `static`.

   (a) Which storage class is used primarily to indicate that a variable or function can be shared by several files?
   (b) Suppose that a variable x is to be shared by several functions in one file but hidden from functions in other files. Which storage class should x be declared to have?
   (c) Which storage classes can affect the storage duration of a variable?

3. List the storage duration (static or automatic), scope (block or file), and linkage (internal, external, or none) of each variable and parameter in the following file:

   ```
   extern float a;

   void f(register double b)
   {
       static int c;
       auto char d;
   }
   ```

4. Let f be the following function. What will be the value of `f(10)` if f has never been called before? What will be the value of `f(10)` if f has been called five times previously?

   ```
   int f(int i)
   {
       static int j = 0;
       return i * j++;
   }
   ```

Section 18.3

5. Suppose that we declare x to be a `const` object. Which one of the following statements about x is *false*?

   (a) If x is of type `int`, it can be used to declare the length of an array.
   (b) The compiler will check that no assignment is made to x.
   (c) x is subject to the same scope rules as variables.
   (d) x can be of any type.

Section 18.4

6. Write a complete description of the type of x as specified by each of the following declarations.

   (a) `char (*x[10])(int);`
   (b) `int (*x(int))[5];`
   (c) `float *(*x(void))(int)[10];`
   (d) `void (*x(int, void (*y)(int)))(int);`

7. Use a series of type definitions to simplify each of the declarations in Exercise 6.

8. Write declarations for the following variables and functions:

    (a) p is a pointer to a function with a character pointer argument that returns a character pointer.

    (b) f is a function with two arguments: p, a pointer to a structure with tag t, and n, a long integer. f returns a pointer to a function that has no arguments and returns nothing.

    (c) a is an array of four pointers to functions that have no arguments and return nothing. The elements of a initially point to functions named `insert`, `search`, `update`, and `print`.

    (d) b is an array of 10 pointers to functions with two `int` arguments that return structures with tag t.

9. In Section 18.4, we saw that the following declarations are illegal:

    ```
    int f(int)[];       /* Functions can't return arrays     */
    int g(int)(int);    /* Functions can't return functions  */
    int a[10](int);     /* Array elements can't be functions */
    ```

    We can, however, achieve similar effects by using pointers: a function can return a *pointer* to the first element in an array, a function can return a *pointer* to a function, and the elements of an array can be *pointers* to functions. Revise each of these declarations accordingly.

Section 18.5   10. Which of the following declarations are legal? (Assume that `PI` is a macro that represents 3.14159.)

    (a) `char c = 65;`
    (b) `static int i = 5, j = i * i;`
    (c) `float f = 2 * PI;`
    (d) `double angles[] = {0, PI/2, PI, 3*PI/2};`

11. Which kind of variables cannot be initialized?

    (a) array variables
    (b) enumeration variables
    (c) structure variables
    (d) union variables
    (e) none of the above

12. What property of a variable determines whether or not it has a default initial value?

    (a) storage duration
    (b) scope
    (c) linkage
    (d) type

19 Program Design

Wherever there is modularity there is the potential for misunderstanding:
Hiding information implies a need to check communication.

It's obvious that real-world programs are larger than the examples in this book, but you may not realize just how much larger. Faster CPUs and larger main memories have made it possible to write programs that would have been impractical just a few years ago. The popularity of graphical user interfaces has added greatly to the average length of a program. Most full-featured programs today are at least 100,000 lines long. Million-line programs are commonplace, and it's not unheard-of for a program to have ten or more million lines.

Q&A   Although C wasn't specifically designed for writing large programs, many large programs have in fact been written in C. It's tricky, and it requires a great deal of care, but it can be done. In this chapter, I'll discuss techniques that have proved to be helpful for writing large programs and show which C features (the `static` storage class, for example) are especially useful.

Writing large programs (often called "programming-in-the-large") is quite different from writing small ones—it's like the difference between writing a term paper (ten pages double-spaced, of course) and a 500-page book. A large program requires more attention to style, since many people will be working on it. It requires careful documentation. It requires planning for maintenance, since it will likely be modified many times.

Above all, a large program requires careful design and much more planning than a small program. As Alan Kay, the designer of the Smalltalk programming language, puts it, "You can build a doghouse out of anything." A doghouse can be built without any particular design, using whatever materials are at hand. A house for humans, on the other hand, is too complex to just throw together.

Chapter 15 discussed writing large programs in C, but it concentrated on language details. In this chapter, we'll revisit the topic, this time focusing on techniques for good program design. A complete discussion of program design issues is obviously beyond the scope of this book. However, I'll try to cover—briefly—

some important concepts in program design and show how to use them to create C programs that are readable and maintainable.

Section 19.1 discusses how to view a C program as a collection of modules that provide services to each other. We'll then see how the concepts of information hiding (Section 19.2) and abstract data types (Section 19.3) can improve modules. In Section 19.4, we'll look at C++, an extended version of C that provides better support for information hiding, abstract data types, and other aspects of programming-in-the-large.

19.1   Modules

When designing a C program (or a program in any other language, for that matter), it's often good to view it as a number of independent *modules.* A module is a collection of services, some of which are made available to other parts of the program (the *clients*). Each module has an *interface* that describes the available services. The details of the module—including the source code for the services themselves—are stored in the module's *implementation*.

In the context of C, "services" are functions. The interface of a module is a header file containing prototypes for the functions that will be made available to other files in the program. The implementation of a module is a source file that contains definitions of the module's functions.

To illustrate this terminology, let's look at the calculator program of Chapter 15. This program consists of the file calc.c, which contains the main function, and a stack module, which is stored in the files stack.h and stack.c (see the figure at the top of the next page). The calc.c file is a *client* of the stack module. The stack.h file is the *interface* of the stack module; it supplies everything the client needs to know about the module. The stack.c file is the *implementation* of the module; it contains definitions of the stack functions and declarations of the variables that make up the stack.

The C library is itself a collection of modules. Each header in the library serves as the interface to a module. <stdio.h>, for example, is the interface to a module containing I/O functions, while <string.h> is the interface to a module containing string-handling functions.

Dividing a program into modules has a number of advantages:

- *Abstraction.* If modules are properly designed, we can treat them as *abstractions*; we know what they do, but we don't worry about the details of how they do it. Thanks to abstraction, it's not necessary to understand how the entire program works in order to make changes to one part of it. What's more, abstraction makes it easier for several members of a team to work on the same program. Once the interfaces for the modules have been agreed upon, the responsibility for implementing each module can be delegated to a particular person. Team members can then work largely independently of one another.

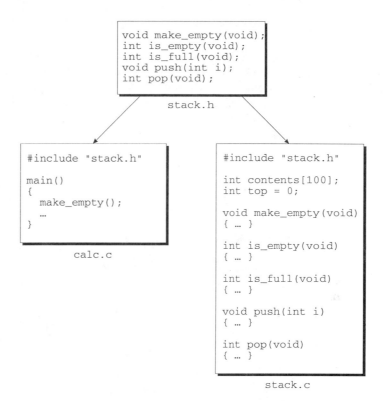

```
void make_empty(void);
int is_empty(void);
int is_full(void);
void push(int i);
int pop(void);
```
stack.h

```
#include "stack.h"

main()
{
  make_empty();
  ...
}
```
calc.c

```
#include "stack.h"

int contents[100];
int top = 0;

void make_empty(void)
{ ... }

int is_empty(void)
{ ... }

int is_full(void)
{ ... }

void push(int i)
{ ... }

int pop(void)
{ ... }
```
stack.c

- **Reusability.** Any module that provides services is potentially reusable in other programs. Our stack module, for example, is reusable. Since it's often hard to anticipate the future uses of a module, it's a good idea to design modules for reusability.

- **Maintainability.** A small bug will usually affect only a single module implementation, making the bug easier to locate and fix. Once the bug has been fixed, rebuilding the program requires only a recompilation of the module implementation (followed by linking the entire program). On a larger scale, we could replace an entire module implementation, perhaps to improve performance or when transporting the program to a different platform.

Although all these issues are important, maintainability is the most critical. Most real-world programs are in service over a period of years, during which bugs are discovered, enhancements are made, and modifications are made to meet changing requirements. Designing a program in a modular fashion makes maintenance much easier. Maintaining a program should be like maintaining a car—fixing a flat tire shouldn't require overhauling the engine.

For an example, we need look no further than the inventory program of Chapters 16 and 17. The original program (Section 16.3) stored part records in an array. Suppose that, after using this program for a while, the customer objects to having a fixed limit on the number of parts that can be stored. To satisfy the customer, we might switch to a linked list (as we did in Section 17.5). Making this change required going through the entire program, looking for all places that depend on the way parts are stored. If we'd designed the program differently in the first place—with a separate module dealing with part storage—we would have only needed to rewrite the implementation of that module, not the entire program.

Once we're convinced that modular design is the way to go, the process of designing a program boils down to deciding what modules it should have, what services each module should provide, and how the modules should be interrelated. We'll now look at these issues briefly. For more information about design, consult a software engineering text. One good choice is *Fundamentals of Software Engineering* by Ghezzi, Jazayeri, and Mandrioli (Englewood Cliffs, N.J.: Prentice-Hall, 1991); I'll use the same terminology they do.

Cohesion and Coupling

Good module interfaces aren't random collections of declarations. In a well-designed program, modules should have two properties:

- *High cohesion.* The elements of each module should be closely related to one another; we might think of them as cooperating toward a common goal. High cohesion makes modules easier to use and makes the entire program easier to understand.
- *Low coupling.* Modules should be as independent of each other as possible. Low coupling makes it easier to modify the program and reuse modules.

Does the calculator program have these properties? The stack module is clearly cohesive: its functions represent operations on a stack. There's little coupling in the program. The `calc.c` file depends on `stack.h` (and `stack.c` depends on `stack.h`, of course), but there are no other apparent dependencies.

Types of Modules

Because of the need for high cohesion and low coupling, modules tend to fall into certain typical categories:

- *Data pools.* A data pool is a collection of related variables and/or constants. In C, a module of this type is often just a header file. From a design standpoint, putting variables in header files isn't usually a good idea, but collecting related constants in a header file can often be desirable. In the C library, `<float.h>` and `<limits.h>` are both data pools.

  `<float.h>` header ➤*23.1*
  `<limits.h>` header ➤*23.2*

- *Libraries.* A library is a collection of related functions. The `<string.h>` header, for example, is the interface to a library of string-handling functions.
- *Abstract objects.* An abstract object is a collection of functions that operate on a hidden data structure. (An "object" is just a collection of data bundled with operations on the data. If the data is hidden, the object is "abstract.") The stack module we've been discussing falls into this category.

- *Abstract data types.* An abstract data type is a type whose representation is hidden. Client modules can use the type to declare variables, but have no knowledge of the structure of those variables. For a client module to perform an operation on a variable, it must call a function provided by the abstract data type module. Abstract data types play a significant role in modern-day programming; we'll return to them in Section 19.3 for a more detailed discussion.

19.2 Information Hiding

A well-designed module often keeps some information secret from its clients. Clients of our stack module, for example, have no need to know whether the stack is stored in an array, in a linked list, or in some other fashion. The technique of deliberately concealing information from the clients of a module is known as *information hiding*. Information hiding has two primary advantages:

- *Security.* If clients don't know how the stack is stored, they won't be able to corrupt it by tampering with its internal workings. To perform operations on the stack, they'll have to call functions that are provided by the module itself—functions that we've written and tested.
- *Flexibility.* Making changes—no matter how large—to a module's internal workings won't be difficult. For example, we could implement the stack as an array at first, then later switch to a linked list or other representation. We'll have to rewrite the implementation of the module, of course, but—if the module was designed properly—we won't have to alter the module's interface.

In C, the major tool for enforcing information hiding is the `static` storage class. Declaring a function to be `static` gives the function internal linkage, thus preventing it from being called from other files (including clients of the module). Declaring a variable with file scope to be `static` has a similar effect—the variable is accessible only to functions in the same file.

`static` storage class ➤ *18.2*

A Stack Module

To see the benefits of information hiding, let's look at two implementations of a stack module, one using an array and the other a linked list. We'll assume that the module's header file has the following appearance:

stack.h
```
#ifndef STACK_H
#define STACK_H

void make_empty(void);
int is_empty(void);
void push(int i);
int pop(void);

#endif
```

Notice that I haven't put a prototype for stack_full in stack.h. Having a stack_full function makes sense when the stack is stored as an array, but not when it's stored as a linked list.

Let's first use an array to implement the stack:

stack1.c

```
#include <stdio.h>
#include <stdlib.h>
#include "stack.h"

#define STACK_SIZE 100

static int contents[STACK_SIZE];
static int top = 0;

void make_empty(void)
{
  top = 0;
}

int is_empty(void)
{
  return top == 0;
}

static int is_full(void)
{
  return top == STACK_SIZE;
}

void push(int i)
{
  if (is_full()) {
    printf("Error in push: stack is full.\n");
    exit(EXIT_FAILURE);
  }
  contents[top++] = i;
}

int pop(void)
{
  if (is_empty()) {
    printf("Error in pop: stack is empty.\n");
    exit(EXIT_FAILURE);
  }
  return contents[--top];
}
```

The variables that make up the stack (contents and top) are both declared static, since there's no reason for the rest of the program to access them directly. I've included an is_full function in stack1.c, but I've made it static so that it's hidden from the rest of the program.

As a matter of style, some programmers use macros to indicate which functions and variables are "public" (accessible elsewhere in the program) and which are "private" (limited to a single file):

```
#define PUBLIC   /* empty */
#define PRIVATE static
```

The reason for writing PRIVATE instead of static is that the latter has more than one use in C; PRIVATE makes it clear that we're using it to enforce information hiding. Here's what the stack implementation would look like if we were to use PUBLIC and PRIVATE:

```
PRIVATE int contents[STACK_SIZE];
PRIVATE int top = 0;

PUBLIC void make_empty(void) { ... }

PUBLIC int is_empty(void) { ... }

PRIVATE int is_full(void) { ... }

PUBLIC void push(int i) { ... }

PUBLIC int pop(void) { ... }
```

Now we'll switch to a linked list:

stack2.c
```
#include <stdio.h>
#include <stdlib.h>
#include "stack.h"

struct node {
  int data;
  struct node *next;
};

static struct node *top = NULL;

void make_empty(void)
{
  top = NULL;
}

int is_empty(void)
{
  return top == NULL;
}

void push(int i)
{
  struct node *new_node;

  new_node = malloc(sizeof(struct node));
```

```
      if (new_node == NULL) {
        printf("Error in push: stack is full.\n");
        exit(EXIT_FAILURE);
      }

    new_node->data = i;
    new_node->next = top;
    top = new_node;
  }

int pop(void)
{
    struct node *old_top;
    int i;

    if (is_empty()) {
      printf("Error in pop: stack is empty.\n");
      exit(EXIT_FAILURE);
    }

    old_top = top;
    i = top->data;
    top = top->next;
    free(old_top);
    return i;
  }
```

There's no need for the `is_full` function anymore, since the stack no longer has a fixed limit on its size. Instead, the `push` function tests whether `malloc` returns a null pointer; if so, there's not enough memory left to push another item on the stack. Fortunately, `is_full` was declared `static` in `stack1.c`, making it impossible for other files to call `is_full`. Since these files were unaware of the existence of `is_full`, removing it can't possibly affect them.

Our stack example shows clearly the advantage of information hiding: it doesn't matter whether we use `stack1.c` or `stack2.c` to implement the module. Both versions match the stack's interface, so we can switch from one to the other without having to make changes elsewhere in the program.

19.3 Abstract Data Types

A module that serves as an abstract object, like the stack module in the previous section, has one disadvantage: there's no way to have multiple instances of the object (more than one stack, in this case). To accomplish this, we'll need to go a step further and create a new *type*.

Once we've defined a `Stack` type, we'll be able to have as many stacks as we want. The following fragment illustrates how we could have two stacks in the same program:

```
#include <stdio.h>
#include "stack.h"

main()
{
  Stack s1, s2;

  make_empty(&s1);
  make_empty(&s2);
  push(&s1, 1);
  push(&s2, 2);
  if (!is_empty(&s1))
    printf("%d\n", pop(&s1));    /* prints "1" */
  ...
}
```

We're not really sure what s1 and s2 are (structures? pointers?), but it doesn't matter. To clients of the stack module, s1 and s2 are *abstractions* that respond to certain operations (make_empty, is_empty, push, and pop).

Let's convert our stack.h header so that it provides a Stack type. Doing so will require adding a Stack (or Stack *) parameter to each function:

```
#define STACK_SIZE 100

typedef struct {
  int contents[STACK_SIZE];
  int top;
} Stack;

void make_empty(Stack *s);
int is_empty(const Stack *s);
void push(Stack *s, int i);
int pop(Stack *s);
```

The stack parameters to make_empty, push, and pop need to be pointers, since these functions modify the stack. The parameter to is_empty doesn't need to be a pointer, but we've made it one anyway. Passing is_empty a Stack *pointer* instead of a Stack *value* is more efficient, since the latter would result in a structure being copied.

Encapsulation

Unfortunately, Stack isn't an *abstract* data type, since stack.h reveals what the Stack type really is. Nothing prevents clients from using a Stack variable as a structure:

```
Stack s1;

s1.top = 0;
s1.contents[top++] = 1;
```

Providing access to the `top` and `contents` members allows clients to corrupt the stack. Worse still, we won't be able to change the way stacks are stored without having to assess the effect of the change on clients.

What we need is a way to prevent clients from knowing how the `Stack` type is represented. Sadly, C has no features designed specifically for *encapsulating* types in this way. Techniques do exist, but they're cumbersome or rely on trickery. The best way to achieve encapsulation is to use C++, which allows us to hide the details of a data type. In fact, C's failure to support abstract data types properly is one of the reasons for the emergence of C++.

C++

19.4   C++

C++

No chapter on program design would be complete without mentioning C++, an extended version of C developed by Bjarne Stroustrup of AT&T Bell Laboratories during the 1980s. C++ is much better than C at supporting modern program design principles, including abstract data types. (C, of course, is a much older language, so we can't really fault it for not supporting newer design techniques.) The most significant feature of C++, the *class*, allows us to achieve the kind of encapsulation that we sought in Section 19.3. Beyond that, C++ provides a cornucopia of new features for programming-in-the-large, including:

- Support for *object-oriented programming,* which offers the promise of greater code reuse by allowing a new class to be "derived" from an existing class instead of written from scratch.
- *Overloaded operators,* which make it possible to give additional meanings to traditional C operators. Overloaded operators allow us to extend the language itself by defining new data types (classes) that are almost indistinguishable from the basic (built-in) types.
- *Templates,* which enable us to write general-purpose, highly reusable classes and functions.
- *Exception handling,* a uniform way of detecting and responding to errors.

One goal of C++ was to retain compatibility with C whenever possible. As a result, all the features of Standard C are also present in C++. That doesn't mean that every C program will compile in C++, however. There are a few minor incompatibilities between the two languages, some of which arise from restrictions that C++ imposes in an effort to achieve greater security than C.

The rest of this section gives an overview of C++. A word of caution: I'll only cover some of the new features in C++, and the description of those won't be very complete. Still, you should be able to get a feel for what C++ programming is like.

Differences between C and C++

Before we tackle the major new features that C++ adds to C—classes, overloading, derivation, virtual functions, templates, and exception handling—we'll need to cover some of the smaller differences between the languages.

comments C++ has single-line comments, which begin with // and end at the first new-line character:

```
// This is a comment.
// So is this.
```

Single-line comments are safer than C-style comments (which are still legal), since they can't accidentally be left unterminated.

tags vs. type names In C++, tags (names identifying a particular kind of structure, union, or enumeration) are automatically type names. Thus, instead of

```
typedef struct { double re, im; } Complex;
```

we can simply write

```
struct Complex { double re, im; };
```

functions with no arguments There's no need to use the word void when declaring or defining a C++ function with no arguments:

```
void draw(void);    // no arguments
void draw();        // no arguments either
```

default arguments C++ allows function arguments to have default values. For example, the following function prints any number of new-line characters. If called with no arguments, it prints a single new-line character.

```
void new_line(int n = 1)    // default argument
{
  while (n-- > 0)
    putchar('\n');
}
```

new_line can be called with or without an argument:

```
new_line(3);    // prints 3 blank lines
new_line();     // prints 1 blank line by default
```

reference arguments C specifies that arguments are passed by value, which makes it difficult to write functions that modify variables (other than arrays) supplied as arguments. To work around this restriction, we end up passing pointers to the variables. A function that exchanges the contents of two variables would have the following appearance in C:

```
void swap(int *a, int *b)
{
  int temp;

  temp = *a;
  *a = *b;
  *b = temp;
}
```

When swap is called, its arguments will be pointers to variables:

```
swap(&i, &j);
```

Although this technique works, it isn't very convenient or especially readable, and it's easy to make a mistake. C++ improves matters somewhat by allowing parameters to be declared as **references** instead of pointers. Here's what the swap function will look like if a and b are references:

```
void swap(int& a, int& b)    // a and b are references
{
  int temp;

  temp = a;
  a = b;
  b = temp;
}
```

When swap is called, the arguments aren't preceded by the & operator:

```
swap(i, j);
```

Inside the body of swap, a and b are understood to be aliases for i and j. The statement temp = a; actually copies the value of i into temp. The statement a = b; actually copies the value of j into i. The statement b = temp; actually copies the value of temp into j.

dynamic storage allocation — C programs can dynamically allocate and release blocks of memory by calling the library functions malloc, calloc, realloc, and free. Although C++ programs have access to these functions, it's better practice to use new and delete, which are *operators*, not functions. new allocates space, while delete releases it. The operand for new is a type specifier:

```
int *int_ptr, *int_array;
int_ptr = new int;           // allocates memory for an int
int_array = new int[10];     // allocates memory for an array
                             //   of ten integers
```

new returns a null pointer if the requested amount of memory can't be allocated. The delete operator requires a pointer as its operand:

```
delete int_ptr;              // releases memory pointed to by
                             //   int_ptr
```

```
delete [] int_array;        // [] required when deallocating
                            //   an array
```

Classes

The most significant difference between C and C++ is the latter's support for *classes.* (The importance of classes is underscored by C++'s original name: "C with Classes.") A class is essentially an abstract data type: a collection of data together with functions that operate on the data. By writing a class, we can create a new data type that—if we're careful—is nearly as powerful as a basic type.

Let's say that we need to store numbers in fractional form: 1/4, 3/7, and so on. If we write a class named Fraction, we'll be able to manipulate fractions with ease. We could declare Fraction variables by writing

```
Fraction f1, f2, f3;
```

We could copy fractions using the = operator, pass them to functions, and write functions that return them.

But that's not all. A feature known as *operator overloading* allows us to use C++ operators as names for operations on Fraction objects. By overloading the * operator so that it multiplies fractions, we'll be able to multiply f1 and f2 by writing

```
f3 = f1 * f2;
```

If f1 has the value 1/2 and f2 has the value 2/3, f3 will be assigned 1/3. Being able to overload operators so that they work with fractions is a big step toward making Fraction as easy to use as the int and float types.

Classes allow us to create any data type that we want. If we need a numeric type that C++ doesn't normally provide (fractions, complex numbers, integers with an unlimited number of digits, and so forth), we can add the type to the language by designing an appropriate class. If we're unhappy with the usual behavior of a C++ type, we can write our own. For example, a variable that belongs to our own Array class could perform a range check when it's subscripted. Our own String variables could expand and shrink as needed. Classes are also ideal for creating complicated data structures that aren't provided as C++ types: queues, sets, stacks, and the like.

What makes classes so useful, however, is that they can model real-world objects, not just the kind of data structures that programmers normally work with. If we're developing a banking application, we might define classes like Account; the Account class could provide operations like deposit and withdraw. Classes like these can make programs much easier both to read and to write, since we'll be performing natural-looking operations on natural-looking objects.

The downside of classes is that they can be difficult to design and implement. That's the price we pay for ease of use. It's the same trade-off that the computer field has made in recent years: as programs become easier to use, they become more complicated internally.

Class Definitions

Defining a class in C++ is a lot like defining a structure in C. In its simplest form, a class definition is almost identical to a structure definition, with the word `class` at the beginning instead of `struct`:

```
class Fraction {
  int numerator;
  int denominator;
};
```

`numerator` and `denominator` are said to be **data members** of the `Fraction` class. By the way, C++ doesn't require that class names begin with capital letter; it's just a convention that many C++ programmers follow.

   Once a class has been defined, we can use its name to declare variables in the same way we'd use a structure name:

```
Fraction f1, f2;
```

(A class tag serves as a type name in C++, so we don't need to write `class Fraction`.) The compiler sets aside space for two variables, `f1` and `f2`, each with its own `numerator` and `denominator` members. C++ has a special name for variables like `f1` and `f2`; they're said to be **instances** of the `Fraction` class. An instance of *any* class is known as an **object**.

   The members of a structure are accessible via the `.` and `->` operators. In a class, on the other hand, the members are hidden within the class by default. As a result, statements like these are illegal:

```
f1.numerator = 0;           // illegal
denom = f2.denominator;     // illegal
```

We say that `numerator` and `denominator` are **private** members of the `Fraction` class.

   If we choose, we can make the members of a class accessible by declaring them to be `public`:

```
class Fraction {
public:
  int numerator;
  int denominator;
};
```

We can even mix public and private members:

```
class Fraction {
public:
  int numerator;       // accessible outside the class
private:
  int denominator;     // hidden within the class
};
```

Note the use of `private:` to indicate that `denominator` is a private member.

Member Functions

If the private members of a class aren't accessible outside the class, how it is possible to change—or even inspect—their values? The answer is ingenious: functions that need access to the data members of a class are themselves declared inside the class! Functions that belong to a class are said to be **member functions**.

Let's make `numerator` and `denominator` private members of `Fraction` and add two member functions to the class:

```
class Fraction {
public:
  void create(int num, int denom);
  void print();
private:
  int numerator;
  int denominator;
};
```

`create` and `print` are public members of `Fraction`, so they can be called outside the class.

Member functions are called from an object, using the same "dot" operator that we use to access a member of a structure:

```
f1.create(1, 2);    // f1 now stores 1/2
f1.print();         // prints "1/2"
```

Admittedly, this looks odd, but you'll quickly get used to it. Here's how to interpret the call of `create`:

> "f1 is a `Fraction` object, so we're calling the `create` function in the `Fraction` class. The `create` function will store 1 in f1's numerator member and 2 in f1's denominator member."

Here's what the call of `print` means:

> "f1 is a `Fraction` object, so we're calling the `print` function in the `Fraction` class. The `print` function will display f1's numerator member, followed by a / character, followed by f2's denominator member."

Note that a member function somehow knows which object called it, even though the object itself isn't one of the function's arguments. We can think of f1 as a sort of argument that goes before the function name instead of being put in the argument list.

Member functions don't have to be public. In the case of the `Fraction` class, we might add `reduce` (which reduces a fraction to lowest terms) as a private member function:

```
class Fraction {
public:
  void create(int num, int denom);
  void print();
```

```
private:
  void reduce();
  int numerator;
  int denominator;
};
```

In practice, data members are usually declared to be private. Member functions are usually declared to be public unless they're intended for use only within the class.

So far we've only *declared* create, print, and reduce; where are they *defined?* One possibility is to define each member function later, outside the class definition. For example, the definition of create might look like this:

```
void Fraction::create(int num, int denom)
{
  numerator = num;
  denominator = denom;
  reduce();
}
```

Notice that Fraction:: precedes the name of the function. This notation is required—without it, the C++ compiler would treat create as an ordinary function, not a member of the Fraction class. Note also that create has direct access to numerator and denominator. In general, a member function has access to all members—public or private—of its class. Finally, note the call of reduce, which looks strange since it's not apparent what object is being reduced. It turns out that when one member function calls another, the latter function assumes that it was called from the same object. In other words, executing the call

```
f1.create(1, 2);
```

is like executing the following statements:

```
f1.numerator = num;
f1.denominator = denom;
f1.reduce();
```

Instead of defining a member function outside its class, we have the option of putting the entire function inside the class definition:

```
class Fraction {
public:
  void create(int num, int denom)
    { numerator = num; denominator = denom; reduce(); }
  ...
};
```

Putting the definition of a member function inside the class definition is advisable only if the definition is very short.

Now let's add a multiply function to the Fraction class. First, we need to declare the function inside the class definition:

```
class Fraction {
public:
  void create(int num, int denom);
  void print();
  Fraction mul(Fraction f);
private:
  void reduce();
  int numerator;
  int denominator;
};
```

Next, we'll need to write the definition of the `mul` function:

```
Fraction Fraction::mul(Fraction f)
{
  Fraction result;

  result.numerator = numerator * f.numerator;
  result.denominator = denominator * f.denominator;
  result.reduce();
  return result;
}
```

At first, the `mul` function looks rather mysterious: `f` is clearly one of the fractions to be multiplied, but where's the other fraction? The answer lies in the way `mul` will be called:

```
f3 = f1.mul(f2);
```

Here's an interpretation of this statement:

> "`f1` is a `Fraction` object, so we're calling the `mul` function in the `Fraction` class. The `mul` function will multiply `f1`'s numerator by `f2`'s numerator, and store the product in `result`'s numerator. Then, `mul` will multiply `f1`'s denominator by `f2`'s denominator, and store the product in `result`'s denominator. Next, `mul` will call `reduce` to reduce the `result` fraction to lowest terms. Finally, `mul` returns `result`, which is copied into `f3`."

Constructors

To ensure that instances of a class are properly initialized, the class may provide a special function known as a *constructor*. A class may also provide a *destructor*—a function that cleans up when an instance of the class is destroyed. The beauty of constructors and destructors (and the danger, as well!) is that they're usually invoked *automatically*, without an explicit function call. In other words, we'll write constructors and destructors for our classes, and the compiler will arrange for them to be called automatically when needed.

Our `Fraction` class already has an initialization function named `create`. Let's replace `create` with a constructor. A constructor looks like a function with the same name as the class itself:

```
class Fraction {
public:
  Fraction(int num, int denom)
    { numerator = num; denominator = denom; reduce(); }
  ...
};
```

Unlike other member functions, a constructor has no specified return type. Notice that constructors go in the `public` part of the class.

Constructors can be called like ordinary functions, but they're usually invoked implicitly in declarations:

```
Fraction f(3, 4);    // declares and initializes f
```

In this declaration of the object `f`, the constructor for the `Fraction` class is called with 3 and 4 as its arguments. As a result, `f` will have 3/4 as its initial value.

Constructors often have default arguments:

```
class Fraction {
public:
  Fraction(int num = 0, int denom = 1)
    { numerator = num; denominator = denom; reduce(); }
  ...
};
```

Since both `num` and `denom` have default values, the `Fraction` constructor can have two arguments:

```
Fraction f(3, 4);
```

one argument:

```
Fraction f(3);       // same as Fraction f(3, 1);
```

or no arguments:

```
Fraction f;          // same as Fraction f(0, 1);
```

Constructors and Dynamic Storage Allocation

Constructors and destructors are especially useful for classes that need dynamic storage allocation and deallocation (via the `new` and `delete` operators). For example, let's say that we get fed up with the limitations of ordinary C strings. Creating our own `String` class offers several advantages:

- `String` objects could contain strings of arbitrary length. In C, a string is limited by the length of its enclosing array.
- The length of a `String` object could be determined quickly. Finding the length of a C string requires calling `strlen`, which searches the entire string to locate its terminating null character.
- Additional operations could be added to the `String` class as needed. In C, we can't easily modify `<string.h>` to contain additional functions.

Here's how we might declare String objects:

```
String s1("abc"), s2("def");
```

s1 would contain "abc" initially, while s2 would contain "def". Of course, the value of either variable could be changed later.

Since there's no limit on the length of a string, a String object will need to contain a pointer to dynamically allocated memory (we'll call this text). For speed, we'll also want a member that stores the length of the string:

```
class String {
  ...
private:
  char *text;    // pointer to string
  int len;       // length of string
};
```

Next, we'll need a constructor that converts an ordinary string to a String object:

```
class String {
public:
  String(const char *s);    // constructor
  ...
private:
  char *text;
  int len;
};
```

Here's what the definition of the constructor might look like:

```
String::String(const char *s)
{
  len = strlen(s);
  text = new char[len+1];
  strcpy(text, s);
}
```

After computing the length of the string that s points to, the constructor uses the new operator to allocate enough space for a copy of the string. Finally, the constructor copies the string into the newly allocated space.

Destructors

Classes that rely on dynamic storage allocation face a challenging problem. Consider what happens to a String object that's local to a function:

```
void f()
{
  String s1("abc");
  ...
}
```

When f is called, the s1 object comes into existence. The constructor for s1 allocates an array of four characters and copies the string "abc" into the array. When f returns, s1 won't exist any more, since it has automatic storage duration. Unfortunately, releasing the space occupied by a String object recovers only the memory used for the text and len members; it doesn't free the memory that text points to. As a result, the program will suffer from a memory leak.

The problem of releasing dynamically allocated memory is one of the reasons that C++ provides *destructors.* A destructor is a function that's called automatically when an object ceases to exist. Constructors and destructors go hand in hand. A constructor initializes an object when it comes into existence; a destructor cleans up when the object ceases to exist. If the constructor for a class allocates memory dynamically, the destructor will most likely free the memory.

A destructor is a member function, just like a constructor is. The name of a destructor is the same as the name of the class, but with the character ~ (tilde) at the beginning. A destructor has no return type and no arguments. Here's what the String class looks like with a destructor added:

```
class String {
public:
  String(const char *s);
  ~String() { delete [] text; }    // destructor
    …
private:
  char *text;
  int len;
};
```

The ~String destructor releases the character array pointed to by text.

Overloading

In C++, two or more functions in the same scope may have the same name. When functions are *overloaded* in this way, the C++ compiler determines which one is called by examining the function's arguments. For example, suppose that two versions of the function f exist in the same scope:

```
void f(int);
void f(double);    // overloading!
```

Here's how calls of f are resolved:

```
f(1);      // a call of f(int)
f(1.0);    // a call of f(double)
```

Overloading has one main advantage: Functions that perform the same operation, but on operands of different types, can be given the same name. As a result, we have fewer names to remember. For example, the following functions both raise x to the power y, but for different types of arguments:

```
int pow(int x, int y);
double pow(double x, double y);
```

Member functions within a class can be overloaded. (In fact, that's probably the most common use of function overloading in C++.) For example, overloading allows us to add another constructor to the String class:

```
class String {
public:
  String(const char *s);
  String() { text = 0; len = 0; }    // overloading
  ~String() { delete [] text; }
  ...
private:
  char *text;
  int len;
};
```

In case you're wondering why text is assigned 0, remember that 0 represents the null pointer. C++ programmers generally prefer 0 over NULL, for reasons we won't go into here.

The new String constructor, known as a ***default constructor*** because it has no arguments, will be invoked when String objects are declared without a specified initial value:

```
String s;    // default constructor is invoked
```

In addition to *function* overloading, C++ also supports *operator* overloading: the same operator symbol can represent different operations, depending on the types of the operands. Operator overloading allows us to redefine the operators of C++ to work with instances of our classes. The result is a more natural-looking, easier-to-read program; clients of the class can perform operations by applying operators instead of calling functions with hard-to-remember names.

For example, the Fraction class would be easier to use if the mul function were replaced by the * operator. Doing so is easy; we just replace the name mul by operator* when we're declaring or defining the function:

```
class Fraction {
public:
  ...
  Fraction operator*(Fraction f);
private:
  ...
};

Fraction Fraction::operator*(Fraction f)
{
  // same body as mul function
}
```

Internally, the function is the same; only the name has changed.

When an operator function is defined as a class member, one of its operands is always implicit. Thus, the * operator that we've just defined is a binary operator, not a unary operator. When we write a statement like

```
f3 = f1 * f2;
```

the compiler notices that f1 is a Fraction object, so it looks in the Fraction class, finds a function named operator*, and converts the statement to:

```
f3 = f1.operator*(f2);
```

After that, execution proceeds as for an ordinary member function.

Input/Output in C++

Although C++ programs can use <stdio.h>, C++ provides an alternative I/O library. The most important header in the new library, <iostream.h>, defines several classes, including istream (input stream) and ostream (output stream). I/O takes place by performing operations on istream and ostream objects. Simple programs that obtain input from the keyboard and display output on the screen use the cin object for input and the cout object for output. cin is an instance of the istream class; cout is an instance of ostream.

<< and >> operators ➤20.1   The istream and ostream classes rely heavily on operator overloading. In particular, the C operators << and >> (left and right shift) are used for most reading and writing operations. The istream class overloads >> so that it obtains input from a stream. The ostream class overloads << so that it writes output to a stream. Using << and >>, an interactive session with the user might look like this:

```
cout << "Enter a number: ";
cin >> n;
cout << "The square is ";
cout << n * n;
cout << "\n";
```

The first statement has the following interpretation: "cout is an ostream object, so we're calling the operator<< function in the ostream class. The operator<< function will take the string "Enter a number" as its argument."

One advantage of the new I/O library is that it can be extended to read and write instances of our own classes. For example, we could create an overloaded << operator that writes a Fraction object:

```
Fraction f(3, 4);

cout << f;    // prints 3/4
```

Being able to write fractions using << takes us another step toward our goal of making the Fraction class as easy to use as the basic types.

Object-Oriented Programming

Although experts still debate the precise requirements for a language to be considered "object-oriented," there's a consensus that such a language must provide at least the following three capabilities:

- *Encapsulation*—the ability to define a new type and a set of operations on that type, without revealing the representation of the type. (Values of the type are the "objects" in "object-oriented.") C++ classes support encapsulation by restricting access to private data members.

- *Inheritance*—the ability to create new types that inherit properties from existing types. C++ supports inheritance through a mechanism known as ***class derivation.***

- *Polymorphism*—the ability of objects that belong to related classes to respond differently to the same operation. In C++, ***virtual functions*** support polymorphism.

We've already looked at classes, so we'll turn now to class derivation and virtual functions.

Derivation

When we need a new class, C++ allows us to ***derive*** it from a previously defined class instead of writing it from scratch. For example, a program that manipulates geometric shapes might need classes named `Circle`, `Square`, and `Triangle`. These could all be derived from a more general class named `Shape`. Properties that are common to all three classes would be defined only once, in the `Shape` class; operations that apply to all shapes would also go in the `Shape` class. If every shape has a color and an *x-y* position on the screen, and if every shape can change its position and color, then `Shape` might look like this:

```
class Shape {
public:
  void change_color(int new_color);
  void move(int x_change, int y_change);
  …
private:
  int x, y;    // coordinates of center
  int color;   // current color
  …
};
```

`Shape` is said to be a ***base class***; `Circle`, `Square`, and `Triangle` are ***derived classes***. The figure at the top of the next page shows the relationships among the classes.

One great advantage of derivation is that it helps us reuse code on a larger scale than would otherwise be possible. If we need to add a `Pentagon` class later, we can derive it from the `Shape` class. That's a lot easier than writing the

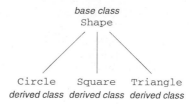

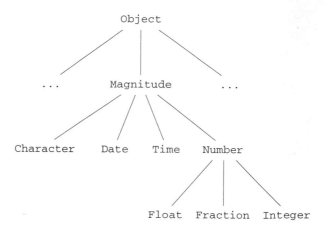

`Pentagon` class from scratch, since `Pentagon` can inherit most of what it needs from `Shape`. We'll only have to write code for those properties that a `Pentagon` doesn't have in common with a `Shape`.

Derivation can also simplify maintenance. If our `Shape` class has a bug, we need only fix it there; there's no need to modify the derived classes. By the same token, if we need to add a new property (or operation) that's relevant for all shapes, we can just put it in the `Shape` class for derived classes to inherit.

Derivation is often used to develop extensive libraries of related classes. In Smalltalk, an object-oriented language that influenced C++, all classes are directly or indirectly derived from a single class named `Object`. The class `Magnitude` (among others) is derived from `Object`, the classes `Character`, `Date`, `Time`, and `Number` are then derived from `Magnitude`, and the classes `Float`, `Fraction`, and `Integer` are derived from `Number`:

Each class has all the properties of its base class, plus some others that are unique to it. Objects that belong to the `Magnitude` class have one feature in common: they can be compared using relational operators (greater than, less than, and so forth). `Number` objects inherit this capability, and have the additional ability to support arithmetic. Arithmetic isn't defined for other `Magnitude` objects. (Comparing dates makes sense; adding dates doesn't.)

Now that we've examined derivation in general terms, let's return to the `Shape` example to illustrate the specifics. To indicate that the `Circle` class is derived from `Shape`, we include a ***derivation list*** in the definition of `Circle`:

```
class Circle: public Shape {
  ...
};
```

Circle **inherits** the members of Shape (with the exception of constructors and destructors); in other words, the members of Shape are also members of Circle.

A derived class may declare additional data members and member functions that aren't present in the base class. For example, Circle will probably need a data member that stores the radius of a circle. The Shape class doesn't have a radius member, so we'll need to put one in Circle:

```
class Circle: public Shape {
public:
  ...
private:
  int radius;    // radius of circle
};
```

In addition to the radius data member, a Circle object will contain members named x, y, and color (inherited from Shape).

When one class is derived from another, C++ allows a base class pointer to point to an instance of the derived class. For example, a variable of type Shape* can point to a Circle, Square, or Triangle object:

```
Circle c;
Shape *p = &c;    // Shape pointer points to a Circle
```

In a similar way, C++ allows a parameter of type Shape* to match an argument that points to a Circle, Square, or Triangle object. A parameter of type Shape& matches any Circle, Square, or Triangle object. The following function appears to require a Shape argument, but in fact could be passed a Circle, Square, or Triangle object instead:

```
void add_to_list(Shape& s)
{
  ...
}
```

add_to_list is a rather versatile function that can handle different kinds of shape arguments.

Virtual Functions

Class derivation becomes even more valuable when combined with *virtual functions*—functions declared in a base class and then implemented differently in each derived class. Consider the Shape class. Every Shape object can increase its size, so the class will need a grow function:

```
class Shape {
public:
  void grow();
  ...
};
```

Unfortunately, the `grow` function will be different for each class derived from `Shape`. To handle this, we'll declare `grow` to be `virtual` in the `Shape` class:

```
class Shape {
public:
  virtual void grow();
  ...
};
```

The `Circle`, `Square`, and `Triangle` classes will now provide their own custom versions of `grow`. The `Circle` version might look like this:

```
class Circle: public Shape {
public:
  void grow() { radius++; }
  ...
private:
  int radius;    // radius of circle
  ...
};
```

Most of the time, a virtual function behaves like an ordinary member function. If `c` is a `Circle` object, the call `c.grow()` increases the radius of `c`. When it's invoked through a pointer (or reference) to a base class, however, a virtual function has a special property: which version of the function is called depends on what kind of object the pointer currently points to.

Let's say that `p` is a pointer to a `Shape` object. Since `Circle` and `Square` are both derived from the `Shape` class, `p` could point to an instance of either one of these classes. When `p` is used to call the `grow` function, `Circle::grow` is called if `p` points to a `Circle` object, but `Square::grow` is called if `p` points to a `Square` object:

```
Shape *p;
Circle c;
Square s;

p = &c;        // p points to a Circle
p->grow();     // calls Circle::grow
p = &s;        // p points to a Square
p->grow();     // calls Square::grow
```

Notice the use of `->` to call `grow`. Calling a member function from a pointer to an object requires `->` instead of the dot operator.

Virtual functions rely on a technique known as ***dynamic binding***, since the compiler can't always determine which version of the function is being called.

(Normal function calls—even calls of overloaded functions—can be resolved by the compiler.) Consider the following example:

```
if (…)
  p = &c;
else
  p = &s;
p->grow();    // calls either Circle::grow or Square::grow
```

There's no way for the compiler to know which version of `grow` is called; that can't be determined until the program is run.

Dynamic binding allows us to create data structures containing objects of different classes—provided that all classes are derived from a common base class—and then apply the same operation to each. Each object can respond differently to the operation, depending on its class. For example, let's say that we keep track of which objects are currently on the screen by storing `Shape` objects in a list. By visiting each object in turn and calling its `grow` function, we can increase its size without knowing what kind of shape it is:

```
while  (not at end of list)  {
    make p point to current shape;
    p->grow();    // calls either Circle::grow, Square::grow,
                  // or Triangle::grow
    advance to next item in list;
}
```

Dynamic binding simplifies our code because we don't need to use a `switch` statement to test an object before performing an operation on it. Also, we can add new classes and remove old ones without modifying the code for processing the data structure. For example, if we add a `Pentagon` class (derived from `Shape`), the loop that makes each shape grow won't need to be changed.

Templates

Templates are "patterns" from which classes can be created. (C++ also has function templates, which we'll ignore.) A template looks much like an ordinary class, except that part of the class definition is left unspecified. Omitting part of the class definition makes the class more general and easier to reuse.

Consider the `Stack` type of Section 19.3. If we translate this type into a C++ class, we might end up with the following definition:

```
class Stack {
public:
  void make_empty();
  int is_empty();
  void push(int);
  int pop();
  …
};
```

Unfortunately, a `Stack` object can only store integers. If we later need a stack that stores some other type of data (`float` values, for example), we could make a copy of the class definition, rename the class, and change `int` to `float` in many places. Creating a `Stack` template is a better idea:

```
template <class T>
class Stack {
public:
  void make_empty();
  int is_empty();
  void push(T);
  T pop();
  ...
};
```

The `Stack` template looks much like the `Stack` class, except for the line

```
template <class T>
```

which indicates that `Stack` is a template that won't be complete until the missing class `T` is filled in. `T` (a "template argument") is a dummy name; any name would do. Notice that `push` now requires an argument of type `T`, and `pop` returns a `T` value. `Stack`'s member functions will have the following appearance:

```
template <class T>
void Stack<T>::push(T x)
{
   ...
}
```

   Class templates are later "instantiated" by filling in the template arguments. Despite the `<class T>` notation, `Stack`'s argument doesn't have to be a class; any C++ type will do. For example, here are three instantiations of the `Stack` class, using `int`, `float`, and `char` as the template arguments:

```
Stack<int> int_stack;        // stack of int values
Stack<float> float_stack;    // stack of float values
Stack<char> char_stack;      // stack of char values
```

The following calls of `push` illustrate how we'd use the three stacks:

```
int_stack.push(10);          // pushes 10 onto int_stack
float_stack.push(1.2);       // pushes 1.2 onto float_stack
char_stack.push('a');        // pushes 'a' onto char_stack
```

Exception Handling

An *exception* is a condition that can arise during the execution of a program, usually as the result of an error. For example, there are two kinds of errors possible when using a `Stack` object: attempting to push an element onto the stack when it's full or attempting to pop an element when it's empty. We could represent these errors by exceptions named `StackFull` and `StackEmpty`.

When an error occurs, a function can "throw" an exception. In the case of the Stack class, the push and pop functions would throw the StackFull and StackEmpty exceptions, respectively:

```
void Stack::push(int i)
{
  if  (no space left)
    throw StackFull();

  ...
}

int Stack::pop()
{
  if  (stack empty)
    throw StackEmpty();

  ...
}
```

Code in which an exception may occur is placed in a "try block." Exceptions are detected by "handlers" ("catch blocks"), which are attached to try blocks. In the following example, a try block that contains calls of push and pop has been followed by two catch blocks. The first catch block handles the StackFull exception by printing Error: Stack full, while the second handles the StackEmpty exception by printing Error: Stack empty.

```
try {
  ...
  s.push(y);

  ...
  z = s.pop();
  ...
}
catch (StackFull) {
  cout << "Error: Stack full\n";
}
catch (StackEmpty) {
  cout << "Error: Stack empty\n";
}
```

After an exception is handled, program execution continues after the last catch block.

If there's no handler for an exception at the end of the current try block, C++ doesn't give up. Instead, it checks enclosing try blocks for a handler. If that search fails, the current function terminates and the exception is propagated to the calling function, then to its caller if necessary, and so on. The worst case is that the exception propagates all the way back to main. If main can't handle the exception, the entire program terminates. This property of exceptions helps prevent errors from accidentally being ignored.

Q & A

Q: You said that C wasn't designed for writing large programs. Isn't UNIX a large program? [p. 419]

A: Not at the time C was designed. In a 1978 paper, Ken Thompson estimated that the UNIX kernel was about 10,000 lines of C code (plus a small amount of assembler). Other components of UNIX were of comparable size; in another 1978 paper, Dennis Ritchie and colleagues put the size of the PDP-11 C compiler at 9660 lines. By today's standards, these are indeed small programs.

Q: Are there any abstract data types in the C library?

FILE type ➤22.1

A: Technically there aren't, but a few come close, including the FILE type (defined in <stdio.h>). Before performing an operation on a file, we must declare a variable of type FILE *:

```
FILE *fp;
```

The fp variable will then be passed to various file-handling functions.

Programmers are expected to treat FILE as an abstraction. It's not necessary to know what a FILE is in order to use the FILE type. Presumably FILE is a structure type, but the C standard doesn't even guarantee that. In fact, it's better not to know too much about how FILE values are stored, since the definition of the FILE type can (and often does) vary from one C compiler to another.

Of course, we can always look in the stdio.h file and see what a FILE is. Having done so, there's nothing to prevent us from writing code to access the internals of a FILE. For example, we might discover that FILE is a structure with a member named bsize (the file's buffer size):

```
typedef struct {
  ...
  int bsize;    /* buffer size */
  ...
} FILE;
```

Once we know about the bsize member, there's nothing to prevent us from accessing the buffer size for a particular file:

```
printf("Buffer size: %d\n", fp->bsize);
```

Doing so isn't a good idea, however, because other C compilers might store the buffer size under a different name, or keep track of it in some other way entirely. Changing the bsize member is an even worse idea:

```
fp->bsize = 1024;
```

Unless we know all the details about how files are stored, this is a dangerous thing to do. Even if we *do* know the details, they may change with a different compiler or the next release of the same compiler.

Q: If C++ is so great, why does anyone still use C?

A: In a sense, this isn't a meaningful question. C++ has all the features of C, so every C++ programmer is "using" C. Let's rephrase the question: "If C++ is so great, why doesn't everyone use the C++ extensions?"

For one thing, C++ is much more complex than C. Since C++ inherits virtually all the features of C while adding a number of new ones, C++ is obviously a larger language. The many ways in which the features of C++ can be combined also add to its complexity. For writing small programs, C is much simpler and works just as well as C++.

The fancy new features of C++ require compilers to do more work. As a result, C++ programs compile somewhat more slowly than C programs. Also, using the new features of C++ may impose a small but measurable run-time performance penalty that's unacceptable in some applications.

Although C++ fixes some of C's most notorious pitfalls, it leaves others intact. And, of course, the new features of C++ introduce some traps that don't exist in C. As Stroustrup himself puts it: "C makes it easy to shoot yourself in the foot. C++ makes it harder, but when do you, it blows away your whole leg."

Don't forget that C has been around a lot longer than C++. Although C++ has begun to stabilize after years of change, it will take some time for C++ compilers to achieve the kind of compatibility that C compilers already enjoy. Moreover, there are a lot more C compilers in existence than C++ compilers, especially for the less popular platforms.

To summarize: For "lean and mean" programs, and for programs that need to be widely portable, C is preferable. For large, full-featured programs—including those with an elaborate graphical user interface—C++ has the edge.

Exercises

Section 19.1

1. A *queue* is similar to a stack, except that items are added at one end but removed from the other in a *FIFO* (first-in, first-out) fashion. Operations on a queue might include:

    inserting an item at the end of the queue
    removing an item from the beginning of the queue
    returning the first item in the queue (without changing the queue)
    returning the last item in the queue (without changing the queue)
    testing whether the queue is empty

    Write an interface for a queue module in the form of a header file named `queue.h`.

Section 19.2

2. Modify the `stack2.c` file to use the PUBLIC and PRIVATE macros.

3. (a) Write an array-based implementation of the queue module described in Exercise 1.

    (b) Write a linked-list implementation of the queue module described in Exercise 1.

Section 19.3   4. (a) Write an implementation of the `Stack` type, using an array representation.

    (b) Redo the `Stack` type, this time using a linked list representation instead of an array. (Show both `stack.h` and `stack.c`.)

5. (a) Convert the `queue.h` header of Exercise 1 so that it defines a `Queue` type. Modify the functions in `queue.h` to take a `Queue` (or `Queue *`) parameter.

    (b) Write an implementation of the `Queue` type, using an array representation.

    (c) Write an implementation of the `Queue` type, using a linked-list representation.

Section 19.4   6. Does the `Fraction` class need a destructor? Justify your answer.

7. Add overloaded operators named +, −, and / to the `Fraction` class. Write definitions for these operators and for the `print` and `reduce` functions.

8. Compared with using C's `printf` and `scanf` functions, what advantages can you see to using the << and >> operators for input and output?

9. Convert the `Queue` type of Exercise 5 into a `Queue` class.

10. Convert the `Queue` class of Exercise 9 into a `Queue` template.

20 Low-Level Programming

A programming language is low level when its programs require attention to the irrelevant.

Previous chapters have described C's high-level, machine-independent features. Although these features are adequate for many applications, some programs need to perform operations at the bit level. Bit manipulation and other low-level operations are especially useful for writing systems programs (including compilers and operating systems), encryption programs, graphics programs, and programs for which fast execution and/or efficient use of space is critical.

Section 20.1 covers C's bitwise operators, which provide easy access to both individual bits and bit-fields. Section 20.2 then shows how to declare structures that contain bit-fields. Finally, Section 20.3 describes how certain ordinary C features (type definitions, unions, and pointers) can help in writing low-level programs. For clarity, I'll rely on 16-bit examples in this chapter; you shouldn't have any trouble extending the examples to 32 bits. The discussion won't depend upon any particular operating system, except for the portions of Section 20.3 that deal with the quirks of DOS programming.

Some of the techniques described in this chapter depend on knowledge of how data is stored in memory, which can vary depending on the machine and the compiler. Relying on these techniques will most likely make a program nonportable, so it's best to avoid them unless absolutely necessary. If you do need them, try to limit their use to certain modules in your program; don't spread them around. And, above all, be sure to document what you're doing!

20.1 Bitwise Operators

C provides six *bitwise operators*, which operate on integers and characters at the bit level. We'll discuss the bitwise shift operators first.

Bitwise Shift Operators

The bitwise shift operators can transform the binary representation of a number by shifting its bits to the left or right. C provides two shift operators, which are shown in Table 20.1.

Table 20.1

Bitwise Shift Operators

Symbol	Meaning
<<	left shift
>>	right shift

The operands for << and >> may be of any integer or character type. The integral promotions are performed on both operands; the result has the type of the left operand after promotion.

The value of i << j is the result when the bits in i are shifted left by j places. For each bit that is "shifted off" the left end of i, a zero bit enters at the right. The value of i >> j is the result when i is shifted right by j places. If i is of an unsigned type or if the value of i is nonnegative, then zeros are added at the left as needed. If i is a negative number, the result is implementation-defined; some implementations add zeros at the left end, while others preserve the sign bit by adding ones.

portability tip   *For portability, it's best to perform shifts only on unsigned numbers.*

The following examples illustrate the effect of applying the shift operators to the number 13:

```
unsigned int i, j;

i = 13;          /* i is now 13 (binary 0000000000001101) */
j = i << 2;      /* j is now 52 (binary 0000000000110100) */
j = i >> 2;      /* j is now  3 (binary 0000000000000011) */
```

As these examples show, neither operator modifies its operands. To modify a variable by shifting its bits, we'd use the compound assignment operators <<= and >>=:

```
i = 13;          /* i is now 13 (binary 0000000000001101) */
i <<= 2;         /* i is now 52 (binary 0000000000110100) */
i >>= 2;         /* i is now 13 (binary 0000000000001101) */
```

 The bitwise shift operators have lower precedence than the arithmetic operators, which can cause surprises. For example, i << 2 + 1 means i << (2 + 1), not (i << 2) + 1.

Bitwise Complement, And, Exclusive Or, and Inclusive Or

Table 20.2 lists the remaining bitwise operators.

Table 20.2
Other Bitwise Operators

Symbol	Meaning
~	bitwise complement
&	bitwise *and*
^	bitwise exclusive *or*
|	bitwise inclusive *or*

The ~ operator is unary; the integral promotions are performed on its operand. The other operators are binary; the usual arithmetic conversions are performed on their operands.

The ~, &, ^, and | operators perform Boolean operations on all bits in their operands. The ~ operator produces the complement of its operand, with zeros replaced by ones and ones replaced by zeros. The & operator performs a Boolean *and* operation on all corresponding bits in its two operands. The ^ and | operators are similar (both perform a Boolean *or* operation on the bits in their operands); however, ^ produces 0 whenever both operands have a 1 bit, whereas | produces 1.

Don't confuse the *bitwise* operators & and | with the *logical* operators && and ||. The bitwise operators sometimes produce the same results as the logical operators, but they're not equivalent.

The following examples illustrate the effect of the ~, &, ^, and | operators:

```
unsigned int i, j, k;

i = 21;       /* i is now     21 (binary 0000000000010101) */
j = 56;       /* j is now     56 (binary 0000000000111000) */
k = ~i;       /* k is now  65514 (binary 1111111111101010) */
k = i & j;    /* k is now     16 (binary 0000000000010000) */
k = i ^ j;    /* k is now     45 (binary 0000000000101101) */
k = i | j;    /* k is now     61 (binary 0000000000111101) */
```

The value shown for ~i is based on the assumption that an `unsigned int` value occupies 16 bits.

The ~ operator deserves special mention, since we can use it to help make even low-level programs more portable. Suppose that we need an integer whose bits are all 1. The preferred technique is to write ~0, which doesn't depend on the number of bits in an integer. In a similar fashion, if we need an integer whose bits are all 1 except for the last five, we could write ~0x001f.

The ~, &, ^, and | operators have different precedence levels:

highest: ~

                &

                ^

lowest: |

As a result, we can combine these operators in expressions without having to use parentheses. For example, we could write i & ~j | k instead of (i & (~j)) | k and i ^ j & ~k instead of i ^ (j & (~k)). Of course, it doesn't hurt to use parentheses to avoid confusion.

The precedence of &, ^, and | is lower than the precedence of the relational and equality operators. As a result, statements like the following one won't have the desired effect:

```
if (status & 0x4000 != 0) …
```

Instead of testing whether status & 0x4000 isn't zero, this statement will evaluate 0x4000 != 0 (which has the value 1), then test whether the value of status & 1 isn't zero.

The compound assignment operators &=, ^=, and |= correspond to the bitwise operators &, ^, and |:

```
i = 21;    /* i is now 21 (binary 0000000000010101) */
j = 56;    /* j is now 56 (binary 0000000000111000) */
i &= j;    /* i is now 16 (binary 0000000000010000) */
i ^= j;    /* i is now 40 (binary 0000000000101000) */
i |= j;    /* i is now 56 (binary 0000000000111000) */
```

Using the Bitwise Operators to Access Bits

When we do low-level programming, we'll often need to store information as single bits or collections of bits. In graphics programming, for example, we may want to squeeze two or more pixels into a single byte. Using the bitwise operators, we can extract or modify data that's stored in a small number of bits.

Let's assume that i is a 16-bit integer variable. Using i as an example, let's see how to perform the most common single-bit operations:

- **Setting a bit.** Suppose that we want to set bit 4 of i. (We'll assume that the most significant bit is numbered 15 and the least significant is numbered 0.) The easiest way to set bit 4 is to *or* the value of i with the constant 0x0010 (a "mask" that contains a 1 bit in position 4):

idiom
```
i = 0x0000;      /* i is now 0000000000000000 */
i |= 0x0010;     /* i is now 0000000000010000 */
```

More generally, if the position of the bit is stored in the variable j, we can use a shift operator to create the mask:

```
i |= 1 << j;          /* sets bit j */
```

For example, if j has the value 3, then 1 << j is 0x0008.

- **Clearing a bit.** To clear bit 4 of i, we'd use a mask with a 0 bit in position 4, and 1 bits everywhere else:

idiom

```
i = 0x00ff;           /* i is now 0000000011111111 */
i &= ~0x0010;         /* i is now 0000000011101111 */
```

Using the same idea, we can easily write a statement that clears a bit whose position is stored in a variable:

```
i &= ~(1 << j);       /* clears bit j */
```

■ *Testing a bit.* The following `if` statement tests whether bit 4 of `i` is set:

idiom

```
if (i & 0x0010) …   /* tests bit 4 */
```

To test whether bit `j` is set, we'd use the following statement:

```
if (i & 1 << j) …   /* tests bit j */
```

To make working with bits easier, we'll often give them names. For example, suppose that we want bits 0, 1, and 2 of a number to correspond to the colors blue, green, and red, respectively. First, we define names that represent the three bit positions:

```
enum {BLUE = 1, GREEN = 2, RED = 4};
```

Defining BLUE, GREEN, and RED as macros would also work, of course. Setting, clearing, and testing the BLUE bit would be done as follows:

```
i |= BLUE;            /* sets BLUE bit   */
i &= ~BLUE;           /* clears BLUE bit */
if (i & BLUE) …       /* tests BLUE bit  */
```

It's also easy to set, clear, or test several bits at time:

```
i |= BLUE | GREEN;            /* sets BLUE and GREEN bits   */
i &= ~(BLUE | GREEN);         /* clears BLUE and GREEN bits */
if (i & (BLUE | GREEN)) …     /* tests BLUE and GREEN bits  */
```

The `if` statement tests whether either the BLUE bit *or* the GREEN bit is set.

Using the Bitwise Operators to Access Bit-Fields

Dealing with a group of several consecutive bits (a *bit-field*) is slightly more complicated than working with single bits. Here are examples of the two most common bit-field operations:

■ *Modifying a bit-field.* Modifying a bit-field requires a bitwise *and* (to clear the bit-field), followed by a bitwise *or* (to store new bits in the bit-field). The following statement shows how we might store the binary value 101 in bits 4–6 of the variable `i`:

```
i = i & ~0x0070 | 0x0050;   /* stores 101 in bits 4-6 */
```

The `&` operator clears bits 4–6 of `i`; the `|` operator then sets bits 6 and 4. Notice that `i |= 0x0050` by itself wouldn't always work: it would set bits 6 and 4 but not change bit 5. To generalize the example a little, let's assume that the variable j contains the value to be stored in bits 4–6 of i. We'll need to shift j into position before performing the bitwise *or*:

```
i = (i & ~0x0070) | (j << 4);    /* stores j in bits 4-6 */
```

The $<<$ operator has higher precedence than $\&$ and $|$, so we can drop the parentheses if we wish:

```
i = i & ~0x0070 | j << 4;
```

- **Retrieving a bit-field.** When the bit-field is at the end of a number (in the low-order bits), fetching its value is easy. For example, the following statement retrieves bits 0–2 in the variable i:

```
j = i & 0x0007;              /* retrieves bits 0-2 */
```

The mask 0x0007 contains 1 bits in each of the desired positions. If the bit-field is somewhere in the middle of i, then we can first shift the bit-field to the right end of the number, then extract the field using the $\&$ operator. To extracts bits 4–6 of i, for example, we could use the following statement:

```
j = (i >> 4) & 0x0007;    /* retrieves bits 4-6 */
```

PROGRAM   **XOR Encryption**

One of the simplest ways to encrypt data is to exclusive-*or* (XOR) each character with a secret key. Suppose that the key is the & character. If we XOR this key with the character z, we'll get the \ character (assuming that we're using the ASCII

ASCII character set ➤*Appendix E*   character set). Here's what happens:

	00100110	(ASCII code for &)
XOR	<u>01111010</u>	(ASCII code for z)
	01011100	(ASCII code for \)

To decrypt a message, we just apply the same algorithm. In other words, by encrypting an already-encrypted message, we'll recover the original message. If we XOR the & character with the \ character, for example, we'll get the original character, z:

	00100110	(ASCII code for &)
XOR	<u>01011100</u>	(ASCII code for \)
	01111010	(ASCII code for z)

The following program, xor.c, encrypts a message by XORing each character with the & character. The original message can be entered by the user or read from a file using input redirection; the encrypted message can be viewed on the

input and output redirection ➤*22.1*   screen or saved in a file using output redirection. For example, suppose that the file msg contains the following lines:

Trust not him with your secrets, who, when left
alone in your room, turns over your papers.
> --Johann Kaspar Lavater (1741-1801)

To encrypt the msg file, saving the encrypted message in newmsg, we'd use the following command:

```
xor <msg >newmsg
```

newmsg will now contain these lines:

```
rTSUR HIR NOK QORN _IST UCETCRU, QNI, QNCH JC@R
GJIHC OH _IST TIIK, RSTHU IPCT _IST VGVCTU.
                --lINGHH mGUVGT jGPGRCT (1741-1801)
```

To recover the original message, we'd use the command

```
xor <newmsg
```

which will display it on the screen.

As the example shows, our program won't change some characters, including digits. XORing these characters with & would produce invisible control characters, which could cause problems with some operating systems. In Chapter 22, we'll see how to avoid problems when reading and writing files that contain control characters. Until then, we'll play it safe by using the iscntrl function to check whether the original character or the new (encrypted) character is a control character. If so, we'll have the program write the original character instead of the new character.

iscntrl function ➤*23.4*

Here's the finished program, which is remarkably short:

xor.c
```c
/* Performs XOR encryption */

#include <ctype.h>
#include <stdio.h>

#define KEY '&'

main()
{
  int orig_char, new_char;

  while ((orig_char = getchar()) != EOF) {
    new_char = orig_char ^ KEY;
    if (iscntrl(orig_char) || iscntrl(new_char))
      putchar(orig_char);
    else
      putchar(new_char);
  }

  return 0;
}
```

20.2 Bit-Fields in Structures

Although the techniques of Section 20.1 allow us to work with bit-fields, these techniques can be tricky to use and potentially confusing. Fortunately, C provides an alternative—declaring structures whose members represent bit-fields.

As an example, let's look at how DOS stores the date at which a file was created or last modified. Since days, months, and years are small numbers, storing them as normal integers would waste space. Instead, DOS allocates only 16 bits for a date, with 5 bits for the day, 4 bits for the month, and 7 bits for the year:

Using bit-fields, we can define a C structure with an identical layout:

```
struct file_date {
  unsigned int day: 5;
  unsigned int month: 4;
  unsigned int year: 7;
};
```

The number after each member indicates its length in bits. Since the members all have the same type, we can condense the declaration if we want:

```
struct file_date {
  unsigned int day: 5, month: 4, year: 7;
};
```

The type of a bit-field must be either `int`, `unsigned int`, or `signed int`. Using `int` is ambiguous; some compilers treat the field's high-order bit as a sign bit, but others don't.

portability tip   *Declare all bit-fields to be either* `unsigned int` *or* `signed int`.

We can use a bit-field just like any other member of a structure, as the following example shows:

```
struct file_date fd;

fd.day = 28;
fd.month = 12;
fd.year = 8;      /* represents 1988 */
```

After these assignments, the `fd` variable will have the following appearance:

We could have used the bitwise operators to accomplish the same effect; using the bitwise operators might even make the program a little faster. However, having a readable program is usually more important than gaining a few microseconds.

Bit-fields do have one restriction that doesn't apply to other members of a structure. Since bit-fields don't have addresses in the usual sense, C doesn't allow us to apply the & operator to a bit-field. Because of this rule, functions such as scanf can't store data directly into a bit-field:

```
scanf("%d", &fd.day);    /*** WRONG ***/
```

Of course, we can always use scanf to read input into an ordinary integer variable, then assign it to fd.day.

How Bit-Fields Are Stored

The C standard allows the compiler some latitude in choosing how it stores bit-fields. Let's take a more detailed look at how a compiler processes the declaration of a structure that has bit-field members.

The rules concerning how the compiler handles bit-fields depend on the notion of "storage units." The size of a storage unit is implementation-defined; typical values are 8 bits, 16 bits, and 32 bits. As it processes a structure declaration, the compiler packs bit-fields one by one into a storage unit, with no gaps between the fields, until there's not enough room for the next field. At that point, some compilers skip to the beginning of the next storage unit, while others split the bit-field across the storage units. (Which one occurs is implementation-defined.) The order in which bit-fields are allocated (left to right or right to left) is also implementation-defined.

Our file_date example assumes that storage units are 16 bits long. (An 8-bit storage unit would also be acceptable, provided that the compiler splits the month field across two storage units.) We also assume that bit-fields are allocated from right to left (with the first bit-field occupying the low-order bits); this is common practice among DOS compilers.

To provide more control over the storage of bit-fields, C allows us to omit the name of any bit-field. Unnamed bit-fields are useful as "padding" to ensure that other bit fields are properly positioned. Consider the time associated with a DOS file, which is stored in the following way:

```
struct file_time {
  unsigned int seconds: 5;
  unsigned int minutes: 6;
  unsigned int hours: 5;
};
```

(You may be wondering how it's possible to store a number between 0 and 59 in a field with only 5 bits. Well, DOS cheats: it divides the number of seconds by 2, so the seconds member is actually between 0 and 29.) If we're not interested in the seconds field, we can leave out its name:

```
struct file_time {
  unsigned int : 5;          /* not used */
  unsigned int minutes: 6;
  unsigned int hours: 5;
};
```

The remaining bit-fields will be aligned as if the seconds field were still present.

Another trick that we can use to control the storage of bit-fields is to specify 0 as the length of an unnamed bit-field:

```
struct s {
  unsigned int a: 4;
  unsigned int : 0;     /* 0-length bit-field */
  unsigned int b: 8;
};
```

A 0-length bit-field is a signal to the compiler to align the following bit-field at the beginning of a storage unit. If storage units are 8 bits long, the compiler will allocate 4 bits for the a member, then skip 4 bits to the next storage unit, and then allocate 8 bits for b. If storage units are 16 bits long, the compiler will allocate 4 bits for a, then skip 12 bits, and then allocate 8 bits for b.

20.3   Other Low-Level Techniques

Some of the language features that we've covered in previous chapters are used often in low-level programming. To wrap up this chapter, we'll take a look at several important examples: defining types that represent units of storage, using unions to bypass normal type-checking, and using pointers as addresses. We'll also cover the volatile type qualifier, which we avoided discussing in Section 18.3 because of its low-level nature.

Defining Machine-Dependent Types

Since the char type—by definition—occupies one byte, we'll sometimes treat characters as bytes, using them to store data that's not necessarily in character form. When we do so, it's a good idea to define a BYTE type:

```
typedef unsigned char BYTE;
```

Depending on the machine, we may want to define additional types, like the following one:

```
typedef unsigned int WORD;
```

We'll use the BYTE and WORD types in later examples.

Using Unions to Provide Multiple Views of Data

Although unions can be used in a portable way—see Section 16.4 for examples—they're often used in C for an entirely different purpose: viewing a block of memory in two or more different ways.

Here's a simple example based on the `file_date` structure described in Section 20.2. Since a `file_date` structure fits into two bytes, we can think of any two-byte value as a `file_date` structure. In particular, we could view an `unsigned int` value as a `file_date` structure (assuming that integers are 16 bits long). The following union allows us to easily convert an integer to a file date or vice versa:

```
union int_date {
  unsigned int i;
  struct file_date fd;
};
```

With the help of this union, we could fetch a file date from disk as two bytes, then extract its `month`, `day`, and `year` fields. Conversely, we could construct a date as a `file_date` structure, then write it to disk as a pair of bytes.

As an example of how we might use the `int_date` union, here's a function that, when passed an integer argument, prints it as a file date:

```
void print_date(unsigned int n)
{
  union int_date u;

  u.i = n;
  printf("%d/%d/%.2d\n", u.fd.month, u.fd.day,
         (u.fd.year+1980)%100);
}
```

To determine the last two digits of the year, we add 1980 to `u.fd.year` (since the year is stored relative to 1980—the year the world began, according to Microsoft) and then compute the remainder when the year is divided by 100.

Using unions to allow multiple views of data is especially useful when working with registers, which are often divided into smaller units. Intel 80x86 processors, for example, have 16-bit registers named AX, BX, CX, and DX. Each of these registers can be treated as two 8-bit registers. AX, for example, is divided into registers named AH and AL.

When writing applications for Intel-based computers, we may need variables that represent the contents of the AX, BX, CX, and DX registers. We want access to both the 16- and 8-bit registers; at the same time, we need to take their relationships into account (a change to AX affects both AH and AL; changing AH modifies AX). The solution is to set up two structures, one containing members that correspond to the 16-bit registers, and the other containing members that match the 8-bit registers. We then create a union that encloses the two structures:

```
union {
  struct {
    WORD ax, bx, cx, dx;
  } word;
  struct {
    BYTE al, ah, bl, bh, cl, ch, dl, dh;
  } byte;
} regs;
```

The members of the `word` structure will be overlaid with the members of the `byte` structure; for example, `ax` will occupy the same memory as `al` and `ah`. And that, of course, is exactly what we wanted. Here's an example showing how the `regs` union might be used:

```
regs.byte.ah = 0x12;
regs.byte.al = 0x34;
printf("AX: %x\n", regs.word.ax);
```

Changing `ah` and `al` affects `ax`, so the output will be

```
AX: 1234
```

Using Pointers as Addresses

We saw in Section 11.1 that a pointer is really some kind of memory address, although we usually don't need to know the details. When we do low-level programming, however, the details matter.

On some computers, an address has the same number of bits as an integer or long integer. Creating a pointer that represents a specific address is easy: we just cast an integer into a pointer. For example, here's how we might store the address 1000 (hex) into a pointer variable:

```
BYTE *p;

p = (BYTE *) 0x1000;    /* p contains address 0x1000 */
```

Other computers are more difficult to deal with. When a computer with an Intel CPU runs in "real mode" (the mode used by DOS), an address consists of two 16-bit numbers: a *segment* and an *offset*. Building a pointer from a specific address is usually done by invoking a macro provided in a nonstandard header. For example, the macro `MK_FP` ("make far pointer")—usually found in the `<dos.h>` header—creates a pointer from a segment/offset pair:

```
BYTE far *p;

p = MK_FP(segment, offset);
```

The word `far` (not a part of Standard C) indicates that `p` is a "far pointer"—in other words, it consists of both a segment and an offset. (A "near pointer" is just an offset.)

PROGRAM   **Toggling the Num Lock Key**

On the IBM PC and compatibles, the Num Lock toggle determines whether the keys on the numeric keypad represent digits or cursor motions. By pressing the Num Lock key, the user can turn Num Lock on or off.

The following programs, `nlockon.c` and `nlockoff.c`, make it possible to change the setting of Num Lock without pressing the Num Lock key. This capability can be useful in a batch file (a file containing a series of DOS commands). For example, we could put the `nlockoff` command in the DOS `autoexec.bat` file to turn Num Lock off whenever the machine is booted.

These programs are actually rather easy to write, since the Num Lock toggle is kept in memory and has the same address on every PC. Bit 5 (the sixth bit from the right) in the byte located at segment 40 (hex), offset 17 (hex), controls Num Lock. Setting this bit turns Num Lock on; clearing it turns Num Lock off. `nlockon.c` and `nlockoff.c` need only store the address of the byte in a pointer, then use the bitwise operators to modify the Num Lock bit within this byte.

The `nlockon.c` and `nlockoff.c` programs were written specifically for DOS compilers that support the `far` keyword and provide the `MK_FP` macro. `nlockon.c` uses the `|=` operator to *set* the Num Lock bit:

nlockon.c
```
/* Turns Num Lock on */

#include <dos.h>

typedef unsigned char BYTE;

main()
{
  BYTE far *p = MK_FP(0x0040, 0x0017);

  *p |= 0x20;    /* sets Num Lock bit */
  return 0;
}
```

`nlockoff.c` uses the `&=` operator to *clear* the Num Lock bit:

nlockoff.c
```
/* Turns Num Lock off */

#include <dos.h>

typedef unsigned char BYTE;

main()
{
  BYTE far *p = MK_FP(0x0040, 0x0017);

  *p &= ~0x20;   /* clears Num Lock bit */
  return 0;
}
```

The `volatile` Type Qualifier

On some computers, certain memory locations are "volatile"; the value stored at such a location can change as a program is running, even though the program doesn't seem to be storing new values there. For example, some memory locations might hold data coming directly from input devices.

The `volatile` type qualifier allows us to inform the compiler if any of the data used in a program is volatile. `volatile` typically appears in the declaration of a pointer variable that will point to a volatile memory location:

```
volatile BYTE *p;   /* p will point to a volatile byte */
```

To see why `volatile` is needed, suppose that p points to a memory location that contains the most recent character typed at the user's keyboard. This location is volatile: its value changes each time the user enters a character. We might use the following loop to obtain characters from the keyboard and store them in a buffer array:

```
while (buffer not full) {
  wait for input;
  buffer[i] = *p;
  if (buffer[i++] == '\n')
    break;
}
```

A sophisticated compiler might notice that this loop changes neither p nor *p, so it could optimize the program by altering it so that *p is fetched just once:

```
store *p in a register;
while (buffer not full) {
  wait for input;
  buffer[i] = value stored in register;
  if (buffer[i++] == '\n')
    break;
}
```

The optimized program will fill the buffer with many copies of the same character—not exactly what we had in mind. Declaring that p points to volatile data avoids this problem by telling the compiler that *p must be fetched from memory each time it's needed.

For additional uses of `volatile`, see the Q&A section in Chapter 24.

Q & A

Q: What do you mean by saying that the & and | operators sometimes produce the same results as the && and || operators, but not always? [p. 453]

A: Let's compare i & j with i && j (similar remarks apply to | and ||). As long as i and j have the value 0 or 1 (in any combination), the two expressions will have the same value. However, if i and j should have other values, the expressions may not always match. If i is 1 and j is 2, for example, then i & j has the value 0 (i and j have no corresponding 1 bits), while i && j has the value 1. If i is 3 and j is 2, then i & j has the value 2, while i && j has the value 1.

Side effects are another problem. Evaluating i & j++ *always* increments j as a side effect, while evaluating i && j++ *sometimes* increments j.

Exercises

Section 20.1

*1. Show the output produced by each of the following code fragments. Assume that i, j, and k are unsigned int variables.

(a) `i = 8; j = 9;`
    `printf("%d", i >> 1 + j >> 1);`

(b) `i = 1;`
    `printf("%d", i & ~i);`

(c) `i = 2; j = 1; k = 0;`
    `printf("%d", ~i & j ^ k);`

(d) `i = 7; j = 8; k = 9;`
    `printf("%d", i ^ j & k);`

2. Describe how to "toggle" a bit (change it from 0 to 1 or from 1 to 0). Illustrate the technique by writing a statement that toggles bit 4 in the variable i.

*3. Explain what effect the following macro has on its arguments. You may assume that the arguments have the same type.

`#define M(x,y)  ((x)^=(y),(y)^=(x),(x)^=(y))`

4. In computer graphics, colors are often stored as three numbers, representing red, green, and blue intensities. Suppose that each number requires eight bits, and we'd like to store all three values in a single long integer. Write a macro named MK_COLOR with three parameters (the red, green, and blue intensities). MK_COLOR should return a long int in which the last three bytes contain the red, green, and blue intensities (in that order), with the red value as the last byte.

5. Write macros named GET_RED, GET_GREEN, and GET_BLUE that, when given a color as an argument (see Exercise 4), return its 8-bit red, green, and blue intensities.

6. (a) Use the bitwise operators to write the following function:

`unsigned short int swap_bytes(unsigned short int i);`

The return value of swap_bytes(i) should be the number that results from swapping the two bytes in i. (Short integers occupy two bytes on most computers.) For example, if i has the value 0x1234 (00010010 00110100 in binary), then swap_bytes(i) should return 0x3412 (00110100 00010010 in binary). Test your function by writing a program that reads a number in hexadecimal, then writes the number with its bytes swapped:

```
Enter a hexadecimal number: 1234
Number with bytes swapped:   3412
```

Hint: Use the %hx conversion to read and write the hex numbers.

(b) Condense the swap_bytes function so that its body is a single statement.

7. Write the following functions:

```
unsigned int rotate_left(unsigned int i, int n);
unsigned int rotate_right(unsigned int i, int n);
```

The value of `rotate_left(i, n)` should be the result of shifting the bits in `i` to the left by n places, with the bits that were "shifted off" moved to the right end of `i`. (For example, `rotate_left(0x1234, 4)` should return `0x2341` if integers are 16 bits long.) `rotate_right` should be similar, but "rotate" bits to the right instead of the left.

8. Let `f` be the following function:

```
unsigned int f(unsigned int i, int m, int n)
{
    return (i >> (m+1-n)) & ~(~0 << n);
}
```

(a) What is the value of `~(~0 << n)`?

(b) What does this function do?

Section 20.2 9. When stored according to the IEEE floating-point standard, a `float` value consists of a 1-bit sign (the leftmost—or most significant—bit), an 8-bit exponent, and a 23-bit fraction, in that order. Design a structure type that occupies 32 bits, with bit-field members corresponding to the sign, exponent, and fraction. Declare the bit-fields to have type `unsigned int`. Check the manual for your compiler to determine the order of the bit-fields. *Warning:* Some compilers limit bit-fields to 16 bits, so you may get an error message if you compile this structure.

Section 20.3 10. Design a union that makes it possible to view a 32-bit value as either a `float` or the structure described in Exercise 9. Write a program that stores 1 in the structure's sign field, 128 in the exponent field, and 0 in the fraction field, then prints the `float` value stored in the union. (The answer should be –2.0 if you've set up the bit-fields correctly.)

21 The Standard Library

Every program is a part of some other program and rarely fits.

In previous chapters we've looked at the C library piecemeal; this chapter focuses on the library as a whole. Section 21.1 lists general guidelines for using the library. It also describes a trick found in some library headers: using a macro to "hide" a function. Section 21.2 gives an overview of each of the library's fifteen headers.

Later chapters cover the library's headers in depth, with related headers grouped together into chapters. One of the headers, `<stddef.h>`, is quite different from the others, so I've chosen to describe it here (Section 21.3).

21.1 Using the Library

The standard library is divided into fifteen parts, with each part described by a header. Most compilers come with a more extensive library that invariably has more than fifteen headers. The extra headers aren't standard, of course, so we can't count on them being available with other compilers. These headers often provide functions that depend on a particular computer or operating system (which explains why they're not standard). They may provide functions that allow more control over the screen and keyboard. Headers that support graphics or a window-based user interface are also common.

The standard headers consist primarily of function prototypes, type definitions, and macro definitions. If one of our files contains a call of a function declared in a header or uses one of the types or macros defined there, we'll need to include the header at the beginning of the file. When a file includes several headers, the order of `#include` directives doesn't matter.

Restrictions on Names Used in the Library

Any file that includes a standard header must obey a couple of rules. First, it can't use the names of macros defined in that header for any other purpose. If a file includes <stdio.h>, for example, it can't reuse NULL, since a macro by that name is already defined in <stdio.h>. Second, library names with file scope (type names, in particular) can't be redefined at the file level. Thus, if a file includes <stdio.h>, it can't define size_t as a identifier with file scope, since <stdio.h> defines size_t to be a type name.

Although these restrictions are pretty obvious, C has other restrictions that you might not expect:

- *Identifiers that begin with an underscore and an upper-case letter or two underscores* are reserved for use within the library; programs should never use names of this form for any purpose.

- *Identifiers that begin with an underscore* are reserved for use as identifiers and tags with file scope. You should never reuse such a name unless it's declared inside a function.

- *Every identifier with external linkage in the standard library* is reserved for use as an identifier with external linkage. In particular, the names of all standard library functions are reserved. Thus, even if a file *doesn't* include <stdio.h>, it shouldn't define an external function named printf, since there's already a function with this name in the library.

These rules apply to *every* file in a program, regardless of which headers the file includes. Although these rules aren't always enforced, failing to obey them can lead to a program that's not portable.

Functions Hidden by Macros

It's common for C programmers to replace small functions by macros. This practice occurs even in the standard library. The C standard allows headers to define macros that have the same names as library functions, but protects the programmer by requiring that a true function be available as well. As a result, it's not unusual for a library header to declare a function *and* define a macro with the same name.

<ctype.h> header ➤*23.4* Examples of function/macro pairs abound in the <ctype.h> header. Consider the isprint function, which tests whether a character is printable. It's common practice for <ctype.h> to declare isprint as a function:

```
int isprint(int c);
```

and also define it as a macro:

```
#define isprint(c) ((c) >= 0x20 && (c) <= 0x7e)
```

By default, a call of isprint will be treated as a macro invocation (since macro names are replaced during preprocessing).

Most of the time, we're happy using a macro instead of a true function, because it will probably make our program run faster. Occasionally, though, we want a genuine function: perhaps we need to minimize the size of the executable code, or maybe we need a pointer to the function.

pointers to functions ➤ *17.7*

If the need arises, we can remove a macro definition (thus gaining access to the true function) by using the #undef directive. For example, the following lines provide access to the isprint function by undefining the isprint macro:

#undef directive ➤ *14.3*

```
#include <ctype.h>
#undef isprint
```

If isprint *isn't* a macro, no harm has been done; #undef has no effect when given a name that's not defined as a macro.

As an alternative, we can disable individual uses of a macro by putting parentheses around its name:

```
(isprint)(c)
```

The preprocessor can't spot a parameterized macro unless its name is followed by a left parenthesis. The compiler isn't so easily fooled, however; it can still recognize isprint as a function.

21.2 Library Overview

We'll now take a quick look at the fifteen headers in the standard library. This section can serve as a "road map" to help you determine which part of the library you need. Each header is described in detail later in this chapter or in a subsequent chapter. For information about a specific library function, consult Appendix D.

<assert.h> *Diagnostics*

<assert.h> header ➤ *24.1*

Contains only the assert macro, which allows us to insert self-checks into a program. If any check fails, the program terminates.

<ctype.h> *Character Handling*

<ctype.h> header ➤ *23.4*

Provides functions for classifying characters and for converting letters from lower to upper case or vice versa.

<errno.h> *Errors*

<errno.h> header ➤ *24.2*

Provides errno ("error number"), an lvalue that can be tested after a call of certain library functions to see if an error occurred during the call.

`<float.h>` *Characteristics of Floating Types*

`<float.h>` header ➤*23.1*   Provides macros that describe the characteristics of floating types, including their range and accuracy.

`<limits.h>` *Sizes of Integral Types*

`<limits.h>` header ➤*23.2*   Provides macros that describe the characteristics of integer and character types, including their maximum and minimum values.

`<locale.h>` *Localization*

`<locale.h>` header ➤*25.1*   Provides functions to help a program adapt its behavior to a country or other geographic region. Locale-specific behavior includes the way numbers are printed (including the character used as the decimal point), the format of monetary values (the currency symbol, for example), the character set, and the appearance of the date and time.

`<math.h>` *Mathematics*

`<math.h>` header ➤*23.3*   Provides a variety of common mathematical functions, including trigonometric, hyperbolic, exponential, logarithmic, power, nearest integer, and absolute value functions. Most functions have `double` arguments and return a `double` value.

`<setjmp.h>` *Nonlocal Jumps*

`<setjmp.h>` header ➤*24.4*   Provides the `setjmp` and `longjmp` functions. `setjmp` "marks" a place in a program; `longjmp` can then be used to return to that place later. These functions make it possible to jump from one function into another, still-active function, bypassing the normal function-return mechanism. `setjmp` and `longjmp` are used primarily for handling serious problems that arise during program execution.

`<signal.h>` *Signal Handling*

`<signal.h>` header ➤*24.3*   Provides functions that deal with exceptional conditions (***signals***), including interrupts and run-time errors. The `signal` function installs a function to be called if a given signal should occur later. The `raise` function causes a signal to occur.

`<stdarg.h>` *Variable Arguments*

`<stdarg.h>` header ➤*26.1*   Provides tools for writing functions that, like `printf` and `scanf`, can have a variable number of arguments.

| `<stddef.h>` | **Common Definitions** |

`<stddef.h>` header ➤21.3 Provides definitions of frequently used types and macros.

| `<stdio.h>` | **Input/Output** |

`<stdio.h>` header ➤22.1–22.8 Provides a large assortment of input/output functions, including operations on both sequential and random-access files.

| `<stdlib.h>` | **General Utilities** |

`<stdlib.h>` header ➤26.2 A catch-all header for functions that don't fit into any of the other headers. The functions in `<stdlib.h>` can convert strings to numbers, generate pseudo-random numbers, perform memory management tasks, communicate with the operating system, do searching and sorting, and perform operations on multibyte characters and strings.

| `<string.h>` | **String Handling** |

`<string.h>` header ➤23.5 Provides functions that perform string operations, including copying, concatenation, comparison, and searching.

| `<time.h>` | **Date and Time** |

`<time.h>` header ➤26.3 Provides functions for determining the time (and date), manipulating times, and displaying times in a variety of ways.

21.3   The `<stddef.h>` Header: Common Definitions

The `<stddef.h>` header provides definitions of frequently used types and macros; it doesn't declare any functions. The types are:

- `ptrdiff_t`. The type of the result when two pointers are subtracted.
- `size_t`. The type returned by the `sizeof` operator.
- `wchar_t`. A type large enough to represent all possible characters in all supported locales.

All three are names for integer types; `ptrdiff_t` must be a signed type, while `size_t` must be an unsigned type. For more information about `wchar_t`, see Section 25.2.

The <stddef.h> header also defines two macros. One of them is NULL, which represents the null pointer. The other macro, offsetof, requires two arguments: *type* (a structure type) and *member-designator* (a member of the structure). offsetof computes the number of bytes between the beginning of the structure and the specified member.

Consider the following structure:

```
struct s {
  char a;
  int b[2];
  float c;
};
```

The value of offsetof(struct s, a) must be 0; C guarantees that the first member of a structure has the same address as the structure itself. We can't say for sure what the offsets of b and c are. One possibility is that offsetof(struct s, b) is 1 (since a is one byte long), and offsetof(struct s, c) is 5 (assuming 16-bit integers). However, some compilers leave holes—unused bytes—in structures (see the Q&A at the end of Chapter 16), which can affect the value produced by offsetof. If a compiler should leave a one-byte hole after a, for example, then the offsets of b and c would be 2 and 6, respectively. But that's the beauty of offsetof: it produces the correct offsets for any compiler, allowing us to write portable programs.

fwrite function ➤22.6 There are various uses for offsetof. For example, suppose that we want to save the first two members of an s structure in a file, ignoring the c member. Instead of having the fwrite function write sizeof(struct s) bytes, which would save the entire structure, we'll tell it to write only offsetof(struct s, c) bytes.

A final remark: Some of the types and macros defined in <stddef.h> appear in other headers as well. (The NULL macro, for example, is also defined in <locale.h>, <stdio.h>, <stdlib.h>, <string.h>, and <time.h>.) As a result, few programs need to include <stddef.h>.

Q & A

Q: I notice that you use the term "standard header" rather than "standard header file." Is there any reason for not using the word "file"?

A: Yes. According to the C standard, a "standard header" need not be a file. Although most compilers do indeed store standard headers as files, the standard opens the door to the possibility that the headers are built into the compiler itself.

Exercises

Section 21.1

1. Locate where header files are kept on your system. Find the nonstandard headers and determine the purpose of each.

2. Having located the header files on your system (see Exercise 1), find a standard header in which a macro hides a function.

3. When a macro hides a function, which must come first in the header file: the macro definition or the function prototype? Justify your answer.

Section 21.2

4. In which standard header would you expect to find each of the following?
   (a) a function that determines the current day of the week
   (b) a function that tests whether a character is a digit
   (c) a macro that gives the largest `unsigned int` value
   (d) a function that rounds a floating-point number to the next higher integer
   (e) a macro that specifies the number of bits in a character
   (f) a macro that specifies the number of significant digits in a `double` value
   (g) a function that searches a string for a particular character
   (h) a function that opens a file for reading

Section 21.3

5. Write a program that declares the s structure (see the text) and prints the sizes and offsets of the a, b, and c members. (Use `sizeof` to find sizes; use `offsetof` to find offsets.) Have the program print the size of the entire structure as well. From this information, determine whether or not the structure has any holes. If it does, describe the location and size of each.

22 Input/Output

*In man-machine symbiosis, it is man
who must adjust: The machines can't.*

C's input/output library, represented by the <stdio.h> header, is the biggest and most important part of the standard library. As befits its lofty status, we'll devote an entire chapter (the biggest, if not one of the most important, in this book) to <stdio.h>.

We've been using <stdio.h> since Chapter 2, and we have experience with the printf, scanf, putchar, getchar, puts, and gets functions. This chapter provides more information about these functions, as well as introducing a number of new functions, most of which deal with files. Fortunately, many of the new functions are closely related to functions with which we're acquainted. fprintf, for instance, is the "file version" of the printf function.

We'll start the chapter with a discussion of some basic issues: the **stream** concept, the FILE type, input and output redirection, and the difference between text files and binary files (Section 22.1). We'll then turn to functions that are designed specifically for use with files, including functions that open and close files (Section 22.2).

After discussing printf, scanf, and related functions for "formatted" input/output (Section 22.3), we'll look at functions that read and write unformatted data:

- getc, putc, and related functions, which read and write one *character* at a time (Section 22.4).
- gets, puts, and related functions, which read and write one *line* at a time (Section 22.5).
- fread and fwrite, which read and write *blocks* of data (Section 22.6).

Section 22.7 then shows how to perform random access operations on files. Finally, Section 22.8 describes the sprintf and sscanf functions, variants of printf and scanf that write to a string or read from a string.

475

perror function ➤24.2

v...printf functions ➤26.1

This chapter covers all but four of the functions in `<stdio.h>`. The omissions are `perror`, `vfprintf`, `vprintf`, and `vsprintf`, which are closely related to other parts of the C library.

22.1   Streams

In C, the term **stream** means any source of input or any destination for output. Many small programs, like the ones in previous chapters, obtain all their input from one stream (usually associated with the keyboard) and write all their output to another stream (usually associated with the screen).

Larger programs may need additional streams. These streams often represent files on magnetic disk, but could be associated with other kinds of devices: modems, network ports, printers, CD-ROM drives, and the like. We'll concentrate on disk files, since they're common and easy to understand. (I may even occasionally use the term *file* when I should say *stream*.) Keep in mind, however, that many of the functions in `<stdio.h>` work equally well with all streams, not just the ones that represent files.

File Pointers

Accessing a stream in a C program is done through **file pointers**, which have type FILE * (the FILE type is defined in `<stdio.h>`). Certain streams are represented by file pointers with standard names; we can declare additional file pointers as needed. For example, if a program needs two streams in addition to the standard ones, it might include the following declaration:

```
FILE *fp1, *fp2;
```

A program may declare any number of FILE * variables, although operating systems usually limit the number of streams that can be open at any one time.

Standard Streams and Redirection

`<stdio.h>` provides three standard streams (Table 22.1). These streams are ready to use—we don't declare them, and we don't open or close them.

Table 22.1
Standard Streams

File Pointer	Stream	Default Meaning
stdin	Standard input	Keyboard
stdout	Standard output	Screen
stderr	Standard error	Screen

The functions that we've used in previous chapters—`printf`, `scanf`, `putchar`, `getchar`, `puts`, and `gets`—obtain input from `stdin` and send output to `stdout`. By default, `stdin` represents the keyboard and `stdout` and stderr represent the screen. Some operating systems, however, allow these default meanings to be changed via a mechanism known as *redirection*.

Under UNIX and DOS, for instance, we can force a program to obtain its input from a file instead of from the keyboard by putting the name of the file on the command line, preceded by the < character:

```
demo <in.dat
```

This technique, known as *input redirection*, essentially makes the stdin stream represent a file (in.dat, in this case) instead of the keyboard. The beauty of redirection is that the demo program doesn't realize that it's reading from in.dat; as far as it knows, any data it obtains from stdin is being entered at the keyboard.

Output redirection is similar. Redirecting the stdout stream in UNIX and DOS is done by putting a file name on the command line, preceded by the > character:

```
demo >out.dat
```

All data written to stdout will now go into the out.dat file instead of appearing on the screen. Incidentally, we can combine output redirection with input redirection:

```
demo <in.dat >out.dat
```

One problem with output redirection is that *everything* written to stdout is put into a file. If the program goes off the rails and begins writing error messages, we won't see them until we look at the file. This is where stderr comes in. By writing error messages to stderr instead of stdout, we can guarantee that those messages will appear on the screen even when stdout has been redirected.

Text Files versus Binary Files

<stdio.h> supports two kinds of files: text and binary. In a *text file*, the bytes represent characters, making it possible for a human to examine the file or edit it. The source code for a C program is stored in a text file, for example. In a *binary file*, on the other hand, bytes don't necessarily represent characters; groups of bytes might represent other types of data, such as integers and floating-point numbers. An executable C program is stored in a binary file, as you'll quickly realize if you try to look at one.

To see the difference between text files and binary files, consider the ways in which we could store the number 32,767 in a file. One option would be to store the number in text form as the characters 3, 2, 7, 6, and 7. If the character set is ASCII, we'd have the following five bytes:

00110011	00110010	00110111	00110110	00110111
'3'	'2'	'7'	'6'	'7'

The other option is to store the number in binary, which would take as few as two bytes:

As this example shows, storing numbers in binary can save quite a bit of space.

Why is it necessary to make a distinction between text files and binary files? A file, after all, is just a sequence of bytes either way. The answer is simple: some operating systems store text files and binary files in different ways. Text files are divided into lines, so there must be some way to mark the end of each line—a special character, for instance. Also, an operating system may use a special character to indicate the end of a text file. Binary files, on the other hand, aren't divided into lines. And since a binary file may legally contain any character, it's impossible to set aside an end-of-file character.

In DOS, there are two differences between a text file and a binary file:

- **End of line.** When a new-line character is written to a *text* file, it is expanded into a pair of characters: a carriage return followed by a line feed. The reverse translation takes place during input. A new-line character written to a *binary* file, however, is a single character (line feed).

- **End of file.** A control-Z character (`\x1a`) in a *text* file is assumed to mark the end of the file. (It's not necessary to have a control-Z character at the end of a text file, but some editors put one there anyway.) A control-Z character in a *binary* file has no special significance; it's treated like any other character.

In contrast, UNIX doesn't differentiate between text files and binary files; they're both stored the same way. A UNIX text file has a single line-feed character at the end of each line; there's no special character to mark the end of the file.

When we're writing a program that reads from a file or writes to a file, we need to take into account whether it's a text file or a binary file. A program that displays the contents of a file on the screen will probably assume it's a text file. A file-copying program, on the other hand, can't assume that the file to be copied is a text file. If it does, binary files containing an end-of-file character won't be copied completely. When we can't say for sure whether a file is text or binary, it's safer to assume that it's binary.

22.2 File Operations

Simplicity is one of the attractions of input and output redirection; there's no need to open a file, close a file, or perform any other explicit file operations. Unfortunately, redirection is too limited for many applications. When a program relies on redirection, it has no control over its files; it doesn't even know their names. Worse still, redirection doesn't help if the program needs to read from two files or write to two files at the same time.

When redirection isn't enough, we'll end up using the file operations that <stdio.h> provides. In this section, we'll explore these operations, which include opening a file, closing a file, changing the way a file is buffered, deleting a file, and renaming a file.

Opening a File

```
FILE *fopen(const char *filename, const char *mode);
```

fopen   Opening a file for use as a stream requires a call of the fopen function. fopen's first argument is a string containing the name of the file to be opened. (A "file name" may include information about the file's location, such as a drive specifier or path.) The second argument is a "mode string" that specifies what operations we intend to perform on the file. The string "r", for instance, indicates that data will be read from the file, but none will be written to it.

---

escape sequences ➤ 7.3

DOS programmers: Be careful when the file name in a call of fopen includes the \ character, since C treats \ as the beginning of an escape sequence. The call

```
fopen("c:\project\test1.dat", "r")
```

will always fail, because the compiler treats \t as a character escape (the meaning of \p is undefined). To avoid the problem, use \\ instead of \:

```
fopen("c:\\project\\test1.dat", "r")
```

---

fopen returns a file pointer that the program can (and usually will) save in a variable and use later whenever it needs to perform an operation on the file. A typical call of fopen looks like this:

```
fp = fopen("in.dat", "r");   /* opens in.dat for reading */
```

When the program calls an input function to read from in.dat later, it will supply fp as an argument.

When it can't open a file, fopen returns a null pointer. Perhaps the file doesn't exist, or it's in the wrong place, or we don't have permission to open it.

Never assume that a file can be opened; always test the return value of fopen to make sure it's not a null pointer.

Modes

Which mode string we'll pass to fopen depends not only on what operations we plan to perform on the file later but also on whether the file contains text or binary data. To open a text file, we'd use one of the mode strings in Table 22.2.

Table 22.2
Mode Strings for
Text Files

String	Meaning
`"r"`	Open for reading
`"w"`	Open for writing (file need not exist)
`"a"`	Open for appending (file need not exist)
`"r+"`	Open for reading and writing, starting at beginning
`"w+"`	Open for reading and writing (truncate if file exists)
`"a+"`	Open for reading and writing (append if file exists)

Q&A   When we use `fopen` to open a binary file, we'll need to include the letter `b` in the mode string. Table 22.3 lists mode strings for binary files.

Table 22.3
Mode Strings for
Binary Files

String	Meaning
`"rb"`	Open for reading
`"wb"`	Open for writing (file need not exist)
`"ab"`	Open for appending (file need not exist)
`"r+b"` or `"rb+"`	Open for reading and writing, starting at beginning
`"w+b"` or `"wb+"`	Open for reading and writing (truncate if file exists)
`"a+b"` or `"ab+"`	Open for reading and writing (append if file exists)

From tables 22.2 and 22.3, we see that `<stdio.h>` distinguishes between *writing* data and *appending* data. When data is written to a file, it normally overwrites what was previously there. When a file is opened for appending, however, attempts to write data to the file actually add it to the end of the file, thus preserving the file's original contents.

By the way, special rules apply when a file is opened for both reading and writing (the mode string contains the + character). We can't switch from reading to writing without first calling a file-positioning function. Also, we can't switch from writing to reading without either calling `fflush` (covered later in this section) or calling a file-positioning function.

file-positioning functions ➤22.7

Closing a File

```
int fclose(FILE *stream);
```

fclose   The `fclose` function allows a program to close a file that it's no longer using. The argument to `fclose` must be a file pointer obtained from a call of `fopen` or `freopen` (discussed later in this section). `fclose` returns zero if the file was closed successfully; otherwise, it returns the error code `EOF` (a macro defined in `<stdio.h>`).

To show how `fopen` and `fclose` are used in practice, here's the outline of a program that opens the file `example.dat` for reading, checks that it was opened successfully, then closes it before terminating:

```
#include <stdio.h>
#include <stdlib.h>

#define FILE_NAME "example.dat"
```

```
main()
{
  FILE *fp;

  fp = fopen(FILE_NAME, "r");
  if (fp == NULL) {
    printf("Can't open %s\n", FILE_NAME);
    exit(EXIT_FAILURE);
  }
  ...
  fclose(fp);
  return 0;
}
```

Of course, C programmers being the way they are, it's not unusual to see the call of fopen combined with the declaration of fp:

```
FILE *fp = fopen(FILE_NAME, "r");
```

or the test against NULL:

```
if ((fp = fopen(FILE_NAME, "r")) == NULL) ...
```

Attaching a File to a Stream

```
FILE *freopen(const char *filename, const char *mode,
              FILE *stream);
```

freopen   freopen attaches a different file to a stream that's already open. The most common use of freopen is to associate a file with one of the standard streams: stdin, stdout, or stderr. To cause a program to begin writing to the file foo, for instance, we could use the following call of freopen:

```
if (freopen("foo", "w", stdout) == NULL) {
  /* error; foo can't be opened */
}
```

After closing any file previously associated with stdout (by command-line redirection or a previous call of freopen), freopen will open foo and associate it with stdout.

freopen's normal return value is its third argument (a file pointer). If it can't open the new file, freopen returns a null pointer. (freopen ignores the error if the old file can't be closed.)

Obtaining File Names from the Command Line

When we're writing a program that will need to open a file, one problem soon becomes apparent: how do we supply the file name to the program? Building file names into the program itself doesn't provide much flexibility, and prompting the user to enter file names can be awkward. Often, the best solution is to have the program obtain file names from the command line entered by the user at the time the program was run. When we execute a program named demo, for example, we might supply it with file names by putting them on the command line:

```
demo names.dat dates.dat
```

In Section 13.7, we saw how to access command-line arguments by defining main as a function with two parameters:

```
main(int argc, char *argv[])
{
   ...
}
```

argc is the number of command-line arguments; argv is an array of pointers to the argument strings. argv[0] points to the program name, argv[1] through argv[argc-1] point to the remaining arguments, and argv[argc] is a null pointer. In the example above, argc is 3, argv[0] points to a string containing the program name, argv[1] points to the string "names.dat", and argv[2] points to the string "dates.dat":

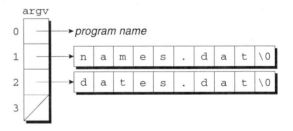

PROGRAM   Checking Whether a File Can Be Opened

The following program determines if a file exists and can be opened for reading. When the program is run, the user will give it a file name to check:

```
canopen f1.dat
```

The program will then print either f1.dat can be opened or f1.dat can't be opened. If the user enters the wrong number of arguments on the command line, the program will print the message usage: canopen filename to remind the user that canopen requires a single file name.

canopen.c
```
/* Checks whether a file can be opened for reading */

#include <stdio.h>

main(int argc, char *argv[])
{
   FILE *fp;
```

```
    if (argc != 2) {
      printf("usage: canopen filename\n");
      return 2;
    }

    if ((fp = fopen(argv[1], "r")) == NULL) {
      printf("%s can't be opened\n", argv[1]);
      return 1;
    }

    printf("%s can be opened\n", argv[1]);
    fclose(fp);
    return 0;
}
```

Note that we can use redirection to discard the output of `canopen` and simply test the status value it returns (0 if the file can be opened; 1 if it can't).

Temporary Files

```
FILE *tmpfile(void);
char *tmpnam(char *s);
```

Real-world programs often need to create temporary files—files that exist only as long as the program is running. C compilers, for instance, often create temporary files. A compiler might first translate a C program to some intermediate form, which it stores in a file. The compiler would then read the file later as it translates the program to object code. Once the program is completely compiled, there's no need to preserve the file containing the program's intermediate form. `<stdio.h>` provides two functions, `tmpfile` and `tmpnam`, for working with temporary files.

tmpfile   `tmpfile` creates a temporary file that will exist until it's closed or the program ends. A call of `tmpfile` returns a file pointer that can be used to access the file later:

```
FILE *tempptr;

tempptr = tmpfile();   /* creates a temporary file */
```

If it fails to create a file, `tmpfile` returns a null pointer.

Although `tmpfile` is easy to use, it has a couple of drawbacks: (1) we don't know the name of the file that `tmpfile` creates, and (2) we can't decide later to make the file permanent. If these restrictions turn out to be a problem, the alternative is to create a temporary file using `fopen`. Of course, we don't want this file to have the same name as a previously existing file, so we need some way to generate new file names; that's where the `tmpnam` function comes in.

tmpnam   `tmpnam` generates a name for a temporary file. If its argument is a null pointer, `tmpnam` stores the file name in a static variable and returns a pointer to it:

```
char *filename;

filename = tmpnam(NULL);    /* creates a temporary file name */
```

Otherwise, tmpnam copies the file name into a character array provided by the programmer:

```
char filename[L_tmpnam];

tmpnam(filename);              /* creates a temporary file name */
```

In the latter case, tmpnam also returns a pointer to the name of the temporary file. L_tmpnam is a macro in <stdio.h> that specifies how long to make a character array that will hold a temporary file name.

When passing a pointer to tmpnam, be sure that it points to an array of at least L_tmpnam characters. Also, be careful not to call tmpnam too often; the TMP_MAX macro (defined in <stdio.h>) specifies the maximum number of temporary file names that can be generated by tmpnam during the execution of a program.

File Buffering

```
int fflush(FILE *stream);
void setbuf(FILE *stream, char *buf);
int setvbuf(FILE *stream, char *buf, int mode,
            size_t size);
```

Transferring information to or from a disk drive is a relatively slow operation. As a result, it isn't feasible for a program to access a disk file directly each time it wants to read or write a character. The secret to achieving acceptable performance is *buffering:* data written to a stream is actually stored in a buffer area in memory; when it's full (or the stream is closed), the buffer is "flushed" (written to the actual output device). Input streams can be buffered in a similar way: the buffer contains data from the input device; input is read from this buffer instead of the device itself. Buffering can result in enormous gains in efficiency, since reading a character from a buffer or storing a character in a buffer takes hardly any time at all. Of course, it takes time to transfer the buffer contents to or from disk, but one large "block move" is much faster than many tiny character moves.

The functions in <stdio.h> perform buffering automatically when it seems advantageous. The buffering takes place behind the scenes, and we usually don't worry about it. On rare occasions, though, we may need to take a more active role. If so, we can use the functions fflush, setbuf, and setvbuf.

fflush   When a program writes output to a file, the data normally goes into a buffer instead. The buffer is flushed automatically when it's full or the file is closed. By calling f flush, however, a program can flush a file's buffer as often as it wishes. The call

```
fflush(fp);      /* flushes buffer for fp */
```

flushes the buffer for the file associated with fp. The call

```
fflush(NULL);    /* flushes all buffers */
```

flushes *all* output streams. fflush returns zero if it's successful and EOF if an error occurs.

setvbuf   setvbuf allows us to change the way a stream is buffered and to control the size and location of the buffer. The function's third argument specifies the kind of buffering desired:

- _IOFBF (full buffering). Data is read from the stream when the buffer is empty or written to the stream when it's full.
- _IOLBF (line buffering). Data is read from the stream or written to the stream one line at a time.
- _IONBF (no buffering). Data is read from the stream or written to the stream directly, without a buffer.

(All three macros are defined in <stdio.h>.)

setvbuf's second argument (if it's not a null pointer) is the address of the desired buffer. The buffer might have static storage duration, automatic storage duration, or even be allocated dynamically. Making the buffer automatic would allow its space to be reclaimed automatically at block exit; allocating it dynamically would enable us to free the buffer as soon as it's no longer needed. setvbuf's last argument is the number of bytes in the buffer. A larger buffer may give better performance; a smaller buffer saves space.

For example, the following call of setvbuf changes the buffering of stream to full buffering, using the N bytes in the buffer array as the buffer:

```
char buffer[N];

setvbuf(stream, buffer, _IOFBF, N);
```

---

  setvbuf must be called after stream is opened but before any other operations are performed on it.

---

setvbuf returns zero if it's successful. It returns a nonzero value if the requested buffering mode is invalid or can't be provided.

setbuf   setbuf is an older function that assumes default values for the buffering mode and buffer size. If buf is a null pointer, the call setbuf(stream, buf) is equivalent to

```
(void) setvbuf(stream, NULL, _IONBF, 0);
```

Otherwise, it's equivalent to

```
(void) setvbuf(stream, buf, _IOFBF, BUFSIZ);
```

where BUFSIZ is a macro defined in <stdio.h>. The setbuf function is considered obsolete; it's not recommended for use in new programs.

 When using setvbuf or setbuf, be sure to close the stream before its buffer is deallocated.

Miscellaneous File Operations

```
int remove(const char *filename);
int rename(const char *old, const char *new);
```

The functions remove and rename allow a program to perform basic file management operations. Unlike most other functions in this section, remove and rename work with file *names* instead of file *pointers*. Both functions return zero if they succeed and a nonzero value if they fail.

remove   remove deletes a file:

```
remove("foo");              /* deletes the file named "foo" */
```

If a program uses fopen (instead of tmpfile) to create a temporary file, it can use remove to delete the file before the program terminates. Be sure that the file to be removed has been closed; the effect of removing a file that's currently open is implementation-defined.

rename   rename changes the name of a file:

```
rename("foo", "bar");   /* renames "foo" to "bar" */
```

rename is handy for renaming a temporary file created using fopen if a program should decide to make it permanent. If a file with the new name already exists, the effect is implementation-defined.

 If the file to be renamed is open, be sure to close it before calling rename; a file can't be renamed if it's open.

22.3 Formatted I/O

In this section, we'll examine library functions that use format strings to control reading and writing. These functions, which include our old friends printf and scanf, have the ability to convert data from character form to numeric form during input and from numeric form to character form during output. None of the other I/O functions can do such conversions.

The ...`printf` Functions

```
int fprintf(FILE *stream, const char *format, ...);
int printf(const char *format, ...);
```

fprintf
printf

ellipsis ➤ 26.1

The `fprintf` and `printf` functions write a variable number of data items to an output stream, using a format string to control the appearance of the output. The prototypes for both functions end with the `. . .` symbol (an ***ellipsis***), which indicates a variable number of additional arguments. Both functions return the number of characters written; a negative return value indicates that an error occurred.

The only difference between `printf` and `fprintf` is that `printf` always writes to `stdout` (the standard output stream), while `fprintf` writes to the stream indicated by its first argument:

```
printf("Total: %d\n", total);        /* writes to stdout */
fprintf(fp, "Total: %d\n", total);   /* writes to fp */
```

A call of `printf` is equivalent to a call of `fprintf` with `stdout` as the first argument.

Don't think of `fprintf` as merely a function that writes data to disk files, though. Like many functions in `<stdio.h>`, `fprintf` works fine with any output stream. In fact, one of the most common uses of `fprintf`—to write error messages to `stderr`, the standard error stream—has nothing to do with disk files. Here's what such a call might look like:

```
fprintf(stderr, "Error: data file can't be opened.\n");
```

Writing the message to `stderr` guarantees that it will appear on the screen even if the user redirects `stdout`.

v...`printf` functions ➤ 26.1

There are two other functions in `<stdio.h>` that can write formatted output to a stream. These functions, named `vfprintf` and `vprintf`, are fairly obscure. Both rely on the `va_list` type, defined in `<stdarg.h>`, so they're discussed along with that header.

...`printf` Conversion Specifications

Both `printf` and `fprintf` require a format string containing ordinary characters and/or ***conversion specifications***. Ordinary characters are printed as is; conversion specifications describe how the remaining arguments are to be converted to character form for display. Section 3.1 described conversion specifications briefly, and we added more details in later chapters. We'll now review what we know about conversion specifications and fill in the remaining gaps.

A ...`printf` conversion specification consists of the % character, followed by as many as five distinct items:

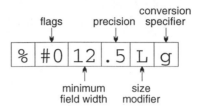

Here's a detailed description of these items, which must appear in the order shown:

- *Flags* (optional; more than one permitted). The – flag causes left justification within a field; the other flags affect the way numbers are printed. Table 22.4 gives a complete list of flags.

Table 22.4

Flags for ...`printf` Functions

Flag	Meaning
–	Left-justify within field.
+	Positive signed numbers begin with +.
space	Positive signed numbers are prefixed by a space. (The + flag overrides the *space* flag.)
#	Octal numbers begin with 0, hex numbers with 0x or 0X. Floating-point numbers always have a decimal point. Trailing zeros aren't removed from numbers printed with the g or G conversions.
0 *(zero)*	Numbers are padded with leading zeros up to the field width. The 0 flag is ignored if the conversion is d, i, o, u, x, or X and a precision is specified. (The – flag overrides the 0 flag.)

- *Minimum field width* (optional). An item that's too small to occupy this number of characters will be padded. (By default, spaces are added to the left of the item, thus right-justifying it within the field.) An item that's too large for the field width will still be displayed in its entirety. The field width is either an integer or the character *. If * is present, the field width is obtained from the next argument.

- *Precision* (optional). The meaning of the precision depends on the conversion:

  d, i, o, u, x, X: minimum number of digits
  (leading zeros are added if the number has fewer digits)
  e, E, f: number of digits after the decimal point
  g, G: maximum number of significant digits
  s: maximum number of characters

The precision is a period (.) followed by an integer or the character *. If * is present, the precision is obtained from the next argument. If only the period is present, the precision is zero.

■ *One of the letters* h, l, *or* L (optional). When used to display an integer, the letter h indicates that it is short; l indicates that the integer is long. When used with e, E, f, g, or G, the letter L indicates a long double argument.

■ *Conversion specifier.* The conversion specifier must be one of the characters listed in Table 22.5. Notice that f, e, E, g, and G are all designed to write double values. However, they work fine with float values as well; thanks to the default argument promotions, float arguments are converted automatically to double when passed to a function with a variable number of arguments. Similarly, a character passed to ...printf is converted automatically to int, so the c conversion works properly.

default argument promotions ➤ *9.3*

Table 22.5
Conversion Specifiers for
...printf Functions

Conversion Specifier	Meaning
d, i	Converts a signed integer to decimal form.
o, u, x, X	Converts an unsigned integer to base 8 (o), base 10 (u), or base 16 (x, X). x displays the hex digits a–f in lower case; X displays them in upper case.
f	Converts a double value to decimal form, putting the decimal point in the correct position. If no precision is specified, displays six digits after the decimal point.
e, E	Converts a double value to scientific notation. If no precision is specified, displays six digits after the decimal point. If e is chosen, the exponent is preceded by the letter e; if E is chosen, the exponent is preceded by E.
g, G	g converts a double value to either f form or e form. e form is selected only if the number's exponent is less than –4 *or* greater than or equal to the precision. Trailing zeros are not displayed; a decimal point appears only when followed by a digit. G chooses between f and E forms.
c	Displays an int value as an unsigned character.
s	Writes the characters pointed to by the argument. Stops writing when the precision (if present) is reached or a null character is encountered.
p	Converts a void * value to printable form.
n	The matching argument must be a pointer to an int (a short int if h precedes n; a long int if l precedes n). Stores into this integer the number of characters written so far by this call of ...printf; produces no output.
%	Writes the character %.

Be careful to follow the rules described here; the effect of using an invalid conversion specification is undefined.

Many plausible-looking conversion specifications (like %le, %lf, and %lg) aren't valid.

Examples of ...`printf` Conversion Specifications

Whew! It's about time for a few examples. We've seen plenty of everyday conversion specifications in previous chapters, so we'll concentrate here on illustrating some of the more advanced ones. As in previous chapters, I'll use • to represent the space character.

Let's start off by examining the effect of flags on the `%d` conversion (they have a similar effect on other conversions). The first line of Table 22.6 shows the effect of `%8d` without any flags. The next four lines show the effect of the `-`, `+`, *space*, and `0` flags (the `#` flag is never used with `%d`). The remaining lines show the effect of combinations of flags.

Table 22.6
Effect of Flags on the `%d` Conversion

Conversion Specification	Result of Applying Conversion to 123	Result of Applying Conversion to –123
`%8d`	•••••123	••••–123
`%-8d`	123•••••	–123••••
`%+8d`	••••+123	••••–123
`% 8d`	•••••123	••••–123
`%08d`	00000123	–0000123
`%-+8d`	+123••••	–123••••
`%- 8d`	•123••••	–123••••
`%+08d`	+0000123	–0000123
`% 08d`	•0000123	–0000123

Table 22.7 shows the effect of the `#` flag on the `o`, `x`, `X`, `g`, and `G` conversions. (`#` can also be used with `e`, `E`, and `f`, but that's extremely rare.)

Table 22.7
Effect of the `#` Flag

Conversion Specification	Result of Applying Conversion to 123	Result of Applying Conversion to 123.0
`%8o`	•••••173	
`%#8o`	••••0173	
`%8x`	••••••7b	
`%#8x`	••••0x7b	
`%8X`	••••••7B	
`%#8X`	••••0X7B	
`%8g`		•••••123
`%#8g`		•123.000
`%8G`		•••••123
`%#8G`		•123.000

In previous chapters, we've used the minimum field width and precision to display numbers, so there's no point in more examples here. Instead, Table 22.8 shows the effect of the minimum field width and precision on the `%s` conversion.

Table 22.9 illustrates how the `%g` conversion displays some numbers in `%e` form and others in `%f` form. All numbers in the table were written using the `%.4g` conversion specification. The first two numbers have exponents of at least 4, so they're displayed in `%e` form. The next eight numbers are displayed in `%f` form. The last two numbers have exponents less than –4, so they're displayed in `%e` form.

Table 22.8
Effect of Minimum Field
Width and Precision on
the %s Conversion

Conversion Specification	Result of Applying Conversion to `"bogus"`	Result of Applying Conversion to `"buzzword"`
%6s	•bogus	buzzword
%-6s	bogus•	buzzword
%.4s	bogu	buzz
%6.4s	••bogu	••buzz
%-6.4s	bogu••	buzz••

Table 22.9
Examples of the %g
Conversion

Number	Result of Applying %.4g Conversion to Number
123456.	1.235e+05
12345.6	1.235e+04
1234.56	1235
123.456	123.5
12.3456	12.35
1.23456	1.235
.123456	0.1235
.0123456	0.01235
.00123456	0.001235
.000123456	0.0001235
.0000123456	1.235e-05
.00000123456	1.235e-06

In the past, we've assumed that the minimum field width and precision were constants embedded in the format string. Putting the * character where either number would normally go allows us to specify it as an argument *after* the format string. For example, the following calls of `printf` all produce the same output:

```
printf("%6.4d", i);
printf("%*.4d", 6, i);
printf("%6.*d", 4, i);
printf("%*.*d", 6, 4, i);
```

Notice that the values to be filled in for the * come just before the value to be displayed. A major advantage of *, by the way, is that it allows us to use a macro to specify the width or precision:

```
printf("%*d", WIDTH, i);
```

We can even compute the width or precision during program execution:

```
printf("%*d", page_width/num_cols, i);
```

The most unusual specifications are %p and %n. The %p conversion allows us to print the value of a pointer:

```
printf("%p\n", (void *) ptr);   /* displays value of ptr */
```

Although %p is occasionally useful during debugging, it's not a feature that most programmers use on a daily basis. The C standard doesn't specify what a pointer looks like when printed using %p, but it's likely to be shown as an octal or hexadecimal number.

The %n conversion is used to find out how many characters have been printed so far by a call of ...printf. For example, after the call

```
printf("%d%n\n", 123, &len);
```

the value of len will be 3, since printf had written 3 characters (123) by the time it reached %n. Notice that & must precede len (since %n requires a pointer), and that len itself isn't printed.

The ...scanf Functions

```
int fscanf(FILE *stream, const char *format, ...);
int scanf(const char *format, ...);
```

fscanf
scanf

fscanf and scanf read data items from an input stream, using a format string to indicate the layout of the input. After the format string, any number of pointers follow as additional arguments. Input items are converted (according to conversion specifications in the format string) and stored at the locations indicated by the pointers.

scanf always reads from stdin (the standard input stream), while fscanf reads from the stream indicated by its first argument:

```
scanf("%d%d", &i, &j);        /* reads from stdin */
fscanf(fp, "%d%d", &i, &j);   /* reads from fp */
```

A call of scanf is equivalent to a call of fscanf with stdin as the first argument.

The ...scanf functions return prematurely if an *input failure* occurs (no more input characters could be read) or if a *matching failure* occurs (the input characters didn't match the format string). Both functions return the number of data items that were read and assigned to arguments; they return EOF if an input failure occurred before any data items could be read.

Loops that test scanf's return value are common in C programs. The following loop, for example, reads a series of integers one by one, stopping at the first sign of trouble:

idiom

```
while (scanf("%d", &i) == 1) {
  ...
}
```

...scanf Format Strings

Calls of the ...scanf functions resemble those of the ...printf functions. That similarity can be misleading, however; the ...scanf functions work quite differently from the ...printf functions. It pays to think of scanf and fscanf as "pattern-matching" functions. The format string represents a pattern that a ...scanf function attempts to match as it reads input. If the input doesn't match the format string, the function returns as soon as it detects the mismatch; the input character that didn't match is "pushed back" to be read in the future.

A ...scanf format string may contain three types of information:

■ *Conversion specifications.* Conversion specifications in a ...scanf format string resemble those in a ...printf format string. Most conversion specifications skip white-space characters at the beginning of an input item (the exceptions are %[, %c, and %n). Conversion specifications never skip *trailing* white-space characters, however. If the input contains •123¤, the %d conversion specification consumes •, 1, 2, and 3, but leaves ¤ unread. (I'm using • to represent the space character and ¤ to represent the new-line character.)

white-space characters ➤ 3.2

■ *White-space characters.* One or more consecutive white-space characters in a ...scanf format string match zero or more white-space characters in the input stream.

■ *Non-white-space characters.* A non-white-space character other than % matches the same character in the input stream.

For example, the format string "ISBN %d-%d-%ld-%d" specifies that the input will consist of:

the letters ISBN
possibly some white-space characters
an integer
the – character
an integer (possibly preceded by white-space characters)
the – character
a long integer (possibly preceded by white-space characters)
the – character
an integer (possibly preceded by white-space characters)

...scanf Conversion Specifications

Conversion specifications for ...scanf functions are actually a little simpler than those for ...printf functions. A ...scanf conversion specification consists of the character % followed by the items listed below (in the order shown).

■ * (optional). The presence of * signifies *assignment suppression:* an input item is read but not assigned to a variable. Items matched using * aren't included in the count that ...scanf returns.

■ *Maximum field width* (optional). The maximum field width limits the number of characters in an input item; conversion of the item ends if this number is reached. White-space characters skipped at the beginning of a conversion don't count.

- *One of the letters* h, l, *or* L (optional). When used to read an integer, the letter h indicates that the matching argument is a pointer to a short integer; l indicates a pointer to a long integer. When used with e, E, f, g, or G, the letter l indicates that the argument is a pointer to double; L indicates a pointer to long double.

- *Conversion specifier.* The conversion specifier must be one of the characters listed in Table 22.10.

Table 22.10

Conversion Specifiers for
...scanf Functions

Conversion Specifier	Meaning
d	Matches a decimal integer.
i	Matches an integer. The number is assumed to be decimal unless it begins with 0 (indicating octal) or with 0x or 0X (hex).
o	Matches an octal integer; the corresponding argument is assumed to be a pointer to unsigned int.
u	Matches a decimal integer; the corresponding argument is assumed to be a pointer to unsigned int.
x, X	Matches a hexadecimal integer; the corresponding argument is assumed to be a pointer to unsigned int.
e, E, f, g, G	Matches a float value.
s	Matches a sequence of non-white-space characters, then adds a null character at the end.
[	Matches a nonempty sequence of characters from a *scanset* (explained later), then adds a null character at the end.
c	Matches *n* characters, where *n* is the maximum field width. If no field width is specified, matches one character. Doesn't add a null character at the end.
p	Matches a pointer value in the form that ...printf might have written it.
n	The corresponding argument must point to a variable of type int (short int if h precedes n; long int if l precedes n). Stores into this variable the number of characters read so far. No input is consumed and the return value of ...scanf isn't affected.
%	Matches the character %.

Numeric data items can always begin with a sign (+ or –). The o, u, x, and X specifiers convert the item to unsigned form, however, so they're not normally used to read negative numbers.

The [specifier is a more complicated (and more flexible) version of the s specifier. A complete conversion specification using [has the form %[*set*] or %[^*set*], where *set* can be any set of characters. (If] is one of the characters in *set*, however, it must come first.) %[*set*] matches any sequence of characters in *set* (the **scanset**). %[^*set*] matches any sequence of characters *not* in *set* (in other words, the scanset consists of all characters not in *set*). For example, %[abc] matches any string containing only the letters a, b, and c, while %[^abc] matches any string that doesn't contain a, b, or c.

string conversion functions ➤26.2

Many of the ...scanf conversion specifiers are closely related to the string conversion functions in <stdlib.h>. These functions convert strings (like "-297") to their equivalent numeric values (–297). The d specifier, for example, looks for an optional + or – sign, followed by a series of decimal digits; this is exactly the same form that the strtol function requires when asked to convert a string to a decimal number. Table 22.11 shows the correspondence between conversion specifiers and string conversion functions.

Table 22.11
Correspondence between
...scanf Conversion
Specifiers and String
Conversion Functions

Conversion Specifier	String Conversion Function
d	strtol with 10 as the base
i	strtol with 0 as the base
o	strtoul with 8 as the base
u	strtoul with 10 as the base
x, X	strtoul with 16 as the base
e, E, f, g, G	strtod

It pays to be careful when writing calls of scanf. An invalid conversion specification in a scanf format string is just as bad as one in a printf format string; either one causes undefined behavior.

scanf Examples

In each of the examples to come, we'll apply a call of scanf to the input characters shown to its right. Characters printed in ~~strikeout~~ are consumed by the call. The values of the variables after the call appear to the right of the input.

The examples in Table 22.12 show the effect of combining conversion specifications, white-space characters, and non-white-space characters. The examples in Table 22.13 show the effect of assignment suppression and specifying a field width. The examples in Table 22.14 illustrate the more esoteric conversion specifiers (i, [, and n).

Table 22.12
scanf Examples
(Group 1)

scanf Call	Input	Variables
n = scanf("%d%d", &i, &j);	~~12•~~•34¤	n: 1 i: 12 j: ?
n = scanf("%d,%d", &i, &j);	~~12•~~,•34¤	n: 1 i: 12 j: ?
n = scanf("%d ,%d", &i, &j);	~~12•,•34~~¤	n: 2 i: 12 j: 34
n = scanf("%d, %d", &i, &j);	~~12•~~,•34¤	n: 1 i: 12 j: ?

Table 22.13
scanf Examples
(Group 2)

scanf *Call*	*Input*	*Variables*
`n = scanf("%*d%d", &i);`	~~12•34~~¤	n: 1 i: 34
`n = scanf("%*s%s", str);`	~~My•Fair~~•Lady¤	n: 1 str: "Fair"
`n = scanf("%1d%2d%3d",` `            &i, &j, &k);`	~~12345~~¤	n: 3 i: 1 j: 23 k: 45
`n = scanf("%2d%2s%2d",` `            &i, str, &j);`	~~123456~~¤	n: 3 i: 12 str: "34" j: 56

Table 22.14
scanf Examples
(Group 3)

scanf *Call*	*Input*	*Variables*
`n = scanf("%i%i%i", &i, &j, &k);`	~~12•012•0x12~~¤	n: 3 i: 12 j: 10 k: 18
`n = scanf("%[0123456789]", str);`	~~123~~abc¤	n: 1 str: "123"
`n = scanf("%[0123456789]", str);`	abc123¤	n: 0 str: ?
`n = scanf("%[^0123456789]", str);`	~~abc~~123¤	n: 1 str: "abc"
`n = scanf("%*d%d%n", &i, &j);`	~~10•20~~•30¤	n: 1 i: 20 j: 5

Detecting End-of-File and Error Conditions

```
void clearerr(FILE *stream);
int feof(FILE *stream);
int ferror(FILE *stream);
```

If we ask a …scanf function to read and store *n* data items, we expect its return value to be *n*. If the return value is less than *n*, something went wrong. There are three possibilities:

- **End of file.** The function encountered end-of-file before matching the format string completely.

- **Error.** An error occurred that was beyond the control of the function.

- **Matching failure.** A data item was in the wrong format. For example, the function might have encountered a letter while searching for the first digit of an integer.

But how can we tell which kind of failure occurred? In many cases, it doesn't matter; something went wrong, and we've got to abandon the program. There may be times, however, when we'll need to pinpoint the reason for the failure.

Every stream has two indicators associated with it: an ***error indicator*** and an ***end-of-file indicator.*** These indicators are cleared when the stream is opened, and one or the other is set when an operation on the stream fails. Not surprisingly, encountering end-of-file sets the end-of-file indicator, and an error sets the error indicator. A matching failure, however, doesn't change either indicator.

clearerr   Once the error or end-of-file indicator is set, it remains in that state until it's explicitly cleared, perhaps by a call of the `clearerr` function. `clearerr` clears both the end-of-file and error indicators:

```
clearerr(fp);     /* clears eof and error indicators for fp */
```

`clearerr` isn't needed often, since some of the other library functions clear one or both indicators as a side effect.

Q&A
feof
ferror   Although we don't have direct access to the error and end-of-file indicators, we can call the `feof` and `ferror` functions to test a stream's indicators to determine why a prior operation on the stream failed. The call `feof(fp)` returns a nonzero value if the end-of-file indicator is set for the stream associated with `fp`. The call `ferror(fp)` returns a nonzero value if the error indicator is set. Both functions return zero otherwise.

When `scanf` returns a smaller-than-expected value, we can use `feof` and `ferror` to determine the problem. If `feof` returns a nonzero value, we've reached the end of the input file. If `ferror` returns a nonzero value, an error occurred during input. If neither returns a nonzero value, a matching failure must have occurred. Regardless of what the problem was, the return value of `scanf` tells us how many data items were read before the problem occurred.

To see how `feof` and `ferror` might be used, let's write a function that searches a file for a line that begins with an integer. Here's how we intend to call the function:

```
n = find_int("foo", &i);
```

`"foo"` is the name of the file to be searched, `i` will be assigned the value of the integer, and `n` will be assigned the line number on which the integer was found. If a problem arises (the file can't be opened, an input error occurs, or no line begins with an integer), `find_int` will return an error code (−1, −2, or −3, respectively).

```
int find_int(const char *filename, int *ptr)
{
  FILE *fp = fopen(filename, "r");
  int line - 1;

  if (fp == NULL)
    return -1;                              /* can't open file */
```

```
      while (fscanf(fp, "%d", ptr) != 1) {
        if (ferror(fp)) {
          fclose(fp);
          return -2;                      /* input error */
        }
        if (feof(fp)) {
          fclose(fp);
          return -3;                      /* integer not found */
        }
        fscanf(fp, "%*[^\n]")             /* skips rest of line */
        line++;
      }

      fclose(fp);
      return line;
    }
```

In the `while` expression, `find_int` calls `fscanf` in an attempt to read an integer from the file. If the attempt fails (`fscanf` returns a value other than 1), `find_int` calls `ferror` and `feof` to see if the problem was an input error or end-of-file. If not, `fscanf` must have failed because of a matching error, so `find_int` skips the rest of the characters on the current line, increments the line count, and tries again. Note the use of the conversion `%*[^\n]` to skip all characters up to the next new-line. (Now that we know about scansets, it's time to show off!)

22.4 Character I/O

In this section, we'll examine library functions that read and write single characters. These functions work equally well with both text streams and binary streams.

You'll notice that the functions in this section treat characters as values of type `int`, not `char`. One reason is that the input functions indicate an end-of-file (or error) condition by returning `EOF`, which is a negative integer constant.

Output Functions

```
int fputc(int c, FILE *stream);
int putc(int c, FILE *stream);
int putchar(int c);
```

putchar `putchar` writes one character to the `stdout` stream:

```
putchar(ch);      /* writes ch to stdout */
```

fputc `fputc` and `putc` are more general versions of `putchar` that write a character to
putc an arbitrary stream:

```
fputc(ch, fp);    /* writes ch to fp */
putc(ch, fp);     /* writes ch to fp */
```

Although `putc` and `fputc` do the same thing, `putc` is usually implemented as a macro and `fputc` as a function. `putchar` is normally a macro as well:

```
#define putchar(c) putc((c), stdout)
```

It may seem odd that the library provides both `putc` and `fputc`. But, as we saw in Section 14.3, macros have several potential problems. Although programmers usually prefer `putc`, which gives a faster program, `fputc` is available as an alternative.

Q&A

If an error occurs, all three functions set the error indicator for the stream and return EOF; otherwise, they return the character that was written.

Input Functions

```
int fgetc(FILE *stream);
int getc(FILE *stream);
int getchar(void);
int ungetc(int c, FILE *stream);
```

getchar   `getchar` reads a character from the `stdin` stream:

```
ch = getchar();    /* reads a character from stdin */
```

fgetc   `fgetc` and `getc` read a character from an arbitrary stream:
getc

```
ch = fgetc(fp);    /* reads a character from fp */
ch = getc(fp);     /* reads a character from fp */
```

Although `getc` and `fgetc` do the same thing, `getc` is usually implemented as a macro, while `fgetc` is a function. `getchar` itself is usually a macro defined in the following way:

```
#define getchar() getc(stdin)
```

For reading characters from a file, programmers usually prefer `getc` over `fgetc`. Since `getc` is a macro, it tends to be faster. `fgetc` is available as a backup if `getc` isn't appropriate.

All three functions behave the same if a problem occurs. At end-of-file, they set the stream's end-of-file indicator and return EOF. If an error occurs, they set the stream's error indicator and return EOF. To differentiate between the two, we can call either `feof` or `ferror`.

One of the most common uses of `fgetc`, `getc`, and `getchar` is to read characters from a file, one by one, until end-of-file occurs. It's customary to use the following `while` loop for that purpose:

idiom
```
while ((ch = getc(fp)) != EOF) {
    ...
}
```

After reading a character from the file associated with `fp` and storing it in the variable `ch` (which must be of type `int`), the test condition compares `ch` with `EOF`. If `ch` isn't equal to `EOF`, we're not at the end of the file yet, so the body of the loop is executed. If `ch` is equal to `EOF`, the loop terminates.

When reading from a file, always store the return value of `fgetc`, `getc`, or `getchar` into an `int` variable, not a `char` variable. Testing a `char` variable against `EOF` may give the wrong result.

---

ungetc

There's one other character input function, `ungetc`, which "puts back" a character read from a stream and clears the stream's end-of-file indicator. This capability can be handy if we need a "lookahead" character during input. For instance, to read a series of digits, stopping at the first nondigit, we could write

isdigit function ➤23.4
```
while (isdigit(ch = getc(fp))) {
    ...
}
ungetc(ch, fp);    /* puts back last value of ch */
```

The number of characters that can be pushed back by consecutive calls of `ungetc`—with no intervening read operations—depends on the implementation and the type of stream involved; only the first call is guaranteed to succeed. Call-

file-positioning functions ➤22.7

ing a file-positioning function (`fseek`, `fsetpos`, or `rewind`) causes the pushed-back characters to be lost.

`ungetc` returns the character it was asked to push back. It returns `EOF` if an attempt is made to push back too many characters before another read or file-positioning operation.

PROGRAM   **Copying a File**

The following program makes a copy of a file. The names of the original file and the new file will be specified on the command line when the program is executed. For example, to copy the file `f1.c` to `f2.c`, we'd use the command

```
fcopy f1.c f2.c
```

`fcopy` will issue an error message if there aren't exactly two file names on the command line or if either file can't be opened.

fcopy.c
```
/* Copies a file */

#include <stdio.h>
#include <stdlib.h>
```

```
main(int argc, char *argv[])
{
  FILE *source_fp, *dest_fp;
  int ch;

  if (argc != 3) {
    fprintf(stderr, "usage: fcopy source dest\n");
    exit(EXIT_FAILURE);
  }

  if ((source_fp = fopen(argv[1], "rb")) == NULL) {
    fprintf(stderr, "Can't open %s\n", argv[1]);
    exit(EXIT_FAILURE);
  }

  if ((dest_fp = fopen(argv[2], "wb")) == NULL) {
    fprintf(stderr, "Can't open %s\n", argv[2]);
    fclose(source_fp);
    exit(EXIT_FAILURE);
  }

  while ((ch = getc(source_fp)) != EOF)
    putc(ch, dest_fp);

  fclose(source_fp);
  fclose(dest_fp);
  return 0;
}
```

Using `"rb"` and `"wb"` as the file modes enables `fcopy` to copy both text and binary files. If we used `"r"` and `"w"` instead, the program wouldn't necessarily be able to copy binary files.

22.5   Line I/O

We'll now turn to library functions that read and write lines. These functions are used mostly with text streams, although it's also legal to use them with binary streams.

Output Functions

```
int fputs(const char *s, FILE *stream);
int puts(const char *s);
```

puts   We encountered the `puts` function in Section 13.3; it writes a string of characters to `stdout`:

```
puts("Hi, there!");          /* writes to stdout */
```

fputs

After it writes the characters in the string, `puts` always adds a new-line character.

`fputs` is a more general version of `puts`. Its second argument indicates the stream to which the output should be written:

```
fputs("Hi, there!", fp);   /* writes to fp */
```

Unlike `puts`, the `fputs` function doesn't write a new-line character unless one is present in the string.

Both functions return `EOF` if an error occurs; otherwise, they return a nonnegative number.

Input Functions

```
char *fgets(char *s, int n, FILE *stream);
char *gets(char *s);
```

gets

We encountered `gets` in Section 13.3; it reads a string of characters from `stdin`:

```
gets(str);                        /* reads a line from stdin */
```

`gets` reads characters one by one, storing them in the string, until it reads a new-line character, which it discards.

fgets

`fgets` is a more general version of `gets` that can read from any stream. `fgets` is also safer than `gets`, since it limits the number of characters that it will store. Here's how we might use `fgets`, assuming that `str` is the name of a character array:

```
fgets(str, sizeof(str), fp);   /* reads a line from fp */
```

In response to this call, `fgets` will read characters one by one, stopping at the first new-line character or when `sizeof(str)` − 1 characters have been read, whichever happens first. If it reads the new-line character, `fgets` stores it along with the other characters. (Thus, `gets` *never* stores the new-line character, but `fgets` *sometimes* does.)

Both `gets` and `fgets` return a null pointer if an error occurs or they reach the end of the input stream before storing any characters. (As usual, we can use `feof` or `ferror` to determine which one it was.) Otherwise, both return a pointer to the string read. As you'd expect, both functions store a null character at the end of the string.

Now that you know about `fgets`, I'd suggest using it instead of `gets` in most situations. With `gets`, there's always the possibility of stepping outside the bounds of the receiving array, so it's safe to use only when the string being read is *guaranteed* to fit into the array. When there's no guarantee (and there usually isn't), it's much safer to use `fgets`. Note that `fgets` will read from the standard input stream if passed `stdin` as its third argument:

```
fgets(str, sizeof(str), stdin);
```

22.6 Block I/O

```
size_t fread(void *ptr, size_t size, size_t nmemb,
             FILE *stream);
size_t fwrite(const void *ptr, size_t size,
              size_t nmemb, FILE *stream);
```

The `fread` and `fwrite` functions allow a program to read and write large blocks of data in a single step. `fread` and `fwrite` are used primarily with binary streams, although—with care—it's possible to use them with text streams as well.

Q&A
fwrite

    `fwrite` is designed to copy an array from memory to a stream. The first argument in a call of `fwrite` is the array's address, the second argument is the size of each array element (in bytes), and the third argument is the number of elements to write. The fourth argument is a file pointer, indicating where the data should be written. To write the entire contents of the array a, for instance, we could use the following call of `fwrite`:

```
fwrite(a, sizeof(a[0]), sizeof(a)/sizeof(a[0]), fp);
```

There's no rule that we have to write the entire array; we could just as easily write any portion of it. `fwrite` returns the number of elements (*not* bytes) actually written. This number will be less than the third argument if a write error occurs.

fread

    `fread` will read the elements of an array from a stream. `fread`'s arguments are similar to `fwrite`'s: the array's address, the size of each element (in bytes), the number of elements to read, and a file pointer. To read the contents of a file into the array a, we might use the following call of `fread`:

```
n = fread(a, sizeof(a[0]), sizeof(a)/sizeof(a[0]), fp);
```

It's important to check `fread`'s return value, which indicates the actual number of elements (*not* bytes) read. This number should equal the third argument unless the end of the input file was reached or an error occurred. The `feof` and `ferror` functions can be used to determine the reason for any shortage.

Be careful not to confuse `fread`'s second and third arguments. Consider the following call of `fread`:

```
fread(a, 1, 100, fp)
```

We're asking `fread` to read 100 one-byte elements, so it will return a value between 0 and 100. The following call asks `fread` to read one block of 100 bytes:

```
fread(a, 100, 1, fp)
```

`fread`'s return value in this case will be either 0 or 1.

---

fwrite is convenient for a program that needs to store data in a file before terminating. Later, the program (or another program, for that matter) can use fread to read the data back into memory. Despite appearances, the data doesn't need to be in array form; fread and fwrite work just as well with variables of all kinds. Structures, in particular, can be read by fread or written by fwrite. To write a structure variable s to a file, for instance, we could use the following call of fwrite:

```
fwrite(&s, sizeof(s), 1, fp);
```

22.7   File Positioning

```
int fgetpos(FILE *stream, fpos_t *pos);
int fseek(FILE *stream, long int offset, int whence);
int fsetpos(FILE *stream, const fpos_t *pos);
long int ftell(FILE *stream);
void rewind(FILE *stream);
```

Every stream has an associated *file position.* When a file is opened, the file position is set either at the beginning of the file or the end, depending on the mode. Then, when a read or write operation is performed, the file position advances automatically, allowing us to move through the file in a sequential manner.

Although sequential access is fine for many applications, some programs need the ability to jump around within a file, accessing some data here and other data there. If a file contains a series of records, for example, we might want to jump directly to a particular record and read it or update it. <stdio.h> supports this form of access by providing five functions that allow a program to determine the current file position or to change it.

fseek   The fseek function changes the file position associated with the first argument (a file pointer). The third argument specifies whether the new position is to be calculated with respect to the beginning of the file, the current position, or the end of the file. <stdio.h> defines three macros for this purpose:

SEEK_SET   beginning of file
SEEK_CUR   current file position
SEEK_END   end of file

The second argument is a (possibly negative) byte count. To move to the beginning of a file, for example, the seek direction would be SEEK_SET and the byte count would be zero:

```
fseek(fp, 0L, SEEK_SET);    /* moves to beginning of file */
```

To move to the end of a file, the seek direction would be SEEK_END:

```
fseek(fp, 0L, SEEK_END);       /* moves to end of file */
```

To move back 10 bytes, the seek direction would be SEEK_CUR and the byte count would be –10:

```
fseek(fp, -10L, SEEK_CUR);   /* moves back 10 bytes */
```

Note that the byte count has type long int, so I've used 0L and –10L as arguments. (0 and –10 would also work, of course, since arguments are converted to the proper type automatically.)

Normally, fseek returns zero. If an error occurs (if the requested position doesn't exist, for example), fseek returns a nonzero value.

The file-positioning functions are best used with binary streams, by the way. C doesn't prohibit programs from using them with text streams, but care is required because of operating system differences. Because of these differences, fseek is sensitive to whether a stream is text or binary. For text streams, either (1) offset (fseek's second argument) must be zero or (2) whence (its third argument) must be SEEK_SET and offset a value obtained by a previous call of ftell. (In other words, we can only use fseek to move to the beginning or end of a file or to return to a place that was visited previously.) For binary streams, fseek isn't required to support calls in which whence is SEEK_END.

ftell   The ftell function returns the current file position as a long integer. (If an error occurs, ftell returns –1L and stores an error code in errno.) The value returned by ftell may be saved and later supplied to a call of fseek, making it possible to return to a previous file position:

```
long int file_pos;
…
file_pos = ftell(fp);          /* saves current position */
…
fseek(fp, file_pos, SEEK_SET); /* returns to old position */
```

If fp is a binary stream, the call ftell(fp) returns the current file position as a byte count, where zero represents the beginning of the file. (If fp is a text stream, however, ftell(fp) isn't necessarily a byte count. As a result, it's best not to perform arithmetic on values returned by ftell. For example, it's not a good idea to subtract values returned by ftell to see how far apart two file positions are.)

rewind   The rewind function sets the file position at the beginning. The call rewind(fp) is nearly equivalent to fseek(fp, 0L, SEEK_SET); the differences are that rewind doesn't return a value, but does clear the error indicator for fp.

fgetpos
fsetpos
Q&A   fseek and ftell have one problem: they're limited to files whose positions can be stored in a long integer. For working with very large files, Standard C provides two additional functions: fgetpos and fsetpos. These functions can handle large files because they use values of type fpos_t to represent file positions. An fpos_t value isn't necessarily an integer; it could be a structure, for instance.

The call `fgetpos(fp, &file_pos)` stores the file position associated with `fp` into the `file_pos` variable. The call `fsetpos(fp, &file_pos)` sets the file position for `fp` to be the value stored in `file_pos`. (This value must have been obtained by a previous call of `fgetpos`.) If a call of `fgetpos` or `fsetpos` fails, it stores an error code in `errno`. Both functions return zero when they succeed and a nonzero value when they fail.

Here's how we might use `fgetpos` and `fsetpos` to save a file position and return to it later:

```
fpos_t file_pos;
...
fgetpos(fp, &file_pos);   /* saves current position */
...
fsetpos(fp, &file_pos);   /* returns to old position */
```

PROGRAM   **Modifying a File of Part Records**

The following program reads a binary file of `part` structures into an array, sets the `on_hand` member of each structure to 0, then writes the structures back to the file. Notice that the file is opened for both reading and writing (`"rb+"`).

invclear.c

```
/* Modifies a file of part records by setting the quantity
   on hand to zero */

#include <stdio.h>
#include <stdlib.h>

#define NAME_LEN 25
#define MAX_PARTS 100

struct part {
  int number;
  char name[NAME_LEN+1];
  int on_hand;
} inventory[MAX_PARTS];

int num_parts;

main()
{
  FILE *fp;
  int i;

  if ((fp = fopen("invent.dat", "rb+")) == NULL) {
    fprintf(stderr, "Can't open inventory file\n");
    exit(EXIT_FAILURE);
  }

  num_parts = fread(inventory, sizeof(struct part),
                    MAX_PARTS, fp);
```

```
      for (i = 0; i < num_parts; i++)
        inventory[i].on_hand = 0;

      rewind(fp);
      fwrite(inventory, sizeof(struct part), num_parts, fp);
      fclose(fp);

      return 0;
    }
```

Calling `rewind` is critical, by the way. After the `fread` call, the file position is at the end of the file. If we were to call `fwrite` without calling `rewind` first, `fwrite` would add new data to the end of the file instead of overwriting the old data.

22.8 String I/O

```
int sprintf(char *s, const char *format, ...);
int sscanf(const char *s, const char *format, ...);
```

The `sprintf` and `sscanf` functions allow us to read and write data using a string as though it were a stream.

sprintf   `sprintf` is similar to `printf` and `fprintf`, except that it writes output into a character array (pointed to by its first argument) instead of a stream. `sprintf`'s second argument is a format string identical to that used by `printf` and `fprintf`. For example, the call

```
sprintf(str, "%d/%d/%d", 9, 20, 94);
```

will copy `9/20/94` into `str`. When it's finished writing into a string, `sprintf` adds a null character and returns the number of characters stored (not counting the null character).

`sprintf` has a variety of uses. Sometimes, for example, we might want to format data for output without actually writing it. We can use `sprintf` to do the formatting, then save the result in a string until it's time to produce output. `sprintf` is also convenient for converting numbers to character form.

sscanf   `sscanf` is similar to `scanf` and `fscanf`, except that it reads from a string (pointed to by its first argument) instead of reading from a stream. `sscanf`'s second argument is a format string identical to that used by `scanf` and `fscanf`.

`sscanf` is handy for extracting data from a string that was read by another input function. For example, we might use `fgets` to obtain a line of input, then pass the line to `sscanf` for further processing:

```
fgets(str, sizeof(str), stdin);   /* reads a line of input */
sscanf(str, "%d%d", &i, &j);      /* extracts two integers */
```

One advantage of using sscanf instead of scanf or fscanf is that we can examine an input line as many times as needed, not just once, making it easier to recognize alternate input forms and to recover from errors. Consider the problem of reading a date that's written either in the form *month / day / year* or *month–day–year*. Assuming that str contains a line of input, we can extract the month, day, and year as follows:

```
if (sscanf(str, "%d /%d /%d", &month, &day, &year) == 3)
  printf("Month: %d, day: %d, year: %d\n", month, day, year);
else if (sscanf(str, "%d -%d -%d", &month, &day, &year) == 3)
  printf("Month: %d, day: %d, year: %d\n", month, day, year);
else
  printf("Date not in the proper form\n");
```

Like the scanf and fscanf functions, sscanf returns the number of data items successfully read and stored. sscanf returns EOF if it reaches the end of the string (marked by a null character) before finding the first item.

vsprintf function ➤26.1   There's one other string I/O function, vsprintf. Since vsprintf relies on the va_list type, defined in <stdarg.h>, it's discussed with that header.

Q & A

Q: **You list only three standard streams—stdin, stdout, and stderr—but my compiler supplies stdaux and stdprn as well. What are these? [p. 476]**

A: stdaux and stdprn aren't part of Standard C, although they're supported by most DOS compilers. stdaux represents the COM (serial) port and stdprn represents the PRN (parallel) port. By performing I/O operations on stdaux, a program can communicate with a device connected to the serial port (a modem, for example). By writing to stdprn, a program can send output directly to a printer.

Q: **If I use input or output redirection, will the redirected file names show up as command-line arguments?**

A: No; the operating system removes them from the command line. Let's say that we run a program by entering

```
demo foo <in_file bar >out_file baz
```

The value of argc will be 4, argv[0] will point to the program name, argv[1] will point to "foo", argv[2] will point to "bar", and argv[3] will point to "baz".

Q: **I'm writing a program that needs to save data in a file, to be read later by another program. Is it better to store the data in text form or binary form?**

A: That depends. If the data is all text to start with, there's not much difference. If the data contains numbers, however, the decision is tougher.

Binary form is usually preferable, since it can be read and written quickly. Numbers are already in binary form when stored in memory, so copying them to a file is easy. Writing numbers in text form is much slower, since each number must be converted (usually by `fprintf`) to character form. Reading the file later will also take more time, since numbers will have to be converted from text form back to binary. Moreover, storing data in binary form often saves space, as we saw in Section 22.1.

Binary files have two disadvantages, however. They're hard for humans to read, which can hamper debugging. Also, binary files generally aren't portable from one system to another, since different kinds of computers store data in different ways. For instance, some machines store integers in two bytes, while others store them in four bytes. Some machines expect the number's high byte to be stored first, while others expect the low byte to come first.

Q: **C programs for UNIX never seem to use the letter b in the mode string, even when the file being opened is binary. What gives? [p. 480]**

A: In UNIX, text files and binary files have exactly the same format, so there's never any need to use `b`. UNIX programmers should still include the `b`, however, so that their programs will be more portable to other operating systems.

Q: **I've seen programs that call `fopen` and put the letter t in the mode string. What does t mean?**

A: The C standard allows additional characters to appear in the mode string, provided that they follow `r`, `w`, `a`, `b`, or `+`. DOS compilers often allow the use of `t` to indicate that a file is to be opened in text mode instead of binary mode. Of course, text mode is the default anyway, so `t` adds nothing. Whenever possible, it's best to avoid using `t` and other nonportable features.

Q: **Why bother to call `fclose` to close a file? Isn't it true that all open files are closed automatically when a program terminates?**

A: That's usually true, but not if the program calls `abort` to terminate. Even when `abort` isn't used, though, there are still good reasons to call `fclose`. First, it reduces the number of open files. Operating systems limit the number of files that a program may have open at the same time; large programs may bump into this limit. (The macro `FOPEN_MAX`, defined in `<stdio.h>`, specifies the minimum number of files that the implementation guarantees can be open simultaneously.) Second, the program becomes easier to understand and modify; by looking for the call of `fclose`, it's easier for the reader to determine the point at which a file is no longer in use. Third, there's the issue of safety. Closing a file ensures that its contents and directory entry are updated properly; if the program should crash later, at least the file will be intact.

abort function ➤26.2

Q: **I'm writing a program that will prompt the user to enter a file name. How long should I make the character array that will hold the file name? [p. 482]**

A: That depends on your operating system. Fortunately, you can use the macro FILENAME_MAX (defined in <stdio.h>) to specify the size of the array. FILENAME_MAX is the length of a string that will hold the longest file name that the implementation guarantees can be opened.

Q: **Can fflush flush a stream that was opened for both reading and writing?**

A: According to the C standard, the effect of calling fflush is defined for a stream that (a) was opened for output, or (b) was opened for updating and whose last operation was not a read. In all other cases, the effect of calling fflush is undefined. When fflush is passed a null pointer, it flushes all streams that satisfy either (a) or (b).

Q: **Can the format string in a call of ...printf or ...scanf be a variable?**

A: Sure; it can be any expression of type char *. This property makes the ...printf and ...scanf functions even more versatile than we've had reason to suspect. Consider the following classic example from Kernighan and Ritchie's *The C Programming Language*, which prints a program's command-line arguments, separated by spaces:

```
while (--argc > 0)
  printf((argc > 1) ? "%s " : "%s", *++argv);
```

The format string is the expression (argc > 1) ? "%s " : "%s", which evaluates to "%s " for all command-line arguments but the last.

Q: **Which library functions—other than clearerr—clear a stream's error and end-of-file indicators? [p. 497]**

A: Calling rewind clears both indicators, as does opening or reopening the stream. Calling ungetc, fseek, or fsetpos clears just the end-of-file indicator.

Q: **I can't get feof to work; it seems to return 0 even at end-of-file. What am I doing wrong?**

A: feof will only return 1 when a previous read operation has failed; you can't use feof to check for end-of-file *before* attempting to read. Instead, you should first attempt to read, then check the return value from the input function. If the return value indicates that the operation was unsuccessful, you can then use feof to determine whether the failure was due to end-of-file. In other words, it's best not to think of calling feof as a way to *detect* end-of-file. Instead, think of it as a way to *confirm* that end-of-file was the reason for the failure of a read operation.

Q: **I still don't understand why the I/O library provides macros named putc and getc in addition to functions named fputc and fgetc. According to Section 21.1, there are already two versions of putc and getc (a macro and a function). If we need a genuine function instead of a macro, we can expose the putc or getc function by undefining the macro. So why do fputc and fgetc exist? [p. 499]**

A: Historical reasons. Prior to the standard, C had no rule that there be a true function to back up each parameterized macro in the library. `putc` and `getc` were traditionally implemented only as macros, while `fputc` and `fgetc` were implemented only as functions.

*Q: **What's wrong with storing the return value of `fgetc`, `getc`, or `getchar` into a `char` variable? I don't see how testing a `char` variable against `EOF` could give the wrong answer. [p. 500]**

A: There are two cases in which this test can give the wrong result. To make the following discussion concrete, I'll assume two's-complement arithmetic.

First, suppose that `char` is an unsigned type. (Recall that some compilers treat `char` as a signed type, while others treat it as an unsigned type.) Now suppose that `getc` returns EOF, which we store into a `char` variable named ch. Since EOF is another name for –1, ch will end up with the value 255. Comparing ch (an unsigned character) with EOF (a signed integer) requires converting ch to a signed integer (255, in this case). The comparison against EOF fails, since 255 is not equal to –1.

Now assume that `char` is a signed type instead. Consider what happens if `getc` reads a byte containing the value 255 from a binary stream. Storing 255 into the ch variable gives it the value –1, since ch is a signed character. Testing whether ch is equal to EOF will (erroneously) give a true result.

Q: **Why doesn't Section 22.4 (Character I/O) say anything about the `getch` and `getche` functions?**

A: Simple—`getch` and `getche` aren't part of the standard I/O library. These functions, which allow a program to capture individual keystrokes, are usually provided by DOS compilers in the nonstandard header `<conio.h>` (console I/O).

The standard input functions `getc`, `fgetc`, and `getchar` are buffered; they don't start to read input until the user has pressed the Enter (Return) key. `getch` and `getche`, on the other hand, return characters as they're entered. The difference between the two functions is that `getch` doesn't echo input characters, while `getche` does. In other words, if we use `getch`, the user won't see the characters that he or she is typing.

`getch` and `getche` can detect when the user has pressed a function key, cursor key, or any of the other special keys on a PC keyboard. When the user presses such a key, these functions return 0. When called the next time, they return a "scan code" indicating which key was pressed. If you're using a DOS compiler, your manual should provide a list of scan codes, or you can consult a book about programming the PC family.

Functions such as `getch` and `getche` are useful for writing certain kinds of programs. First, they allow the construction of interactive programs—editors, for example—that must be able to respond instantly to user input. Second, they allow programs to tell when the user has pressed a special key. Third, `getch` allows a program to read input without having to echo it, a definite advantage in some situations (reading a password, say).

getch and getche have their problems as well. They don't give the user a chance to backspace and correct errors. And since they're nonstandard, programs that call these functions won't be portable to UNIX or other operating systems.

Q: When I'm reading user input, how can I skip all characters left on the current input line?

A: One possibility is to write a small function that reads and ignores all characters up to (and including) the first new-line character:

```
void skip_line(void)
{
  while (getchar() != '\n')
    ;
}
```

Another possibility is to ask scanf to skip all characters up to the first new-line character:

```
scanf("%*[^\n]");    /* skips characters up to new-line */
```

scanf will read all characters up to the first new-line character, but not store them anywhere (the * indicates assignment suppression). The only problem with using scanf is that it leaves the new-line character unread, so you may have to discard it separately.

Whatever you do, don't call the fflush function:

```
fflush(stdin);    /* effect is undefined */
```

Although some implementations allow the use of fflush to "flush" unread input, it's not a good idea to assume that all do. fflush is designed to flush *output* streams; the C standard states that its effect on input streams is undefined.

Q: Why is it not a good idea to use `fread` and `fwrite` with text streams? [p. 503]

A: One difficulty is that, under some operating systems, the new-line character becomes a pair of characters when written to a text file (see Section 22.1 for details). We must take this expansion into account, or else we're likely to lose track of our data. For example, if we use fwrite to write blocks of 80 characters, some of the blocks may end up occupying more than 80 bytes in the file because of new-line characters that were expanded.

Q: Why are there two sets of file-positioning functions (`fseek`/`ftell` and `fsetpos`/`fgetpos`)? Wouldn't one set be enough? [p. 505]

A: fseek and ftell have been part of the C library for eons, so they had to be included in the C standard. Unfortunately, these functions don't work for very large files (which weren't common at the time C was designed), so fsetpos and fgetpos were added during standardization.

Q: **Why doesn't this chapter discuss screen control: moving the cursor, changing the colors of characters on the screen, and so on?**

A: Standard C provides no functions for screen control. The standard addresses only issues that can reasonably be standardized across a wide range of computers and operating systems; screen control is outside this realm. If you're working under DOS, you have several options for screen control, including calling the functions in <conio.h>, a header provided by most DOS compilers. UNIX programmers face the problem that their programs need to work with a variety of terminals. The customary way to handle this problem is to use the UNIX curses library, which supports screen control in a terminal-independent manner.

Q: **What about standard functions for graphics?**

A: There are no standard functions for graphics—see the answer to the previous question. If your program needs graphics capabilities, you have several choices. Your compiler may come with a graphics library. You could obtain a graphics library written by a third party. Or, as a last resort, you could write your own library.

Exercises

Section 22.1

1. Indicate whether each of the following files is more likely to contain text data or binary data:
   (a) a file of object code produced by a C compiler
   (b) a program listing produced by a C compiler
   (c) an e-mail message sent from one computer to another
   (d) a file containing a graphics image

Section 22.2

2. Indicate which mode string is most likely to be passed to fopen in each of the following situations:
   (a) A database management system opens a file containing records to be updated.
   (b) A mail program opens a file of saved messages so that it can add additional messages to the end.
   (c) A graphics program opens a file containing a picture to be displayed on the screen.
   (d) An operating system command interpreter opens a "batch file" (or "shell script") containing commands to be executed.

3. Extend the canopen program so that the user may put any number of file names on the command line:

```
canopen foo bar baz
```

   The program should print a separate can be opened or can't be opened message for each file. It should return 2 if there were no arguments on the command line, 1 if any of the files couldn't be opened, or 0 if all files could be opened.

Section 22.3

4. Show how each of the following numbers would look if printed by printf with %#012.5g as the conversion specification:

(a) 83.7361
(b) 29748.6607
(c) 1054932234.0
(d) 0.0000235218

5. Is there any difference between the printf conversion specifications %.4d and %04d? If so, explain what it is.

*6. Write a call of printf that prints

1 widget

if the widget variable (of type int) has the value 1, and

n widgets

if its value is *n*. You are not allowed to use the if statement or any other statement; the answer must be a single call of printf.

*7. Suppose that we call scanf as follows:

n = scanf("%d%f%d", &i, &x, &j);

(i, j, and n are int variables and x is a float variable.) Assuming that the input stream contains the characters shown, give the values of i, j, n, and x after the call. In addition, indicate which characters were consumed by the call.

(a) 10•20•30¤
(b) 1.0•2.0•3.0¤
(c) 0.1•0.2•0.3¤
(d) .1•.2•.3¤

8. In previous chapters, we've used the scanf format string " %c" when we wanted to skip white-space characters and read a nonblank character. Some programmers use "%1s" instead. Are the two techniques equivalent? If not, what are the differences?

Section 22.4   9. Which one of the following calls is *not* a valid way of reading one character from the standard input stream?

(a) getch()
(b) getchar()
(c) getc(stdin)
(d) fgetc(stdin)

10. The fcopy program has one minor flaw: it doesn't check for errors as it's writing to the destination file. Errors during writing are rare, but do occasionally occur (the disk might become full, for example). Show how to add the missing error check to fcopy.c, assuming that we want the program to write a message and terminate immediately if an error occurs.

11. The following loop appears in the fcopy program:

```
while ((ch = getc(source_fp)) != EOF)
    putc(ch, dest_fp);
```

Suppose that we neglected to put parentheses around ch = getc(source_fp):

```
while (ch = getc(source_fp) != EOF)
    putc(ch, dest_fp);
```

Would the program compile without an error? If so, what would the program do when it's run?

12. Write a program named `toupper` that converts all letters in a file to upper case. (Characters other than letters shouldn't be changed.) The user will supply the name of the input file on the command line:

    ```
    toupper test.doc
    ```

    Have `toupper` write its output to `stdout`.

13. Write a program named `fcat` that "concatenates" any number of files by writing them to standard output, one after the other, with no break between files. For example, the following command will display the files `f1.c`, `f2.c`, and `f3.c` on the screen:

    ```
    fcat f1.c f2.c f3.c
    ```

    `fcat` should issue an error message if any file can't be opened. *Hint:* Since it has no more than one file open at a time, `fcat` needs only a single file pointer variable. Once it's finished with a file, `fcat` can use the same file pointer variable when it opens the next file.

14. (a) Write a program named `cntchar` that counts the number of characters in a text file.

    (b) Write a program named `cntword` that counts the number of words in a text file (a "word" is any sequence of non-white-space characters).

    (c) Write a program named `cntline` that counts the number of lines in a text file.

    Have each program obtain the file name from the command line and write its output to `stdout`.

15. The `xor` program of Section 20.1 refuses to encrypt bytes that—in original or encrypted form—are control characters. We can now remove this restriction. Modify the program so that the names of the input and output files are command-line arguments. Open both files in binary mode, and remove the test that checks whether the original or encrypted character is a control character.

16. Write a program named `hexdump` that displays the bytes in a file as a series of hexadecimal codes, printed 20 per line:

    ```
    43 68 61 69 72 6d 61 6e 20 42 69 6c 6c 20 6c 65 61 64 73 20
    74 68 65 20 68 61 70 70 79 20 77 6f 72 6b 65 72 73 20 69 6e
    20 73 6f 6e 67 21 0d 0a
    ```

    Have the user specify the file name on the command line. Be sure to open the file in `"rb"` mode.

17. Of the many techniques for compressing the contents of a file, one of the simplest and fastest is known as ***run-length encoding***. This technique compresses a file by replacing sequences of identical bytes by a pair of bytes: a repetition count followed by a byte to be repeated. For example, suppose that the file to be compressed begins with the following sequence of bytes (shown in hex):

    ```
    46 6f 6f 20 62 61 72 21 21 21 20 20 20 20 20
    ```

    The compressed file will contain the following bytes:

    ```
    01 46 02 6f 01 20 01 62 01 61 01 72 03 21 05 20
    ```

    Run-length encoding works well if the original file contains many long sequences of identical bytes. In the worst case (a file with no repeated bytes), run-length encoding can actually double the length of the file.

    (a) Write a program named `comp` that uses run-length encoding to compress a file. To run `comp`, we'd use a command of the form

    `comp` *original-file compressed-file*

If *compressed-file* has no extension, comp will add the extension .rle. For example, the command

```
comp foo bar
```

will cause comp to create a file named bar.rle and write a compressed version of foo to that file. (comp will save foo's name at the beginning of the bar.rle file.) *Hint:* The hexdump program of Exercise 16 could be useful for debugging.

(b) Write a program named uncomp that reverses the compression performed by the comp program. The uncomp command will have the form

```
uncomp compressed-file
```

If *compressed-file* has no extension, uncomp adds the extension .rle. For example, the command

```
uncomp bar
```

will cause uncomp to open the file bar.rle and write an uncompressed version of its contents to the file whose name is stored at the beginning of bar.rle.

Section 22.5 18. (a) Write your own version of the fgets function. Make it behave as much like the real fgets function as possible; in particular, make sure that it has the proper return value. To avoid conflicts with the standard library, don't name your function fgets.

(b) Write your own version of fputs, following the same rules as in part (a).

Section 22.6 19. Modify the invent program of Section 16.3 by adding two new operations:

- Save the database in a specified file.
- Load the database from a specified file.

Use the codes d (dump) and r (restore), respectively, to represent these operations. The interaction with the user should have the following appearance:

```
Enter operation code: d
Enter name of output file: invent.dat

Enter operation code: r
Enter name of input file: invent.dat
```

20. Write a program that merges two files containing part records stored by the invent program (see Exercise 19). Assume that the records in each file are sorted by part number, and that we want the resulting file to be sorted as well. If both files have a part with the same number, combine the quantities stored in the records. (As a consistency check, have the program compare the part names and print an error message if they don't match.) Have the program obtain the names of the input files and the merged file from the command line.

*21. Modify the invent2 program of Section 17.5 by adding the d (dump) and r (restore) operations described in Exercise 19. Since the part structures aren't stored in an array, the d operation can't save them all by a single call of fwrite. Instead, it will need to visit each node in the linked list, saving the part number, name, and quantity on hand to a file. (Don't save the next pointer; it won't be valid once the program terminates.) As it reads parts from the file, the r operation will rebuild the list one node at a time.

Section 22.7 22. Write calls of fseek that perform the following file-positioning operations on a binary file whose data is arranged in 64-byte "records." Use fp as the file pointer in each case.

(a) Move to the beginning of record n. (Assume that the first record in the file is record 0.)
(b) Move to the beginning of the last record in the file.

(c) Move forward one record.

(d) Move backward two records.

Section 22.8   23.   Write a program named `dispdate` that reads a date from the command line and displays it in the following form:

`September 13, 1995`

Allow the user to enter the date as either `9-13-95` or `9/13/95`; you may assume that there are no spaces in the date. Print an error message if the date doesn't have one of the specified forms. *Hint:* Use `sscanf` to extract the month, day, and year from the command-line argument.

23 Library Support for Numbers and Character Data

Prolonged contact with the computer turns mathematicians into clerks and vice versa.

This chapter describes the five library headers that provide support for working with numbers, characters, and character strings. Sections 23.1 and 23.2 cover the <float.h> and <limits.h> headers, which contain macros describing the characteristics of numeric and character types. Sections 23.3 through 23.5 discuss the remaining headers: <math.h> (mathematical functions), <ctype.h> (character functions), and <string.h> (string functions).

23.1 The <float.h> Header: Characteristics of Floating Types

The <float.h> header provides macros that define the range and accuracy of the floating types. There are no types or functions in <float.h>.

Two macros apply to all floating types. The FLT_ROUNDS macro specifies the rounding mode for floating-point addition. Table 23.1 shows the possible values of FLT_ROUNDS. The FLT_RADIX macro specifies the radix of exponent representation; it has a minimum value of 2 (binary).

Table 23.1
Rounding Modes

Value	Meaning
−1	Indeterminable
0	Toward zero
1	To nearest
2	Toward positive infinity
3	Toward negative infinity

The remaining macros, which I'll present in a series of tables, describe the characteristics of specific types. Each macro begins with either FLT, DBL, or

LDBL, depending on whether it refers to the `float`, `double`, or `long double` type. The C standard provides extremely detailed definitions of these macros; my descriptions will be less precise but easier to understand. The tables indicate maximum or minimum values for some macros, as specified in the C standard.

Table 23.2 lists macros having to do with the number of significant digits in a number.

Table 23.2
Significant Digit Macros in <float.h>

Name	Value	Description
FLT_MANT_DIG DBL_MANT_DIG LDBL_MANT_DIG		Number of significant digits (base FLT_RADIX)
FLT_DIG DBL_DIG LDBL_DIG	≥ 6 ≥ 10 ≥ 10	Number of significant digits (base 10)

Table 23.3 lists macros having to do with exponents.

Table 23.3
Exponent Macros in <float.h>

Name	Value	Description
FLT_MIN_EXP DBL_MIN_EXP LDBL_MIN_EXP		Smallest (most negative) power to which FLT_RADIX can be raised
FLT_MIN_10_EXP DBL_MIN_10_EXP LDBL_MIN_10_EXP	≤ -37 ≤ -37 ≤ -37	Smallest (most negative) power to which 10 can be raised
FLT_MAX_EXP DBL_MAX_EXP LDBL_MAX_EXP		Largest power to which FLT_RADIX can be raised
FLT_MAX_10_EXP DBL_MAX_10_EXP LDBL_MAX_10_EXP	$\geq +37$ $\geq +37$ $\geq +37$	Largest power to which 10 can be raised

Table 23.4 lists the remaining macros, which describe how large numbers can be, how close to zero they can get, and how close two consecutive numbers can be.

Table 23.4
Max, Min, and Epsilon Macros in <float.h>

Name	Value	Description
FLT_MAX DBL_MAX LDBL_MAX	$\geq 10^{+37}$ $\geq 10^{+37}$ $\geq 10^{+37}$	Largest value
FLT_MIN DBL_MIN LDBL_MIN	$\leq 10^{-37}$ $\leq 10^{-37}$ $\leq 10^{-37}$	Smallest positive value
FLT_EPSILON DBL_EPSILON LDBL_EPSILON	$\leq 10^{-5}$ $\leq 10^{-9}$ $\leq 10^{-9}$	Smallest representable difference between two numbers

Since most of the macros in <float.h> are of interest only to experts in numerical analysis, it's probably one of the least-used headers in the standard library.

23.2   The `<limits.h>` Header: Sizes of Integral Types

The `<limits.h>` header provides macros that define the range of each integer and character type. There are no types or functions in `<limits.h>`.

One set of macros in `<limits.h>` deals with the character types: `char`, `signed char`, and `unsigned char`. Table 23.5 lists these macros and shows the maximum or minimum value of each.

Table 23.5
Character Macros in
`<limits.h>`

Name	Value	Description
CHAR_BIT	≥8	Number of bits per character
SCHAR_MIN	≤–127	Minimum signed character
SCHAR_MAX	≥+127	Maximum signed character
UCHAR_MAX	≥255	Maximum unsigned character
CHAR_MIN	*	Minimum character
CHAR_MAX	**	Maximum character
MB_LEN_MAX	≥1	Maximum number of bytes per multibyte character

*CHAR_MIN is equal to SCHAR_MIN if char is treated as a signed type; otherwise, CHAR_MIN is 0.
**CHAR_MAX has the same value as either SCHAR_MAX or UCHAR_MAX, depending on whether char is treated as a signed type or an unsigned type.

The remaining macros in `<limits.h>` deal with the integer types: `short int`, `unsigned short int`, `int`, `unsigned int`, `long int`, and `unsigned long int`. Table 23.6 lists these macros and shows the maximum or minimum value of each.

Table 23.6
Integer Macros in
`<limits.h>`

Name	Value	Description
SHRT_MIN	≤–32767	Minimum short integer
SHRT_MAX	≥+32767	Maximum short integer
USHRT_MAX	≥65535	Maximum unsigned short integer
INT_MIN	≤–32767	Minimum integer
INT_MAX	≥+32767	Maximum integer
UINT_MAX	≥65535	Maximum unsigned integer
LONG_MIN	≤–2147483647	Minimum long integer
LONG_MAX	≥+2147483647	Maximum long integer
ULONG_MAX	≥4294967295	Maximum unsigned long integer

The macros in `<limits.h>` are handy for checking whether a compiler supports integers of a particular size. For example, to determine whether the `int` type can store numbers as large as 100,000, we might use the following preprocessor directives:

```
#if INT MAX < 100000
#error int type is too small
#endif
```

#error directive ➤ 14.5   If the `int` type isn't adequate, the `#error` directive will abort compilation.

Going a step further, we might use the macros in `<limits.h>` to help a program *choose* how to represent a type. Let's say that variables of type `Quantity` must be able to hold integers as large as 100,000. If `INT_MAX` is at least 100,000, we can define `Quantity` to be `int`; otherwise, we'll need to make it `long int`:

```
#if INT_MAX >= 100000
typedef int Quantity;
#else
typedef long int Quantity;
#endif
```

23.3 The `<math.h>` Header: Mathematics

The functions in `<math.h>` fall into five groups:

> Trigonometric functions
> Hyperbolic functions
> Exponential and logarithmic functions
> Power functions
> Nearest integer, absolute value, and remainder functions

Before we delve into these groups, let's take a brief look at how the functions in `<math.h>` deal with errors.

Errors

The `<math.h>` functions handle errors in a way that's different from other library functions. When an error occurs, most `<math.h>` functions store an error code in a special variable named `errno` (from the `<errno.h>` header). In addition, when the return value of a function would be larger than the largest `double` value, the functions in `<math.h>` return a special value, represented by the macro `HUGE_VAL` (defined in `<math.h>`). `HUGE_VAL` is of type `double`, but it isn't necessarily an ordinary number. (The IEEE standard for floating-point arithmetic defines a value named "infinity"—a logical choice for `HUGE_VAL`.)

`<errno.h>` header ➤24.2

IEEE floating-point standard ➤7.2

The functions in `<math.h>` primarily detect two kinds of errors:

- **Domain error:** An argument is outside a function's domain. If a domain error occurs, the function's return value is implementation-defined and `EDOM` ("domain error") is stored in `errno`. In some implementations of `<math.h>`, functions return the value *NAN* ("not-a-number") when a domain error occurs. NAN is another special value (like "infinity") defined in the IEEE standard.

- **Range error:** The return value of a function is outside the range of `double` values. If the return value's magnitude is too large (overflow), the function returns positive or negative `HUGE_VAL`, depending on the sign of the correct result. In addition, `ERANGE` ("range error") is stored in `errno`. If the return value's magnitude is too small to represent (underflow), the function returns zero; some implementations may also store `ERANGE` in `errno`.

We'll ignore the possibility of error for the remainder of this section. However, the function descriptions in Appendix D explain the circumstances that lead to each type of error.

Trigonometric Functions

```
double acos(double x);
double asin(double x);
double atan(double x);
double atan2(double y, double x);
double cos(double x);
double sin(double x);
double tan(double x);
```

cos
sin
tan

The `cos`, `sin`, and `tan` functions compute the cosine, sine, and tangent, respectively. If PI is defined to be `3.14159265`, passing `PI/4` to `cos`, `sin`, and `tan` produces the following results:

```
cos(PI/4)  ⇒  0.707107
sin(PI/4)  ⇒  0.707107
tan(PI/4)  ⇒  1.0
```

Note that arguments to `cos`, `sin`, and `tan` are expressed in radians, not degrees.

acos
asin
atan

`acos`, `asin`, and `atan` compute the arc cosine, arc sine, and arc tangent:

```
acos(1.0)  ⇒  0.0
asin(1.0)  ⇒  1.5708
atan(1.0)  ⇒  0.785398
```

Applying `acos` to a value returned by `cos` won't necessarily yield the original argument to `cos`, since `acos` always returns a value between 0 and π. `asin` and `atan` return a value between $-\pi/2$ and $\pi/2$.

atan2

`atan2` computes the arc tangent of `y/x`, where `y` is the function's first argument and `x` is its second. The return value of `atan2` is between $-\pi$ and π. The call `atan(x)` is equivalent to `atan2(x, 1.0)`.

Hyperbolic Functions

```
double cosh(double x);
double sinh(double x);
double tanh(double x);
```

cosh
sinh
tanh

The `cosh`, `sinh`, and `tanh` functions compute the hyperbolic cosine, sine, and tangent:

```
cosh(0.5)  ⇒  1.12763
sinh(0.5)  ⇒  0.521095
tanh(0.5)  ⇒  0.462117
```

Arguments to cosh, sinh, and tanh must be expressed in radians, not degrees.

Exponential and Logarithmic Functions

```
double exp(double x);
double frexp(double value, int *exp);
double ldexp(double x, int exp);
double log(double x);
double log10(double x);
double modf(double value, double *iptr);
```

exp The exp function returns *e* raised to a power:

$$exp(3.0) ⇒ 20.0855$$

log
log10   log is the inverse of exp—it computes the logarithm of a number to the base *e*. log10 computes the "common" (base 10) logarithm:

```
log(20.0855)  ⇒  3.0
log10(1000)   ⇒  3.0
```

Computing the logarithm to a base other than *e* or 10 isn't difficult. The following function, for example, computes the logarithm of x to the base b, for arbitrary x and b:

```
double logb(double x, double b)
{
  return log(x) / log(b);
}
```

modf   The modf and frexp functions decompose a double value into two parts. modf splits its first argument into integer and fractional parts. It returns the fractional part and stores the integer part into the variable pointed to by the second argument:

modf(3.14159, &int_part) ⇒ 0.14159 (int_part is assigned 3.0)

Although int_part must have type double, we can always cast it to int or long int later.

frexp   frexp splits a floating-point number into a fractional part *f* and an exponent *n* in such a way that the original number equals $f \times 2^n$, where either $0.5 \leq f < 1$ or $f = 0$. It returns *f* and stores *n* into the (integer) variable pointed to by the second argument:

frexp(12.0, &exp) $\Rightarrow$ .75 (exp is assigned 4)
frexp(0.25, &exp) $\Rightarrow$ 0.5 (exp is assigned –1)

ldexp   ldexp undoes the work of frexp by combining a fraction and an exponent into a single number:

ldexp(.75, 4) $\Rightarrow$ 12.0
ldexp(0.5, -1) $\Rightarrow$ 0.25

In general, the call ldexp(x, exp) returns $x \times 2^{exp}$.

Power Functions

```
double pow(double x, double y);
double sqrt(double x);
```

pow   The pow function raises its first argument to the power specified by its second argument:

pow(3.0, 2.0) $\Rightarrow$ 9.0
pow(3.0, 0.5) $\Rightarrow$ 1.73205
pow(3.0, -3.0) $\Rightarrow$ 0.037037

sqrt   sqrt computes the square root:

sqrt(3.0) $\Rightarrow$ 1.73205

Using sqrt to find square roots is preferable to calling pow, by the way, since sqrt is usually a much faster function.

Nearest Integer, Absolute Value, and Remainder Functions

```
double ceil(double x);
double fabs(double x);
double floor(double x);
double fmod(double x, double y);
```

ceil
floor   The ceil ("ceiling") function returns—as a double value—the smallest integer that's greater than or equal to its argument. floor returns the largest integer that's less than or equal to its argument:

ceil(7.1) $\Rightarrow$ 8.0
ceil(7.9) $\Rightarrow$ 8.0
ceil(-7.1) $\Rightarrow$ –7.0
ceil(-7.9) $\Rightarrow$ –7.0

```
floor(7.1)   ⇒   7.0
floor(7.9)   ⇒   7.0
floor(-7.1)  ⇒  -8.0
floor(-7.9)  ⇒  -8.0
```

In other words, ceil "rounds up" to the nearest integer, while floor "rounds down." There's no standard function that rounds to the nearest integer, but we can easily use ceil and floor to write our own:

```
double round(double x)
{
   return x < 0.0 ? ceil(x-0.5) : floor(x+0.5);
}
```

fabs   fabs computes the absolute value of a number:

```
fabs(7.1)   ⇒  7.1
fabs(-7.1)  ⇒  7.1
```

fmod   fmod returns the remainder when its first argument is divided by its second argument:

```
fmod(5.5, 2.2)  ⇒  1.1
```

C doesn't allow the % operator to have floating operands, but fmod is a more-than-adequate substitute.

23.4   The `<ctype.h>` Header: Character Handling

The <ctype.h> header provides two kinds of functions: character-testing functions (like isdigit, which tests whether a character is a digit) and character case-mapping functions (like toupper, which converts a lower-case letter to upper case).

Although C doesn't require that we use the functions in <ctype.h> to test characters and perform case conversions, it's a good idea to do so. First, these functions have been optimized for speed (in fact, many are implemented as macros). Second, we'll end up with a more portable program, since these functions work with any character set. Third, the <ctype.h> functions adjust their behavior when the locale is changed, which helps us write programs that run properly in different parts of the world.

locales ➤ 25.1

The functions in <ctype.h> all take int arguments and return int values. We can usually ignore this detail, however—when necessary, C can automatically convert char arguments to int and int return values to char.

Character-Testing Functions

isalnum	`int isalnum(int c);`
isalpha	`int isalpha(int c);`
iscntrl	`int iscntrl(int c);`
isdigit	`int isdigit(int c);`
isgraph	`int isgraph(int c);`
islower	`int islower(int c);`
isprint	`int isprint(int c);`
ispunct	`int ispunct(int c);`
isspace	`int isspace(int c);`
isupper	`int isupper(int c);`
isxdigit	`int isxdigit(int c);`

Each character-testing function returns 1 or 0 depending on whether or not its argument has a particular property. Table 23.7 lists the property that each function tests.

Table 23.7
Character-Testing
Functions

Name	*Test*
`isalnum(c)`	Is c alphanumeric?
`isalpha(c)`	Is c alphabetic?
`iscntrl(c)`	Is c a control character?*
`isdigit(c)`	Is c a decimal digit?
`isgraph(c)`	Is c a printing character (other than a space)?
`islower(c)`	Is c a lower-case letter?
`isprint(c)`	Is c a printing character (including a space)?
`ispunct(c)`	Is c punctuation?**
`isspace(c)`	Is c a white-space character?***
`isupper(c)`	Is c an upper-case letter?
`isxdigit(c)`	Is c a hexadecimal digit?

*In ASCII, the control characters are `\x00` through `\x1f` plus `\x7f`.
**All printing characters except the space and the alphanumeric characters are considered punctuation.
***The white-space characters are space, form feed (`\f`), new-line (`\n`), carriage return (`\r`), horizontal tab (`\t`), and vertical tab (`\v`).

PROGRAM   **Testing the Character-Testing Functions**

The following program demonstrates the character-testing functions by applying them to the characters in the string `"azAZ0 !\t"`.

tchrtest.c

```
/* Tests the character-testing functions */

#include <ctype.h>
#include <stdio.h>

#define TEST(f) printf("  %c  ", f(*p) ? 'x' : ' ');
```

```
main()
{
  char *p;

  printf("      alnum      cntrl      graph      print"
         "      space     xdigit\n"
         "           alpha      digit      lower      punct"
         "      upper\n");

  for (p = "azAZ0 !\t"; *p != '\0'; p++) {
    if (iscntrl(*p))
      printf("\\x%02x:", *p);
    else
      printf("    %c:", *p);
    TEST(isalnum);
    TEST(isalpha);
    TEST(iscntrl);
    TEST(isdigit);
    TEST(isgraph);
    TEST(islower);
    TEST(isprint);
    TEST(ispunct);
    TEST(isspace);
    TEST(isupper);
    TEST(isxdigit);
    printf("\n");
  }

  return 0;
}
```

The program produces the following output:

	alnum		cntrl		graph		print		space		xdigit
		alpha		digit		lower		punct		upper	
a:	x	x			x	x	x				x
z:	x	x			x	x	x				
A:	x	x			x		x			x	x
Z:	x	x			x		x			x	
0:	x			x	x		x				x
:							x		x		
!:					x		x	x			
\x09:				x					x		

Character Case-Mapping Functions

```
int tolower(int c);
int toupper(int c);
```

tolower
toupper
The `tolower` function returns the lower-case version of a letter passed to it as an argument, while `toupper` returns the upper-case version. If the argument to either function is not a letter, it returns the character unchanged.

PROGRAM   **Testing the Case-Mapping Functions**

The following program applies the case-mapping functions to the characters in the string `"aA0!"`.

tcasemap.c

```
/* Tests the case-mapping functions */

#include <ctype.h>
#include <stdio.h>

main()
{
  char *p;

  for (p = "aA0!"; *p != '\0'; p++) {
    printf("tolower('%c') is '%c'; ", *p, tolower(*p));
    printf("toupper('%c') is '%c'\n", *p, toupper(*p));
  }
  return 0;
}
```

The program produces the following output:

```
tolower('a') is 'a'; toupper('a') is 'A'
tolower('A') is 'a'; toupper('A') is 'A'
tolower('0') is '0'; toupper('0') is '0'
tolower('!') is '!'; toupper('!') is '!'
```

23.5 The `<string.h>` Header: String Handling

We first encountered the `<string.h>` header in Section 13.5, which covered the most basic string operations: `strcpy` (string copy), `strcat` (string concatenate), `strcmp` (string compare), and `strlen` (string length). As we'll see now, there are quite a few other string-handling functions in `<string.h>`, as well as functions that operate on character arrays that aren't necessarily null-terminated.

`<string.h>` provides five kinds of functions:

- *Copying functions.* Functions that copy characters from one place in memory to another place.
- *Concatenation functions.* Functions that add characters to the end of a string.
- *Comparison functions.* Functions that compare character arrays.
- *Search functions.* Functions that search an array for a particular character, a set of characters, or a string.
- *Miscellaneous functions.* Functions that initialize a character array or compute the length of a string.

We'll now tackle these functions, one group at a time.

Copying Functions

```
void *memcpy(void *s1, const void *s2, size_t n);
void *memmove(void *s1, const void *s2, size_t n);
char *strcpy(char *s1, const char *s2);
char *strncpy(char *s1, const char *s2, size_t n);
```

Q&A

The four copying functions move characters (bytes) from one place in memory (the *source*) to another (the ***destination***). Each function requires that the first argument point to the destination and the second point to the source. All copying functions return the first argument (a pointer to the destination).

memcpy
memmove

memcpy copies n characters from the source to the destination, where n is the function's third argument. If the source and destination overlap, the behavior of memcpy is undefined. memmove is the same as memcpy, except that it works correctly when the source and destination overlap.

strcpy
strncpy

strcpy copies a null-terminated string from the source to the destination. strncpy is similar to strcpy, but it won't copy more than n characters, where n is the function's third argument. (If n is too small, strncpy won't be able to copy a terminating null character.) If it encounters a null character in the source, strncpy adds null characters to the destination until it has written a total of n characters. strcpy and strncpy, like memcpy, aren't guaranteed to work if the source and destination overlap.

The following examples illustrate the copying functions; the comments show which characters are copied.

```
char source[] = {'h', 'o', 't', '\0', 't', 'e', 'a'};
char dest[7];

memcpy(dest, source, 3);    /* h, o, t                 */
memcpy(dest, source, 4);    /* h, o, t, \0             */
memcpy(dest, source, 7);    /* h, o, t, \0, t, e, a    */

memmove(dest, source, 3);   /* h, o, t                 */
memmove(dest, source, 4);   /* h, o, t, \0             */
memmove(dest, source, 7);   /* h, o, t, \0, t, e, a    */

strcpy(dest, source);       /* h, o, t, \0             */

strncpy(dest, source, 3);   /* h, o, t                 */
strncpy(dest, source, 4);   /* h, o, t, \0             */
strncpy(dest, source, 7);   /* h, o, t, \0, \0, \0, \0 */
```

Note that memcpy, memmove, and strncpy don't require a null-terminated string; they work just as well with any block of memory. The strcpy function, on the other hand, doesn't stop copying until it reaches a null character, so it works only with null-terminated strings.

Concatenation Functions

```
char *strcat(char *s1, const char *s2);
char *strncat(char *s1, const char *s2, size_t n);
```

strcat   strcat appends its second argument to the end of the first argument. Both arguments must be null-terminated strings; strcat puts a null character at the end of the concatenated string. Consider the following example:

```
char str[7] = "tea";

strcat(str, "bag");   /* adds b, a, g, \0 to end of str */
```

The letter b overwrites the null character after a, so that str now contains the string "teabag". strcat returns its first argument (a pointer).

strncat   strncat is the same as strcat, except that its third argument limits the number of characters it will copy:

```
char str[7] = "tea";

strncat(str, "bag", 2);   /* adds b, a, \0 to str       */
strncat(str, "bag", 3);   /* adds b, a, g, \0 to str */
strncat(str, "bag", 4);   /* adds b, a, g, \0 to str */
```

As these examples show, strncat always leaves the resulting string properly null-terminated.

Comparison Functions

```
int memcmp(const void *s1, const void *s2, size_t n);
int strcmp(const char *s1, const char *s2);
int strcoll(const char *s1, const char *s2);
int strncmp(const char *s1, const char *s2,
            size_t n);
size_t strxfrm(char *s1, const char *s2, size_t n);
```

We'll tackle the comparison functions in two groups. Functions in the first group (memcmp, strcmp, and strncmp) compare two character arrays. The comparison is done character by character, using the computer's normal collating sequence (typically ASCII). Functions in the second group (strcoll and strxfrm) are used if the locale needs to be taken into account.

locales ▶25.1
memcmp
strcmp
strncmp

The memcmp, strcmp, and strncmp functions have much in common. All three expect to be passed pointers to character arrays. The characters in the first array are then compared one by one with the characters in the second array. All three functions return as soon as a mismatch is found. Also, all three return a negative, zero, or positive integer, depending on whether the stopping character in the first array was less than, equal to, or greater than the stopping character in the second.

The differences among the three functions have to do with when to stop if the arrays are equal. The memcmp function is passed a third argument, n, that limits the number of comparisons performed; it pays no particular attention to null characters. strcmp doesn't have a preset limit, stopping instead when it reaches a null character in either array. (As a result, strcmp can be used only with null-terminated strings.) strncmp is a blend of memcmp and strcmp; it stops when n comparisons have been performed or a null character is reached in either array.

The following examples illustrate memcmp, strcmp, and strncmp:

```
char s1[] = {'b', 'i', 'g', '\0', 'c', 'a', 'r'};
char s2[] = {'b', 'i', 'g', '\0', 'c', 'a', 't'};

if (memcmp(s1, s2, 3) == 0) …   /* true  */
if (memcmp(s1, s2, 4) == 0) …   /* true  */
if (memcmp(s1, s2, 7) == 0) …   /* false */

if (strcmp(s1, s2) == 0) …      /* true  */

if (strncmp(s1, s2, 3) == 0) … /* true  */
if (strncmp(s1, s2, 4) == 0) … /* true  */
if (strncmp(s1, s2, 7) == 0) … /* true  */
```

strcoll

setlocale function ➤25.1

The strcoll function is similar to strcmp, but the outcome of the comparison depends on the current locale (set by calling the setlocale function). strcoll is useful for programs that need to perform comparisons differently depending on where the program is running.

strxfrm

Most of time, strcoll is fine for performing a locale-dependent string comparison. Occasionally, however, we might need to perform the comparison more than once (a potential problem, since strcoll isn't especially fast) or change the locale without affecting the outcome of the comparison. In these situations, the strxfrm ("string transform") function is available as an alternative to strcoll.

strxfrm transforms its second argument (a string), placing the result in the array pointed to by the first argument. The third argument limits the number of characters written to the array. Calling strcmp with two transformed strings should produce the same outcome (negative, zero, or positive) as calling strcoll with the original strings.

strxfrm returns the length of the transformed string. As a result, strxfrm is typically called twice: once to determine the length of the transformed string and once to perform the transformation. Here's an example:

```
size_t len;
char *transformed;

len = strxfrm(NULL, original, 0);
transformed = malloc(len+1);
strxfrm(transformed, original, len);
```

Search Functions

```
void *memchr(const void *s, int c, size_t n);
char *strchr(const char *s, int c);
size_t strcspn(const char *s1, const char *s2);
char *strpbrk(const char *s1, const char *s2);
char *strrchr(const char *s, int c);
size_t strspn(const char *s1, const char *s2);
char *strstr(const char *s1, const char *s2);
char *strtok(char *s1, const char *s2);
```

strchr   The `strchr` function searches a string for a particular character. The following example shows how we might use `strchr` to search a string for the letter `f`.

```
char *p, str[] = "Form follows function.";

p = strchr(str, 'f');   /* finds first 'f' */
```

`strchr` returns a pointer to the first occurrence of `f` in `str` (the one in `follows`). Locating multiple occurrences of a character is easy; for example, the call

```
p = strchr(p+1, 'f');   /* finds next 'f' */
```

finds the second `f` in `str` (the one in `function`).

memchr   `memchr` is similar to `strchr`, but it stops searching after a set number of characters instead of stopping at the first null character. `memchr`'s third argument limits the number of characters it can examine—a useful capability if we don't want to search an entire string or if we're searching a block of memory that's not terminated by a null character. The following example uses `memchr` to search an array of characters that lacks a null character at the end:

```
char *p, str[22] = "Form follows function.";

p = memchr(str, 'f', sizeof(str));
```

Like the `strchr` function, `memchr` returns a pointer to the first occurrence of the character. If they can't locate the desired character, both functions return a null pointer.

strrchr   `strrchr` is similar to `strchr`, but it searches the string in *reverse* order:

```
char *p, str[] = "Form follows function.";

p = strrchr(str, 'f');   /* finds last 'f' */
```

In this example, `strrchr` will first search for the null character at the end of the string, then go backwards to locate the letter `f` (the one in `function`). `strrchr` returns a null pointer if it fails to find the desired character.

strpbrk   `strpbrk` is more general than `strchr`; it returns a pointer to the leftmost character in the first argument that matches *any* character in the second argument:

```
char *p, str[] = "Form follows function.";

p = strpbrk(str, "mn");    /* finds first 'm' or 'n' */
```

In this example, p will point to the letter m in Form. Like the other search functions, strpbrk returns a null pointer if no match is found.

strspn
strcspn
Q&A

The strspn and strcspn functions, unlike the other search functions, return an integer (of type size_t), representing a position within a string. When given a string to search and a set of characters to look for, strspn returns the index of the first character that's *not* in the set. When passed similar arguments, strcspn returns the index of the first character that's *in* the set. Here are examples of both functions:

```
size_t len;
char str[] = "Form follows function.";

len = strspn(str, "morF");     /* len = 4 */
len = strspn(str, " \t\n");    /* len = 0 */
len = strcspn(str, "morF");    /* len = 0 */
len = strcspn(str, " \t\n");   /* len = 4 */
```

strstr

strstr searches its first argument (a string) for a match with its second argument (also a string). In the following example, strstr searches for the word fun:

```
char *p, str[] = "Form follows function.";

p = strstr(str, "fun");    /* locates "fun" in str */
```

strstr returns a pointer to the first occurrence of the search string; it returns a null pointer if it can't locate the string. After the call above, p will point to the letter f in function.

strtok

strtok is the most complicated of the search functions. It's designed to search a string for a "token"—a sequence of characters that doesn't include certain delimiting characters. The call strtok(s1, s2) scans the s1 string for a nonempty sequence of characters that are *not* in the s2 string. strtok marks the end of the token by storing a null character in s1 just after the last character in the token; it then returns a pointer to the first character in the token.

What makes strtok especially useful is that later calls can find additional tokens in the same string. The call strtok(NULL, s2) continues the search begun by the previous strtok call. As before, strtok marks the end of the token with a null character, then returns a pointer to the beginning of the token. The process can be repeated until strtok returns a null pointer, indicating that no token was found.

To see how strtok works, we'll use it to extract a month, day, and year from a date written in the form

month day, year

where spaces and/or tabs separate the month from the day and the day from the year. In addition, spaces and tabs may precede the comma. Let's say that the string `str` has the following appearance to start with:

After the call

```
p = strtok(str, " \t");
```

`str` will have the following appearance:

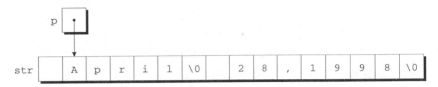

`p` points to the first character in the month string, which is now terminated by a null character. Calling `strtok` with a null pointer as its first argument causes it to resume the search from where it left off:

```
p = strtok(NULL, " \t");
```

After this call, `p` points to the first character in the day:

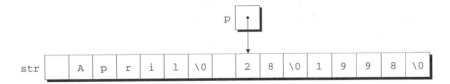

A final call of `strtok` locates the year:

```
p = strtok(NULL, " \t,");
```

After this call, `str` will have the following appearance:

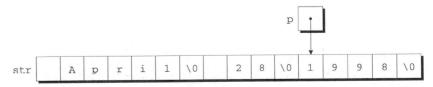

When `strtok` is called repeatedly to break a string into tokens, the second argument isn't required to be the same in each call. In our example, the final call of `strtok` has the argument `" \t,"` instead of `" \t"`.

Miscellaneous Functions

```
void *memset(void *s, int c, size_t n);
size_t strlen(const char *s);
```

memset   `memset` stores multiple copies of a character into a specified area of memory. If p points to a block of N bytes, for example, the call

```
memset(p, ' ', N);
```

will store a space in every byte of the block. One of `memset`'s uses is initializing an array to zero bits:

```
memset(a, 0, sizeof(a));
```

`memset` returns its first argument (a pointer).

strlen   `strlen` returns the length of a string, not counting the null character. See Section 13.5 for examples of `strlen` calls.

strerror function ➤24.2   There's one other miscellaneous string function, `strerror`, which is covered along with the `<errno.h>` header.

Q & A

Q: **Why does `<string.h>` provide so many ways to do the same thing? Do we really need four copy functions (`memcpy`, `memmove`, `strcpy`, and `strncpy`)? [p. 530]**

A: Let's start with `memcpy` and `strcpy`. These functions are used for different purposes. `strcpy` will only copy a character array that's terminated with a null character (a string, in other words); `memcpy` can copy a memory block that lacks such a terminator (an array of integers, for example).

The other functions allow us to choose between safety and performance. `strncpy` is safer than `strcpy`, since it limits the number of characters copied. We pay a price for safety, however, since `strncpy` is likely to be slower than `strcpy`. Using `memmove` involves a similar trade-off. `memmove` will copy characters from one region of memory into a possibly overlapping region. `memcpy` isn't guaranteed to work properly in this situation; however, if we can guarantee no overlap, `memcpy` is likely to be faster than `memmove`.

Q: **Why does the `strspn` function have such an odd name? [p. 534]**

A: Instead of thinking of `strspn`'s return value as the index of the first character that's *not* in a specified set, we could think of it as the length of the longest "span" of characters that *are* in the set.

Exercises

Section 23.3

1. Write a program that finds the roots of the equation $ax^2 + bx + c = 0$ using the formula

$$x = \frac{-b \pm \sqrt{b^2 - 4ac}}{2a}$$

   Have the program prompt for the values of a, b, and c, then print both values of x. (If $b^2 - 4ac$ is negative, the program should instead print a message to the effect that the roots are imaginary.)

2. Extend the `round` function so that it rounds x to n digits after the decimal point. For example, the call `round(3.14159, 3)` would return 3.142. *Hint:* Multiply x by 10^n, round to the nearest integer, then divide by 10^n. Be sure that your function works correctly for both positive and negative values of x.

Section 23.4

3. Using `isalpha` and `isalnum`, write a function that checks whether a string has the syntax of a C identifier (that is, it consists of letters, digits, and underscores, with a letter or underscore at the beginning).

4. Write a program that copies a file from standard input to standard output, removing all blank lines (lines containing only white-space characters).

5. Write a program that copies a file from standard input to standard output, capitalizing the first letter in each word.

Section 23.5

6. In each of the following cases, indicate which function would be the best to use: `memcpy`, `memmove`, `strcpy`, or `strncpy`. Assume that the indicated action is to be performed by a single function call.

   (a) Moving all elements of an array "down" one position in order to leave room for a new element in position 0.
   (b) Deleting the first character in a null-terminated string by moving all other characters back one position.
   (c) Copying a string into a character array that may not be large enough to hold it. If the array is too small, assume that the string is to be truncated; no null character is necessary at the end.
   (d) Copying the contents of one array variable into another.

7. Section 23.5 explains how to call `strchr` repeatedly to locate all occurrences of a character within a string. Is it possible to locate all occurrences *in reverse order* by calling `strrchr` repeatedly?

8. Use `strchr` to write the following function:

   ```
   int numchar(const char *s, char ch);
   ```

   `numchar` returns the number of times the character `ch` occurs in the string `s`.

9. Replace the test condition in the following `if` statement by a single call of `strchr`:

   ```
   if (ch == 'a' || ch == 'b' || ch == 'c') ...
   ```

10. Replace the test condition in the following `if` statement by a single call of `strstr`:

    ```
    if (strcmp(str, "foo") == 0 || strcmp(str, "bar") == 0 ||
        strcmp(str, "baz") == 0) ...
    ```

    Hint: Combine the string literals into a single string, separating them with a special character. Does your solution assume anything about the contents of `str`?

11. Write a program that prompts the user to enter a series of words, then prints the words in reverse order. Read the input as a string, and then use `strtok` to break it into words.

12. Write a call of `memset` that replaces the last `n` characters in a null-terminated string `s` with `!` characters.

13. Many versions of `<string.h>` provide additional (nonstandard) functions, such as those listed below. Write each function using only the features of Standard C.

    (a) `strdup(s)` — Returns a pointer to a copy of s stored in memory obtained by calling `malloc`. Returns a null pointer if enough memory couldn't be allocated.

    (b) `stricmp(s1, s2)` — Similar to `strcmp`, but ignores the case of letters.

    (c) `strlwr(s)` — Converts upper-case letters in s to lower case, leaving other characters unchanged; returns s.

    (d) `strrev(s)` — Reverses the characters in s (except the null character); returns s.

    (e) `strset(s, ch)` — Fills s with copies of the character ch; returns s.

24 Error Handling

*There are two ways to write error-free
programs; only the third one works.*

Although student programs often fail when subjected to unexpected input, commercial programs need to be "bulletproof"—able to recover gracefully from errors instead of crashing. Making programs bulletproof requires that we anticipate errors that might arise during the execution of the program, include a check for each error, and provide a suitable action for the program to perform if the error should occur.

This chapter explores two ways for programs to check for errors: by calling assert (Section 24.1) and by checking the errno variable (Section 24.2). Section 24.3 explains how programs can detect and handle conditions known as *signals*, some of which represent errors. Finally, Section 24.4 explores the setjmp/longjmp mechanism, which is often used for responding to errors.

Error detection and handling aren't among C's strengths. C indicates run-time errors in a variety of ways rather than in a single, uniform way. Furthermore, it's the programmer's responsibility to include code to test for errors. As a result, it's easy to overlook potential errors; if one of these should actually occur, the program often continues running, albeit not very well. C++ tackles C's weaknesses head-on by providing an improved way to deal with errors known as *exception handling*.

exception handling in C++ ➤ 19.4

24.1 The <assert.h> Header: Diagnostics

```
void assert(int expression);
```

assert   assert, which is declared in the <assert.h> header, allows a program to monitor its own behavior and detect possible problems at an early stage.

Although `assert` is actually a macro, it's designed to be used like a function. It has one argument, which must be an "assertion"—an expression that we expect to be true under normal circumstances. Each time `assert` is executed, it checks the value of its argument. If the argument has a nonzero value, `assert` does nothing; if its value is zero, `assert` prints a message (to `stderr`, the standard error stream) and calls the `abort` function to terminate program execution.

stderr stream ➤22.1
abort function ➤26.2

For example, let's say that the file `demo.c` declares an array `a` of length `N`. We're concerned that the statement

```
a[i] = 0;
```

in `demo.c` might cause the program to fail because `i` is not between 0 and N–1. We can use `assert` to check this condition before we perform the assignment to `a[i]`:

```
assert(0 <= i && i < N);    /* checks subscript first */
a[i] = 0;                   /* now does the assignment */
```

If `i`'s value is less than 0 or greater than or equal to `N`, the program will terminate after displaying a message like the following one:

```
Assertion failed: 0 <= i && i < N, file DEMO.C, line 109
```

Standard C doesn't require that the message have exactly this form. However, it does require that the message specify the argument that was passed to `assert` (in text form), the name of the source file containing the `assert`, and the line number of the `assert`.

`assert` has one disadvantage: it increases the running time of a program because of the extra check it performs. Using `assert` once in a while probably won't have a great effect on a program's speed, but in time-critical applications, the increase in running time may not be acceptable. As a result, many programmers use `assert` during testing, then disable it when the program is finished. Disabling `assert` is easy: we need only define the macro `NDEBUG` prior to including the `<assert.h>` header:

```
#define NDEBUG
#include <assert.h>
```

The value of `NDEBUG` doesn't matter, just the fact that it's defined. If the program should fail later, we can reactivate `assert` by removing `NDEBUG`'s definition.

 Avoid putting an expression that has a side effect—including a function call—inside an `assert`; if `assert` is disabled at a later date, the expression won't be evaluated. Consider the following example:

```
assert((p = malloc(n+1)) != NULL);
```

If `NDEBUG` is defined, `assert` will be ignored and `malloc` won't be called.

24.2 The `<errno.h>` Header: Errors

lvalues ➤4.2

Some functions in the standard library indicate failure by storing an error code (a positive integer) in the `errno` variable, declared in `<errno.h>`. (`errno` may actually be a macro. If so, the C standard requires that it represent an lvalue, allowing us to use it like a variable.) Most of the functions that rely on `errno` belong to `<math.h>`, but there are a few in other parts of the library.

sqrt function ➤23.3

Let's say that we need to use a library function that signals an error by storing a value in `errno`. After calling the function, we can check whether the value of `errno` is nonzero; if so, an error occurred during the function call. For example, suppose that we want to check whether a call of the `sqrt` (square root) function has failed. Here's what the code would look like:

```
errno = 0;
y = sqrt(x);
if (errno != 0) {
  fprintf(stderr, "sqrt error; program terminated.\n");
  exit(EXIT_FAILURE);
}
```

It's important to store zero in `errno` before calling a library function—like `sqrt`—that may change it. Although `errno` is zero at the beginning of program execution, it could have been altered by a later function call. Library functions never clear `errno`; that's the program's responsibility.

Q&A

The value stored in `errno` when an error occurs is usually either EDOM or ERANGE. (Both are macros defined in `<errno.h>`.) These values reflect the two kinds of errors that can occur when a math function is called:

- ■ *Domain errors* (EDOM): An argument passed to a function is outside the function's domain. For example, passing a negative number to `sqrt` causes a domain error.

exp function ➤23.3

- ■ *Range errors* (ERANGE): A function's return value is too large to be represented as a `double` value. For example, passing 1000 to the `exp` function often causes a range error, because e^{1000} is too large to represent as a `double` on many computers.

Some functions can experience both kinds of errors; by comparing `errno` to EDOM or ERANGE, we can determine which error occurred.

The `perror` and `strerror` Functions

```
void perror(const char *s);
char *strerror(int errnum);
```

perror   When a library function stores a nonzero value in errno, we may want to display a message that indicates the nature of the error. One way to do this is to call the perror function (declared in <stdio.h>), which prints the following items, in the order shown: (1) its argument, (2) a colon, (3) a space, (4) an error message determined by the value of errno, and (5) a new-line character. The output of perror goes to the stderr stream, not to standard output.

stderr stream ➤22.1

Here's how we might use perror:

```
errno = 0;
y = sqrt(x);
if (errno != 0) {
  perror("sqrt error");
  exit(EXIT_FAILURE);
}
```

The error message that perror prints after sqrt error is implementation-defined. Here's one possibility:

```
sqrt error: Math argument
```

We're assuming that Math argument is the message that corresponds to the EDOM error. An ERANGE error usually produces a different message, such as Result too large.

strerror   The strerror function, which belongs to <string.h>, is closely related to perror. When passed an error code, strerror returns a pointer to a string describing the error. For example, the call

```
puts(strerror(EDOM));
```

might print

```
Math argument
```

The error message that perror displays is the same message that strerror would return if passed errno as its argument.

24.3   The <signal.h> Header: Signal Handling

<signal.h> provides facilities for handling exceptional conditions, known as *signals*. Signals fall into two categories: run-time errors (such as division by zero) and events caused outside the program. Many operating systems, for example, allow users to interrupt or kill running programs; these events are treated as signals in C. When an error or external event occurs, we say that a signal has been *raised*. Many signals are *asynchronous:* they can happen at any time during program execution, not just at certain points that are known to the programmer. Since signals may occur at unexpected times, they have to be dealt with in a unique way.

Signal Macros

<signal.h> defines a number of macros that represent signals; Table 24.1 lists these macros and their meanings. C implementations are allowed to provide other signal macros, as long as their names begin with SIG followed by an upper-case letter.

Table 24.1
Signals

Name	Meaning
SIGABRT	Abnormal termination (possibly caused by a call of abort)
SIGFPE	Error during an arithmetic operation (possibly division by zero or overflow)
SIGILL	Illegal instruction
SIGINT	Interrupt
SIGSEGV	Invalid storage access
SIGTERM	Termination request

The C standard doesn't require that the signals in Table 24.1 be raised automatically, since not all of them may be meaningful for a particular computer and operating system. Most implementations support at least some of these signals.

The **signal** Function

```
void (*signal(int sig, void (*func)(int)))(int);
```

signal   The most important function in <signal.h> is signal, which installs a signal-handling function for use later if a given signal should occur. signal is much easier to use than you might expect from its prototype. Its first argument is the code for a particular signal; the second argument is a pointer to a function that will handle the signal if it's raised later in the program. For example, the following call of signal installs a handler for the SIGINT signal:

```
signal(SIGINT, handler);
```

handler is the name of a signal-handling function. If the SIGINT signal occurs later during program execution, handler will be called automatically.

Every signal-handling function must have an int argument. When a particular signal is raised and its handler is called, the handler will be passed the code for the signal. Knowing which signal caused a handler to be called can be useful; in particular, it allows us to use the same handler for several different signals.

A signal-handling function can do almost anything it wants to. Possibilities include ignoring the signal, performing some sort of error recovery, or terminating *abort function* ➤ 26.2 the program. Unless it's invoked by abort or raise, however, a signal handler shouldn't call a library function or attempt to use a variable with static storage duration.

If a signal-handling function returns, the program resumes executing from the point at which the signal occurred. There are a couple of special cases, however. If the signal was SIGABRT, the program will terminate (abnormally) when the handler returns. The effect of returning from a function that has handled `SIGFPE` is undefined. (In other words, don't do it.)

Although `signal` has a return value, it's often discarded. The return value, a pointer to the previous handler for the specified signal, can be saved in a variable if desired. In particular, if we plan to restore the original signal handler later, we need to save `signal`'s return value:

```
void (*orig_handler)(int);    /* function pointer */

orig_handler = signal(SIGINT, handler);
```

This call installs `handler` as the handler for `SIGINT`, and saves a pointer to the original handler in the `orig_handler` variable. To restore the original handler later, we'd write

```
signal(SIGINT, orig_handler); /* restores original handler */
```

Predefined Signal Handlers

Instead of writing our own signal handlers, we have the option of using one of the predefined handlers that `<signal.h>` provides. There are two of these, each represented by a macro:

- **SIG_DFL.** SIG_DFL handles signals in a "default" way. To install SIG_DFL, we'd use a call such as

  ```
  signal(SIGINT, SIG_DFL);    /* use default handler */
  ```

  The effect of calling `SIG_DFL` is implementation-defined, but in most cases it causes program termination.
- **SIG_IGN.** The call

  ```
  signal(SIGINT, SIG_IGN);    /* ignore SIGINT signal */
  ```

  specifies that `SIGINT` is to be ignored if it should be raised later.

In addition to `SIG_DFL` and `SIG_IGN`, the `<signal.h>` header may provide other signal handlers; their names must begin with `SIG_` followed by an upper-case letter. At the beginning of program execution, the handler for each signal is initialized to either `SIG_DFL` or `SIG_IGN`, depending on the implementation.

`<signal.h>` defines another macro, `SIG_ERR`, that looks like it should be a signal handler. Actually, `SIG_ERR` isn't a handler at all; it's used to test for an error when installing a signal handler. If a call of `signal` is unsuccessful—it can't install a handler for the specified signal—it returns `SIG_ERR` and stores a positive value in `errno`. Thus, to test whether `signal` has failed, we could write

```
if (signal(SIGINT, handler) == SIG_ERR) {
  /* error; can't install handler for SIGINT */
}
```

There's one tricky aspect to the entire signal-handling mechanism: what happens if a signal is raised by the function that handles that signal? To prevent infinite recursion, the C standard requires that, when a handler is called for a signal other than SIGILL, the handler for that signal be reset to SIG_DFL (the default handler) or blocked in some other way. (We have no control over this process; it's all done behind the scenes.)

After a signal has been handled, it can't be handled a second time by the same function unless the handler is re-installed. One way to do that, of course, is to have the handler call signal before it returns.

The **raise** Function

```
int raise(int sig);
```

raise   Although signals usually arise spontaneously, it's occasionally handy for a program to cause a signal to occur. The raise function, which is also part of <signal.h>, does just that. The argument to raise specifies the code for the desired signal:

```
raise(SIGABRT);   /* raises the SIGABRT signal */
```

The return value of raise can be used to test whether the call was successful: zero indicates success, while a nonzero value indicates failure.

PROGRAM   **Testing Signals**

The following program illustrates the use of signals. First, it installs a custom handler for the SIGILL signal (carefully saving the original handler), then calls raise_sig to raise that signal. Next, it installs SIG_IGN as the handler for the SIGILL signal and calls raise_sig again. Finally, it reinstalls the original handler for SIGILL, then calls raise_sig one last time.

tsignal.c
```
/* Tests signals */

#include <signal.h>
#include <stdio.h>

void handler(int sig);
void raise_sig(void);

main()
{
  void (*orig_handler)(int);
```

```
    printf("Installing handler for signal %d\n", SIGILL);
    orig_handler = signal(SIGILL, handler);
    raise_sig();

    printf("Changing handler to SIG_IGN\n");
    signal(SIGILL, SIG_IGN);
    raise_sig();

    printf("Restoring original handler\n");
    signal(SIGILL, orig_handler);
    raise_sig();

    printf("Program terminates normally\n");
    return 0;
}

void handler(int sig)
{
    printf("Handler called for signal %d\n", sig);
}

void raise_sig(void)
{
    raise(SIGILL);
}
```

Incidentally, the call of raise doesn't need to be in a separate function. I defined raise_sig simply to make a point: regardless of where a signal is raised—whether it's in main or in some other function—it will be caught by the handler that was installed most recently.

The output of this program can vary somewhat, since a large part of the signal-handling mechanism is left undefined in the C standard. Here's one possibility:

```
Installing handler for signal 4
Handler called for signal 4
Changing handler to SIG_IGN
Restoring original handler
```

From this output, we see that SIGILL has the value 4 and that the original handler for SIGILL must have been SIG_DFL. (If it had been SIG_IGN, we'd see the message Program terminates normally.) Finally, we observe that SIG_DFL causes the program to terminate, but doesn't print an error message.

24.4   The `<setjmp.h>` Header: Nonlocal Jumps

```
int setjmp(jmp_buf env);
void longjmp(jmp_buf env, int val);
```

goto statement ➤6.4 Normally, a function returns to the point at which it was called. We can't use a goto statement to make it go elsewhere, because a goto can jump only to a label within the same function. The <setjmp.h> header, however, makes it possible for one function to jump directly to another function without returning.

The most important items in <setjmp.h> are the setjmp macro and the longjmp function. setjmp "marks" a place in a program; longjmp can then be used to return to that place later. Although this powerful mechanism has a variety of potential applications, it's used primarily for error handling.

setjmp
To mark the target of a future jump, we call setjmp, passing it a variable of type jmp_buf (defined in <setjmp.h>). setjmp stores the current "environ-

ment" (including a pointer to the location of the setjmp itself) in the variable for later use in a call of longjmp; it then returns zero.

longjmp
Returning to the point of the setjmp is done by calling longjmp, passing it the same jmp_buf variable that we passed to setjmp. After restoring the environment in the jmp_buf variable, longjmp will—here's where it gets tricky—*return from the* setjmp *call.* setjmp's return value this time is val, the second argument to longjmp. (If val is 0, however, setjmp returns 1.)

⚠ Be sure that the argument to longjmp was previously initialized by a call of setjmp. Otherwise, calling longjmp results in undefined behavior. (The program will probably crash.)

To summarize, setjmp returns zero the first time it's called; later, longjmp transfers control back to the original call of setjmp, which this time returns a nonzero value. Got it? Perhaps we need an example...

PROGRAM **Testing setjmp/longjmp**

The following program uses setjmp to mark a place in main; the function f2 later returns to that place by calling longjmp.

tsetjmp.c
```
/* Tests setjmp/longjmp */

#include <setjmp.h>
#include <stdio.h>

static jmp_buf env;

void f1(void);
void f2(void);

main()
{
  int ret;

  ret = setjmp(env);
  printf("setjmp returned %d\n", ret);
```

```
      if (ret != 0) {
        printf("Program terminates: longjmp called\n");
        return 0;
      }
      f1();
      printf("Program terminates normally\n");
      return 0;
    }

    void f1(void)
    {
      printf("f1 begins\n");
      f2();
      printf("f1 returns\n");
    }

    void f2(void)
    {
      printf("f2 begins\n");
      longjmp(env, 1);
      printf("f2 returns\n");
    }
```

The output of this program will be

```
setjmp returned 0
f1 begins
f2 begins
setjmp returned 1
Program terminates: longjmp called
```

The original call of setjmp returns 0, so main calls f1. Next, f1 calls f2, which uses longjmp to transfer control back to main instead of returning to f1. When longjmp is executed, control goes back to the setjmp call. This time, setjmp returns 1 (the value specified in the longjmp call).

Q & A

Q: **My version of `<errno.h>` defines other macros in addition to EDOM and ERANGE. Is this practice legal? [p. 541]**

A: Yes. The C standard allows macros that represent other error conditions, provided that their names begin with the letter E followed by a digit or an upper-case letter.

Q: **Some of the macros that represent signals have cryptic names, like SIGFPE and SIGSEGV. Where do these names come from? [p. 543]**

A: The names of signals date back to the early C compilers, which ran on a DEC PDP-11. The PDP-11 hardware could detect errors with names like "Floating Point Exception" and "Segmentation Violation."

*Q: I noticed a type named `sig_atomic_t` in the `<signal.h>` header. What's the purpose of this type?

A: `sig_atomic_t` is an integer type that can be accessed "as an atomic entity," according to the C standard. In other words, the CPU can fetch a `sig_atomic_t` value from memory or store one in memory with a single machine instruction, rather than using two or more machine instructions. `sig_atomic_t` is often defined to be `int`, since most CPUs can load or store an integer in one instruction.

Normally, a signal-handling function isn't supposed to access variables with static storage duration. However, the C standard allows one exception: a signal handler may store a value in a `sig_atomic_t` variable, provided that it's declared `volatile`. To see the reason for this arcane rule, consider what might happen if a signal-handler were to modify a static variable that's of a type larger than `sig_atomic_t`. If the program had fetched part of the variable from memory just before the signal occurred, then completed the fetch after the signal is handled, it could end up with a garbage value. `sig_atomic_t` variables can be fetched in a single step, and `volatile` variables must be fetched each time they're used, so the problem doesn't occur.

`volatile` type qualifier ➤ 20.3

Q: If signal-handling functions aren't supposed to call library functions, how can a signal handler call `signal` to re-install itself? [p. 545]

A: The C standard makes an exception for this case. A signal-handling function can legally call `signal`, provided that the first argument is the signal that it's handling at the moment.

Q: The `tsignal` program calls `printf` from inside a signal handler. Isn't that illegal?

A: There's another exception in the C standard: a signal-handling function invoked as a result of `raise` or `abort` may call library functions.

Q: How can `setjmp` modify the argument that's passed to it? I thought that C always passed arguments by value. [p. 547]

A: The C standard says that `jmp_buf` must be an array type, so `setjmp` is actually being passed a pointer.

Q: Sometimes my program won't compile when I use `setjmp`. What's the problem?

A: According to Standard C, there are only two legal ways to use `setjmp`:

- As an expression statement (possibly cast to `void`).
- As part of the controlling expression in an `if`, `switch`, `while`, `do`, or `for`. The entire controlling expression must have one of the following forms. (*constexp* is a constant expression that evaluates to an integer, and *op* is a relational or equality operator.)

```
setjmp(...)
!setjmp(...)
```

constexp op `setjmp(…)`
`setjmp(…)` *op constexp*

Some compilers allow calls of `setjmp` that don't follow these rules. But if you don't follow the rules, your program won't be portable.

Q: **After a call of `longjmp`, what are the values of variables in the program?**

A: Most variables retain the values they had at the time of the `longjmp`. However, an automatic variable inside the function that contains the `setjmp` doesn't have a definite value unless it was declared `volatile` or it hasn't been modified since the `setjmp` was performed.

Q: **Is it legal to call `longjmp` inside a signal handler?**

A: Yes, provided that the signal handler wasn't invoked because of a signal raised during the execution of a signal handler.

Exercises

Section 24.1

1. (a) Assertions can be used to test for two kinds of problems: (1) problems that should never occur if the program is correct, and (2) problems that are beyond the control of the program. Explain why `assert` is best suited for problems that fall into the first category.

    (b) Give three examples of problems that are beyond the control of the program.

Section 24.2

2. (a) Write a "wrapper" function named `try_math_fcn` that calls a math function (assumed to have a `double` argument and return a `double` value) and then checks whether the call succeeded. Here's how we might use `try_math_fcn`:

    ```
    y = try_math_fcn(sqrt, x, "Error in call of sqrt");
    ```

    If the call `sqrt(x)` is successful, `try_math_fcn` returns the value computed by `sqrt`. If the call fails, `try_math_fcn` calls `perror` to print the message `Error in call of sqrt`, then calls `exit` to terminate the program.

    (b) Write a macro that has the same effect as `try_math_fcn` but builds the error message from the function's name:

    ```
    y = TRY_MATH_FCN(sqrt, x);
    ```

    If the call of `sqrt` fails, the message will be `Error in call of sqrt`. *Hint:* Have `TRY_MATH_FCN` call `try_math_fcn`.

Section 24.3

3. Write a signal handler for `SIGINT` that keeps track of how many times it's been called. The handler must ignore the signal the first two times it occurs, but terminate the program (by calling `exit`) when it occurs for the third time.

Section 24.4

4. In the `invent` program (Section 16.3), the `main` function has a `for` loop that prompts the user to enter an operation code, reads the code, and then calls either `insert`, `search`, `update`, or `print`. Add a call of `setjmp` to `main` in such a way that a subsequent call of `longjmp` will return to the `for` loop. (After the `longjmp`, the user will be prompted for an operation code, and the program will continue normally.) `setjmp` will need a `jmp_buf` variable; where should it be declared?

25 **International Features**

*If your computer speaks English
it was probably made in Japan.*

As originally designed, C wasn't especially suitable for use in many countries. Classic C assumes that characters are single bytes and that all computers recognize the characters #, [, \,], ^, {, |, }, and ~, which are needed to write C programs. Unfortunately, these assumptions aren't valid in all parts of the world. The experts who created Standard C in the 1980s saw the importance of making C an international language. This chapter describes the features they added to the language and library for the benefit of international programmers.

The <locale.h> header (Section 25.1) provides functions that allow a program to tailor its behavior to a particular "locale"—perhaps a country, a state or province, or a particular culture. Multibyte characters and wide characters (Section 25.2) enable programs to work with large character sets like those found in Asian countries. Trigraph sequences (Section 25.3) make it possible to write programs on computers that lack some of the characters normally used in C programming.

The importance of C to the international community was underscored in 1994 with the approval of Amendment 1 to the ISO C standard. This amendment describes additional library support for international programming, including the new headers <iso646.h>, <wctype.h>, and <wchar.h>. Since it's not yet in widespread use (and this book is already too long), I won't go into the details of Amendment 1. For additional information, see Harbison and Steele, *C: A Reference Manual*, Fourth Edition (Englewood Cliffs, N.J.: Prentice-Hall, 1995).

25.1 The `<locale.h>` Header: Localization

The <locale.h> header provides functions to control aspects of the library that vary from one locale to another. A *locale* is often a country, but it need not be. Different regions of a country could be treated as separate locales, for example; locales could even represent different cultures within a single region.

Locale-dependent aspects of the library include:

- ■ *Formatting of numerical values.* In some locales, for example, the decimal point is a period (297.48), while in others it's a comma (297,48).
- ■ *Formatting of monetary values.* For example, the currency symbol varies from country to country.
- ■ *Character set.* The character set often depends on the language in a particular locale. Asian countries usually require a much larger character set than Western countries.
- ■ *Appearance of date and time.* In some locales, for example, it's customary to put the month first when writing a date (8/24/97); in others, the day goes first (24/8/97).

Categories

By changing locale, a program can adapt its behavior to different parts of the world. But a locale change can affect many aspects of the library, some of which we might prefer not to alter. Fortunately, we're not required to change all aspects of a locale at the same time. Instead, we can use one of the following macros to specify a *category:*

<string.h> header ➤23.5
- ■ LC_COLLATE. Affects the behavior of two string-comparison functions, strcoll and strxfrm. (Both functions are declared in <string.h>).

<ctype.h> header ➤23.4

multibyte functions ➤25.2
- ■ LC_CTYPE. Affects the behavior of the functions in <ctype.h> (except isdigit and isxdigit). Also affects the multibyte functions in <stdlib.h>.
- ■ LC_MONETARY. Affects the monetary formatting information returned by the localeconv function. Doesn't affect the behavior of any library functions.

string conversion functions ➤26.2
- ■ LC_NUMERIC. Affects the decimal-point character used by formatted I/O functions (like printf and scanf) and the string conversion functions (atof and strtod) in <stdlib.h>. Also affects the nonmonetary formatting information returned by localeconv.

strftime function ➤26.3
- ■ LC_TIME. Affects the behavior of the strftime function (declared in <time.h>), which converts a time into a character string.

Implementations are free to provide other categories and define LC_ macros not listed above.

The **setlocale** Function

```
char *setlocale(int category, const char *locale);
```

setlocale   The `setlocale` function changes the current locale, either for a single category or for all categories. If the first argument is one of the macros `LC_COLLATE`, `LC_CTYPE`, `LC_MONETARY`, `LC_NUMERIC`, or `LC_TIME`, a call of `setlocale` affects only a single category. If the first argument is `LC_ALL`, the call affects all categories. The C standard defines only two values for the second argument: `"C"` and `""`. Other locales, if any, depend on the implementation.

At the beginning of every program's execution, the call

```
setlocale(LC_ALL, "C");
```

occurs behind the scenes. In the `"C"` locale, library functions behave in the "normal" way, and the decimal point is a period.

Changing locale after the program has begun execution requires an explicit call of `setlocale`. Calling `setlocale` with `""` as the second argument switches to the *native locale,* allowing the program to adapt its behavior to the local environment. The C standard doesn't define the exact effect of switching to the native locale. Some implementations of `setlocale` check the execution environment (in the same way as `getenv`) for an environment variable with a particular name (perhaps the same as the category macro). Some don't do anything at all. (The standard doesn't require `setlocale` to have any effect. Of course, a library whose version of `setlocale` does nothing isn't likely to sell too well in some parts of the world.)

getenv function ➤26.2

We can't say much about locales other than `"C"` and `""`, since they vary considerably from one compiler to another. Some implementations may not provide any other locales. Others may provide locales with names like `"Germany"`. One popular compiler uses cryptic strings like `"en_GB.WIN1252"` to represent locales. `en` indicates the language (English), `GB` the country (Great Britain), and `WIN1252` the character set (Windows multilingual).

When a call of `setlocale` succeeds, it returns a pointer to a string associated with the category in the new locale. (The string might be the locale name itself, for example.) On failure, `setlocale` returns a null pointer.

`setlocale` can also be used as a query function. If its second argument is a null pointer, `setlocale` returns a pointer to a string associated with the category in the *current* locale. This feature is especially useful if the first argument is `LC_ALL`, since it allows us to fetch the current settings for all categories. A string returned by `setlocale` can be saved (by copying it into a variable) and then used in a later call of `setlocale`.

Q&A

The `localeconv` Function

```
struct lconv *localeconv(void);
```

localeconv   Although we can ask `setlocale` about the current locale, the information that it returns isn't necessarily in the most useful form. To find out highly specific information about the current locale (What's the decimal-point character? What's the currency symbol?), we need `localeconv`, the only other function declared in `<locale.h>`.

`localeconv` returns a pointer to a structure of type `struct lconv`, which contains detailed information about the current locale. This structure has static storage duration and may be modified by a later call of `localeconv` or `setlocale`. Be sure to extract the desired information from the `lconv` structure before it's wiped out by one of these functions.

Some members of the `lconv` structure have `char *` type; other members have `char` type. Table 25.1 lists the `char *` members. The first three members deal with the formatting of nonmonetary values, while the others have to do with monetary values. The table also shows the value of each member in the `"C"` locale (the default); a value of `" "` means "not available."

Table 25.1

`char *` Members of `lconv` Structure

	Name	Value in "C" Locale	Description
Nonmonetary	decimal_point	" . "	Decimal-point character
	thousands_sep	" "	Character used to separate groups of digits before decimal point
	grouping	" "	Sizes of digit groups
Monetary	int_curr_symbol	" "	International currency symbol*
	currency_symbol	" "	Local currency symbol
	mon_decimal_point	" "	Decimal-point character
	mon_thousands_sep	" "	Character used to separate groups of digits before decimal point
	mon_grouping	" "	Sizes of digit groups
	positive_sign	" "	String indicating nonnegative value
	negative_sign	" "	String indicating negative value

*A three-letter abbreviation followed by a separator (often a space or a period). For example, the international currency symbols for Italy, Netherlands, Norway, and Switzerland are `"ITL. "`, `"NLG  "`, `"NOK  "`, and `"CHF  "`, respectively.

The `grouping` and `mon_grouping` members deserve special mention. Each character in these strings specifies the size of one group of digits. (Grouping takes place from right to left, starting at the decimal point.) A value of `CHAR_MAX` indicates that no further grouping is to be performed; 0 indicates that the previous element should be used for the remaining digits. For example, the string `"\3 "` (`\3` followed by `\0`) indicates that the first group should have 3 digits, then all other digits should be grouped in 3's as well.

Table 25.2 lists the `char` members of the `lconv` structure and shows the value of each member in the `"C"` locale; a value of `CHAR_MAX` means "not available." All members in Table 25.2 have to do with the formatting of monetary values. Table 25.3 shows how to interpret the values of the `p_sign_posn` and `n_sign_posn` members.

Table 25.2
char Members of
lconv Structure

Name	Value in "C" Locale	Description
int_frac_digits	CHAR_MAX	Number of digits after decimal point (international formatting)
frac_digits	CHAR_MAX	Number of digits after decimal point (local formatting)
p_cs_precedes	CHAR_MAX	1 if currency_symbol precedes nonnegative value; 0 if it succeeds value
p_sep_by_space	CHAR_MAX	1 if currency_symbol is separated by space from nonnegative value; 0 if not
n_cs_precedes	CHAR_MAX	1 if currency_symbol precedes negative value; 0 if it succeeds value
n_sep_by_space	CHAR_MAX	1 if currency_symbol is separated by space from negative value; 0 if not
p_sign_posn	CHAR_MAX	Position of positive_sign for nonnegative value (see Table 25.3)
n_sign_posn	CHAR_MAX	Position of negative_sign for negative value (see Table 25.3)

Table 25.3
Values of
p_sign_posn and
n_sign_posn

Value	Meaning
0	Parentheses surround quantity and currency_symbol
1	Sign precedes quantity and currency_symbol
2	Sign succeeds quantity and currency_symbol
3	Sign immediately precedes currency_symbol
4	Sign immediately succeeds currency_symbol

To see how the members of the lconv structure might vary from one locale to another, let's compare two hypothetical examples. Table 25.4 shows typical values of the monetary lconv members for the USA and Italy (the latter example is from the C standard itself).

Table 25.4
Typical Values of
Monetary lconv
Members for
USA and Italy

Member	USA	Italy
int_curr_symbol	"USD "	"ITL."
currency_symbol	"$"	"L."
mon_decimal_point	"."	""
mon_thousands_sep	","	"."
mon_grouping	"\3"	"\3"
positive_sign	""	""
negative_sign	"-"	"-"
int_frac_digits	2	0
frac_digits	2	0
p_cs_precedes	1	1
p_sep_by_space	0	0
n_cs_precedes	1	1
n_sep_by_space	0	0
p_sign_posn	4	1
n_sign_posn	4	1

Here's how the monetary amount 7593 would be formatted in the two locales:

	USA	*Italy*
Positive format	$7,593.00	L.7.593
Negative format	$-7,593.00	-L.7.593
International format	USD 7,593.00	ITL.7.593

Keep in mind that none of C's library functions are able to format monetary values automatically. It's up to each program to use the information in the lconv structure to accomplish the formatting.

25.2 Multibyte Characters and Wide Characters

One of the biggest problems in adapting programs to different locales is the character set issue. In the U.S., the majority of computers use the ASCII character set, and most of the others use EBCDIC. Outside the U.S., the situation is more complicated. In many countries, computers employ character sets that are similar to ASCII, but lack certain characters; we'll discuss this issue further in Section 25.3. Other countries, especially those in Asia, face a different problem: written languages that require a very large character set, usually numbering in the thousands.

Changing the meaning of type char to handle larger character sets isn't possible, since char values, by definition, are limited to single bytes. Instead, C allows compilers to provide an ***extended*** character set. This character set may be used for writing C programs (in comments and strings, for example), in the environment in which the program is run, or in both places. C provides two encodings for an extended character set: ***multibyte characters*** and ***wide characters.*** It also provides functions that convert from one encoding to the other.

Multibyte Characters

In a ***multibyte character*** encoding, one or more bytes represent each extended character. Any extended character set must include the essential characters that C requires (letters, digits, operators, punctuation, and white-space characters); these characters are required to be single bytes. Other bytes can be interpreted as the beginning of a multibyte character.

Japanese Character Sets

The Japanese employ four different writing systems. The most complex, *kanji*, consists of thousands of symbols—far too many to represent in a one-byte encoding. (*Kanji* symbols actually come from Chinese, which has a similar problem with large character sets.) There's no single way to encode *kanji*; common encodings include JIS (Japan Industrial Standard), Shift-JIS, and EUC (Extended UNIX Code).

Some multibyte character sets rely on a ***state-dependent encoding.*** In this kind of encoding, each sequence of multibyte characters begins in an ***initial shift state.*** Certain multibyte characters encountered later in the sequence change the shift state, affecting the meaning of subsequent bytes. Japan's JIS encoding, for example, mixes one-byte codes with two-byte codes; "escape sequences" embedded in strings indicate when to switch between one-byte and two-byte modes. (In contrast, the Shift-JIS encoding is not state-dependent. Each character requires either one or two bytes, but the first byte of a two-byte character can always be distinguished from a one-byte character.)

In any encoding, the C standard requires that a zero byte always represent a null character, regardless of shift state. Also, a zero byte can't be the second (or later) byte of a multibyte character.

The C library provides two macros, MB_LEN_MAX and MB_CUR_MAX, related to multibyte characters. Both macros specify the maximum number of bytes in a multibyte character. MB_LEN_MAX (defined in <limits.h>) gives the maximum for *any* supported locale, while MB_CUR_MAX (defined in <stdlib.h>) gives the maximum for the *current* locale. (Changing locales may affect the interpretation of multibyte characters.) Obviously, MB_CUR_MAX can't be larger than MB_LEN_MAX.

Wide Characters

The other way to encode an extended character set is to use ***wide characters.*** A wide character is an integer whose value represents a character. Unlike multibyte characters, which may vary in length, all wide characters supported by a particular implementation require the same number of bytes.

Wide characters have the type wchar_t (defined in <stddef.h> and <stdlib.h>), which must be an integral type able to represent the largest extended character set for any supported locale. For example, if two bytes are enough to represent any extended character set, then wchar_t could be defined as unsigned short int.

One advantage of using wide characters is that C supports wide character constants and wide string literals. Wide character constants resemble ordinary character constants but are prefixed by the letter L:

```
L'a'
```

Wide string literals are also prefixed by L:

```
L"abc"
```

This string represents an array containing the wide characters L'a', L'b', and L'c', followed by a wide character whose code is zero.

Unicode

Wide characters are well-suited for character sets with a fixed-length encoding. An important example is **Unicode,** an attempt at a universal character set—one that every country can use. Unicode is currently supported by Windows NT; in time, it will likely become a feature of other operating systems as well. Each Unicode character occupies two bytes, so Unicode can represent as many as 65,536 characters, leaving plenty of room for the alphabets required by all modern languages, as well as some archaic languages (Sanskrit, for example). Unicode also includes a number of specialized symbols, such as those used in mathematics.

Multibyte Character Functions

```
int mblen(const char *s, size_t n);
int mbtowc(wchar_t *pwc, const char *s, size_t n);
int wctomb(char *s, wchar_t wchar);
```

mblen   The mblen function checks whether its first argument points to a series of bytes that form a valid multibyte character. If so, the function returns the number of bytes in the character; if not, it returns –1. As a special case, mblen returns 0 if the first argument points to a null character. The second argument limits the number of bytes that mblen will examine; typically, we'll pass MB_CUR_MAX.

The following function uses mblen to determine whether a string consists of valid multibyte characters. (This example and the wccheck example later in the section are from P. J. Plauger's *The Standard C Library* (Englewood Cliffs, N.J.: Prentice-Hall, 1992).) The function returns zero if s points to a valid string:

```
int mbcheck(const char *s)
{
  int n;

  for (mblen(NULL, 0); ; s += n)
    if ((n = mblen(s, MB_CUR_MAX)) <= 0)
      return n;
}
```

Two aspects of the mbcheck function deserve special mention. First, there's the mysterious call mblen(NULL, 0). It turns out that mblen keeps track of the shift state in a static variable. The call mblen(NULL, 0) sets this variable to its initial state so that characters later in the string will be interpreted properly. (Passing a null pointer to mbtowc or wctomb has a similar effect. Each function has its own shift state, by the way.) Later calls of mblen may change the shift state. Second, there's the matter of termination. Keep in mind that s points to an ordinary character string, which is assumed to end with a null character. mblen will return zero when it reaches this null character, causing mbcheck to return.

mbtowc   The mbtowc function converts a multibyte character (pointed to by the second argument) into a wide character. The first argument points to the variable into which the function will store the result. The third argument limits the number of bytes that mbtowc will examine. mbtowc returns the same value as mblen: the number of bytes in the character if it's valid, −1 if it's not, and zero if the second argument points to a null character.

wctomb   The wctomb function converts a wide character (the second argument) into a multibyte character, which it stores into the array pointed to by the first argument. wctomb may store as many as MB_LEN_MAX characters into the array, but doesn't append a null character. The conversion takes the current shift state into account, and updates the shift state if needed. wctomb returns the number of bytes in the character if it's valid, −1 if it's not. (Note that wctomb returns 1 if asked to convert a null wide character.)

The following function uses wctomb to determine whether a string of wide characters can be converted to valid multibyte characters:

```
int wccheck(wchar_t *wcs)
{
  char buf[MB_LEN_MAX];
  int n;

  for (wctomb(NULL, 0); ; ++wcs)
    if ((n = wctomb(buf, *wcs)) <= 0)
      return -1;                  /* invalid character */
    else if (buf[n-1] == '\0')
      return 0;                   /* all characters are valid */
}
```

Incidentally, all three functions—mblen, mbtowc, and wctomb—can be used to test whether a multibyte encoding is state-dependent. When passed a null pointer as its char * argument, each function returns a nonzero value if multibyte characters have state-dependent encodings or zero if they don't.

Multibyte String Functions

```
size_t mbstowcs(wchar_t *pwcs, const char *s,
                size_t n);
size_t wcstombs(char *s, const wchar_t *pwcs,
                size_t n);
```

mbstowcs   The mbstowcs function converts a multibyte string into a sequence of wide characters. The second argument points to the multibyte string, while the first argument points to an array of wide characters. The third argument limits the number of wide characters that can be stored in the array. mbstowcs stops when it reaches the limit or encounters a null character (which it stores in the wide character array). It returns the number of array elements modified, not including the terminating zero code, if any. mbstowcs returns −1 if it encounters an invalid multibyte character.

wcstombs   The wcstombs function is the opposite of mbstowcs: it converts a string of wide characters into multibyte characters. The second argument points to the wide character string. The first argument points to the array in which the multibyte characters are to be stored. The third argument limits the number of bytes that can be stored in the array. wcstombs stops when it reaches the limit or encounters a null character (which it stores). It returns the number of bytes stored, not including the terminating null character, if any. wcstombs returns −1 if it encounters a wide character that doesn't correspond to any multibyte character.

The mbstowcs function assumes that the string to be converted begins in the initial shift state. The string created by wcstombs always begins in the initial shift state.

25.3 Trigraph Sequences

A *trigraph sequence* (or simply, a "trigraph") is a three-character code that can be used as an alternative to an ASCII character. The problem that trigraphs address is simple: C programs require the characters #, [, \,], ^, {, |, }, and ~. Many European countries use variants of ASCII that lack some of these characters. In Germany, for example, the characters [, \,], {, |, }, and ~ are replaced by Ä, Ö, Ü, ä, ö, ü, and ß, respectively. Trigraphs provide a way to write valid C programs without using any of the missing characters.

Table 25.5 gives a complete list of trigraphs. All trigraphs begin with ??, which makes them, if not exactly attractive, at least easy to spot.

Table 25.5
Trigraph Sequences

Trigraph Sequence	ASCII Equivalent
??=	#
??(	[
??/	\
??)	]
??'	^
??<	{
??!	|
??>	}
??-	~

Trigraphs can be freely substituted for their ASCII equivalents. For example, the program

```
#include <stdio.h>

main()
{
  printf("hello, world\n");
  return 0;
}
```

could be written

```
??=include <stdio.h>

main()
??<
  printf("hello, world??/n");
  return 0;
??>
```

All Standard C compilers are required to accept trigraphs, even though they're not always needed. Occasionally, this feature can cause problems.

Be careful about putting ?? in a string—it's possible that the compiler will treat it as the beginning of a trigraph. If this should happen, turn the second ? character into an escape sequence by preceding it with a \ character. The resulting ?\? combination can't be mistaken for the beginning of a trigraph.

Q & A

Q: **How long is the locale information string returned by `setlocale`? [p. 553]**

A: There's no maximum length, which raises a question: how can we set aside space for the string if we don't know how long it will be? The answer, of course, is dynamic storage allocation. The following example (based on a similar example in Harbison and Steele's *C: A Reference Manual*) shows how to determine the amount of space needed, then copy the locale information into that space:

```
char *temp, *old_locale;

temp = setlocale(LC_ALL, NULL);
if (temp == NULL) {
  /* locale information not available */
}
old_locale = malloc(strlen(temp) + 1);
if (old_locale == NULL) {
  /* memory allocation failed */
}
strcpy(old_locale, temp);
```

To restore the old locale information, we'd first switch to the native locale, then restore the old locale:

```
setlocale(LC_ALL, "");          /* switch to native locale */
setlocale(LC_ALL, old_locale); /* restore old locale */
```

Q: **Why does C provide both multibyte characters and wide characters? Wouldn't either one be enough by itself? [p. 556]**

A: The two encodings serve different purposes. Multibyte characters are handy for input/output purposes, since I/O devices are often byte-oriented. Wide characters, on the other hand, are more convenient to work with inside a program, since every wide character occupies the same amount of space. Thus, a program might read multibyte input, convert it to wide character form for manipulation within the program, and then convert it back to multibyte form for output.

Exercises

Section 25.1

1.   Determine which locales are supported by your compiler.

2.   Write a program that tests whether your compiler's `" "` (native) locale is the same as its `"C"` locale.

Section 25.2

3.   The Shift-JIS encoding for *kanji* requires either one or two bytes per character. If the first byte of a character is between `0x81` and `0x9f` or between `0xe0` and `0xef`, a second byte is required. (Any other byte is treated as a whole character.) The second byte must be between `0x40` and `0x7e` or between `0x80` and `0xfc`. (All ranges are inclusive.) For each of the following strings, give the value that the `mbcheck` function of Section 25.2 will return when passed that string as its argument.

   (a) `"\x05\x87\x80\x36\xed\xaa"`
   (b) `"\x20\xe4\x50\x88\x3f"`
   (c) `"\xde\xad\xbe\xef"`
   (d) `"\x8a\x60\x92\x74\x41"`

Section 25.3

4.   Modify the following program fragment by replacing as many characters as possible by trigraphs.

```
while ((orig_char = getchar()) != EOF) {
  new_char = orig_char ^ KEY;
  if (iscntrl(orig_char) || iscntrl(new_char))
    putchar(orig_char);
  else
    putchar(new_char);
}
```

26 Miscellaneous Library Functions

It is the user who should parametrize
procedures, not their creators.

Our final chapter looks at the three remaining headers in the standard library: <stdarg.h>, <stdlib.h>, and <time.h>. These headers are unlike any others in the library, so I've saved them for last. The <stdarg.h> header (Section 26.1) makes it possible to write functions with a variable number of arguments. The <stdlib.h> header (Section 26.2) is an assortment of functions that don't fit into one of the other library headers. The <time.h> header (Section 26.3) allows programs to work with dates and times.

26.1 The `<stdarg.h>` Header: Variable Arguments

```
void va_start(va_list ap, parmN);
type va_arg(va_list ap, type);
void va_end(va_list ap);
```

We've seen that functions such as printf and scanf have no fixed limit on the number of arguments they accept. The ability to handle a variable number of arguments isn't limited to library functions, however. The <stdarg.h> header provides the tools we'll need to write our own functions with variable-length argument lists. <stdarg.h> defines one type, va_list, and three macros. These macros, named va_start, va_arg, and va_end, can be thought of as functions with the prototypes shown above.

To see how these macros work, we'll use them to write a function named max_int that finds the maximum of *any* number of integer arguments. Here's how we might call the function:

```
max_int(3, 10, 30, 20)
```

The first argument specifies how many additional arguments follow. This call of max_int will return 30 (the largest of the numbers 10, 30, and 20).

Here's the definition of the max_int function:

```
int max_int(int n, ...)    /* n must be at least 1 */
{
  va_list ap;
  int i, current, largest;

  va_start(ap, n);
  largest = va_arg(ap, int);

  for (i = 1; i < n; i++) {
    current = va_arg(ap, int);
    if (current > largest)
      largest = current;
  }

  va_end(ap);
  return largest;
}
```

The ... symbol in the parameter list (known as an ***ellipsis***) indicates that the parameter n is followed by a variable number of additional parameters.

The body of max_int begins with the declaration of a variable of type va_list:

```
va_list ap;
```

Declaring such a variable is mandatory for max_int to be able to access the arguments that follow n.

va_start   The statement

```
va_start(ap, n);
```

indicates where the variable-length part of the argument list begins (in this case, after n). A function with a variable number of arguments must have at least one "normal" parameter; the ellipsis always goes at the end of the parameter list, after the last normal parameter.

va_arg   The statement

```
largest = va_arg(ap, int);
```

fetches max_int's second argument (the one after n), assigns it to largest, and automatically advances to the next argument. The word int indicates that we expect max_int's second argument to have int type. The statement

```
current = va_arg(ap, int);
```

fetches `max_int`'s remaining arguments, one by one, as it is executed inside a loop.

Don't forget that `va_arg` always advances to the next argument after fetching the current one. Because of this property, we couldn't have written `max_int`'s loop in the following way:

```
for (i = 1; i < n; i++)
  if (va_arg(ap, int) > largest)    /*** WRONG ***/
    largest = va_arg(ap, int);
```

va_end   The statement

```
va_end(ap);
```

is required to "clean up" before the function returns. (Instead of returning, the function might call `va_start` and traverse the argument list again.)

default argument promotions ➤9.3   When a function with a variable argument list is called, the compiler performs the default argument promotions on all arguments that match the ellipsis: character values are promoted to integers, and `float` values are promoted to `double`. Consequently, it doesn't make sense to pass a character type or `float` to `va_arg`, since arguments—after promotion—will never have one of those types.

Calling a Function with a Variable Argument List

Calling a function with a variable argument list is an inherently risky proposition. As far back as Chapter 3, we saw how dangerous it can be to pass the wrong arguments to `printf` and `scanf`. Other functions with variable argument lists are equally sensitive. The primary difficulty is that a function with a variable argument list has no easy way to determine how many arguments were passed or what their types are. This information must be passed into the function and/or assumed by the function. `max_int` relies on the first argument to specify how many additional arguments follow; it assumes that the arguments are of type `int`. Functions like `printf` and `scanf` rely on the format string, which describes the number of additional arguments and the type of each.

Another problem has to do with passing NULL as an argument. NULL is usually defined to represent 0. When 0 is passed to a function with a variable argument list, the compiler assumes that it represents an integer—there's no way it can tell that we want it to represent the null pointer. The solution is to add a cast, writing `(void *) NULL` instead of NULL. (See the Q&A section at the end of Chapter 17 for more discussion of this point.)

The v...printf Functions

```
int vfprintf(FILE *stream, const char *format,
             va_list arg);
int vprintf(const char *format, va_list arg);
int vsprintf(char *s, const char *format,
             va_list arg);
```

vfprintf
vprintf
vsprintf

The vfprintf, vprintf, and vsprintf functions (the "v...printf func-tions") belong to <stdio.h>. We're discussing them in this section because they're invariably used in conjunction with the macros in <stdarg.h>.

The v...printf functions are closely related to fprintf, printf, and sprintf. Unlike these functions, however, the v...printf functions have a fixed number of arguments. Each function's last argument is a va_list value, which implies that it will be called by a function with a variable argument list. In practice, the v...printf functions are used primarily for writing "wrapper" func-tions that accept a variable number of arguments, which are then passed to a v...printf function.

As an example, let's say that we're working on a program that needs to dis-play error messages from time to time. We'd like each message to begin with a prefix of the form

```
** Error n:
```

where *n* is 1 for the first error message and increases by one for each subsequent error. To make it easier to produce error messages, we'll write a function named errorf that's similar to printf, but adds ** Error n: to the beginning of its output and always writes to stderr instead of stdout. We'll have errorf call vfprintf to do most of the actual output. Here's what errorf might look like:

```
int errorf(const char *format, ...)
{
  static int num_errors = 0;
  int n;
  va_list ap;

  num_errors++;
  fprintf(stderr, "** Error %d: ", num_errors);
  va_start(ap, format);
  n = vfprintf(stderr, format, ap);
  va_end(ap);
  fprintf(stderr, "\n");
  return n;
}
```

26.2   The `<stdlib.h>` Header: General Utilities

`<stdlib.h>` serves as a catch-all for functions that don't fit into any of the other headers. The functions in `<stdlib.h>` fall into seven unrelated groups:

> String conversion functions
> Pseudo-random sequence generation functions
> Memory management functions
> Communication with the environment
> Searching and sorting utilities
> Integer arithmetic functions
> Multibyte character and string functions

We'll look at each group in turn, with two exceptions: the memory management functions and the multibyte character and string functions.

The memory management functions (`malloc`, `calloc`, `realloc`, and `free`) permit a program to allocate a block of memory and then later release it or change its size. Chapter 17 describes all four functions in some detail.

The multibyte character and string functions allow programs to manipulate characters that are more than one byte long. Section 25.2 discusses multibyte characters and explains what the multibyte functions do.

String Conversion Functions

```
double atof(const char *nptr);
int atoi(const char *nptr);
long int atol(const char *nptr);
double strtod(const char *nptr, char **endptr);
long int strtol(const char *nptr, char **endptr,
                int base);
unsigned long int strtoul(const char *nptr,
                          char **endptr, int base);
```

The functions in this group convert strings containing numbers in character form to their equivalent numeric values. Three of these functions are fairly old, while the other three were added during the standardization of C.

atof
atoi
atol

The old functions (`atof`, `atoi`, and `atol`) convert a string to a `double`, `int`, or `long int` value, respectively. Each function skips white-space characters at the beginning of the string, treats subsequent characters as part of a number, and stops at the first character that can't be part of the number.

strtod
strtol
strtoul

The new functions (`strtod`, `strtol`, and `strtoul`) are more sophisticated. For one thing, they indicate where the conversion stopped by modifying the variable that `endptr` points to. (The second argument can be a null pointer if we're not interested in where the conversion ended.) To check whether a function was able to consume the entire string, we can just test whether this variable points to a null character. What's more, `strtol` and `strtoul` have a `base` argument that specifies the base of the number being converted. All bases between 2 and 36 (inclusive) are supported.

Besides being more versatile than the old functions, the new functions are better at handling errors. The old functions lack any way to indicate how much of the string was consumed during a conversion. Moreover, the old functions return zero if they can't locate a number to convert; they return an undefined value if the number is too large. As a result, neither problem can be detected by checking the function's return value. The new functions store `ERANGE` in `errno` if a conversion produces a value that's too large (or too small) to represent.

<errno.h> header ➤24.2

With the addition of `strtod`, `strtol`, and `strtoul`, the `atof`, `atoi`, and `atol` functions are redundant. They remain in the library for the benefit of older C programs, but `strtod`, `strtol`, and `strtoul` are recommended for new programs.

PROGRAM   **Testing the String Conversion Functions**

The following program converts a string to numeric form by applying each of the six string conversion functions. After calling the `strtod`, `strtol`, and `strtoul` functions, the program also displays an indication of whether each conversion produced a valid result and whether it was able to consume the entire string. The program obtains the input string from the command line.

tstrconv.c

```
/* Tests string conversion functions */

#include <errno.h>
#include <stdio.h>
#include <stdlib.h>

#define CHK_VALID  printf("      %s              %s\n",           \
                          errno != ERANGE ? "Yes" : "No ", \
                          *ptr == '\0' ? "Yes" : "No");

main(int argc, char *argv[])
{
  char *ptr;

  if (argc != 2) {
    printf("usage: tstrconv string\n");
    exit(EXIT_FAILURE);
  }

  printf("Function    Return Value\n");
  printf("--------    ------------\n");
  printf("atof        %g\n", atof(argv[1]));
  printf("atoi        %d\n", atoi(argv[1]));
  printf("atol        %ld\n\n", atol(argv[1]));
```

```
    printf("Function    Return Value    Valid?    "
           "String Consumed?\n"
           "--------    ------------    ------    "
           "----------------\n");

    errno = 0;
    printf("strtod     %-12g", strtod(argv[1], &ptr));
    CHK_VALID;

    errno = 0;
    printf("strtol     %-12ld", strtol(argv[1], &ptr, 10));
    CHK_VALID;

    errno = 0;
    printf("strtoul    %-12lu", strtoul(argv[1], &ptr, 10));
    CHK_VALID;

    return 0;
}
```

If 3000000000 is the command-line argument, the output of tstrconv might have the following appearance:

```
Function    Return Value
--------    ------------
atof        3e+09
atoi        24064
atol        -1294967296

Function    Return Value    Valid?    String Consumed?
--------    ------------    ------    ----------------
strtod      3e+09           Yes       Yes
strtol      2147483647      No        Yes
strtoul     3000000000      Yes       Yes
```

On many machines, the number 3000000000 is too large to represent as a long integer, although it's valid as an unsigned long integer. The atoi and atol functions can't detect the problem, and end up returning strange values. The strtoul function performs the conversion correctly, while strtol returns 2147483647 (the largest long integer) and stores ERANGE in errno.

If 123.456 is the command-line argument, the output will be

```
Function    Return Value
--------    ------------
atof        123.456
atoi        123
atol        123

Function    Return Value    Valid?    String Consumed?
--------    ------------    ------    ----------------
strtod      123.456         Yes       Yes
strtol      123             Yes       No
strtoul     123             Yes       No
```

All functions treated this input as a valid number, although the integer functions stopped at the decimal point. The `strtol` and `strtoul` functions failed to consume the input completely, however, so we know there's a problem.

If `foo` is the command-line argument, the output will be

```
Function    Return Value
--------    ------------
atof        0
atoi        0
atol        0


Function    Return Value    Valid?    String Consumed?
--------    ------------    ------    ----------------
strtod      0               Yes            No
strtol      0               Yes            No
strtoul     0               Yes            No
```

All the functions look at the letter `f` and immediately return zero. The `str...` functions don't change `errno`, but we can tell that something went wrong from the fact that the functions didn't consume the string.

Pseudo-Random Sequence Generation Functions

```
int rand(void);
void srand(unsigned int seed);
```

The `rand` and `srand` functions support the generation of pseudo-random numbers. These functions are useful in simulation programs and game-playing programs (to simulate a dice roll or the deal in a card game, for example).

rand Each time it's called, `rand` returns a number between 0 and `RAND_MAX` (a macro defined in `<stdlib.h>`). The numbers returned by `rand` aren't actually random; they're generated from a "seed" value. To the casual observer, however, `rand` appears to produce an unrelated sequence of numbers.

srand Calling `srand` supplies the seed value for `rand`. If `rand` is called prior to `srand`, the seed value is assumed to be 1. Each seed value determines a particular sequence of "random" numbers; `srand` allows us to select which sequence we want.

A program that always uses the same seed value will always get the same sequence of numbers from `rand`. This property can sometimes be useful: the program behaves the same way each time it's run, making testing easier. However, we usually want `rand` to produce a *different* sequence each time the program is run. (A poker-playing program that always deals the same cards isn't likely to be popular.) The easiest way to "randomize" the seed values is to call the `time` function, which returns a number that encodes the current date and time. Passing `time`'s return value to `srand` makes the behavior of `rand` vary from one run to the next. See the `guess.c` and `guess2.c` programs in Section 10.2 for examples of this technique.

time function ➤26.3

PROGRAM **Testing the Pseudo-Random Sequence Generation Functions**

The following program displays the first ten values returned by the rand function, then allows the user to choose a new seed value. The process repeats until the user enters zero as the seed.

trand.c
```
/* Tests the pseudo-random sequence generation functions */

#include <stdio.h>
#include <stdlib.h>

main()
{
  int i, seed;

  printf("This program displays the first ten values of "
         "rand.\n");

  for (;;) {
    for (i = 0; i < 10; i++)
      printf("%d ", rand());
    printf("\n\n");
    printf("Enter new seed value (0 to terminate): ");
    scanf("%d", &seed);
    if (seed == 0)
      break;
    srand(seed);
  }

  return 0;
}
```

Here's how a session with the program might look:

```
This program displays the first ten values of rand.
346 130 10982 1090 11656 7117 17595 6415 22948 31126

Enter new seed value (0 to terminate): 100
1862 11548 3973 4846 9095 16503 6335 13684 21357 21505

Enter new seed value (0 to terminate): 1
346 130 10982 1090 11656 7117 17595 6415 22948 31126

Enter new seed value (0 to terminate): 0
```

There are many ways to write the rand function, so there's no guarantee that every version of rand will generate the numbers shown here. Note that choosing 1 as the seed gives the same sequence of numbers as not specifying the seed at all.

Communication with the Environment

```
void abort(void);
int atexit(void (*func)(void));
void exit(int status);
char *getenv(const char *name);
int system(const char *string);
```

The functions in this group provide a simple interface to the operating system, allowing programs to (1) terminate, either normally or abnormally, and return a status code to the operating system, (2) fetch information from the user's environment, and (3) execute operating system commands.

exit   Performing the call exit(*n*) anywhere in a program is equivalent to executing the statement return *n*; in main: the program terminates, and *n* is returned to the operating system as a status code. The <stdlib.h> header defines the macros EXIT_FAILURE and EXIT_SUCCESS, which can be used as arguments to exit. The only other portable argument to exit is 0, which has the same meaning as EXIT_SUCCESS. Returning status codes other than these is legal, but not necessarily portable to all operating systems.

atexit   When a program terminates, it normally performs a few final actions behind the scenes, including flushing output buffers, closing open streams, and deleting temporary files. We may have other "clean-up" actions that we'd like a program to perform at termination. The atexit function allows us to "register" a function to be called upon program termination. To register a function named cleanup, for example, we could call atexit as follows:

```
atexit(cleanup);
```

When we pass a function pointer to atexit, it stores the pointer away for future reference. Later, when the program terminates, any function registered with atexit will be called automatically. (If several functions have been registered, the one registered most recently is called first.)

abort   abort is similar to exit, but causes abnormal program termination. Functions registered with atexit aren't called. Depending on the implementation, it may be the case that file buffers aren't flushed, streams aren't closed, and temporary files aren't deleted. abort returns an implementation-defined status code indicating "unsuccessful termination."

Q&A

getenv   Many operating systems provide an "environment": a set of strings that describe the user's characteristics. These strings typically include the path to be searched when the user runs a program, the type of the user's terminal (in the case of a multi-user system), and so on. For example, a UNIX search path might look something like this:

```
PATH=~:~/bin:/bin:/usr/bin:.
```

DOS paths have a similar appearance:

```
PATH=C:\;C:\DOS;C:\WINDOWS
```

getenv provides access to any string in the user's environment. To find the current value of the PATH string, for example, we would write

```
p = getenv("PATH");
```

After this statement has been executed, p points to a string such as `"~:~/bin:/ bin:/usr/bin:."` or `"C:\;C:\DOS;C:\WINDOWS"`. The string returned by getenv is statically allocated and may be changed by a later call of the function.

system   The system function allows a C program to run another program (possibly an operating system command). The argument to system is a command line, similar to one that we'd enter at the operating system prompt. For example, suppose that we're writing a program that needs a listing of the files in the current directory. A UNIX program would call system in the following way:

```
system("ls >myfiles");
```

A DOS program would use a slightly different call:

```
system("dir >myfiles");
```

After either call, myfiles will contain a directory listing. The value returned by system is implementation-defined. Typically, system returns the termination status code from the program that we asked system to run; testing this value allows us to check whether the program worked properly. Calling system with a null pointer has a special meaning: the function returns a nonzero value if a command processor is available.

Searching and Sorting Utilities

```
void *bsearch(const void *key, const void *base,
              size_t nmemb, size_t size,
              int (*compar)(const void *,
                            const void *));
void qsort(void *base, size_t nmemb, size_t size,
           int (*compar)(const void *, const void *));
```

bsearch   The bsearch function searches a sorted array for a particular value (the **key**). When bsearch is called, the key parameter points to the key, base points to the array, nmemb is the number of elements in the array, size is the size of each element (in bytes), and compar is a pointer to a comparison function. The comparison function is similar to the one required by qsort: when passed pointers to the key and an array element (in that order), the function must return a negative, zero, or positive integer depending on whether the key is smaller than, equal to, or greater than the array element. bsearch returns a pointer to an element that matches the key; if it doesn't find a match, bsearch returns a null pointer.

Although Standard C doesn't require it to, `bsearch` normally uses the "binary search" algorithm to search the array. `bsearch` first compares the key with the element in the middle of the array; if there's a match, the function returns. If the key is smaller than the middle element, `bsearch` limits its search to the first half of the array; if the key is larger, `bsearch` searches only the last half of the array. `bsearch` repeats this strategy until it finds the key or runs out of elements to search. Thanks to this technique, `bsearch` is quite fast—searching an array of 1000 elements requires only 10 comparisons at most; searching an array of 1,000,000 elements requires no more than 20 comparisons.

qsort   Section 17.7 discusses the `qsort` function, which can sort any array. `bsearch` works only for sorted arrays, but we can always use `qsort` to sort an array prior to asking `bsearch` to search it.

PROGRAM   Determining Air Mileage

Our next program computes the air mileage from New York City to various international cities. The program first asks the user to enter a city name, then displays the mileage to that city:

```
Enter city name: Frankfurt
Frankfurt is 3851 miles from New York City.
```

The program will store city/mileage pairs in an array. By using `bsearch` to search the array for a city name, the program can easily find the corresponding mileage. (Mileages are from *The New York Public Library Desk Reference*, Second Edition (New York: Prentice-Hall, 1993).)

airmiles.c

```c
/* Determines air mileage from New York to other cities */

#include <stdio.h>
#include <stdlib.h>
#include <string.h>

struct city_info {
  char *city;
  int miles;
};

int compare_cities(const void *key_ptr,
                   const void *element_ptr);

main()
{
  char city_name[81];
  struct city_info *ptr;
  const struct city_info mileage[] =
    {{"Acapulco",        2260}, {"Amsterdam",        3639},
     {"Antigua",         1783}, {"Aruba",            1963},
     {"Athens",          4927}, {"Barbados",         2100},
     {"Bermuda",          771}, {"Bogota",           2487},
```

```
        {"Brussels",        3662}, {"Buenos Aires",    5302},
        {"Caracas",         2123}, {"Copenhagen",      3849},
        {"Curacao",         1993}, {"Frankfurt",       3851},
        {"Geneva",          3859}, {"Glasgow",         3211},
        {"Hamburg",         3806}, {"Kingston",        1583},
        {"Lima",            3651}, {"Lisbon",          3366},
        {"London",          3456}, {"Madrid",          3588},
        {"Manchester",      3336}, {"Mexico City",     2086},
        {"Milan",           4004}, {"Nassau",          1101},
        {"Oslo",            3671}, {"Paris",           3628},
        {"Reykjavik",       2600}, {"Rio de Janeiro",  4816},
        {"Rome",            4280}, {"San Juan",        1609},
        {"Santo Domingo",   1560}, {"St. Croix",       1680},
        {"Tel Aviv",        5672}, {"Zurich",          3926}};

  printf("Enter city name: ");
  scanf("%80[^\n]", city_name);
  ptr = bsearch(city_name, mileage,
                sizeof(mileage)/sizeof(mileage[0]),
                sizeof(mileage[0]), compare_cities);
  if (ptr != NULL)
    printf("%s is %d miles from New York City.\n",
           city_name, ptr->miles);
  else
    printf("%s wasn't found.\n", city_name);

  return 0;
}

int compare_cities(const void *key_ptr,
                   const void *element_ptr)
{
  return strcmp((char *) key_ptr,
                ((struct city_info *) element_ptr)->city);
}
```

Integer Arithmetic Functions

```
int abs(int j);
div_t div(int numer, int denom);
long int labs(long int j);
ldiv_t ldiv(long int numer, long int denom);
```

abs
labs
The abs function returns the absolute value of an int value; the labs function returns the absolute value of a long int value.

div
The div function divides its first argument by its second, returning a div_t value. div_t is a structure that contains both a quotient member (named quot) and a remainder member (rem). For example, if ans is a div_t variable, we could write

```
ans = div(5, 2);
printf("Quotient: %d Remainder: %d\n", ans.quot, ans.rem);
```

ldiv

Q&A

The `ldiv` function is similar but works with long integers; it returns an `ldiv_t` structure, which also has `quot` and `rem` members. (The `div_t` and `ldiv_t` types are defined in `<stdlib.h>`.)

26.3   The `<time.h>` Header: Date and Time

The `<time.h>` header provides functions for determining the time (and date), performing arithmetic on time values, and formatting times for display. Before we explore these functions, however, we need to discuss how times are stored. `<time.h>` provides three types, each of which represents a different way to store a time:

- `clock_t`: A time value measured in "clock ticks."
- `time_t`: A compact, encoded time and date (a *calendar time*).
- `struct tm`: A time that has been "broken down" into seconds, minutes, hours, and so on. A value of type `struct tm` is often called a *broken-down time.* Table 26.1 shows the members of the `tm` structure. All members are of type `int`.

Table 26.1
Members of the tm Structure

Name	Description	Minimum Value	Maximum Value
tm_sec	Seconds after the minute	0	61**
tm_min	Minutes after the hour	0	59
tm_hour	Hours since midnight	0	23
tm_mday	Day of the month	1	31
tm_mon	Months since January	0	11
tm_year	Years since 1900	0	–
tm_wday	Days since Sunday	0	6
tm_yday	Days since January 1	0	365
tm_isdst	Daylight Saving Time flag	*	*

*Positive if Daylight Saving Time is in effect, zero if it's not in effect, and negative if this information is unknown.
**Allows for two extra "leap seconds."

These types are used for different purposes. A `clock_t` value is good only for representing a time duration; `time_t` and `struct tm` values can store an entire date and time. `time_t` values are tightly encoded, so they occupy little space. `struct tm` values require much more space, but they're often easier to work with. The C standard states that `clock_t` and `time_t` must be "arithmetic types," by the way, but leaves it at that. As a result, we don't know if `clock_t` and `time_t` values are stored as integers or floating-point numbers.

We're now ready to look at the functions in `<time.h>`, which fall into two groups: time manipulation functions and time conversion functions.

Time Manipulation Functions

```
clock_t clock(void);
double difftime(time_t time1, time_t time0);
time_t mktime(struct tm *timeptr);
time_t time(time_t *timer);
```

clock The clock function returns a clock_t value representing the processor time used by the program since execution began. To convert this value to seconds, we would divide it by CLOCKS_PER_SEC, a macro defined in <time.h>.

When clock is used to determine how long a program has been running, it's customary to call it twice: once at the beginning of main and once just before the program terminates:

```
#include <time.h>

main()
{
  clock_t start_clock = clock();
  …
  printf("Processor time used: %g sec.\n",
         (clock() - start_clock) / (double) CLOCKS_PER_SEC);
  return 0;
}
```

The reason for the initial call of clock is that the program will use some processor time before it reaches main, thanks to hidden "start-up" code. Calling clock at the beginning of main determines how much time the start-up code requires so that we can subtract it later.

The C standard doesn't say whether clock_t is an integer type or a floating type; the type of CLOCKS_PER_SEC is also unknown. As a result, we don't know the type of the expression

```
(clock() - start_time) / CLOCKS_PER_SEC
```

making it difficult to display using printf. To solve the problem, our example casts CLOCKS_PER_SEC to double, forcing the entire expression to have type double.

time The time function returns the current calendar time. If its argument isn't a null pointer, time also stores the calendar time in the object that the argument points to. time's ability to return a time in two different ways is an historical quirk, but it gives us the option of writing either

```
curtime = timc(NULL);
```

or

```
time(&cur_time);
```

where cur_time is a variable of type time_t.

difftime   The `difftime` function returns the difference between `time0` (the earlier time) and `time1`, measured in seconds. Thus, to compute the actual running time of a program (not the processor time), we might use the following code:

```
#include <time.h>

main()
{
  time_t start_time = time(NULL);
  …
  printf("Running time: %g sec.\n",
          difftime(time(NULL), start_time));
  return 0;
}
```

mktime   The `mktime` function converts a broken-down time (stored in the structure that its argument points to) into a calendar time, which it then returns. As a side effect, `mktime` adjusts the members of the structure according to the following rules:

- `mktime` changes any members whose values aren't within their legal ranges (Table 26.1). Those alterations may in turn require changes to other members. If `tm_sec` is too large, for example, `mktime` reduces it to the proper range (0–59), adding the extra minutes to `tm_min`. If `tm_min` is now too large, `mktime` reduces it and adds the extra hours to `tm_hour`. If necessary, the process will continue to the `tm_mday`, `tm_mon`, and `tm_year` members.
- After adjusting the other members of the structure (if necessary), `mktime` sets `tm_wday` (day of the week) and `tm_yday` (day of the year) to their correct values. There's never any need to initialize the values of `tm_wday` and `tm_yday` before calling `mktime`, since it ignores the original values of these members.

`mktime`'s ability to adjust the members of a `tm` structure makes it useful for time-related arithmetic. As a example, let's use `mktime` to answer the following question: If the 1996 Olympics begin on July 19 and end 16 days later, what is the ending date? We'll start by storing July 19, 1996 into a `tm` structure:

```
struct tm t;

t.tm_mday = 19;
t.tm_mon = 6;      /* July */
t.tm_year = 96;    /* 1996 */
```

We'll also initialize the other members of the structure (except `tm_wday` and `tm_yday`) to ensure that they don't contain garbage values that could affect the answer:

```
t.tm_sec = 0;
t.tm_min = 0;
t.tm_hour = 0;
t.tm_isdst = -1;
```

Next, we'll add 16 to the `tm_mday` member:

```
t.tm_mday += 16;
```

That leaves 35 in `tm_mday`, which is out of range for that member. Calling `mktime` will bring the members of the structure back into their proper ranges:

```
mktime(&t);
```

We'll discard `mktime`'s return value, since we're interested only in the function's effect on `t`. The relevant members of `t` now have the following values:

Member	Value	Meaning
tm_mday	4	4
tm_mon	7	August
tm_year	96	1996
tm_wday	0	Sunday
tm_yday	216	217th day of the year

Time Conversion Functions

```
char *asctime(const struct tm *timeptr);
char *ctime(const time_t *timer);
struct tm *gmtime(const time_t *timer);
struct tm *localtime(const time_t *timer);
size_t strftime(char *s, size_t maxsize,
                const char *format,
                const struct tm *timeptr);
```

The time conversion functions make it possible to convert calendar times to broken-down times. They can also convert times (calendar or broken-down) to string form. The following figure shows how these functions are related:

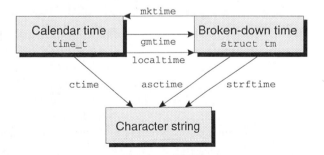

The figure includes the `mktime` function, which the C standard classifies as a "manipulation" function rather than a "conversion" function.

gmtime
localtime

asctime

The gmtime and localtime functions are similar. When passed a pointer to a calendar time, both return a pointer to a structure containing the equivalent broken-down time. localtime produces a local time, while gmtime's return value is expressed in UTC (Coordinated Universal Time).

The asctime (ASCII time) function returns a pointer to a string of the form

```
Tue Aug 30 17:07:12 1994\n
```

constructed from the broken-down time pointed to by its argument. The string is stored in a static variable that's modified by each call of asctime.

ctime

The ctime function returns a pointer to a string describing a local time; the call

```
ctime(&t)
```

is equivalent to

```
asctime(localtime(&t))
```

strftime

sprintf function ➤22.8

The strftime function, like the asctime function, converts a broken-down time to string form. Unlike asctime, however, it gives us a great deal of control over how the time is formatted. In fact, strftime resembles sprintf in that it "writes" characters into a string s (the first argument) according to a format string (the third argument). The format string may contain ordinary characters, which are copied into s unchanged, and the conversion specifiers shown in Table 26.2. The last argument points to a tm structure, which is used as the source of date and time information. The second argument is a limit on the number of characters that can be stored in s.

locales ➤25.1

The strftime function, unlike the other functions in <time.h>, is sensitive to the current locale. Changing the LC_TIME category may affect the behavior of the conversion specifiers. The examples in Table 26.2 are strictly for the "C" locale; in a German locale, %A might produce Dienstag instead of Tuesday.

PROGRAM   **Displaying the Date and Time**

Let's say we need a program that displays the current date and time. The program's first step, of course, is to call the time function to obtain the calendar time. The second step is to convert the time to string form and print it. The easiest way to do the second step is to call ctime, which returns a pointer to a string containing a date and time, then pass this pointer to puts or printf.

So far, so good. But what if we want the program to display the date and time in a particular way? Let's assume that we need the following format:

```
08-30-94    5:07p
```

The ctime function always uses the same format for the date and time, so it's no help. The strftime function is better; using it, we can almost achieve the appearance that we want. Unfortunately, strftime won't let us display a one-

Table 26.2

Conversion Specifiers for the `strftime` Function

Conversion	Replacement
%a	Abbreviated weekday name (e.g., `Tue`)
%A	Full weekday name (e.g., `Tuesday`)
%b	Abbreviated month name (e.g., `Aug`)
%B	Full month name (e.g., `August`)
%c	Complete day and time (e.g., `Aug 30 17:07:12 1994`)
%d	Day of the month (`01–31`)
%H	Hour on 24-hour clock (`00–23`)
%I	Hour on 12-hour clock (`01–12`)
%j	Day of the year (`001–366`)
%m	Month (`01–12`)
%M	Minute (`00–59`)
%p	AM/PM designator (AM or PM)
%S	Second (`00–61`)*
%U	Week number (`00–53`)**
%w	Weekday (`0–6`)
%W	Week number (`00–53`)***
%x	Complete date (e.g., `Aug 30 1994`)
%X	Complete time (e.g., `17:07:12`)
%y	Year without century (`00–99`)
%Y	Year with century (e.g., `1994`)
%Z	Time zone name or abbreviation (e.g., `EST`)
%%	%

*Allows for two extra "leap seconds."
**Treats the first Sunday as the beginning of week 1.
***Treats the first Monday as the beginning of week 1.

digit hour without a leading zero. Also, `strftime` uses AM and PM instead of a and p.

When `strftime` isn't good enough, we have another alternative: convert the calendar time to a broken-down time, then extract the relevant information from the structure and format it ourselves using `printf` or a similar function. We might even use `strftime` to do some of the formatting, then have other functions complete the job.

The following program illustrates the options. It displays the current date and time in three ways: the format used by `ctime`, one close to what we want (created by `strftime`), and the correct format (created by `printf`). The `ctime` version is easy to do, the `strftime` version is a little harder, and the `printf` version is even more difficult.

datetime.c

```
/* Displays the current date and time in three formats */

#include <stdio.h>
#include <time.h>

main()
{
  time_t current = time(NULL);
  struct tm *ptr;
  char date_time[19];
  int hour;
  char am_or_pm;
```

```
     /* print date and time in default format */
  puts(ctime(&current));

     /* print date and time using strftime to format */
  strftime(date_time, sizeof(date_time),
           "%m-%d-%y  %I:%M%p\n", localtime(&current));
  puts(date_time);

     /* print date and time using custom formatting */
  ptr = localtime(&current);
  hour = ptr->tm_hour;
  if (hour <= 11)
    am_or_pm = 'a';
  else {
    hour -= 12;
    am_or_pm = 'p';
  }
  if (hour == 0)
    hour = 12;
  printf("%.2d-%.2d-%.2d  %2d:%.2d%c\n", ptr->tm_mon+1,
         ptr->tm_mday, ptr->tm_year, hour, ptr->tm_min,
         am_or_pm);

  return 0;
}
```

The output of `datetime.c` will have the following appearance:

```
Tue Aug 30 17:07:12 1994

08-30-94  05:07PM

08-30-94   5:07p
```

Q & A

Q: **Although `<stdlib.h>` provides six functions that convert strings to numbers, there don't appear to be any functions that convert numbers to strings. What gives?**

A: Some C libraries supply functions with names like `itoa` that convert numbers to strings. Using these functions isn't a great idea, though, since they aren't part of the C standard and won't be portable. The best way to convert a number to a string is to call `sprintf`:

sprintf function ➤22.8

```
char s[10];
int i;

sprintf(s, "%d", i);   /* stores i in the string s */
```

Not only is sprintf portable, but it also provides a great deal of control over the appearance of the number.

*Q: Is there a relationship between the abort function and SIGABRT signal? [p. 572]

A: Yes. When called, abort actually raises the SIGABRT signal. If there's no handler for SIGABRT, the program terminates abnormally as described in Section 26.2. If a handler has been installed for SIGABRT (by a call of the signal function), the handler is called. If the handler returns, the program then terminates abnormally. However, if the handler *doesn't* return (it calls longjmp, for example), then the program doesn't terminate.

signal function ➤24.3

longjmp function ➤24.4

Q: Isn't there some way to avoid all the ugly casting in the comparison function for bsearch or qsort?

A: Yes, although it involves casting elsewhere in the program. Let's look at the comparison function used in airmiles.c:

```
int compare_cities(const void *key_ptr,
                   const void *element_ptr)
{
  return strcmp((char *) key_ptr,
                ((struct city_info *) element_ptr)->city);
}
```

We can write this function in a more natural way, without the casts:

```
int compare_cities(const char *key_ptr,
                   const struct city_info *element_ptr)
{
  return strcmp(key_ptr, element_ptr->city);
}
```

Unfortunately, we can't pass the new version of compare_cities to bsearch, which expects a pointer to a function with two void * arguments. The solution is to add a cast to the bsearch call:

```
ptr = bsearch(city_name, mileage,
              sizeof(mileage)/sizeof(mileage[0]),
              sizeof(mileage[0]),
              (int (*) (const void *, const void *))
                compare_cities);
```

Does this technique make the program more readable? You be the judge.

Q: Why do the div and ldiv functions exist? Can't we just use the / and % operators? [p. 576]

A: div and ldiv aren't quite the same as / and %. Recall from Section 4.1 that applying / and % to negative operands doesn't give a portable result. If i or j is negative, whether the value of i / j is rounded up or down is implementation-defined, as is the sign of i % j. The answers computed by div and ldiv, on the other hand, don't depend on the implementation. The quotient is rounded toward zero; the remainder is computed according to the formula $n = q \times d + r$, where n is the original number, q is the quotient, d is the divisor, and r is the remainder. Here are a few examples:

n	d	q	r
7	3	2	1
−7	3	−2	−1
7	−3	−2	1
−7	−3	2	−1

Efficiency is the other reason that `div` and `ldiv` exist. Many machines can compute both the quotient and remainder in a single instruction, so calling `div` or `ldiv` may be faster than using the `/` and `%` operators separately.

Q: **Where does the name of the `gmtime` function come from? [p. 580]**

A: Programming languages aren't the only things that have been standardized. International time was standardized in 1883 with the creation of 24 time zones. Since some people (navigators and astronomers, in particular) needed a way to state times in absolute terms, rather than relative to a time zone, Greenwich Mean Time was established, based on the meridian running through Greenwich, England. More recently, Greenwich Mean Time was renamed Coordinated Universal Time, but the `gmtime` function was already in widespread use.

Exercises

Section 26.1

1. Rewrite the `max_int` function so that, instead of passing the number of integers as the first argument, we must supply 0 as the last argument. *Hint:* `max_int` must have at least one "normal" argument, so you can't remove the argument `n`. Instead, assume that it's one of the numbers to be compared.

2. Write a simplified version of `printf` in which the only conversion specification is `%d`, and all arguments after the first must be of type `int`.

3. Write the following function:

    ```
    char *vstrcat(const char *first, ...);
    ```

    All arguments of `vstrcat` are assumed to be strings, except for the last argument, which must be a null pointer (cast to `char *` type). The function returns a pointer to a dynamically allocated string containing the concatenation of the arguments. `vstrcat` should return a null pointer if not enough memory is available. *Hint:* Have `vstrcat` go through the arguments twice: once to determine the amount of memory required for the returned string and once to copy the arguments into the string.

Section 26.2

4. Explain the meaning of the following statement, assuming that `value` is a variable of type `long int` and `p` is a variable of type `char *`:

    ```
    value = strtol(p, &p, 10);
    ```

5. Write a statement that randomly assigns one of the numbers 7, 11, 15, or 19 to the variable n.

6. Write a function that returns a random double value *d* in the range $0.0 \leq d < 1.0$.

7. Write a program that simulates the dice game known as "craps." The program should "roll" a pair of simulated dice by randomly selecting two numbers between 1 and 6. If the sum of the numbers is 7 or 11, have the program print the message Player wins. If the sum is 2, 3, or 12, have it print Player loses. Otherwise, have the program repeatedly roll the dice until the original sum is reached a second time (Player wins) or the dice add up to 7 (Player loses). Have the program display the values of the dice after each simulated roll.

8. (a) Write a program that calls the rand function 1000 times, printing the low-order bit of each value it returns (0 if the return value is even, 1 if it's odd). Do you see any patterns? (Often, the last few bits of rand's return value aren't especially random.)

   (b) How can we improve the randomness of rand for generating numbers within a small range?

9. Test the atexit function by writing two functions, one of which prints That's all, and the other folks!. Use the atexit function to register both to be called at program termination. Make sure they're called in the proper order, so that we see the message That's all, folks! on the screen.

Section 26.3

10. Write a program that uses the clock function to measure how long it takes qsort to sort an array of 100 integers that are originally in reverse order. Run the program for arrays of 1000 and 10000 integers as well.

11. Write a function that, when passed a year (1996, for example), returns a time_t value representing the beginning of that year (the first second of the first minute of the first hour...).

12. Write a program that prompts the user for a date (month, day, and year) and an integer n, then prints the date that's n days later.

13. Write a program that prompts the user to enter two dates, then prints the number of days between them. *Hint:* Use the mktime and difftime functions.

14. Write programs that display the current date and time in each of the following formats. Use strftime to do all or most of the formatting.

   (a) Tuesday, August 30, 1994   05:07p
   (b) Tue, 30 Aug 94   17:07
   (c) 08/30/94   5:07:12 PM

APPENDIX A
C Syntax

Annex B of the ISO standard for C gives a complete set of syntax rules for the language. This appendix reproduces these rules, which I've reworked for readability.* In each rule, the name of a syntax item appears in the left margin, followed by its definition. Names of syntax items are shown in *italic*. The |, *, +, [,], (, and) symbols have the following meanings:

> *item*₁ | *item*₂ indicates that *item₁* and *item₂* are alternatives.
>
> *item** indicates that *item* may be repeated zero or more times.
>
> *item*⁺ indicates that *item* may be repeated one or more times.
>
> [*item*] indicates that *item* is optional.
>
> (and) are used to group alternatives.

When set in **Courier bold**, however, these symbols have their usual C meaning. Although most of the rules are reasonably clear, some require further explanation. Where necessary, I've included commentary.

Tokens

token   *keyword* | *identifier* | *constant* | *string-literal* | *operator* | *punctuator*

preprocessing-token   *header-name* | *identifier* | *pp-number* | *character-constant* | *string-literal* | *operator* | *punctuator* | each non-white-space character that cannot be one of the above

> "Tokens" are the indivisible symbols that make up a program. The preprocessor recognizes some tokens that the compiler doesn't, hence the distinction between a *token* and a *preprocessing-token*.

---

*This material is adapted from American National Standards Institute ANSI/ISO 9899 © 1990 with permission by ANSI. Copies of this standard may be purchased from ANSI, 11 West 42nd Street, New York, NY 10036.

Keywords

keyword   `auto` | `break` | `case` | `char` | `const` | `continue` | `default` | `do` | `double` | `else` | `enum` | `extern` | `float` | `for` | `goto` | `if` | `int` | `long` | `register` | `return` | `short` | `signed` | `sizeof` | `static` | `struct` | `switch` | `typedef` | `union` | `unsigned` | `void` | `volatile` | `while`

Identifiers

identifier   *nondigit* (*nondigit* | *digit*)*

nondigit   `_` | `a` | `b` | `c` | `d` | `e` | `f` | `g` | `h` | `i` | `j` | `k` | `l` | `m` | `n` | `o` | `p` | `q` | `r` | `s` | `t` | `u` | `v` | `w` | `x` | `y` | `z` | `A` | `B` | `C` | `D` | `E` | `F` | `G` | `H` | `I` | `J` | `K` | `L` | `M` | `N` | `O` | `P` | `Q` | `R` | `S` | `T` | `U` | `V` | `W` | `X` | `Y` | `Z`

digit   `0` | `1` | `2` | `3` | `4` | `5` | `6` | `7` | `8` | `9`

Constants

constant   *floating-constant* | *integer-constant* | *enumeration-constant* | *character-constant*

floating-constant   *fractional-constant* [*exponent-part*] [*floating-suffix*] | *digit*$^+$ *exponent-part* [*floating-suffix*]

fractional-constant   *digit** `.` *digit*$^+$ | *digit*$^+$ `.`

exponent-part   (`e` | `E`) [`+` | `-`] *digit*$^+$

floating-suffix   `f` | `l` | `F` | `L`

> By default, a floating constant is stored in `double` form. The letter `f` or `F` at the end of a floating constant tells the compiler to store it as a `float`; `l` or `L` stores it as a `long double`.

integer-constant   *decimal-constant* [*integer-suffix*] | *octal-constant* [*integer-suffix*] | *hexadecimal-constant* [*integer-suffix*]

decimal-constant   *nonzero-digit* *digit**

octal-constant   `0` *octal-digit**

> Note that `0` is officially classified as an octal constant, not a decimal constant. This oddity makes no difference, of course, since `0` has the same meaning in any base.

hexadecimal-constant   (`0x` | `0X`) *hexadecimal-digit*$^+$

nonzero-digit   `1` | `2` | `3` | `4` | `5` | `6` | `7` | `8` | `9`

octal-digit   `0` | `1` | `2` | `3` | `4` | `5` | `6` | `7`

hexadecimal-digit   `0` | `1` | `2` | `3` | `4` | `5` | `6` | `7` | `8` | `9` | `a` | `b` | `c` | `d` | `e` | `f` | `A` | `B` | `C` | `D` | `E` | `F`

integer-suffix   *unsigned-suffix* [*long-suffix*] | *long-suffix* [*unsigned-suffix*]

unsigned-suffix   `u` | `U`

long-suffix	`l` | `L`
	The letter `u` or `U` at the end of an integer constant tells the compiler to store it as an `unsigned int`; `l` or `L` stores it as a `long int`. When followed by both letters (in either order), the constant is stored as an `unsigned long int`.
enumeration-constant	*identifier*
|	*enumeration-constant* is used in the *enumerator* rule (see **Declarations**).
character-constant	`'`*c-char*⁺`'` | `L'`*c-char*⁺`'`
|	If `L` is present, the constant represents a wide character.
c-char	any character except `'`, `\`, or new-line | *escape-sequence*
	Be careful to interpret the preceding rule correctly. It *does* say that a character constant can't contain the new-line character, but it *doesn't* say that a character constant can't contain a `'` or `\` character; both can still appear in a character constant as part of an escape sequence.
escape-sequence	*simple-escape-sequence* | *octal-escape-sequence* | *hex-escape-sequence*
simple-escape-sequence	`\'` | `\"` | `\?` | `\\` | `\a` | `\b` | `\f` | `\n` | `\r` | `\t` | `\v`
octal-escape-sequence	`\` *octal-digit* [*octal-digit*] [*octal-digit*]
hex-escape-sequence	`\x` *hexadecimal-digit*⁺
	For historical reasons, an octal escape sequence is limited to three digits. A hex escape sequence, on the other hand, may have any number of digits.

String Literals

string-literal	`"`*s-char**`"` | `L"`*s-char**`"`
|	If `L` is present, the literal represents a wide string.
s-char	any character except `"`, `\`, or new-line | *escape-sequence*
	This rule *doesn't* say that a string constant can't contain a `"` or `\` character; both can still appear as part of an escape sequence.

Operators

operator	`[` | `]` | `(` | `)` | `.` | `->` | `++` | `--` | `&` | `*` | `+` | `-` | `~` | `!` | `sizeof` | `/` | `%` | `<<` | `>>` | `<` | `>` | `<=` | `>=` | `==` | `!=` | `^` | `|` | `&&` | `||` | `?` | `:` | `=` | `*=` | `/=` | `%=` | `+=` | `-=` | `<<=` | `>>=` | `&=` | `^=` | `|=` | `,` | `#` | `##`
	For convenience, the preprocessor operators `#` and `##` are grouped with C's ordinary operators.

Punctuators

punctuator	`[` | `]` | `(` | `)` | `{` | `}` | `*` | `,` | `:` | `=` | `;` | `...` | `#`
	Some punctuators are also operators, depending on context. The `=` token, for example, is a punctuator when used in a declaration to separate a variable from its initializer or an enumeration constant from its value; when used in an expression, it's the assignment operator. The `...` token (*ellipsis*) is used for writing functions with variable-length argument lists.

Header Names

header-name   <h-char⁺> | "q-char⁺"

h-char   any character except new-line and >

q-char   any character except new-line and "

> A header name can contain almost any character. The reason for allowing so much flexibility is that header names often contain operating-system-dependent information (a path, for example).

Preprocessing Numbers

pp-number   [.] *digit* (*digit* | *nondigit* | (**e** | **E**) (**+** | **-**) | **.**)*

> During preprocessing, numbers are detected using this simple rule, which allows some illegal numbers (0x0y, for example) to slip through. They'll be detected later by the compiler, though, so no harm is done.

Expressions

primary-expression   *identifier* | *constant* | *string-literal* | **(** *expression* **)**

> A primary expression is an expression that's indivisible, either because it's a single identifier, constant, or string literal or because it's enclosed in parentheses. All other expressions are subject to C's rules of precedence and associativity, which are embodied in the 19 rules that follow.

postfix-expression   *primary-expression* (**[** *expression* **]** | **(** [*argument-expression-list*] **)** | **.** *identifier* | **->** *identifier* | **++** | **--**)*

argument-expression-list   *assignment-expression* (**,** *assignment-expression*)*

> The arguments in a function call must be "assignment expressions," not arbitrary expressions, to avoid confusion between the comma *punctuator,* which separates arguments, and the comma *operator.*

unary-expression   (**++** | **--** | **sizeof**)* (*postfix-expression* | *unary-operator cast-expression* | **sizeof** **(** *type-name* **)**)

unary-operator   **&** | ***** | **+** | **-** | **~** | **!**

cast-expression   (**(** *type-name* **)**)* *unary-expression*

multiplicative-expression   *cast-expression* ((***** | **/** | **%**) *cast-expression*)*

additive-expression   *multiplicative-expression* ((**+** | **-**) *multiplicative-expression*)*

shift-expression   *additive-expression* ((**<<** | **>>**) *additive-expression*)*

relational-expression   *shift-expression* ((**<** | **>** | **<=** | **>=**) *shift-expression*)*

equality-expression   *relational-expression* ((**==** | **!=**) *relational-expression*)*

AND-expression   *equality-expression* (**&** *equality-expression*)*

exclusive-OR-expression   *AND-expression* (**^** *AND-expression*)*

inclusive-OR-expression	*exclusive-OR-expression* (**|** *exclusive-OR-expression*)*
logical-AND-expression	*inclusive-OR-expression* (**&&** *inclusive-OR-expression*)*
logical-OR-expression	*logical-AND-expression* (**||** *logical-AND-expression*)*
conditional-expression	*logical-OR-expression* (**?** *expression* **:** *conditional-expression*)*
assignment-expression	(*unary-expression assignment-operator*)* *conditional-expression*
assignment-operator	**=**	***=**	**/=**	**%=**	**+=**	**-=**	**<<=**	**>>=**	**&=**	**^=**	**|=**
expression	*assignment-expression* (**,** *assignment-expression*)*
constant-expression	*conditional-expression*

A constant expression is defined to be a *conditional-expression*, not an *expression* in general, since C prohibits assignment and comma operators in constant expressions. (C also disallows increment and decrement operators and function calls, although that's not shown in the syntax rules.)

Declarations

declaration	*declaration-specifiers* [*init-declarator-list*] **;**
declaration-specifiers	(*storage-class-specifier* | *type-specifier* | *type-qualifier*)+

The preceding rule is misleading, since it shows that a declaration may contain more than one storage class specifier. Actually, only one genuine storage class is allowed, and it must precede type specifiers and type qualifiers. The justification for the rule is that a declaration may begin with typedef (considered a storage class specifier for syntax purposes), followed by a storage class. Type specifiers and type qualifiers may indeed be mixed, as the rule shows, leading to strange combinations like int const unsigned volatile long.

init-declarator-list	*init-declarator* (**,** *init-declarator*)*
init-declarator	*declarator* [**=** *initializer*]
storage-class-specifier	**typedef**	**extern**	**static**	**auto**	**register**

To simplify the syntax rules, typedef is lumped with the genuine storage classes.

type-specifier	**void**	**char**	**short**	**int**	**long**	**float**	**double**	**signed**	**unsigned**	*struct-or-union-specifier*	*enum-specifier*	*typedef-name*
struct-or-union-specifier	(**struct** | **union**) (*identifier* | [*identifier*] **{** *struct-declaration*+ **}**)
struct-declaration	*specifier-qualifier-list struct-declarator-list* **;**
specifier-qualifier-list	(*type-specifier* | *type-qualifier*)+
struct-declarator-list	*struct-declarator* (**,** *struct-declarator*)*
struct-declarator	*declarator*	[*declarator*] **:** *constant-expression*

The constant expression in the preceding rule specifies the width of a bit-field. If the constant expression is present, the declarator can be omitted, creating an unnamed bit-field.

enum-specifier	**enum** (*identifier* | [*identifier*] **{** *enumerator-list* **}**)
enumerator-list	*enumerator* (**,** *enumerator*)*

enumerator	*enumeration-constant* [**=** *constant-expression*]
type-qualifier	**const**	**volatile**
declarator	(***** *type-qualifier**)* *direct-declarator*
direct-declarator	(*identifier*	**(** *declarator* **)**) (**[** [*constant-expression*] **]**	**(** *parameter-type-list* **)**	**(** [*identifier-list*] **)**)*
parameter-type-list	*parameter-declaration* (**,** *parameter-declaration*)* [**,** **...**]

> The presence of **, . . .** at the end of a parameter list indicates that a variable number of additional parameters may follow.

parameter-declaration	*declaration-specifiers* [*declarator*	*abstract-declarator*]
identifier-list	*identifier* (**,** *identifier*)*
type-name	*specifier-qualifier-list* [*abstractor-declarator*]

> *type-name* is used in the *unary-expression* and *cast-expression* rules (see **Expressions**).

abstract-declarator	(***** *type-qualifier**)⁺	(***** *type-qualifier**)* *direct-abstract-declarator*

> An ordinary declarator includes both a name and information about the properties of that name; an abstract declarator specifies properties, but omits the name. The function prototype
>
> ```
> void f(int **, float []);
> ```
>
> uses the abstract declarators ** and [] to help describe the types of f's parameters.

direct-abstract-declarator	**(** *abstract-declarator* **)**	[**(** *abstract-declarator* **)**] (**[** [*constant-expression*] **]**	**(** [*parameter-type-list*] **)**)⁺
typedef-name	*identifier*
initializer	*assignment-expression*	**{** *initializer-list* [**,**] **}**

> No, this isn't a mistake; an initializer list may indeed be followed by a (superfluous) comma.

initializer-list	*initializer* (**,** *initializer*)*

Statements

statement	*labeled-statement*	*compound-statement*	*expression-statement*	*selection-statement*	*iteration-statement*	*jump-statement*
labeled-statement	*identifier* **:** *statement*	**case** *constant-expression* **:** *statement*	**default** **:** *statement*

> The latter two forms of *labeled-statement* are allowed only inside a switch statement.

compound-statement	**{** *declaration** *statement** **}**
expression-statement	[*expression*] **;**

> For syntax purposes, the null statement is treated as an expression statement in which the expression is missing.

selection-statement	**if (** *expression* **)** *statement* [**else** *statement*]	**switch (** *expression* **)** *statement*

The body of a `switch` statement is virtually always a compound statement, although that's not strictly required. That compound statement may have declarations, although initializers in those declarations will be ignored.

iteration-statement   `while (` *expression* `)` *statement* |
`do` *statement* `while (` *expression* `) ;` |
`for ( [` *expression* `] ; [` *expression* `] ; [` *expression* `] )` *statement*

jump-statement   `goto` *identifier* `;` | `continue ;` | `break ;` | `return [` *expression* `] ;`

External Definitions

translation-unit   *external-declaration*[+]

external-declaration   *function-definition* | *declaration*

function-definition   `[` *declaration-specifiers* `]` *declarator* *declaration** *compound-statement*

The declaration specifiers describe the function's return type; the declarator gives its name and parameter list. The declarations (present only in the Classic C style of function definition) specify the types of the parameters. The compound statement is the function's body.

Preprocessing Directives

preprocessing-file   `[` *group* `]`

group   `( [` *pp-tokens* `]` *new-line* | *if-section* | *control-line* `)`[+]

if-section   *if-group* *elif-group** `[` *else-group* `]` *endif-line*

if-group   `# if` *constant-expression* *new-line* `[` *group* `]` |
`# ifdef` *identifier* *new-line* `[` *group* `]` |
`# ifndef` *identifier* *new-line* `[` *group* `]`

elif-group   `# elif` *constant-expression* *new-line* `[` *group* `]`

else-group   `# else` *new-line* `[` *group* `]`

endif-line   `# endif` *new-line*

control-line   `# include` *pp-tokens* *new-line* |
`# define` *identifier* *replacement-list* *new-line* |
`# define` *identifier* *lparen* `[` *identifier-list* `] )` *replacement-list* *new-line* |
`# undef` *identifier* *new-line* |
`# line` *pp-tokens* *new-line* |
`# error [` *pp-tokens* `]` *new-line* |
`# pragma [` *pp-tokens* `]` *new-line* |
`#` *new-line*

lparen   the left-parenthesis character without preceding white space

replacement-list   `[` *pp-tokens* `]`

pp-tokens   *preprocessing-token*[+]

new-line   the new-line character

APPENDIX B
C Operators

Precedence	Name	Symbol(s)	Associativity
1	array subscripting	[ ]	left
1	function call	( )	left
1	structure and union member	. ->	left
1	increment (postfix)	++	left
1	decrement (postfix)	--	left
2	increment (prefix)	++	right
2	decrement (prefix)	--	right
2	address of	&	right
2	indirection	*	right
2	unary plus	+	right
2	unary minus	-	right
2	bitwise complement	~	right
2	logical negation	!	right
2	size	sizeof	right
3	cast	( )	right
4	multiplicative	* / %	left
5	additive	+ -	left
6	bitwise shift	<< >>	left
7	relational	< > <= >=	left
8	equality	== !=	left
9	bitwise *and*	&	left
10	bitwise exclusive *or*	^	left
11	bitwise inclusive *or*	|	left
12	logical *and*	&&	left
13	logical *or*	||	left
14	conditional	? :	right
15	assignment	= *= /= %= += -= <<= >>= &= ^= |=	right
16	comma	,	left

APPENDIX C
Standard C versus Classic C

This appendix lists most of the significant differences between Standard C and Classic C (the language described in the first edition of Kernighan and Ritchie's *The C Programming Language*). The headings indicate which chapter of this book discusses each Standard C feature. This appendix doesn't address the C library, which has changed much over the years.

If your compiler doesn't claim to be "standard," it's a good idea to check its manual to see how many Standard C features the compiler provides. Virtually all C compilers can handle at least some of the newer features.

For other (less important) differences between Standard C and Classic C, consult Appendices A and C in K&R (Second Edition).

2 C Fundamentals

identifiers   In Classic C, only the first eight characters of an identifier are significant.

keywords   Classic C lacks the keywords `const`, `enum`, `signed`, `void`, and `volatile`. In Classic C, the word `entry` is a keyword.

4 Expressions

unary +   Classic C doesn't provide the unary + operator.

5 Selection Statements

switch   In Classic C, the controlling expression (and case labels) in a `switch` statement must have type `int` after promotion. In Standard C, the expression and labels may be of any integral type, including `unsigned int` and `long int`.

7   Basic Types

unsigned types   Classic C provides only one unsigned type (`unsigned int`).

`signed`   Classic C doesn't support the `signed` type specifier.

number suffixes   Classic C doesn't provide the `U` (or `u`) suffix to specify that an integer constant is unsigned, nor does it provide the `F` (or `f`) suffix to indicate that a floating constant is to be stored as a `float` value instead of a `double` value. In Classic C, the `L` (or `l`) suffix can't be used with floating constants.

`long float`   Classic C allows the use of `long float` as a synonym for `double`; this usage isn't legal in Standard C.

`long double`   Classic C doesn't provide the `long double` type.

escape sequences   The escape sequences `\a`, `\v`, and `\?` don't exist in Classic C. Also, Classic C doesn't provide hexadecimal escape sequences.

`size_t`   In Classic C, the `sizeof` operator returns a value of type `int`; in Standard C, it returns a value of type `size_t`.

usual arithmetic conversions   Classic C requires that `float` operands be converted to `double`. Also, Classic C specifies that combining a shorter unsigned integer with a longer signed integer always produces an unsigned result.

9   Functions

function definitions   In a Standard C function definition, the types of the parameters are included in the parameter list:

```
double square(double x)
{
  return x * x;
}
```

Classic C requires that the types of parameters be specified in separate lists:

```
double square(x)
double x;
{
  return x * x;
}
```

function declarations   A Standard C function declaration (prototype) specifies the types of the function's parameters (and the names as well, if desired):

```
double square(double x);
double square(double);      /* alternate form */
int rand(void);             /* no parameters  */
```

A Classic C function declaration omits all information about parameters:

```
double square();
int rand();
```

function calls   When a Classic C definition or declaration is used, the compiler doesn't check that the function is called with arguments of the proper number and type. Furthermore, the arguments aren't automatically converted to the types of the corresponding parameters. Instead, the integral promotions are performed, and `float` arguments are converted to `double`.

void   Classic C doesn't support the `void` type.

12   Pointers and Arrays

pointer subtraction   Subtracting two pointers produces an `int` value in Classic C but a `ptrdiff_t` value in Standard C.

13   Strings

string literals   In Classic C, adjacent string literals aren't concatenated. Also, Classic C doesn't prohibit the modification of string literals.

string initialization   In Classic C, an initializer for a character array of length n is limited to $n - 1$ characters (leaving room for a null character at the end). Standard C allows the initializer to have length n.

14   The Preprocessor

#elif, #error,   Classic C doesn't provide the `#elif`, `#error`, and `#pragma` directives.
#pragma

#, ##, defined   Classic C doesn't provide the `#`, `##`, and `defined` operators.

16   Structures, Unions, and Enumerations

structure and union   In Standard C, each structure and union has its own name space for members;
members and tags   structure and union tags are kept in a separate name space. Classic C uses a single name space for members and tags, so members can't have the same name (with some exceptions), and members and tags can't overlap.

whole-structure   Classic C doesn't allow structures to be assigned, passed as arguments, or returned
operations   by functions.

enumerations   Classic C doesn't support enumerations.

17   Advanced Uses of Pointers

`void *`   In Standard C, `void *` is used as a "generic" pointer type; for example, `malloc` returns a value of type `void *`. In Classic C, `char *` is used for this purpose.

pointer mixing   Classic C allows pointers of different types to be mixed in assignments and comparisons. In Standard C, pointers of type `void *` can be mixed with pointers of other types, but any other mixing isn't allowed without casting. Similarly, Classic C allows the mixing of integers and pointers in assignments and comparisons; Standard C requires casting.

pointers to functions   If `pf` is a pointer to a function, Standard C permits using either `(*pf)(...)` or `pf(...)` to call the function. Classic C allows only `(*pf)(...)`.

18   Declarations

`const` *and* `volatile`   Classic C doesn't provide the `const` and `volatile` type qualifiers.

initialization of arrays, structures, and unions   Classic C doesn't allow the initialization of automatic arrays and structures, nor does it allow initialization of unions (regardless of storage duration).

25   International Features

wide characters   Classic C doesn't support wide character constants and wide string literals.

trigraph sequences   Classic C doesn't support trigraph sequences.

26   Miscellaneous Library Functions

variable arguments   Classic C doesn't provide a portable way to write functions with a variable number of arguments, and lacks the . . . (ellipsis) notation.

APPENDIX D
Standard Library Functions

This appendix describes the library functions supported by Standard C.* When using this appendix, please keep the following points in mind:

- In the interest of brevity and clarity, I've omitted a few details; for the full story, see the standard. Some functions (notably `printf`, `scanf`, and their variants) are covered in detail elsewhere in the book, so their descriptions here are minimal. For more information about a function (including examples of how it's used), see the section(s) listed in italic at the lower right corner of the function's description.

- Each function description ends with lists of other relevant functions. **Similar** functions closely resemble the function being described. **Related** functions are often used in conjunction with the function being described. (For example, `calloc` and `realloc` are "similar" to `malloc`, while `free` is "related.") **See also** functions aren't as closely related to the function being described but might be of interest.

- If some aspect of a function's behavior is described as **implementation-defined,** that means that it depends on how the C library is implemented. The function will always behave consistently, but the results may vary from one system to another. (In other words, check the manual to see what happens.) **Undefined** behavior, on the other hand, is bad news: not only may the behavior vary between systems, but the program may act strangely or even crash.

- The descriptions of many of the functions in <math.h> refer to **domain error** and **range error**, which are defined at the end of this appendix.

---

*This material is adapted from American National Standards Institute ANSI/ISO 9899 © 1990 with permission by ANSI. Copies of this standard may be purchased from ANSI, 11 West 42nd Street, New York, NY 10036.

- The behavior of the following library functions is affected by the current locale:

Character-handling functions (except `isdigit` and `isxdigit`)
Formatted input/output functions
Multibyte character and string functions
String conversion functions
`strcoll`, `strftime`, and `strxfrm`

The `isalpha` function, for example, usually checks whether a character lies between a and z or A and Z. In some locales, other characters are considered alphabetic as well. This appendix describes how the library functions behave in the `"C"` (default) locale.

- A few library functions are actually macros. They're used in the same way as functions, however, so I don't treat them differently.

---

abort   *Abort Program*   `<stdlib.h>`

```
void abort(void);
```

Raises the SIGABRT signal. If the signal isn't caught (or if the signal handler returns), the program terminates abnormally and returns an implementation-defined code indicating unsuccessful termination. Whether output buffers are flushed, open streams closed, or temporary files removed is implementation-defined.

Similar functions   `exit, raise`
Related functions   `assert, signal`
See also   `atexit`   *26.2*

---

abs   *Absolute Value of Integer*   `<stdlib.h>`

```
int abs(int j);
```

Returns   Absolute value of j. The behavior is undefined if the absolute value of j can't be represented.

Similar functions   `fabs, labs`   *26.2*

---

acos   *Arc Cosine*   `<math.h>`

```
double acos(double x);
```

Returns   Arc cosine of x; the return value is in the range 0 to π. A *domain error* occurs if x isn't between −1 and +1.

Related functions   `asin, atan, atan2, cos, sin, tan`   *23.3*

---

asctime   *Convert Date and Time to ASCII*   `<time.h>`

```
char *asctime(const struct tm *timeptr);
```

Returns   A pointer to a null-terminated string of the form

```
Mon Jul 15 12:30:45 1996\n
```

constructed from the broken-down time in the structure pointed to by `timeptr`.

Similar functions   `ctime, strftime`
Related functions   `difftime, gmtime, localtime, mktime, time`   *26.3*

---

asin   *Arc Sine*   `<math.h>`

```
double asin(double x);
```

Returns   Arc sine of x; the return value is in the range $-\pi/2$ to $\pi/2$. A *domain error* occurs if x isn't between -1 and $+1$.

Related functions   `acos, atan, atan2, cos, sin, tan`   *23.3*

---

assert   *Assert Truth of Expression*   `<assert.h>`

```
void assert(int expression);
```

If the value of `expression` is nonzero, `assert` does nothing. If the value of `expression` is zero, `assert` writes a message to `stderr` (specifying the text of `expression`, the name of the source file containing the `assert`, and the line number of the `assert`); it then terminates the program by calling `abort`. To disable `assert`, define the macro `NDEBUG` before including `<assert.h>`.

Related functions   `abort`   *24.1*

---

atan   *Arc Tangent*   `<math.h>`

```
double atan(double x);
```

Returns   Arc tangent of x; the return value is in the range $-\pi/2$ to $\pi/2$.

Similar functions   `atan2`
Related functions   `acos, asin, cos, sin, tan`   *23.3*

---

atan2   *Arc Tangent of Quotient*   `<math.h>`

```
double atan2(double y, double x);
```

Returns   Arc tangent of `y/x`; the return value is in the range $-\pi$ to π. A *domain error* may occur if x and y are both zero.

Similar functions   `atan`
Related functions   `acos, asin, cos, sin, tan`   *23.3*

atexit   *Register Function to be Called at Program Exit*   `<stdlib.h>`

```
int atexit(void (*func)(void));
```

Registers the function pointed to by `func` as a termination function. The function will be called if the program terminates normally (via `return` or `exit` but not `abort`). `atexit` can be called repeatedly to register multiple termination functions. The last function to be registered is the first called upon termination.

Returns   Zero if successful, nonzero if unsuccessful (an implementation-dependent limit has been reached).

Related functions   `exit`
See also   `abort`   *26.2*

---

atof   *Convert String to Floating-Point*   `<stdlib.h>`

```
double atof(const char *nptr);
```

Returns   A `double` value corresponding to the longest initial part of the string pointed to by `nptr` that has the form of a floating-point number. The behavior is undefined if the number can't be represented.

Similar functions   `strtod`
Related functions   `atoi, atol`
See also   `strtol, strtoul`   *26.2*

---

atoi   *Convert String to Integer*   `<stdlib.h>`

```
int atoi(const char *nptr);
```

Returns   An integer corresponding to the longest initial part of the string pointed to by `nptr` that has the form of an integer. The behavior is undefined if the number can't be represented.

Similar functions   `atol, strtol, strtoul`
Related functions   `atof`
See also   `strtod`   *26.2*

---

atol   *Convert String to Long Integer*   `<stdlib.h>`

```
long int atol(const char *nptr);
```

Returns   A long integer corresponding to the longest initial part of the string pointed to by `nptr` that has the form of an integer. The behavior is undefined if the number can't be represented.

Similar functions   `atoi, strtol, strtoul`
Related functions   `atof`
See also   `strtod`   *26.2*

bsearch   *Binary Search*   `<stdlib.h>`

```
void *bsearch(const void *key, const void *base,
              size_t memb, size_t size,
              int (*compar)(const void *,
                            const void *));
```

Searches for the value pointed to by `key` in the sorted array stored at address `base`, which has nmemb elements, each with `size` bytes. `compar` is a pointer to a "comparison function." When passed pointers to the key and an array element, in that order, the comparison function must return a negative, zero, or positive integer, depending on whether the key is less than, equal to, or greater than the array element.

Returns   A pointer to an array element that tests equal to the key. Returns a null pointer if the key isn't found.

Related functions   `qsort`   *26.2*

---

calloc   *Allocate and Clear Memory Block*   `<stdlib.h>`

```
void *calloc(size_t nmemb, size_t size);
```

Allocates a block of memory for an array with nmemb elements, each with `size` bytes. The block is cleared by setting all bits to zero.

Returns   A pointer to the beginning of the block. Returns a null pointer if a block of the requested size can't be allocated.

Similar functions   `malloc, realloc`
Related functions   `free`   *17.3*

---

ceil   *Ceiling*   `<math.h>`

```
double ceil(double x);
```

Returns   Smallest integer that's greater than or equal to x.

Similar functions   `floor`   *23.3*

---

clearerr   *Clear Stream Error*   `<stdio.h>`

```
void clearerr(FILE *stream);
```

Clears the end-of-file and error indicators for the stream pointed to by `stream`.

Related functions   `feof, ferror, rewind`   *22.3*

---

clock   *Processor Clock*   <time.h>

```
clock_t clock(void);
```

Returns   Elapsed processor time (measured in "clock ticks") since the beginning of program execution. (To convert to seconds, divide by CLOCKS_PER_SEC.) Returns (clock_t)-1 if the time is unavailable or can't be represented.

Similar functions   time
See also   difftime   *26.3*

---

cos   *Cosine*   <math.h>

```
double cos(double x);
```

Returns   Cosine of x (measured in radians).

Related functions   acos, asin, atan, atan2, sin, tan   *23.3*

---

cosh   *Hyperbolic Cosine*   <math.h>

```
double cosh(double x);
```

Returns   Hyperbolic cosine of x. A *range error* occurs if the magnitude of x is too large.

Related functions   sinh, tanh
See also   acos, asin, atan, atan2, cos, sin, tan   *23.3*

---

ctime   *Convert Date and Time to String*   <time.h>

```
char *ctime(const time_t *timer);
```

Returns   A pointer to a string describing a local time equivalent to the calendar time pointed to by timer. Equivalent to asctime(localtime(timer)).

Similar functions   asctime, strftime
Related functions   difftime, gmtime, localtime, mktime, time   *26.3*

---

difftime   *Time Difference*   <time.h>

```
double difftime(time_t time1, time_t time0);
```

Returns   Difference between time0 (the earlier time) and time1, measured in seconds.

Related functions   asctime, ctime, gmtime, localtime, mktime, strftime, time
See also   clock   *26.3*

---

div   *Integer Division*   <stdlib.h>

```
div_t div(int numer, int denom);
```

Returns	A structure containing `quot` (the quotient when `numer` is divided by `denom`) and `rem` (the remainder). The behavior is undefined if the result can't be represented.
Similar functions	`ldiv` 26.2

---

exit   *Exit from Program*   <stdlib.h>

```
void exit(int status);
```

Calls all functions registered with `atexit`, flushes all output buffers, closes all open streams, removes any files created by `tmpfile`, and terminates the program. The value of `status` indicates whether the program terminated normally. The only portable values for `status` are `0` and `EXIT_SUCCESS` (both indicate successful termination) plus `EXIT_FAILURE` (unsuccessful termination). Other values of `status` are implementation-defined.

Similar functions	`abort`
Related functions	`atexit` 9.5, 26.2

---

exp   *Exponential*   <math.h>

```
double exp(double x);
```

Returns	*e* raised to the power x. A *range error* occurs if the magnitude of x is too large.
Similar functions	`pow`
Related functions	`log`
See also	`log10` 23.3

---

fabs   *Absolute Value of Floating-Point Number*   <math.h>

```
double fabs(double x);
```

Returns	Absolute value of x.
Similar functions	`abs`, `labs` 23.3

---

fclose   *Close File*   <stdio.h>

```
int fclose(FILE *stream);
```

Closes the stream pointed to by `stream`. Flushes any unwritten output remaining in the stream's buffer. Deallocates the buffer if it was allocated automatically.

Returns	Zero if successful, `EOF` if an error was detected.
Related functions	`fopen`, `freopen`
See also	`fflush` 22.2

---

feof   *Test for End-of-File*   `<stdio.h>`

```
int feof(FILE *stream);
```

Returns   A nonzero value if the end-of-file indicator is set for the stream pointed to by `stream`; otherwise, returns zero.

Similar functions   `ferror`
Related functions   `clearerr, fseek, rewind`   *22.3*

---

ferror   *Test for File Error*   `<stdio.h>`

```
int ferror(FILE *stream);
```

Returns   A nonzero value if the error indicator is set for the stream pointed to by `stream`; otherwise, returns zero.

Similar functions   `feof`
Related functions   `clearerr, rewind`   *22.3*

---

fflush   *Flush File Buffer*   `<stdio.h>`

```
int fflush(FILE *stream);
```

Writes any unwritten data in the buffer associated with `stream`, which points to a stream that was opened for output or updating. If `stream` is a null pointer, `fflush` flushes all streams that have unwritten data stored in a buffer.

Returns   Zero if successful, `EOF` if an error was detected.

See also   `fclose, setbuf, setvbuf`   *22.2*

---

fgetc   *Read Character from File*   `<stdio.h>`

```
int fgetc(FILE *stream);
```

Reads a character from the stream pointed to by `stream`.

Returns   The character read. If `fgetc` encounters the end of the stream, it sets the stream's end-of-file indicator and returns `EOF`. If a read error occurs, `fgetc` sets the stream's error indicator and returns `EOF`.

Similar functions   `getc, getchar`
Related functions   `fputc, putc, ungetc`
See also   `putchar`   *22.4*

---

fgetpos   *Get File Position*   `<stdio.h>`

```
int fgetpos(FILE *stream, fpos_t *pos);
```

Stores the current position of the stream pointed to by `stream` into the object pointed to by `pos`.

Returns   Zero if successful. If the call fails, returns a nonzero value and stores an implementation-defined error code in `errno`.

Similar functions   `ftell`
Related functions   `fsetpos`
See also   `fseek`, `rewind`   *22.7*

---

fgets   *Read String from File*   `<stdio.h>`

```
char *fgets(char *s, int n, FILE *stream);
```

Reads characters from the stream pointed to by `stream` and stores them into the array pointed to by `s`. Reading stops at the first new-line character (which is stored in the string), when $n - 1$ characters have been read, or at end-of-file. `fgets` appends a null character to the string.

Returns   `s` (a pointer to the array in which the input is stored). Returns a null pointer if a read error occurs or `fgets` encounters the end of the stream before it has stored any characters.

Similar functions   `gets`
Related functions   `fputs`
See also   `puts`   *22.5*

---

floor   *Floor*   `<math.h>`

```
double floor(double x);
```

Returns   Largest integer that's less than or equal to `x`.

Similar functions   `ceil`   *23.3*

---

fmod   *Floating Modulus*   `<math.h>`

```
double fmod(double x, double y);
```

Returns   Remainder when `x` is divided by `y`. If `y` is zero, whether a *domain error* occurs or `fmod` returns zero is implementation-defined.

See also   `div`, `ldiv`   *23.3*

---

fopen   *Open File*   `<stdio.h>`

```
FILE *fopen(const char *filename, const char *mode);
```

Opens the file whose name is pointed to by `filename` and associates it with a stream. `mode` specifies the mode in which the file is to be opened. Clears the error and end-of-file indicators for the stream.

Returns	A file pointer to be used when performing subsequent operations on the file. Returns a null pointer if the file can't be opened.
Similar functions	`freopen`
Related functions	`fclose`, `setbuf`, `setvbuf` *22.2*

---

fprintf   *Formatted File Write*   `<stdio.h>`

```
int fprintf(FILE *stream, const char *format, ...);
```

Writes output to the stream pointed to by `stream`. The string pointed to by `format` specifies how subsequent arguments will be displayed.

Returns	Number of characters written. Returns a negative value if an error occurs.
Similar functions	`printf`, `sprintf`, `vfprintf`, `vprintf`, `vsprintf`
Related functions	`fscanf`
See also	`scanf`, `sscanf` *22.3*

---

fputc   *Write Character to File*   `<stdio.h>`

```
int fputc(int c, FILE *stream);
```

Writes the character `c` to the stream pointed to by `stream`.

Returns	`c` (the character written). If a write error occurs, `fputc` sets the error indicator for `stream` and returns `EOF`.
Similar functions	`putc`, `putchar`
Related functions	`fgetc`, `getc`
See also	`getchar` *22.4*

---

fputs   *Write String to File*   `<stdio.h>`

```
int fputs(const char *s, FILE *stream);
```

Writes the string pointed to by `s` to the stream pointed to by `stream`.

Returns	A nonnegative value if successful. Returns `EOF` if a write error occurs.
Similar functions	`puts`
Related functions	`fgets`
See also	`gets` *22.5*

---

fread   *Read Block from File*   `<stdio.h>`

```
size_t fread(void *ptr, size_t size, size_t nmemb,
             FILE *stream);
```

Attempts to read `nmemb` elements, each `size` bytes long, from the stream pointed to by `stream` and store them in the array pointed to by `ptr`.

Returns   Number of elements (*not* characters) actually read. This number will be less than nmemb if fread encounters end-of-file or detects a read error. The return value is zero if either nmemb or size is zero.

Related functions   fwrite   *22.6*

---

free   *Free Memory Block*   `<stdlib.h>`

```
void free(void *ptr);
```

Releases the memory block whose address is ptr (unless ptr is a null pointer, in which case the call has no effect). The block must have been allocated by a call of calloc, malloc, or realloc.

Related functions   calloc, malloc, realloc   *17.4*

---

freopen   *Reopen File*   `<stdio.h>`

```
FILE *freopen(const char *filename, const char *mode,
              FILE *stream);
```

After freopen closes the file associated with stream, it opens the file whose name is filename and associates it with stream. The mode parameter has the same meaning as in a call of fopen.

Returns   Value of stream if the operation succeeds. Returns a null pointer if the file can't be opened.

Similar functions   fopen
Related functions   fclose, setbuf, setvbuf   *22.2*

---

frexp   *Split into Fraction and Exponent*   `<math.h>`

```
double frexp(double value, int *exp);
```

Splits value into a fractional part f and an exponent n in such a way that

$$value = f \times 2^n$$

f is normalized so that either $0.5 \le f < 1$ or $f = 0$. Stores n into the integer that exp points to.

Returns f, the fractional part of value.

Related functions   ldexp
See also   modf   *23.3*

---

fscanf   *Formatted File Read*   `<stdio.h>`

```
int fscanf(FILE *stream, const char *format, ...);
```

Reads any number of data items from the stream pointed to by `stream`. The string pointed to by `format` specifies the format of the items to be read. The arguments that follow `format` point to locations where the items are to be stored.

Returns   Number of data items successfully read and stored. Returns `EOF` if an error occurs or end-of-file is reached before any items could be read.

Similar functions	`scanf, sscanf`
Related functions	`fprintf, vfprintf`
See also	`printf, sprintf, vprintf, vsprintf` *22.3*

---

fseek   *File Seek*   `<stdio.h>`

```
int fseek(FILE *stream, long int offset, int whence);
```

Changes the file position indicator for the stream pointed to by `stream`. If `whence` is SEEK_SET, the new position is the beginning of the file plus `offset` bytes. If `whence` is SEEK_CUR, the new position is the current position plus `offset` bytes. If `whence` is SEEK_END, the new position is the end of the file plus `offset` bytes.

For text streams, either `offset` must be zero or `whence` must be SEEK_SET and `offset` a value obtained by a previous call of `ftell`. For binary streams, `fseek` may not support calls in which `whence` is SEEK_END.

Returns   Zero if the operation is successful, nonzero otherwise.

Similar functions	`fsetpos, rewind`
Related functions	`ftell`
See also	`fgetpos` *22.7*

---

fsetpos   *Set File Position*   `<stdio.h>`

```
int fsetpos(FILE *stream, const fpos_t *pos);
```

Sets the file position indicator for the stream pointed to by `stream` according to the value pointed to by `pos` (obtained from a previous call of `fgetpos`).

Returns   Zero if successful. If the call fails, returns a nonzero value and stores an implementation-defined error code in `errno`.

Similar functions	`fseek, rewind`
Related functions	`fgetpos`
See also	`ftell` *22.7*

---

ftell   *Determine File Position*   `<stdio.h>`

```
long int ftell(FILE *stream);
```

Returns   Returns the current file position indicator for the stream pointed to by `stream`. If the call fails, returns −1L and stores an implementation-defined error code in `errno`.

Similar functions	`fgetpos`
Related functions	`fseek`
See also	`fsetpos, rewind` *22.7*

`fwrite`   *Write Block to File*   `<stdio.h>`

```
size_t fwrite(const void *ptr, size_t size,
              size_t nmemb, FILE *stream);
```

Writes `nmemb` elements, each `size` bytes long, from the array pointed to by `ptr` to the stream pointed to by `stream`.

Returns   Number of elements (*not* characters) actually written. This number will be less than `nmemb` if `fwrite` detects a write error.

Related functions   `fread`   *22.6*

`getc`   *Read Character from File*   `<stdio.h>`

```
int getc(FILE *stream);
```

Reads a character from the stream pointed to by `stream`. *Note:* `getc` is normally implemented as a macro; it may evaluate `stream` more than once.

Returns   The character read. If `getc` encounters the end of the stream, it sets the stream's end-of-file indicator and returns EOF. If a read error occurs, `getc` sets the stream's error indicator and returns EOF.

Similar functions	`fgetc, getchar`
Related functions	`fputc, putc, ungetc`
See also	`putchar` *22.4*

`getchar`   *Read Character*   `<stdio.h>`

```
int getchar(void);
```

Reads a character from the `stdin` stream. *Note:* `getchar` is normally implemented as a macro.

Returns   The character read. If `getchar` encounters the end of the input stream, it sets `stdin`'s end-of-file indicator and returns EOF. If a read error occurs, `getchar` sets `stdin`'s error indicator and returns EOF.

Similar functions	`fgetc, getc`
Related functions	`putchar, ungetc`
See also	`fputc, putc` *7.3, 22.4*

`getenv`   *Get Environment String*   `<stdlib.h>`

```
char *getenv(const char *name);
```

Searches the operating system's environment list to see if any string matches the one pointed to by name.

Returns   A pointer to the string associated with the matching name. Returns a null pointer if no match is found.

See also   `system`   *26.2*

---

gets   *Read String*   `<stdio.h>`

```
char *gets(char *s);
```

Reads characters from the `stdin` stream and stores them into the array pointed to by `s`. Reading stops at the first new-line character (which is discarded) or at end-of-file. `gets` appends a null character to the string.

Returns   `s` (a pointer to the array in which the input is stored). Returns a null pointer if a read error occurs or `gets` encounters the end of the stream before it has stored any characters.

Similar functions   `fgets`
Related functions   `puts`
See also   `fputs`   *13.3, 22.5*

---

gmtime   *Convert to Greenwich Mean Time*   `<time.h>`

```
struct tm *gmtime(const time_t *timer);
```

Returns   A pointer to a structure containing a broken-down UTC (Coordinated Universal Time—formerly Greenwich Mean Time) value equivalent to the calendar time pointed to by `timer`. Returns a null pointer if UTC isn't available.

Similar functions   `localtime`
Related functions   `asctime, ctime, difftime, mktime, strftime, time`   *26.3*

---

isalnum   *Test for Alphanumeric*   `<ctype.h>`

```
int isalnum(int c);
```

Returns   A nonzero value if `c` is alphanumeric and zero otherwise. (`c` is alphanumeric if either `isalpha(c)` or `isdigit(c)` is true.)

Related functions   `isalpha, isdigit`
See also   `islower, isupper`   *23.4*

---

isalpha   *Test for Alphabetic*   `<ctype.h>`

```
int isalpha(int c);
```

Returns   A nonzero value if `c` is alphabetic and zero otherwise. (`c` is alphabetic if either `islower(c)` or `isupper(c)` is true.)

Similar functions	`islower, isupper`	
Related functions	`isalnum`	
See also	`tolower, toupper`	*23.4*

---

iscntrl   *Test for Control Character*   `<ctype.h>`

```
int iscntrl(int c);
```

Returns   A nonzero value if `c` is a control character and zero otherwise.

Related functions   `isgraph, isprint, isspace`   *23.4*

---

isdigit   *Test for Digit*   `<ctype.h>`

```
int isdigit(int c);
```

Returns   A nonzero value if `c` is a digit and zero otherwise.

Similar functions   `isxdigit`
See also   `isalnum`   *23.4*

---

isgraph   *Test for Graphical Character*   `<ctype.h>`

```
int isgraph(int c);
```

Returns   A nonzero value if `c` is a printing character (except a space) and zero otherwise.

Similar functions   `isprint`
Related functions   `iscntrl, isspace`   *23.4*

---

islower   *Test for Lower-Case Letter*   `<ctype.h>`

```
int islower(int c);
```

Returns   A nonzero value if `c` is a lower-case letter and zero otherwise.

Similar functions   `isalpha, isupper`
Related functions   `tolower, toupper`
See also   `isalnum`   *23.4*

---

isprint   *Test for Printing Character*   `<ctype.h>`

```
int isprint(int c);
```

Returns   A nonzero value if `c` is a printing character (including a space) and zero otherwise.

Similar functions   `isgraph`
Related functions   `iscntrl, isspace`   *23.4*

ispunct	*Test for Punctuation Character*	`<ctype.h>`

`int ispunct(int c);`

Returns   A nonzero value if `c` is a punctuation character and zero otherwise. All printing characters except the space and the alphanumeric characters are considered punctuation.

See also   `isalnum, isgraph, isprint`   *23.4*

---

isspace	*Test for White-Space Character*	`<ctype.h>`

`int isspace(int c);`

Returns   A nonzero value if `c` is a white-space character and zero otherwise. The white-space characters are space (`' '`), form feed (`'\f'`), new-line (`'\n'`), carriage return (`'\r'`), horizontal tab (`'\t'`), and vertical tab (`'\v'`).

See also   `iscntrl, isgraph, isprint`   *23.4*

---

isupper	*Test for Upper-Case Letter*	`<ctype.h>`

`int isupper(int c);`

Returns   A nonzero value if `c` is an upper-case letter and zero otherwise.

Similar functions   `isalpha, islower`
See also   `tolower, toupper`   *23.4*

---

isxdigit	*Test for Hex Digit*	`<ctype.h>`

`int isxdigit(int c);`

Returns   A nonzero value if `c` is a hexadecimal digit (0–9, a–f, A–F) and zero otherwise.

Similar functions   `isdigit`   *23.4*

---

labs	*Absolute Value of Long Integer*	`<stdlib.h>`

`long int labs(long int j);`

Returns   Absolute value of `j`. The behavior is undefined if the absolute value of `j` can't be represented.

Similar functions   `abs, fabs`   *26.2*

---

ldexp	*Combine Fraction and Exponent*	`<math.h>`

`double ldexp(double x, int exp);`

Returns	$x \times 2^{exp}$. A *range error* may occur.
Related functions	`frexp` *23.3*

`ldiv`   *Long Integer Division*   `<stdlib.h>`

`ldiv_t ldiv(long int numer, long int denom);`

Returns	A structure containing `quot` (the quotient when `numer` is divided by `denom`) and `rem` (the remainder). The behavior is undefined if the result can't be represented.
Similar functions	`div` *26.2*

`localeconv`   *Get Locale Conventions*   `<locale.h>`

`struct lconv *localeconv(void);`

Returns	A pointer to a structure containing information about the current locale.
Related functions	`setlocale` *25.1*

`localtime`   *Convert to Local Time*   `<time.h>`

`struct tm *localtime(const time_t *timer);`

Returns	A pointer to a structure containing a broken-down local time equivalent to the calendar time pointed to by `timer`.
Similar functions	`gmtime`
Related functions	`asctime`, `ctime`, `difftime`, `mktime`, `strftime`, `time` *26.3*

`log`   *Natural Logarithm*   `<math.h>`

`double log(double x);`

Returns	Logarithm of x to the base *e*. A *domain error* occurs if x is negative. A *range error* may occur if x is zero.
Similar functions	`log10`
Related functions	`exp`
See also	`pow` *23.3*

`log10`   *Common Logarithm*   `<math.h>`

`double log10(double x);`

Returns	Logarithm of x to the base 10. A *domain error* occurs if x is negative. A *range error* may occur if x is zero.
Similar functions	`log`
See also	`exp`, `pow` *23.3*

longjmp   *Nonlocal Jump*   `<setjmp.h>`

`void longjmp(jmp_buf env, int val);`

Restores the environment stored in `env` and returns from the call of `setjmp` that originally saved env. If `val` is nonzero, it will be `setjmp`'s return value; if `val` is 0, `setjmp` returns 1.

Related functions   `setjmp`
See also   `signal`   *24.4*

---

malloc   *Allocate Memory Block*   `<stdlib.h>`

`void *malloc(size_t size);`

Allocates a block of memory with `size` bytes. The block is not cleared.

Returns   A pointer to the beginning of the block. Returns a null pointer if a block of the requested size can't be allocated.

Similar functions   `calloc, realloc`
Related functions   `free`   *17.2*

---

mblen   *Compute Length of Multibyte Character*   `<stdlib.h>`

`int mblen(const char *s, size_t n);`

If `s` is a null pointer, initializes the shift state.

Returns   If `s` is a null pointer, returns a nonzero or zero value, depending on whether or not multibyte characters have state-dependent encodings. If `s` points to a null character, returns zero. Returns the number of bytes in the multibyte character pointed to by `s`, if the next `n` or fewer bytes form a valid character. If not, returns −1.

Related functions   `mbtowc, wctomb`
See also   `mbstowcs, setlocale, wcstombs`   *25.2*

---

mbstowcs   *Convert Multibyte String to Wide Character String*   `<stdlib.h>`

`size_t mbstowcs(wchar_t *pwcs, const char *s,`
`                size_t n);`

Converts the sequence of multibyte characters that `s` points to into a sequence of wide character codes and stores not more than `n` codes into the array pointed to by `pwcs`. Conversion ends if a null character is encountered; it is converted into a code with the value zero.

Returns   Number of array elements modified, not including the terminating code, if any. Returns `(size_t)-1` if an invalid multibyte character is encountered.

Related functions   `wcstombs`
See also   `mblen, mbtowc, setlocale, wctomb`   *25.2*

---

mbtowc   *Convert Multibyte Character to Wide Character*   `<stdlib.h>`

`int mbtowc(wchar_t *pwc, const char *s, size_t n);`

If s is a null pointer, initializes the shift state. If s isn't a null pointer, converts the multibyte character that s points to into the code for a wide character; at most n bytes of the multibyte character will be examined. If the multibyte character is valid and pwc isn't a null pointer, stores the code into the object that pwc points to.

Returns   If s is a null pointer, returns a nonzero or zero value, depending on whether or not multibyte characters have state-dependent encodings. If s points to a null character, returns zero. Returns the number of bytes in the multibyte character pointed to by s, if the next n or fewer bytes form a valid character. If not, returns –1.

Related functions   `mblen, wctomb`
See also   `mbstowcs, setlocale, wcstombs`   *25.2*

---

memchr   *Search Memory Block for Character*   `<string.h>`

`void *memchr(const void *s, int c, size_t n);`

Returns   A pointer to the first occurrence of the character c among the first n characters of the object pointed to by s. Returns a null pointer if c isn't found.

Similar functions   `strchr`
See also   `strpbrk, strrchr, strstr`   *23.5*

---

memcmp   *Compare Memory Blocks*   `<string.h>`

`int memcmp(const void *s1, const void *s2, size_t n);`

Returns   A negative, zero, or positive integer, depending on whether the first n characters of the object pointed to by s1 are less than, equal to, or greater than the first n characters of the object pointed to by s2.

Similar functions   `strcmp, strcoll, strncmp`   *23.5*

---

memcpy   *Copy Memory Block*   `<string.h>`

`void *memcpy(void *s1, const void *s2, size_t n);`

Copies n characters from the object pointed to by s2 into the object pointed to by s1. May not work properly if the objects overlap.

Returns   s1 (a pointer to the destination).

Similar functions   `memmove, strcpy, strncpy`   *23.5*

---

memmove   *Copy Memory Block*   `<string.h>`

`void *memmove(void *s1, const void *s2, size_t n);`

Copies n characters from the object pointed to by `s2` into the object pointed to by `s1`. Will work properly if the objects overlap, although it may be slower than `memcpy`.

Returns   `s1` (a pointer to the destination).

Similar functions   `memcpy`, `strcpy`, `strncpy`   *23.5*

---

memset   *Initialize Memory Block*   `<string.h>`

`void *memset(void *s, int c, size_t n);`

Stores c into the first n characters of the memory block pointed to by `s`.

Returns   `s` (a pointer to the memory block).

See also   `memcpy`, `memmove`   *23.5*

---

mktime   *Convert to Calendar Time*   `<time.h>`

`time_t mktime(struct tm *timeptr);`

Converts a broken-down local time (stored in the structure that `timeptr` points to) into a calendar time. The members of the structure aren't required to be within their legal ranges; also, the values of tm_wday (day of the week) and tm_yday (day of the year) are ignored. `mktime` stores values in tm_wday and tm_yday after adjusting the other members to bring them into their proper ranges.

Returns   A calendar time corresponding to the structure that `timeptr` points to. Returns `(time_t)-1` if the calendar time can't be represented.

Related functions   `asctime`, `ctime`, `difftime`, `gmtime`, `localtime`, `strftime`, `time` *26.3*

---

modf   *Split into Integer and Fractional Parts*   `<math.h>`

`double modf(double value, double *iptr);`

Splits `value` into integer and fractional parts; stores the integer part into the `double` object pointed to by `iptr`.

Returns   Fractional part of `value`.

See also   `frexp`   *23.3*

perror   *Print Error Message*   `<stdio.h>`

`void perror(const char *s);`

Writes the following message to the `stderr` stream:

string : *error-message*

where *string* is the string pointed to by `s` and *error-message* is an implementation-defined message that matches the one returned by the call `strerror(errno)`.

Related functions   `strerror`   *24.2*

---

pow   *Power*   `<math.h>`

`double pow(double x, double y);`

Returns   `x` raised to the power `y`. A *domain error* occurs if (1) `x` is negative and `y`'s value isn't an integer or (2) the result can't be represented when `x` is zero and `y` is less than or equal to zero. A *range error* is also possible.

Similar functions   `exp, sqrt`
See also   `log, log10`   *23.3*

---

printf   *Formatted Write*   `<stdio.h>`

`int printf(const char *format, ...);`

Writes output to the `stdout` stream. The string pointed to by `format` specifies how subsequent arguments will be displayed.

Returns   Number of characters written. Returns a negative value if an error occurs.

Similar functions   `fprintf, sprintf, vfprintf, vprintf, vsprintf`
Related functions   `scanf`
See also   `fscanf, sscanf`   *3.1, 22.3*

---

putc   *Write Character to File*   `<stdio.h>`

`int putc(int c, FILE *stream);`

Writes the character `c` to the stream pointed to by `stream`. *Note:* `putc` is normally implemented as a macro; it may evaluate `stream` more than once.

Returns   `c` (the character written). If a write error occurs, `fputc` sets the stream's error indicator and returns EOF.

Similar functions   `fputc, putchar`
Related functions   `fgetc, getc`
See also   `getchar`   *22.4*

---

putchar   *Write Character*   `<stdio.h>`

`int putchar(int c);`

Writes the character c to the `stdout` stream. *Note:* `putchar` is normally implemented as a macro.

Returns   c (the character written). If a write error occurs, `putchar` sets `stdout`'s error indicator and returns EOF.

Similar functions   `fputc, putc`
Related functions   `getchar`
See also   `fgetc, getc`   *7.3, 22.4*

---

puts   *Write String*   `<stdio.h>`

`int puts(const char *s);`

Writes the string pointed to by s to the `stdout` stream, then writes a new-line character.

Returns   A nonnegative value if successful. Returns EOF if a write error occurs.

Similar functions   `fputs`
Related functions   `gets`
See also   `fgets`   *13.3, 22.5*

---

qsort   *Sort Array*   `<stdlib.h>`

```
void qsort(void *base, size_t nmemb, size_t size,
           int (*compar)(const void *, const void *));
```

Sorts the array pointed to by base. The array has nmemb elements, each size bytes long. compar is a pointer to a "comparison function." When passed pointers to two array elements, the function must return a negative, zero, or positive integer, depending on whether the first array element is less than, equal to, or greater than the second.

Related functions   `bsearch`   *17.7, 26.2*

---

raise   *Raise Signal*   `<signal.h>`

`int raise(int sig);`

Raises the signal whose number is sig.

Returns   Zero if successful, nonzero otherwise.

Similar functions   `abort`
Related functions   `signal`   *24.3*

rand   *Generate Pseudo-Random Number*   `<stdlib.h>`

```
int rand(void);
```

Returns   A pseudo-random integer between 0 and RAND_MAX (inclusive).

Related functions   `srand`   *26.2*

---

realloc   *Resize Memory Block*   `<stdlib.h>`

```
void *realloc(void *ptr, size_t size);
```

`ptr` is assumed to point to a block of memory previously obtained from `calloc`, `malloc`, or `realloc`. `realloc` allocates a block of `size` bytes, copying the contents of the old block if necessary.

Returns   A pointer to the beginning of the new memory block. Returns a null pointer if a block of the requested size can't be allocated.

Similar functions   `calloc, malloc`
Related functions   `free`   *17.3*

---

remove   *Remove File*   `<stdio.h>`

```
int remove(const char *filename);
```

Deletes the file whose name is pointed to by `filename`.

Returns   Zero if successful, nonzero otherwise.

See also   `rename`   *22.2*

---

rename   *Rename File*   `<stdio.h>`

```
int rename(const char *old, const char *new);
```

Changes the name of a file. `old` and `new` point to strings containing the old name and new name, respectively.

Returns   Zero if the renaming is successful. Returns a nonzero value if the operation fails (perhaps because the old file is currently open).

See also   `remove`   *22.2*

---

rewind   *Rewind File*   `<stdio.h>`

```
void rewind(FILE *stream);
```

Sets the file position indicator for the stream pointed to by `stream` to the beginning of the file. Clears the error and end-of-file indicators for the stream.

---

scanf   *Formatted Read*   `<stdio.h>`

```
int scanf(const char *format, ...);
```

Reads any number of data items from the `stdin` stream. The string pointed to by `format` specifies the format of the items to be read. The arguments that follow `format` point to locations where the items are to be stored.

Returns   Number of data items successfully read and stored. Returns `EOF` if an error occurs or end-of-file is reached before any items could be read.

---

setbuf   *Set Buffer*   `<stdio.h>`

```
void setbuf(FILE *stream, char *buf);
```

If `buf` isn't a null pointer, a call of `setbuf` is equivalent to:

```
(void) setvbuf(stream, buf, _IOFBF, BUFSIZ);
```

(`BUFSIZ` is a macro defined in `<stdio.h>`.) Otherwise, it's equivalent to:

```
(void) setvbuf(stream, NULL, _IONBF, 0);
```

---

setjmp   *Prepare for Nonlocal Jump*   `<setjmp.h>`

```
int setjmp(jmp_buf env);
```

Stores the current environment in `env` for use in a later call of `longjmp`.

Returns   Zero when called directly. Returns a nonzero value when returning from a call of `longjmp`.

---

setlocale   *Set Locale*   `<locale.h>`

```
char *setlocale(int category, const char *locale);
```

Sets a portion of the program's locale. `category` indicates which portion is affected. `locale` points to a string representing the new locale.

Returns	If locale is a null pointer, returns a pointer to the string associated with category for the current locale. Otherwise, returns a pointer to the string associated with category for the new locale. Returns a null pointer if the operation fails.
Related functions	localeconv *25.1*

---

setvbuf   *Set Buffer*   <stdio.h>

```
int setvbuf(FILE *stream, char *buf, int mode,
            size_t size);
```

Changes the buffering of the stream pointed to by stream. The value of mode can be either _IOFBF (full buffering), _IOLBF (line buffering), or _IONBF (no buffering). If buf is a null pointer, a buffer is automatically allocated if needed. Otherwise, buf points to a memory block that can be used as the buffer; size is the number of bytes in the block. *Note:* setvbuf must be called after the stream is opened but before any other operations are performed on it.

Returns	Zero if the operation is successful. Returns a nonzero value if mode is invalid or the request can't be honored.
Similar functions	setbuf
Related functions	fopen, freopen
See also	fflush *22.2*

---

signal   *Install Signal Handler*   <signal.h>

```
void (*signal(int sig, void (*func)(int)))(int);
```

Installs the function that func points to as the handler for the signal whose number is sig.

Returns	A pointer to the previous handler for this signal; returns SIG_ERR if the handler can't be installed.
Related functions	abort, raise *24.3*

---

sin   *Sine*   <math.h>

```
double sin(double x);
```

Returns	Sine of x (measured in radians).
Related functions	acos, asin, atan, atan2, cos, tan *23.3*

---

sinh   *Hyperbolic Sine*   <math.h>

```
double sinh(double x);
```

Returns	Hyperbolic sine of x. A *range error* occurs if the magnitude of x is too large.

Related functions	`cosh, tanh`	
See also	`acos, asin, atan, atan2, cos, sin, tan`	*23.3*

`sprintf`   *Formatted String Write*   `<stdio.h>`

```
int sprintf(char *s, const char *format, ...);
```

Similar to `fprintf` and `printf`, but stores characters in the array pointed to by s instead of writing them to a stream. The string pointed to by `format` specifies how subsequent arguments will be displayed. Stores a null character in the array at the end of output.

Returns   Number of characters stored in the array, not counting the null character.

Similar functions	`fprintf, printf, vfprintf, vprintf, vsprintf`	
Related functions	`sscanf`	
See also	`fscanf, scanf`	*22.8*

`sqrt`   *Square Root*   `<math.h>`

```
double sqrt(double x);
```

Returns   Square root of x. A *domain error* occurs if x is negative.

Similar functions	`pow`	*23.3*

`srand`   *Seed Pseudo-Random Number Generator*   `<stdlib.h>`

```
void srand(unsigned int seed);
```

Uses `seed` to initialize the sequence of pseudo-random numbers produced by calling `rand`.

Related functions	`rand`	*26.2*

`sscanf`   *Formatted String Read*   `<stdio.h>`

```
int sscanf(const char *s, const char *format, ...);
```

Similar to `fscanf` and `scanf`, but reads characters from the string pointed to by s instead of reading them from a stream. The string pointed to by `format` specifies the format of the items to be read. The arguments that follow `format` point to locations where the items are to be stored.

Returns   Number of data items successfully read and stored. Returns `EOF` if the end of the string is reached before any items could be read.

Similar functions	`fscanf, scanf`	
Related functions	`sprintf, vsprintf`	
See also	`fprintf, printf, vfprintf, vprintf`	*22.8*

---

strcat   *String Concatenation*   `<string.h>`

`char *strcat(char *s1, const char *s2);`

Appends characters from the string pointed to by `s2` to the string pointed to by `s1`.

Returns   `s1` (a pointer to the concatenated string).

Similar functions   `strncat`   *13.5, 23.5*

---

strchr   *Search String for Character*   `<string.h>`

`char *strchr(const char *s, int c);`

Returns   A pointer to the first occurrence of the character `c` in the string pointed to by `s`. Returns a null pointer if `c` isn't found.

Similar functions   `memchr`
See also   `strpbrk, strrchr, strstr`   *23.5*

---

strcmp   *String Compare*   `<string.h>`

`int strcmp(const char *s1, const char *s2);`

Returns   A negative, zero, or positive integer, depending on whether the string pointed to by `s1` is less than, equal to, or greater than the string pointed to by `s2`.

Similar functions   `memcmp, strcoll, strncmp`   *13.5, 23.5*

---

strcoll   *String Compare Using Locale-Specific Collating Sequence*   `<string.h>`

`int strcoll(const char *s1, const char *s2);`

Returns   A negative, zero, or positive integer, depending on whether the string pointed to by `s1` is less than, equal to, or greater than the string pointed to by `s2`. The comparison is performed according to the rules of the current locale's `LC_COLLATE` category.

Similar functions   `memcmp, strcmp, strncmp`
Related functions   `strxfrm`   *23.5*

---

strcpy   *String Copy*   `<string.h>`

`char *strcpy(char *s1, const char *s2);`

Copies the string pointed to by `s2` into the array pointed to by `s1`.

Returns   `s1` (a pointer to the destination).

Similar functions   `memcpy, memmove, strncpy`   *13.5, 23.5*

strcspn   *Search String for Initial Span of Characters Not in Set*   <string.h>

```
size_t strcspn(const char *s1, const char *s2);
```

Returns   Length of the longest initial segment of the string pointed to by s1 that doesn't contain any character in the string pointed to by s2.

Related functions   strspn   *23.5*

---

strerror   *Convert Error Number to String*   <string.h>

```
char *strerror(int errnum);
```

Returns   A pointer to a string containing an error message corresponding to the value of errnum.

Related functions   perror   *24.2*

---

strftime   *Write Formatted Date and Time to String*   <time.h>

```
size_t strftime(char *s, size_t maxsize,
                const char *format,
                const struct tm *timeptr);
```

Stores characters into the array pointed to by s under control of the string pointed to by format. The format string may contain ordinary characters, which are copied unchanged, and conversion specifiers, which are replaced by values from the structure pointed to by timeptr. The maxsize parameter limits the number of characters (including the null character) that can be stored.

Returns   Zero if the number of characters to be stored (including the null character) exceeds maxsize. Otherwise, returns the number of characters stored (not including the null character).

Similar functions   asctime, ctime
Related functions   difftime, gmtime, localtime, mktime, time   *26.3*

---

strlen   *String Length*   <string.h>

```
size_t strlen(const char *s);
```

Returns   The length of the string pointed to by s, not including the null character.

13.5, 23.5

---

strncat   *Bounded String Concatenation*   <string.h>

```
char *strncat(char *s1, const char *s2, size_t n);
```

Appends characters from the array pointed to by s2 to the string pointed to by s1. Copying stops when a null character is encountered or n characters have been copied.

Returns   s1 (a pointer to the concatenated string).

Similar functions   strcat   *23.5*

---

strncmp   *Bounded String Compare*   <string.h>

`int strncmp(const char *s1, const char *s2, size_t n);`

Returns   A negative, zero, or positive integer, depending on whether the first n characters of the array pointed to by s1 are less than, equal to, or greater than the first n characters of the array pointed to by s2. Comparison stops if a null character is encountered in either array.

Similar functions   memcmp, strcmp, strcoll   *23.5*

---

strncpy   *Bounded String Copy*   <string.h>

`char *strncpy(char *s1, const char *s2, size_t n);`

Copies the first n characters of the array pointed to by s2 into the array pointed to by s1. If it encounters a null character in the array pointed to by s2, strncpy adds null characters to the array pointed to by s1 until a total of n characters have been written.

Returns   s1 (a pointer to the destination).

Similar functions   memcpy, memmove, strcpy   *23.5*

---

strpbrk   *Search String for One of a Set of Characters*   <string.h>

`char *strpbrk(const char *s1, const char *s2);`

Returns   A pointer to the leftmost character in the string pointed to by s1 that matches any character in the string pointed to by s2. Returns a null pointer if no match is found.

See also   memchr, strchr, strrchr, strstr   *23.5*

---

strrchr   *Search String in Reverse for Character*   <string.h>

`char *strrchr(const char *s, int c);`

Heturns   A pointer to the last occurrence of the character c in the string pointed to by s. Returns a null pointer if c isn't found.

See also   memchr, strchr, strpbrk, strstr   *23.5*

`strspn`   *Search String for Initial Span of Characters in Set*   `<string.h>`

`size_t strspn(const char *s1, const char *s2);`

Returns   Length of the longest initial segment in the string pointed to by `s1` that consists entirely of characters in the string pointed to by `s2`.

Related functions   `strcspn`   *23.5*

`strstr`   *Search String for Substring*   `<string.h>`

`char *strstr(const char *s1, const char *s2);`

Returns   A pointer to the first occurrence in the string pointed to by `s1` of the characters in the string pointed to by `s2`. Returns a null pointer if no match is found.

See also   `memchr, strchr, strpbrk, strrchr`   *23.5*

`strtod`   *Convert String to Double*   `<stdlib.h>`

`double strtod(const char *nptr, char **endptr);`

Skips white-space characters in the string that `nptr` points to, then converts subsequent characters into a `double` value. If `endptr` isn't a null pointer, `strtod` modifies the object pointed to by `endptr` so that it points to the first leftover character. If no `double` value is found, or if it has the wrong form, `strtod` stores `nptr` into the object pointed to by `endptr`. If the number is too large or small to represent, it stores `ERANGE` in `errno`.

Returns   Converted number. Returns zero if no conversion could be performed. If the number is too large to represent, returns plus or minus `HUGE_VAL`, depending on the number's sign. Returns zero if the number is too small to represent.

Similar functions   `atof`
Related functions   `strtol, strtoul`
See also   `atoi, atol`   *26.2*

`strtok`   *Search String for Token*   `<string.h>`

`char *strtok(char *s1, const char *s2);`

Searches the string pointed to by `s1` for a "token" consisting of characters not in the string pointed to by `s2`. If a token exists, the character following it is changed to a null character. If `s1` is a null pointer, a search begun by the most recent call of `strtok` is continued; the search begins immediately after the null character at the end of the previous token.

Returns   A pointer to the first character of the token. Returns a null pointer if no token could be found.

See also   `memchr, strchr, strpbrk, strrchr, strstr`   *23.5*

strtol   *Convert String to Long Integer*   `<stdlib.h>`

```
long int strtol(const char *nptr, char **endptr,
                int base);
```

Skips white-space characters in the string that `nptr` points to, then converts subsequent characters into a `long int` value. If `base` is between 2 and 36, it is used as the radix of the number. If `base` is zero, the number is assumed to be decimal unless it begins with `0` (octal) or with `0x` or `0X` (hex). If `endptr` isn't a null pointer, `strtol` modifies the object pointed to by `endptr` so that it points to the first leftover character. If no `long int` value is found, or if it has the wrong form, `strtol` stores `nptr` into the object pointed to by `endptr`. If the number can't be represented, it stores `ERANGE` in `errno`.

Returns   Converted number. Returns zero if no conversion could be performed. If the number can't be represented, returns `LONG_MAX` or `LONG_MIN`, depending on the number's sign.

Similar functions   `atoi, atol, strtoul`
Related functions   `strtod`
See also   `atof`   *26.2*

---

strtoul   *Convert String to Unsigned Long Integer*   `<stdlib.h>`

```
unsigned long int strtoul(const char *nptr,
                          char **endptr, int base);
```

`strtoul` is identical to `strtol`, except that it converts a string to an unsigned long integer.

Returns   Converted number. Returns zero if no conversion could be performed. If the number can't be represented, returns `ULONG_MAX`.

Similar functions   `atoi, atol, strtol`
Related functions   `strtod`
See also   `atof`   *26.2*

---

strxfrm   *Transform Locale-Specific String*   `<string.h>`

```
size_t strxfrm(char *s1, const char *s2, size_t n);
```

Transforms the string pointed to by `s2`, placing the first `n` characters of the result—including the null character—in the array pointed to by `s1`. Calling `strcmp` with two transformed strings should produce the same outcome (negative, zero, or positive) as calling `strcoll` with the original strings.

Returns   Length of the transformed string (which may exceed `n`).

Related functions   `strcmp, strcoll`   *23.5*

system   *Perform Operating System Command*   `<stdlib.h>`

`int system(const char *string);`

Passes the string pointed to by `string` to the operating system's command processor (shell) to be executed.

Returns   When `string` is a null pointer, returns a nonzero value if a command processor is available. If `string` isn't a null pointer, returns an implementation-defined value.

See also   `getenv`   *26.2*

---

tan   *Tangent*   `<math.h>`

`double tan(double x);`

Returns   Tangent of x (measured in radians).

Related functions   `acos, asin, atan, atan2, cos, sin`   *23.3*

---

tanh   *Hyperbolic Tangent*   `<math.h>`

`double tanh(double x);`

Returns   Hyperbolic tangent of x.

Related functions   `cosh, sinh`
See also   `acos, asin, atan, atan2, cos, sin, tan`   *23.3*

---

time   *Current Time*   `<time.h>`

`time_t time(time_t *timer);`

Returns   The current calendar time. Returns `(time_t)-1` if the calendar time isn't available. If `timer` isn't a null pointer, also stores the return value in the object that `timer` points to.

Similar functions   `clock`
Related functions   `asctime, ctime, difftime, gmtime, localtime, mktime, strftime`
    26.3

---

tmpfile   *Create Temporary File*   `<stdio.h>`

`FILE *tmpfile(void);`

Creates a temporary file that will automatically be removed when it's closed or the program ends. Opens the file in `"wb+"` mode.

Returns   A file pointer to be used when performing subsequent operations on the file. Returns a null pointer if a file can't be created.

Related functions   `tmpnam, fopen`   *22.2*

---

tmpnam *Generate Temporary File Name*   `<stdio.h>`

`char *tmpnam(char *s);`

Generates a name for a temporary file. If `s` is a null pointer, `tmpnam` stores the file name in a static variable. Otherwise, it copies the file name into the character array pointed to by `s`. (The array must be long enough to store `L_tmpnam` characters, where `L_tmpnam` is a macro defined in `<stdio.h>`.)

Returns   A pointer to the file name.

Related functions   `tmpfile`   *22.2*

---

tolower *Convert to Lower Case*   `<ctype.h>`

`int tolower(int c);`

Returns   If `c` is an upper-case letter, returns the corresponding lower-case letter. If `c` isn't an upper-case letter, returns `c` unchanged.

Similar functions   `toupper`
Related functions   `islower, isupper`
See also   `isalpha`   *23.4*

---

toupper *Convert to Upper Case*   `<ctype.h>`

`int toupper(int c);`

Returns   If `c` is a lower-case letter, returns the corresponding upper-case letter. If `c` isn't a lower-case letter, returns `c` unchanged.

Similar functions   `tolower`
Related functions   `islower, isupper`
See also   `isalpha`   *23.4*

---

ungetc *Unread Character*   `<stdio.h>`

`int ungetc(int c, FILE *stream);`

Pushes the character `c` back onto the stream pointed to by `stream` and clears the stream's end-of-file indicator. The number of characters that can be pushed back by consecutive calls of `ungetc` varies; only the first call is guaranteed to succeed. Calling a file positioning function (`fseek`, `fsetpos`, or `rewind`) causes the pushed-back character(s) to be lost.

Returns   `c` (the pushed-back character). Returns `EOF` if an attempt is made to push back too many characters without a read or file positioning operation.

Related functions   `fgetc, getc, getchar`   *22.4*

va_arg   *Fetch Argument from Variable Argument List*   <stdarg.h>

type va_arg(va_list ap, *type*);

Fetches an argument in a variable argument list, then modifies ap so that the next use of va_arg fetches the following argument. ap must have been initialized by va_start prior to the first use of va_arg.

Returns   Value of the argument, assuming that its type (after the default argument promotions have been applied) is compatible with *type*.

Related functions   va_end, va_start
See also   vfprintf, vprintf, vsprintf   *26.1*

---

va_end   *End Processing of Variable Argument List*   <stdarg.h>

void va_end(va_list ap);

Ends the processing of the variable argument list associated with ap.

Related functions   va_arg, va_start
See also   vfprintf, vprintf, vsprintf   *26.1*

---

va_start   *Start Processing of Variable Argument List*   <stdarg.h>

void va_start(va_list ap, *parmN*);

Must be invoked before accessing a variable argument list. Initializes ap for later use by va_arg and va_end. *parmN* is the name of the last ordinary parameter (the one followed by , ...).

Related functions   va_arg, va_end
See also   vfprintf, vprintf, vsprintf   *26.1*

---

vfprintf   *Formatted File Write Using Variable Argument List*   <stdio.h>

int vfprintf(FILE *stream, const char *format,
                va_list arg);

Equivalent to fprintf with the variable argument list replaced by arg.

Returns   Number of characters written. Returns a negative value if an error occurs.

Similar functions   fprintf, printf, sprintf, vprintf, vsprintf
See also   va_arg, va_end, va_start   *26.1*

---

vprintf   *Formatted Write Using Variable Argument List*   <stdio.h>

int vprintf(const char *format, va_list arg);

Equivalent to `printf` with the variable argument list replaced by `arg`.

Returns   Number of characters written. Returns a negative value if an error occurs.

Similar functions   `fprintf`, `printf`, `sprintf`, `vfprintf`, `vsprintf`
See also   `va_arg`, `va_end`, `va_start`   *26.1*

---

vsprintf   *Formatted String Write Using Variable Argument List*   `<stdio.h>`

```
int vsprintf(char *s, const char *format,
             va_list arg);
```

Equivalent to `sprintf` with the variable argument list replaced by `arg`.

Returns   Number of characters stored, not counting the null character.

Similar functions   `fprintf`, `printf`, `sprintf`, `vfprintf`, `vprintf`
See also   `va_arg`, `va_end`, `va_start`   *26.1*

---

wcstombs   *Convert Wide Character String to Multibyte String*   `<stdlib.h>`

```
size_t wcstombs(char *s, const wchar_t *pwcs,
                size_t n);
```

Converts a sequence of wide character codes into the corresponding multibyte characters. `pwcs` points to an array containing the wide characters. The multibyte characters are stored into the array pointed to by `s`. Conversion ends if a null character is stored or if storing a multibyte character would exceed the limit of `n` bytes.

Returns   Number of bytes stored, not including the null character. Returns `(size_t)-1` if a code that doesn't correspond to a valid multibyte character is encountered.

Related functions   `mbstowcs`
See also   `mblen`, `mbtowc`, `setlocale`, `wctomb`   *25.2*

---

wctomb   *Convert Wide Character to Multibyte Character*   `<stdlib.h>`

```
int wctomb(char *s, wchar_t wchar);
```

Converts the wide character whose code is `wchar` into a multibyte character. If `s` isn't a null pointer, stores the result into the array that `s` points to. If `s` is a null pointer, initializes the shift state.

Returns   If `s` is a null pointer, returns a nonzero or zero value, depending on whether or not multibyte characters have state-dependent encodings. If `wchar` corresponds to a valid multibyte character, returns the number of bytes in the character; if not, returns −1.

Related functions   `mblen`, `mbtowc`
See also   `mbstowcs`, `setlocale`, `wcstombs`   *25.2*

Errors for <math.h> *Functions*

Domain Error   An argument is outside the domain of the function. If a domain error occurs, the function's return value is implementation-defined and EDOM is stored in errno.

Range Error   The return value of a function is outside the range of double values. If the return value's magnitude is too large to represent (overflow), the function returns positive or negative HUGE_VAL, depending on the sign of the correct result. In addition, ERANGE is stored in errno. If the return value's magnitude is too small to represent (underflow), the function returns zero; some implementations may also store ERANGE in errno.

ASCII Character Set

Decimal	Escape Sequence Oct	Escape Sequence Hex	Escape Sequence Char	Character							
0	\0	\x00		*nul*	32		64	@	96	`
1	\1	\x01		*soh* (^A)	33	!	65	A	97	a
2	\2	\x02		*stx* (^B)	34	"	66	B	98	b
3	\3	\x03		*etx* (^C)	35	#	67	C	99	c
4	\4	\x04		*eot* (^D)	36	$	68	D	100	d
5	\5	\x05		*enq* (^E)	37	%	69	E	101	e
6	\6	\x06		*ack* (^F)	38	&	70	F	102	f
7	\7	\x07	\a	*bel* (^G)	39	'	71	G	103	g
8	\10	\x08	\b	*bs* (^H)	40	(	72	H	104	h
9	\11	\x09	\t	*ht* (^I)	41	)	73	I	105	i
10	\12	\x0a	\n	*lf* (^J)	42	*	74	J	106	j
11	\13	\x0b	\v	*vt* (^K)	43	+	75	K	107	k
12	\14	\x0c	\f	*ff* (^L)	44	,	76	L	108	l
13	\15	\x0d	\r	*cr* (^M)	45	-	77	M	109	m
14	\16	\x0e		*so* (^N)	46	.	78	N	110	n
15	\17	\x0f		*si* (^O)	47	/	79	O	111	o
16	\20	\x10		*dle* (^P)	48	0	80	P	112	p
17	\21	\x11		*dc1* (^Q)	49	1	81	Q	113	q
18	\22	\x12		*dc2* (^R)	50	2	82	R	114	r
19	\23	\x13		*dc3* (^S)	51	3	83	S	115	s
20	\24	\x14		*dc4* (^T)	52	4	84	T	116	t
21	\25	\x15		*nak* (^U)	53	5	85	U	117	u
22	\26	\x16		*syn* (^V)	54	6	86	V	118	v
23	\27	\x17		*etb* (^W)	55	7	87	W	119	w
24	\30	\x18		*can* (^X)	56	8	88	X	120	x
25	\31	\x19		*em* (^Y)	57	9	89	Y	121	y
26	\32	\x1a		*sub* (^Z)	58	:	90	Z	122	z
27	\33	\x1b		*esc*	59	;	91	[	123	{
28	\34	\x1c		*fs*	60	<	92	\	124		
29	\35	\x1d		*gs*	61	=	93	]	125	}
30	\36	\x1e		*rs*	62	>	94	^	126	~
31	\37	\x1f		*us*	63	?	95	_	127	*del*

BIBLIOGRAPHY

The best book on programming for the layman is
"Alice in Wonderland"; but that's because it's
the best book on anything for the layman.

American National Standard for Information Systems—Programming Language—
C, Document Number X3.159–1989. Now superseded by the ISO standard
(ISO/IEC 9899:1990), which is the same except for formatting differences.

Obtaining the C Standard

Although the C standard is an important document that most serious programmers
will want to own, it's not obvious how to obtain a copy. One possibility is to order the
original standard (X3.159–1989) from ANSI. Call (212) 642-4900 or write to

American National Standards Institute
11 West 42nd Street, 13th Floor
New York, NY 10036

The price, as of this writing, is $215.00. Before you rush to order a copy, however,
be aware that the ANSI standard has been superseded by the ISO standard, which
is available from ANSI for $130.00. (Outside the U.S., contact ISO at 1, rue de
Varembi, Case postale 56, CH-1211 Geneve 20, Switzerland or send e-mail to
central@isocs.iso.ch.) Why the price difference? The ANSI standard is bundled
with the Rationale, a document that explains some of the decisions made during the
creation of the standard.

If the price is still a bit high, consider buying a copy of *The Annotated ANSI C
Standard* (Berkeley: Osborne McGraw-Hill, 1993), which sells for about $40.
(Despite its title, this book actually reprints the international standard.) The book
includes annotations by Herbert Schildt, but lacks the Rationale.

Since standards organizations support themselves by selling documents, you
can't get either the ANSI or the ISO standard via the Internet. You can, however,
obtain the Rationale from *ftp.uu.net* in directory *doc/standards/ansi/X3.159-1989*.

Bentley, J., *Programming Pearls*, Addison-Wesley, Reading, Mass., 1986, and *More Programming Pearls*, Addison-Wesley, Reading, Mass., 1988. Although they aren't about C, these books will be of great interest to C programmers. The author emphasizes writing efficient programs, but he touches on other topics that are crucial for the professional programmer. His light touch makes the books as enjoyable to read as they are informative.

Feuer, A. R., *The C Puzzle Book*, Second Edition, Prentice-Hall, Englewood Cliffs, N.J., 1989. Contains numerous "puzzles"—small C programs whose output the reader is asked to predict. Good for testing your C knowledge and reviewing the fine points of the language.

Ghezzi, C., M. Jazayeri, and D. Mandrioli, *Fundamentals of Software Engineering*, Prentice-Hall, Englewood Cliffs, N.J., 1991. An excellent software engineering text that clearly shows the relationship between programming languages and software engineering. The book to turn to for more information on modularity, abstraction, and other software design principles.

Harbison, S. P., and G. L. Steele, Jr., *C: A Reference Manual*, Fourth Edition, Prentice-Hall, Englewood Cliffs, N.J., 1995. The ultimate C reference—essential reading for the would-be C expert. Covers both Standard C and Classic C in considerable detail, with frequent discussions of implementation differences found in C compilers. Not a tutorial—assumes that the reader is already well versed in C.

Horton, M. R., *Portable C Software*, Prentice-Hall, Englewood Cliffs, N.J., 1990. Covers all aspects of program portability, including hardware and operating system dependencies. Especially valuable for making programs portable among different versions of UNIX.

Kernighan, B. W., and D. M. Ritchie, *The C Programming Language*, Second Edition, Prentice-Hall, Englewood Cliffs, N.J., 1988. The original C book, affectionately known as K&R or simply "the White Book." Includes both a tutorial and a complete C reference manual. The second edition reflects the changes made in Standard C. The first edition is sometimes called the "Old Testament"; the second edition, of course, is the "New Testament."

Koenig, A., *C Traps and Pitfalls*, Addison-Wesley, Reading, Mass., 1989. An excellent compendium of common (and some not-so-common) C pitfalls. Forewarned is forearmed.

Libes, D., *Obfuscated C and Other Mysteries*, Wiley, New York, 1993. A collection of essays about various aspects of C. Notable for providing (and explaining) winning programs from the annual International Obfuscated C Code Contest.

Lunde, K., *Understanding Japanese Information Processing*, O'Reilly & Associates, Sebastopol, Calif., 1993. A fine introduction to the intricacies of writing software for the Japanese market. If you're not sure why C provides multibyte characters, read this book.

Plauger, P. J., *The Standard C Library*, Prentice-Hall, Englewood Cliffs, N.J., 1992. Not only explains all aspects of the standard library, but provides complete source code! There's no better way to learn the library than to study this book. Even if your interest in the library is minimal, the book is worth getting just for the opportunity to study C code written by a master.

Raymond, E. S., ed., *The New Hacker's Dictionary*, Second Edition, MIT Press, Cambridge, Mass., 1993. Although this isn't a C book, it explains much of the jargon that C programmers use.

Ritchie, D. M. The development of the C language, *Preprints, Second ACM SIGPLAN History of Programming Languages Conference*, 201–208. Published as *ACM SIGPLAN Notices* **28**, 3 (March 1993). A recent look back by the designer of C.

Ritchie, D. M., S. C. Johnson, M. E. Lesk, and B. W. Kernighan. UNIX time-sharing system: the C programming language, *Bell System Technical Journal* **57**, 6 (July–August 1978), 1991–2019. A famous article that discusses the origins of C and describes the language as it looked in 1978.

Rosler, L. The UNIX system: the evolution of C—past and future, *AT&T Bell Laboratories Technical Journal* **63**, 8 (October 1984), 1685–1699. Traces the evolution of C from 1978 to 1984 and beyond.

Stevens, W. R., *Advanced Programming in the UNIX Environment*, Addison-Wesley, Reading, Mass., 1992. An excellent follow-up to this book for programmers working under the UNIX operating system. Focuses on using the library functions that are provided in UNIX, including Standard C functions as well as functions that are specific to UNIX.

Straker, D., *C Style: Standards and Guidelines*, Prentice-Hall, Englewood Cliffs, N.J., 1992. A collection of style guidelines. In most cases, provides alternatives for the reader to choose from rather than recommending a single style.

Stroustrup, B., *The C++ Programming Language*, Second Edition, Addison-Wesley, Reading, Mass., 1991. The latest revision of the first C++ book, written by the designer of C++.

Summit, S., *C Programming FAQs: Frequently Asked Questions*, Addison-Wesley, Reading, Mass., 1996. An expanded version of the FAQ list that has appeared for years in the Usenet *comp.lang.c* newsgroup.

Tondo, C. L., and S. E. Gimpel, *The C Answer Book*, Second Edition, Prentice-Hall, Englewood Cliffs, N.J., 1988. Contains answers to the exercises in the second edition of K&R.

Tondo, C. L., A. Nathanson, and E. Yount, *Mastering MAKE*, Second Edition, Prentice-Hall, Englewood Cliffs, N.J., 1994. A comprehensive guide to using the `make` utility on a variety of platforms.

van der Linden, P., *Expert C Programming*, Prentice-Hall, Englewood Cliffs, N.J., 1994. Written by one of the C wizards at Sun Microsystems, this book manages to entertain and inform in equal amounts. With its profusion of anecdotes and jokes, it makes learning the fine points of C seem almost fun.